ALTERED
STATES

ALTERED STATES

A Reader in the New World Order

Edited by
Phyllis Bennis and Michel Moushabeck

Introduction by Noam Chomsky

OLIVE
BRANCH
PRESS

An imprint of Interlink Publishing Group, Inc
NEW YORK

First published in 1993 by
OLIVE BRANCH PRESS
An imprint of Interlink Publishing Group, Inc.
99 Seventh Avenue ● Brooklyn, New York 11215

The essay entitled "Marginalization or Renewal? Africa in the New World Order," (original title: "Africa and the New World Disorder") by William Minter appeared in the October 19, 1992 issue of *Christianity and Crisis*. Copyright © 1992 by Christianity and Crisis, Inc. Reprinted by permission. The essay entitled "Coming in From the Cold? The CIA After the Collapse of the Soviet Union," (original title: "Let's Terminate the C.I.A.") by Marcus Raskin appeared in the June 8, 1992 issue of the *The Nation*. Copyright © 1992 by The Nation Co., Inc. Reprinted by permission. The essay entitled "Why Palestine Should Stand Up for Itself," by Edward W. Said appeared in the September 30, 1992 issue of *The Guardian*. Copyright © 1992 by Edward W. Said. Reprinted by permission.

Library of Congress Cataloging-in-Publication Data

Altered states : a reader in the new world order / edited by Phyllis Bennis,
Michel Moushabeck ; introduction by Noam Chomsky.
p. cm.
Includes bibliographical references (p.) and index.
ISBN 1–56656–115–9—ISBN 1–56656–112–4 (pbk.)
1. World politics—1989–   I. Bennis, Phyllis, 1951–
II. Moushabeck, Michel, 1955–
D2009.A45   1993
909.82'9—dc20   93–4299
                                                                             CIP

Printed and bound in the United States of America

10 9 8   7   6 5 4 3 2 1

Contents

PART NINE ▪ Europe

Contributors

As'ad AbuKhalil is a Scholar-in-Residence at the Middle East Institute, Washington, D.C., and an adjunct Professor of Arab Politics at Georgetown University.

Naseer H. Aruri is Professor of Political Science at the University of Massachusetts, Dartmouth. He is a member of the Palestine National Council, and a three-term member of the Board of Directors of Amnesty International.

Alejandro Bendaña is Director of the Centro de Estudios Internacionales in Managua, Nicaragua. He was Secretary-General of the Foreign Ministry in the Sandinista government.

Medea Benjamin is Executive Director of Global Exchange, an organization promoting ties between First and Third World citizens. She worked in Cuba from 1979–1983 and is the author of *No Free Lunch: Food and Revolution in Cuba Today*.

Tony Benn is a long time Labor Party member of the British Parliament. He formerly represented the UK in the European Parliament. His most recent book is *A Future for Socialism*.

Phyllis Bennis is United Nations and Middle East correspondent for Pacifica Radio. She is the author of *From Stones to Statehood: The Palestinian Uprising* and co-editor of *Beyond the Storm: A Gulf Crisis Reader*.

Praful Bidwai is Senior Editor at *The Times of India*. He is a fellow of the Amsterdam-based Transnational Institute, and is working on a book on the impact of IMF "structural adjustment" in large Third World economies. He is a frequent contributor to *The Nation*.

John Borneman is Assistant Professor of Anthropology, Cornell University. His most recent book is *Belonging in the Two Berlins: Kin, State, Nation*.

Robert S. Browne is former staff director of the Sub-Committee on

International Development, Finance, Trade and Monetary Policy of the House Banking Committee. He is currently Resident Scholar at Howard University.

Jo-Marie Burt is a Ph.D. candidate in Political Science at Columbia University. She is co-author of *Peru Caught in the Crossfire*.

Noam Chomsky is Institute Professor of Linguistics and Philosophy at the Massachusetts Institute of Technology (MIT). He has written numerous books and articles on linguistics, philosophy, intellectual history and contemporary issues, including U.S. foreign policy. His most recent book is *Year 501: The Conquest Continues*.

Alexander Cockburn is a regular columnist for *The Nation*. He is co-author of *The Fate of the Forest: Developers, Destroyers and Defenders of the Amazon*.

Bogdan Denitch is the Michael Harrington Professor of Social Science at Queens College and Graduate School, CUNY. He chairs the annual Socialist Scholars Conference. His latest book is *After the Flood: Politics and Democracy After Communism*.

Joseph Diescho is a Namibian academic and activist with a Ph. D. in Political Science from Columbia University. He currently heads the New York-based Fund for the University of Namibia, and intends to return to teach in the near future.

Richard Falk is Albert G. Milbank Professor of International Law and Practice at Princeton University. He represented Ethiopia and Liberia before the International Court of Justice, and was Vice-President of the American Society of International Law. He has written extensively on human rights and international law issues; his most recent book is *Explorations at the Edge of Time*.

Bill Frelick is a senior policy analyst with the U.S. Committee for Refugees. He visited Kurdish refugee camps in Iran in April 1992, and is the author of *Yugoslavia Torn Asunder: Lessons for Protecting Refugees from Civil War*.

John Fieno is an intern at the Center of Concern from the Helen Kellogg Institute of International Studies at the University of Notre Dame.

Chris Giannou is a physician who has worked for 20 years in the developing world. He is the author of *Besieged: A Doctor's Story of Life and Death in Beirut*. He spent most of 1992 as Surgical Director for the International Committee of the Red Cross in Somalia.

Leanne Grossman is Managing Editor of *Surviving Together*, a journal on relations with the former Soviet Union and Baltic States, published by ISAR. The views stated here are expressly her own.

Ana Guadalupe Martinez is a member of the political-diplomatic commission of the FMLN. She was a member of the delegation to the United Nations-sponsored negotiations to end El Salvador's civil war.

Yvonne Yazbeck Haddad is Professor of Islamic History at the University of Massachusetts in Amherst. She is the author of *Contemporary Islam and the Challenge of History* and co-author of *Mission to America: Five Islamic Sects in North America*.

Susanna Hecht teaches in UCLA's Graduate School of Planning. She is co-author of *The Fate of The Forest: Developers, Destroyers, and Defenders of the Amazon*.

Paul Hockenos is the Central and Eastern Europe correspondent for *In These Times*. He is the author of *Free to Hate: The Rise of the Right in Post-Communist Eastern Europe*.

Mehrdad Izady received his Ph.D. from Columbia University, and is now teaching Kurdish and Persian at Harvard University. He is author of *The Kurds: A Concise Handbook* (1992), and the forthcoming *Historical Dictionary of Kurdistan*.

Yanique Joseph is a researcher with the Cambridge Forecast Group. She is coordinator of the Haitian Initiative on Environment and Development, and is active in The Other Economic Summit/Americas.

Michio Kaku is Professor of Theoretical Physics at the Graduate Center of the City University of New York. He is the author of *To Win a Nuclear War: The Pentagon's Secret War Plans* and *Beyond Einstein: The Cosmic Quest for the Theory of the Universe*.

Mary Kaldor is co-chair of the Helsinki Citizens Assembly and the author of *Imaginary War*.

Farhad Karim is a graduate student at Columbia University.

Rami G. Khouri is former Editor-in-Chief of the *Jordan Times*. He is a columnist and television commentator in Amman, Jordan, and is the author of a forthcoming book on the contemporary Middle East.

Ben Kiernan is Associate Professor of History at Yale University. He is the author of *How Pol Pot Came to Power*. An earlier version of his article appeared in *Beyond the Cold War*, edited by George W. Breslauer.

Michael T. Klare is Director of the Five College Program in Peace and World Security Studies at Hampshire College. He is a noted analyst of U.S. strategy and foreign relations issues.

Law Wing-Sang teaches at the Department of Social Studies at Hong Kong Polytechnic. He is a co-founder of TAMUD (Inauguration Overseas of the Tian-An-Men University of Democracy), and editor of its journal *Tiananmen Review*.

Sonja Licht is co-chair of the Helsinki Citizens Assembly. She works at the Institute for European Studies in Belgrade, and is a MacArthur Fellow.

Ngô Vĩnh Long is Associate Professor of History at the University of Maine, teaching Chinese, Japanese and Southeast Asian history. He is a noted scholar of Vietnam and U.S.-Vietnamese relations.

Bernard Magubane is Professor of Anthropology at the University of Connecticut. He is a well-known scholar of South African history and political developments in the region.

Arjun Makhijani is President of the Institute for Energy and Environmental Research in Takoma Park, Maryland. He is the author of *From Global Capitalism to Economic Justice* from which this article was drawn.

Clovis Maksoud is Director of the Center for the Global South at the School of International Studies at American University in Washington. He is the former Ambassador of the League of Arab States to the United Nations and the U.S.

William Minter is Scholar-in-Residence at the American University and Associate Director for Education of the Washington Office on Africa. He has edited a collection of documents, *Africa's Problems . . . African Initiatives*, for the Washington Office on Africa.

Michel Moushabeck is the founder and publisher of Interlink Publishing Group in New York and co-editor of *Beyond the Storm: A Gulf Crisis Reader*.

James A. Paul is a writer and consultant on Middle East issues based in New York. He is a contributing editor to MERIP's *Middle East Report*.

Major-General Mattiyhau Peled (ret.) is Professor of Arabic Literature at Tel Aviv University. He is the author of *Religion, My Own: The Literary Works of Najib Mahfouz*, and is a long-time activist in Israel's peace movement.

John Prendergast is a research associate at the Center of Concern in Washington, and co-ordinator of the Coalition for Peace in the Horn of Africa. He is the author of *Peace, Development and People in the Horn of Africa*.

Marcus Raskin is a co-founder of the Institute for Policy Studies and a member of the editorial board of *The Nation*. He is author of books on political theory, international relations and government. His most recent book is *Abolishing the War System*.

Edward W. Said is University Professor at Columbia University. He is a renowned Middle East scholar and critic, a former member of the Palestine National Council, and author of numerous books including *Orientalism*, *The Question of Palestine*, and *Culture and Imperialism*.

Ricardo Soberón is a lawyer and director of the Andean Commission of Jurists' program on Drugs, Security and Human Rights in Lima, and is an adviser to the Andean Council of Coca Producers.

Joe Stork is editor of the *Middle East Report* published by MERIP.

Tatiana Vorozheikina is senior research fellow at the Center for Developing Countries of the Institute of the World Economy and International Relations of the Russian Academy of Sciences in Moscow.

Hilbourne A. Watson is Professor of Political Science at Howard University. His most recent book is the forthcoming *The Caribbean in the Global Political Economy*.

Tim Watson is a graduate student in English and Comparative Literature at Columbia University, and an editor at Olive Branch Press.

Fred Weir is Moscow correspondent for the Canadian *Tribune*. He also works for the Canadian Broadcasting Company.

Editors' Preface

Looking North: The New Challenge to the South

Michel Moushabeck and Phyllis Bennis

> We stand at a defining hour. Halfway around the world, we are engaged in a great struggle . . . We know why we're there. We are Americans . . . What is at stake is more than one small country, it's a big idea — a new world order . . . Only the United States of America has had both the moral standing, and the means to back it up . . . The winds of change are with us now . . .
> —George Bush, 1991 State of the Union Address

Throughout the Gulf crisis and the U.S.-allied invasion of Iraq in 1991 — one of the most wretched episodes in American imperial history — we heard a lot of talk about George Bush's vision of a "new world order." Having reduced southern Iraq to rubble, and having inflicted six-figure casualties on a people with whom he said "we" had no quarrel, George Bush felt uniquely qualified to lecture the American people on the values of democracy, though it was and remained unclear what was meant by the term, and where and for whom it should apply. (In Kuwait, the U.S. fought to restore autocracy; in Algeria, it hailed democracy's ruin; in Angola, it failed to support the outcome of democratic elections; in Somalia, it spent a decade propping up the anti-democratic regime of Mohammad Siad Barre; in Israel, it finances illegal settlement and occupation of the West Bank and Gaza by the Middle East's "only democracy"; in Haiti, it simply looked the other way.)

Clearly the war in the Persian/Arabian Gulf was not the noble cause that George Bush said it was. And all the talk about a new era of freedom and democracy, about decency and humanity, about prosperity, equality and social justice, about a new world order — amounts to one thing and only one thing: U.S. hegemony and dominance in what Bush called "the New American Century," because in it the U.S. is "the dominant force for good in the world." (In fact, that "dominant force" was born in the end of the Cold War and the collapse of Soviet influence in the Arab world, making it possible for the U.S. and its allies to launch a devastating war against Iraq.)

While the groundwork was laid from 1989, it was the year 1991 that marked the beginning of this new world order, and it was filled with the kind of moments when history stands still, moments that remain embedded in our individual and collective memory. Where were you, what were you doing, when you saw the first explosions over Baghdad's skies on CNN? When you first saw the enormous Russian flag carried through Moscow's streets in an image repeated for months in champagne and credit card commercials? When you first heard of the August coup? When you first saw Palestinian, Arab state and Israeli negotiators in Madrid sitting down to talk? When you first saw the red flag of the Soviet Union lowered for the last time over the Kremlin?

The changes shook the world, economically, politically, militarily, strategically. Alliances were made and broken, old enemies became new friends, and longtime allies were eyed with new suspicions. It was indeed the beginning of a new world order.

It was not, however, a very orderly new world. The collapse of the Soviet Union and the end of the Cold War rendered obsolete the old global bipolar order. Over the past four decades, superpower contention acted as a stabilizing agent in some regions and in global spheres of influence, thereby producing the longest period of peace — *in Europe* — since World War II.

Suddenly, a volcano of change erupted with what Václav Havel called the "lava of post-communist surprises." The organization of the world into the nation-states decreed by colonial powers in the early twentieth century was rapidly deconstructing; it seemed the center could not hold. It was not that nationalism had faded from the global stage; quite the contrary, new nationalisms, new xenophobias, new chauvinisms sprouted like mushrooms after a rain. Nationalism, and its derivatives in racism and ethnic/religious hatreds, became dominant ideologies dividing pocket-sized populations from their neighbors, often within existing states. States began to crumble, and the new nationalisms emerged to challenge existing political institutions. As states fell, they divided into new "national" statelets, vying for economic and political survival in a newly-opened global playing field. As nations fell, micro-nationalisms rose to new heights.

In the wake of the Gulf War (the first test of the new world order and the U.S.'s role as unchallenged world policeman), the collapse of the Soviet Union (and with it its role as strategic contender with Washington), and the new weakness of the broader international community in the now unipolar world, it is certain that many things will never be the same again. Most of all, these new realities will impact the impoverished, underfed, over-indebted peoples of the South, the developing countries of the Third World. In the West, those images of the crumbling Cold War era had to do mostly with the Soviet Union and Europe — the fall of European socialism, the end of nuclear nightmares. But for much of the world, the emerging new world order was something very different: the triumphant West, and its former enemy, the defeated wannabe-West, joining to become the North — asserting economic and political domination over the poor and marginalized South, over Africa, the Middle East/West Asia, Latin America, Southeast Asia.

In the past, Washington used the Cold War to justify its longtime economic, political and military intervention in the Third World. Soviet strategic interest in blocking U.S. hegemony in the Third World matched the South's own interest in opposing Washington's interventions. In that context, Soviet assistance to the countries of the South was often instrumental in their uneven battles against U.S. and other Western control. But as the new order takes hold, the world is witnessing an intensification of the North-South conflict. The absence of the USSR as a strategic counterweight in diplomatic and military affairs, Russia's financial dependency on the West, and Western Europe's inability to challenge U.S. domination (a hopeful myth shattered by U.S. strongarm actions during the Gulf crisis) together create a dangerously lopsided unipolarity.

It carries with it a sobering message to the hungry and disempowered populations of the South, who are already paying a heavy price in political isolation and economic hardship. The U.S. is in a position to create and exploit more "villains," and to reward and protect more "friends," so long as they pay for such protection by following the policies chosen by Washington. (Quite apart from securing generous contracts and massive arms sales to its Gulf clients, the U.S. made quite a substantial profit after the various nations had paid their due towards the cost of Desert Storm. It remains to be seen whether Washington, ostensibly concerned about weapons proliferation in the Third World, is embarrassed about attaining its Number One Arms Dealer to the Third World position, with $18.5 billion in military sales to those regions in 1990 alone.)

An important aspect of the new world order with a special impact on the South is the new role for the United Nations as a key tool of U.S. foreign policy. During the Gulf crisis, the UN, designed to preserve peace and security throughout the world, was transformed into an instrument of intervention and legitimation of war. Not only was the military action authorized by the UN (though carried out by Washington and its allies) an excessive response to the Iraqi invasion of Kuwait, but it violated the UN Charter's own principle of exhausting all peaceful means before resorting to armed force. Further, the decision to use force was taken in an utterly discriminatory manner. If the same standards were used to enforce compliance of other binding UN resolutions by member states, Israel (who invaded and still occupies territories in Lebanon, Syria and Palestine), Indonesia (who invaded and occupied East Timor, killing nearly a third of the local population), the Serbs (whose savage slaughter of Bosnian civilians highlighted their campaign of ethnic cleansing), and of course the U.S. itself (who violated international law in its invasions of Panama and Grenada), would top the list of candidates for strong UN action. But the Security Council, structured to give its powerful Northern members veto power over the will of the majority of the nations of the world, made the application of such double standards not only possible but legal.

The same can be said about other UN agencies and multilateral institutions: the International Monetary Fund (IMF), the World Bank, and the General Agreement on Tariffs and Trade (GATT), key vehicles in enforcing the U.S.-dominated new economic order, are designed to reflect and strengthen the interests of the North — the transnational corporations, banks and investment companies capable of orchestrating the North-South economic divide. Their political/economic influence along this North-South faultline is directly proportional to the level of debt owed by the countries of the South. Writing in *The Nation* (March 29, 1993), Noam Chomsky noted "the U.S. International Trade Commission estimates that American companies stand to gain $61 billion a year from the Third World if U.S. protectionist demands are satisfied at GATT (as they are in NAFTA, the North American Free Trade Agreement), at a cost to the South that will dwarf the current huge flow of debt-service capital from South to North."

In the struggle between North and South, the role of technology and mass communications are central. Advanced technologies, which might have led to a more informed world, instead have become ingenious tools of control by the North. The exclusive access to satellites and telecommunications guarantees that the overwhelming majority of world news is created and transmitted by the North to the developing countries of the South. Deprived of technology and their own channels of communication, the peoples of the South find it frustratingly difficult to get their voices heard abroad. Such imbalance resulting from the growth of the American (and, to a lesser degree, British) media's domination of international broadcasting means that the South continues to be limited to American news shaped by an American perspective. The "global village" has given way to the global CNN/BBC-ization of information.

Despite the end of the Cold War, there are no signs to encourage the belief that real peace is just around the corner. We still live in a world divided into nation-states defined, more or less, by national identities. But increasingly those identities are being reshaped, and the new passions they engender are creating the basis for long-term dissidence and conflict of a very different nature than in earlier periods.

The post-World War II years (before and during the Cold War) were the era of decolonization. Anti-colonial struggles, some of them genuinely revolutionary, were the defining events of the time. In many of those battles, the struggle against colonial domination (or in the later years, the slightly more subtle forms of neo-colonial control) was waged in concert with the fight for economic and social justice. The intersection of national rights and an end to economic exploitation by outside countries created a progressive rallying cry in the demand for national self-determination.

Today, in both the North and South, nationalism looks very different. It has re-emerged, not as a defense or standard bearer against colonial or colonial-style domination, but as a backward, inward-directed ethnic isolationism. In Somalia, for example, factional fighting within an unusually homogenous society in which virtually all Somalis share an ethnic and linguistic identity, brought much of the country to its knees. The ethnic power rivalry was waged among narrowly-distinct rival clans and sub-clans. And as a result, the capital and much of the rest of the country were brought to the brink of starvation and social collapse. Outside of the eyes of much of the North, ethnic persecution is also underway in the Sudan, Liberia, Zaire, Cambodia, Rwanda and elsewhere.

But increasingly it is in Europe that the rivalries of ethnic/religious and nationalist hatreds are played out most viciously. The images of Bosnia, from the rape of Muslim women by Serbian thugs to the intensification of air and artillery attacks on Bosnian civilians as part of Serb and Croatian campaigns of "ethnic cleansing," have shocked the people of the industrialized North, unused to scenes of wanton destruction outside the Third World (at least since World War II). The destruction of the ancient historic city of Sarajevo by Serbian gunners on the hills ringing the town, has come to symbolize the brutality of ethnic conflict. It is not an accident that much of the most brutal nationalist strife has emerged in the formerly socialist countries of Eastern Europe and the former Soviet Union. The manifestations were suppressed during 40 years of socialism, but at least part of the post-Cold War nationalist fever seems to have arisen from state socialism's failure to change ideas. As well, the new economic pressures and social crises have created a political terrain ripe for scapegoating and nationalist demagoguery. Once the socialist lid was lifted, renewed ethnic and nationalist hatreds flourished in the newly open atmosphere.

Certainly this phenomenon is not limited to the new states built on the ruins of the Soviet Union and the formerly socialist countries of Eastern Europe. The anti-immigrant hysteria gripping France, Germany and even the traditionally more tolerant countries of Northern Europe, reflects the same reality. Attacks against "foreigners" (Turks, Arabs, Gypsies, Bulgarians, Romanians, etc.) and their homes by right-wing and neo-Nazi groups have become almost daily occurrences in Germany. Jean-Marie Le Pen's racist movement against Algerians, Moroccans and other "foreigners" in France, as well as similar movements across the continent, signal the ascendancy of the new definition of "nationalism."

That is not to say that no old-style nationalist movements remain within the countries of the South. One of the last truly anti-colonial nationalist movements, aimed directly against colonial occupation, is that of Palestine. Other examples include independence movements in Ethiopia and the Western Sahara aimed at the now-independent African governments of those countries. However, overwhelmingly they still reflect the legacies of colonial control by the North.

Since the end of World War II, there has not been a moment when so many people worldwide were desperately fleeing terror. According to the UN High Commissioner for Refugees, over 18 million people across the globe are displaced in their own country or stateless refugees across borders. Contrary to the xenophobic complaints of Northern pundits, the vast majority of refugees fleeing countries of the South seek sanctuary in other Southern states — not in the far less accessible North. George Bush's dark vision of a "defining moment" does reflect (whatever his intention) these facts — facts that must be dealt with by his successor.

The Clinton administration came to power while much of the world is hungry, poor, and vastly exploited; much of it is armed. In the industrialized North, the birthrates continue to decline; in the impoverished South populations skyrocket in the opposite direction. The gap between wealth and poverty that prevailed during the Cold War is widening to a chasm. Famine and communal war sweeping through regions of Africa no longer commanding superpower attention limned by the search for regional clients in the Cold War, continue to escalate.

With such a state of world affairs, the Clinton administration faces heightened anti-American resentment around the world, especially in the South, and increased suspicion of the new administration's universalist and humanitarian claims. So far, the Clinton White House has been unwilling to challenge the Cold War strategy of building and enhancing America's dominance in a — now — unipolar world.

Upon taking office Bill Clinton warned the South that "while the Soviet Union is gone, a president must still be ready to defy and to defeat those who threaten us . . . As we scale down our military, we must also keep up our guard." One hundred days into the new administration, Alexander Cockburn (*The Nation*, May 3, 1993) detailed its accomplishments so far: Clinton had "sold out the Haitian refugees; . . . let a Bush appointee, Herman Cohen, run Africa policy, essentially giving a green light to Savimbi in Angola to butcher thousands; put Israel's lobbyists in charge of Mideast policy; bolstered the arms industry with a budget in which projected spending for '93 is higher in constant dollars than average spending during the cold war from 1950; increased secret intelligence spending . . ."

And that was only the first 100 days.

· · · · · · ·

The idea of putting together this anthology emerged in early 1992, a few months after the publication of our earlier work, *Beyond the Storm: A Gulf Crisis Reader*. That book's widespread use and adoption as a text by more than 60 colleges and universities prompted us to take the debate a step further, by examining the broader notion of the new world order in the post-Cold War, post-Gulf War, post-Soviet world.

This collection, therefore, attempts to examine and make sense of that changing world — from the often ignored vantage point of the South. It functions as a history and analysis of the political, economic, and military relations being reshaped around the globe by a now strategically unchallenged U.S. Although a number of worthwhile studies on various aspects of the new world order are already in existence, what has been lacking, in our view, is a thorough evaluation of the effects of these global changes on the nations and peoples of the South. Hence, this effort to capture the breadth of issues involved, and offer the reader a glimpse of some of the major forces at work in the creation and projection of post-Cold War U.S. power abroad.

That is what this anthology is all about. Of course, it is by no means an exhaustive study of the subject. First, we wouldn't dare. Second, our main objectives are to encourage informed debate on a set of issues vital to world peace, to expose the ills and reality of the U.S. government's foreign policy (which has been unusually prone to propaganda and double-speak), and to lead the reader to the point where she or he may want to seek further information.

It is important to mention at least some of the issues which, to our regret, are not covered in this book, primarily due to the constraints of space and deadlines. Those include the shifting balance of power among the Arab states, and the economic impact on the Third World of the decline of Soviet support. Regional conflicts we could not address include those in Afghanistan, Armenia-Azerbaijan, Angola, East Timor and Guatemala. Additionally, we did not include analyses of the impact of the new world order on the peoples of the global South here in the U.S. itself — chief among them disempowered communities of color, women, gays and lesbians, undocumented workers, the un- and under-employed.

We are indebted to a large number of friends and colleagues who provided us with intellectual stimulation, advice and guidance that were critical to the completion of this book. We wish to thank, above all, the contributors to this volume for their insightful analyses and incalculable general support. Our deepest appreciation must also be extended to our colleague Tim Watson for his sensitivity, commitment, understanding and friendship, as well as for being a thoughtful and thorough editor. Special thanks should go to the wonderfully supportive staff of Olive Branch Press who worked round the clock to get this book out on time. We are also grateful to Rick Schneider of Dialog Design for his superb cover design and illustration.

The following are some of the people who generously shared ideas, contacts and other crucial assistance, as well as providing encouragement and valuable support: Ping Ferry, Carol Bernstein, Ethan Young, Samori Marksman, Max Elbaum, Ruth and Stan Cohen, Victor Mashabele, Susanne Riveles, Jaime Hermida, Laura Flanders, Stuart Schaar, Vivian Stromberg, Stephen Chan, Gustavo Acosta, Zillah Eisenstein, Roberta Goodman, Zeineb Istrabadi, Aijaz Ahmad, Eric Canepa, Mario Murillo, Victor Navasky, Barbara Ehrenreich, Eqbal Ahmad, Colleen Lye, Qadri Ismail. We had translation assistance from Ted Kuster and Michel Shehadeh. Finally, thanks are due to our families for having been a constant source of encouragement, and especially for their tolerance of our long absences and distracted moods.

—Brooklyn
June 1993

Introduction

World Orders, Old and New

*Noam Chomsky**

$\mathbf{T}$he South Commission study *Challenge to the South* closes with a call for a "new world order" that will respond to "the South's plea for justice, equity, and democracy in the global society." The rulers of that society, however, adhere to quite a different conception of world order, expressed by Winston Churchill: "the government of the world must be entrusted to the satisfied nations," the "rich men dwelling at peace within their habitations" whose power places them "above the rest," not the "hungry nations" who "seek more" and thus endanger tranquility. The global rulers can hardly be expected to heed the pleas of the South, any more than rights were granted to the general population, as a gift from above, within the rich societies themselves. Those assigned the status of spectators from below can afford no illusions on these matters.

The realities are illustrated in the Commission study. Thus, it observes that gestures to Third World concerns in the 1970s were "undoubtedly spurred" by concern over "the newly found assertiveness of the South after the rise in oil prices in 1973." As the threat abated, the rich men lost interest and turned to "a new form of neo-colonialism," monopolizing control over the world economy, undermining the more democratic elements of the United Nations, and in general proceeding to institutionalize "the South's second class status." The pattern is consistent; it would be remarkable if it were otherwise.

A few years before Churchill's forthright articulation of the vision of the powerful, a British War Department study transmitted by Secretary Henry Stimson to the State Department warned of the "rising tide all over the world wherein the common man aspires to higher and wider horizons" (July 1945). It was in this context that a potential Soviet threat to the post-war order was perceived. There is no proof that Russia has "flirted with the thought" of

---

* This article is based on Chomsky's "A View From Below," *Diplomatic History*, Winter 1992, and "World Orders, Old and New," prepared for the South Commission.

1

supporting the rising tide of aspirations of the common man [sic], the study observed, but it might do so. Taking no chances, the U.S. must therefore defend itself by surrounding the potential criminal with military force aimed at its heartland. The common man's aspirations posed a particularly severe threat because, as director of the Office of Strategic Services William Donovan had informed the President, the U.S. had "no political or social philosophy equally dynamic or alluring" to counter the "strong drawing card in the proletarian philosophy of Communism," particularly attractive at that historical moment, with empires in disarray, the traditional conservative order discredited by its fascist associations, and the resistance, popular-based and with radical democratic tendencies, enjoying much prestige.[1] The threat was countered by a worldwide campaign to destroy the anti-fascist resistance and restore the conservative business-ruled order, chapter 1 of post-war history.

The threat, however, did not end. A decade later, President Eisenhower complained that unlike us, the communists could "appeal directly to the masses." His Secretary of State, John Foster Dulles, deplored their "ability to get control of mass movements," "something we have no capacity to duplicate." "The poor people are the ones they appeal to and they have always wanted to plunder the rich," he observed to his brother, CIA director Allen Dulles, in 1958. The "social philosophy" that the rich should plunder the poor lacks popular appeal, a public relations problem that the rich rulers have never been able to overcome. The same concerns extended to "the preferential option for the poor" of the Latin American bishops and other commitments to social justice or democracy in more than form. The basic threat is loss of control.

Much the same was true of relations with the USSR. It was not Stalin's crimes that troubled Western leaders. Truman noted in his diary that "I can deal with Stalin," agreeing with Eisenhower and others; what went on in Russia was not his concern, Truman declared. Stalin's death would be a "real catastrophe," he felt. But cooperation was contingent on the U.S. getting its way 85% of the time, Truman made clear. In the leading scholarly study of U.S. security planning in the early post-war period, Melvyn Leffler observes that, "Rarely does a sense of real compassion and/or moral fervor emerge from the documents and diaries of high officials. These men were concerned primarily with power and self-interest, not with real people facing real problems in the world that had just gone through fifteen years of economic strife, Stalinist terror, and Nazi genocide."[2]

The animating concern was not Stalin's enormous crimes, but the apparent successes in development and the appeal of the "proletarian philosophy" to the "common man" in the West and to subjugated and oppressed people everywhere. The failure of Eastern Europe to return to its traditional role of providing food and raw materials to the West compounded these concerns.[3] The problem is not crimes, but insubordination, a fact illustrated once again in the case of Saddam Hussein, a favored friend and trading partner of the U.S. and its allies right through the period of his worst atrocities. As the Berlin Wall fell in 1989, the White House intervened directly, in a highly secret meeting, to ensure that Iraq would receive another $1 billion in loan guarantees, overcoming Treasury and Commerce Department objections that Iraq was not creditworthy. The reason, the State Department explained, was that Iraq was "very important to U.S. interests in the Middle East"; it was "influential in the peace process" and was a "key to maintaining stability in the region, offering great trade opportunities for U.S. companies."[4] As in the case of Stalin, Saddam Hussein's crimes were of no account, until he committed the crime of disobedience on August 2, 1990.

Whatever its political coloration, an independent course is unacceptable, successes that might provide a model to others still more so. The miscreant is then termed a "rotten apple" that is spoiling the barrel, a "virus" that must be exterminated. It is a "threat to stability." Thus, when a successful CIA operation overturned the democratic capitalist government of Guatemala in 1954, an internal State Department report explained that Guatemala had "become an increasing threat to the stability of Honduras and El Salvador. Its agrarian reform is a powerful propaganda weapon; its broad social program of aiding the workers and peasants in a victorious struggle against the upper classes and large foreign enterprises has a strong appeal to the populations of Central American neighbors where similar conditions prevail." In the operative sense of the term, "stability" means security for "the upper classes and large foreign enterprises," and it must naturally be preserved. These are crucial features of the old world order, well-documented in the internal record, regularly illustrated in historical practice, bound to persist as contingencies change.

Writing on world order in 1992, one can hardly overlook the fact that we are approaching the end of the first 500 years of a world order in which the major theme has been Europe's conquest of most of the world. The cast of characters has changed somewhat: a European-settled colony leads the crusade, and Japan, one of the few regions of the South to escape subjugation, was able to join the club of rich men. In contrast, parts of Western Europe that were colonized retain Third World features. One notable example is Ireland, violently conquered, then barred from development by the standard "free trade" doctrines selectively applied to ensure subordination of the South — today called "structural adjustment," "neoliberalism," or "our noble ideals," from which the rich men, to be sure, are exempt.

Throughout the Colombian era, the South has been assigned a service role: to provide resources, cheap labor, markets, opportunities for investment and export of pollution. For the past half-century, the U.S. has been the global enforcer, protecting the interests of the rich. Accordingly, the primary threat to U.S. interests is depicted in high-level planning documents as "radical and nationalistic regimes" that are responsive to popular pressures for "immediate improvement in the low living standards of the masses" and for diversification of their economies, tendencies that conflict with the need to protect U.S. control of raw materials and "a political and economic climate conducive to private investment" (NSC 5432/1, 1954). The basic themes of internal planning sometimes reach the public record, as when the editors of the *New York Times*, applauding the overthrow of the parliamentary Mossadegh regime in Iran in 1953, observed that, "Underdeveloped countries with rich resources now have an object lesson in the heavy cost that must be paid by one of their number which goes berserk with fanatical nationalism." Most important, the historical record conforms to this understanding of the role of the South.

Within the rich men's club, order must also reign. The lesser members are to pursue their "regional interests" within the "overall framework of order" managed by the United States, the only power with "global interests and responsibilities," as Kissinger admonished Europe in 1973. In the early post-war years, a European third force could not be tolerated. Neutralism would be "a shortcut to suicide," Dean Acheson held. The formation of NATO was in large part motivated by the need "to integrate Western Europe and England into an orbit amenable to American leadership," Leffler observes.[5] With U.S. economic domination in decline, those strictures might become harder to enforce. For the moment, they remain fairly well in place in the loose framework of world government (G7, the IMF and World Bank, etc.).

Standard reasoning is developed in a secret February 1992 Pentagon draft of Defense Planning Guidance, which describes itself as "definitive guidance from the Secretary of Defense" for budgetary policy to the year 2000.[6] The U.S. must hold "global power" and a monopoly of force. It will then "protect" the "new order" while allowing others to pursue "their legitimate interests," as the U.S. defines them. The U.S. "must account sufficiently for the interests of the advanced industrial nations to discourage them from challenging our leadership or seeking to overturn the established political and economic order," or even "aspiring to a larger regional or global role." There must be no independent European security system; rather, U.S.-dominated NATO must remain the "primary instrument of Western defense and security, as well as the channel for U.S. influence and participation in European security affairs." "We will retain the pre-eminent responsibility for addressing selectively those wrongs which threaten not only our interests, but also those of our allies or friends"; the U.S. alone will determine what are "wrongs" and when they are to be selectively "righted." As in the past, the Middle East is a particular concern. Here "our overall objective is to remain the predominant outside power in the region and preserve U.S. and Western access to the region's oil" while deterring aggression (selectively), maintaining strategic control and "regional stability" (in the technical sense), and protecting "U.S. nationals and property." In Latin America, a crucial threat is Cuban "military provocation against the U.S. or an American ally" — the standard Orwellian reference to the escalating U.S. war against Cuban independence.

The case of Cuba well illustrates the persistence of traditional themes and the basic logic of the North-South conflict. 170 years ago, the U.S. was unsympathetic to the liberation of Latin America, adopting Thomas Jefferson's precept that it is best for Spain to rule until "our population can be sufficiently advanced to gain it from them piece by piece." Opposition to Cuban independence was particularly strong. Secretary of State John Quincy Adams, the author of the Monroe Doctrine, described Cuba as "an object of transcendent importance to the commercial and political interests of our

Union." Expressing the dominant elite view, he urged Spanish sovereignty until Cuba would fall into U.S. hands by "the laws of political . . . gravitation," a "ripe fruit" for harvest. One prime concern was the democratic tendencies in the Cuban independence movement, which advocated abolition of slavery and equal rights for all. In the rhetoric of contemporary planners, there was a threat that "the rot might spread," even to U.S. shores.

By the end of the nineteenth century, the British deterrent was gone and the U.S. was powerful enough to conquer Cuba, just in time to prevent the success of the indigenous liberation struggle. Cuba was effectively placed under the rule of the white propertied classes and U.S. firms. In the 1930s, President Roosevelt revoked the "good neighbor policy" to overturn a civilian government regarded as a threat to U.S. commercial interests. The Batista dictatorship served those interests loyally, thus enjoying full support.

Castro's overthrow of the dictatorship in January 1959 soon elicited U.S. hostility. By late 1959, Washington had conluded that Castro was unacceptable. One reason, State Department liberals explained, was that "our business interests in Cuba have been seriously affected." A second was the threat to "stability": "The United States cannot hope to encourage and support sound economic policies in other Latin American countries and promote necessary private investments in Latin America if it is or appears to be simultaneously cooperating with the Castro program." Studies of Cuban opinion provided to the White House concluded that most Cubans were optimistic about the future and supported Castro, while only 7% expressed concern about communism. Soviet presence was nil.

By October 1959, U.S.-based planes were attacking Cuba. CIA subversion included supply of arms to guerrilla bands and sabotage of sugar mills and other economic targets. In March 1960, the Eisenhower administration formally adopted a plan to overthrow Castro in favor of a regime "more devoted to the true interests of the Cuban people and more acceptable to the U.S.," though it must be done "in such a manner as to avoid any appearance of U.S. intervention."

Sabotage, terror, and aggression were escalated further by the Kennedy administration, along with the kind of economic warfare that no small country within the U.S. sphere can long endure.

After the Bay of Pigs failure, Kennedy's international terrorist campaign escalated further, reaching quite remarkable dimensions. The operations were formally called off by President Lyndon Johnson. They continued, however, and were escalated by Nixon. Subsequent terrorist actions are attributed to renegades beyond CIA control, whether accurately or not, we do not know; one high Pentagon official through the 1960s, Roswell Gilpatric, has expressed his doubts. The Carter administration, with the support of U.S. courts, condoned hijacking of Cuban ships in violation of the anti-hijacking convention that Castro was respecting. The Reaganites rejected Cuban initiatives for a diplomatic settlement and imposed new sanctions on the most outlandish pretexts, a record reviewed by Wayne Smith, who resigned as head of the U.S. Interests Section in Havana in protest.

In the 1980s the embargo was tightened, and again in mid-1991, while the

U.S. resumed Caribbean military maneuvers, a standard technique of intimidation. As in the 1820s, such policies are supported across the spectrum of articulate opinion. Interestingly, there is no effort to conceal the fact that Washington is exploiting the disappearance of the Soviet deterrent and the decline of East bloc economic relations with Cuba to achieve its longstanding aims, through economic warfare or other means. Similarly, throughout the 1980s, the liberal press scoffed at Gorbachev's "new thinking" because he had not yet offered the U.S. a free hand to attain its objectives in Central America.

The Cuban record demonstrates with great clarity that the Cold War framework was scarcely more than a pretext to conceal the standard refusal to tolerate Third World independence, whatever its political cast. From 1917 through the 1980s, virtually every U.S. act of subversion, violence, or economic warfare in the Third World was justified on grounds of defense from the Russians. Woodrow Wilson needed other pretexts when he invaded Haiti and the Dominican Republic, just as George Bush had to seek new ones after the demise of the Soviet Union. But the basic realities do not change.

The Cold War itself had many of the features of North-South conflict. The Third World first appeared in Eastern Europe, which began to provide raw materials for workshops of the West as far back as the fourteenth century, and then followed the (now familiar) path towards underdevelopment as trade and investment patterns took their natural course. For reasons of scale, Russian economic subordination to the West was delayed, but by the nineteenth century the process was well underway. The Bolshevik takeover in October 1917, which quickly aborted incipient socialist tendencies and destroyed any semblance of working class or other popular organization, extricated the USSR from the Western-dominated periphery, setting off the inevitable reaction, beginning with immediate military intervention. These were, from the outset, some of the basic contours of the Cold War.

The logic was not fundamentally different from the case of Grenada or Guatemala, but the scale of the problem was. It was enhanced after Russia's leading role in defeating Hitler enabled it to isolate Eastern and parts of Central Europe from Western control. A tiny departure from subordination is intolerable, a huge one much less so, particularly when it threatens "stability" through the rotten apple effect.

No less ominous was the ability of the Soviet Union to lend support to targets of U.S. subversion or destruction, and its military capacity, so enormous as to deter U.S. intervention elsewhere. Under such circumstances, "coexistence" was even more out of the question than in the case of Guatemala, Chile, Grenada, Nicaragua, and so on. Though by no means the whole story of the Cold War, this was a major theme, and a very familiar one.

The USSR reached the peak of its power by the late 1950s, always far behind the West. The Cuban missile crisis, revealing extreme Soviet vulnerability, led to a huge increase in military spending, leveling off by the late 1970s. The economy was then stagnating and the autocracy unable to control internal dissidence. The command economy had carried out basic industrial development but was unable to proceed to more advanced stages,[7] and also suffered from the global recession that devastated much of the South. By the 1980s, the system had collapsed, and the core countries, always far richer and more powerful, "won the Cold War." Much of the Soviet empire will probably return to its traditional Third World status, with the ex-*nomenklatura* taking on the role of the Third World elites linked to international business and financial interests. But the U.S. is deeply in debt at every level (federal, state, corporate, household) after a decade of Reagan-Bush economic mismanagement. It is thus not well-placed to compete with its rivals for domination of these restored Third World domains, one of the sources of tension within the rich men's club.

A further consequence of the Soviet collapse is that a new framework is needed for intervention. The problem arose through the 1980s, requiring a propaganda shift to international terrorists, Hispanic narcotraffickers, crazed Arabs, and other chimeras. Yet another consequence is that the collapse of the Soviet deterrent "makes military power more useful as a United States foreign policy instrument . . . against those who contemplate challenging important American interests" (Dimitri Simes of the Carnegie Endowment for International Peace), an insight echoed by Reaganite Latin America planner Elliott Abrams during the invasion of Panama and by commentators throughout the Gulf crisis, who noted that the U.S. and Britain could now use force without limit against a defenseless enemy.

The first years of the post-Cold War era reveal how little has changed, tactical adjustments aside. With Gorbachev's "new thinking" (that is, the decline of Soviet support for targets of U.S. attack, and of the Soviet deterrent), overt intervention became a more feasible option, but on condition that it be "decisive and rapid" and accompanied by massive propaganda campaigns of demonization. Immediately after the fall of the Berlin Wall, symbolically ending the Cold War, President Bush inaugurated the new era by invading Panama, restoring the rule of the tiny white minority and returning the security forces to U.S. control. The United States vetoed two Security Council condemnations, joined in one case by the United Kingdom and France. All of this is so familiar as barely to merit a footnote in history, but there were some novelties. Even the most fertile imagination could not conjure up a Soviet threat, so new pretexts were needed. And, as noted, there was no concern over a Soviet response.

Reactions to the invasion north and south of the Rio Grande differed sharply. In the United States, opinion hailed "Operation Just Cause." In contrast, the Group of Eight Latin American democracies, which had suspended Panama because of Noriega's crimes, expelled it permanently as a country under military occupation. In August 1990, a Panamanian presidential commission called for an end to the "occupation of the State and its territory by U.S. troops" and the reestablishment of national sovereignty. A leading Honduran journal denounced the "international totalitarianism" of George Bush "in the guise of 'democracy.'" Bush, it said, had "declared plainly to Latin America that for the North American government, there is no law — only its will — when imposing its designs on the hemisphere." "We live in a climate of aggression and disrespect," "hurt by our poverty, our weakness, our naked dependence, the absolute submission of our feeble nations to the service of an implacable superpower. Latin America is in pain."[8]

The second act of post-Cold War aggression was Iraq's invasion of Kuwait, shifting Saddam Hussein overnight from friend and favored trading partner to reincarnation of Attila the Hun, the familiar pattern when some murderous tyrant steps out of line. The United States and United Kingdom moved quickly to bar the diplomatic track, for fear that peaceful means might "defuse the crisis" with "a few token gains" for their former friend, as the administration position was outlined by *New York Times* diplomatic correspondent Thomas Friedman.[9] The war policy was strongly opposed by the population in the region. The Iraqi democratic opposition, always rebuffed by Washington, opposed U.S. policy throughout: the pre-August 1990 support for the Iraqi dictator, the resort to war rather than peaceful means, and finally the tacit support for Saddam Hussein as he crushed the Shi'ite and Kurdish rebellions. One leading spokesman, banker Ahmad Chalabi, who described the outcome of the war as "the worst of all possible worlds" for the Iraqi people, attributed the U.S. stand to its traditional policy of "supporting dictatorships to maintain stability."[10]

The United Nations suffered further blows. Since it fell "out of control" by the 1960s, the United States has been far in the lead in vetoing Security Council resolutions and hampering UN activities generally. The invasion of Kuwait was unusual in that the United States and the United Kingdom opposed an act of international violence, and thus did not block the usual condemnations and efforts to reverse the crime. But under U.S. pressure, the Security Council was compelled to wash its hands of the matter, radically violating the UN Charter by leaving individual states free to respond to the aggression as they chose. Further U.S. pressures prevented the Council from responding to the call of member states for meetings, as stipulated by Council rules that the United States had vigorously upheld when they served its interests. That Washington has little use for diplomatic means or institutions of world order, unless they can be used as instruments of its own power, has been dramatically illustrated in Southeast Asia, the Middle East, Central America, and elsewhere. Nothing is likely to change in this regard.

Hostility to meaningful democracy also continued without change. As the Berlin Wall fell, elections were held in Honduras in "an inspiring example of the democratic promise that today is spreading throughout the Americas," in George Bush's words.[11] The candidates represented large landowners and wealthy industrialists, with close ties to the military, the effective rulers, under U.S. control. Their political programs were virtually identical, and the campaign was largely restricted to insults and entertainment. Human rights abuses by the security forces escalated before the election. Starvation and misery were rampant, having increased during the "decade of democracy," along with capital flight and the debt burden. But there was no major threat to order, or to investors.

At the same time, the electoral campaign opened in Nicaragua. Its 1984 elections do not exist in U.S. commentary, though they were favorably described by a host of observers, including Western government and parliamentary delegations and a study group of the Latin American Studies Association. The elections could not be controlled, and therefore are not an inspiring example of democracy. Taking no chances with the long-scheduled 1990 elections, Bush announced as the campaign opened that the embargo would be lifted if his candidate won. The White House and Congress renewed their support for the contra forces in violation of the agreement of the Central American presidents and the judgement of the World Court. Nicaraguans were thus informed that only a vote for the U.S. candidate would end the terror and illegal economic warfare. In Latin America, the electoral results were generally interpreted as a victory for George Bush, even by those who celebrated the outcome. In a typical reaction, a Guatemala City journal attributed the result to "ten years of economic and military aggressions waged by a government with unlimited resources": "It was a vote in search of peace by a people that, inevitably, were fed up with violence, . . . a vote from a hungry people that, more than any idea, need to eat." In the United States, in contrast, the result was hailed as a "Victory for U.S. Fair Play," with "Americans United in Joy," as *New York Times* headlines put it.[12]

Again expressing traditional attitudes, a Latin American Strategy Development Workshop at the Pentagon in September 1990 concludes that current relations with the Mexican dictatorship are "extraordinarily positive," untroubled by stolen elections, death squads, endemic torture, scandalous treatment of workers and peasants, and so forth. But "a 'democracy opening' in Mexico could test the special relationship by bringing into office a government more interested in challenging the U.S. on economic and nationalist grounds," the fundamental concern over many years.[13]

The National Security Strategy report sent to Congress in March 1990, recognized that military power must target the Third World, primarily the Middle East, where the "threats to our interests" that have required force "could not be laid at the Kremlin's door," a fact now acknowledged. Furthermore, the Soviet pretext for military spending having disappeared, the threat now becomes "the growing technological sophistication of Third World conflicts." The United States must therefore strengthen its "defense industrial base," with incentives "to invest in new facilities and equipment as well as in research and development," and develop further forward basing and counterinsurgency and low-intensity conflict capacities.[14] In brief, the prime concerns continue to be control of the South and support for high tech industry at home, with the ideological framework adapted to new contingencies.

Other factors, however, are likely to inhibit the U.S. resort to force to control the South. Among them are the successes of the past years in crushing popular nationalist and reform tendencies, the elimination of the "communist" appeal to those who hope to "plunder the rich," and the economic catastrophes of the last decade. In the light of these developments, limited forms of diversity and independence can be tolerated with less concern that they will lead to a challenge to ruling business interests. Control can be exercised by economic measures: structural adjustment, the IMF regimen, selective resort to free trade measures, and so forth. Quite generally, democratic forms are tolerable as long as "stability" is ensured. If this dominant value is threatened — by popular uprisings in Iraq, the electoral victory of a radical priest in Haiti, an Islamic movement in Algeria, or any uncontrolled popular force — then the iron fist must strike.

Another inhibiting factor is that the domestic base for foreign adventures has eroded. A leaked fragment of an early Bush administration national security review observes that "much weaker enemies" must be defeated "decisively and rapidly"; any other outcome might "undercut political support." The Reagan administration was compelled to resort to clandestine terror and proxy forces because political support for violent intervention was so thin. And it has been necessary to whip up impressive propaganda campaigns to portray "much weaker enemies" as threats to our very existence, so as to mobilize a frightened population to at least temporary support for decisive and rapid action.

Still another problem is that the other two centers of economic power — German-led Europe and Japan — have their own interests, though the Defense Planning study cited earlier is correct in noting that basic interests are shared; notably, the concern that the Third World fulfil its service function. Furthermore, the internationalization of capital that has accelerated since Nixon dismantled the Bretton Woods system gives a somewhat new cast to competition among national states. Merely to cite one indication, while the U.S. share in world manufactured exports declined 3.5% from 1966 to 1984, the share of U.S.-based transnational corporations (TNCs) slightly increased.[15] And international trade patterns yield a very different picture if imports from overseas subsidiaries are counted as domestic production. These are factors of growing importance in the new world order.

Furthermore, the U.S. no longer has the economic base for intervention. Recognition of this fact has led to proposals in the business press that the U.S. become a "mercenary" state, using its "monopoly power" in the "security market" to maintain its "control over the world economic system," selling "protection" to other wealthy powers who will pay a "war premium" (*Chicago Tribune* financial editor William Neikirk). Nearly half of a substantial decline in the U.S. current account deficit for 1991 is attributed to foreign payments for the Gulf War, much of the rest by exports to Middle East oil producers, including billions of dollars in weapons.[16] The profits of Gulf oil production, in particular, must continue to be available to support the economies of the U.S. and its British associate, who are to carry out the enforcer role.

The use of force to control the Third World is a last resort. Economic weapons are more efficient. Some of the newer mechanisms can be seen in the GATT negotiations. One major U.S. concern is the "new themes": guarantees for "intellectual property rights," such as patents and software, that will enable TNCs to monopolize new technology; and removal of constraints on services and investment, which will undermine national development programs in the Third World and effectively place investment decisions in the hands of TNCs and the financial institutions of the North. These are "issues of greater magnitude" than the more publicized conflict over agricultural subsidies, according to William Brock, head of the Multilateral Trade Negotiations Coalition of major U.S. corporations. In the latter sphere, the U.S. objects to a GATT provision that allows countries to restrict food exports in times of need, demanding that U.S. agribusiness must control raw materials no matter what the human cost.[17] In general, each of the wealthy industrial powers advocates a mixture of liberalization and protection designed for the interests of dominant domestic forces, and particularly for the TNCs that are to dominate the world economy.

The effects would be to reduce Third World governments to a police function, with the task of controlling their own working classes and super-fluous population while TNCs gain free access to their resources and control new technology and global investment — and, of course, are granted the central planning and management functions denied to governments, which are unacceptable agents because they might fall under the influence of popu-lar pressures reflecting domestic needs, the "radical nationalism" of the internal planning record. The outcome is called "free trade," but some have more accurately described it as a kind of "corporate mercantilism," with managed commercial interactions among corporate groupings and con-tinuing state intervention in the North to subsidize and protect domestically-based corporations and financial institutions.[18]

The Latin Americanization of the East follows the familiar course. Thus Poland, adopting the doctrines professed by the rich, liberalized its economy. In reaction, the EC raised import barriers to protect its own industry and agriculture. EC chemical and steel industries warned that "restructuring" must not harm Western industry. The World Bank estimates that the protec-tionist measures of the industrial countries — keeping pace with free market bombast — reduce the national income of the "developing societies" by about twice the amount provided by official "development assistance," much of it a form of export promotion.[19]

There are many familiar reasons why wealth and power tend to reproduce. It should, then, come as little surprise that the Third World continues to fall behind the North. UN statistics indicate that as a percentage of developed countries, Africa's GDP per capita (minus South Africa) declined by about 50% from 1960 to 1987. The decline was almost as great in Latin America.[20] For similar reasons, within the rich societies themselves large sectors of the population are becoming superfluous by the reigning values and must be marginalized or suppressed, increasingly so in the past 20-year period of economic stagnation and pressures on corporate profit. Societies of the North — notably the United States — are taking on certain Third World aspects, as wealth and power is increasingly concentrated among investors and professionals who benefit from internationalization of capital flow and communication.

Like the domestic poor in the developed societies, the South has little bargaining power in its dealings with the club of rich men. The prospects for "justice, equity and democracy" (in a meaningful sense) are not auspicious. But they are not hopeless. The South Commission study mentions several directions that should be pursued, though I think the analysis is too optimis-tic in expecting these to influence the policies and attitudes of the rulers. One direction is internal change leading to meaningful democracy, social justice and improvement of conditions of life, and popular control over capital and investment so that such resources as are available will be used for constructive development rather than investment abroad or enriching TNCs and small wealthy sectors linked to them. If, for example, Latin America could control its own wealthy classes, preventing capital flight, much of the debt would be wiped out. A related need is South-South cooperation to address common economic, social, and cultural needs.

But the crucial factor can only be internal changes in the core countries. This prospect is not to be dismissed. Throughout the North, notably in the U.S., there have been significant changes in the past 30 years, at least at the cultural if not the institutional level. Had the quincentennial of the old world order been in 1962, it would have been celebrated as the liberation of the hemisphere. In 1992 large sectors demanded recognition of the fact that the "liberation" set off the two worst demographic catastrophes in human history, in the Western hemisphere and Africa. The domestic constraints on state violence, noted earlier, are another case in point. Perhaps the most striking example is the Third World solidarity movements that developed through the 1980s in the United States, to a large extent based in churches and with broad social roots. This process of democratization and concern for social justice threatens power, and is therefore minimized or dismissed in the doctrinal system, but it has large significance, I believe.

Democratization and social reform in the South are values in themselves. But there is little reason to suppose that steps towards internal freedom and justice will appeal to elite opinion in the West; on the contrary, they will be no less frightening than the so-called "crisis of democracy" within the rich societies (that is, the efforts of large parts of the population, since the 1960s, to enter the political arena). But in this way, the South can move towards mutually supportive relations with liberatory tendencies within Western societies. Such developments will naturally be regarded by the powerful as dangerous and subversive. However, they offer the only real hope for the great mass of people in the world, even for the survival of the human species in the era of environmental and other global problems that cannot be faced by primitive social and cultural structures that are driven by short term material gain, and that consider human beings to be instruments, not ends.

Notes

1. War Department Study and OSS cited in Melvyn P. Leffler, *A Preponderance of Power*, Stanford, 1992, pp. 78, 60.
2. Ibid., pp. 52–3, 15.
3. Ibid., p. 35.
4. Lionel Barber and Alan Friedman, *Financial Times* (London), May 3, 1991. See also *Los Angeles Times*, February 23, 25, 26, 1992.
5. Op. cit., p. 17.
6. Excerpts, *New York Times*, March 8, 1992; Patrick Tyler, *New York Times*, March 10, 1992; Barton Gellman, *Washington Post Weekly Edition*, March 16–22, 1992.
7. Charles S. Maier, *Why Did Communism Collapse in 1989?*, Program on Central and Eastern Europe, Working Paper Series #7, Jan. 1991.
8. Noam Chomsky, *Deterring Democracy*, 1991, Hill and Wang, New York. See chapter 5.

9. Friedman, "Behind Bush's Hard Line," *New York Times*, August 22, 1991.
10. Chomsky, op. cit.; chapter 6 and Afterword.
11. Associated Press, April 17, 1990.
12. Chomsky, op. cit.; chapter 10.
13. *Latin America Strategy Development Workshop*, September 26 and 27, 1990, minutes, p. 3. Andrew Reding, "Mexico's Democratic Challenge," *World Policy Journal* (Spring 1991).
14. *National Security Strategy of the United States*, the White House, March 1990.
15. Arthur MacEwan, *Socialist Review*, July–Dec. 1991.
16. AP, *New York Times*, p. D21, March 18, 1991; Barry Schweid, AP, *Boston Globe*, February 15, 1991.
17. Mark Ritchie, "GATT, Agriculture and the Environment," *The Ecologist*, Nov./Dec. 1990.
18. Peter Phillips, *Challenge*, Jan./Feb. 1992.
19. World Bank Response to NGO Working Group Position Paper on the World Bank, in *Trócaire Development Review* (Catholic Agency for World Development, Dublin, 1990).
20. *Monthly Review*, March 1992.

■ PART ONE ■

After the Gulf War

1

Democratic Disguise:
Post-Cold War Authoritarianism

Richard Falk

It has been widely assumed that the collapse of the Soviet Union was also a victory for democracy as the basis for legitimate state-society relations. Francis Fukuyama's infamous article "The End of History?" obviously captured this mood of celebration, arguing that the democratic idea was not only ascendent, given the failures of Marxism-Leninism, but that it was likely to remain so forever, that "democracy" in its liberal capitalist form was the final and ultimate form of governance.[1] Fukuyama's article itself was less significant than the extraordinary response it evoked, which suggested a strongly felt ideological need in anti-communist circles to represent the victory of the West in the Cold War in terms of ideas and ideals.

Whether this endorsement of capitalist democracy as the only form of government is worthy of celebration, or more appropriately an occasion for caution and reflection, is the basic theme of this essay. In my view, the abrupt way the Cold War ended in 1989–90 was ambiguous in relation to the well-being of the peoples of the world, especially those living in the countries of the South, and those in the North who were poor and non-white. On the positive side was the removal of the threat of World War III and the recurrent danger and experience of competitive military intervention, including support for the sort of civil wars that devastated Mozambique and Angola in the 1980s.[2] Also helpful, in most respects, was the tendency to associate the Soviet collapse with authoritarianism and the denial of human rights.

But such positive effects are far from the whole story. The ideological gatekeepers in the West, especially the United States, emphasized the extent to which the Soviet failure should be regarded as a death certificate for socialism, in general, including socialist values; that is, a subordination of economic policy to the aims of social justice, including an ideal of equality and the responsibility of the state for meeting the basic needs of its entire citizenry. In essence, "democracy" was endorsed, but only in its capitalist

17

forms. Even the most successful welfare or social democratic states were put on the defensive, warned that the socialist content of welfare policies was a corrupting element that had deteriorated their competitive position in the world economy. Sweden, in particular, reacted to this pressure by rolling back aspects of its welfare state.

A further negative effect of this insistence that democracy was the only proper way to govern, was to encourage authoritarian states to appear to trim their sails, but not to give up their basic reliance on coercion and intimidation. In an age where some claim "the image is everything," democracy has been frequently reduced to an image, associated with rituals: elections, political parties, human rights associations and reports. In some settings, this embrace of a democratic imagery has indeed usefully increased the political space available for oppositional politics and citizen initiatives. But in others, democratization has obscured the persistence of authoritarian structures and practices, and has fastened an exploitative and painful capitalist discipline upon an impoverished people as if preordained in heaven. The insistence that "democracy" implies economic liberalism has also reinforced the interventionary claims of the International Monetary Fund (IMF) and the World Bank, leaving governments in the South with little room for the adoption of more compassionate development policies with beneficial social content, especially in relation to their own poor.

In this essay, my intention is to consider Turkey as a country caught up in the pressure to democratize up to a certain point, but not beyond. The Turkish case is emblematic of a far wider array of specific responses to the ideological pressures of "the new world order." In general, these responses lead authoritarian states to alter their language and style, but not to abandon their core reliance on violence and intimidation in relation to "enemies" within their borders. If the state is also "socialist" in its orientation — which has not been the case, of course, with Turkey — then it will be obliged to open its economy up to market forces (as China, North Korea, Vietnam, and Cuba are each doing to a degree, and with sharply varying success). Arguably, the decisive test of "legitimacy," and even democracy, has become the market, with issues of democratic political life being of minor relevance, especially if democratic rituals are observed. Turkey, already capitalist and in some superficial senses "democratic," experiences this pressure to democratize mainly in relation to human rights and, to some extent, with respect to the assurance of civilian rule. Nevertheless, the effectiveness of the pressure is related to economic policy; specifically, whether Turkey will gain admission to the European Community, and thereby improve its prospects for growth and capital expansion. That is, the political content of legitimacy is greater in Turkey's case because of its economic motivations within the special context of Europe.

I. Concealed Authoritarianism

We need to begin by connecting political developments in Turkey over the course of the last five years with this broader pattern of adaptation at work in international political life: the pragmatic subordination of authoritarian rule to the new cosmetic requirements of geopolitics. Such states as the Philippines, Chile, South Korea, Thailand, Argentina, Brazil, Indonesia, Pakistan, Egypt, Nigeria and Mexico illustrate variations on this same basic theme.[3] Each of these instances of incomplete democratization is significantly distinctive, yet the pattern is notable both for exhibiting common characteristics and for confirming a trend in state-society restructuring that is becoming a main feature of contemporary international relations, and seems driven, above all, by the requirements of a more closely integrated world economy.

In its broadest contours the pattern consists of a democratizing foreground in the midst of a persisting, if officially unacknowledged, authoritarian structure. The pattern is significantly associated with an emphasis on public relations and appearances by governing elites, but these appearances of democracy to achieve their goals need to be presented to and perceived by the world as part of an ongoing process of deepening democracy. Free and fair, periodic elections are often no longer enough to satisfy international expectations, even if complemented by multi-party rivalry and a generalized atmosphere of freedom for opposition politics.[4] The key additional factor, especially in and around Europe, is now the observance of human rights, including the toleration of domestic and transnational monitoring and protest activities by independent citizen groups rooted in civil society and by reasonably apolitical supervisory scrutiny at the regional and global level. The human rights dimension of democratization has had its impact on geopolitics, including the manner by which U.S. foreign policy reconciles its interventionary objectives with its commitment to "democracy."[5] On the one side, "friends" are under more pressure to correct human rights abuses; but, on the other, justifications for intervention cluster now around humanitarian rationales rather than rest on strategic and ideological claims. A renewed concern with principles guiding "humanitarian intervention" is an expression of this most recent phase of interventionary diplomacy.

The contradictory realities of Turkey provide a fascinating "text" by which to appraise this emergent pattern of hidden authoritarianism, combining both the reality of at least limited democratization as an encouraging development on the surface, and the ugly manifestations of persisting authoritarianism that limit what is needed to liberate society from oppressive circumstances. Under such conditions, knowing "the rules of the game" may be a literal key to survival for those citizens who are taking advantage of Turkey's expanding democratic space.[6] It is important to appreciate that despite the public relations motivations of governing elites, hidden authoritarianism creates *real* new democratic opportunities, including the possibility to test, and possibly to extend, limits. A new equation of struggle between democratic and authoritarian forces emerges, the outcome of which remains uncertain. Social forces are released that cannot be entirely stage-managed by elites (or outside forces) to ensure a "safe" quantum of democratization.[7] The situation in Turkey is complex and obscure, but there is no clear indication as yet that democratic tendencies are sufficiently threatening to the authoritarian elites to suggest the imminence of "a Fujimora solution," but neither can such a possibility be entirely ruled out, especially if political violence associated with Kurdish militancy intensifies.[8]

The Turkish situation, then, is one of uncertainty: real, albeit limited and uneven, progress in relation to human rights and a struggle over the definition of the new rules of the game.[9] At the same time, the degree of Turkish democratization seems modest enough and under sufficient state control, to make extremely unlikely a serious challenge directed at the authoritarian underpinnings of Turkish political life in the foreseeable future.

One manifestation of the emergent Turkish tension between democratic openings and authoritarian constraints concerned human rights activities themselves. For instance, a human rights group in Turkey has been organizing an annual film festival on human rights themes, but it has not yet been allowed to include films made in Turkey or that deal with Turkey, although it presses the authorities for permission to do so. This same group publishes a daily newsletter and a yearbook summarizing human rights abuses of the government. More dramatically, the group was sponsoring torture rehabilitation centers in Istanbul, Ankara, Izmir, and was expecting to open a fourth such facility in the Kurdish southeast city of Diyarbakir. As far as I know, Turkey is the only country that *both* allows such centers *and* needs them.[10] We were told that about 200 doctors and psychiatrists were involved in the work of these centers on a voluntary basis. The intriguing question is why the Turkish state tolerates such discrediting activities and yet continues to practice torture on a widespread basis. No satisfactory answers have emerged.

II. A Quest for Legitimacy

The true rationale for democratization is rarely acknowledged by the Turkish political leadership, but must be surmised from circumstances. In Turkey's case that means a convergence of regional and global developments, as well as the mutual reinforcement of political and economic considerations. The Turkish government seeks to enhance its international reputation, first of all, to gain admission to the European Community, which in many policy and business circles is regarded as essential for Turkish success in the world economy; and, secondly, as a respected participant in wider diplomatic relationships in the Middle East and beyond. These bear especially on Turkish trade and investment prospects, as well as its capacity to serve as a role model for the newly independent Turkic states in Central Asia, formerly Soviet republics.

To achieve such results in the present European and global atmosphere seems to require evidence that Turkey is deepening its democratic experience in a number of crucial respects. A key element, in light of past takeovers by the Turkish military, is the willingness of the military to professionalize its role in Turkish society, refraining from overt interferences with civilian rule, thereby stabilizing expectations about the continuity of civilian governance and respect for party competition and electoral outcomes.[11] Sustaining civilian governance is a minimum expectation of statist legitimacy in the intermediate zone of the global hierarchy — a prerequisite for full access to purely Northern arenas of political and economic interaction.[12]

In addition to civilianization, human rights progress is required in two different respects: a commitment at the highest official levels to end gross abuses of human rights and a toleration (without harassment) of a range of human rights activities rooted in civilian society; that is, activities by citizens and political associations not subject to the direct control of the state. The Turkish political leadership appears to recognize that the litmus test of democratic credibility will be its willingness and ability to improve upon the situation of the large Kurdish minority (numbering some 12 million, but about equally divided between Kurds living throughout Turkey in varying degrees of assimilation and Kurds in southeast Turkey, where they exist as a regional majority harboring strong nationalist, ethnic, and economic aspirations and grievances), and to allow independent human rights groups to criticize the government for abuses of Kurdish rights. Both of these developments are precedent-shattering for Turkey, signifying the influence of new domestic and international factors.

Why has this quest for legitimacy accelerated in recent years? One factor is the end of the Cold War, and the falling away of any ideological adversary to market-oriented constitutionalism (other than a resurgence of religious traditionalism, an instance of what is usually called "Islamic fundamentalism"). Closely related, the collapse of the Soviet Union, and the Western tilt of the successor Russian government, removes the main external security pretext for anxiety about the quality of internal security. It also makes it more difficult to merge anti-Kurdish oppressive policies with oppressive policies directed against that portion of the internal Turkish opposition that is Marxist-oriented. Furthermore, regional and international awareness and sympathy for the Kurdish plight has been greatly increased by the developments in the Kurdish regions of northern Iraq following the Gulf War, with inevitable concern about the relationship of the various Kurdish minorities in the region, especially in contiguous Turkey with its large Kurdish population.[13]

As long as Turkey was perceived as an important NATO ally in the strategic rivalry with the Soviet Union, these human rights problems were mainly screened out by the mainstream media, by public opinion, and by Western governments. In the new setting, normative factors associated with the rule of law and public morality are perceived as more important for the stability of a country. Many scholars now believe that the Soviet collapse was connected with a terrible record of human rights abuses, and that this denial is associated in turn with its miserable economic performance.

As pointed out earlier, states in the European area are under greater democratizing pressures than in the Asian area partly because of a regional political tradition and partly because capitalist success is being correlated more directly with genuine democratization in Europe. China, North Korea, and Vietnam continue to be treated by the United States and its Asian allies as posing varying degrees of threat to regional security interests; whether these dangers are real or imagined is a complex matter, and is linked to U.S.-Japan relations and to the U.S. drive to retain its hegemonic role in the region despite the disappearance of any Soviet challenge. There is also a reluctance to raise issues of democracy and human rights given U.S. strategic relations with South Korea, Taiwan, Thailand, and Singapore, and their uneven realization of even limited democratic governance. Even by objecting to the practices of, say, Vietnam one calls attention to the comparable failures of these "friends" of the West. There are some Asian pressures to democratize, but not on a scale comparable to Europe. Furthermore, China, North Korea, and Vietnam are treated circumspectly, as regional challengers, giving security arguments in the area somewhat greater weight, particularly for South Korea and Taiwan; the economic performance of authoritarian systems in Asian settings is so dismayingly impressive as to blunt criticisms from other perspectives. Also, there is nothing comparable in Asia to the European Community, with its pretension that a shared commitment to constitutional democracy and human rights has built the foundations of a peaceful and harmonious region, that imposes formal membership criteria, a highly evolved framework for the promotion and protection of human rights, and includes a new conception of political identity based on being "European."[14] As argued earlier, much of the democratizing pressure felt by Turkey is related to the perceived economic advantages of EC membership.

In addition, the democratization imperative is reinforced by several recent variants of modernization thinking, especially in its more market-oriented forms. Individualism is an ingredient of advanced capitalism, and requires, at the very least, a range of freedoms for an expanding middle class. It also means a more cosmopolitan frame of reference as tourism, travel, and TV help shape a consumerist lifestyle that includes access to world news and freedom of choice. This sense of being modern is very central to Turkish political identity; it helped provide the foundational ideology for Turkey as an emergent post-Ottoman sovereign state in the immediate aftermath of World War I. Such an identity differentiates Turkey as secular from the main traditionalist regional alternatives.

III. Obstacles on the Road to Legitimacy

Yet not all current pressures favor further democratization within the Turkish setting. There are significant counter-pressures that confine democratic prospects, and disclose several indications that authoritarian practices are being increasingly relied upon, causing serious abuses of human rights.

Perhaps the most pervasive counter-pressure arises from the Turkish political culture, heavily laden with layers of authoritarian tradition. There is no hallowed past in Turkey that emphasizes the rights of individuals; on the contrary, there is a long imperial and militarist tradition associated with Ottoman rule that regards the people as "subjects" rather than as "citizens." Kemal Ataturk, the charismatic founding figure, glorified as the father of modern Turkey, also stood for strong central government reinforced by police and military tactics. Socialization patterns from infancy in Turkish families reinforce these authoritarian tendencies, giving political identity a rigidly patriarchal twist, conditioning leaders to subordinate women and to rely on force when opposed as an indispensable certification of their

manhood.[15] With little experience of democracy, and with Ataturk's modernism having the further effect of confining the influence of Islam to private
realms and to the rural poor, the Turkish state has operated in a virtual moral
vacuum. Turkish civil society has been weak and submissive.

This sketch of Turkish civil society helps explain the tendency of the
military to intervene, and regard themselves as more appropriate guardians of
Turkish well-being and security than "the politicians," stereotyped as indeci-
sive and venal, portrayed as bickering among themselves in the search for
influence and wealth rather than dealing effectively with the enemies of
Turkey. A country often receives the politics it deserves, and the perception
of mainstream political forces as passive and helpless in relation to this
authoritarian setting has led in the past to more fundamental political challenges directed at the established order in Turkey assuming a revolutionary
and violent form. The opposition is as likely to reflect the political culture as
are entrenched elites, and hence it is hardly surprising that revolutionary
Turkish politics has also almost always embraced militarist tactics and relied
upon an authoritarian organizational structure. Thus, political behavior
across the whole of the ideological spectrum in Turkey has tended to be
anti-democratic, especially during periods of crisis.

Another intersecting source of resistance to democratization arises from
the growth and assertiveness of a Kurdish political movement, both a militant
Kurdish opposition internal to Turkey and an even more dedicated separatist
Kurdish movement directed and guided from without. It is difficult to assess
the strength and unity of radical Kurdish oppositional forces currently challenging the Turkish status quo, and to what extent a grander vision of a
reunion of Kurdish peoples living in several countries in the region is covertly
and existentially endorsed as the real goal of Kurdish oppositional activity
even while it is overtly renounced to avoid threatening Turkish political
leaders.

Similarly, it is difficult to interpret the interactions between the PKK
(Kurdish Workers Party) and the Turkish government. Despite a clear disparity of power, both are seemingly violent, and each blames the rigidity of
the other for its refusal to work within a political and democratic framework.
In the background are Kurdish memories of oppression and atrocity, extending even to prohibitions on the use of the Kurdish language or maintaining
Kurdish traditions, as well as a long period of utter frustration in the political
domain. For the Turkish elite and public there is the essential Ataturk
insistence on territorial nationality and unity as an absolute political value,
making any separatist tendency invalid and a subversive challenge to the
sacred ethos at the core of Turkish identity. Such Turkish hyper-statism has
been reinforced by credible fears that outsiders, in the aftermath of the
Ottoman collapse, were interested in weakening Turkey by lending support
to dissident minorities dedicated, it was believed, to the dismemberment of
the Turkish state. These fears and concerns tend to reinforce a paranoid
response by both the Turkish state and majority public sentiments to Kurdish
efforts to achieve group rights and some form of internal self-determination.
This Turkish inability to comprehend the Kurdish movement in non-

maximalist terms is seemingly having a self-fulfilling impact, driving many Kurdish moderates to despair or convincing them that only Kurdish extremism can achieve results. Hence, as is common in such circumstances, a vicious circle is generated, with each party to the conflict feeling that their worst apprehensions of the other are being vindicated.

Finally, the Turkish security establishment has remained in place, occupying the commanding bureaucratic heights within state structures, and has not been supplanted by more democratic orientations. An essential insight of Leninism is the extreme difficulty of reforming state policy without destroying the old state apparatus and replacing its personnel. The Turkish state has not been transformed by democratic tendencies, which have only achieved a marginal and precarious relationship to Turkish political style and identity.

IV. The Turkish Compromise

Regardless of motivation at elite levels, Turkish moves toward democratization have, temporarily at least, created new political space for initiatives rooted in civil society. More convincingly than in the past, Turkish political leaders have allowed, and even encouraged, these developments without being confronted by a strong prospect of direct military interference. Indeed, if the Turkish military were to take over from the elected leaders in the months ahead, it would be perceived as a serious blow to Turkey's reputation, and would effectively end any hope of closer affiliation with the European Community for the foreseeable future.[16] At the same time, if high levels of political violence were to persist in Turkey, and if Kurdish militancy is regarded by both the public and security forces as a serious threat to the unity of the Turkish state, explicitly authoritarian policies could be expected to re-emerge. If the politicians did not effectively support such developments, a military takeover, including the suspension of elections and even martial law, would be likely, and, what is more, would be welcomed by the mainstream media and by the majority of Turkish citizens. It is this authoritarian climate that draws on both the bureaucratic prominence of security forces and the particular Ataturk-Ottoman heritage that continues to form the basis of Turkish political identity and dominates Turkish political culture. Such a heritage sets Turkey apart from such other superficially similar cases as Chile, the Philippines, even Egypt and Mexico. For these reasons, the democratization project seems especially important to carry forward in Turkey, hopefully far enough to exert a real impact upon evolving Turkish political culture. For the present, however, democratization in Turkey, although impressive, remains particularly vulnerable to collapse, and reversal.

At this time, there exists an implicit compromise between what might be called "the government" and "the state" in Turkey: the elected civilian government is committed to pushing ahead with the democratization project, but it refuses to challenge the permanent bureaucratic apparatus of the state that embodies the authoritarian heritage and engages in oppressive practices that are not effectively challenged.[17] The alliances of big business bear significantly on this relationship between government and state in Turkey, but seem currently ambivalent on issues of democratization in the face of a rising Kurdish challenge.

In one crucial respect, the Turkish compromise obviates the need for the military to intervene explicitly in the political process. Whether such tactics succeed in the longer run depends on whether the Turkish government can sell the world on the story that the Kurdish movement is basically a terrorist challenge directed at the stability of the state and whether the Kurdish people can mount a sufficient non-violent challenge that is differentiated from the PKK and that cannot be ignored.[18]

V. A Concluding Note

Will the Turkish compromise work in Turkey? Is it present to varying degrees in other countries? Such questions are forms of inquiry about the depth and sustainability of the turn toward democracy and human rights by many countries in recent years. Is this turn superficial and temporary, or can it be strengthened and made cumulative in its effects? Market and statist forces are ambivalent, caught between their convictions that some degree of civilianization and democratization is necessary for economic growth and stability, and their deep-seated distrust of the people and populist politics, especially in Third World conditions where class consciousness is inevitably strong and basic needs of the vast majority are not being met. A crucial factor is the transnationalization of civil society and democratization. In this regard, the fate of the Helsinki Citizens Assembly on a regional level and in relation to its Turkish presence has crucial symbolic significance.[19] Only by establishing social forces committed to democracy and human rights can the debilitating effects of the Turkish compromise be effectively challenged through creating countervailing forces to those mounted by the security establishment and its media and business allies. It is evident that traditional radical opposition, based on armed struggle and resistant to negotiated compromises, has never worked in Turkey. Whether this emergent approach to democratization can over time achieve a mass base that is able to challenge and defeat authoritarianism in Turkey, and elsewhere, remains to be seen.

What is here described in a Turkish setting is being replicated to varying degrees elsewhere. This pattern of accommodating democratizing pressures without genuinely supplanting authoritarian structures and practices is surprisingly widespread, suggesting structural factors at a global level. Each instance is significantly distinctive, yet there are also wider trends taking place. Successes and failures in one place influence the political learning in other places. And it is not only elites that learn, it is also social movements of resistance and transformation. It is a main task of progressive intellectuals throughout the world to help identify the political space to strengthen genuine democratizing tendencies in various specific circumstances. The future of democracy — as an outcome of pressures from below — is increasingly dependent on transnational contributions to indigenous efforts.

There is reason to consider the particular problems associated with democratizing previously authoritarian states, especially when the challenge to authoritarianism has taken the form of a mutual accomodation. As the Turkish example highlights, the accommodation may be very limited in its effects, especially if the political culture reinforces authoritarian practices and sensibilities. The successful transition to democracy may begin with the acceptance of rituals and mechanisms — elections and parties — but it will remain superficial, and essentially irrelevant to those most victimized, until it addresses directly and effectively both state violence and minority grievances.

Notes

1. Francis Fukuyama, "The End of History?" *The National Interest* 16:3–18 (1989); for the longer argument see Fukuyama, *The End of History and the Last Man* (New York: Free Press, 1992).
2. For a vivid account see Victoria Brittain, *Hidden Lives, Hidden Deaths: South Africa's Crippling of a Continent* (Boston: Faber and Faber, 1988).
3. C.f. the parallel discussion of "low intensity democracy" as pertaining to five illustrative countries by Barry Gills and Joel Rocamora, "Low Intensity Democracy," University of Sheffield, Sheffield Papers in International Studies, No. 11, 1992, 39 pp.; for an influential and illuminating analysis of the U.S. role in promoting cosmetic democracy while opposing more authentic expressions of political democracy, especially in North/South contexts, see Noam Chomsky, *Deterring Democracy* (New York: Hill & Wang, paper edition, 1992); valuable analysis is found in Eqbal Ahmad's essay, "The Neo-Fascist State: Notes on the Pathology of Power in the Third World," in Falk, Samuel S. Kim, and Saul H. Mendlovitz, eds., *Toward a Just World Order* (Boulder, Colo.: Westview, 1982), 74–83. For conservative skepticism about U.S. promotion of "democracy" in foreign policy see Graham E. Fuller, *The Democracy Trap: Perils of the Post-Cold War World* (New York: Dutton, 1991). For country studies that disclose patterns of deep authoritarianism, see Alicia Ely-Yamin, "Justice Corrupted, Justice Denied: Unmasking the Untouchables of the Mexican Federal Judicial Police," paper of The Mexico Project, World Policy Institute, New York, November 20, 1992; R. William Liddle, "Indonesia's Threefold Challenge," *Democracy* 3:60–74 (1992).
4. In other words, this pattern challenges the creative capacities of authoritarian forces far more than did the long-standing pressures exerted by the United States on its Third World allies in Cold War settings to establish the formalistic electoral trappings of democracy, but no more; this earlier pattern was manifest in the U.S. relationship to South Vietnam during the Vietnam War, especially during Lyndon Johnson's presidency (1963–1968), and seemed characteristic of democratizing pressures placed by the Reagan administration on the leadership of El Salvador in the 1980s.
5. Even the Reagan administration was "embarrassed" by death squad activity in "democratic" El Salvador, but bipartisan aid kept flowing from the United States because of the trappings of formal democracy, the anti-Marxist orientation of the Duarte government, and above all, the Cold War logic of treating local political struggles as matters of strategic relevance to the East/West balance.
6. I recall a conversation in April 1990 with human rights lawyers in the Filipino city of Ilo-Ilo in which the claim was made that it was more dangerous for them to defend human rights in the Aquino period than during the time of more blatant authoritarianism that characterized Marcos' rule. The contention was that Marcos controlled the armed forces from the center, set the rules of the game, whereas Aquino was unable to impose limits, giving a far freer rein to local militarist pressures that were more drastic and less predictable.
7. If the quantum becomes unsafe, then the possibility exists of either an overt reversal of direction, as occurred in Peru, or as an encouraging erosion of authoritarian influence as some observers contend is happening in Chile during the early 1990s; the experience of radical democratization in the Gorbachev era is instructive, unleashing forces within the bloc that could not be contained, spilling over to engulf Gorbachev himself.
8. Temporary takeovers of government by the military have been a staple feature of Turkish political life during the Cold War, occurring in 1960, 1971, and 1980, but whether the military is still potentially inclined to set such crude limits on the political process is unknown. For an analysis arguing that the military in Turkey is no longer inclined to play such a role see Metin Heper, "Consolidating Turkish Democracy," *Democracy*, 3:105–117, at 114, 1992. The argument here is that post-Cold War moves toward democratization are deeper, offering more hope, harder to derail, and are increasingly linked to a successful accommodation with the world economy, especially in the European setting.
9. Heper also stresses the democratizing effects of a more assertive legislative branch, offsetting to a

degree the emergence of a strong presidential system with close ties to the military and the internal security apparatus; see note 8, 107–09.

10. Denmark, for instance, has long maintained such a center, but for victims of torture elsewhere.

11. As already mentioned, Heper claims that the Turkish military leadership is itself disillusioned by its efforts to shape Turkish politics, and is more inclined to disavow its past role as guardian of the Ataturk state, opting instead for professionalism and low visibility; note 8, 106–07.

12. Such expectations are lower for countries without First World aspirations, as in sub-Saharan Africa; Chile's recent expression of interest in becoming a part of the enlarged NAFTA framework is indicative of its intention to qualify for formal linkage to the First World; notably, The Report of the South Commission linked positive development in the Third World with a democratizing dynamic: "Democratic institutions and popular participation in decision-making are . . . essential to genuine development. Only when there is effective political freedom can the people's interests become paramount within nations. The people must be able to determine the system of government, who forms their government, and in broad terms what the government does in their name and on their behalf. Respect for human rights, the rule of law, and the possibility to change governments through peaceful means are among the basic constituents of a democratic polity." *The Challenge to the South* (Oxford: Oxford University Press, 1990), 11–12; appropriately, the South Commission's conception of democracy is not tied to the market and to privatization, whereas, for the Turkish elite, it is their preoccupation with market success that makes them willing to embrace democratic forms in a largely instrumental spirit.

13. Recent events involving Iraqi Kurds fighting side-by-side with Turkish security forces against the Kurdish guerrilla presence in Iraq dramatically confirm the impression that there is not a single Kurdish political movement, but that statist affiliations and ideological orientations may be more important than Kurdish solidarity in certain circumstances. Chris Hedges, "An Odd Alliance Subdues Turkey's Kurdish Rebels," *New York Times*, November 24, 1992.

14. On the other hand, some countries seeking foreign investment and international credit feel pressures of a comparable character — the Philippines is a good illustration; during Aquino's six years of presidency there were seven attempted military coups, suggesting both the precariousness of even minimum democracy and the difficulty of achieving civilianization.

15. Even now, women play only minor roles in Turkish political life, although this too is changing somewhat as a result of democratizing pressures from within and without.

16. With the collapse of the Soviet Union, Turkey is both released as a security partner and given an option to exert influence over the Turkic former republics, new Central Asian states; there is speculation that pursuing such an option is not dependent on deepening democracy, and could relieve the kind of pressure that arises from the view that Turkish economic growth depends on its ability to form a part of the new Europe; political obstacles to the European direction may also be arising in this post-Cold War period in the form of racist tensions expressed by way of anti-Turkish violence in Germany and genocidal tactics against the Muslim population in Bosnia.

17. Terminology here is not entirely satisfactory. One might alternatively distinguish that portion of the state or government that is civilian and elected from that portion that is not. Because the authoritarian behavior is not fully admitted, it is difficult to evaluate.

18. For instance, a Kurdish "*intifada*" in the southeast that captures worldwide attention, and renders more transparent Turkish reliance on state violence to destroy democratic practices and demands by a large, victimized minority. It should not be overlooked that the Kurdish people — those who have not been assimilated — continue in many settings to be denied even the right to speak Kurdish or to celebrate Kurdish holidays; that is, the level of oppression is blatant and extreme, and in direct violation of minimum international human rights standards.

19. The HCA recently formed a Turkish chapter, whose work focuses on opposing the government's authoritarian practices and supporting Kurdish rights, while obeying the restrictions of Turkey's current democratic game.

2

Redefining Non-Alignment:
The Global South in the New Global Equation

Clovis Maksoud

As the rumblings of glasnost and perestroika were sending shockwaves throughout Eastern Europe, the democratic project, both in the former Soviet Union and in Eastern Europe, began to show signs of resilience and irreversibility. From then onwards this was reflected in the growing congeniality of relations between the United States and the Soviet Union, manifesting itself in cooperation between the superpowers within and outside the United Nations. The process of democratization in Eastern Europe, and growing signs of introversion in the former Soviet Union gave rise to a sharper contradiction between North and South; replacing the endemic tensions between East and West. The Global South, otherwise known during the Cold War as the Third World, welcomed the surge of freedom in Eastern Europe, but sensed that its margin of maneuver on the world scene and influence in the United Nations was being gradually reduced and eroded. The policy known as Non-Alignment was, on the level of essence, becoming less relevant, while the motives and objectives of the movement continued to be necessary, constructive, and useful. This undoubtedly necessitated a restatement of the policy in a manner that would emphasize South-South relations and recast the South in a way that would enable it to withstand the transitional phase in which international relations were being constructed after the Cold War.

For this reason, it was premature to describe what was taking place, as President Bush did in the euphoria of triumphalism after the Gulf War, as the "New World Order." A more precise description would be that what was emerging was a new global equation; a term which avoids rendering a moral judgement on an emerging situation. Needless to say, this equation has given rise to new political prescriptions and economic panaceas, setting in motion ethnic and sectarian developments that, while affirming self-determination, have also brought in civil strife, ethnic antagonisms and untold human tragedies. This is why the term "order" is misplaced; equally the question must be asked whether this global equation can be called "new" at a time when we have witnessed a revival of ethnic medievalism and early colonial tendencies and developments.

While the Cold War froze some of these negative tendencies, the fragmentation that followed the fall of communism demonstrated the flaws and vulnerability of the "democrats." This led to a fall back on ethnic and absolutist concepts of nationalism that brought in their wake the destruction of many civil societies and the breakdown of long established communities. As in former Yugoslavia, in Georgia, Azerbaijan, Armenia, and other regions, crisis management became complex and costly. In many instances the United Nations had to be involved, which meant that its peacekeeping functions had to be redefined. While the enforcement measures used during the Gulf crisis were authorized by the UN Security Council, as in its Resolution 678 on November 29, 1990 authorizing the use of force, the subsequent implementation of the resolutions were not undertaken by the UN itself. The looseness of language in some of these resolutions allowed exclusive interpretations by the Western powers, as the countervailing role of the Soviet Union no longer existed.

Of course, the end of the Cold War made the UN Security Council more operational and active; yet with the new global equation, a perception that the U.S. was setting the agenda became widespread. There was evidence of growing Western assertiveness. This led the Global South to treat the UN Security Council more as an adversary rather than a protector. Perhaps this perception was overblown, and in certain instances gave rise to exaggerated and unreasonable anxieties; the fact remains, however, that a measure of alienation developed which in turn increased the intensity of the already existing North-South tensions.

To the countries of the Global South, the Western powers' historic shift — from their dismissal of the UN during the Cold War, ignoring its resolutions for more than a quarter of a century, to their sudden celebration of the UN's new role, and their need to dominate its proceedings and deliberations — was, to put it mildly, dizzying. We were and still are, it seems, witnessing the pains of adjustment; some adjustments might appear unrelated while others could lead to rational reorganization within the framework of the Global South.

Evidence of oddity falls into the realm of political and psychological reflexes existent, but not necessarily inherent, in any process of adjustment. They express themselves in defiance; acceptance of defeats but never of surrender, coping with being humbled but rejecting humiliation. Perhaps this explains the phenomenon, for example, of Saddam Hussein's sustained defiance and the Global South's general reaction to it. While most of the Arab world and the Global South condemned the coerciveness of Hussein's regime — its blatant and obvious violations of human rights, its bloody and useless war against Iran, its invasion of Kuwait, and its obliviousness to prevailing realities and opinions — the Arabs and the people of the Global South profoundly resented the haughtiness of Western diktat, the clear double standards, and the West's dealing with Hussein's infractions as if more eager to project hegemonic power in the region than to correct the infractions and redress the actual grievances.

This resentment was reinforced by the crude exploitation of Iraq's intransigence to bolster the fortunes of political leaders in the U.S. and other Western powers.[1] Even when this alleged opportunism was categorically denied there was in the background sufficient historical experience to justify some of the Global South's wild and perhaps farfetched conclusions; i.e., Iran/contra, the "failed policy" which President Bush admitted towards Iraq prior to the invasion of Kuwait, etc. The chasm that has existed between the West and the Global South has, in many instances, been exacerbated by a Western discourse oblivious to Southern sensitivities, concerns, and dignity. It is this power consciousness that has permeated Western parlance, and lent credence to the assumption that the West is against the rights, aspirations, and interests of the Global South. This in turn has clogged the channels of communication between the West and the South, and at times interrupted consequential dialogue, introducing obstacles to a genuine understanding and balanced relations. True, mastery of the technological revolution by Western — especially U.S. — media has rendered Western terms of reference prevalent and at times dominant. These terms, however, should not be considered as if they have been readily accepted or necessarily approved. In many instances the asymmetry in communication capabilities has pushed political elites in the South to recoil into cultural assertiveness for fear of being easily coopted; thus leading to a tendency — maybe a trend — to mystify historical roots as a means of compensating for technical inability and the paucity of access to the most advanced and empowering scientific and technological opportunities. It follows that the political constituency in many countries of the Global South has become susceptible to movements that seek to fill their lives with pride while knowledge declines.

Inequality in any form, and in most circumstances, is a prescription for the insurrection of the spirit. In such an atmosphere, extreme ethnic and/or religious fundamentalist approaches find fertile ground and hit a responsive chord. What follows is a dethronement of reason and a concomitant absence of scrutiny and accountability. Many sectors of the population become mesmerized by the challenge to their collective sense of dignity rather than acquire a collective commitment to struggle for their human rights. A derailment of energies follows and the chances for a thorough advancement diminish. The Global South, although conscious of its predicament has found itself in the grip of false choices, unable to converse with the West — and North — or to cooperate on equitable terms, and thus pushed to confrontation, only to be penalized or ostracized.

While the Global South has been grappling with this predicament, the North has been preoccupied with reconstituting its broader framework, reasserting its primacy and harnessing the consequences of a new and enlarged, albeit turbulent, Europe. In pursuing this endeavor, the North has been dealing with problems that are similar and, as in the case of Yugoslavia, identical to those facing many Southern societies. These problems, however, are far more acute in the South. This is not to underestimate the seriousness of the fragmentation that took place in the former USSR and Eastern Europe, but to highlight the sense of *instant* responsibility that the West felt towards its eastern counterpart, while responsibility towards the Global South has remained distant, patronizing, and selective. The South thus has found itself in a transformed world, echoing policies of the past that, while redundant and repetitive, have remained relevant and useful at a fundamental level. These policies, however, need to be restated in a manner indicating that they have been updated and are being practiced in different circumstances and conditions.

The policies of Non-Alignment were the product of the South's will to exercise independent judgement over and above enjoying the fruits of independence from colonial and imperial rule. Non-alignment became the policy direction of developing countries as they sought to expand the area of peace and avoid being coopted into either the U.S.-led Western bloc or the Soviet-led Eastern bloc. While not belonging to an organized "third force," non-aligned countries considered their position as contributing to relaxing international tensions, enabling them access to both superpowers, and signaling that the countries of the Global South would not forfeit their new freedom to accommodate the logic and requirements of the Cold War. What the Non-Aligned Movement assumed was that the imperatives of the Cold War, in terms of military priorities, invariably hampered the urgent needs for expeditious economic development.

This assumption was correct, but the readiness to act accordingly was not uniform among all non-aligned states. Pivotal states in the Non-Aligned Movement, such as India, Egypt, Indonesia, and Yugoslavia during the 1950s and 1960s, could not prevent cracks in the movement as they began to surface in the 1970s due, in part, to a loosening of the criteria of non-alignment which enabled, for example, Saudi Arabia and Cuba to be included, and to the concomitant amorphousness that ensued. The strains within the movement that followed eroded its effectiveness and weakened its credibility. Despite these handicaps, non-alignment continued to provide countries that adhered to it a sense of association and solidarity that proved serviceable, sustaining a modicum of mobility on the world stage and thus exercising a restraining influence on the dangers of a bi-polar world.

With the removal of the Soviet Union as a counterbalance to the U.S., the bipolar world began to be replaced by what is termed a unipolar system. This description, logical on the surface, is not precise. The new global equation that followed the fall of communism and the breakdown of the Soviet Union is more complex. The question of whether the world has become unipolar could only be asked if we assume that the previous system was exclusively a bipolar one. True, if the possession of overwhelming nuclear and long range missiles are the primary determinants of what constitute a "pole," then we must all acquiesce to this definition. It was this outlandish acquiescence that rendered the Non-Aligned Movement insistent on convening a Summit Conference in September 1992 in Indonesia, although many recognized it might be necessary to change the term "non-alignment" as it was no longer applicable (see below). However, the bonds of similarity of conditions, interests and objectives render the need for an ongoing grouping essential and crucial. Most of the non-aligned countries are all in the Global South and from this optic their status in the world is distinct and distinguishable from the profound and substantial changes taking place in the Global North.

In the early days of non-alignment, the countries that subscribed to it were emerging from Western hegemony, fulfilling long denied national rights and aspirations. To most of these countries, the West was associated with capitalist exploitation of their resources, raw material and economic potential. Nationalist movements considered the process of decolonization to be simultaneously one of freedom from capitalist control. But while independence from the West was the paramount motivating force, there was no inclination — indeed there was prevailing rejection — to fall under the control of the Soviet Union, economically, militarily, or ideologically.

India's Jawaharlal Nehru, trained in the Western liberal tradition and also a socialist, was the principal architect of the policy of non-alignment. India, the backbone and pioneer of non-alignment, persuaded other newly independent countries to join the movement. The term "non-alignment" did not mean neutrality; it was distinct in that it adhered to an objectivity of judgement. Non-alignment could be neutral, but neutrality was not inherent. It was a political concept that consciously chose to remain separate from the spheres of influence of both Western and Soviet blocs. In this sense it was an outer projection of an inner search for direction; insisting on an independent ideological judgement, i.e., socialism with varying democratic structures. Non-alignment was an activist, judgmental policy, aligned with — when necessary — progressive, democratizing forces within both blocs, and seeking economic policies that enhanced the role of the public sector but not to the exclusion of the private sector.

The Bandung Conference of April 1955 prefaced the Non-Aligned Movement, accentuated cooperation between African and Asian countries, and highlighted the need to find peaceful solutions to tensions within the two regions, the Pauch Sheel. The conference expressed its concern with poverty, and decided to pressure for the rapid decolonization of Africa. It also upheld a position to maintain relations with both superpowers.

Krushchev's ascendance to power reduced the tension that had built up between the Soviet Union and the Non-Aligned Movement under Stalin; prompting the U.S. to reevaluate its position as well. The late 1950s and early 1960s saw a tacit recognition of the movement by the two superpowers, in contrast to their earlier contempt. The rise in the political stature of non-alignment was accompanied by an increase in membership as most African countries, upon achieving independence, joined; Latin American countries showed increased interest and participation. Of particular importance was the ideological difference within the movement that came to the fore at the 1961 Belgrade conference. Nasser and Tito wanted to see a strict and refined definition of "non-alignment," while Nehru maintained that it should be a looser and more open concept. It was this latter view that prevailed, and opened the movement to a variety of members, making it increasingly difficult to articulate coherent overall policy objectives.

The influence of the Non-Aligned Movement in the 1960s began to manifest itself in the UN General Assembly. India became a key player as neither East nor West would trust each other on sensitive political issues. Although the U.S. and the Soviet Union respected the independent role of the movement, both wanted to intrude on it by creating alliances within it. This became manifest in the 1962 conflict between India and China. China's attack on India related to its desire to play the dominant role in the movement, although it was not a member. Despite Nasser's successful mediation between the two countries, India's position within the movement was substantially weakened by these events, and was further eroded by the war between India and Pakistan in 1965. Egypt began to play a more central role in the movement, and the development of a more radical and Africanized consciousness of non-alignment focused on Israel as the projection of the West in the Middle East, and on the eradication of apartheid in South Africa. In Asia, the political focus became internalized as the region struggled with its developmental problems and regional conflicts.

In the 1970s, the NAM receded as a global movement, but maintained a position of strength within the UN General Assembly, using this forum to articulate independent judgements on a variety of issues. This decade represented non-alignment's peak of moral influence, but also the beginning of the erosion of the concept itself. There were several reasons for this. Central was the inclusiveness of the definition. Attempts to synchronize diverse interests resulted in watering down policy decisions to such a degree that they became vague, redundant, and at times meaningless.

The prevailing ideological orientation sought by the movement was to align with the progressive and sympathetic forces within the two blocs, seeking to liberalize communism, while at the same time making capitalist societies more socially conscious and sensitized to Third World problems and concerns. It was hoped that such an evolutionary process would result in a convergence of interests including a commitment to freedom, equality and human rights. The proliferation of non-aligned members resulted, however, in a loss of focus and vitality of purpose. The 1980s saw the position of the Non-Aligned Movement reduced still further, as the UN began to lose influence in world affairs; especially during President Reagan's administrations.

After the collapse of communism in the Eastern bloc and the Soviet Union, the Non-Aligned Movement had to reassess its position in world politics, and to question its relevance in a new global equation. It was in this context, then, that the Tenth Summit of Non-Aligned Countries was held in Jakarta on September 1–6, 1992. In many ways the summit was the last hurrah of a movement that united developing countries at a time when the bipolar system sought to determine and dominate their policies and destinies. The terms "non-alignment" and "Third World" are no longer germane to the discourse in the new global equation. The motives and objectives that impelled the developing countries to act together, however, remain valid and relevant. Changes in the international order have rendered a regrouping of the developing countries necessary and a redefinition of their purpose inevitable. The summit was a significant effort in this direction. In the Summit Declaration the leaders of 128 states affirmed that the next era in international relations would be determined by the North-South paradigm, as opposed to the old East-West Cold War axis. And indeed, while an attachment to the term "non-alignment" has persisted, it is more a lingering nostalgia, circumventing the immediate need for a semantic and psychological adjustment to new and emerging realities. In fact, the Jakarta Declaration implicitly recognized the dawn of a new era, in which the terms "Third World" and "non-aligned" have been subsumed by the term "Global South."

Historically, the sense of collective consciousness that imbued the Non-Aligned Movement was prompted by a determination to remain distinct and apart from the Western and Soviet blocs. The same consciousness has continued as the countries of the Global South seek to remain immune from the hegemonic propensities within the new unipolar system. The Jakarta Declaration articulated the anxieties of the developing countries by stating that "the dominance of a few countries, which has become prominent, could result in further inequities, uncertainties and instabilities. The failure to redress the widening gap between the affluent North and the impoverished South is looming as the central issue that could threaten international security and stability."

The Jakarta Summit recognized the changed contours of the international landscape. On the one hand, the leaders of the Non-Aligned Movement showed themselves eager to avoid precipitating any unnecessary confrontations with the North. On the other hand, they underlined a multitude of legitimate grievances, both political and economic, nurtured by patterns of patronizing behavior and insensitive policies. In a strategy that reflected these new realities, the summit leaders sought to deter Northern hegemony by advocating a strengthened and more powerful United Nations. In particular, they called for enhancing the powers of the secretary general and restoring the authority of the General Assembly. The exercise of excessive power by the Security Council, leading to unacceptable imbalances in the international order, was a matter of explicit concern.

It was no surprise that the summit should have called for a formula to redress the imbalances within the UN system, and to ensure that the countries of the South restore to themselves a credible and effective collective solidarity. The summit sought a breathing space — a measured distance from the North — to allow the countries of the Global South to set their own agendas and to negotiate their economic and developmental priorities without being forced into suffocating strategic and economic dependencies on the developed North.

The goal was to fashion a strategy which avoided confrontation but put the dialogue with the North on firmer ground. The Declaration stated that "the Heads of State or Government were of the view that, as an indispensable corollary to the North and South context, some South-South cooperation based on the concept of collective self-reliance must also be intensified. [This cooperation] not only opens up new avenues for growth and reduces undue dependence vis-a-vis the North, but also constitutes an integral element of any strategy towards the restructuring of international economic cooperation. They emphasized that success in South-South cooperation will lend greater credibility and added strength to efforts in obtaining a new, more rational and equitable international economic order . . . The South needs the resources, markets and technology of the North to realize its development aspirations. The developed countries cannot be the sole engine of growth for the world economy, particularly in the context of recessionary conditions."

The developing South has shown itself fully cognizant of its economic and political potentialities and liabilities. Recognition and articulation of these factors imparted a certain historical significance to the Jakarta Summit. For these reasons alone the gathering deserved more serious attention from the media and political establishments in the North. The South's insistence on recovering its independence of judgement and its own terms of reference has become evident. The legacy of forty years of non-alignment reinforces this determination, manifest in the movement's assertion of independence from the bipolar system of power. The Global South's distinct and independent position provides a means to share in the construction of a genuinely interdependent world, thus avoiding the debilitating consequences of perpetuated dependencies on the North. We may be witnessing the end of non-alignment as the term becomes outdated; yet, the Jakarta Summit may have signaled the beginning of the mobilization of the peoples and nations of the Global South.

Perhaps this is the time to explain more precisely what we mean by "Global South," and to define its quest for a consequential presence on the world stage in order to respond to the legitimate demands and requirements of the peoples and societies that constitute it.

It is obvious that the terms "non-alignment" and "Third World" are no longer descriptive of the South; the motives and the conditions that led these countries to consider themselves as parts of a "Third World" were due to a conviction that they were clearly distinct from the two worlds led by the two superpowers. What the term the "Third World" meant to these countries was that they, as newly independent states, were both an integral part of the world, and also independent of the two hegemonic military blocs that repeatedly sought to dominate the global scene. The insistence on being distinct from these two "worlds" was not a declaration of separation from them, but a declaration of independence in dealing and interacting with them. For this reason, as we have observed, the policy of non-alignment was pursued and both terms, non-alignment and Third World, were inextricably linked. Now the changes in the overall world situation require a more appropriate term — the Global South — in order to define, in more precise terms, the context of the international situation and the proper juxtaposition of regional groupings.

The Earth Summit in Rio in June 1992 underlined clearly the new relationship between the North and South, with the Group of 77[2] playing a pivotal role in rallying the countries of the South, based on common concerns in the economic, environmental, developmental and social arenas. A definition of the South was spelled out:

Three and a half billion people, three-quarters of humanity, live in the developing
countries of the South. These countries vary greatly in size, in levels of development, in economic, social and political structures. Yet they share a fundamental
trait; they exist on the periphery of the developed countries of the North. Most of
their people are poor; their economies are mostly weak and defenseless; they are
generally powerless in the world arena.[3]

It is noticeable that the most distinguishable characteristic of the South is
that the large majority of humankind live in the developing South. The term
"developing" indicates a process of catching up with levels obtainable but not
achieved; of opportunities available but in most instances denied or fore-
closed; of potentialities existent but, either deliberately or through neglect,
unexplored. What a South consciousness seeks is to address the urgent need
to accelerate the pace of South-South relations in order to interface with the
industrial North in a manner that prevents the divisiveness inherent in the
proliferation of regional political, strategic and economic dependencies.
What follows is a requirement that the countries of the South should project
the South as a collective grouping on the global scene. The Non-Aligned
Movement thus becomes subsumed in the Global South. This is the *new* that
emerges in international relations.

Although the term Global South connotes a broad geographic area of
former colonial and presently developing countries, this does not mean that
within the Global South there are no pockets of affluence and developmental
achievement akin to those in the North. Similarly in the North there are to be
found pockets of poverty, of disenfranchised populations and institutional
and social decay. Having stated this proviso, and the fact the South is fully
aware of this reality, it remains necessary, however, that the Global South
continue to be defined as a distinct and distinguishable group of nations and
societies.

But what about areas which, prior to the collapse of the Soviet Union,
were integrated within its superpower framework, only to be revealed as
fragments of an empire with many facets of vulnerability, impoverishment,
untutored and frustrated ethnic tendencies? Are they to be included in the
Global South? There is also yet another category of states and societies which
objectively fit into the broad definition of the South but are reluctant to be
included, except on their own terms as a "leader," i.e., China; or eager to be
considered fully part of the North but unable because of cultural and religious restraints, i.e., Turkey.

While China and Turkey might be gray zones in the North-South divide,
the issue concerning the newly independent Central Asian Republics remains
an issue that should be addressed in light of their special circumstances as well
as their socio-economic conditions, which in many aspects are similar to
those obtaining in the countries of the Global South.

Positing the Global South in an emerging new equation requires an
understanding of the dynamics of change that the international community is
undergoing. These changes are either sudden or expected. The sudden
changes require that the nations of the Global South construct mechanisms
that provide them with the ability to mesh the expected with the sudden. In

other words, we must be cognizant of the reality that in the new global equation the sudden must be expected. This should not be too difficult, as most of the changes — both sudden and expected — continue to take place in the North. This in turn has engaged the North in what might be described as "North-centrism." What follows is a growing realization that the characteristic Northern propensity to marginalize the Global South has acquired a life of its own. This became inevitable as the oppressive regimes in both the Soviet Union and Yugoslavia collapsed, unleashing xenophobic forces whose paramountcy destroyed the glue that preserved the aspects of their civil societies (however coercively).

The preoccupation of the Western powers with this complex series of problems, in addition to the economic dislocations that free market economies have brought about, has rendered the treatment of critical problems in the Global South secondary, to be neglected if not ignored. Thus, while the North has sought to get its eastern house in order, the Global South has been slow in doing the same.

The South, however, must not allow the North's indifference and neglect to prevent it from developing and promoting its own agenda in the new global equation, whether this takes place through a rejuvenated Non-Aligned Movement, through the United Nations, or by other means. Ultimately, if co-existence was the optimum objective during the Cold War, co-discovery between North and South should become the inspiring incentive for genuinely new international relations.

Notes

1. *New York Times*, August 16, 1992.
2. The Group of 77 (G77 — which now numbers 124) came into being during the United Nations Conference on Trade and Development, held in Geneva in 1964. The G77 "sprang to prominence in the 1970s with the onset of the New International Economic Order (NIEO) negotiations . . . (it) is the central instrument through which the developing countries have attempted to transform international regimes in trade and payments. The G77 not only articulates and aggregates the interests of over 100 countries, it also functions as the principal collective negotiating instrument of the developing world in international development diplomacy." Marc Williams, *Third World Cooperation: The Group of 77 in UNCTAD* (New York: St. Martin's Press, 1991) p. 1.
3. *The Challenge to the South: An Overview and Summary of the South Commission Report* (New York: Oxford University Press, 1990) p. 1.

3

Command and Control:
Politics and Power in the Post-Cold War
United Nations

Phyllis Bennis

From its 1990 star turn in the buildup to the Gulf War, the United Nations has remained a central figure in Washington's foreign policy. Part independent player, part multifaceted tool of U.S. diplomacy, the international organization has served as a forum for winning both support (coerced or not) and legitimacy (however legally shaky) for U.S. goals ranging from Desert Storm to the anti-Libya embargo to sending the Marines to Somalia to the fierce missile attacks against Iraq in the last days of the Bush administration.

With the organization's prominence in the new world order reaffirmed by the punishing ceasefire it imposed on Iraq, the UN became mirror as well as venue for the vast changes sweeping the world. When the Soviet flag was pulled down for the last time at UN headquarters in New York, no one challenged the new Russian Federation's announcement that it was taking over its predecessor's veto-wielding seat on the Security Council. With Cold War gridlock a thing of the past, U.S. vetoes (let alone any by the subordinate powers of the "Perm Five," Britain, France, China or Russia) ended in May 1990.

President Bush's emphasis on the UN's significance, so starkly contrary to Reagan's dismissive, often condemnatory attitude towards the world body, reflects Washington's goal of creating an international consensus (or the illusion thereof) to legitimate its international domination. The U.S. claim remains based on its unchallenged military-strategic superiority; while Japan and the EC, especially Germany, compete with it economically, U.S. strategic superiority remains undisputed.

Double Standards

That superiority also ensured Washington's power to determine not only how, but whether and when the world organization would respond to emerging crises. In the two years following the Gulf War, the accusations of Western and especially U.S. double standards, not a new issue but newly public, became a permanent cloud hovering over the UN. When Iraq violated international law with its invasion of Kuwait, the U.S. took the UN to war to reverse the wrong and punish Baghdad. When even questionable allegations arose regarding Libyan involvement in the terrorist attack on Pan Am flight 103 over Lockerbie, the U.S. rammed through punishing sanctions against the Arab state.

But other countries, including Serbia and most notably Israel, violated UN resolutions with impunity, including Security Council demands that carry the force of international law, and the U.S. did nothing, and allowed the UN to do nothing, to enforce them.

When the crisis in Somalia saturated Western television screens in the summer of 1992, the Security Council finally did take action. But the UN deployment of 500 Pakistani peacekeeping troops was far too small and its mandate far too limited to accomplish anything against the civil war and famine ravaging Somalia. The Council members, including the most powerful, did nothing to ensure the deployment would be able to function. To no one's surprise, it failed — and provided a dramatic triumph-by-contrast to the U.S. Marines' media-enshrined landing at Mogadishu six months later.

The double standard showed up even more overtly when Israel expelled over 400 Palestinians to a no-man's-land on the border of Israel's self-styled "security zone" in south Lebanon in December 1992. Washington prevented the inclusion of any enforcement mechanism in the Council resolution condemning the expulsions and demanding that Israel allow them to return. At first Tel Aviv ignored the demand. Then, faced with unexpected Lebanese resistance and widespread international condemnation of Israel, Washington jumped to orchestrate a "compromise." Israel announced it would allow 110 of the exiles to return right away, the other 300 in one year. President Clinton's Secretary of State Warren Christopher announced the arrangement during his first appearance at the United Nations in February 1993, claiming that the expulsion of 300 instead of 400 for one year instead of two somehow was "consistent" with the Council resolution's explicit demand to allow the *immediate* return of *all* expellees.

The deal included a U.S. promise to veto any sanctions resolution against Israel, and Washington made it perfectly clear it would view with extreme disfavor any move by Non-Aligned or other Council members even to discuss such an idea. As a result, the draft sanctions resolution even then being discussed in the non-aligned Caucus of the Security Council was shelved. Led by its Muslim members, Morocco, Pakistan and Djibouti, the Caucus agreed that the Council would simply express its belief that the U.S.-Israeli compromise represented a positive step, and its hope that all the expellees would be returned soon.[1] In what many observers believed to be a craven effort to win points from the Clinton administration, Morocco's ambassador, as Council president, took the lead in arranging the diplomatic steps, and relayed the message to his Israeli counterpart.

In some conflicts, Washington's double standards meant aggressive action to deny the UN any involvement at all. For the Madrid Arab-Israeli peace talks, for example, the U.S. accepted Israel's demand that the negotiations deliberately circumvent a decades-old UN consensus enshrined in numerous resolutions, calling for an international peace conference under UN auspices. Madrid was instead shaped as a regional conference under U.S. and then-Soviet sponsorship, with UN involvement reduced to a silent "observer." According to a draft Memorandum of Understanding jointly prepared by U.S. and Israeli officials only weeks before Madrid, the "UN representative will have no authority. He may hold talks only in the hallways, note down the content of the talks, and report to the secretary general . . ."[2]

The cry of double standards greeted the new Clinton administration in the United Nations. It was not a new phenomenon; but the end of the Cold War, and the emergence of a U.S. domination strategically unchallenged, meant it had become more blatant than ever before.

Superpower Lives Here

Despite the end of the Cold War and the collapse of the Soviet Union, the U.S. remained committed to retaining its superpower status — with or without a superpower contender. This meant a continued commitment to global reach, the capability of fielding military forces around the world, changing only the justifying rhetoric. "Containment of communism" doesn't work any more, but "defending international peace and security" is a seductive new pretext.

Its appeal lies partly in the stark reality that in the chaos of the post-Cold War world, international as well as national "peace and security" *is* threatened in many places. Justifying military intervention on humanitarian grounds sounds less oxymoronic in a new world order where ferocious nationalist, ethnic and racist hostilities, once constrained by socialism and the Cold War, now rage unchecked. In this global disorder, Washington and its allies can pick and choose where, when and how to intervene — and whether the UN will be allowed or coerced to play a role.

It was in orchestrating this new superpower-without-a-sparring-partner era, that the United Nations emerged as a major weapon in Washington's diplomatic arsenal after the Gulf War. After years of dismissing the UN as a backwater of socialist bombast and rampant Third Worldism, the world body suddenly emerged as the Bush administration's favorite multilateral institution. The UN, especially the Security Council, was invested with unprecedented status, and a heady scent of power filled the halls and conference rooms of UN headquarters.

It began on August 2, 1990, the day Saddam Hussein's army invaded Kuwait. As the days of the Gulf crisis turned into months, the U.S. kept the Security Council in virtual round-the-clock session, relentlessly ratcheting up the anti-Iraq stakes from condemnation to sanctions to the ultimate prize: a UN declaration of war to be waged at Washington's command.

But the illusion of United Nations decision-making was never transformed into a true shift in power; Washington held the reins, and the UN was turned into a compliant tool for Bush administration policy. But for a price. In preparation for the crucial vote authorizing the U.S. war against Iraq, diplomatic carrots and sticks were tossed with abandon. Some of the economic bribes were dispensed to countries not even on the Security Council, apparently to win the support of the recipients' *allies* to vote with the U.S. The $7 billion in debt relief to Egypt was one such example.

Virtually every developing country on the Security Council was offered new economic perks in return for a vote in favor of the U.S. war: Colombia, impoverished Ethiopia, Zaire (already fully in thrall to the U.S.) were all offered new aid packages, access to World Bank credits or rearrangements of International Monetary Fund grants or loans.

Military deals were cut as well. Ethiopia's government was given access to new military aid after a long denial of arms to that civil war-wrecked nation. Colombia was also offered a new package of military assistance.

China was the sole member of the Perm Five not toeing the U.S. line. It was common knowledge among UN-based journalists that China was looking for two major concessions in return for not opposing the U.S. war resolution. One was Washington's support for Beijing's return to international diplomatic legitimacy after 18 months of post-Tiananmen Square massacre isolation. The second was economic development aid. On November 28, 1990, the day before the vote authorizing the use of force against Iraq, the White House announced a high-profile meeting between President Bush and Chinese Foreign Minister Qian Qichen, the first since Tiananmen Square, to be held the day after the vote. It was designed officially to welcome Beijing back into legitimate international diplomacy. China abstained on the resolution. And less than one week later, the World Bank announced that China would be given access to $114 million in economic aid.

But carrots were not the only tool; sticks were used too. The U.S. would see that those countries who opposed the U.S. resolution, Cuba and Yemen, the sole Arab member of the Council, would, as much as possible, pay a high and very public price.

Against Cuba the U.S. had few options. Washington's 30-year-old diplomatic and economic blockade against Havana meant the State Department had few new diplomatic or economic weapons available to it.

But Yemen was different. Despite its history of cordial ties with the U.S. since reunification in the late 1980s, the small and impoverished country was to become an example to the world of the consequences of violating a U.S.-ordered consensus. Within minutes of voting "no" on Resolution 678, authorizing war, Yemen's Ambassador Abdallah Saleh al-Ashtal was informed, in full earshot of the world via the UN broadcasting system, that "that will be the most expensive 'no' vote you ever cast."

Three days later the U.S. cut its $70 million aid package to Yemen, one of the poorest countries in the region.

Points on the Compass

The double standard issue pinpointed the process of transforming the once-overarching East-West framework that shaped the UN, into an explicit North-South divide. With 15 new formerly Soviet republics joining the

General Assembly, the divisions emerged as the European and Slavic republics positioned themselves as poorer cousins of the (largely white) North, while Iran and Turkey (with NATO backing) contended for influence in the Muslim and Asian republics. Russia, especially, empowered by its Security Council veto, emerged as the chief Western wannabe, competing with the poorest of Africa and Asia for aid funds even while begging for admission to the G7 power club.

The North-South tension came to a head at the June 1992 Earth Summit in Rio, in the conflict between two conflicting agendas on environment and development issues. In what the *Los Angeles Times* called a "tactical tour de force," the Bush administration beat back the environmental concerns of Europe and the developing countries alike. Washington held the limits of its commitment to environmental goals, and, in doing so, reasserted U.S. hegemony over the countries of the South.

On the eve of the summit, Washington made official its long-anticipated refusal to sign the treaty on biodiversity and habitat protection set to be finalized in Rio. The move came less than a month after Bush succeeded in forcing the Europeans to abandon their commitment to set timetables for the industrialized countries to roll back global warming-causing emissions.

The five years of preparatory work for the Rio summit often brought the U.S. head to head against its erstwhile allies in the European Community, and, more fundamentally, against the interests of the South. The European position, reflecting the increasing influence of Green movements in European politics, acknowledged some responsibility of the industrialized countries to scale back environmentally catastrophic emissions. The U.S. admitted no such thing.

For the countries of the South, the issue was even more fundamental. Pressure was mounting on those nations to create environmentally-correct strategies for economic development. But, facing endemic poverty and the legacy of centuries of colonial domination by the North, Third World governments were reluctant to abandon efforts to improve the living standards of their impoverished populations, and instead demanded economic compensation and the large-scale transfer of environment-friendly technology to improve, rather than abandon, their commitment to development. It would cost billions of dollars — and logic and Earth Summit organizers called for it to be paid by the North. But the U.S. was not on board.

Following a pattern established 20 years before, the Earth Summit left many promises unmet. At the first UN Conference on the Human Environment, held in Stockholm in 1972, the late Swedish Prime Minister Olaf Palme denounced the U.S. for its massive defoliation in Vietnam, and demanded that "ecological warfare cease immediately."[3] Twenty years later, his demand remained on the South's agenda.

Spin-Doctors

For the U.S., a key task of the new world order was to re-orchestrate and recast the United Nations as a respected part of U.S. diplomacy. During the

Gulf crisis, Washington raised the organization's stature, but it remained unclear whether that rehabilitation was to be a one-time tactic to gain support for the war against Iraq, or if it reflected a long-range shift in strategic U.S. planning for the UN.

Towards the end of 1991, the five-year term of the lackluster Secretary General Javier Perez de Cuellar was coming to a close. By tradition, the SG cannot be a citizen of one of the five veto-wielding members of the Security Council. Also by tradition, the regional groups within the UN rotate the right to nominate from among their own member states the new candidate.

Following the Peruvian Perez de Cuellar, Austrian Kurt Waldheim, and Burmese U Thant, it was understood to be Africa's turn. But not everyone liked that idea. A Third World-oriented secretary general, speaking from and for the Non-Aligned countries, could do much to thwart U.S. efforts to achieve the appearance of unanimity in the UN behind its grand coalitions. Early lists of candidates, headed by the OAU's venerable Tanzanian advocate of non-alignment, Salim Salim, were all found unacceptable by the U.S. and its allies.

By the fall, Washington had settled on Egypt's former foreign minister Boutros Boutros Ghali. Developing his political position in the post-Nasser period in Egypt, Boutros Ghali reflected the strong pro-Western orientation of Anwar Sadat, his mentor. The U.S. claimed Boutros Ghali's candidacy answered the demand for an African SG. Despite the fact that most African diplomats believed that a truly African-based and African-accountable SG must be from sub-Saharan Africa, Egypt's geography provided a free gift for U.S. spin-masters. Washington was also thus able to promote a pro-U.S. Arab candidate to bolster its post-Gulf War credibility among some allies in the Middle East and other developing countries. And Egypt's post-Camp David foreign policy, buttressed by billions of dollars a year in U.S. aid, loyally defended U.S. Middle East interests. Who could be better trusted to continue that same political trajectory from the SG's office on the UN's 38th floor?

Boutros Ghali also found strong support from France, which played the role of his sponsor in the Security Council. His election was assured, and U.S. influence in the organization seemed higher than ever.

The General Assembly session that began in September 1991 saw a succession of heads of state and foreign ministers, including George Bush, extolling the UN's role in the new, post-Cold War and post-Gulf War world order.

Bush called for changes in the UN to reflect new world realities, and he demanded quick repeal of the 1975 General Assembly resolution that identified Zionism as a form of racism and racial discrimination. The U.S. letter of assurance to Israel prior to the Madrid peace conference included a commitment to accomplish that repeal. So by mid-November, U.S. diplomats crisscrossed the globe, using Gulf War-tested methods of bribing and threatening other nations to win support for the repeal efforts.[4] By mid-December the campaigning was over, and the December 16 repeal vote surpassed Washington's wildest expectations, with 111 countries voting for repeal. The ability of the U.S. to remake the UN in its own image seemed assured.

Thus, by early 1992, while its own dues remained in arrears to the tune of hundreds of millions of dollars, the U.S. endorsement of the UN reached its zenith. The announcement of a high-profile Security Council summit was a clear indication that the UN had proved itself far too valuable a weapon in Washington's diplomatic arsenal to be tossed aside after the Gulf War.

The unprecedented summit brought together the heads of state of the 15 members of the Security Council to discuss the future of the United Nations. On the practical level it was not much more than a photo op. (The imperial British ambassador, Sir David Hannay, rotating president of the Security Council for January, insisted that the hastily called meeting be held by January 31. A less diplomatic British diplomat, asked why the telegenic conference couldn't be delayed till February, when the U.S. would be presiding over the Council, reportedly quipped, "because our elections come before yours.") But beyond the hype, the UN summit was designed to cement the transformation of the world body into a credible implementor of U.S. policy.

Washington Reaches for the Globe

As countries fell and new nationalist passions rose with the massive changes of 1991, the UN remained at centerstage of global clean-up operations. The UN's apparent centrality in the Gulf War segued to newly prominent roles in efforts to resolve civil and inter-ethnic wars and conflicts, some of long-standing duration, often rooted in Cold War realities (El Salvador, Cambodia, Angola, Afghanistan), others creating newly "cleansed" swaths of death and destruction (Croatia, Bosnia, Nagorno-Karabakh, Somalia).

In the U.S., military leaders reacting to the end of the Cold War reiterated the primacy of "global reach" to defend U.S. interests and maintain U.S. superpower status. The UN was part of the mechanism of asserting global reach.

In the spring of 1992, the U.S. reactivated its simmering anti-Libya crusade. The pretext was Washington's effort to force Libya to turn over two of its nationals for trial in the U.S. or Britain on charges of involvement in the 1988 Lockerbie disaster. Noting its lack of bilateral extradition treaties with London and Washington, Libya refused to send the two for trial there. Instead, as required by the 1970 anti-hijacking Montreal Convention, Libya volunteered either to put the men on trial itself, or send them for trial in Malta or another neutral country. Tripoli asked the International Court of Justice to determine whether its proposed action was sufficient. But despite the pending case already being heard before the ICJ, the U.S. forced the Security Council to endorse preemptive, punitive sanctions against Libya.

Despite a new flurry of diplomatic carrots and sticks, the U.S. faced widespread unease, in many cases downright opposition, from Council members.[5] But Washington expended far less political capital on the anti-Libya crusade than it had to gain support for Desert Storm, and the results were far from definitive. Only ten of the 15 Council members voted for sanctions, just one more than the minimum required for passage. Five non-aligned countries abstained.

Whispered fears grew louder that the U.S. effort was designed to concentrate UN power solely in the hands of the North-weighted Security Council, stripping the authority of all other UN institutions — even of the International Court, let alone the sometimes unruly democracy of the General Assembly. Zimbabwe's Ambassador Simbarashe Mumbengegwi noted the threat to UN integrity posed by that concentration of power. "The Security Council only consists of 15 members," he said after the Libyan sanctions vote. "There are 160 [UN] members who are not part of the Security Council. Therefore it would be a serious mistake to want to create a situation where 15 members can want to argue that they are much stronger as a body than the 160 who are not in that body. That would really undermine the very basis of the United Nations, which is basically democratic, [and based on] equality of states. And if the Security Council were to be seen in that light, it would undermine its authority for the rest of the members' confidence in it as an institution which can protect their interests."[6]

As Washington moved to tighten its own grip, its hand-picked secretary general, while remaining generally in tune with the West's agenda, began exerting a more independent role. First criticized for an "aloof" and "arrogant" posture, Boutros Ghali soon angered some of his erstwhile sponsors by refusing to remain silent in the face of Council inaction. As Somalia's crisis worsened with no UN response, the secretary general's famous condemnation of the Council's narrow focus on "the rich man's war" in Bosnia further antagonized the West (although it did help spur international public opinion). Additionally, whatever combination of half-hidden Arab-African solidarity and frustration with the Council's stalemate over Bosnia may have motivated Boutros Ghali, his remark served to further undermine UN credibility in the war-torn former Yugoslav republics. But Boutros Ghali remained a key player in the U.S. and Western effort to remake the UN into a newly central player in post-Cold War diplomacy.

Peacekeeping, Peace-Making, Peace-Enforcing

Throughout 1992, UN activism remained at an all-time high. Despite continuing criticism of double standards of enforcement, peacekeeping missions expanded. Debates proliferated over the nature of the UN's military role. The French heated up the debate by suggesting the legitimacy of "humanitarian intervention," that would bypass considerations of national sovereignty and send troops without the consent of governments to protect populations deemed by some outside force to be at risk. By early 1993, the UN was fielding 13 separate peacekeeping operations, more than ever before. Some, like the operations in Cambodia and the former Yugoslavia, involved tens of thousands of UN military and civilian staff.

Boutros Ghali played a central role in the effort to redefine the nature of peacekeeping, at times going beyond what even his Council backers were prepared to accept. In his *Agenda for Peace*, drafted at the request of the January Council summit, he outlined a bold plan to dramatically expand UN interventions. While traditional UN peacekeeping was based on troops deployed to monitor ceasefire lines with the consent of both parties, Boutros Ghali's 1992 plan called for preemptive UN deployments to prevent or limit disputes: peace-making, designed to force parties to agreement, if possible through peaceful means such as boycotts (and presumably through military means if not); peacekeeping, identified as "hitherto" requiring the consent of all parties; and peace-building following conflicts.

Perhaps most contentious, he also called for a permanent UN military force to be established and placed under the command of the Security Council, noting that the end of the Cold War had created the political environment to make such a multilateral force possible. His call inevitably drew new attention to the long-standing refusal of the U.S. ever to place its troops under any UN or multilateral command. Even during the Gulf War, the SG reminded the world, the Council only authorized member states to go to war against Iraq; it did not call for a direct UN attack.

As the organization's resources were spread thin in peacekeeping and peace-making efforts around the globe, failures emerged from the shadows. After a high-profile claim of success in ending the 13-year civil war in Afghanistan, the UN withdrew, leaving behind an even more brutal intra-mujahedeen war. The hard-fought UN-brokered peace agreement in El Salvador was threatened by the government's refusal to demobilize the worst human rights violators within the military. Cambodia's UN-imposed peace accord, threatened from the beginning by U.S. and UN acquiescence to Khmer Rouge "legitimacy," was undermined even further by Pol Pot's organization's refusal to participate in UN-sanctioned elections. And in Angola, despite a clear victory for the ruling MPLA in UN-sponsored elections, long-time U.S. ally Jonas Savimbi's UNITA rebels rejected the results and reignited the civil war.

At the same time, a massive UN troop deployment and joint UN-EC sponsored talks to resolve the war of "ethnic cleansing" in Bosnia-Herzegovina did nothing to staunch the brutality of wanton rape and murder. The UN's credibility there, already perilously low, dipped even further with the murder by Serbian militiamen of a ranking Bosnian government official while he was under UN protection.

Whose Command, Whose Control?

The visibility of UN failures, however, along with the growing international disfavor in which the UN was viewed in the countries where it was deployed, often masked the real power relations behind the UN decisions and deployment. Since its origins almost fifty years ago, the United Nations was created, and continues, to reflect, not challenge, the power relationships of its member states. The Perm Five gave themselves veto-power in the Council not because they were the most representative of nations, but because they were the most powerful — and the UN was designed to perpetuate the power of the victorious World War II allies.

There was a popular notion that Desert Storm was a "UN war," ignoring Washington's stranglehold on real power. Similarly, as the UN is stretched thinner and thinner in hot spots around the world, it becomes easy to blame "the UN" for peacekeeping failures; praising instead, for example, the arrival of a few platoons of red-blooded young U.S. Marines.

What gets lost is the issue of who determines success or failure for the UN. Certainly the 500 Pakistani troops sent to Somalia in the summer of 1992 arrived too late, stayed too close to the airport, accomplished very little and quickly failed. But who determined that their mandate should only include defense of the Mogadishu airport? Who decided only 500 should be sent? Why did they have to wait over six weeks because their own logistics people did not have the requisite equipment and no other country would provide it? And given the predominance of U.S. influence in the Council, can a full distinction between "UN" and "U.S." responsibility be made?

The ambitious profile of the UN has spurred new interest in many countries in following Washington's lead and seeking out a center of power within the global organization. Japan, for example, has staked out a leading position in humanitarian operations, despite its constitutional ban on sending troops abroad. Visiting Tokyo in February 1993, Boutros Ghali urged Japan to reverse its long-standing ban to participate fully in UN peacekeeping, implying it would help Japan's goal of securing a permanent seat on the Council.

This was not the only such move. The myriad of failures and/or uncertain outcomes brought new visibility to once-whispered calls for a variety of structural changes designed to rework the UN's relations of authority. Because the locus of real power in the United Nations, the power to wage war or impose peace, lies in the Security Council, most reform proposals focus on expanding its membership.

Both Germany and Japan claim the right to permanent Council seats, by virtue of their economic clout. The Non-Aligned Movement, seeking to redress the Council's historic North-South imbalance, has discussed adding three of the largest and most powerful countries of the Southern continents — usually mentioning India, Nigeria and Brazil — to the Council's permanent members. The U.S. has been on record (albeit quietly) since 1974 in support of Germany's claim; Japan used its two-year rotating stint on the Council in 1992–93 and its escalating financial support of peacekeeping operations to lobby for a similar position.

The key challenge facing the South in the new UN is the question of democracy. As long as the democratic side of the organization, the General Assembly, is kept strategically powerless, and the least democratic organ, the Security Council, remains the real center of power, the UN will be unable to retain independence of action in the face of U.S. decisions. Structural changes to integrate power and democracy are required.

An important, though unlikely, start would be a move to realize and empower the Assembly's role of overseeing all Council activity. Democratizing the Council itself requires ensuring a permanent voice for the countries of the South — not expanding and consolidating the North's grip by adding Germany and Japan to the permanent members.

The Clinton administration entered a UN in which Washington was both preeminently powerful, and the target of deep-rooted antagonism for its heavy-handed enforced consensuses and its double standards. It entered a UN desperately short of cash, while the U.S. still owed hundreds of millions in back dues. It entered the UN to direct the organization's multilateral forms of diplomacy towards the legitimation of its own unipolar projection of power.

But despite its new credibility in Washington, in certain aspects the UN has not changed since its founding: it continues to reflect, rather than challenge, the basic priorities and power relations of its strongest member states. Resources are still scarce, and the stark reality is that the only UN programs being expanded are those involving peacekeeping forces.

But key changes are taking place in the broadening definition of international peacekeeping efforts. Historically, international involvement was balanced against the right of nations to maintain their sovereignty. Now, with a notion gaining wider acceptance that national sovereignty might be just a bit passé, UN activism is becoming more and more explicitly interventionist — on the side of the North.

In a world where the vast majority of conflicts now rage *within*, rather than between nations, increased UN activism may at times be the only viable alternative to the world standing in mute witness to mass slaughter. But that activism cannot be defined solely in military terms, and success in the long term will depend on a currently out-of-reach independence of action on the part of the UN. If its role in the world is to defend democracy, the UN's own democracy must be reclaimed. Otherwise, with the reality of a U.S.-dominated United Nations torn by North-South divisions, UN intervention, under the guise of peacekeeping, peacemaking or peace-enforcing, will be indistinguishable from the U.S. interventions it is so often used to legitimate.

Notes

1. *New York Times*, February 13, 1993.
2. *Ma'ariv* (Israel), August 4, 1991, quoted in *Journal of Palestine Studies* #81, Autumn 1991, p. 182.
3. *Los Angeles Times*, June 1992.
4. Reports from UN-based Non-Aligned diplomatic sources.
5. Non-Aligned and other Council members confided their dismay to UN reporters only on a not-for-attribution basis.
6. Statement to author.

4

Pax Americana: U.S. Military Policy in the Post-Cold War Era

Michael T. Klare

The Persian Gulf War of January-February 1991 was the first major crisis of the post-Cold War era, and for many analysts represents a watershed in the evolution of U.S. military strategy. "The second of August 1990 will be remembered for generations to come as a turning point for the United States in its conduct of foreign affairs," General Carl E. Vuono of the U.S. Army observed in 1991 — "the day America announced the end of containment and embarked upon the strategy of power projection."[1] But while it is certainly true that the Gulf War will have a substantial and long-lasting impact on U.S. military thinking, it is important to recognize that the process of reshaping U.S. grand strategy for the post-Cold War era began well before the onset of the Persian Gulf crisis, and arose as much for domestic considerations – in particular, from a need to articulate a viable rationale for maintaining a large military establishment in the absence of a credible Soviet threat – as it did from international developments. In evaluating this process, two key developments require particular attention.

First, the Gulf War institutionalized *a new paradigm of combat* that will in all likelihood govern U.S. military planning for a generation to come. To describe this new paradigm, we can use the term "mid-intensity conflict," meaning conflict that falls below the level of "high-intensity conflict" (or all-out global war between the United States and the Soviet Union), and above the level of "low-intensity conflict" (or counter-insurgency and small-scale military operations such as those conducted in Grenada and Panama).

Second, the Gulf War legitimized *a new assertion of pax Americana*, or the discretionary use of U.S. military power by the president to protect and enforce certain rules of international behavior that have been dictated by Washington. This posture is often confused — sometimes intentionally —

with the concept of a "New World Order," but, as I will argue, these are two very different concepts.

The New Military Paradigm

Until 1990, the United States military had only two clear paradigms to guide its strategic thinking — the paradigm of high-intensity conflict (HIC), or all-out war with the Warsaw Pact on the plains of Europe, and the paradigm of low-intensity conflict (LIC), or counter-insurgency and police-type operations in underdeveloped Third World areas. The first, HIC, was developed in response to the threat posed by massive Soviet forces in Eastern Europe. This paradigm envisioned the use of heavy tank forces backed by artillery and airpower in sustained, massive battles stretching across Germany, Czechoslovakia, Poland, and adjacent countries. Although the United States was prepared to fight such a war with non-nuclear weapons, it also reserved the right to employ nuclear weapons on a first-use basis to avert defeat in such a conflict.

The second paradigm was developed in the late 1950s and early 1960s in response to an upsurge of guerrilla warfare (or "wars of national liberation," as they were known at the time) in the colonial and ex-colonial areas of Africa, Asia, and Latin America. The LIC or "counter-insurgency" paradigm involved U.S. military and economic aid to threatened Third World regimes and, *in extremis*, direct U.S. military intervention (as in Vietnam and the Dominican Republic). The strategy of counter-insurgency was discredited by the U.S. defeat in Vietnam, but was revived again in the Reagan era under the banner of low-intensity conflict. In line with current U.S. military doctrine, LIC also includes counter-terrorism, narcotics interdiction, pro-insurgency (or support for anti-communist insurgencies in the Third World), and small-scale "contingency" operations like those conducted in Grenada and Panama.[2]

These two paradigms effectively governed the organization and "armamentation" of U.S. military forces (what the military calls *force structure*), as well as the strategies and doctrines governing the actual use of U.S. forces, for most of the Cold War era. Thus, in response to the HIC threat, the United States maintained "heavy" forces equipped with large numbers of tanks, rockets, artillery pieces, and support aircraft; for LIC, it established "light" forces that could be rapidly deployed to distant locations. Each of these sets of forces, moreover, had their own sets of strategies, tactics, and doctrines.

This was where things stood in December 1989 when, for all practical purposes, the Cold War came to an end. For many people, the end of the Cold War was viewed as a great blessing, allowing for the reallocation of resources from the military to the civilian sector; for the U.S. military establishment, however, it was seen as an unmitigated disaster. Why is this so? The answer lies in the fact that the two paradigms described above provided no rationale for the continued maintenance of large military forces in the post-Cold War era, and thus the Pentagon faced massive cutbacks in military appropriations. There was no such rationale because the end of the

Cold War swept away the likelihood of a high-intensity conflict in Europe, and with it, the sole justification for maintenance of heavy, well-equipped forces. All that was left, it appeared, was the LIC paradigm — and this mission could easily be performed by a force one-tenth the size of the existing U.S. military establishment. And it doesn't take much imagination to realize that the reduction of the U.S. military to a force one-tenth its present size would produce enormous pain and hardship for the professional military class, for U.S. defense contractors, for the legions of think-tank analysts, and for all the other groups and institutions that depend for their livelihood on high levels of military spending.

Needless to say, this powerful collection of constituencies did not respond passively to this impending disaster. Rather, they sought to invent a new enemy and a new paradigm that would justify retention of large military units in the post-Cold War era. And, not surprisingly, they *did* discover a new enemy: emerging Third World powers equipped with large, modern conventional forces and the rudiments of a nuclear/chemical/missile capability. To combat these powers, they argued, a new military paradigm was needed — what they called "mid-intensity conflict."[3]

The selection of emerging Third World powers as the U.S.'s new adversary was influenced to some degree by a number of studies conducted in the late 1980s on U.S. strategy options in the 1990s. Most prominent of these was *Discriminate Deterrence*, the 1988 report of the U.S. Commission on Integrated Long-Term Strategy. Although focused largely on the alleged threat from the USSR, the Commission warned against over-emphasis on the Soviet threat and called for greater attention to Third World threats. "An emphasis on massive Soviet attacks leads to tunnel vision among defense planners," the report noted. "Apocalyptic show-downs between the United States and the Soviet Union are certainly conceivable . . . but they are much less probable than other forms of conflict." Most worrisome of these other forms of conflict, the report argues, are regional conflicts in the Third World. Because future adversaries in such conflicts are likely to be armed with increasingly potent weapons, any American efforts to prevail in such encounters "will call for use of our most sophisticated weaponry."[4]

This image of U.S. forces engaged in intense combat with regional Third World powers was explored in much greater detail by a task force assembled in 1989 by the Center for Strategic and International Studies (CSIS) of Washington, D.C. In their final report, *Conventional Combat Priorities*, the task force identified such encounters as the most significant contingency facing U.S. forces in the 1990s and beyond. "With the decline of the Soviet military threat to Europe, conflicts that might be termed 'mid-intensity' will dominate U.S. planning concerns," the report noted. The growing likelihood of such encounters "will provide a key justification for military budgets during the 1990s and will establish most of the threats against which U.S. forces are sized, trained, and equipped."[5]

Analysts began to reassess U.S. strategic assumptions and press for a military doctrine for full-scale combat with emerging powers. Essential to their arguments is the view that mid-intensity conflict (MIC) is not just a

Central American military action writ large, but a new ballgame. Compare, for instance, Operation Just Cause (the December 1989 invasion of Panama) and Operation Desert Storm. In Panama, the United States faced a glorified police force of perhaps 10,000 troops equipped with zero tanks and missiles and four propeller-driven planes. In response, Washington committed 25,000 infantry troops. In Iraq, the United States faced a battle-tested army of 1 million equipped with some 5,500 tanks, 700 modern planes, and a vast supply of guided missiles. To overpower this force, Washington deployed 500,000 combat troops backed by some 1,800 aircraft and 150 warships.

The clear distinction between the encounters reflects a growing differentiation between smaller and poorer Third World countries like Panama and a dozen or so regional powers that have acquired modern arsenals and the ability to produce nuclear or chemical munitions. That select group includes Argentina, Brazil, Egypt, India, Iran, Iraq, Israel, Pakistan, South Africa, Syria, Taiwan, Turkey, and the two Koreas. Such nations stand out as military leviathans in the Third World.

The identification of emerging Third World powers as the new adversary had many attractions for the U.S. military in 1990. These countries possess large forces with modern weapons, including ballistic missiles and high-performance aircraft, and thus any war against them would require the use of large, well-equipped American forces. Also, because they possess (or are thought to possess) weapons of mass destruction, they could be portrayed as a genuine threat to regional and international stability — and thus Washington could argue that military action is needed to crush their nuclear and/or chemical capabilities.

This perception of the new adversary was already fully entrenched in Washington prior to the Iraqi invasion of Kuwait in August 1990. Indeed, we can trace the emergence of the new paradigm to President Bush's first major speech on national security affairs, at the U.S. Coast Guard Academy in May 1989: "The security challenges we face today do not come from the East alone," he noted. "The emergence of regional powers is rapidly changing the strategic landscape. In the Middle East, in South Asia, in our own hemisphere, a growing number of nations are acquiring advanced and highly destructive capabilities — in some cases, weapons of mass destruction, and the means to deliver them." In response to this threat, he argued, the United States must adopt new anti-proliferation measures and, if necessary, "must check the aggressive ambitions of renegade regimes."[6]

This notion of combat against "renegade regimes" armed with modern conventional weapons and nuclear or chemical capabilities became the new planning model for the U.S. military. Thus, in January 1990, Secretary of Defense Dick Cheney told Congress that the United States must "recognize the challenges beyond Europe that may place significant demands on our defense capabilities." In face of these challenges, he argued, the Pentagon must adopt strategies "that rely more heavily on mobile, highly ready, well-equipped forces and solid, power-projection capabilities."[7]

This perspective was developed even more fully in an April 1990 article by General Vuono, the Army Chief of Staff:

Because the United States is a global power with vital interests that must be protected throughout an increasingly turbulent world, we must look beyond the European continent and consider other threats to our national security. The proliferation of military power in what is often called the "Third World" presents a troubling picture. Many Third World nations now possess mounting arsenals of tanks, heavy artillery, ballistic missiles, and chemical weapons . . . The proliferation of advanced military capabilities has given an increasing number of countries in the developing world the ability to wage sustained, mechanized land warfare. The United States cannot ignore the expanding military power of these countries, and the Army must retain the capability to defeat potential threats wherever they occur. *This could mean confronting a well-equipped army in the Third World.*[8] (Emphasis added.)

This prophetic statement is just one of many such remarks made by high-ranking U.S. military officers in the spring of 1990, suggesting that senior officials had reached consensus on a new, MIC-oriented military posture months before the Iraqi invasion of Kuwait. Consistent with this posture, the Department of Defense and the individual military services began to reconfigure U.S. capabilities from an HIC-oriented force to an MIC-oriented force. Moreover, in the spring of 1990, the Pentagon conducted an elaborate, computerized war game, "Operation Internal Look '90," featuring Iraq as the hypothetical enemy.[9] Now, in reporting these developments, I do not mean to suggest that the United States was actively looking for a fight with Iraq; but I do believe that the adoption of this paradigm by U.S. military officials led the Pentagon leadership to welcome a war with Iraq once the prospect of such an engagement presented itself. In the words of General Colin Powell, "It was nice to have Desert Storm come along now," before Iraq had fully developed its military capabilities. "Not that it's nice to have a war, but if it was going to come, this was a good time for it."[10]

Once the war began, U.S. forces employed the strategies and doctrines that had already been developed for such a contingency — i.e., the use of superior firepower and technology to crush a numerically superior but technologically inferior opponent. This approach had originally been developed to ensure a NATO victory in any major conventional conflict with the Soviet Union. As spelled out in NATO's "Follow-on Force Attack" (FOFA) strategy and the U.S. Army's "Airland Battle Doctrine" (ABD), the new approach called for simultaneous allied attacks on the enemy's first, second, and third echelons of troops, along with the prodigious use of "smart" weapons to destroy enemy communications systems, radars, air bases, road systems, and other vital facilities.[11]

After the Gulf War, this strategic approach is now being standardized as the new U.S. military posture for the 1990s. To quote Secretary Cheney from his testimony before the House Foreign Affairs Committee on March 19, 1991:

The Gulf War presaged very much the type of conflict we are most likely to confront again in this new era – major regional contingencies against foes well-armed with advanced conventional and non-conventional weaponry. In addition to Southwest Asia, we have important interests in Europe, Asia, the Pacific and

Central and Latin America. In each of these regions there are opportunities and potential future threats to our interests. We must configure our policies and our forces to effectively deter, or quickly defeat, such regional threats.[12]

It is apparent from such statements that MIC is consciously intended to overcome what U.S. military officers see as the mistakes of Vietnam. From their perspective, the principal error of that conflict was to apply firepower gradually in the belief that the enemy would sue for peace at a low level of escalation, whereas, in fact, North Vietnam took advantage of "gradualism" to build up its own military. The new doctrine calls for the use of fast, concentrated firepower to destroy an enemy and crush its will to fight.

One can, of course, draw other lessons from Vietnam — for instance, lessons about the need for political clarity and cohesion when committing a democracy to a conflict abroad. It would be a mistake, moreover, to view Vietnam as a "limited" conflict, given the years of steady bombing by B-52s and other aircraft of North Vietnam, Laos, and Viet Cong positions in the South. Still, the aversion to gradualism governs the thinking of current Pentagon leaders. "Many of us here who are in this position now were in Vietnam, and that has left a profound impact on our feelings about how our nation ought to conduct its business," explains Gen. Charles Horner, commander of U.S. Air Force units in Saudi Arabia. "We think that war is a very serious business and it should not be dragged out in an effort to achieve some political objective."[13]

Central to the notion of winning quickly is the belief that every advantage in technology should be employed to stun, cripple, and defeat an enemy. The army of the future "must be lethal," Gen. Vuono wrote in 1990. "Lethality results from quality soldiers . . . equipped with weapons that are superior to those of any adversary and available in numbers adequate to defeat potential enemies."[14] Gen. Norman Schwarzkopf accentuated the point in September 1990 when discussing U.S. plans for a war with Iraq: "We would be using capabilities that are far more lethal, far more accurate, and far more effective than anything we've ever used."[15]

The implication is clear: there will be no gradualism, no restraint on firepower. The president underlined the precept in November 1990: "Should military action be required, this will not be another Vietnam; this will not be a protracted, drawn-out war. . . . If one American soldier has to go into battle, that soldier will have enough force behind him to win, and then get out as soon as possible."[16]

In line with this outlook, senior U.S. strategists have begun to hammer out a blueprint for the combination of weapons and forces that would best serve U.S. needs for the mid-intensity conflicts of the future. Based on the record of Operation Desert Storm, and what is known of the Pentagon's evolving plans for MIC, we can identify some of the weapons and forces that are likely to dominate the Pentagon's "wish list" for U.S. military capabilities in the mid- to late 1990s:

* *Strategic mobility*: If U.S. forces are to prevail in future regional conflicts,

they will have to arrive quickly and in sufficient strength to overcome formidable local forces — and this, in turn, means possessing adequate numbers of long-range ships and aircraft to transport and sustain a substantial U.S. force in distant areas.

* *Mobile firepower*: Once U.S. troops arrive at distant battlefields, they must be capable of fighting and defeating well-equipped, professional armies. To prevail in such confrontations, U.S. forces must come equipped with large numbers of weapons that pack a mighty punch, but that can be moved quickly to distant battlefields.

* *Advanced tactical aircraft*: Because many Third World countries possess modern fighters and air defense systems of Soviet or Western European manufacture, U.S. combat planes must be capable of overcoming enemy defenses and delivering their ordinance when and where needed.

* *Advanced "standoff" missiles*: Given the growing sophistication of Third World artillery and air defense systems, it is considered essential that American forces be able to fire highly accurate missiles at critical enemy targets (air bases, command centers, military factories, tank formations, and so on) from distant, out-of-sight locations.[17]

* *"Middleweight" combat formations*: Ultimately, the successful conduct of MIC operations will require the introduction of new combat formations (brigades, divisions, and so on) that can be sufficiently powerful to defend themselves against well-armed Third World adversaries.

These, and other such systems, are likely to dominate Pentagon spending programs in the 1990s. And while *total* U.S. military spending is likely to decline, spending on MIC-oriented programs can be expected to increase.

The Reassertion of *Pax Americana*

The second major outcome of the Persian Gulf conflict is the renewed assertion of *pax Americana*, which I would define as the unbridled use of military force in the protection of strategic U.S. assets abroad and in enforcing certain rules of international behavior deemed beneficial to the continued political and economic paramountcy of the U.S.

Here, too, one can see the emergence of this outlook in U.S. military thought before the outbreak of the Persian Gulf conflict. In essence, this outlook holds that the United States is a global power with vital economic interests in many parts of the world — interests that are shared in many cases by the Western industrial powers with which the United States is closely aligned. This outlook further holds that these interests are threatened by social, economic, and political disorder in the Third World, and that, for lack of any suitable alternative, the United States must shoulder responsibility for the protection of such interests and for the maintenance of global law and order.

This outlook is clearly articulated in President Bush's important address on national security policy of February 7, 1990. America's post-Cold War strategy, he noted, assumes that "new threats are emerging beyond the traditional East-West antagonism of the last 45 years." These threats must now receive the same attention once accorded to the Soviet threat. "Clearly, in the future we will need to be able to thwart aggression, repel a missile, or protect a seaplane, or stop a drug lord." To do so, moreover, "we will need forces adaptable to conditions everywhere. And we will need agility, readiness, sustainability. We will need speed and stealth."[18]

Essential to this mode of thinking is the conviction that the United States must be prepared to use force when necessary to carry out the missions described by President Bush. As suggested by General A.M. Gray, the Commandant of the Marine Corps:

> The international security environment is in the midst of changing from a bipolar balance to a multipolar one with polycentric dimensions. The restructuring of the international environment has the potential to create regional power vacuums that could result in instability and conflict. We cannot permit these voids to develop through disinterest, benign neglect, or lack of capability if we are to maintain our position as a world leader and protect our global interests. This requires that we maintain our capability to respond to likely regions of conflict.[19]

For students of history, this will read a great deal like the concept of "world policeman" espoused by President Teddy Roosevelt and other American policymakers at the turn of the century. And while current U.S. leaders are reluctant to employ this particular term, it is clear that they were beginning to think this way in 1989 and early 1990, months before the outbreak of the Persian Gulf crisis. Thus, in a January 1990 article on U.S. strategy in "The New Post-War Era," Senator John McCain of Arizona wrote that:

> If anything, the global conditions that led us to make these uses of force [in Korea, Vietnam, Grenada, and Libya] are likely to be even more important in the future. "Glasnost" does not change the fact that there has been an average of more than 25 civil and international conflicts in the developing world every year since the end of World War II [and that] the U.S. economy is critically dependent on the smooth flow of world trade. . . .
> Our strategy and force mix must reflect the fact that our friends and allies are even more dependent on global stability and the free flow of trade than we are. At the same time, it must reflect the fact that no other allied or friendly nation will suddenly develop power projection forces, and that it would not be in our interest to encourage other nations to assume this role. *The U.S. may not be the "world's policeman," but its power projection forces will remain the free world's insurance policy.*[20] (Emphasis added.)

Essential to this outlook is the belief that the United States — and *only* the United States — has the capacity to employ military force on a global basis in the protection of vital Western interests. This, in fact, has become the central premise of post-Cold War U.S. military posture. As noted by Dick Cheney in a remarkable speech before the National Press Club on March 22, 1990, what distinguishes the United States from other Western powers, "is that we're willing to put U.S. troops on the ground. The message to friends and enemies alike is that *Americans are willing to risk their lives to insure the security of our friends and allies.*"[21] (Emphasis added.)

General Colin Powell put this in more vivid terms: "I like to say that we're not the superpower or super-policeman of the world, but when there is trouble somewhere in the world that we least expect, it's the United States that gets called on to perform the role of being the cop on the beat."[22]

When and where will the United States next serve as "the cop on the beat"? That is, of course, very hard to predict in advance. When questioned on this point in April 1991, General Powell replied, "Think hard about it. I'm running out of demons. I'm running out of villains. I'm down to Castro and Kim Il Sung."[23] The fact is, however, that the United States is not likely to "run out of villains" any time soon. Given the likelihood of political and social disorder in a world of grossly uneven economic development *and* resurgent ethnic and religious loyalties, there is no end to possible threats to U.S. interests around the world. There are, however, a number of potential impediments to the full implementation of this new American strategy.

The first of these impediments is largely economic in nature: the costs of fighting high-tech wars keep going up, while the ability of the United States to sustain such costly endeavors appears to be going down. President Bush was able to sidestep this contradiction in the Gulf crisis by arm-twisting U.S. allies into paying most of the costs of the war. It is unlikely, however, that the allies will always be willing to do this in the future — Iraq was an unusual adversary in that Saddam Hussein's designs on Kuwait and the Gulf threatened the interests of so many countries. When contemplating military action against an enemy considered less threatening by the world community, therefore, the United States may find that its allies will balk at providing the necessary cash, and thus, faced with the prospects of going it alone, may conclude that the financial costs (if not the costs in human lives) are just too high.

The second major impediment is of a more conceptual — or if you will, of a moral nature. To appreciate this, it is necessary to recall that the reassertion of *pax Americana* began to occur at the same time that President Bush and Secretary of State Baker were attempting to articulate the concept of a "New World Order" based on international peace and cooperation. Although admittedly vague, the concept does entail certain idealistic goals and themes that are probably shared by a large proportion of the world's population.

Consider the president's words: The new world order, he says, implies "the peaceful settlement of disputes, solidarity against aggression, reduced and controlled arsenals, and the just treatment of all peoples."[24] As I understand these words, this would mean the use of sanctions and diplomacy to end the Gulf crisis, not the use of force as implied by *pax Americana*; it would mean solidarity against all aggressions, including those by friends of the U.S. (e.g., Morocco in the Western Sahara, Indonesia in East Timor, Israel in southern Lebanon), and not just those by its long-term adversaries; it would mean a moratorium on U.S. arms transfers to the Middle East, not the current U.S. rush to sell billions of dollars' worth of new high-tech weapons to its allies in the region; and it would mean respect for the human rights of all oppressed peoples, not just those in countries ruled by the U.S.'s adversaries.

These are important distinctions, and they are increasingly evident as such to significant segments of the American population. True, there is a large reservoir of jingoism in the population that can be tapped by the president to mobilize support for adventuristic military operations abroad, as demonstrated by the Panama invasion and Operation Desert Storm. But the U.S. public also expects Washington at least to appear to behave in an ethical and even *noble* fashion abroad; and increasingly the dictates of morality seem to imply the superiority of negotiations over combat and of collective action (via the United Nations) over unilateralism. While U.S. behavior in the Persian Gulf can be seen as a triumph of unilateralism, it is also true that Bush worked very hard to cloak U.S. action through a barrage of UN resolutions. And, having established this precedent, it will be very hard for Washington to intervene abroad — even in the manner of the Panama operation — without first gaining international support. The need to act in accordance with the presumptions of a new world order (or to give the *appearance* of doing so) could, therefore, act as an inhibition on any adventuristic use of force by the U.S. government.

At this point, it is still too early to predict how these contrary trends — the reassertion of *pax Americana* on one hand and the inhibitionary pressures of economics and morality on the other — will play themselves out in the years ahead. Nevertheless, it appears that the paradigm of mid-intensity conflict is firmly entrenched in official thinking, and that the principle of presidential war-making has received a significant boost. It is also apparent that these precepts enjoy considerable support in the U.S. Congress and among those Americans who take comfort in America's status as a military superpower at a time of declining economic vigor. In the absence of any substantial challenges to these two precepts, therefore, it is likely that they will dominate U.S. foreign and military policy for the indefinite future.

Notes

1. Carl E. Vuono, "National Strategy and the Army of the 1990s," *Parameters*, Summer 1991, p. 12.
2. For discussion of U.S. doctrine of counter-insurgency and LIC, see: Michael Klare and Peter Kornbluh, eds., *Low-Intensity Warfare* (New York: Pantheon, 1988), esp. chaps. 1–4.
3. The author first discussed the concept of MIC in "The New Military Paradigm," *Technology Review*, May-June 1991, pp. 28–36.
4. U.S. Commission on Integrated Long-Term Strategy, *Discriminate Deterrence* (Washington: Government Printing Office, 1988), pp. 10, 13, 33–34.
5. *Conventional Combat Priorities: An Approach for the New Strategic Era*, Report of the CSIS Conventional Combat 2002 Project (Washington: Center for Strategic and International Studies, May 1990), p. 23.
6. Presidential address at U.S. Coast Guard Academy, New London, Conn., May 24, 1989 (White House transcript).
7. *Department of Defense Annual Report*, January 1990, p. v.
8. Carl E. Vuono, "Versatile, Deployable, and Lethal," *Sea Power*, April 1990, pp. 57–63.
9. See *Atlanta Constitution*, October 25, 1991.
10. Quoted in *Air Force Times*, April 15, 1991.
11. For discussion of the new NATO strategy and the weapons technologies involved, see Klare, "NATO's Improved Conventional Weapons," *Technology Review*, May-June 1985, pp. 34–40, 73.
12. Statement of Dick Cheney before the House Foreign Affairs Committee, March 19, 1991 (Dept. of Defense transcript).
13. *New York Times*, August 25, 1990.
14. Vuono, "Versatile, Deployable, and Lethal."
15. *Wall Street Journal*, September 6, 1990.

16. *New York Times*, December 1, 1990.
17. For further discussion of the high-tech bombs and missiles used by Coalition forces in the Persian Gulf War, see: Klare, "High-Death Weapons of the Gulf War," *The Nation*, June 3, 1991, pp. 722, 738–42; and Dave Walker and Eric Stambler, ". . . And the Dirty Little Weapons," *Bulletin of the Atomic Scientists*, May 1991, pp. 20–24.
18. Speech before the Commonwealth Club of San Francisco, February 7, 1991 (White House transcript).
19. Gen. A.M. Gray, "Defense Policy for the 1990s," *Marine Corps Gazette*, May 1990, p. 18.
20. John McCain, "The Need for Strategy in the New Postwar Era," *Armed Forces Journal* (January 1990), p. 44.
21. Statement of Dick Cheney before the National Press Club, Washington, D.C., March 22, 1990 (Dept. of Defense transcript).
22. Quoted in *Dallas Morning News*, March 3, 1991.
23. Interview in *Air Force Times*, April 15, 1991.
24. Statement at the Air University, Maxwell Air Force Base, Ala., April 13, 1991 (White House transcript).

5

Contingency Plans:
Nuclear Weapons After the Cold War

Michio Kaku

Since time immemorial, the rise of empires has been closely accompanied by their aggressive use of superior weaponry. Whether it was the British gun-boat of the 1800s, the machine guns and tanks of the Great Powers in the early 1900s, or the nuclear weapons of the superpowers in the mid-1900s, weapons have always been the backbone of imperial power, playing an intimate role in their rise and fall. Whether it was the routing of the Persian forces by Alexander the Great, the sacking of Carthage by Rome, or the defeat of the Spanish Armada by the British, such pivotal, epoch-making events in world history have often hinged upon the decisive and critical use of military force.

However, with the collapse of the Soviet Union and the rise of the "New World Order," it is widely believed that nuclear weapons have become largely obsolete and have finally outlived their purpose. A nuclear "deterrent" is unnecessary if there is nothing left to deter. A nuclear "containment" policy is unnecessary if there is nothing left to contain. Indeed, the willingness of the Russians to sell perhaps several hundred tons of weapons-grade uranium and plutonium to the U.S. seemed to herald a diminished role for nuclear weapons.

If "deterrence" was the primary purpose of nuclear weapons, then all this is correct. Then future historians will record that nuclear weapons were finally banned during the New World Order. However, contrary to the prevailing myth, deterring an attack from the Soviet Union was never really the primary purpose of nuclear weapons. Hence they will continue to play a crucial role for decades to come.

Unknown to the American people, the primary strategy of the Pentagon has always been *nuclear warfighting*, i.e. controlling conventional confrontations with the use of nuclear threats, up to and including first strike.[1] To the Pentagon, nuclear weapons were always treated like any other conventional

60

weapon, obeying the classic, universal laws of military strategy laid down by von Clausewitz in the last century. The only difference was that they were a million times more powerful than conventional weaponry. As stated by nuclear strategist Paul Nitze, nuclear warfighting implies being prepared to unleash "the utmost levels of violence" to gain control over conventional conflicts.

For example, a robber pointing a gun to a teller's head is using a potent threat used to control the conflict. The robber may not intend actually to pull the trigger. However, the threat is credible only if the robber is physically and mentally prepared to blow the teller's head off. The robbery is successful only if the teller believes that the robber is capable of controlled violence and murder.

In this way, nuclear weapons are used every day. They are used whenever nuclear-equipped battleships are sent conspicuously to sail off the coast of Lebanon, Nicaragua, Libya, etc. For example, approximately 300 nuclear weapons were aboard battleships and aircraft carriers patrolling the Persian Gulf during the height of the Gulf War. This policy was stated most eloquently by Henry Kissinger, who first rose to fame among policymakers with the publication of his watershed book, *Nuclear Weapons and Foreign Policy*. In that book, nuclear weapons were identified as the cornerstone of U.S. foreign policy during the Cold War.

In this article, we will investigate how nuclear weapons will continue their role in the New World Order, including

1) third generation nuclear weapons and the Third World
2) selective proliferation and nuclear threats
3) Star Wars and first strike.

Third Generation Nuclear Weapons

President Bush strenuously prevented any Congressional move to ban the testing of nuclear weapons in Nevada. This seemed puzzling if deterrence was his primary goal. Testing is unnecessary if there is nothing that has to be tested.

However, the real purpose of nuclear testing has been to ensure the deployment of third generation nuclear weapons, which were only reaching maturity in the early nineties. These third generation nuclear weapons are designed specifically to control conventional conflicts, especially in the Third World.

First generation nuclear weapons, like the first hydrogen bomb called "Mike," were large, bulky, weighing as much as a railroad car. They could barely fit in the bomb bay of a B-52. They were strictly indiscriminate weapons of mass murder. Second generation hydrogen bombs were called MIRVs, which were small enough so that several of them could be packed into the nose cose of a Minuteman missile, raising the possibility of attaining disarming first strike capability, i.e. the ability to capture enemy missiles in their silos, bombers on their airfields, and submarines in their ports in one disarming strike.

However, third generation hydrogen bombs are called "designer hydrogen bombs," i.e. weapons designed to perform sophisticated tasks on the battlefield. The world got its first glimpse of these third generation weapons with the Star Wars program, which was originally designed to deploy X-ray lasers energized by the force of a third generation hydrogen bomb.

In actual warfare, these third generation devices first surfaced in public in January 1991, the week before the bombing of Baghdad began. The Pentagon leaked to *Newsweek* magazine the details of how these weapons could be used to pulverize the Iraqis.[2] First, a hydrogen bomb might be detonated over their capital. The resulting electromagnetic shock wave would blind their extensive anti-aircraft radar systems. Then the Iraqi army would be vaporized in their hardened bunker positions by firing neutron bombs and "earth penetrators" which would explode deep below the surface of the desert.

Third generation hydrogen bombs have been made possible by recent advances in nuclear physics. Today, hydrogen warheads are designed like a Swiss watch; physicists know, microsecond-by-microsecond, precisely how the nuclear shock wave expands within the core of the bomb during the various stages of a nuclear detonation. As a result, they can now tinker with these ingredients and design warheads with a specific yield, energy spectrum, fallout, etc. Like a tailor making a suit to fit the demands of a customer, nuclear physicists can now make hydrogen bombs to order.

Recently, internal documents of the Los Alamos National Laboratory, which developed the first atomic bomb, were made public, giving us a rare insight into how these weapons could be used against Third World countries.[3] It was revealed that the lab was accelerating efforts at developing these advanced weapons, which would be sophisticated, precision guided nuclear warheads. One important weapon designed to control conventional conflicts is called the "tinynuke," with an explosive yield one twentieth of the original Hiroshima bomb. Like its cousin, the neutron bomb, the tinynuke would be used directly to immobilize ground troops. With a force of only 1,000 tons of TNT and producing limited fallout, the U.S. could rapidly occupy battlefields which were originally irradiated by these weapons only hours or days earlier. Using precision guidance and controlling the explosive yield of this battlefield weapon, the Pentagon hopes to reduce political opposition to these weapons by limiting "collateral" damage to civilians.

For warfare in the desert and jungles, the laboratory has been developing the "micronuke," a warhead with a thousandth of the power of the Hiroshima bomb, but still ten times the force of the 2,000-pound bombs dropped on Iraq. This weapon could be fired with a missile equipped with an earth penetrating warhead, capable of striking underground command-and-control centers. Since ordinary hydrogen warheads have limited use against bunkers deep in the earth, these earth penetrators are to be used against a heavily fortified, dug-in force.

In the event that the enemy has a fledging missile force, the laboratory has been developing a "mininuke," with a force a hundredth that of the Hiroshima bomb. This weapon is designed to destroy enemy missiles in flight by detonating a nuclear shock wave. Rather than relying on direct hits (like the

Patriot missile), these missiles may even miss their target by a wide margin yet still have a "kill" because of the nuclear shock wave.

The Bush Doctrine

Nuclear policy in the New World Order, however, will differ from the Cold War in one important way. The "Bush Doctrine" states that the U.S. would go to war against any Third World adversary that was developing nuclear weapons. This Doctrine was developed before the Gulf War began, when President Bush had difficulty persuading the American people of the necessity to go to war. Opinion polls showed that the public was split evenly 45%– 45% on the question of war. What apparently tipped the scales was the inflammatory statement that the Iraqis could produce a atomic bomb within a "few months," even though this flatly contradicted the estimates of most nuclear physicists that it would take about 10 years.[4] After the Gulf War, the most accurate estimate was that Iraq was still several years away from nuclear weapons because of serious bottlenecks in their program.

Although the Iraqis were years away from developing even a primitive nuclear force, it is ironic that disclosures have shown that the relatively primitive Iraqi nuclear infrastructure was developed largely by the West. Under President Bush, generous exchanges of high technology were made to the Iraqis, some of which were subsequently diverted to the nuclear program, an issue which began to surface during the 1992 presidential campaign.

For example, more than $1.5 billion of sensitive high technology for Iraq was licensed by the U.S. Commerce Department before the Gulf War, including sensitive equipment from 200 major companies in the West: Hewlett-Packard, Honeywell, Unisys, International Computer Systems, Rockwell, and Tektronix.[5] All signed lucrative trade agreements with the Iraqi Atomic Energy Commission and Saad 16, Iraq's missile research center. Honeywell even did a study of a gasoline bomb warhead for the Iraqi military. It is therefore not surprising that much of the high technology seen being blown up on CNN during the Gulf War came from the U.S. and West Germany.

On the surface, this policy towards Iraq, first arming it with billions in high technology and then reducing much of its industrial infrastructure to useless rubble, seems schizophrenic. However, this zig-zag in the U.S. treatment of Iraq can be explained if we understand two long-standing U.S. policies: divide-and-conquer, and selective proliferation.

Under President Nixon, the Shah of Iran was chosen to become the U.S. surrogate, the policeman of the Gulf. As a consequence, he was propped up with generous arms shipments and his murderous security force SAVAK was trained by the CIA. The Shah then obediently carried out U.S. interests in this vital but volatile area. When the Shah fell and the Iranian fundamentalists took over, the U.S. needed a counterweight to Iran in order to maintain its balance of power, so it tilted toward Iraq, especially during the Iran-Iraq war. That was the reason why the Bush administration willingly allowed nuclear-related technology into Iraq.

However, when Iraq invaded Kuwait and the Iraqis were defeated, the

U.S. deliberately refrained from backing Kurdish and Shi'ite separatists, because a dismembered Iraq would allow Iran to reassert its dominance in the Gulf.

Selective Proliferation

Most Americans believe the U.S. government has consistently tried to prevent the proliferation of nuclear weapons technology around the world. The American people willingly supported President Bush's pledge to use force to stop the spread of nuclear weapons to Iraq.

The true U.S. policy is selective proliferation, i.e. selectively proliferating bomb technology to your Cold War friends and denying it to your enemies. This policy was explained by Kissinger, who once said that if a nation was going to build a bomb anyway, why not provide certain assistance in order to influence its foreign policy?

This policy, originating in the Cold War, has remained in effect. It is no accident that the newest members of the nuclear club include South Africa, Israel, and Pakistan, all of whom attained nuclear status with the direct and/or indirect help of the U.S. In 1988, interviews with top U.S. intelligence experts indicated that the number of atomic bombs possessed by these new nations were: Israel — at least 100; South Africa — up to 20; Pakistan — 4; India — 12 to 20.[6] Since then, these countries have steadily increased the number of bombs in their nuclear stockpiles.

For example, it takes about 1,000 ultracentrifuges operating continuously for one year to produce enough nuclear material for one atomic bomb (roughly 20 pounds of enriched uranium). In 1992 the Pakistanis had about 14,000 ultra-centrifuges, or enough, in principle, to make 10–15 atomic bombs per year.[7] The U.S. was fully aware of this, but has winked at the Pakistanis because of their crucial role in supplying the anti-communist rebels in Afghanistan.

In 1992, the Pakistani government publicly admitted, after years of adamant denials, that it had the capability of building the atomic bomb. This work was conducted in secret at their facility at Kahuta, near Rawalpindi, with the tacit blessing of the U.S. When the U.S. Congress passed a bill requiring that U.S. aid be stopped to those nations building nuclear weapons, the Reagan administration intervened directly on behalf of the Pakistanis, stating that Pakistan was exempt from the ban because it had not yet built such a bomb. However, as some analysts have stated in public, this argument was specious because the Pakistanis where only "one screw-turn away" from technically assembling an atomic bomb.

Dr. A.Q. Kahn, sometimes called the "father of the Pakistani bomb," who apparently helped assemble the first Pakistani atomic bomb in 1986, was quoted as saying, "America knows it. What the CIA has been saying about our possessing the bomb is correct." The Pakistanis were apparently even capable of producing an advanced, light-weight atomic bomb, weighing no more than 400 pounds, that could be strapped onto the belly of a U.S.-made F-16 fighter-bomber.[8]

The South African Bomb

The most striking example of the nuclear double standard is the way in which the U.S., while condemning the Iraqi nuclear project, has carefully nurtured the vast South African nuclear complex, centered at Valindaba and Pelindaba, which dwarfs the puny Iraqi program by several orders of magnitude.

As early as 1968, the U.S. gave 230 pounds of enriched uranium to the South Africans in order to power up the 20 megawatt U.S.-made Safari-I nuclear power plant, which operates on 90% enriched (weapons grade) uranium. In 1973, the South African government proudly announced that it had refined several tons of weapons-grade fuel for its Pelindaba reactor. In 1975, a rather astonishing statement was made by Dr. Pieter Koornhof, the Minister of Mines for South Africa. He announced the plan for a $4.5 billion new facility which would eventually have the capability of producing 5,000 tons of enriched uranium per year.[9]

Because South Africa has large natural deposits of uranium ore, it is essentially self-sufficient in uranium and has operated as an outcast from the International Atomic Energy Agency (IAEA) for decades. Although it had secured its own independent source of weapons grade uranium, it lacked one key commodity: the technical help necessary to fabricate an actual bomb. This technical know-how apparently came from Israel.

On September 22, 1979, the U.S. Vela satellite (specifically sent into orbit to photograph unauthorized nuclear detonations) detected a mysterious, brilliant flash of light off the coast of South Africa, near Prince Edward's Island. Nearby were two Israeli warships. Although the Carter administration tried to dismiss this as an anomaly, probably caused by random meteorites, a special Pentagon scientific task-force, in a rare event, contradicted the official position by maintaining that the mysterious flash was a "double flash," the unique fingerprint of a nuclear detonation.

According to Seymour Hersh of the *New York Times*,[10] this was actually the third nuclear test conducted jointly by the South African government and the Israel Defense Force to test a low-yield nuclear bomb that was to be standardized by the Israeli military. They carefully detonated the first two atomic bombs in heavy cloud cover in order to fool the Vela satellite. However, on the third test, they apparently miscalculated and fired the atomic bomb when there was a break in the cloud cover.

Hersh quoted one Israeli official, who was involved with the test, who said, "It was a fuck-up. There was a storm and we figured it would block Vela, but there was a gap in the weather — a window — and Vela got blinded by the flash."

According to Israeli defector Mordechai Vanunu, who worked at the top secret Dimona nuclear plant, the Israeli military possesses several hundred atomic bombs. Mr. Vanunu even sent color photographs of the nuclear bomb cores to the London *Sunday Times*. According to Vanunu, the Israelis at Dimona produce 1.2 kilograms of pure plutonium per week, or enough to manufacture 4 to 12 atomic bombs per year.[11, 12] When photographs of these bomb cores where shown to U.S. weapons designers, they identified them as being from advanced nuclear weaponry, most probably sophisticated "enhanced radiation weapons," commonly known as the neutron bomb.

If correct, this would make Israel the sixth largest nuclear arsenal in the world, with about 300 atomic bombs. According to Hersh, the Israelis were even poised to fire their nuclear weapons at the Arabs during one tense moment during the 1973 war. After the war, the Israel Defense Force established three nuclear-capable battalions, each with 12 self-propelled 175 mm nuclear cannons. Three nuclear artillery shells were stockpiled for each weapon, making a total of 108 warheads for these nuclear cannons alone for a future battle fought in the desert.[10]

This cooperation between the South African government and the Israelis also extends to testing intermediate range missiles. The Overberg South African testing range is used by the Israelis to test their Shavit (Comet) missile, which uses the Jericho-2B missile for the first two stages. The Shavit is powerful enough to send a 2,000-pound bomb a distance of 1,700 miles. It was, in fact, used to send the first Israeli satellite into orbit in 1988. One top U.S. administration official, commenting on the close relationship between Israel and South Africa in developing these weapons, said, "We know everything — names, dates, everything. We don't have any evidence that it's a plain uranium-for-missiles deal. Think of the relationship as a whole series of deals."[13]

First Strike

To understand nuclear weapons in the New World Order, one must understand the principles behind nuclear warfighting, based on the work of the mathematician John von Neumann. Although he was recognized as being one of the world's great mathematicians, he was also an anti-communist who used his creation, Game Theory, to change the Pentagon policy on nuclear weapons, laying the foundations for nuclear warfighting.

There are at least three key principles behind nuclear warfighting. First, said von Neumann, was the threat. One can control a conventional conflict, he theorized, by using a slowly escalating series of nuclear threats against the enemy. If the enemy refused to back down at one level, then these nuclear threats must be escalated to the next level. To make the threat credible, one must have weapons at every level of escalation and be prepared to fight at each level. Finally, if the enemy refused to back down after all these threats, then one must possess the trump card, the highest level of escalation: first strike capability. By controlling the "highest level of violence," one controlled all lower levels of violence in the conflict.

In nuclear warfare, this is called Escalation Dominance, i.e. controlling each level of escalation up to and including first strike. This is the reason why the bulk of the U.S. nuclear arsenal is *not* in the form of ICBMs, but in a bewildering variety of forms: nuclear artillery, shells, torpedoes, and cruise missiles on board ships, carriers, jet fighters, bombers, submarines, and battleships. In this fashion, the Pentagon can control a conventional conflict by threatening to escalate to nuclear weapons on any level of intensity.

For example, as early as 1954, the U.S. threatened to unleash Operation Vulture on the Vietnamese people at the battle of Dien Bien Phu. One plan was to drop two to six 31 kiloton atomic bombs on the Vietnamese people.[1] The strike was to be limited, so that it would not embroil the Soviets, but decisive enough to prop up the collapsing French empire in French Indochina.

In 1968, after months of escalating the conflict on the battlefield, President Nixon raised the level of escalation by threatening the Vietnamese with the November Ultimatum. Operation Duck Hook would have escalated the conflict by bombing the dikes of North Vietnam, flooding key areas of the country. If that failed, then the appendix to Operation Duck Hook would be executed, hitting the Vietnamese with two tactical nuclear weapons near the border with China.[1]

The second principle behind nuclear warfighting is uncertainty. The enemy must always be uncertain as to whether you are willing to escalate the nuclear conflict.

This is the official reason why the U.S. has for decades refused to sign a No First Use pledge in Europe, i.e. agreeing not to strike first with nuclear weapons. If the U.S. signed a pledge not to fire, then the enemy would know for certain that the U.S. would never escalate to nuclear weapons. This violates von Neumann's principle of uncertainty. Then tactical nuclear weapons lose their "threat value."

In early 1992, there was a classified Pentagon study which was leaked to the *New York Times*, stating that the primary goal of U.S. power should be to prevent the rise of any rival military power. The report went on and listed seven possible future challenges to U.S. power. Although this document was soon repudiated, the leak had, intentionally or unintentionally, served a definite purpose: to create uncertainty in the minds of potential adversaries that the U.S. might strike at future rivals to its power.

The third principle of nuclear warfighting is that one must be prepared to fire first, and possess the weapons of first strike. Most people, however, believe that nuclear weapons are "unusable" because they are too destructive. The key to nuclear warfighting, therefore, is to make nuclear weapons usable once again. This is the purpose of the Star Wars system: to make the world safe for nuclear weapons.

The purpose of a Star Wars system cannot be a purely defensive one, since a completely leak-proof shield violates the laws of physics. However, even a leaky shield is effective if one strikes first. This was most clearly stated by President Nixon, who once compared this to gladiators armed with swords. There is a stalemate if they possess the same weapons. However, if one of the gladiators suddenly grabs a shield, then the stalemate is instantly broken. The gladiator with the shield can strike first, weakening the enemy. If the wounded gladiator retaliates with a feeble second strike, then this is easily deflected by the shield.

In other words, the Star Wars system has its greatest (and perhaps only) military value in a first strike. During the Cold War, with the Soviets possessing 10,000 strategic nuclear weapons which could strike the U.S. in

30 minutes, even a massive commitment to Star Wars would have had limited threat value. However, after the demise of the Soviet Union, a Star Wars system has become much more practical and useful against a smaller adversary.

Will This Backfire?

Even though the Pentagon wishes to use nuclear weapons as the foundation for the New World Order, there are indications that this policy will eventually backfire.

First, selective proliferation has dispersed nuclear technology to unstable areas around the world (e.g., the border between India and Pakistan, the Middle East, South Africa) which may easily spiral out of U.S. control if a conflict flares up.

Second, third generation nuclear weapons reduce the "fire break" or threshold for conventional conflicts escalating to nuclear ones.

Third, maintaining this vast nuclear infrastructure accelerates the economic decline of the United States. A vast armada of ships and gunboats did not save the British empire, and nuclear weapons may not save the American one either. Nuclear weapons, instead of insuring U.S. hegemony in the "American Century," may very well contribute to its accelerating decline.

This is because continued military spending is perhaps the most serious threat to U.S. economic vigor. About 30% of the U.S. budget goes into the military, primarily to maintain a vast network of hundreds of nuclear military bases around the world to enforce the policy of containment and encirclement of communism. However, if we include hidden military costs in the civilian sector (e.g. the Department of Energy, which manufactures nuclear weapons, and interest on the national debt which is used to pay off the Vietnam War and Reagan's re-militarization policy), then almost 50% of the U.S. budget goes towards non-productive, parasitic military spending which does not contribute to economic vigor and which saps U.S. competitiveness.

A case can be made, in fact, that the astonishing rise of German and Japanese economic strength is due to their near-total absence of military spending. The Japanese, for example, spend only 1% of their GNP on weapons, which is much smaller than the generous amount they spend on research, development, planning, and modernization. It is the reverse in the U.S.

In a thesis developed by Yale professor Paul Kennedy, empires exist in three stages: economic empire, military empire, to inevitable decline of the empire. In what Kennedy calls "imperial overreach," the economy is sacrificed to maintain the military empire. The U.S., in 1992, is at stage three.

For example, in 1945, the U.S. controlled 50% of the world's wealth. In 1992, that number has declined to 25%, and is still falling. Most of that wealth was squandered maintaining a world-spanning network of 395 foreign military bases in 35 countries, which costs over $210 billion annually to maintain. With such a colossal military burden, the United States has undergone a remarkable de-industrialization process, which the world has not seen since England began to de-industrialize around 1900.

A journalist who once interviewed Ronald Reagan asked an interesting question: could the policy of "spending the Russians into a depression" eventually backfire. Was it possible that the U.S. would also be pauperized by its vast military spending during the Cold War? Mr. Reagan's response was quite surprising. He admitted that there was such a danger, but then he said confidently, "But they'll bust first."

Perhaps Mr. Reagan was correct in his first prediction. The Soviets have indeed bust first. But the U.S. is apparently not far behind.

Notes

1. M. Kaku and D. Axelrod, *To Win a Nuclear War: The Pentagon's Secret War Plans*, South End Press, Boston, 1987.
2. *Newsweek*, January 14, 1991.
3. "Little Nuclear Secrets," *New York Times*, September 9, 1992.
4. "Unless Stopped, Iraq Could Have A-Arms in 10 Years, Experts Say," *New York Times*, November 18, 1990, p. 1.
5. "Building Saddam Hussein's Bomb," *New York Times Magazine*, March 8, 1992, p. 30.
6. "Bombs in the Basement," *Newsweek*, July 11, 1988, pp. 42–45.
7. Ibid., see 4.
8. Ibid., see 6.
9. Ronald Walters, *South Africa and the Bomb*, Lexington Books, 1987.
10. Seymour Hersh, *The Sampson Option: Israel's Nuclear Arsenal and American Foreign Policy*, Random House, New York, 1992.
11. "Revealed: The Secrets of Israel's Nuclear Arsenal," London *Sunday Times*, October 5, 1986.
12. Frank Barnaby, *The Invisible Bomb*, I.B. Tauris, London, 1989.
13. "Israel's Deal with the Devil?" *Newsweek*, November 6, 1989, p. 52.

6

Coming in From the Cold?
The CIA After the Collapse of the Soviet Union

Marcus Raskin

The end of the Cold War and the collapse of the U.S.'s chief adversary in that conflict has challenged the very existence of the national security state, which has dominated American society for almost a half-century. A pillar of that apparatus is the nation's intelligence community — the Central Intelligence Agency, the National Security Agency and related agencies.[1] With an annual secret budget estimated at between $30 billion and $40 billion, these agencies, led by the CIA, have been in the forefront of the "secret war" for forty-five years. Aside from rare official inquiries such as the Church committee's investigations in 1975 and periodic exposés in the media, they have operated virtually exempt from public scrutiny. Only when the not uncommon disaster — such as Iran/contra — breaks into the headlines do Americans get a glimmer of what is being done in their name by the secret services.

Now that the Cold War is over, it's time for a far-reaching public debate on the future role of the intelligence agencies. In my view they should be dismantled or transformed, not merely reorganized. At the confirmation hearings of Robert Gates as Bush's Director of Central Intelligence, and in subsequent debates in the Senate, the question of the CIA's future was raised, but only a few legislators, most notably Senator Daniel Patrick Moynihan, have challenged its Cold War premises or questioned its future usefulness. Rather, the approach has been to try to think up new jobs for the CIA. The Senate Select Committee on Intelligence entertained such ideas as using the agency to help multinational corporations compete in the global economy or to wage stepped-up antiterrorist campaigns or to collect environmental intelligence.

On February 5, 1992, the chairmen of the Senate and House Intelligence Committees, David Boren and Dave McCurdy, respectively, introduced parallel bills on reorganizing the "intelligence community." But these legislative efforts merely sanctify into law the Cold War traditions of U.S. intelligence — covert operations, a threat mentality, a presumption for military intervention and the continuing need for the intelligence community. The "new" intelligence community would be led by a Director of National Intelligence, who would serve as the president's chief adviser on intelligence. Under both bills, the organization and decision-making would remain under the executive branch. As Senator Ernest Hollings said in committee, the intelligence community should maintain the capacity "to keep policymakers abreast of the great variety of threats the nation faces . . . proliferation of high-technology weapons, regional threats, terrorism, drug trafficking, economic and business developments among our trade rivals, and environmental change."

The fact that the senators were still thinking of the intelligence community in terms of the Cold War model was obvious in their performance during Gates's confirmation hearings in 1991. During his career, Gates had been involved in a variety of covert activities, cover-ups and "plausible denials." He claimed that he knew nothing about the Iran/contra affair, although he was deputy director at the time. As Senator Edward Kennedy, one of the CIA's few critics, pointed out on the Senate floor, "Mr. Gates's record is one of a cold warrior who skewed intelligence to fit his or his superiors' view of the world. He ignored the biggest scandal of the decade, intimidated those who disagreed with his views, and ignored the crumbling of the Soviet Union long after it began."

The CIA's failure to predict and analyze the likely consequences of a Soviet collapse was an egregious example of its Cold War mindset — its fiercely ideological cast and its belief in the value of stability over change (except when it is doing the destabilizing).

Despite Gates's involvement in these agency-wide failings and the testimony of other agency officials that he "cooked" intelligence reports to suit the Reagan administration, he was confirmed. The Gates hearings produced evidence that the CIA's activities were often counterproductive, useless or even criminal. Yet most senators professed themselves satisfied by Gates's *mea culpas* and accepted as acts of contrition his pledges never to lie to them, to be more open with the public and to clean up the agency's image.

In May 1991, seeking to increase Congressional control over the CIA, Senator John Glenn introduced a bill requiring that top officials of the agency, in addition to the director, be confirmed by the Senate, but this bill, which was tacked onto the Intelligence Authorization Act of 1991, was voted down by the Senate, 59 to 38. Opponents of Glenn's amendment argued that secrecy and czarlike power for the director were still necessary. The Senate's main concerns were about waste and duplication of effort. By April 1992 the Senate Intelligence Committee returned to its traditional role of covering for the CIA, even though the agency lied at least twice to the committee about the transfer of intelligence information to Iraq. After the end of the Gulf War, the CIA told the Intelligence Committee that the agency had stopped giving intelligence to the Iraqis two years before Iraq's August 1990 invasion of Kuwait. During the Gates nomination hearings the agency changed its tune and said it had ceased cooperating with the Iraqis in early 1990. After the nomination was approved, the CIA said it gave intelligence for another three to four months beyond early 1990. Then further information was released that suggested that the agency continued to give information until August 1990. Senator Boren did not seem bothered by these contradictions.

Reform efforts in Congress have been timid and marginal and seemed likely to remain dormant until another intelligence scandal surfaced. The opportunity to restructure U.S. intelligence for the post-Cold War world has been temporarily lost. Nevertheless, transforming the Cold War intelligence apparatus should be a topic of public debate for the rest of this century, just as U.S. national defense assumptions must be continually re-examined and revised in the light of realities of the post-Cold War world. The debate over American and world security has just begun. The purpose of this essay is to contribute to that debate by reconsidering the root assumptions and policy alternatives of national security.

In my view, such a reappraisal will show that the Cold War mission of the intelligence community has ended and that it should be dismantled, along with the atmosphere of paranoia and conflict that it fed and propagated at home and abroad. The history of U.S. intelligence over the past forty-five years teaches us what needs to be done if it is to serve democratic ends.

I.

During the Cold War years, U.S. intelligence operations were carried out according to a conflict/threat model of international relations. Within that model, American policymakers assumed that the United States was under continuous siege from enemies real or potential, but mostly conjured. It assumed that the U.S.'s place in the world was primarily achieved through military and covert means. And it assumed that the United States could never be at peace, that it must always be involved in some kind of military or paramilitary activity that it initiated and controlled.

American leaders believed that the state required an extensive covert intelligence operation that would assure the nation's superiority in the conflict with its chief enemy, the Soviet Union. Also needed were internal security controls to insure a compliant citizenry. The role of the intelligence community was to perceive the world through the lens of distrust. Institutionalized paranoia was the prescription for the American people, not only against enemies abroad but against their fellow Americans as well.

In addition to exaggerated fears of Soviet power and intentions, the conflict/threat model presumed a world inhabited by Enemy Others. The U.S.'s competitive spirit accepted cooperation in military alliances only when it was the leading partner. The Soviet Union was portrayed as the archrival, an enduring, pervasive threat that was behind all mischief in the world. To combat it, the United States had to engage in a variety of dirty tricks in the "back alleys" of the world, in Secretary of State Dean Rusk's phrase.

As a recent Pentagon working paper ("Defense Planning Guidance: 1994–1999") indicated, the conflict/threat model is far from dead. Under this Defense Department proposal the United States would preside over a *pax*

Americana and "discourage" advanced industrial nations from "challenging our leadership," as well as deter "potential competitors from even aspiring to a larger or global role." This country, the Pentagon said, "will retain the preeminent responsibility for addressing selectively those wrongs which threaten not only our interests, but those of our allies or friends, or which could seriously unsettle international relations." Such a policy of world dominance has failure written all over it. As Quincy Wright, a leading international lawyer of the post-World War II era, pointed out, "The effort to achieve ideological and political unification by the French Revolution and Napoleon, by the Fascist revolution and the Axis, and by the communist revolution and Stalin failed and again indicated that co-existence and co-operation among independent nations is the only basis for peace, order, and justice in the world of varied nationalities and ideologies." This reasoning is especially compelling in the aftermath of the collapse of the Soviet Union.

We tend to forget that there is an alternative to the conflict/threat model — the cooperation model. It calls for international cooperation, with nations working through international bodies, adhering to international norms and settling disputes peacefully. The cooperation model gives high priority to finding solutions to the difficult problem of squaring national sovereignty with a code of international human rights, eschewing unilateral intervention and pursuing a comprehensive disarmament program while establishing an international security arrangement through the Military Staff Committee of the United Nations.

During World War II and immediately after, the cooperation model enjoyed a brief ascendancy, reflecting the U.S.-Soviet alliance, the hopes for the newly formed UN, the people's yearning for peace. But with the defeat of Henry Wallace's Progressive Party in the 1948 election; the death of two-time GOP presidential candidate Wendell L. Willkie, whose internationalist ideas dominated the liberal wing of the Republican Party; the rise of McCarthyism; the victory of the Maoists in China; the economic recession of 1949; and the escalation of border skirmishes between the forces of North and South Korea into full-scale war the following year, the cooperation model died, eclipsed by the Cold War. The conflict/threat model dominated government policy and other institutions as well — cultural, educational, economic.

The bureaucratic rationale for the CIA emerged from fears of officials in the Office of Strategic Services (the war-time precursor to the CIA) that the United States was too dependent on British intelligence, that the Soviet Union was seeking control over Eastern Europe and that adequate information was needed to counterbalance Soviet attempts at expansion. According to Anthony Cave Brown in his book *Wild Bill Donovan: The Last Hero*, a paper, "The Basis for a World-Wide Intelligence Service," was prepared by Lieut. Col. Otto Doering for the chief of the OSS, Maj. Gen. William Donovan, in 1944. Doering recommended that such an intelligence service be given, among other things, "access to vouchered and unvouchered funds . . . its own communications systems . . . [responsibility] for all secret activity, including secret intelligence, counterespionage, cryptanalysis, and subversive operations." He hoped that it would grow out of the OSS and would be directly responsible to the president. It would not have any police function.

Donovan revised Doering's paper and sent it to President Roosevelt in November 1944. It presented a comprehensive plan for an intelligence service that "would coordinate, collect and produce finished intelligence, its coordination extended to all government intelligence agencies." Collection would include espionage and counterespionage. The proposed service would also conduct extensive subversive operations abroad and "perform such other functions and duties relating to intelligence" as the president might direct. The production of intelligence would relate to "national planning and security in peace and war," and the new service would have access "to the intelligence production of all other services."

The Donovan paper was leaked to *Chicago Tribune* reporter Walter Trohan, an influential conservative journalist of the period. In a story on the Donovan-Doering plan, he charged that it would create a "super-gestapo agency" to spy on the world. The public and Congressional outcry was immediate. Congressional members referred to the proposed agency as the New Deal version of the Soviet OGPU (the forerunner of the KGB). The leak, which according to Trohan was initiated by Roosevelt through his press secretary, Steve Early, had the effect of sinking Donovan's chances to head the new intelligence agency. Indeed, Congress disbanded the OSS, and under the terms of the National Security Act of 1947 set up a new organization to supersede it. The CIA was not much of an improvement over Donovan's model. The major civil liberties safeguard imposed on the CIA was that it was barred from carrying out internal police functions. Those functions were left to the noted civil libertarian J. Edgar Hoover. Soon enough, the CIA — and other intelligence units within the armed forces as well — would compete with the FBI in domestic spying by infiltrating political groups, often for disruptive purposes. The classic cases of such CIA and NSA activities were Operations Chaos and Minaret, which were illegal spying programs against Americans that used warrantless electronic surveillance and human intelligence.

A Game Without Rules

In 1954, a commission appointed by President Eisenhower and chaired by Lieut. Gen. James Doolittle formulated an official rationale to justify intelligence activities already underway. In a key statement, the commission said: "It is now clear that we are facing an implacable enemy whose avowed objective is world domination by whatever means and at whatever cost. There are no rules in such a game. Hitherto acceptable norms of human conduct do not apply. If the United States is to survive, long-standing American concepts of 'fair play' must be reconsidered. We must . . . learn to subvert, sabotage and destroy our enemies by more clever, more sophisticated and more effective methods than those used against us." It also concluded, "Another important requirement is an aggressive covert psychological, political and paramilitary organization more effective, more unique and, if necessary, more ruthless than that employed by the enemy. No one should be permitted to stand in the way of the prompt, efficient and secure accomplishment of this mission."

Spying was indeed a dirty business. The operations of the CIA and other agencies were often immoral, unconstitutional and criminal. Such activities would have made the public uneasy, so they had to be shrouded by the arts of secrecy and plausible denial. Since the CIA often operated as the president's private army, the executive branch became a kind of front for illegal covert actions. The president gave them a patina of legitimacy, thereby turning the office into a switching point between criminal and lawful activities. Sometimes, of course, presidents or their subordinates were caught flat-footed participating in criminal activities, as when Howard Hunt, a former CIA agent working for the White House, used the agency to help him break into the office of Daniel Ellsberg's psychiatrist.

Secrecy also served to shield the intelligence establishment (and its hefty budgets) from Congressional and media scrutiny. It insulated the CIA from public examination that might have prevented it from launching disastrous operations like the Bay of Pigs invasion or Operation Phoenix in Vietnam, in which some 20,000 innocent people and suspected Vietcong supporters were murdered. Without outside criticism of its past mistakes, the CIA was doomed to repeat them.

And so for decades it conducted interventions worldwide, subverting governments, arming insurgencies, spreading black propaganda. Often these actions produced harmful consequences. The "victorious coup" in Iran that expelled Mossadegh brought back the Shah, whose misrule paved the way for the Ayatollah Khomeini. The 1954 coup that overthrew Guatemala's democratically elected government produced decades of cruel dictatorship. The glorious putsch that expelled Sukarno in Indonesia brought in its wake the murder or imprisonment of hundreds of thousands of Indonesians. Back in Washington, the exaggerations of Soviet capabilities and intentions by various elements of the intelligence community fed and sustained the arms race.

"Scholars and Spies"

The benign view of itself the CIA projected — as a mere gatherer and dispenser of information to the president from its "campus" at Langley, Virginia, where strolled professorial, pipe-smoking types — was gradually eroded by belated revelations that some of these men had conducted experiments on unwilling subjects with mind-altering drugs, had used germ warfare agents against poor nations and had planned and executed coups.

As the Gates hearings showed, the CIA's "scholars and spies" were hardly dedicated to independent inquiry. Often their analyses were slanted to pander to the desires of the policymakers and the predilections of the national security curia. To advance their careers, junior analysts skewed their reports to harmonize with what the "hierarchic other," or superiors in the organization, wanted.

Secrecy invariably assumes a priesthood dealing in fixed truths and essences. It is the antithesis of the spirit of free inquiry exemplified in the teachings of pragmatism, the leading twentieth-century school of social thought. As John Dewey pointed out, "intelligence," in its full meaning as a powerful instrument of social action, can work only as a *public* activity, in settings where judgements and conclusions can be cross-examined and verified through open inquiry and further discourse. "The one fact," he wrote in *Ethics*, "which is most certain is that throughout social life as a whole the older idea and practice which made knowledge a monopolistic possession still persists in a way which prevents the realization and even the fair trial of the democratic ideal. . . . The problem of bringing about an effective socialization of intelligence is probably the greatest problem of democracy today."

A secret bureaucracy, a policy of secrets within secrets, disclosed only to those with "a need to know," by its very nature engenders paranoia, institutional ignorance and control by a handful of executives, especially in the context of the conflict/threat mindset. The career of James Jesus Angleton, the poet *manqué* and former head of CIA counterintelligence, exemplified this tendency toward paranoia at the highest levels. Angleton apparently concluded that William Colby, a former Director of Central Intelligence and the head of Operation Phoenix, was a mole for the Soviet Union. Angleton's malign suspicions, fed by a Soviet defector, rocked the agency for more than a decade.

Angleton's case is perhaps extreme. In the closed society of the intelligence community, what the analyst concludes may be distorted by institutional pressures and a deep-seated policy that goes unquestioned but that distorts analysts' structuring of the data. In an intelligence agency millions of pieces of data are processed daily. As in any scientific inquiry, this flux must be arranged into some order, and the task of the analyst is to make an existential judgement of what he or she believes to be true or authentic. But what is found to be authentic in the closed society of intelligence may derive from a desire or a vested interest simply to please the boss. Undeniably, these factors are at work in other, nonsecret agencies of government. But there is an important difference: "Open" governmental agencies operate with some degree of accountability to Congress, the courts and, through the media, the public.

Covert Wars

But intelligence collection and analysis sometimes seemed the least of the CIA's purposes. The agency has generally been more interested in carrying out direct paramilitary interventions with the sanction of Congress or the president or, sometimes, on its own motion. In September 1970 President Nixon ordered CIA Director Richard Helms to take measures to make the Chilean economy "scream" in order to destabilize the government of socialist President Salvador Allende. Assassination attempts were made against unwanted foreign leaders, usually leftists like Patrice Lumumba in the Congo. Cuba's Fidel Castro has been a favorite target since the Eisenhower administration. But rightists were not immune. In the Dominican Republic, Rafael

Trujillo, a right-wing dictator who had lost the confidence of Washington, was assassinated in 1961. CIA "assets" who became leaders of their country and showed some independence, like Panama's Manuel Noriega, were cut down to size. Under the Reagan administration CIA-backed surrogates, or "freedom fighters," waged wars in Nicaragua, El Salvador, Afghanistan, Angola, Cambodia and Chad. Covert support to diverse elements in Eastern Europe was stepped up, sometimes with the help of Pope John Paul II.

CIA Director William Casey served as the field marshal of a worldwide system of covert wars. No area of the world was immune from intervention by the CIA, NSA and other agencies. All of these escapades flowed from what Frank Wisner, former Deputy Director of the CIA, once called "the mighty Wurlitzer" — the ten aspects of intelligence work. Each activity is inextricably linked to the others; like an onion, peel away one layer and you reach another, more dangerous layer. The ten are:

1. The gathering of information by overt or covert means (if the information is gathered by covert means, then as likely as not, another nation's laws are violated).

2. Evaluating, analyzing and storing information; finding assets (covert sources) and establishing proprietaries (dummy companies) to undertake specific tasks.

3. Advising and disseminating information that is often false and self-deceiving; getting U.S. government consumers to use the information, developing a market for it and fashioning information and facts that are custom-made for particular clients in the government. The market may want truthful information or lies.

4. Persuading government consumers to use information they may not ordinarily be interested in (an organization dependent on the whim of a president must provide him with what he wants, but he may bore easily, and so irrelevant or tabloidlike information has to be generated to keep presidential interest).

5. Organizing more covert activities to obtain information, verify conclusions and answer new requests of policymakers. This is accomplished by expanding the asset and informant network within the United States and abroad; reading intelligence material from other nations and other agencies within the government or from corporations; finding, then relying on, more intelligence material that is gathered secretly or through technical means; bribing and paying assets who are members of other governments.

6. Organizing clandestine activities to obtain classified information of other nations as well as undertaking disinformation campaigns in which material is manufactured to promote either the position of the CIA, the official policies of the United States, the agendas of specific groups within the intelligence community or policies that are contrary to those stated to Congress or that violate American law (it should be noted that such disinformation has often found itself blown back into the United States, where it was used to whip up political support for positions that had no factual predicate).

7. Organizing black operations of a complex nature such as economic and political destabilization, mining harbors, funding third-party nations to do

the bidding of the United States (as in the case of Israel) as well as receiving and organizing proxy funds.

8. Employing scientific and technological means to undercut the development or abort or inhibit the activities of an adversary nation; developing technical intelligence capacity, cryptography and topographic analysis through satellites.

9. Recruiting local armies and guerrilla groups and developing and guiding them so they can be used for the national objectives of the United States. Covertly sponsoring labor unions, women's groups and paying for crowds and demonstrators.

10. Using force — assassination teams when necessary — to assert the considered (or ill-considered) policy. Fighting small wars that are kept out of the U.S. media. Shielding the president by offering plausible denial and cover for illegal and criminal actions he ordered.

These activities form the foundation stones of the intelligence community. The entire project of this community helped to make the government of the United States into an Orwellian nightmare, in which "intelligence" became synonymous with massive self-deception and treachery. Force and fraud had found a home base in the intelligence community and in the Cold War conception of intelligence.

II.

The United States has reached a turning point: it must decide what sort of nation it wants to be. The future role of the intelligence community will have a direct bearing on the character of the nation, for the intelligence community helps determine the policymakers' perception of the world. It can sustain myths, generate and authenticate "threats," and give the color of rationality to force and fraud.

The struggles smoldering in Eastern Europe and the former Soviet Union, the clan animosities raging from Angola to Croatia, the endemic tensions in the Middle East and elsewhere in the world provide plenty of potential stages for future intelligence actions should the U.S. decide to continue playing the dirty game of back-alley wars.

But there is an alternative: adopting the cooperation model. This would mean dismantling the present intelligence community, abandoning those functions that served the Cold War state and reassigning to other agencies the functions that can be integrated into the cooperation model of international relations. In this scheme, intelligence analysis would be used as a communications bridge among nations rather than as a tool for power and control.

The cooperation model would be based on the premise that the problems of our world at the close of the twentieth century cannot be resolved by a single nation, the United States, pursuing its own ends. The environment, immigration, disarmament, economic justice and health, as well as the need for mediating regional and international disputes, are matters of world concern requiring the public exchange of ideas and information among a wide array of very different national cultures. A shift away from the conflict/ threat paradigm, which means demilitarization and the shifting of budget expenditures away from militarized national security policies, would free badly needed resources to deal with the United States's pressing domestic problems.

The United States is in the best position to lead the shift to the cooperation model because its military security problems can be dealt with through a worldwide general disarmament process in tandem with the strengthening of UN peacekeeping functions.

Under the cooperation model, intelligence would of course cease to be a clandestine enterprise. Instead it would operate as an international social project, in tandem with a new foreign policy agenda dedicated to environmental protection, scientific understanding, improved communications and information dispersal, worldwide economic development, health improvement and military disarmament.

Steps to an Open Society

What changes should be made in the intelligence community so that it could serve a nation that acts within the cooperation model of international politics? I would propose the following steps:

Step One. There should be a comprehensive revision of the National Security Act of 1947 to insure that the United States pursues policies of cooperation with the UN and respect for international law and human rights. The act's purpose, to "provide a comprehensive program for the future security of the United States," cannot be achieved under its current philosophy of militarization of governmental thought, command and organization, and of the employment of resources for war and conflict. The language of a revised National Security Act would emphasize global disarmament, stimulation of international communication, reinvestment in the U.S. infrastructure, preservation of the environment, protection of human rights and cooperation on common problems among nations in the post-Cold War world. Intelligence activities would be harnessed to achieving those ends.

Step Two. There should be a review of all laws and executive orders that give the intelligence community special status. The most relevant examples are laws that exempt various agencies from systematic review of their operations, from the federal pay scale and from federal labor-management relations statutes. We should also abolish the law exempting the CIA retirement system from public scrutiny and the CIA, NSA, Defense Intelligence Agency and certain other intelligence units from public financial disclosure requirements.

Several other Cold War laws should be repealed or revised, including those making intelligence agencies only vaguely accountable for how they spend their money. There are statutes that protect members of the CIA from false identification laws, computer fraud statutes, as well as those that allow interference with satellite transmissions. These laws violate the elementary principles of openness, democracy and cooperation that are necessary to international cooperation in the post-Cold War world.

Step Three. The CIA's analytic functions should be transferred to noncovert agencies of government. This would affect some nongovernmental sectors of society as well — universities, international corporations, labor unions and media that have maintained a symbiotic relationship with the national security state, including the intelligence agencies, since World War II.

The idea that knowledge and information know no boundaries, which dominated the scientific community before World War II, should be revived. The data-collection and analysis functions of the CIA and NSA should be internationalized much in the manner that medical information is now exchanged internationally and publicly. The information could be made available as part of an international information agency that would establish regional centers. The United States, with the assent of the UN Security Council and General Assembly, could form a worldwide consortium of intelligence agencies, served by a worldwide community of scholars and analysts whose researches would be made public and distributed widely through regional centers. It would be understood that this consortium would operate under the UN. Just as no nation can afford not to trade internationally, so no nation or society can afford not to share information for the common good.

The specific areas on which this consortium would concentrate are scientific and data gathering and dissemination; economic justice reporting; conflict resolution/environmental enhancement; the state of human rights; and the state of international agreements, especially in the disarmament area.

Step Four. The paramilitary functions that the CIA performed during the Cold War should be placed under the control of the uniformed military services, where they would be subjected to public scrutiny and civilian control. The War Powers Act and Article I, Section 8 of the Constitution, which gives Congress the power to declare war, govern the president's use of military power except when the United States is attacked. CIA covert actions under the military would be publicly accountable. To underscore this point, the laws on mercenaries should be amended so that they apply directly to government officials or their agents. These sections of the law now make it a crime for individuals to conspire on U.S. soil to destroy the property of or to organize a military expedition against a nation with which the United States is at peace. But penalties are relatively light, no more than three years in prison and/or a $5,000 fine. They should be substantially increased. Throughout the Cold War, covert activities, many of them unauthorized, took place under the color of bureaucratic legality. In the future, rogue operators or those who otherwise transgress legal authority would be subject to criminal prosecution.

In other words, military interventions, economic destabilization and other covert actions would be deemed criminal offenses. A president who sought to avoid the constitutional constraints by running a secret war or intervention would face impeachment. It should be noted that when the House Judiciary Committee drew up impeachment charges against President Nixon it did not include the invasion and bombing of Cambodia, a nation with which the United States was at peace. The ostensible reason for the committee's failure to act was that U.S. troops in Vietnam were threatened by North Vietnamese forces thought to be in Cambodia.

Step Five. The secretary of state should set forth a needs and requirements report to Congress in order to improve the political reporting of the State Department. The secretary would make clear that the department will absorb analysts from the CIA, but that it will not countenance being used as a cover for covert and clandestine activities.

Step Six. A Protection of Records Act should be crafted to insure that no records of the CIA or other intelligence agencies are destroyed. In this way a true account of the history of the Cold War period could be written. These records should be made public as quickly as possible after being transferred to the Archivist of the United States. Substantial penalties should apply to those government officials who attempt to forge or rewrite the record.

Step Seven. Except for that part of the National Security Agency that would be given over to the Arms Control and Disarmament Agency and, for specific and narrowly defined purposes, the Defense Department, the NSA would become an international public library under the control of the Librarian of Congress and secondarily the Archivist of the United States.

Any residual activities of the NSA should be subjected to rigorous public scrutiny by Congress in order to assure that its information be made publicly available, and to assure that its various activities are in fact constitutionally sanctioned. (For example, monitoring telephone calls is an invasion of privacy when those on the phone are not informed and have not given their permission.)

The use of technical intelligence to assure compliance with arms control and disarmament agreements should be strengthened. The NSA could link up with similar agencies throughout the world for the specific purpose of observing military maneuvers and the production and shipment of arms, as well as adhering to the disarmament process. All activities having to do with monitoring arms control and disarmament arrangements could be supervised by the Arms Control and Disarmament Agency and could be publicly conducted, with the NSA serving as the technical arm.

Step Eight. Throughout the Cold War, security procedures and surveillance of government officials have been used as an *in terrorem* policy to protect secrets and enforce loyalty. These secrets, as often as not, have reflected two types of material. The first broad category is related to technical scientific matters and military plans. The second is related to operations that were in violation of American law or the law of other nations and international law. Security procedures that in fact have been thinly veiled cover-up schemes (for example, Iran/contra) should now be forbidden by executive order.

Matters that pertain to the defense of the United States would continue to be secret. Such secrecy is warranted so long as classification is carried out by the Defense Department as part of its constitutional mandate and pertains to defensive measures permitted by the UN Charter, international law and the laws of the United States. However, the entire system of classifying documents would require comprehensive revision so that it would conform to the revised National Security Act described in Step One.

Step Nine. Under Article I, Section 5 of the Constitution, "each House may determine the rules of its proceedings" and "each house shall keep a journal of its proceedings, and from time to time publish the same, excepting such parts as may in their judgement require secrecy." This section would appear to give ample support to the idea of secret hearings (executive session). However, during the Cold War this rule of prudence of the Constitution was severely abused. Secrecy was used as a way of coopting various members of Congress and committees into intelligence activities that would ordinarily be subject to legal challenge, criticism and debate.

The end of the Cold War is the right time to restore a rule that is clearly contemplated by the Constitution, namely, that secrecy in government is the exception and not the normal way of doing business. Congress itself should now revise its own organizational structure on national security matters. It should re-examine its own assumptions regarding secrecy and the harm caused by its failure to be an independent and disinterested public guardian over the intelligence agencies. House Rule XLVIII, which governs the House Permanent Select Committee on Intelligence, begins from the assumption of secrecy and nondisclosure of information. Senate Resolution 400, which established its Select Committee on Intelligence, also assumes that its work is primarily secret. The irony is that concern about leaks by Congressional members is greater than concern about the actual practices of the intelligence agencies.

The United States is a protean organism; it can change its shape and purpose. And it can assist in giving birth to a cooperative world civilization that recognizes the importance of cultures and nations outside Europe. If American leaders attempt to control a messy, recalcitrant reality through military and covert means, if the nation does not take stock of itself and initiate its own internal reconstruction, then the future will indeed be a nightmare of decline and continuous war, with the covert agencies leading the way. The U.S. will continue to mistake paranoia for intelligence, and American leaders will be seeking new Enemy Others to justify the national security state. Without substantial changes in attitudes and direction, the intelligence community will be a willing accomplice, supplying or inventing new threats to an insecure leadership and nation. This year the threat could be the Japanese and next year the Germans, or perhaps it is Iraq or Iran or Libya, or Croatians, North Koreans, African-Americans or immigrants, that justify covert operations.

It is time for the executive and Congress to come in from the cold. It is time for knowledge workers inside and outside governments to work together and fashion a world cooperation model that could help humanity transcend the horrible follies of the twentieth century.

Notes

1. The U.S. "intelligence community" properly includes the intelligence units in each branch of the armed services, as well as those in the State Department, the Energy Department, the Drug Enforcement Administration, the Justice and Treasury Departments and the National Imaging Agency.

7

The "New Enemy"?
Islam and Islamists After the Cold War

Yvonne Yazbeck Haddad

President Bush's remarks in his address to Congress, that ". . . [a] new world order is struggling to be born . . . a world where the rule of law supplants the rule of the jungle" has elicited a great deal of comment from Islamists. Their hope was that with the end of the Cold War, a new era would be inaugurated where the interests of Islamic countries would be taken into consideration. One writer even hoped that Muslims would be represented as one of the five permanent members of the Security Council of the United Nations. Operations Desert Shield and Desert Storm appear to have put an end to such speculation. Where they had hoped for a world in which dialogue among equals could bring about resolution of conflict, Islamists now describe the American utilization of force and the threat of force in the area as "the law of the jungle which is called international legitimacy, as long as there is one great power dominating with its policies and values."[1]

The Islamist literature identifies three "new world orders" that have been imposed on the Middle East during this century. All three orders were decreed by superpowers and are perceived to be marked by hypocrisy, proclaiming ethical principles and universal values that are contradicted by the policies that are implemented. All three ultimately have operated to the detriment of the people in the area.[2]

The first "new world order" was proclaimed at the end of the First World War as a result of the Sykes-Picot Agreement, which codified the dismemberment of the three Muslim empires (Ottoman, Safavid and Moghul), placing the majority of Muslim people under European rule (except for Turkey, Saudi Arabia and parts of Iran). It brought about the League of Nations which provided an international sanction for European nations to rule over Muslim states. The highly acclaimed Wilson Doctrine promising self-determination to all people denied that very right to the Palestinian people, who constituted the overwhelming majority in Palestine. It also legitimated the usurpation of Arab land for Jewish colonization. The dismemberment of the Ottoman empire was aided by the alliance forged between some of the Arabs and the British. The paramount ideology became that of Arab nationalism.[3]

The second world order was the product of the post-Second World War period. It brought into being the United Nations and created the context for the Cold War. It institutionalized the fragmentation of the Muslim world into nation-states, providing them with national boundaries, constitutions, flags and national anthems. (In 1969, forty-two independent states that identified themselves as Islamic created the Organization of the Islamic Conference. The breakdown of the Soviet Union has added six more states with Islamic majorities.) The United Nations sanctioned the creation of a Jewish state in Palestine. It affirmed the values of secularism and respect for the state system, yet soon after, the United States helped engineer the overthrow of the nationalist Mohammad Mossadegh in Iran and Dhu al-Fiqar Ali Bhutto in Pakistan, and attempted to undermine Gamal Abdel Nasser in Egypt precisely because it found secular nationalism inimical to its hegemonic interest in the area.[4]

The third world order proclaimed by Bush after the end of the Cold War brought an end to what had obtained since the end of the Second World War and "moved it [the Cold War] from the realm of politics to the domain of history."[5] It was marked by the Gulf War, which some Islamists dubbed World War III because of the coalition of nations that fought against Iraq. It led to a fragmentation in the Arab League and the acknowledgement of a new Arab world order, albeit one which is fractured along many lines. These fractures include divisions between the haves and the have-nots, between the Gulfies (*Khalijis*) and the Arab expatriates they call mercenaries (*Murtaziqa*), and between the Arabs and the Arabized (*Musta'riba*).[6]

For Islamists, the new world order proclaimed by President Bush marked a new shift in the role of the United Nations. They believe that it has been transformed from an agency for the peaceful resolution of conflict into an instrument of war. They note with great concern the decline of the power of the General Assembly and the enhancement of the strength of the Security Council. The unipolar world of United States hegemony which was created by the collapse of the Soviet Union appears to initiate a shift in policy instituting a significant change in military strategy in the area. This American strategy is seen as insisting on the subjugation and disempowerment of the people in the area in favor of the empowerment of the state of Israel.[7] Consequently, some go as far as to dismiss the new world order as illegitimate, "a name for a non-existent entity," because it does not represent the collective free will of the nations of the world. It is depicted as proclaimed by the "arrogant" West in an effort to safeguard its own interests and rejuvenate its own foundations by ascribing universal values to justify its actions that are inspired by greed.[8]

In the understanding of the Islamists, during the second world order Israel fought proxy wars for the benefit of the West to punish those who refused to be pliant clients. Now they see Bush's world order as one in which the United

States and its allies fought a massive proxy war for the benefit of Israel, all the while affirming the necessity of maintaining the disempowerment of all Arab countries combined.

During the summer and fall of 1992, the Bush administration provided a reassessment of the parameters of American foreign policy vis-a-vis the Middle East in the post-Cold War era. Assistant Secretary of State for Near Eastern and South Asian Affairs Edward P. Djerejian gave a series of speeches (at the Meridian House,[9] the National Association of Arab-Americans,[10] and the Middle East Institute[11]) that addressed the context of the relationship between the United States and the Middle East, outlined U.S. goals in the area, and identified the "fundamental values" that undergird American foreign policy. All quotations in this paper, unless otherwise identified, are from the Meridian text.

The miracle of modern technology has made the Middle East closer than ever before. In a very real sense, American declarations engender an immediate response from all Middle Eastern intellectuals regardless of their ideological affiliation. The CNN-ization of the world has made "instant reply" the order of the day. Rashid al-Ghannoushi of the Renaissance Party of Tunisia reported in a speech in London that he had, by October 6, sent a letter to Assistant Secretary Djerejian welcoming some aspects of his speech. He also addressed a variety of issues raised in its content.[12] His concerns are echoed in the speeches and writings of a number of Islamists who are attempting to contextualize the relationship, goals, values and policies outlined by the Bush administration and the perception that governs their response to its affirmations. This paper will deal with some of these attempts.

In his speech at the Middle East Institute, Djerejian agreed with Bernard Lewis that colonialism is over. A hopeful declaration, it nonetheless did not announce a major change in American policies in the area. While Islamists would be the first to welcome such a turn of events, American goals in the area as outlined in the text, though couched in new language, affirmed that the United States government continues to claim authority over the oil resources of the region and to provide unequivocal support for the state of Israel. Both of these goals are perceived by Islamists as a continuation of colonialism. "The persistence of unrestrained American support for Israel will enhance the Arab perception that America is the enemy of the Arabs."[13] Thus Islamists see decolonization as still in process. They continue to long for the day they will be in control of their own resources and their own future. Islamists see their governments as under intrusive constraints placed on them by what is termed "American interests" in the area and recognize that the U.S. government has control over their destiny in the economic, political and military spheres.[14]

In the Meridian speech, Djerejian noted that a cooperative world has replaced the conflict and competition of the Cold War as evidenced in the American response to Saddam Hussein's invasion of Kuwait. He cited the new "collective engagement" as the example of cooperation to prevent future crises. For Islamists, Operation Desert Storm was anything but the end of colonialism. Rather it was perceived as a reassertion of neo-colonialism and a confirmation of traditional imperial values and policies. American intervention is thought to be motivated by its imperial-Crusader-Zionist nature and its enmity to the *umma* (the Islamic worldwide community). "The United States did not act in order to support Kuwait or to defend Saudi Arabia; rather its aim was to implement the American-Israeli goals of destroying Iraqi military power."[15] Rashid al-Ghannoushi put it in these words:

> This inherent desire to dominate motivated the recent Western campaign in the Gulf. International law was a convenient tool, rather than a universal dictum to be applied even-handedly. Apparently, enforcement of these legal doctrines is dependent on the geopolitical nature of the countries involved, i.e. whether they are Western or Third World. The Gulf campaign objectives were threefold: 1) control of oil resources, 2) protection of Israel, and 3) the attainment of U.S. hegemony, not only over the Middle East, but also over the Western world.[16]

In the first place, Islamists perceive that the war against Iraq not only sanctified the lines drawn in the sand by Britain and France after the First World War, but was also a deliberate policy to maintain the division and fragmentation of the Arabs and Muslims in order to maintain Western imperialism.[17] While their initial response to the Iraqi invasion of Kuwait was negative, "The occupation of Kuwait is aggression and a crime,"[18] some were willing to tolerate it as a necessary sacrifice on the road to unity of the *umma*, a first step in erasing the artificial lines of division imposed on the area by Europe.

Second, from the Islamist perspective Operation Desert Storm guaranteed continued American domination of the economic resources of the region, not only by affirming American authority over the oil, but also by making Gulf regimes dependent on American protection. Furthermore, for several decades the inter-alia reflections in the region were to assess whether oil revenues belonged solely to the Gulf states or whether they should be shared with the Arab nation and/or the Islamic *umma*. The debate was over whether Gulf oil revenues should be for the private enjoyment of Saudis, Kuwaitis, and Qataris, or whether the wealth should be shared with the poorer countries of the Arab world such as Syria, Jordan and Yemen or with the poorer non-Arab Muslim nations such as Somalia and Bangladesh. Operation Desert Storm affirmed that the oil is not Gulf oil, Arab oil or Muslim oil, but is in fact American oil.[19]

Third, for Islamists, Operation Desert Storm demonstrated that colonialism is thriving by providing a public demonstration of the way the U.S. demands the subservience of client states in the region. Both Jordan and Yemen, who heeded the will of their people by refusing to participate in Operation Desert Storm, were punished through the withholding of aid.

Fourth, for Islamist observers colonialism is perceived as being alive and well since Operation Desert Storm guaranteed Israeli military dominance of the region. No effort has been made by the United States or the United Nations to eliminate Israel's stockpiles of weapons of mass destruction, whether nuclear, chemical, or biological. Rather, the United States continues to empower Israel and enhance its arsenal.[20]

Fifth, colonialism in its classical sense as usurpation of land for the settlement of an alien people at the expence of indigenous inhabitants is thriving since Operation Desert Storm has also facilitated the continued settlement of Palestine by Russian Jews, financed by the United States, while keeping the original people of the land (both Christians and Muslims) in exile or diaspora:

> While celebrating the end of the Cold War, a war on the Arabs and the Muslims has been declared through this enormous emigration . . . It is impossible for anyone, whatever their good intentions towards the United States, to see this immigration of millions as anything but an extremely hostile act against Palestine, the Arabs and the Muslims, comparable to the Balfour Declaration.[21]

The Meridian speech affirmed that the United States government does "not view Islam as the next 'ism' confronting the West or threatening world peace."[22] This statement was welcomed by al-Ghannoushi as one of the signs of positive developments in the relationship of Islam with the West. He also recognized the efforts of some scholars, some sectors of the media, and human rights organizations.[23] While Islamists have welcomed this affirmation, they continue to seek additional reassurance of consistency, not only in the statements that are issued, but also in the implementation of American policy in the region.

Several domestic agendas appear to profit from the demonization of Islam, giving the impression that Americans not only hate Islam but fear what they see as its irrational power:

1. The American press has had a field day depicting Islam as reactionary, obscurantist, prone to violence, oppressive of its women and intolerant of its minorities. Some Islamists go as far as to portray this as an intellectual, media and civilizational war waged against the Islamist ideology.[24] Of particular concern has been the image of Islam projected by the press, often seeming to echo the rhetoric of Israel's leaders. Whether through the writings of scholars such as Daniel Pipes and Bernard Lewis, or in the editorial comments of opinion makers such as Charles Krauthamer and Mortimer Zuckerman, or in policy considerations by talking heads or think tank experts such as Martin Indyk and Peter Rodman, the intention appears to be to depict Islam and Muslims as irrational and unreliable and with proclivities toward terrorism.[25]

2. Other detractors of Islamist movements have come from within the Republican administration. President Reagan after his election in 1980 gave an interview to *Time* magazine in which he said he feared that the Muslims were going back to their belief that unless they killed a Christian or a Jew they would not go to heaven. A decade later, Vice President Dan Quayle in a 1990 address to the graduating class of the United States Naval Academy at Annapolis said "the world is still a dangerous place . . . We have been surprised this past century by the rise of communism, the rise of Nazism, and the rise of Islamic radical fundamentalism . . ." Among the Islamists there is currently a suspicion that many employees of the State Department and "denizens of the beltway think tanks" are not only in search of an "ism" to attack in order to maintain their positions, but that they have indeed already

found in Islamism an enemy worthy to replace the collapsed "evil empire" of communism.[26]

3. The third American source of anti-Islamism verbiage has been the American political right, both secular and Christian. This includes such commentators as George Will and Pat Buchanan.[27] Since the Arab-Israeli War of 1967, the Christian right has found theological and Biblical justification to identify Islam as a menace. Pat Robertson has appeared on television and not only solicited funds for support of his telecast from Israeli-occupied south Lebanon, but also asked people to pray for the destruction of the Aqsa Mosque in Jerusalem, in order to rebuild the Temple and hasten the second coming of Christ. The Temple Mount Foundation has reportedly collected over a million dollars for the building of the Temple.

4. Palpable American fear of Islam has helped several Middle East and North African governments use the threat of Islamic movements as a ploy in seeking American support against Islamic opposition. The oppression of Islamists in Tunisia and Algeria has been justified by the fear of fundamentalism.[28]

Western fear of Islam has been very important in providing an impetus for the recruitment of people into the Islamic movement. Zionist and American concerns about the power of Islam are quoted by Islamists as proof of its efficacy. Political recruits to Islamism are told that various Israeli leaders have affirmed that they fear the power of Islam much more than that of Arab nationalism. Ben Gurion is reported to have said, "We do not fear except Islam"; Shimon Peres warned, "We will not feel secure until Islam puts away its sword"; and Yitzhak Rabin declared, "The religion of Islam is our only enemy."[29]

If the professed fear of Islamism by the West continues to expedite the recruitment of young people into the Islamic movements, the perception of American hypocrisy in its dealings with the people of the region helps maintain them in the cause. Despite American denial of a linkage between the Iraqi occupation of Kuwait and the Israeli occupation of Palestine and parts of Syria and Lebanon, Islamists have seen a strong parallel. Operation Desert Storm has clearly demonstrated for them the double standard of the U.S., which condemns the Iraqi occupation of Kuwait while it supports the Israeli occupation of Arab territory.[30]

Djerejian's Meridian speech once again reiterated the "fundamental values" that the United States promulgates as undergirding its foreign policy in the area:

> Reviewing the main thrusts of our policy in the Middle East reminds us that, even in the 1990s, our national security interests in the region continue to exert a powerful claim on our attention. But there is more to our policy agenda than protection of vital resources and conflict resolution. Another pillar of U.S. policy is our support for human rights, pluralism, women's and minority rights and popular participation in government, and our rejection of extremism, oppression and terrorism. These worldwide issues constitute an essential part of the foundation for America's engagement with the countries of the Near East — from the Maghreb to Iran and beyond.[31]

The resurgence of the issue of values as the major divide between Islamists and the West taps into a perception of the West as bent on divesting Muslims of Islam, at times projected as a civilizational war since Islamists lay claim to alternate values which they understand as truly universal.[32] That Muslims reject the American list of "fundamental values" is explained not as the inability to adjust to the modern progressive world; instead the act of rejection is seen as the necessary means of preserving the Islamic *umma* from disintegration.[33] From this perspective even the Palestinian-Israeli conflict in the Islamist discourse is seen not so much within the context of political, geographic or national concerns but is cast as the latest round between the world of Islam and the West, a struggle for cultural dominance.[34] The "fundamental values" are seen by Islamists as "a perpetuation of the general Western mode of tarnishing the image of political Islam . . . This has traditionally taken the form of portraying the Islamic trend as the antithesis of humanity's achievement — democracy, freedom, women's rights, the arts, tolerance, progress and plurality. Such negativism is manifest in the pejorative use of terms such as fundamentalism, radicalism and extremism which embody the misperception of an Islamic threat."[35]

It is important to note that colonialism during the last century was justified by a set of values which were declared to be universal, ones that should apply to the whole world. The British called their endeavor "the white man's burden," trying to elevate the colored peoples of the world to the standards of the white man. The French referred to their colonial adventure as the "civilizing mission," since they were spreading their hegemony over areas of the world that needed the civilization of the Enlightenment and the French Revolution. The American venture into colonial expansion was called "manifest destiny." Islamists understand the Western attitude towards native, non-European cultures to be still characterized by these very descriptions, and believe it to be condescending and contemptuous of other cultures as "not measuring up."

Islamists looking at the values proclaimed as undergirding American policy in 1992 — Bush's "new world order" — continue to see a double standard, or what they call *nifaq* (hypocrisy). They also note that while the United States government has identified human rights as a priority, it appears to make a difference whose human rights are being violated. The U.S. has been vocal and forthright concerning Iraqi human rights violations, while it has been silent about the incarceration of thousands of Islamists in Tunisia and Algeria, perceived by the Islamists as prisoners of conscience. The U.S. has also been silent about the persistent human rights violations by Israel against the Palestinian population.[36] Thousands are in jail, and in administrative custody without being charged with any crimes.

Islamists welcomed the State Department's affirmation that one of the underlying values of American policy is pluralism. Djerejian defined it in these words:

Americans recognize Islam as one of the world's great faiths, it is practiced on every continent; it counts among its adherents millions of citizens of the United States. As Westerners we acknowledge Islam as an historic civilizing force among the many that have influenced and enriched our culture. The legacy of the Muslim culture which reached the Iberian peninsula in the eighth century is a rich one in the sciences, arts, and culture, and in tolerance of Judaism and Christianity.[37]

Al-Ghannoushi considered this statement a major positive development since it provides a recognition of Muslim contributions to world civilization, as well as the presence of millions of Muslim citizens in the United States. It moves beyond the common identification of the United States as a Judeo-Christian country, and appears to allow for Muslim participation and input in defining the American future.

The affirmation of the rights of minorities was one of the foundational principles of British and French colonialism, which periodically justified intervention in the internal politics of the region. Both governments pressured the Ottoman Sultan at different times to grant equal rights to religious minorities in his empire. Islamists know that one of the objections Westerners continue to have to an Islamic state is that they expect that under an Islamic system Muslims would discriminate against religious minorities. The question they ask, then, is "Why is the United States silent about Israeli violations of the minority rights of its Christian and Muslim population?" Islamists point to the fact that the state of Israel, which discriminates by law against its Christian and Muslim citizens, depriving them of housing, land and other resources made available for Jewish citizens, is subsidized by some four billion dollars a year. Furthermore, the recent American action of establishing a "no fly zone" over Iraq in order to protect the Shi'ites of Iraq from an oppressive Saddam Hussein has raised questions by Islamists from Indonesia to Nigeria. They wonder both about the newly found "American love for Shi'ites" and about the apparent inconsistency of American policies: Why not establish a "no-fly zone" over South Lebanon where the Israeli air force as well as its surrogate Lebanese militia have been pounding at Shi'ites since 1978?[38]

Despite efforts to censor press reports surrounding Operation Desert Storm, Islamists throughout the world watched the progress of the war on CNN. They raised and continue to raise serious questions about whether or not Americans have any concern over the death of Muslims. During Operation Desert Storm, seventeen Palestinians were "massacred" at the Aqsa Mosque by the Israeli police.[39] At the same time Muslims observed "the concern index" in relation to the deaths of seven Israelis as a consequence of Iraqi Scud missile attacks. While Muslims worldwide watched American public celebration of the victory over Iraq, they wondered why Americans were jubilant at the death of 100,000 Muslims in that country. And they continue to ask, "Why is there a difference in the way Americans value Jewish life and Muslim life?" Concerning the present strife in Eastern Europe they ask, "Had the ethnic cleansing going on in Bosnia been targeting the Jewish population, would there have been a difference in the American response?" If so, "Why?"

Nevertheless, the West remains guilty of hypocrisy at the very least. . . . Bosnia, unlike Kuwait, does not contain invaluable oil wells that demand immediate, decisive Western acts of bravery. Since no tangible spoils will be gained, the neo-fascist Serbian genocide of the Muslims will find no "lines drawn in the sand." International law seems either to be inoperative in Bosnia or its tenets view the butchery as insufficient cause for intervention. Why, one must ask, do Western agencies insist on concentrating their efforts only on the delivery of humanitarian aid to the beleaguered Bosnians? For all intents and purposes, it appears as though they are fattening the prey for the slaughter. The international laws written by Western powers are applicable only to their own self-interests at the expense of aspirations, cultures and civilizations of other nations. . . . Thus the values which Western powers claim to apply even-handedly have been exposed to the Muslim world, which in turn has lost faith in a corrupt value system.[40]

The issue of the role and status of women reiterated in Djerejian's Meridian speech echoes some of the concern expressed by colonial officials at the beginning of the century. Muslims were told that their women were oppressed, their society was licentious and their practices of polygamy and easy divorce were reprehensible. Currently, Islamists are faulted because their women are too modest and do not emulate the new Western fashions in dress and lifestyle. Islamists cannot understand why the West seems to be obsessed with Muslim women. They wonder why Westerners think that Muslim women would ever want to be treated with the lack of respect that is shown to their American counterparts. Why would they want to be reduced to wage earners, only to be divorced and abandoned with their children to join the ranks of those under the poverty level. They are puzzled by the insistence that they should restructure their society and social agenda in order for women to become sex objects. They question the efficacy of adopting Western family values that would emulate what they see on television programs such as *Dallas*, *Loveboat* and *Dynasty*, values that are deemed unacceptable even by many of the leaders in the United States:

Despite the fact that the Muslim woman has emulated the European woman, her problems have not been solved. The problem of the European woman persists in being dangerous. Her earlier perception of herself was of gentleness and rectitude in society and of a righteous wife. In her new consciousness, her clothing uncovers her private parts in order to affirm the body in a society that is dominated by instant pleasure.[41]

As for support for popular participation in government for the "democratic way," Muslims throughout the world, whether nationalists, humanists, secularists or Islamists, are asking about U.S. silence concerning the Algerian elections and the repression of the Renaissance Party in Tunisia. The Meridian speech appears to justify American support of the Algerian suspension of the election in the following words: "While we believe in the principle of 'one person, one vote,' we do not support one person, one vote, one time." U.S. silence is construed as support for the Algerian junta's "hijacking of democracy." The United States is seen as the supporter of illegitimate autocratic governments.[42] Furthermore, Islamists ask why the United States has maintained silence over Israel's invalidation of the 1978 election in the Occupied Territories, at the time hailed as the freest ever held in the region.

Does the United States support elections only when they guarantee that the winners will be supporters of American policy? As al-Ghannoushi put it:

> The double standards are clearest when two revolutionary trends, occurring simultaneously in Eastern Europe and the Muslim world, are treated with a markedly bipolar attitude. The democratic drive was given full support in the former — not due to its sacredness, but because it was politically prudent in combating the spread of socialism by fragmenting it. Conversely, democracy in the Muslim world would unify its people, topple autocratic regimes and ignite an irreversible trend of progress. Such a synthesis would pose, by Western definitions, serious obstacles to their interests, which are tied to the current dictatorships. For this reason, the falsification of elections and mass, farcical trials in Tunisia, as well as the theft and oppression of the Algerian freedom of choice, is met with insincere objections.[43]

Islamists welcome the American rejection of extremism, oppression and terrorism, yet they perceive that the United States has refrained from condemning Israeli state terrorism as well as repressive measures on the West Bank and Gaza. They still await the freeing of the hostage Sheikh Obeid abducted from his home in South Lebanon by the Israeli forces. "The post-Cold War era, far from initiating justice based on truth rather than power-politics, has furthered suspicions within the Muslim *umma* that the international legal system, embodied in the United Nations' charter, is aimed at their subjugation rather than their emancipation."[44]

Affirmations that colonialism and the Crusades are over are not sufficient to allay Islamist fears that American policy in the region continues to be intrusive, subjecting the people of the area to the whims and needs of the United States. The justification of American foreign policy as based on superior values and its packaging in the cloak of righteousness is seen not only as hypocritical, but also as an insult to the intelligence of the people of the Middle East.

Notes

1. Munir Shafiq, "al-Istratijiyya al-Amerikiyya wa-Athar 'al-Nizam al-'Alami al-Jadid' 'Ala al-'Alam al-'Arabi," *Qira'at Siyasiyya*, 2; 1 (Winter 1992), p. 19.
2. 'Adel Mahdi, "al-Nizam al-Duwali al-Jadid wa-Atharuhu al-Wad' al-'Arabi wa-al-Islam," *Qira'at Siyasiyya*, 1; 2–3 (Spring-Summer 1991), p. 5; c.f. Khalil al-Shiqaqi, "al-Mustaqbal al-'Arabi wa al-Filastini ba'd Harb al-Khalij," *Qira'at Siyasiyya*, 1; 2-3 (Spring-Summer 1991), pp. 27–80.
3. al-Shaqiqi, "al-Mustaqbal," p. 28.
4. Mahdi, "al-Nizam," pp. 13–14.
5. Mahdi, "al-Nizam," p. 5.
6. It appears that a growing number of Gulf Arabs are questioning the authenticity of the "Arabness" of the people of the Northern tier and increasingly referring to them as Arabized and therefore of questionable stock.
7. This view is shared by other observers. "The linkage of this war to a supposed 'new world order' is serious, because it demonstrates for all to see that this 'new' 'order' is being initiated and constructed, and then is to be maintained, through the wanton destruction of the weak by the military force of the powerful." Andre Gunder Frank, "Third World War: A Political Economy of the Gulf War and the New World Order," *Third World Quarterly*, 13; 1 (1992), p. 279.
8. Mahdi, "al-Nizam," pp. 5–10; Ahmad Shawqi al-Hafani, "Azmat al-Khalij wa al-Amn al-'Arabi," *Risalat al-Jihad*, 10; 96 (February 1991), p. 30.
9. Edward P. Djerejian, "The United States and the Middle East in a Changing World: Diversity, Interaction and Common Aspirations," June 2, 1992.

10. Edward P. Djerejian, "The United States and the Middle East in a Changing World," September 11, 1992.

11. October 16, 1992.

12. Rashid al-Ghannoushi, "Islam and the West: Realities and Potentialities," paper presented at a seminar sponsored by the Centre for Democratic Studies, University of Westminster, London, October 6, 1992. (Trans. by Azzam el-Tamimi, revised by Ahmad AbulJobain, in Ahmad Yousef and Ahmad AbulJobain, *Politics of the Islamic Resurgence Through Western Eyes*, United Association for Studies and Research (forthcoming).

13. al-Shiqaqi, "al-Mustaqbal," p. 68.

14. Abu Zaid, "al-Islam," p. 36.

15. "Malhuzat 'ala Hamish Azmat al-Khalij," *al-Insan*, 3 (December 1990), p. 4.

16. Ghannoushi, "Islam and the West," p. 2; c.f. Muhammad Khalifa, "Harb al-Khalij Uwla Hurub al-Qarn al-Hadi wa al-'Ishrin," *Risalat al-Jihad*, 10; 99 (May 1991), pp. 30–35.

17. A Jordanian is reported to have said: "While the West saw its military intervention as a means to assure the emergence of a stable, just 'new world order' in the post-Cold War era, we saw it as a cruel attempt by the West to reinforce the unjust, untenable order which the West created in the early years of the century and from which we have suffered for three generations." Gabriel Habib, "New World Order: View from the Middle East," *Christianity and Crisis*, May 27, 1991; c.f. "'al-Wajh akhar li-Harb al-Khalij al-Thaniya," *Risalat al-Jihad*, 20 (June 1991), p. 16.

18. "Waqafat ma' Azmat al-Khalij," *al-Sunna*, 7 (November 1990), p. 37.

19. "The oil is not for the inhabitants of the Gulf alone, while other Muslims die of hunger." "al-Dual al-Khalijiyya wa al-Tahaddiyat," *Risalat al-Haramayn*, 20 (June 1991), p. 7.

20. Mahdi, "al-Nizam," p. 20; c.f. 'Atwani, "Itayqidhu," p. 79; "al-Wajh al-Akhar li-Harb al-Khalij," *Risalat al-Haramayn*, 20 (June 1991), p. 16.

21. Shafiq, "al-Istratijiyya," p. 10; c.f. Nasr 'Alwani, "Lakum fina Shuraka' ya Ahl al-Kahf," *Risalat al-Jihad*, 10; 99 (May 1991), pp. 96–98.

22. Djerejian, "The United States," p. 6.

23. Ghannoushi, "Islam and the West," p. 5.

24. Mahdi, "al-Nizam," p. 22.

25. Daniel Pipes, "The Muslims Are Coming, The Muslims Are Coming!" *National Review* (November 19, 1990) pp. 28–31; Bernard Lewis, "Roots of Muslim Rage," *Atlantic Monthly*, 226:3 (September 1990) pp. 47ff.; Charles Krauthammer, "The New Crescent of Crisis: Global Intifada," *Washington Post*, February 16, 1990; Mortimer Zuckerman, "Beware of Religious Stalinists," *U.S. News and World Report*, March 22, 1993, 80.

26. The idea for the dismemberment of the Muslim world is attributed to a European conference convened in 1907 to discuss the disintegration of European civilization. The conference reportedly decided that Muslims constituted the greatest danger. See Ahmad Mahmud Abu Zaid, "al-Islam bayn Quwwat al-A'da' wa-Jahl al-Abna'," *Risalat al-Jihad*, 10; 99 (May 1991), p. 37.

27. Patrick J. Buchanan, "Rising Islam May Overwhelm the West," *New Hampshire Sunday News*, August 20, 1989.

28. "The authoritarian regimes invoked the image of fundamentalism to secure Western backing. Thus ancient fears, anxieties and illusions surfaced when faced with the mythical 'fundamentalism threat.'" Ghannoushi, "Islam and the West," p. 3.

29. Ziyad Muhammad 'Ali, *'Ida' al-Yahud li al-Haraka al-Islamiyya* (Amman: Dar al-Furqan, 1982), pp. 45–6.

30. al-Hanafi, "Azmat al-Khalij," pp. 28–31.

31. Djerejian, "The United States," p. 5.

32. "After dismantling Islamic unity, Crusaderism in cooperation with other enemy powers uses a variety of means to distance Muslims from their religion and sever their relationship with God in order to loosen them from the bonds of the Islamic system and enlist them in apostasy and licentiousness." Abu Zaid, "al-Islam," p. 37.

33. Mahdi, "al-Nizam," p. 17.

34. Bashir Nafi', "al-Mashru' al-Watani al-Filastini Nahwa Marhala Jadida: Ay Dawr li al-Islamiyyin," *Qira'at Siyasiyya*, 2; 1 (Winter 1992), p. 59.

35. Ghannoushi, "Islam and the West," p. 3.

36. Khalid Baig, "The Carnage in Jerusalem: Facts vs. Israeli Lies," *The Message*, 14; 6 (November 1990), pp. 19–20.

37. Djerejian, "The United States," p. 6.

38. "What of the Kurds in Turkey who are systematically massacred in their homes and villages? What of the Palestinians in their refugee camps being raided regularly? And what of the Lebanese Shi'a civilians who are constantly attacked and raided, since the Zionist state invaded their villages and transformed those who escaped with their lives into refugees? How do they differ from the Shi'a of Iraq? All those groups are being murdered with American weapons, money, and sometimes even personnel." "Editorial" *The Arab Review* (October 1992), p. 3.

39. Baig, "The Carnage," pp. 19–20; c.f. "Al-Wajh al-Akhar," p. 17.

40. Ghannoushi, "Islam and the West," p. 4.
41. Malik Bennabi, "Shurut al-Nahda . . . wa-Mushkilat al-Hadara," *Risalat al-Jihad*, 10; 96 (February 1991), p. 111.
42. 'Abd al-Sabur Marzuq, "al-Ab'ad al-Gha'iba fi Azmat al-Khalij," *Risalat al-Jihad*, 10; 96 (February 1991), pp. 8–10.
43. Ghannoushi, "Islam and the West," p. 4; c.f. Ziyad Abu 'Amr, "al-Filastiniyyun wa-Tahadiyat 'al-Nizam al-'Arabi al-Jadid," *Qira'at Siyasiyya*, 2; 1 (Winter 1992), pp. 77–89.
44. Ghannoushi, "Islam and the West," p. 4; c.f. al-Hafani, "Azmat al-Khalij," p. 28.

8

Eco-Tiers:
Rio and Environmentalism After the Cold War

Susanna Hecht and Alexander Cockburn

As Rio prepared for the Earth Summit of June 1992 by paving the road to the airport and placing in detention the young street kids regularly assassinated by death squads, the inhabitants of Rio, one of Brazil's most depressed cities in a disintegrating economy, positioned themselves for the windfall of 30,000 participants in need of services ranging from taxis to transvestites. The Rio conference was one where the average citizen was rigorously excluded from the formal conference by phalanxes of Brazilian troops and UN peacekeeping forces. The *"cordon militaire"* and physical isolation of the Rio Centro conference site reflected the larger social and economic contours of the current environmental arena.

The realities of the Rio conference were resumed in its social geometry. There was the official ECO 92 conference, where national delegations and formal emissaries from international agencies like the World Bank cloaked *realpolitik* in the meliorist argot of environmentalism. In spite of their unparalleled weight in Rio, the G7, the group of the world's seven richest countries, had excised global ecological terms from their vocabulary less than a month later, when their economic summit proceeded as though the Rio conclave had never been. A separate forum was that of the Non-Governmental Organizations (NGOs), a term giving institutional expression to groups as diverse in their power, funding and social complexion as the World Wildlife Fund, the Methodist Church, peasant organizations, and women's cooperatives. More than one thousand of these NGOs had been involved in the long preparations for the Rio Summit. Finally, there was the Earth Parliament, largely composed of modest grassroots and indigenous peoples' organizations; those who bear the brunt of environmental degradation most directly, deploying the least power, but with the most extensive knowledge of sustainable resource management. Views of the dynamics and the responsibilities for greenhouse gas emissions, destruction of tropical forests, and intellectual

95

ownership depend powerfully upon one's position in these "eco-tiers." These divisions also underlie the relentless downgrading of Rio agreements from potential conventions and treaties, to "non-binding principles."

The original purpose of the Earth Summit was to arrive at a series of legally binding international accords on issues including climate change, forests, toxic wastes, and biodiversity, and to elaborate Agenda 21 (the Earth Summit's final document), and an Earth Charter. Oriented to the concerns of the developed world, climate and forests were the most prominent issues. Most of the features of these agreements were to be signed with smiles of triumph and bonhomie after the language had been worked out in a series of four "prep comms" and several ancillary working group meetings, the arenas in which the real politics were to unfold away from the glare and embarrassment of public scrutiny. But in this, the last decade of the twentieth century, there can be no pretense of a universal, mutually-agreed-upon agenda. At the end of the day, the largest document, Agenda 21, weighed in at 800 pages of non-binding normative principles. A late agreement endorsing the need for a convention on desert lands was mainly a sop to African countries who gained little from the conference (and who were usually exiled to roofless, phoneless booths at the ECO 92 site). The legally binding documents were so eviscerated as to have no practical impact. President Bush coyly resisted committing himself to a Rio appearance until after the CO_2 accords had been cleansed of any binding language about levels of emissions and timetables for their reduction. (This prompted the boycott of the meeting by the environmental minister of the European Parliament.) The treaty itself was reduced to a "framework convention," in which no targets or timetables were agreed upon. The U.S. government announced its resistance to the biodiversity treaty on the grounds that the U.S. would not pay for preservation outside its borders, nor hamper its biotechnology industries.

The transcendental rhetoric associated with major UN conferences scarcely does justice to either the agenda of such major players at Rio as the World Bank, or to the day-to-day struggles of native peoples, farmers, and poor urbanites agitating for such minimal considerations as potable water. The Earth Summit was, after all, the UN Conference on Environment and Development, and for many Third World nations the substantive controversies surrounding the latter term are the key to any strategy on the environment. Thus, in Rio issues that remain critical to any reconstruction of a development agenda were carefully avoided, in spite of considerable agitation by developing countries. All attempts at the summit to provide environmental guidelines to GATT (the General Agreement on Tariffs and Trade), which had viciously parried any environmental guidance as eco-imperialism, were scuttled. Norms for multinational companies were also jettisoned. Self-regulation in the matters of business was the position adopted by Western governments, in spite of the rigorous concerns of many environmental groups and NGOs.

More to the point, no debt relief was really forthcoming, except to countries like Brazil with huge debts and large biodiversity, which could then be parlayed into debt-for-nature swaps. Current interest flows from developing countries to First World institutions now amount to $40–50 billion a year, roughly half the $120 billion in aid requested by developing countries. Efforts to increase aid were met with the usual flurry of vague promises from industrialized countries (not including the U.S.) committed only to the hazy terrain of allocating 0.7% of GNP "by the year 2000 or as soon as possible."

From Earthday to Doomsday

The road to Rio really began 20 years earlier with the Stockholm conference, in a world more rosy and optimistic with everyone pulling forward at the task. There was the new green revolution, promising increased agricultural yields in the Third World, whose underbelly of social inequality, genetic erosion and environmental damage was yet to be widely revealed. Countries like Brazil seemed to have soundly embarked upon Walter Rostow's "take-off," with growth rates of 8%/year.

The agenda of Stockholm was profoundly influenced by a sharp re-emergence of Malthusian thought in the developed world. The ideas of Paul Ehrlich's *Population Bomb* and Garrett Hardin's *Tragedy of the Commons* — basically blaming population increase and non-private forms of property for environmental degradation — fueled fears that the gains of the post-war development period would be swamped in an overwhelming tide of humans. The Club of Rome's *Limits to Growth*, extending the Malthusian premises of Ehrlich and coupling them to a critique of industrial development, stressed that pollution as well as food was another global constraint. It argued that population pressed up against the limits of resources, and as it did so it also generated more and more pollution that began to poison the planet. Population and pollution control, and capitalist property were the only means of avoiding doom.

Armed with this model of the future, the Stockholm conference concentrated primarily on First World concerns, pollution and population. Not surprisingly, the preparatory meetings were characterized by tremendous indifference and even hostility from Third World nations, viewing environmentalism as a concern for the well-fed, and population and pollution controls as means for continuing and indeed enhancing unequal economic relations and technical dependence, and trapping the developing world forever in penury. Poverty rather than pollution was viewed as the central global problem, and growth rates such as Brazil's of over 8% were a good deal more relevant than toxic eels in the Rhine.

The two positions reflected the clash between a developmentalist ideology that had been in place for more than 25 years in the Third World, against a new-minted set of U.S./European concerns like "no growth," population control, limited industrial development and a romanticized view of village life (the same village life that had been reviled as stifling and un-modern by a generation of development theorists). Environmental ideas resonated poorly in the Third World, where neither the social context, institutional organization, or even the basic premises were shared.

To mollify the emerging Third World fury, a preliminary conference in

Switzerland was undertaken to assure the success of the Stockholm conference. Here, environmental concerns were placed in the context of development, and it was argued that the lack of development as well as the
development process were responsible for environmental degradation, and
indeed could limit development options over the long run.

At Stockholm, discussions of population and pollution followed predictable North-South divisions, but a new unexpected terrain of contest surfaced:
that of genetic resources and biotechnology.

Biodiversity and Biotechnology

Most of the world's biodiversity resides in the South and includes land races,
minor cultivars and wild cousins of the major food crops on the planet. In
addition, some $20 billion/annum of medicinal germplasm is marketed or
uses tropical plants as templates for synthetic drugs. This form of biodiversity
has traditionally been seen in the First World as a global heritage, and
arguments usually advanced for the conservation of biodiversity by environmentalists take a decidedly ethical-scientific or aesthetic tone. The developing countries were assumed to share this "global heritage" interpretation even
as private patents on improved crops and medicines resulted in substantial
private royalty payments flowing out of the Third World. But arguments that
the raw materials for these products are cultural artifacts, and represent
intellectual effort and property on a par with those of white-coated geneti-
cists, have increasingly been advanced by indigenous peoples and small
farmers, the stewards of most of the world's crop biodiversity. The emergence of this debate (tagged "intellectual property rights" in Rio) very early on
in the international setting presaged the creation of markets for "common"
goods, and the battles over real ownership and obligation and the losers and
winners from technology transfers. As tropical countries saw the value of
their raw materials plummet, the germplasm of their botanical endowments
became yet another market bid from the international arena, and one of
interesting economic potential; however, this raised extraordinarily complex
issues of ownership, detention and distribution of the royalties, and enflamed
the regular tensions between Third World states and their peasant and forest
peoples, who had suddenly becomes masters of a valuable resource.

In terms of international agreements, Stockholm was not without results.
It resulted in the creation of the United Nations Environment Program
(UNEP), and the signing of conventions on marine pollution by dumping
from ships, on world cultural and natural heritage sites, and on arctic seals. As
such things go, these initiatives were relatively non-contentious. Seals have
almost as much purchase on human sympathy as pandas, heritage sites ensure
glorious tourist venues, and the marine dumping would be impossible to
monitor. The following year saw the signing of the convention that prohibited trade in endangered species of wild fauna and flora, which set up a
system of trade sanctions and a worldwide reporting network to curb the
trade in endangered species. This convention used existing frontier and
customs monitoring, and as such was relatively easy to implement, unlike the

later proposed climate and biodiversity accords, which require profound structural shifts in economies and the creation of new international and national institutions.

The real response to Stockholm from the Third World was that elaborated in the 1974 NIEO (New International Economic Order) proclamation articulated at the UN General Assembly meeting. Here the issues revolved around straightforward economic concerns: increased real transfers of funds from the North to the South, enhancing developing country capacities in science and technology, more financing of technology transfer, and changes in patent laws to facilitate it. The counter-attack from conservatives in the First World was not long in coming, and if the uproar over Third World "arrogance" and "blackmail" at last subsided, it was only because the New International Order was regarded as a slogan from the dead past.

From Our House to Greenhouse

Concerns over pollution at the international level focused primarily on the atmosphere: the 1979 First World Climate Conference warned about the destruction of the ozone layer, northern European and northeastern U.S. forests were blighted by acid rain, and there were murmurings about the greenhouse effect. The same year the first convention on Long Range Transboundary pollution was signed. These debates were consummately First World since the main sources of the atmospheric degradation were localized in the First World, and the discourse was initially seen as one of industrialized nations. Later, modeling of climate would begin to place recent Third World emitters in the same ranks as those who had spewed pollutants into the atmosphere for more than a hundred years. In much of the popular literature the impact of more than a hundred years of fossil fuel combustion was effectively deflated to current annual emissions, and Third World biomass burning was catapulted into the role of major climate villain.

In 1980, the first systematic document on environmental degradation was published: the World Conservation Strategy. It identified development processes that were a menace to the world's ecosystems, and emphasized the three objectives of resource conservation: maintenance of essential environmental processes, preservation of genetic diversity, and sustainable use of species and ecosystems — all very laudable objectives. The document places the blame for environmental destruction on population pressures, inappropriate decisions and technologies. The only historical analysis revolves around population increase, which, as is so often the case, is viewed as the ultimate driver of environmental degradation.

The most widely noted document of the later part of the 1980s was the Bruntland Report. Focusing on the idea of "One World, Common Futures," it sought to frame development issues as environmental ones, and to emphasize that the model advanced by the First World was not sustainable. Equity issues make an appearance. The report critiques the "conservation" agenda of much of the environmental arena, the separation of environmental issues from larger production processes, and emphasizes that environmental issues are now a focus for international security; indeed the document attacks the armament industry directly. But this document was viewed as "soft," providing virtuous nostrums which had little real bite. But even as the rhetoric was improving, a new economic ice age was swiftly converting the landscape into a neo-liberal tundra.

The Frazzled State

The Third World national delegations that congregated in Rio had a mien very different from the spirited profile apparent in the mid-1970s, when calls for a new international economic order were at their zenith. Amid collapsing economies, stratospheric debt, stringent austerity programs imposed by the International Monetary Fund, these governments had been brought to heel. Simultaneously, their very standing as sovereign states has been increasingly compromised in the eyes of their own civil societies, which see them as predatory and corrupt domestically, and internationally as servile executors of First World economic agendas. The Earth Summit's host country, Brazil, is testimony to these developments.

With the highest absolute levels of deforestation on the planet, cities shrouded in pollution, a populace of which less than 8% has access to potable water, serious problems of industrial and agricultural pollution, Brazil has environmental problems of enormous proportions. But its environmental problems pale in daily life in comparison with those of its economy, social equity and justice. A country with one of the worst income distributions in the world, it has seen a decline in real wages and negative growth. More than 15% of its heads of households are without employment; in São Paulo alone more than 186,000 jobs were eliminated in March. Levels of unemployment in Brazil are now higher than they have been in eight years and more than 40% of its population lives in absolute poverty. In 1991, while environmental bureaucrats pored over their documents in Geneva and New York, the Catholic Land Commission in Brazil reported that some 242,196 people were involved in land struggles over rights to more than 17 million acres, a number that does not include the 15 million acre Yanomami struggle. Some 54 peasant organizers and rural workers were killed. Brazil's native population was reduced by 27 murders, 21 suicides as a result of cultural dislocation, and 206 deaths from epidemics.

Meanwhile, Brazil's government was wracked with accusations of corruption. Between President Collor's inauguration in May 1990 until his resignation in January 1993, more than 150 denunciations of corruption per month were filed, with the lion's share charged against the administration. By the spring of 1992, Collor had to dismiss virtually his entire cabinet. Indeed, even First Lady Rosanne Collor was charged with misappropriation of funds, having made a typo confusing *carentes* (the needy) with *parentes* (her relatives), and allocated staggering sums to the latter. Eventually the scandal forced Collor himself to step down to avoid imminent impeachment.

What the case of Brazil exemplifies so thoroughly is the decline in state leadership in economic development. Dancing to the tune of international donors, the Third World state has become less the provider of benefits (except to its corrupt beneficiaries) than an enforcer of stabilization and structural adjustment reforms. Many Third World states, especially in Latin America and Africa, are now very limited in their ability to set the terms for economic and political interactions in society, and to carry out the activities assigned to them. Weakened, corrupt, delegitimized, their impotence has opened up considerable room for elaborating new civil society-state relations, particularly as the new states have "democratized."

This collapse in state capacity must be understood very clearly going into the Rio meetings. It is here that the origins of the "alternative" Rio lie, and why there is now such suspicion about state-to-state agreements, when the state has become at best irrelevant and at worst inimical to welfare in most people's lives.

The erosion of state capacity has also been coupled to a tremendous ideological attack on the state, where neo-liberal and monetarist economic reformers have blamed the erratic performance of the Third World econo- mies on policy or "government failures" that have distorted the free function- ing of markets. On the left, the governments' craven response to IMF austerity programs and the worsening economic and social conditions have also provided substantive and ideological grist to further discredit the state.

International laws and agreements such as those proposed in Rio assume a neutrality of law and the ability of the nation-state to implement these laws no matter what the social, cultural and environmental settings. As the more radical elements of the NGO community reiterated time and time again in the Rio preparations, goals of resource management presented in such agree- ments are rooted in the values and perceptions of Western or Western-trained professionals which are not universally shared and which presume that states can everywhere enforce them in a just, non-violent and equitable manner. The widespread distrust of the state, along with the proposals that govern- ments were compelled by economic duress to endorse has pushed the Rio debates into a few basic camps.

Big Bank Theory

In the formal meetings of ECO 92 the most visible strategy was the creation of markets through such neo-liberal instruments as pollution rights, and reliance on markets as the ultimate arbiters of value for forests and intellectual property. Thus, environmental concerns are transported into a "non-political" arena where market forces hold sway. Nowhere is such market optimism more in evidence than in the 1992 World Bank Development Report focus- ing on the environment and compiled under the authority of Lawrence Summers, the Bank's then-chief economist and vice president and later assistant treasury secretary for international affairs, a suitable position given his environmental posture. Written by economists, the report has already caused tremendous consternation within the Bank's own environmental staff. The document shows a tenuous contact with reality, not to mention a staggering lack of familiarity with the environment and development literature, even that generated by the Bank's own staff, and views market mechanisms as being central to elaborating long-term strategies of environmental sustainability with high rates of global economic growth.

The World Bank views environmental problems as the outcome of the "three Ps" — population, pricing problems, and (faulty) property rights. Hence the solutions offered pivot on the reduction of population through accelerated urbanization and expanding labor markets for women; the elimination of pricing distortions by creating tradable pollution permits; and the eradication of common property. Familiar patterns of Malthusian thinking (pollution is the outcome of numbers of people rather than a reflection of patterns of consumption) are harnessed to data-free analysis — even a cursory examination of, for example, deforestation in Brazil would reveal that the highest destruction occurs in areas of private property; in countries such as Malaysia, traditions of commonly-held property have kept forests intact until these are replaced by impeccably private logging concessions that destroy.

The World Bank report is a benchmark in that it presents with savage clarity its posture on global issues concerning development and the environment. The Bank tilts away from social programs and back toward infrastructural schemes. The funds for growth and for environmental reform in the Third World would, in the Bank's vision, largely be generated by increased trade rather than direct First World transfers. Such a perspective ignores the existing dynamics of very large transfers from the Third World to the First, and also the inequalities in the terms of trade. If the substance of the official UNCED in Rio could be evoked by any one document, it would be this one, just as the spirit of the report is best distilled in Summers' offhand note in one memo that many Third World countries are in fact underpolluted, and should be hospitable to industries causing, say, prostate cancer because life expectancy rates make it unlikely that workers would last long enough to fall prey to this older man's affliction.

If there was a "winner" at Rio, it was the World Bank. Through the dismantling of UNEP, and the undermining of several UN bureaucracies, the Bank was able to shift political and financial control of international environmental issues away from the relatively open UN structure, to its own more covert practices. The Bank also emerged as the new manager of the three to four billion dollars that the rich nations will eventually pledge to the Global Environmental Facility (GEF) and the Bank-affiliated International Development Association which, with its budget of roughly six billion dollars a year, will assume a greater role in environmental affairs.

The most critical new environmental initiative, however, revolves around the Global Environmental Facility elaborated by the G7 and administered through the World Bank. An idea of what one might expect from the GEF is given by looking at the Amazon Pilot Project, a potential investment of some $1.5 billion over the next 5 years in Amazonian conservation projects. This is the single largest environmental program ever, and the largest tropical forest/biodiversity initiative. Its current status is instructive, and suggests why the forest and biodiversity initiatives remain stymied, and why many NGOs and forest peoples deplore this option.

The Amazon project, which focuses on the enhancement of research organizations, the elaboration of regional conservation programs, and "sustainable development" efforts, has specifically excluded the participation of non-governmental entities in the project, thus assuring conflictive, expensive and probably sabotaged programs. It rather summed up for many the kinds of results that could be expected from ECO 92: exclusion of civil society, World Bank control of the major resources, and the funds basically fueling corrupt national bureaucracies.

The Global Environmental Facility has become even further embroiled in controversy, with the Amazon Pilot project appearing sensitive and progressive compared with the GEF's later forays. The GEF is increasingly viewed as the agency that picks up the tab for the social and environmental costs of Bank development initiatives, thus permitting projects to excise these expensive "side issues" from project budgets.

Conservation Strategies: Consumer Choice and Big Bureaucracy

The formal conference of Rio offered three main strategies. One salient trend in the discussions at Rio and after has been the elimination of the state altogether and the emphasis on individualized consumption patterns — a sort of consumer choice model of conservation. Most elaborated for tropical forest issues, the arguments run something like this: if eating hamburgers causes forests to fall, and Brazil nut snacks keep them standing, then consumer decisions lie at the heart of environmental salvation. Careful consolidated purchases including those of large tracts of land for conservation in tropical countries, perfecting markets (if the forests are correctly assessed in market terms they will not be destroyed) and deft marketing strategies (the Body Shop, Ben and Jerry's Rainforest Crunch, etc.) create the economic conditions through which beneficial environmental results can be most effectively achieved. This kind of strategy is ideologically fashionable, anti-statist, and ignores any possible underlying structural dynamic that might be at play. Its popular appeal lies in the "what you can do to save the world" realm, and in "unproblematic" market solutions.

The second central strategy deflects efforts away from action and into large scientific bureaucracies. Here the efforts focus on assessment, research, zoning exercises and agreeing to think about things profoundly and for well-funded periods of time. Thus, the U.S. position on CO_2 emissions — it agrees to assess its emissions — is a typical response.

At the other end of the spectrum lie the overarching international institutional structures and monitoring bodies. Regulatory powers seem to be lacking at almost any level of structure, and primarily tugged along by international purse strings. Moreover, the long-standing resistance of the U.S. to the UN could compromise any enforcement powers. As the U.S. does not obey World Court decisions that it finds distasteful, there is no a priori reason to believe that any kinds of enforcement or sanctions would have much effect, whether or not the U.S. is a signatory.

If Third World states have ceded much of the initiative to First World institutions, their frailty has made possible more positive perspectives for political action. This terrain has increasingly come to be occupied by civic associations or by finding solutions to collective problems without the intercession of the state. With more formal democratic structures, more participatory forms of decision-making and reduced (but still considerable) levels of repression, local communities — often using formal NGO structures — are attempting to improve deteriorating economic and social conditions.

The structure of environmental debates and the "solutions" to the environmental crises of the tropical world remain embedded in an ideological framework about conservation and development which is largely excised from the historical and economic realities of most of the Third World. In response to this oversight, and to the declining conditions of life for many of the rural poor, national political and social movements have increasingly moved into the "political ecology" sphere, in which social movements and NGOs increasingly hope to define the environmental agenda in terms that address the more general questions of resource distribution and access, political rights and processes, as well as larger philosophical issues of the nature of property (ranging from harvesting rights to intellectual property rights), the nature of nature (untrammeled Eden or artifact and habitat), and technical and development alternatives. Their expression and practice emphasizes development and equity concerns in which environmental issues are but one subset of a broader range of activities; most of their efforts focus on concerns of social justice. While there is an argument to be made about the value of indigenous knowledge and management of tropical resources, the environmental dimensions of these concerns have largely been appropriated by mainstream environmental movements, while international concern over the pressing legitimacy of claims for social justice has remained poorly developed. It is this disjuncture that underlay the three conferences at Rio.

■ PART TWO ■

The North-South Economic Divide

9

Economic Apartheid in the New World Order

Arjun Makhijani*

The collapse of Soviet-style centralized socialism has been so complete and its failings so glaring and public that by 1992 frequent declarations of victory by votaries of the capitalist order were no longer necessary, hardly three years after the collapse of the Berlin Wall. Rather, they contented themselves in assisting the conversion of the former Soviet Union to capitalism, though for the most part this amounted to presiding over a disorganized and utter collapse. The world of the Cold War had two military superpowers; in 1990, President Bush set out to define the "New World Order" in which there would be only one — the United States.

In reality, there was only one superpower all along, if one takes all aspects of world domination into account. While the Soviet Union was a power in the sense that it could, like the United States, destroy the world at any time, only the United States presided over an enormous international economic alliance and coalition, across race and nationality, but consisting first of all of peoples of European descent. This alliance could use the economic machinery of multinational corporations and the international monetary system dominated by the U.S. dollar to continue to extract resources and cheap labor from the Third World, even as formal political colonialism was declining. In that respect, the New World Order is only a military one in which the United States has gotten rid of the threat of complete destruction at the hands of a rival military power, but with the old economic order still intact. The old economic order is structured much like South African apartheid.

Nationalism and Racism

The military subjugation of the economically deprived by the privileged, both between countries and within them, is an essential element of the war

* This essay is drawn from the author's *From Global Capitalism to Economic Justice* (Apex Press, 1992).

system. The naked use of force to maintain inequalities and exploitation is not how capitalism has been "marketed," however, either nationally or internationally.

For many years capitalism was sold domestically as anti-communism, clothed in God and Country. Such propaganda was made easier by the violent reality of the repression under Stalin, but it was only the newest form of an older propaganda and rationalization. Before there were any socialist countries, similar policies of economic exploitation were clothed in arguments of extending the benefits of European civilization to the backward peoples of the Third World. Exploitation was sold as the "White Man's burden." In the United States, the use of force by some groups to oppress others has been sold as the maintenance of law and order, as the romantic image of the conquest of the West, as scientific progress, and as racial superiority. Here we consider two ideologies commonly used to justify oppression: racism and nationalism. In most capitalist countries, nationalism is overall a "respectable" ideology. Racism is not. Yet the way the two are used to justify oppression are very similar.

The global reality of capitalism, as opposed to its mythology, is that, as an economic system, it is approximately like South Africa in its dynamic and divisions, and in its violence and inequalities.[1] The facts of apartheid and the global economy are similar. There are even similarities in the history of the political-economic alignments between capitalist countries in their relations with the Third World with the racial alignments in South Africa. In South Africa, the two main groups of Whites — the English and the Boers — fought a very bitter and violent war (the "Boer War"). But right after it, they compromised so as to establish common dominance over the non-White people of South Africa. There was an analogous result in global capitalism after the two world wars. In exchange for markets, an open door for U.S. capital, and bases for Cold War military strategy, the U.S. became the military guarantor of a continued flow of cheap resources and labor to Germany and Japan (as well as other capitalist countries), providing precisely what the Nazis and Japanese militarists had sought to obtain through war. Thus, despite tensions resulting from trade, employment and other issues, capitalist countries as a group have tended to resemble one country in many ways, especially as regards their relatively coordinated economic policies and their very similar rules for dealing with the Third World.

The South African system of pass laws is reproduced on an international scale by the system of passports and visas by which mobility is easy for a minority and difficult for a majority. This reality is graphically illustrated by the difference between the heavily policed U.S.-Mexican border and the quite open, non-militarized U.S.-Canadian border. Similarly, the proposed elimination of borders within the European Community has been accompanied by a hardening of the European border to people from the Third World. As one EC official put it: "The principle of free movement within the [EC] region is built around having solid external borders, so the internal frontiers cannot come down until measures are taken to secure the external borders."[2]

That hardening of external borders is now being played out to the tune of neo-Nazi and other right-wing violence in Germany and elsewhere in the European Community.

The European governments have tried to prevent people from the Third World from coming to settle on their continent. By contrast, the cheap labor, markets, land, and resources of the Third World have long been welcome, and extracted by force if necessary. Trade is governed by international rules of "free trade" and free capital movement, and International Monetary Fund "conditionalities." But the people are not free to move.

South Africa, like the capitalist countries, can also be said to have a "liberal democracy" — but only for a portion of its population. Similarly, in the global capitalist system, liberal democracy prevails mainly in the capitalist countries, excluding the vast majority of the people in the system who live in the Third World. Even the statistics match — the same divisions of White and non-White; similar differences of income; similar differences in infant mortality; similar expropriation of land and resources; similar rules giving mobility to the minority and denying it to the majority; and the similar immense and forcible marginalization of a vast number of people who are not involved in any essential way in the monetized economy, but are ruled and daily oppressed by it. And within each community, there exist many kinds of divisions, including those of class and gender.

The similarities between apartheid and Third World oppression do not stop with their practical impacts. The *ideologies* which support the two systems are also roughly parallel. *In order to rationalize exploitation, characteristics of inferiority are ascribed to the dominated peoples, which sets up the dynamic of racism.* Both racism and oppressor nationalism have arisen as ideologies out of the economic demands of the capitalist system.

Both race and nationality strongly manifest themselves primarily in the social interaction of the dominating and the dominated; they are not phenomena internal to a particular group. "White" is defined by "Black" much as "Black" is defined by "White," for as soon as "Whites" are out of the context of that social setting then they themselves take on diverse characteristics. A peasant in Brittany is Breton when confronted with a Parisian, French when confronted with a German, European when confronted with a Russian, and White in the face of a Moroccan or Algerian or Senegalese.

The strength and passions associated with these identities are volatile and dependent, in part, on the individual's judgement about economic prospects of the particular group relative to the others. In the case of racism and oppressor nationalism, the ideologies generally come to be shared by the working people of the dominant nationality to a great extent, despite their evident long-term interest lying in solidarity with workers of other nationalities. It is a social and economic reality that the poor and oppressed standing at the door of relative privilege can be quite prejudiced and ready to do violence to protect it. For example, overt racial prejudices are often strongly held by White European and U.S. blue collar workers.

Of course, despite the critical similarities between oppressor nationalism and apartheid, there are also many differences. Some stem from the reality that South Africa is set within the overall context of global capitalism and some from the fact that in South Africa the Whites and non-Whites live within the boundaries of the same state. Thus, while the overall analogy is useful, important aspects of both oppressive systems need to be addressed separately. But it is plain that violence inheres in both global capitalism and in South African apartheid and that a principal motive for both is economic exploitation.

Capitalist Geography

The successes of capitalism tend to get judged in terms of the conditions within capitalist countries alone. But the reality of the capitalist economy has always been far larger. The tradition of European colonial exploitation began with capitalism and, in diverse ways, has continued to be a powerful force, with the active participation of elites in the Third World. A violent economic history lies at the root of present-day global inequalities and violence.

From the Iberian quest for gold in Africa and the Americas to the vast expansion of lands the Europeans occupied into the present century, the economic "lifeline" of capitalism has run outside the boundaries of Europe. Contrary to both capitalist and Marxist theory, capitalism has never had a purely internal dynamic. The marginalization of vast areas and large numbers of people in the money-economy has been as integral to its course as the glitter and the riches. Exploitation of the many has accompanied the development of "liberal democracy." Let us consider one example in some detail.

The Volta Aluminum Company

The raw material for aluminum, bauxite, is mined mainly in a few Third World countries. It is refined into alumina. The alumina is smelted into aluminum ingots by electrolysis, which is very energy-intensive. One large aluminum ingot production plant, called the Volta Aluminum Company (Valco) is owned by two multinational corporations, Kaiser and Reynolds. It is located at Tema in Ghana, near the Akosombo dam.

The Akosombo dam was built with a World Bank loan soon after Ghana's independence in 1961. It was to be Ghana's proud project of modernization and independence. It also happened to be a project of great interest to Kaiser Aluminum and Reynolds. Most of the electricity was to be dedicated to the production of aluminum by Valco.

The dam flooded roughly two million acres of Ghanaian land, much of it forested, creating Volta Lake. The flooding displaced large numbers of people, many of whom were not properly resettled. The huge lake divided the country north-to-south making transportation difficult and costly. Soon schistosomiasis, a debilitating parasitic disease which had not been much in evidence before, and river blindness became endemic around Volta Lake.

Valco in the meantime got some of the cheapest electricity in the world. The contract was guaranteed; and the government could not change the price. (However, in a modern version of *noblesse oblige*, the company did, along the way, increase the rate it was paying from the initial quarter of a cent a kilowatt hour to half a cent.)

As Ghana's own electricity needs grew, it had to build far more costly hydroelectric and fossil fuel generating stations. The situation became stark in energy terms in the early 1980s, when Ghana was selling a huge amount of electricity on a firm basis to Valco for only $14 million, while at the same time importing oil equivalent to the same amount of energy for $180 million, though the oil was used mainly for transport and not for electricity generation.

While Valco paid only half a cent per kilowatt hour for firm power, most other industries and people of Ghana paid four to sixteen times as much for unreliable and interruptible power.

Valco's profits in Ghana under these favorable operating conditions were immense. Based on 1982 prevailing prices of aluminum, and operation of the plant at 80% capacity (4 potlines out of 5) my approximate estimates of Valco's operations in Ghana for 1982 are that total sales would have been on the order of $270 million, costs, including taxes, $145 million, and profits $125 million.

While Kaiser and Reynolds reaped large profits in Ghana, the costs to Ghana itself were substantial. For example, the revenue which Ghana lost due to underpriced electricity, relative to prices in Europe and Japan for aluminum production, was roughly $50 million per year. Additional losses to the economy arose from the necessity of supplying uninterrupted power to Valco, and disrupting domestic production instead. Further, as noted, the costs to Ghanaians for electric power were higher than the cost to Valco.

Along the way, short of foreign exchange, Ghana fell into debt. To fill the exchange gap, cocoa was cultivated on an ever wider scale, taking up large amounts of land. Gold, bauxite, and other extractive export-oriented industries were developed or expanded. They consumed more electricity. Thus, oil consumption was increased, as were foreign exchange bills, debts, pollution and greenhouse gas emissions.

If one included all the quantifiable costs, including loss of production, the costs of diseases, underpricing of electricity, etc., the annual losses to Ghana might well amount to several hundred million dollars. These direct costs exclude significant items such as an industrial structure skewed towards exports to pay for foreign exchange losses from additional imports and debt payments. Ghana succeeded in raising the electricity rate to about 2¢ a kilowatt hour in 1985.

Capitalist Governments, Corporations, Third World Elites and Military Power

Exploitation of the Third World is rooted in the close relationships which exist between capitalist governments, corporations and multinational banks, and Third World elites. Exploitation would not be possible in its current form were it not for the way these groups and institutions interact and the immense financial and military power which they are able to exert.

Multinational corporations (including multinational banks) collectively represent the most powerful economic forces in the world today. Annual sales of the largest corporations are around $100 billion, a sum which exceeds the gross national products of all but half a dozen Third World countries and many relatively wealthy capitalist nations as well. Multinational banks control assets of hundreds of billions of dollars. Moreover, they have much more concentrated control of these sums of money. They generate revenues in "hard currency," which is generally in short supply in Third World countries. Large portions of their holdings are liquid assets or convertible to liquid assets. They can move capital around the world with the speed of computers; they can invest in or divest from communities and countries. They are responsible for the extraction of vast quantities of the earth's natural resources. They chart the course of much of the world's technological development, and they determine, to a considerable degree, the prices of large numbers of products around the world.

Their policies are not internally restrained or guided by any logic of the well-being of the community or of the environment. They are institutions avowedly and unabashedly devoted to the pursuit of profit.

Government failures adequately to regulate corporations or hold them accountable are manifestations of the close ties between capitalist governments and the corporate world. *The nexus between capitalist-country governments and large corporations (including banks) is perhaps the single most important structural element of the war system* because the military, political and financial power of governments is used to protect the property and prerogatives of large corporations.

Government support for corporate activities expresses itself in innumerable ways, from pressure to maintain high military production, to an unconscionable trade in armaments, to the economic raison d'être of the Cold War.

In the last two hundred years, the wars of colonial conquest in Asia and Africa, the genocide of tribal peoples in North America and Australia, and the many interventions to resubjugate the people of Latin America have all relied on military force. A principal purpose of these actions by governments has been to enable the pursuit of private profit.

The exploitation of resources, environmental destruction, and impoverishment in the Third World would not be possible without violence and the threat of violence. For instance, Japan's rise as a capitalist power, like that of the Europeans, was based upon imperialist expansion and cheap foreign resources. The Japanese invasion of China beginning in 1931 (which marked the beginning of the Second World War as much as later European events) was economic in origin. The conflict between Japan and the U.S. which led up to the Japanese attack on Pearl Harbor also involved colonial resources, such as Indonesian oil. Japan, like the European powers and the U.S., went to war over controlling resources, labor and markets outside of its borders. Similarly, German aggression in Eastern Europe and the Soviet Union was for control of resources and cheap labor, in the absence of which it could not establish itself securely as an economic and military power in Europe.[3]

The mythology of capitalism is that of the "free market," in which "government intervention" is regarded as undesirable. In reality, governments of capitalist countries have had a central role in providing the military force which has enabled capitalism to exist at all. More than any "invisible hand" guiding the functioning of the marketplace where goods are bought and sold, the *military hand of the capitalist state has been central to the economic development of capitalism.*

The ties between corporate economic interests and military violence have seldom been as clear as in the years succeeding World War II. As the Second World War came to a close, the chairman of General Electric suggested the creation of a "permanent war economy" to maintain purchasing power. Those who hoped for a "permanent war economy" after World War II were looking for more than the maintenance of internal domestic purchasing power. American plans for its economic future were based on capturing the markets of Europe and former European markets in the Third World.

This in turn necessitated two things. First, the Soviets with their supposed and actual antagonism to multinational corporations, had to be kept out of as much of Europe as possible after World War II. Second, in a Europe bereft of resources and devastated by war, the U.S. had to take over Europe's imperialist role, keeping the Third World in the capitalist orbit through economic and military influence. In explaining post-war policy in testimony to Congress in 1944, Dean Acheson firmly linked jobs and even the rule of the Constitution in the U.S. to foreign markets:

> When we look at the problem of [full employment] we may say that it is a problem of foreign markets . . . [Y]ou could fix it so that everything produced here would be consumed here. That would completely change our Constitution, our relations to property, human liberty, our very conceptions of law . . . and nobody contemplates that. Therefore you must look to other markets and those markets are abroad.[4]

These considerations were at the heart of the U.S. strategy of containment which was spelled out in National Security memorandum NSC-68, which guided post-war policy to a successful conclusion for capitalism. To quote it directly:

> Fostering a world environment in which the American system can flourish . . . embraces two subsidiary policies. One is a policy which we would probably pursue even if there were no Soviet threat. It is a policy of attempting to create a healthy international community. The other is a policy of "containing" the Soviet system. These two policies are closely interrelated and interact on one another.[5]

The way in which U.S. military power and corporate economic interests were to be maintained was by violence and the threat of violence. Deterrence did not mean merely preventing an equally armed Soviet Union from attacking the U.S. It meant the superior assertion of U.S. power to keep the Soviet Union out of areas in which the U.S. or other capitalist powers exercised dominance. The theory behind NSC-68 provided for violence both directly against the Soviet Union and in the Third World. The success of the Marshall

Plan in post-war Western Europe not only grew out of U.S. capital, it was founded on continued control of cheap Third World resources.

Subjugation at Home: Military Power *within* Countries

The military power of the state is also important domestically. The inequalities and impoverishment occasioned by the pursuit of profit are so immense that the threat of armed force and its use have been needed to forestall popular resistance. The state may use military force to break a strike and enforce the prerogatives of the property owner. It does not usually come to the aid of the worker who has unjustly lost his or her job with the same force or alacrity.

Military subjugation within Third World countries has changed in form since the end of direct colonial rule. Revolts and revolutions in capitalism have been centered in precisely the areas which were the most relentlessly and violently impoverished by capitalist practice. Indeed, one might say that most of the people rendered utterly propertyless by capitalism, the truly impoverished "with nothing to lose," have been the women and men who are landless rural workers, poor peasants (whose property is usually at the mercy of moneylenders), unorganized workers in small industry and the unemployed in the Third World.

The first phase of these revolts (and the imperialist reaction to them) resulted in three broadly different outcomes:

1. Socialist revolutions, in which nationalist, Marxist, and Leninist ideas were joined in uneasy theories, ideologies and practice. These generally occurred when resistance movements were confronted with wars, or violent internal repression, as well as impoverishment produced by imperialism.
2. Nationalist movements of varying intensity in which local ruling classes (capitalists, bureaucrats, landowners) secured political independence from imperialist rule, but where economic connections to imperialism remained strong, as for example India, Ghana and Algeria.
3. More or less pliant regimes or puppet governments put in place by imperialist rulers to avoid more nationalist or leftist governments. Such pliant governments were also imposed at the point of the U.S. gun in many of the countries in Latin America which achieved independence from Spain in the nineteenth century.

Though struggles for independence from colonial rule stemmed from a desire to reduce oppression, that has not been the general result for the majority of people in the Third World, who remain poor and oppressed. Violent repression of the people in Third World countries remains very strong. It works to maintain the prerogatives of local elites, and, in most cases, also of multinational corporations and banks within the Third World. Immense and growing class divisions have allowed a common purpose to emerge between the military structures of repression in the Third World and the protection of local and foreign corporate property. These phenomena occur to a large extent irrespective of whether Third World countries are ruled by elected or non-elected governments. Today, it is not only the armed forces of the capitalist countries which are engaged in the service of capitalism; they have, in effect, been joined by most of the armed forces of the Third World.

An Economic Principle for a New World Order

Restructuring the world economy so that it is both just and equitable will require that we discard old ideas that have led to the apartheid structure of the global economy and put new principles in their place. One capitalist idea that has led to the present state of affairs has been the assumption that wages across borders would equalize themselves if goods and capital moved freely, even if people were not free to move. That has turned out to be a false assumption so far as the Third World (largely former colonies) is concerned. This idea must be replaced by a new principle: *the movement of capital and goods shall not be more free than the movement of people.* This does not necessarily mean restraints on capital and goods, but only that freedom extend to people also, since it will not automatically come from the movement of commodities and money.

We can see the need for such a principle clearly if we look at the North American economy. The flows of capital, goods and people between the U.S. and Canada are all relatively free. The border is *open, secure and non-militarized.* In contrast the movement of goods and capital between the U.S. and Mexico is free, but the movement of people is free only from the U.S. to Mexico. Traveling in the other direction, Mexicans face searchlights, barbed wire, vigilantes and armed forces.

At the same time, large corporations have a vested interest in maintaining the militarized border, because confining labor in Mexico keeps wages low there and allows companies to pay people far below the amounts they would be paid in the U.S. for the same labor productivity. This lack of connection between wages and labor productivity is one of the driving forces in the apartheid nature of the global economy. The international monetary system, dominated by the U.S. dollar, is the principal financial mechanism that perpetuates these unjust wage differences, since exchange rates of currencies are driven by international capital movements and not by relative labor productivity.

The North American Free Trade Agreement (NAFTA), which would further free capital and goods movement, would benefit mainly large multinational corporations while aggravating wage issues for U.S. workers and leaving immigration issues for Mexicans unresolved. And even if it achieves wildly improbable success in making most Mexicans as well-off as the average person in the rest of North America, its main result for the global economy would be to shift the border of global apartheid southward to Central

America in the process. The process might even split Mexico apart internally, since a relatively prosperous northern Mexico might begin to set up stiff barriers against other parts of the country.

In conclusion, therefore, such examples show the urgent need for restraints on capital movement through regulation of multinational corporations and through reform of the international monetary system, and additional freedom of movement for workers from the Third World, that are essential if the New World Order is to represent a decisive move away from the present reality of global apartheid, towards real economic justice.

Notes

1. The earliest publication which I have come across which explores the parallel between capitalism and South Africa is an essay by Gernot Kohler, *Global Apartheid*, World Order Models Project, Working Paper Number Seven, 1978.
2. EC official quoted by Alan Riding, "Rifts Imperil Europe's No-Border Plan," *New York Times*, April 16, 1990, p. 19.
3. Arjun Makhijani, *Monetary Crises in Twentieth Century Capitalism*, unpublished, written in 1981.
4. Dean Acheson, Congressional testimony in 1944, quoted by William Appleman Williams in "Large Corporations and American Foreign Policy," in *Corporations and the Cold War*, Monthly Review Press, New York, 1969; pp. 95–6.
5. National Security Council memorandum 68, as cited in Thomas Etzold and John L. Gaddis, *Containment: Documents on American Foreign Policy and Strategy 1945–50*, Columbia University Press, New York, 1979; p. 401.

10

The IMF and the World Bank in the New World Order

Robert S. Browne

The abrupt collapse of the centrally planned economies of Eastern Europe meant essentially two things to the two venerable financial behemoths which face one another across Washington's 19th Street, three blocks west of the White House: a long awaited opportunity for the achievement of universality in their membership, and the prospect of an unobstructed road toward their goal of installing orthodox capitalism as the uncontested economic system for our planet. At the same time, a growing public appreciation for the planet's environmental frailty and ecological unity was thrusting upon the World Bank a new burden of global responsibility which threatened to overshadow its other concerns.

Although at the time of their creation, both the IMF (International Monetary Fund) and the World Bank held their membership open to all countries which wished to join, the undisguised pro-capitalist bias of the institutions, coinciding with the emergence of the Cold War, rendered such membership unattractive to the Soviet Union and to most of the managed economies. Those countries which did choose membership soon discovered — despite the institutions' self-definition as strictly economic, non-ideologically driven organizations — that members which persisted in demonstrating too strong a commitment to socialism found it extremely difficult to obtain loans (e.g., post-Batista Cuba and post-Somoza Nicaragua). In the case of Vietnam, once a communist government was in place, the U.S. actively saw to it that new loans were cut off, although the motivation in this instance was probably as much punitive as ideological.

A major milestone in the Bretton Woods institutions' pursuit of the twin objectives of universality of membership and the spreading of capitalism was achieved in 1980 when the People's Republic of China took its seat in the IMF. With the recent adherence to the IMF of the Eastern European nations, including the components of the ex-Soviet Union, membership coverage has become virtually total. The quantitative goal having been achieved, the focus will henceforth be entirely qualitative in nature — insuring that member countries pursue policies which are maximally supportive of current capitalist economic orthodoxy. Although this emphasis clearly predates the ending of the Cold War, it is now being pursued with a single-mindedness which may offer some insight into the "New World Order" concept which yawns before us.

Origins

The IMF and the World Bank were created simultaneously, at an international conference held in 1944 in Bretton Woods, New Hampshire. Economists from the United Kingdom and the U.S. were the basic architects of the two institutions, with the views of the American, Harry Dexter White (who later became a celebrated victim of McCarthyism), largely winning out over the views of British economist John Maynard Keynes.

Convened while World War II was still raging, but after the allies had finally begun to feel some assurance that ultimate victory would be theirs, the conference reflected the widely held concern that it was important for the victors to reach some agreement on how the post-war global economy should be structured. The international economic behavior which had characterized the inter-war period had left much to be desired (indeed, many scholars attributed the roots of the war to the faulty international economic relationships instituted after World War I) and it was felt that wisdom dictated that the most propitious moment for reaching an accommodation on new arrangements was before the cooperative atmosphere of the allied war effort had given way to the narrow nationalistic concerns likely to reemerge once peace was established.

The stated objectives of the IMF were to promote and maintain high levels of employment and income through the expansion of international trade and the achievement and maintenance of exchange rate stability and currency convertibility.

The World Bank's objectives, as suggested by its formal name (the International Bank for Reconstruction and Development), were to assist in the reconstruction of the global infrastructure which had been destroyed by the war, and to facilitate the development of the economies of the other member countries. The development thrust was clearly subordinate to the reconstruction priority.

In those days, the concept of the "Third World" had not yet crystallized, and most countries of Asia and Africa were still involuntary appendages to the great Western industrialized powers. It requires little imagination, of course, to think of other considerations which may have lain behind the creation of the Bank and Fund. As indicated earlier, for example, little effort was made to disguise the fact that the Bretton Woods institutions were firmly rooted in the capitalist conception of how the world economy should function; while both institutions were later regularly vilified, by a handful of vituperative conservative American politicians, as tools for perpetuating strong governments and socialist experiments, the reality is that, from the outset, the overwhelming bias of the Bretton Woods institutions was toward capitalism. As the Third World countries emerged from colonial status, the Bretton Woods institutions stood ready to assist them, but with their ideological preferences easily discernible beneath a facade of political neutrality.

Structure

The basic structure of the IMF is somewhat suggestive of a credit union to which member countries make contributions (in gold and national currency) of a size determined by the magnitude of their national wealth and economic activity, and from which they may borrow should their national finances deteriorate to the point where a threat exists to their ability to maintain the rate of exchange which has been agreed for their currency. The monetary system originally formulated by the IMF designated the U.S. dollar, backed by gold, as the anchor currency against which all exchange rates were calibrated. Because IMF loans were principally intended to provide funding to enable borrowers to work out short-term imbalances in their current accounts, the loans were generally of short maturity and were conditioned on the borrower making whatever adjustments (short of a change in the exchange rate) might be called for to enable its economy to return to a stable position. Should a member country find that it was facing a payments imbalance of such severity that, even with a loan, it could not possibly continue to function with the prevailing exchange rate, the IMF could agree to a permanent change in that country's exchange rate. In its early years, the industrialized countries were the principal borrowers at the IMF.

The World Bank is structured more along the lines of a conventional corporation, with the member countries subscribing to shares of the Bank's capital and paying for their contribution with a nominal cash payment (payable in gold and national currency) and a sizeable promissory note. The promissory notes (referred to as "callable capital") are then used as a base against which the Bank goes into the private capital market and obtains long-term, favorably priced loans, which money it then relends to borrowing members on long-term and at rates of interest slightly below market rates.

Theoretically, all members of both organizations are eligible to borrow from both institutions (membership in the IMF is a prerequisite for membership in the Bank). In fact, however, once Europe and Japan had been largely rebuilt, the Bank's membership effectively regrouped into two categories, borrowing countries and non-borrowers. By 1960, with the wave of newly independent countries rapidly expanding the numbers of potential borrowers, and with a significant number of these new borrowers lacking the most basic forms of infrastructure, the Bank created a second window, the International Development Association (IDA), which was funded by grants from the non-borrowing countries and which made "soft" (i.e., very long-term and virtually interest-free) loans to the poorer countries.

The ultimate power in both the Fund and the Bank rested in a board of governors consisting of a representative from each member government, but with voting power based on the size of each member's contribution or subscription. The U.S. was by far the largest subscriber and contributor to both institutions and consequently held the largest number of votes, a situation which still prevails, although by a greatly diminished margin. Within the IMF, the current U.S. share of about 17% is still sufficient to give the U.S. veto power over critical matters, which require an 85% vote for approval. Loan approvals are by simple majority in both organizations, however, so the U.S. does not enjoy veto power over loans.

Evolution

In terms of its stated objectives, the IMF's performance can be generally rated as favorable over its first 25 years. Exchange rates were kept reasonably stable and international trade enjoyed an era of unprecedented growth. The poorer countries complained, with some justification, that the international monetary system was loaded against them, and even the developed countries, as their economies were restored to normalcy, became restive over the advantages which flowed to the U.S. as a result of the system's use of the dollar as the anchor, or reserve currency. These grumblings became louder as the U.S. chose to run up an astronomical budget deficit in order to wage the Vietnam War, a war which had little support among the other industrialized nations. These nations complained that they were, in effect, involuntarily helping to finance that war because of their obligation to maintain their currencies in a fixed relationship with a dollar which was clearly being rapidly depreciated in terms of the gold into which it was allegedly convertible.

By 1971 this fictitious relationship between gold and the dollar had become so untenable that President Nixon abruptly closed the gold window — i.e., he ended the dollar's convertibility into gold and later decreased its gold content. As a result, the IMF formally ended the era of fixed exchange rates and introduced floating rate options for all members. The net effect of these radical alterations in the exchange rate system was to leave the IMF with a very indistinct mandate. Deprived of its principal compass, stable exchange rates, it was not clear just how the vessel was to be steered or indeed whether there was any further need for the vessel at all, for the major Western powers, utilizing the format of an informal grouping of their finance ministers (Group of 7) gradually worked out an informal cooperative arrangement for the management of their monetary relationships. At annual Economic Summit meetings and ad hoc interim consultations, these seven powerful nations effectively determined what global monetary arrangements were to be. The role of the IMF had clearly been eclipsed, if not totally usurped.

In August 1982, Mexico stunned the world and brought panic to the banking community by defaulting on its international debt, merely the first of a number of Third World countries eventually to do so. As the atmosphere filled with rumors of the imminent collapse of some of the giant international banking houses, the managing director of the IMF saw an opportunity for a powerful new role for this increasingly irrelevant institution. With breathtaking courage, the IMF thrust itself into the debt crisis, extending loans, offering advice, and imposing conditionalities. It was highly risky business, because the bulk of the Third World debtors were soon seen to be suffering from problems of insolvency rather than of liquidity. That is, they were facing serious funding imbalances which would require long-term solutions, rather than facing temporary cash shortage problems which could be expected to correct themselves within the short to medium term. The IMF's money was not long-term money; normally its loans were to be repaid within three years, for the IMF was simply a revolving fund, which needed prompt repayment of its loans so that the money could be lent to someone else. The IMF thus found itself in the anomalous position of extending loans to debt defaulting countries and demanding that they stabilize their economies sufficiently to enable them *to resume payments on old loans and repay the new loan,* all within three years.

To ensure that the borrowers met these objectives, the IMF imposed extremely austere conditionalities on them, obliging them to introduce spending reductions and other contractionary measures of such severity that social upheaval broke out in many of the borrowing countries. Furthermore, this IMF-imposed austerity quickly translated into reduced imports from the industrialized countries, whose economies were already stagnating. A chorus of complaints arose against these stabilization programs, seriously damaging the IMF's reputation among both its debtor and its creditor members. Its debtor members accused it of serving as the bill collector for the private banks, and of inflicting massive suffering and political and economic insecurity in the process.

Meanwhile, the World Bank, which did have long-term loan funds, gradually began to make its funds available for debt reduction; as it did, the panic in the financial markets gradually subsided and the IMF began to ease its conditionalities. It also organized a fund of money which could be lent out at medium-term — loans of 5 to 10 years maturity. The private banking system had tottered, but it survived the crisis; in the eyes of many, it was the IMF which deserved the credit for perhaps saving the international banking system from collapse. Although its reputation among the poorer countries remained sullied, it had clearly found a raison d'être. It had shed its aura of irrelevance.

The World Bank, which had been slow to react to the debt crisis, shaped its response with greater deliberation. It chose to modify its traditional practice of extending loans only for specific, well defined projects by offering a species of nonproject-specific loans which could be used for meeting current expenditures including debt service payments. Countries receiving such loans were, however, obliged to introduce major reforms in their internal policies or face cancelation of the loan. Such loans came to be known as structural adjustment loans (SALs) and the World Bank was soon earmarking as much as a quarter of its total new lending for them. Virtually indistinguishable from the IMF's stabilization loans except by their longer maturity, the Bank's

SALs were highly controversial from their inception and remain so until this day. They must be understood within the larger framework of where the Bretton Woods institutions seem to be headed in the 1990s.

Policy Reform vs. National Sovereignty

From its inception, the IMF has had the right to impose conditions on the loans which it extends to its members. This is not an unreasonable demand. Lenders generally exercise some degree of control over the conduct of borrowers, most commonly by restricting the borrower's freedom to incur additional debt. Prior to the debt crisis, IMF conditionalities traditionally took the form of gently nudging the borrower to reduce its budget and/or balance of payments deficit, and most of the major industrialized countries routinely acquiesced in such conditionalities when they sought IMF loans. Although onerous, the conditions were normally accepted without notable protest because there was general agreement that the policy prescriptions being urged were the correct ones for restoring economic stability to the borrower's economy.

With the advent of the debt crisis and the emergence of structural adjustment lending, however, the nature of the policy reforms being demanded became far more pervasive than heretofore. The routine directive instructing a borrower to reduce its deficits was replaced by strictly drawn agreements committing the borrower to meet numerical targets by specific dates or face the cancelation of the undisbursed portion of the loan. Typical conditionalities might be: the borrower's budget or balance of payments deficit must be reduced by x per cent within one year; similar reductions might be exacted for the money supply and the rate of inflation; the currency must be devalued by x per cent within six months, etc. In addition to these quantitative targets, a number of qualitative changes are usually also requested, such as liberalizing the trade regime, reducing the size of the public sector and/or privatizing those portions of it not deemed by the Bretton Woods officials to be appropriate for public ownership.

Not surprisingly, these conditionalities are resisted vigorously by many of the borrowers. "A brazen violation of national sovereignty" was the initial complaint to be widely articulated by Third World nations, who were shocked to see the multilateral financial institutions taking it upon themselves to dictate the internal policies of their member countries. These alleged affronts to national sovereignty were, however, soon overshadowed by the social disruptions which occurred in the wake of some of these severe structural adjustment programs (SAPs). The IMF, particularly, was vilified, not only for overstepping its authority by imposing these conditions but also because the conditionalities were proving to be harmful rather than helpful. Devaluation, for example, often led to inflation; other conditionalities also produced unanticipated negative side effects.

As experience with the structural adjustment programs mounted, the criticisms became more sophisticated, for it was noted that the hardship visited upon the borrowing countries did not fall equitably across the entire population, but rather fell with disproportionate weight on the poorest, the most defenseless elements of society. Such inequity, of course, was not a deliberate goal but rather an inescapable by-product of the development approach which was being propagated. It is possible that no alternative means exist for rationalizing some of the imbalances in national economies which yield a better mixture of results than the SAPs do, but the structural adjustment approach continues to be viewed with considerable skepticism by development experts from all factions of the ideological spectrum. Even within the staff of the Bank and the Fund there are stark differences of opinion as to the relative merits of the SAPs, despite the strong positive claims for them regularly made by the two institutions. More recently, both institutions have reluctantly admitted that they have made mistakes in the design and timing of some of their SAPs.

The Africans have been particularly critical of certain aspects of the SAPs. The routine insistence by the Bretton Woods institutions that borrowers receiving SALs must liberalize their trade regimes has too often destroyed local industries and flooded the borrower country with unnecessary imported goods — hardly a felicitous outcome. Further aggravating the Africans' complaint has been the World Bank's dogged persistence in obliging its African borrowers (not solely those receiving SALs) to pursue strategies of export-led development despite the Africans' protestations (and the supporting evidence) that an over-dependence on an export-led development strategy has been largely responsible for Africa's current deplorable predicament. Even more egregious is the Bank's policy of pushing for further expansion in Africa's production of commodities which are already in excess global supply (e.g., coffee and other tropical beverages, expanded production of which the Bank has also been pushing in Asia and Latin America), thus leading to collapsing commodity prices and serious resource mis-allocation.

Toward the end of the eighties a totally new type of conditionality was almost imperceptibly added to the eligibility criteria for official loans to Third World countries: human rights. First enshrined in the charter of the European Development Bank (created in 1989), the idea of requiring World Bank and IMF borrowers to meet minimal human rights criteria had been percolating for some time within the U.S. bureaucracy but had garnered only desultory support from the other donor nations. The eruption of democratic forces in Eastern Europe, however, provided a natural opening for the adoption of such criteria. The official addition of such "non-economic" factors to the loan eligibility criteria constituted a radical policy change for the Bretton Woods institutions, although as we have noted earlier, the "ideological neutrality" of the institutions had always been more theoretical than real. The unabashed push for "privatization" under the SAPs had removed any remaining pretense of their ideological neutrality, and the recent introduction of environmental impact testing for World Bank projects, had already weakened the Bank's resistance to the adoption of new types of additional criteria for evaluating loan requests. (Currently on the horizon: limits on military spending by countries seeking to obtain loans from the Bretton Woods institutions.)

Despite their objections to both the old and the new conditionalities, an ever-increasing number of countries are seeking to participate in such programs. Perhaps this is none too surprising when one realizes that, short of outright debt repudiation, it is now virtually the only game in town for heavily indebted Third World countries. The World Bank and the IMF, whose competitiveness and jealousies are common knowledge within the development community, are currently cooperating on an unprecedented scale in the shaping of joint IMF/World Bank structural adjustment loan packages, which now constitute almost the sole access to large scale official funding for most of the poor and highly indebted countries. The major bilateral lenders, both public and private, are now rarely willing to lend to a debt-burdened country unless it has negotiated a structural adjustment program with the IMF/World Bank nexus, and the regional development banks are increasingly patterning their lending programs after those of the Bretton Woods institutions. The IMF and the World Bank are thus effectively the gatekeepers to whatever stock of development capital the world community is willing to make available for the Third World.

Conclusion

It is fairly apparent then, that the financial Goliaths of 19th Street are the point men in the struggle to lock the Third World into the Western dominated capitalist development mode. They control the major pot of public development capital, exercise veto power over access to most other sources of development monies, and are widely regarded as the gurus of capitalist economic development. There is little in their histories or structures, however, to suggest that they are democratically administered. The large contributors control the voting power, and their interests are likely to remain paramount so long as no serious dissension arises among them. While the possibility of such dissension certainly cannot be ruled out, especially in view of the increasing competitiveness of the global community and the proliferation of regional trading blocs, the likelihood is that the rich/poor nation split will remain the dominant global dichotomy for the foreseeable future, and the Bretton Woods institutions, and especially the IMF, are likely to continue to function as the agents for the wealthier nations.

This is not meant to suggest that there is total polarization between the have and the have-not nations. For different reasons there is a widely shared interest in the overcoming of poverty and the achievement of higher living standards for the less developed nations. On the other hand, there are starkly different views as to how this can best be done, as well as on what the ultimate global landscape should be. It is noteworthy that the industrial and economic success of the highly touted "four tigers" of Asia (Taiwan, South Korea, Hong Kong and Singapore), and of Malaysia, Thailand, Brazil and Mexico, has not been viewed with equanimity by all elements in the American population. As U.S. plants flee to these low-wage areas, and as American consumers choose the lower-priced goods pouring in from low-wage countries, workers and other vulnerable sectors of American society may increasingly view the Third World nations as latent economic enemies, and implicitly challenge the wisdom of assisting these countries. U.S. bilateral aid programs are already restrained from providing assistance which might create competition with American production, and the Congress has made repeated efforts to introduce such restrictions into the World Bank's lending program.

Simultaneously, the countries of the South, viewing the prevailing global economic arrangements imposed on the world by the developed countries of the North, complain bitterly at the injustices which are inflicted upon them, and condemn the unwillingness of the big powers to submit to their en-treaties for a more democratic approach to global financial arrangements.

The lack of symmetry in the IMF's disciplinary procedures is one of the more visible of these inequities. As part of its effort to maintain a stable and prosperous international economy, the IMF staff reviews the performance of its members on a regular basis and is not timid about informing a country if its policies are believed to be harmful to itself or to the global economy. For several years now the IMF has urged the U.S. to reduce its budget deficit because of the negative effect it is having on the global economy, but the U.S. has consistently ignored this advice, with impunity. This defiance has not gone unnoticed and unenvied by the smaller nations who, because their financial survival often depends on compliance with the IMF's wishes, cannot afford to defy its directives.

Another systemic complaint about the Bretton Woods institutions, and about the IMF in particular, goes to its link between money and power. In its mildest form, the criticism is simply that IMF voting strength is directly proportional to the value of a country's production and trade, a practice which marginalizes the voice of the poorer nations. A more profound variant of this criticism goes on to challenge the equity of utilizing Western currency arrangements as the foundation for the global monetary system. This is seen as further handicapping countries which can obtain such currencies only through a payments surplus with the hard currency countries, a difficult achievement which is replete with its own gross inequities.

It should be noted that virtually the only counterpoint to the Bretton Woods institutions' vast agglomeration of power in the development field lies with the United Nations and some of its specialized agencies such as the UNDP, UNICEF, FAO, UNEP, etc. But this grouping can hardly be termed a competitive force, for the UN and its agencies tend to be congeni-tally strapped for funds and at their best dispose of far fewer development-oriented resources than do the Bretton Woods institutions. The importance of having at least one major alternative nexus to the IMF-World Bank establishment is, however, a view which is being articulated with increasing sympathy, as the possible implications of the Bretton Woods monopoly becomes more apparent.

The overriding characteristic of the global economy continues to be the vast disparities in wealth and income amongst various peoples, countries and regions — disparities which are closely paralleled by stunning differentials in technological expertise and in rates of population growth. In some regions the economic disparities are growing and in others they are narrowing. The

Bretton Woods institutions are supposed to know why this is so, but they have persuaded few people that they do.

There is a growing perception that the development process is closely linked to a host of other global societal concerns, such as the preservation of the planet's biological diversity and of its ecological unity. There is widespread concern for the earth's diminishing resource base, and for the speed with which environmental deterioration appears to be taking place across the globe. Harmonious resolution of the developmental imperatives on the one hand, with the environmental concerns on the other, is arguably the first order of business of the Bretton Woods institutions in the New World Order. Such harmony is not likely to become a reality, however, until these institutions are subjected to a more democratic method of governance, one which balances the narrow self-interests and ideological biases of the major industrial countries with a stronger voice for the multitudinous but largely powerless populations of the South. Without such balance in their deliberations, the prospects for an attractive New World Order are slim indeed.

11

Economic Globalization: NAFTA and Its Consequences

Hilbourne A. Watson

This essay situates the North American Free Trade Agreement (NAFTA) in the context of the fundamental changes transpiring in capitalism today: globalization, industrial restructuring and the new model of global capitalist accumulation based on the new computer-based technological paradigms. This process has unprecedented implications for geography and sovereignty (nations and nation-states), democracy, classes, groups and individuals, and the ability of the nation-state to design and manage economic policies in conventional ways. Developments necessitating the new technologies to sustain the new accumulation model include: the collapse of mass production, the falling rate of profit, need for a model that rationalizes allocation of resources on a global scale and the intensification of global competition. This approach allows us to capture NAFTA as a dynamic and contradictory process reflecting liberalization, regionalization, and globalization.

The Reality of Globalization

Globalization, a process of the transformation of the world economy, is not reducible to terms like international, multinational, cross-border, or offshore. It refers to "operations within an integral whole"; globalization is a tendency since "a truly global service . . . knows no internal boundaries, can be offered throughout the globe, and pays scant attention to national aspects. The closer we get to a global, integral whole, the closer we get to the end of geography."[1] Ohmae insists that it "is a twenty-first century fact that any institution that does business and pays taxes within a country is a legitimate citizen of that country. It is a full dues-paying participant in the economy, with all the rights and all the obligations that entails."[2] These statements capture the drift of thinking by capital and leading international technocrats about globalization and the declining significance of geography and sovereignty.

The end of the Cold War and chronic national debt and budget deficits are weakening the productive base of the U.S. economy: the withdrawal of U.S. troops from Europe and the shake out in the military-industrial complex, including cuts in defense and aerospace production, are resulting in acute hardships in many U.S. communities. The functioning of the U.S. job market is also affected by the unrelenting thrust of high technology R&D and industrial restructuring to enhance global competitiveness and raise the rate of profit. The structure and composition of U.S. trade has changed considerably in recent years, with its share of world exports declining relative to an increase in its share of world imports — due in part to rising levels of foreign investment in the economy and declining competitiveness.[3] Not only is growing trade dependency a function of globalization and restructuring, but it also makes economic activity in the U.S. more dependent on international economic and political developments.

U.S. Interests and NAFTA in a Global Context

Regional economic integration strategies are integral to globalization in the contemporary period. NAFTA is a regional economic integration strategy designed to enhance the competitive position of the United States within North America, especially vis-a-vis Japan and Europe. The deepening of regional economic integration in North America and in Europe is central to the global industrial restructuring process: this makes regionalization the most advanced attempt at globalization to date.

But regionalization is a contradictory process in that it is limited to a group of economies based on rules that tend to exclude others from the benefits offered to members of the bloc. Capital is relying on this strategy to transcend the impediments in the cybernetic process of governmental decision-making and in multilateral organizations like the General Agreement on Tariffs and Trade (GATT). The deepening of global financial, industrial and market integration linking Europe, North America and Japan in alliances in industries like banking, automobiles, pharmaceuticals and computers advances globalization.[4] In other words, the trade blocs are deeply allied to one another in competitive and complementary ways; as such, they cannot afford to create industry-wide barriers to block access against one another.[5]

The U.S. is also interested in NAFTA as an export strategy: U.S. exports increased from 7.5% of GDP in 1985 to 11.5% of GDP in 1992.[6] NAFTA is a subset of the Enterprise of the Americas Initiative (EAI) strategy for deepening links between Washington and the rest of the hemisphere. By forming separate bilateral trade agreements with individual countries in Latin America and the Caribbean, the U.S. takes the initiative to define the imperatives of hemispheric economic integration according to its own priorities. A major objective is to stem the competitive drive of the EC bloc and Japan in the hemisphere.

Under NAFTA, national economic priorities, social needs, and global priorities of profit maximization are on a collision course as capital shifts investment and production to low-wage sites like Mexico, where skilled workers can produce typewriters, automobile parts, vehicles, and textiles and garments for the U.S. market at a fraction — an average of one-fifth to one-tenth — of wage costs in the U.S.[7] This means that profits are more important to capital than expanding production at home and creating jobs for Americans. The restructuring of Mexico's industrial base shows how the new technologies make it possible to create world market factories in selected least developed countries based on globally defined scientific and manufacturing standards and achieve rates of productivity comparable in some areas of production with those in North America.

Basic Themes and Key Elements in NAFTA[8]

The proposed date for the implementation of NAFTA is January 1, 1994. From Washington's outlook, the central themes in NAFTA are: U.S. global competitiveness; creation of new high-paying jobs for Americans; expansion of the Mexican economy to stimulate economic growth in the United States; and safeguards for American workers and the environment. The integration of the three markets via trade liberalization will make it the largest and richest market in the world. Since the U.S.-Canada FTA took effect in January 1989, U.S. exports to Canada have risen by 19% from $72 billion to $85 billion. About 85% of U.S. exports to Mexico are manufactured goods, and since 1987 exports there have almost tripled to $44 billion.

The argument that NAFTA will create new high-paying jobs for Americans is based on factors including the findings of a number of academic studies,[9] the fact that more than 2 million Americans now owe their jobs to exports to Mexico and Canada, and the argument that wages in export-related jobs are 17% higher than in non-export jobs. The phased elimination of tariff and non-tariff barriers over 15 years will allow 65% of U.S. exports of industrial and manufactured goods to Mexico to enter duty-free with the implementation of NAFTA or within five years of inception. U.S. banks, insurance, trucking, and telecommunications companies are eager to exploit Mexico's services market, which is worth $146 billion. NAFTA should also give American companies greater access to Canada's $285 billion services market.

The liberalization of Mexico's auto market is expected to deepen the development of "Detroit South," as national content requirements are replaced by continental requirements.[10] The dominant position held by U.S. capital in the vital area of intellectual property rights will be further enhanced by NAFTA's provisions. The Office of the U.S. Trade Representative assumes that since "70 cents of each Mexican import dollar is spent on U.S. goods," regional economic growth will strengthen the economy and stimulate U.S. exports to Mexico.[11] It is stressed that NAFTA environmental provisions build on existing U.S. policies by allowing for tougher standards and encouraging Canada and Mexico to strengthen theirs. There are provisions to strengthen critical infrastructure in the U.S.-Mexico border region to benefit interests on both sides of the border.

U.S. workers are to be protected from injury from imports by means of the gradual phasing out of tariffs on sensitive products over a fifteen-year period and through the provision of "effective adjustment assistance to help displaced workers." It is expected that the growth stimulated by NAFTA in Mexico's economy will "diminish pressure to emigrate to the United States by creating new jobs and higher wages for Mexicans at home." This view underscores Washington's commitment to the free movement of capital and its opposition to the free movement of labor across national borders. An aspect of the competitive nature of NAFTA is its tough rules of origin (ROR) and local content provisions to prevent non-NAFTA countries from shipping goods into the U.S. via Canada and Mexico to exploit NAFTA.[12]

NAFTA objectives are consistent with the GATT in seeking to "eliminate barriers to trade, promote conditions of fair competition, increase investment opportunities, provide adequate protection for intellectual property rights, establish effective procedures for the implementation and application of the Agreement and for the resolution of disputes and to further trilateral, regional and multilateral cooperation."[13]

NAFTA builds on a number of bilateral agreements in force between the U.S. and Canada, the United States and Mexico, and Canada and Mexico since 1985 including the U.S.-Canada FTA. NAFTA members share other characteristics that make economic integration necessary: large current account deficits, foreign debts, and the need for an export-led growth strategy.[14] Canada and Mexico conduct between two-thirds and three-quarters of their trade with the U.S., which does about a quarter of its trade with the two of them combined. There are high levels of foreign direct investment (FDI) and portfolio investment across the three borders which set the context for deepening trade and investment liberalization.

NAFTA is designed to achieve trade liberalization (freer trade), not free trade per se. In this sense it is quite different from the EC, which is a comprehensive economic union. The EC model is based on the transfer of sovereignty to the central regional authority. NAFTA does not endorse a common external tariff. Whereas the EC has reached the stage of free labor mobility, NAFTA is not likely to move in that direction (though it provides for limited cross-border entry of white-collar business persons). In contrast with the EC, NAFTA does not cover monetary and exchange rate issues. The history and political realities that led Europe toward full integration are not replicated in North America.

Importance of NAFTA to Canada and Mexico

Long before the Canada-U.S. FTA (CFTA) was signed, Canada's economy was highly integrated into the U.S. economy. Ottawa sees membership in NAFTA as necessary to preserve benefits under the FTA and maintain its role as a major player in global economic affairs beyond its economic size and weight. Canada attaches considerable importance to access to Mexico's market, and is counting on NAFTA to strengthen its foreign direct investment thrust in the region, expand its banking industry and increase agricultural trade with Mexico. One of the major challenges NAFTA will pose for Canada is the intensification of competition in import-sensitive areas, including auto parts, textiles, and apparel, a situation that could intensify worker displacement and other social problems.[15] NAFTA also extends to intellectual property and land transportation that were not included in the CFTA, with implications for Canada's weak secondary manufacturing sector.

Mexico expects to increase its bilateral trade with United States and hopes that liberalization will improve industrial efficiency. Mexico is counting on NAFTA to raise the level of foreign confidence in the economy and increase foreign direct investment while returning "flight capital" to finance the external debt and stabilize the peso. Broadly, Mexico hopes NAFTA will help control inflation, increase exports, strengthen industrial competitiveness and reduce its staggering foreign debt — which was about $100 billion in 1990.

U.S. Labor and NAFTA

The problem for U.S. workers is too few jobs, especially too few good jobs. Economic recovery cannot guarantee a rapid expansion of employment nor the growth of good jobs. Restructuring reduces the demand for labor as capital shifts to a global strategy for allocating productive resources. The position of organized labor in the U.S. on NAFTA is informed by its understanding of the structural problems in the U.S. economy: namely the decline in real wages for U.S. workers since 1978 from a weekly average of $401 to $341 (in 1990$); the widening gap between rich and poor; the rapid increase in the number of low-wage jobs, especially in the services sector, from 12% of the workforce or 6.6 million employees in 1979 to 18% or 14 million in 1990; the loss of 2.8 million well-paid manufacturing jobs since 1979, with 1.3 million such jobs lost since January 1989; and the deepening of U.S. status as a debtor economy.[16] The median wage for U.S. workers in food, textiles, apparel, paper, rubber and plastics, fabricated metals, machinery, aircraft, and automobiles fell between 1979–89.[17]

The AFL-CIO contends that, barring remedial action, both NAFTA and GATT will inflict more serious economic damage on the U.S. economy in the form of higher unemployment, erosion of the industrial base, lower environmental standards, harm to farmers, and higher U.S. FDI abroad.[18] In this light, labor focuses on economic, income and wage disparities among the U.S., Canada and Mexico. In 1990, average hourly manufacturing wages in the U.S. were $14.77, in Canada $16.02, and in Mexico $1.80. Differences in environmental standards and protection provisions and the lack of careful planning are also noted. Labor's point is that U.S. workers could lose since NAFTA would have the effect of further reducing their average wages and the disparity in wages, incomes, and standards of living between the two countries, and Mexico's chronic external debt problem will undermine its ability to increase imports from the U.S., as projected by the Office of the U.S. Trade Representative.

A fact weakening Washington's argument about the projected growth in exports to Mexico is that a large part of U.S.-Mexico trade has already been liberalized. Labor recommends implementation of a plan to improve the standard of living for Mexicans, toward leveling the playing field and keeping U.S. capital at home. It draws attention to the Maquila program to suggest the types of problems some U.S. and Mexican workers could face under NAFTA. In addition, labor analysts question the commitment of the U.S. government to adjustment assistance to U.S. workers displaced by NAFTA.[19] Hufbauer and Schott draw on a number of studies which analyze the potential impact of NAFTA on workers in North America. Most of these studies predict a bleak future for unskilled workers in the U.S. and Canada. Moreover, data show that wages for Mexican workers in the Maquiladoras and production workers in other manufacturing declined during the 1980s.[20]

NAFTA is defended on the grounds that it will add a net gain of between 64,000 and 150,000 jobs to the U.S. economy by 2000.[21] However, Faux and Spriggs are extremely critical of the assumptions and methodology that inform these studies cited by the Bush administration. They argue that these studies make unrealistic assumptions about full employment — the idea that no U.S. jobs will be lost — and investment — that no investment will shift from the high-wage U.S. economy to the low-wage Mexican economy. Faux and Spriggs stress that the U.S. economy could lose 550,000 jobs and $36 billion in GDP within ten years of NAFTA.[22]

One recent study concludes that NAFTA — by increasing U.S. and Canadian grain imports — will undermine grain production in Mexico and increase unemployment and encourage the migration to the cities of between 800,000 and 2,000,000 Mexican corn producers, including highly vulnerable peasant and small farming families.[23] These authors also project that the export of U.S. capital to Mexico will increase unemployment in the United States. Such an outcome could add a potential 700,000 new illegal Mexican immigrants to the U.S. Job creation in Mexico from NAFTA is not expected to have any significant impact on unemployment in that country. Koechlin et al. estimate that rising U.S. investment in Mexico between 1992–2000 will cost the U.S. between 290,000 and 490,000 jobs, while creating between 400,000 and 680,000 jobs in Mexico. But the lost agricultural jobs will be even higher in number. Their estimate of a net increase in unemployment in Mexico also questions the claim that NAFTA will result in a significant increase in Mexican imports of U.S. goods. It should also be noted that low wages in Mexico tend to disguise hidden social compensation costs and mask net increases in wage rates.[24] There is no definitive or reliable estimate of the real effects of NAFTA on jobs and investments in the three economies; therefore, it is impossible to be definitive about wage and employment effects of NAFTA.

Washington looks to NAFTA to strengthen competitiveness in industries like autos and to alleviate some structural problems in the economy. In 1991, yearly average total compensation including wages and benefits for manufacturing workers in the seven leading capitalist economies were as follows: Germany ($36,857); Canada ($34,935); Japan ($34,263); Italy ($31,537); France ($30,019); United States ($27,606); and Britain ($26,084).[25] Even the most skilled Mexican manufacturing workers earn an average of only $5,625. The U.S. and Canada are counting on NAFTA to lower wages and other production costs to achieve or maintain competitiveness with Japan and Germany.[26]

NAFTA, National Debt and U.S. Workers

The structural problems affecting the U.S. economy and American workers are aggravated by the enervating effects of the national debt and massive interest payments on that debt on the quality of life of the population: the national debt erodes the standard of living by reducing real wages and income. The debt affects and constrains resource allocation, consumer spending and confidence, fixed investment, home mortgages, employment, labor mobility, and productivity. In 1981, every American family of four held a $17,000 share of the $1.5 trillion national debt; in 1992, that same family's estimated share was $65,000 based on a $4.5 trillion national debt. In 1970, the federal debt was 40% of GDP; by 1990 it had risen to 70% of GDP.[27]

At least $3 trillion of the national debt accrued in the 1980s. For years to come, as Americans ponder basic and vital issues like healthcare, education, saving, tax reform, urban renewal, productivity, and democracy, they will do so under the crippling weight of this debt. As cities struggle to survive, some of them will have to restructure by merging to create larger and more viable entities to meet obligations in the face of the economic crisis. This could alter the geography of local politics.

The new technologies are redefining standards of capitalist productivity, and companies must adjust to these imperatives or face marginalization or extinction. This requires them to lower the cost of inputs of capital and labor via regional and global alliances. The NAFTA agreement is such a strategy whose justification links overcoming the national debt crisis with immediate concerns of global competitiveness.

Organized labor calls for protection of workers' rights and workplace standards, higher wages for Mexican workers, environmental standards and infrastructure development, and other related requirements. The AFL-CIO frustration with the logic of global capital is reflected in a call for legislation to "deny trade benefits to companies that transfer production from the United States to Mexico."[28] Labor's challenge is to design an appropriate strategy for American workers to survive in the new post-Cold War global environment, characterized by unrelenting technological change and the decline of U.S. hegemony.

Canada and Mexico: Contradictions of Constrained Liberalization

For more than a century Canadians have had a trade phobia, especially when dealing with the United States. This preoccupation lies at the intersection of Canadianization (economic nationalism) and continentalism (integration with the U.S. economy). The anti-free trade sentiment is so strong in some sections of the society that many Canadians tend to attribute most of the country's current economic problems to the CFTA. The recession has led to an increase in unemployment from 7.8 to 11.4% from 1988 to 1992. Canadians are as divided over NAFTA as they are about the CFTA. Canada conducts only 1% of its trade with Mexico and many Canadians feel the economy will reap few direct benefits from NAFTA. In 1991, Canada imported $1.2 billion in goods from Mexico but exported only $400 million. In the same year, U.S. domestic exports to Canada amounted to $79 billion and domestic imports from Canada were $91 billion, accounting for 19.7 and 18.7% of all U.S. domestic exports and imports of selected goods. In 1991, the value of U.S. direct investment in Canadian manufacturing, petroleum and finance was nearly $67 billion, or 17.9% of all U.S. foreign investment in these areas. This situation makes Canadians disenchanted with free trade and the extent of the integration of their economy into the U.S. economy.[29]

Canada and Mexico are bent on strengthening textile and garment production. There is a related matter about textiles and apparel that could hurt U.S. and Canadian workers while creating jobs in Mexico. It stems from the implications of global competition and NAFTA for the U.S. textile industry complex and the financial health of several of the companies in the industry. A number of leading textile companies, including Burlington, West Point Pepperell, Field Crest Cannon, and J.P. Stevens Textile Group, could abandon production or even collapse: some of the leading apparel makers are considering abandoning the garment business altogether at considerable cost to American jobs and offshore operations and employment in the Caribbean.[30] Some of these companies might relocate their operations in Mexico to remain competitive.

Rules of origin (ROR) under NAFTA will have the effect of deepening the integration of Mexico's textile and apparel industry into the U.S. economy. The reason is that ROR tend to restrict investment from third party sources. Mexico may feel justified in demanding a larger share of the U.S. market for textiles and apparel since it now contributes only about 3% of U.S. imports of textiles and clothing.[31] As mentioned above, Mexico's domestic agricultural production could contract in the face of rising grain exports from the U.S. Still, the extent to which NAFTA helps to improve investor confidence in Mexico, thereby reducing the economic and financial risks of investing there, could increase its appeal as an investment site for textiles relative to Canada. The U.S. textile industry complex and its effectiveness in influencing government policy are related to the contribution of the industry to employment; the strategic importance of states where the industry is located; its links to military production and national security; the nature of the employment it generates; and the sheer value of its output. The future of this industry, which is one of the most protected industries in the U.S. (with a particularly negative impact on many Third World textile exporters), may weigh in the scales of GATT reforms, restructuring, and NAFTA.[32]

Implications for the Caribbean

A recent World Bank study concludes that Latin American countries, with the exception of Mexico and Brazil, have little or nothing to gain in terms of trade and investment from signing FTAs with the U.S.[33] However, the U.S. is using the Enterprise of the Americas Initiative (EAI) to force Latin American and Caribbean economies into bilateral FTAs to deal with investment, trade and debt problems. The Caribbean, in particular, faces very serious implications from NAFTA. The region could suffer from the diversion of investment, technology, jobs and trade to Mexico. The most concrete case comes from exports of wearing apparel which several Caribbean Basin Initiatives (CBI) like the Dominican Republic, Haiti, and Jamaica assemble from U.S.-cut and -formed materials for re-export to the U.S.

A study by the United States International Trade Commission concludes that NAFTA would increase Mexico's market share of these goods at the expense of the Caribbean.[34] U.S. officials have already warned the Caribbean not to expect any special treatment such as parity with Mexico under NAFTA. The message is that the region must use the phase-in period of NAFTA to restructure its productive base and rely on market forces to drive its competitiveness.

Not even Puerto Rico is safe from the potential negative effects of NAFTA. Puerto Rico will have to fight very hard to prevent many of the Fortune 500 companies doing business there from shifting to Mexico. While it is true that many of the U.S. companies doing business in Puerto Rico are also already well established in Mexico, the elimination of tariffs on a number of products might entice some of these companies to expand in Mexico at Puerto Rico's expense. Closer proximity, lower wages, a larger labor force, a more complex industrial base, and the removal of tariffs will give Mexico a distinct competitive advantage. Puerto Rico's access to tax-free profits of Fortune 500 companies under Internal Revenue Section 936 provisions helps to finance development at home and in other CBI economies. A loss for Puerto Rico would amount to a loss for some of these other Caribbean economies, where considerable amounts of 936 monies have been invested. The fact that Puerto Ricans elected a pro-statehood party in the 1992 elections may signal that a majority of Puerto Ricans are concerned about NAFTA and other economic issues, and are choosing between independence and what they may see as economic protection under statehood. The Caribbean as a whole stands to lose a lot unless NAFTA is made more responsive to the region's special needs.

Conclusion

NAFTA, which is about trade liberalization — not free trade — is simultaneously a regional response to the intensification of global competition and a moment in the globalization process. ROR aspects of NAFTA have the effect of constraining the trade liberalization process. Still, capital and the state approach it as a strategy to lower the cost of production, partly by reducing the real wage rate and the cost of capital inputs in the free trade zone. There is no definitive or reliable estimate of the real effects of NAFTA on jobs and investments in the three economies; therefore, it is impossible to be definitive about wage and employment effects of NAFTA.

The provisions of NAFTA also reveal the weakening of the post-war nation-state system. The global restructuring of investment, technology and labor shifts its effects to nations, classes, groups and individuals and the capitalist democratic process. While the NAFTA signatories hope to exploit its provisions, there are no guarantees that equity will be achieved, because capitalism is based on competition and private accumulation, rather than on the fiction of a level playing field. Workers across the employment spectrum in North America are vulnerable to the strategy of lowering the wage rate.

Large numbers of women, so-called minorities (especially blacks and Latinos), and working class whites are concentrated in the wage groups with marginal education, training and skills — the ones who will be most severely hurt by NAFTA. It is important for workers — especially women workers — and those concerned with the protection of the environment to understand that the geography of struggle is shifting. The new geography of struggle demands new strategies of transformation to deal with the contradictions of capitalism at the regional and global level: foreign policy and the economics of trade cannot be left to capital and the state in the age of globalization and the decline of the nation-state and sovereignty; for these are also the legitimate concerns of civil society.

Notes

1. R. O'Brien, *Global Financial Integration: The End of Geography* (New York: Council on Foreign Relations, 1992), p. 5.
2. K. Ohmae, "The Boundaries of Business: The Perils of Protectionism," *Harvard Business Review* (July/August 1991), p. 127.
3. Office of Technology Assessment, *Competing Economies: America, Europe and the Pacific Rim* (Washington, D.C.: U.S. Congress, Office of Technology Assessment, 1991).
4. See H.A. Watson, "The Canada-United States Free Trade Agreement and Semiconductors with a Case Study of Electronics Assembly Production in Barbados," *Social and Economic Studies* 41;4 (December 1992).
5. An excellent case of global integration exists in the automobile industry in which U.S. and Japanese manufacturers share technology, finance, design and engineering, but compete for market share.
6. *Wall Street Journal*, September 14, 1992, p. A1.
7. According to a Roper Organization 1992 poll of 455 senior executives of U.S. manufacturing companies, 34% of U.S. manufacturers strongly favor and 47% mostly favor NAFTA; 40% are inclined to move business to Mexico; 60% favor a free trade agreement with all of Latin America; 75% of U.S. companies with sales of $1 billion or more approve NAFTA; 70% of companies with fewer than 500 workers support it; and 33% think NAFTA will hurt U.S. workers. See *Wall Street Journal Reports*, September 24, 1992, p. R1.
8. The main sources for this section include *Description of the Proposed North American Free Trade Agreement*, prepared by the governments of Canada, Mexico, and the United States, August 12, 1992; *Key Points: North American Free Trade Agreement* (United States Trade Representative, August 12, 1992); *NAFTA Themes* (United States Trade Representative, August 12, 1992).
9. See G.C. Hufbauer and J. Schott, *North American Free Trade: Issues and Recommendations* (Washington, D.C.: Institute of International Economics, 1992), pp. 57–61.
10. "Detroit South" refers to the development of an automobile production industry across Mexico by U.S., European and Japanese auto makers.
11. *NAFTA Themes*, op. cit.

12. *Key Points*, op. cit.
13. Ibid.
14. Hufbauer and Schott, op. cit., p. 4.
15. Ibid., p. 21.
16. American Federation of Labor & Congress of Industrial Organizations, *International Trade: Where We Stand* (Washington, D.C.: AFL-CIO, 1992), pp. 1–2.
17. *Fortune*, August 24, 1992, pp. 62–74.
18. There are domestic and international areas of concern where NAFTA could shift power from the domestic to the international arena with negative implications for democracy. The effect would be to undermine national institutions including unions, political parties, and governments. See AFL-CIO, op. cit., pp. 11–12.
19. J. Faux and W. Spriggs, *U.S. Jobs and the Mexico Trade Proposal* (Washington, D.C.: Economic Policy Institute, 1992).
20. Hufbauer and Schott, op. cit., pp. 122–23.
21. Ibid., pp. 107–13.
22. Faux and Spriggs, op. cit.
23. T. Koechlin, M. Larudee, S. Bowles, and G. Epstein, *Effect of NAFTA on Investment, Employment and Wages in Mexico and the U.S.* (mimeo, February 1992).
24. *Business Latin America*, April 27, 1992, p. 134.
25. *Wall Street Journal*, October 12, 1992, p. B1.
26. The decision by BMW to build an auto manufacturing plant in South Carolina also reflects the gap in blue collar wage rates between Germany and the U.S.
27. *Washington Post*, September 27, 1992, p. A1.
28. AFL-CIO, op. cit., p. 10.
29. *Wall Street Journal Reports*, September 24, 1992, p. R12.
30. *Business Week*, September 1, 1991, p. 117.
31. G. Bannister and P. Low, *Textiles and NAFTA: A Case of Constrained Liberalization* (World Bank Policy Research Working Papers, International Trade Division, 1992), pp. 31–32.
32. H.A. Watson, "Global Restructuring and Prospects for Restructuring and Export Competitiveness in the Caribbean," in Watson (ed.), *The Caribbean in the Global Political Economy* (Boulder: Lynne Rienner, 1993).
33. R. Erzan and A. Yeats, *Free Trade Agreements with the U.S.: What's in It for Latin America?* (Washington, D.C.: World Bank Policy Research Working Papers, 1992).
34. *Potential Effects of NAFTA on Apparel Investment in CBERA Countries: Report to the U.S. Trade Representative on Investigation, No. 332–321* (Washington, D.C.: U.S. International Trade Commission Publication 2541, July 1992). The Caribbean has major concerns about the trade and investment diversion implications of NAFTA for apparel assembly activities in the region. The countries most affected are the Dominican Republic, Jamaica, Haiti, and a few countries in Central America. All are beneficiaries under the Caribbean Basin Economic Recovery Act. Caribbean apparel exports to the U.S. earned over $2 billion in 1990 or 24% of the value of all exports to the U.S., and created 200,000 jobs. See also Watson, "Global Restructuring . . .," op. cit.

The Transformation of Nationalism:

From Anti-Colonialism to

Ethnic Cleansing

12

The New Nationalism in Europe

Mary Kaldor

$\mathbf{F}$ar from ending, history seems to have speeded up since the revolutions of 1989. Germany has unified; the Soviet Union, Yugoslavia, and Czechoslovakia have fallen apart. A major war is taking place in the middle of the continent, with tens of thousands of deaths, millions of refugees, and the destruction of whole villages, towns, and historic buildings. Anti-Semitism, anti-gypsyism, and other forms of xenophobia are on the rise again almost everywhere in Europe.

Did those of us who devoted so much of our lives to the goal of ending the Cold War make a mistake? Was it worth being a dissident or a peace activist if this was to be the final outcome? Why did we assume that everything could be solved if the division of Europe were removed? Cold War apologists, like John Lewis Gaddis or John Mearsheimer told us that future generations would look back nostalgically on the period of the Cold War as a golden era of stability — the "Long Peace," they called it.[1] East European officials used to warn us that democracy was impossible because nationalist and racist feelings would be revived. Were they right after all? Was nationalism kept in check, "deep frozen" as many commentators would have it, only to reemerge when the Cold War ended?

I do not think the dissidents and peace activists were wrong. People's behavior is conditioned by their immediate experience, not by memories of what happened to previous generations. Of course, those memories are rekindled and used in every nationalist conflict, but it is the current context that determines the power of memory to shape politics. In this essay, I want to put forward two propositions. First, far from having been suppressed by the Cold War, the new nationalism is a direct consequence of the Cold War experience. Without the Cold War, it can be argued, the current wave of nationalism would not have happened; at least, not in the same way and with the same virulence. Secondly, the new nationalism that is sweeping through Central and Eastern Europe is a different phenomenon from the nationalism

141

of previous epochs, although it may share some common features. It is a contemporary phenomenon, not a throwback to the past. Before developing this argument a few preliminary remarks need to be made about the nature of nationalism.

What is Nationalism?

"Nationalism," according to Ernest Gellner, "is primarily a political principle, which holds that the political and national unit should be congruent. Nationalism as a sentiment, or as a movement, can best be defined in terms of this principle. Nationalist *sentiment* is the feeling of anger aroused by the violation of the principle, or the feeling of satisfaction aroused by its fulfilment. A nationalist *movement* is one actuated by a sentiment of this kind."[2]

Nationalism is a relatively recent phenomenon that came into being in the late eighteenth century. It is extremely difficult to disentangle the concept of a nation from the concept of a nation-state. Definitions of a nation vary: a common linguistic group, inhabitants of a particular territory, an ethnic group, a group with shared cultural traditions, religion or values. In practice, a group of human beings that define themselves as a nation usually do so because they are citizens of a particular state, because they are discriminated against by a state, or because of their interest in establishing their own state.

All nationalisms share two common features. One is the notion of citizenship — the idea that sovereignty, i.e. control of the state, should be vested in the nation rather than, say, the monarch as in eighteenth century Western Europe or nineteenth century Central Europe, or foreign oppressors, as in the U.S.-controlled Third World or in the Soviet empire. This idea is linked to the expansion of the territorial and administrative reach of the state. Before the eighteenth century, the state was a rather remote affair that hardly impinged on everyday life. As state functions expanded, it became harder to gain legitimacy for monarchic rule.

Of course, concepts of citizenship varied. Historians often distinguish between Western and Eastern nationalism — in particular, the French and German variants of citizenship. In France, the citizens were the inhabitants of French territory. There was a notion that being French was associated with French language and culture. But this could be acquired; immigrants and minorities could assimilate. By contrast, the German notion of citizenship was ethnic. Even today, anyone of German ethnic origin can claim German citizenship.

Secondly, nationalism always involves a sense of distinct group identity which is defined in contrast to other groups. The rise of nationalism was linked to the rise of written vernacular languages which, in turn, was linked to the expansion of the intellectual class. The discovery of print technology made the written word far more widely accessible. New publications, for example novels and newspapers, gave rise to new identities and new communicative networks. Benedict Anderson uses the term "imagined community" to describe the way in which people who had never met or who were not related could develop a sense of community because they read the same newspapers or novels.[3]

History, literature, folk songs and other symbols all play a central role in the construction of an "imagined community." The intellectuals rediscover significant battles, mythic episodes in the nation's past, national costumes, lullabies, holy places. The Scottish kilt, to take one example, was a nineteenth century invention. But it is in war that the idea of a nation is substantiated. The existence of an enemy, real or imagined, is a crucial element in forging a sense of national identity.

During the Cold War years, it seemed as though national sentiment was being superseded by bloc sentiment, at least in Europe. In the East, the language of Marxism-Leninism displaced the language of nationalism as a legitimizing principle. And in the West, vague commitments to democracy and the Western way of life seemed more important than national interest. The idea of an ideological enemy seemed more convincing than a national enemy. Many commentators talked about the post-1945 European era as "post-nationalist." This turned out to be wishful thinking.

The Roots of the New Nationalism

The current wave of nationalism in Eastern Europe has to be understood in terms of the collapse of the communist state. Weber defined the state as an organization "that (successfully) claims the monopoly of the legitimate use of physical force."[4] Pierre Bourdieu, the French sociologist, has extended that definition to cover what he calls symbolic violence as well as physical violence. By symbolic violence, he means the use of language as a form of domination.[5] It is in both these senses that the state has collapsed or is collapsing in much of the post-communist world.

First of all, the language of domination, the Marxist-Leninist discourse has been totally discredited. More importantly, no alternative language exists which is capable of reconstructing legitimacy, i.e. mobilizing a consensus about the political rules of the game. During the communist period, there were no public political debates and no autonomous political movements or parties. There was no mechanism through which political ideas, principles or values, political groups or even individuals could gain respect or trust in society. Any individual who succeeded in a career or who established himself or herself as a public figure did so through some form of collaboration or compromise with the regime.

There were, of course, private intellectual debates in universities and institutes and across the kitchen table. (Russian dissidents used to talk about kitchen table diplomacy.) And these debates were often far-reaching, especially in the former Yugoslavia, Hungary and Poland. Nevertheless, they were private and confined to a marginal stratum in society. There were also dissidents, and some of these, like Vaclav Havel, George Konrad, or Milovan Djilas, were very famous. But dissidents are troublesome, ambiguous figures. In societies where everyone has to collaborate in order to survive, the dissident is a guilty reminder of complicity. They are seen as idiosyncratic individualists not reassuring leaders.

To some extent, Europe, understood as a haven of peace, prosperity and democracy and identified with the European Community, constituted a political alternative. But it soon became clear that only rich countries could join the European Community. And the experience of market reform, which was associated with Western countries, especially in the former Yugoslavia, Poland, and Slovakia, quickly dispelled the mobilizing potential of the European idea. Moreover, since all politicians made use of the language of democracy, markets, and Europe, and nobody understood what it signified, it lacked the substantive content on which to base new forms of authority.

In the aftermath of the 1989 revolutions, many people decided to enter politics and many new parties were formed. There was no basis to choose between one party rather than another or one individual rather than another. In a sense, all politicians were like Ross Perot or Stanislav Tyminski. There were no tried and tested politicians, no established routes to power. Rather, there was a generalized distrust of politicians and parties. Given the huge expectations generated by the 1989 revolutions, every politician was bound to be disappointing.

In these circumstances, the appeal to an untainted uncompromised ethnic, religious or linguistic identity proved to be one of the most effective ways to win power. In large parts of the post-communist world, it is nationalist parties which have won elections. You vote for a politician because he (and it almost always is he and not she) is a Serb or a Slovak or whatever, like you. And the mobilization of fear, the notion that you and your people are threatened, the creation of a war psychosis in the time-honored communist tradition, are all mechanisms to stay in power, to reestablish authority, to reclaim control over the means of symbolic violence. Both communist and nationalist discourse require an Other — imperialism or an enemy nation. But the communist rhetoric could claim a monopoly over discourse because it was based on universalist values. The problem with the nationalist rhetoric is that it is inherently exclusionary. Of its nature, it is fragmentary — stimulating counterclaims to the control of symbolic violence.

Of course, there were differences among nationalist parties. Some were anti-communist and called themselves democratic. Others were simply revamped communist parties, as in Serbia or Azerbaijan. Some nationalist parties made efforts to include minorities in their nationalist project, as in the Ukraine. Others were openly exclusivist. Many commentators suggested that these differences were important. Nationalism is said to be Janus-faced. A sense of national identity is a necessary precondition for democracy, for opposing totalitarianism, and for rebuilding a sense of civic responsibility. The movements in Poland, the Baltic states, or Slovenia were compared to liberation movements in the Third World. Yet sadly, the ugly face of nationalism seems to have shown itself much more frequently than the pleasing face. In Slovenia and Croatia, and in the Baltic states, ethnically based citizenship laws have been introduced. Everywhere xenophobia and chauvinism is on the increase. In many places, paranoia about the Other is whipped up and human rights are violated in the name of national security.

Secondly, the Cold War machines are disintegrating. The arms buildup over the last forty years was an extensive process profoundly influencing economies and societies. It was naive to suppose that this process could be reversed merely by cutting defense budgets. Large parts of the post-communist world are flooded with surplus weapons, unemployed soldiers and arms producers. It is easy enough to form a paramilitary group by putting on a home-made uniform, buying weapons on the black market, and perhaps even employing an ex-soldier or two in a mercenary capacity. The wars in the former Yugoslavia or the Transcaucasian region are being fought by paramilitary groups of this kind.

In the Croatian-occupied part of Bosnia-Herzogovina, known as the "Croatian Community of Herzog-Bosne," there are, for example, several military groupings. There is the official Croatian-Bosnian army, the HVO; there is the Muslim territorial defense force known as "Armija"; there is the extreme right-wing Hos, who wear black in memory of the Ustashe (Croatian Nazis) who ruled Croatia in 1941–5; and there are a number of smaller freelance armies like the Croatian "Falcons" or the "Yellow Ants." Each group has its own chain of command, its own sources of supply, its own registered license plates and its own roadblocks. The same plethora of groups can be found in the Serbian parts of Bosnia-Herzogovina and, with the breakdown of lines of command as a consequence of the collapse of the Communist Party, the Yugoslav Army, the JNA, has come to look more and more like a collection of paramilitary groups.

Much the same situation is to be found in the Transcaucasian region. In Georgia, all the political parties, except the Greens, have their own militias. The Georgian leader, Eduard Shevardnadze, has tried to reestablish the monopoly over the means of violence by trying to weld together these militias into a regular army. It is this ragbag of armed bands that is currently facing defeat at the hands of the Abkhazian National Guard. In Ngorno Karabakh, you see everywhere young men in a wide variety of uniforms lolling around waiting to be sent to the front. They are all unpaid volunteers. The minister of defense of Ngorno Karabakh, himself a former Intourist guide, told me that he thought it would become easier to create a regular army now that there was a "a real war." "In a real war with tanks and helicopters, formerly independent military forces are more willing to join together." In Azerbaijan, the government is employing Russian ex-Soviet Army officers on yearly contracts to create a regular army. All the same, the Ministry of Defense official spokesman described the war with Armenia as a "citizens' struggle." "We have no army and they have no army — this is a citizens' struggle. All the fighting is done by irregular troops."

The point is not simply that private armies exist as in feudal times. It is also that no single grouping has the legitimacy to reestablish a monopoly. No single group, be it an elected government or a disaffected minority, can command widespread trust in society. In these circumstances, government troops become just another paramilitary group.

In societies where the state controlled every aspect of social and economic life, the collapse of the state means anarchy. The introduction of markets actually means the absence of any kind of regulation. The kind of self-organized market institutions that are the precondition for a market economy simply do not exist and have not been allowed to exist. The market does not, by and large, mean new autonomous productive enterprises. It means corruption, speculation and crime. Many of these paramilitary groups are engaged in a struggle for survival. They use the language of nationalism to legitimize a kind of primitive accumulation — a grab for land or for capital. The nationalist conflicts in the former Yugoslavia and the former Soviet Union cannot be understood in terms of traditional power politics, that is to say, in terms of conflicting political objectives defined by parties to the conflict, which are in principle amenable to some kind of compromise solution. Rather, they have to be understood as a social condition — a condition of laissez-faire violence.

Characteristics of the New Nationalism

The new nationalism is different from earlier nationalism in a number of respects. First of all, it can be said that the new nationalism is anti-modern, whereas earlier nationalisms were part of the modern project. This statement needs both elaboration and qualification. Nationalism has, of course, always harked back to some idea of a romantic past, but nevertheless nationalism was an essential component of what we call modernity; it was linked to the rise of the modern state and to industrialization. Indeed, the early nationalists were rather functionalist. Nationalism, for them, was part of the march towards progress. They viewed the nation-state as a viable political unit for democracy and industry; not as a natural institution for an historically established national community, but as a stage in human evolution, from local to national and eventually to global society. Mazzini, for example, did not support the independence of Ireland because he thought that Ireland was not viable as a nation-state. In much the same way, nationalists in the Third World envisaged national liberation as a precondition for modernization and development.

The new nationalism is anti-modern not only in the sense that it is a reaction to modernity but also in the sense that it is not a viable political project — it is out of tune with the times. This is why I use the term anti-modern rather than post-modern. The rediscovery of cultural identity is often considered an element of post-modernism. The term post-modern implies some possibility of moving beyond modernity, whatever that may involve. The new nationalism offers no such prospect. In a world of growing economic, ecological, and even social interdependence, the new nationalism proposes to create ever smaller political units. Earlier nationalisms were unifying rather than fragmentative, often in very oppressive ways. In the eighteenth century, there were some 300 German states; they were unified by German nationalism. The rediscovery of Scottish traditions in the nineteenth century was part of the process of creating a British, not a Scottish, national identity; some Scots liked to call themselves North Britons. In many Third

World countries, nationalism was a way of overcoming ancient tribal or religious feuds.

Earlier nationalisms incorporated different cultural traditions. The new nationalism is culturally separatist. It is often said that Yugoslavia was an artificial creation because it contained so many different linguistic, religious and cultural traditions. But all modern nations were artificial. The national language was usually based on a dominant dialect which was spread through the written word and through education. At the time of Italian unification, only between 2 and 3% of Italians spoke Italian. At the first sitting of the newly created Italian National Assembly, Massimo d'Azeglio said: "We have made Italy, now we have to make Italians."[6] The Yugoslav project was simply less successful than earlier national projects, perhaps because it was attempted too late or too quickly. The new nationalism is a reaction to the cultural hegemony of earlier nationalisms. It is an attempt to preserve and to reconstruct pre-existing cultural traditions, said to be national, at the expense of other traditions.

The new nationalism puts a lot of emphasis on *ethnos*. Cultural traditions are a birthright; they cannot be acquired. This is reflected in the citizenship laws in the Baltic countries or in Slovenia and Croatia, which exclude certain minorities and which distinguish between autochthonous, i.e. indigenous, and other minorities. There were, of course, elements of ethnicity in earlier nationalisms, especially in Germany. But the current emphasis on *ethnos* combined with cultural separatism contains an inherent tendency to fragmentation. Every excluded minority discovers it is a nation. The former Yugoslavia is not only divided into Slovenia, Croatia, and Bosnia-Herzogovina, etc. Croatia is divided into a Crotian and Serbian part, in Bosnia and Herzegovina, there is now a Bosnian Croatian state and a Bosnian Serbian state, and there are now distinctions between Bosnian Muslims who were once Croat and Bosnian Muslims who were once Serbs.

The anti-modern nature of the new nationalist movements is also reflected in their social composition. The earlier nationalist movements tended to be urban and middle class although they did become mass movements in the twentieth century. While it is difficult to generalize, the new movements often include an important rural element. Susan Woodward has characterized the war in Bosnia-Herzegovina as a socio-economic war, in which rural nationalists confront multi-ethnic townspeople.[7] In Serbia, the main support for Slobodan Milosevic comes from industrial workers who live in the countryside and maintain their own smallholdings. In the nineteenth century and in Third World national liberation movements, intellectuals were extremely important. There are still, of course, nationalist intellectuals, but in today's world where the opportunities to travel and to collaborate with intellectuals in other countries have greatly increased, it is much more common to find intellectuals in green, peace and human rights movements which have a globalist consciousness. The expansion of education and of scientific and office jobs has greatly increased the number of people who can be called intellectuals and who have international horizons. In Serbia, it is the students and the Academy of Sciences that constitute the main opposition to

Milosevic. In the Transcaucasian region, it is Armenian and Azerbaijani intellectuals, supported by Russian intellectuals, that are making the main efforts to overcome the national conflicts.

A post-modern project would be integrating rather than unifying or fragmentative. It would emphasize cultural diversity rather than cultural homogeneity or cultural divisiveness. It would encompass the growing educated strata in society. Some people argue that the new nationalism has the potential to be integrating. Scottish nationalists talk about Scotland in Europe. Likewise, the new nation-states in Eastern Europe all say that they want to "join Europe." Indeed, it is often said that a major motivation for nationalism in Slovenia and Croatia and also the Baltic states was that people in these countries believed that their chances of joining the European Community were greater if they were unencumbered by their large backward neighbors, i.e. Russia and Serbia. Fashionable European concepts like "subsidiarity" or "Europe of the Regions" offer the possibility of combining local and regional autonomy with Europe-wide cooperation. But this kind of concept is completely at odds with the ethnic principle of citizenship and even, I would argue, with the notion of territorial sovereignty which is an essential element of all nationalisms. And, in practice, the new nationalism has shown itself to be closed and not open to the outside world. New nationalist governments are reimposing control over the media, especially television; they are renationalizing rather than privatizing industry; they are introducing new barriers to travel, trade and communication with the multiplication of frontiers. As such, the new nationalist project is unviable; it is incapable of solving economic and environmental problems and it is a recipe for violent unrest and frequent wars.

The second feature of the new nationalism that is different from earlier nationalisms is the use of new technology. If the new nationalism is anti-modern in philosophy, it is modern or even post-modern in technique. In place of the novels and newspapers that provided the medium for the construction of an earlier nationalism, the new nationalism is based on new communicative networks involving television, videos, telephone, faxes, and computers. These new techniques greatly extend the possibilities for mobilizing, manipulating and controlling public opinion. The neo-Nazis in Germany circulate anti-Semitic videos and they use CB radios to orchestrate their demonstrations.

A particularly important aspect of the use of new technology is the emergence of transnational "imagined communities." Groups of exiles in Paris, London or Zurich have often played an important role in national movements. But ease of communication, as well as the expansion of expatriate communities in new countries like the United States, Canada, or Australia, have transformed the new national movements into transnational networks. In almost every significant national movement, money, arms and ideas are provided by expatriates abroad. Irish-American support for the IRA has been well documented. Other examples include Canadian mercenaries in Croatia; American Macedonians calling for the unification of Macedonia and Bulgaria; the Armenian diaspora supporting the claim to Ngorno Karabakh.

The new nationalism is, in part, a consequence of the loss of cultural identity in the anonymous melting pot nations of the new world. The dreams of the expatriates, the longing for a "homeland" that does not exist, are dangerously superimposed on the anti-modern chaotic reality which they have left behind. Radha Kumar has described the support given by Indians living in the United States to the Hindu nationalist movement: "Separated from their countries of origin, often living as aliens in a foreign land, simultaneously feeling stripped of their culture and guilty for having escaped the troubles 'back home,' expatriates turn to diaspora nationalism without understanding the violence that their actions might inadvertently trigger."[8]

Another aspect of the new technology is, of course, modern weapons. Modern military technology is immensely destructive. Even without the most up-to-date systems, villages and towns in Croatia and Bosnia-Herzogovina have been razed to the ground. It is the combination of an anti-modern philosophy with modern technology, in both military and communicative terms, that makes the new nationalism so dangerous.

Alternatives to Nationalism

The new nationalism is a dead-end phenomenon. It is a reaction to the oppressive nature of modernity, especially its statist East European variant, and a rationale for the new gangsterism. It will lead, at best, to small, autarchic, authoritarian, poor states, and, at worst, to endemic, continuous violence. The conflict in Northern Ireland can be viewed as a foretaste of the new nationalism. It is a mistake to interpret what is happening in Ulster as a reversion to the past, although the various parties to the conflict, especially the various paramilitary groups make use of tradition; rather it is a contemporary anti-modern phenomenon with many similarities to the new nationalisms in Eastern Europe.

The reason why the new nationalism is unviable lies in the fact that the nation-state as a form of organization, with extensive administrative control over a clearly defined territory, is no longer an effective instrument for the management of modern societies. In my view, this was already the case before World War I. The bloc system, which came into being after the Second World War as a result of the Cold War, succeeded in establishing some sort of stability, albeit oppressive, for a while because it was able to overcome some of the shortcomings of the nation-state.

The nation-state is both too large and too small. It is too small to cope with economic interdependence, global environmental problems, destructive military technologies. It is too large to allow for democratic accountability, cultural diversity, and the complex decision-making needed in economic and environmental fields. The blocs offered a method of dealing with the problems that arose from the fact that nations were too small. But they greatly exacerbated the problems that arose from the fact that nation-states were too large. The new nationalism is a reaction to these problems, through attempting to make ever smaller nation-states.

What is needed now is a break with the idea of territorial sovereignty —

the notion of more or less absolute control by a centralized administrative unit over a specific geographic area. There is a need for greater autonomy at local and regional levels in order to enhance democracy, to increase people's ability to influence their own lives, to foster cultural traditions and diversity and to overcome the sense of anonymity engendered by modernity, and to make sensible decisions about local economic and environmental problems. But there is also a need for international institutions with the right and the real power to intervene and interfere at local levels in order to protect human rights and democratic practices, to uphold environmental and social standards, and to prevent war. In other words, there need to be layers of political organization, criss-crossing both territory and fields of activity.

Is this a utopian concept? In fact, elements of this approach already exist. The most important example is the European Community. In my view, the European Community is not the forerunner of a European nation-state, although that is what many people would like it to be. It is a much more interesting animal. It is a new type of political institution with certain elements of supranationality, i.e. sovereignty in certain fields of activity, which enable it to interfere in the affairs of member states, to overrule member states on some issues. The EC could become an institution capable of dealing with Europe-wide problems and, at the same time, enhancing local and regional autonomies. And the same kind of evolution could be envisaged for other international institutions like the United Nations or the CSCE (Conference on Security and Cooperation in Europe). At present, these organizations derive their power from the nation-states, and this constitutes a severe limitation on what they can achieve. If their roles are to be extended, this will have to come about as a result of new forms of transnational political pressure.

New forms of communication have given rise to new transnational networks. In certain fields of activity, especially intellectual and managerial activity, people communicate more, through telephone, fax and frequent travel, and relate more to others in the same field all over the world than to their neighbors or to their fellow nationals. If these networks have created transnational "imagined communities" based on ethnicity, they have also created other kinds of more globally conscious "imagined communities." There are, in particular, two types of networks which have a common interest, together with international institutions, in curbing the administrative sway of nation-states.

One type of network relates to local layers of government — municipalities and regional governments. Since the early 1980s, local governments have become much more involved with foreign policy issues through twinning arrangements, nuclear-free or violence-free zones, and other initiatives. Organizations like the Association of Nuclear-Free Authorities, the Standing Council of Local Authorities of the Council of Europe or the Association of European Regions potentially constitute new types of transnational pressure groups.

A second type of network arises out of the single issue social movements that became so important in the 1970s and 1980s. These groups were much more successful at local and transnational levels than at national levels. While they were unable to break the grip of traditional political parties on national politics, they were much more effective than political parties at creating transnational constituencies. Organizations like Greenpeace, Helsinki Watch, Amnesty International, Oxfam, or the Helsinki Citizens Assembly are able to cross national boundaries and to operate in an international context. To these groups should be added trades unions, churches and academic institutions which have greatly increased international networking in recent years. Together, they are forming what could be called a transnational civil society.

Throughout Eastern Europe and especially in areas of conflict, it is possible to find brave groups of individuals, often intellectuals, who are struggling to provide an alternative to violence and to ethnic nationalism. They use the language of citizenship, civil society, non-violence, internationalism. And they are supported by transnational networks of the kind described above. The main hope for an alternative to nationalism lies in the construction of a new political culture, a new legitimate language, that might be based on an alliance between this emerging transnational civil society and international institutions.

The Balkan War provides an example of what could be done. At the moment, the activities of international institutions are greatly hampered by their intergovernmental nature, which essentially means they are seeking solutions "from above." This is both because they can only make decisions based on compromise between member states, and very often the compromises satisfy no one, and because they consider that their negotiating partners are the representatives of states or embryo states and these are people, aggressive nationalists, who are breaking all the norms of international behavior. As a consequence, international institutions are becoming parties to ethnic partition which, among other tragic consequences, could mean a loss of legitimacy for the institutions themselves.

As I have argued, the new nationalism is a social condition arising from the collapse of communist state structures. The new politicians may have been elected, but they do not have the legitimacy to be said to "represent" the people because of their exclusionary policies. There are also, in the Balkan region, municipalities, civic groups and individuals who are doing whatever they can to keep multi-ethnic communities together, to prevent the war from spreading, to support refugees and deserters, to provide humanitarian aid. These groups are helped by municipal and civic transnational networks, although their resources are extremely meager. If international institutions could identify those groups and institutions who uphold international standards as their primary partners and could take actions to condemn *all* those who violate international norms, this could be the beginning of a reconstruction of legitimate political culture "from below."

The forerunners of the new groups in Eastern Europe are the dissidents of the 1970s and 1980s, and their political discourse can be traced back to the dialogue between peace groups and democracy groups across the East-West divide. In the long run, it is to be hoped that the dialogue will be remembered not for its role in ending the Cold War and ushering in a new period of turbulent nationalism, but rather as the beginning of a new way of thinking about politics and political institutions.

Notes

1. See John Lewis Gaddis, "The Long Peace," *International Security* (Spring 1986); John Mearsheimer, "The Long Peace," *International Security* (Summer 1990).
2. Ernest Gellner, *Nations and Nationalism*, Blackwell (1990).
3. Benedict Anderson, *Imagined Communities*, Verso (1991).
4. See Max Weber, "Politics as a Vocation," in *From Max Weber: Essays in Sociology*, Routledge (1991, first published in English in 1948).
5. For an introduction to the concept of symbolic violence, see *Réponses: Pour une anthropologie reflexive*, Seuil (1992).
6. Quoted in Eric Hobsbawm, *Nations and Nationalism since 1870; Programme, Myth and Reality*, Cambridge University Press (1990).
7. Paper presented to the Women in International Security conference on ethnic conflict, Stirin, Czechoslovakia, September, 1992.
8. "Nationalism, Nationalities and Civil Society," in *Nationalism and European Integration: Civil Society Perspectives*, Helsinki Citizens Assembly Publication Series 2 (1992).

13

Uncivil Society:
The Return of the European Right

Paul Hockenos

When the "democratic revolutions" toppled the communist regimes in 1989, the peoples of the East bloc seemed unanimous in their will to "return to Europe," to become the full citizens of a democratic, integrated European House. But while overnight they won the right to freedom of expression, many of their first impulses toward a new political identity were strikingly less than democratic. Throughout Central and Eastern Europe, exclusive nationalisms quickly filled the vacuum that the single-party states had left behind. The horrifying war in former Yugoslavia was only the most spectacular, chilling evidence of the threat that nationalist ideology posed to democracy throughout Central and Eastern Europe. Simultaneously, the resurgence of right-wing, national populist, neo-fascist and even pro-Nazi movements in the East coincided with the startling successes of ultra-right political parties in Western Europe. Despite the many differences between the vast array of undemocratic movements from the Atlantic to the Urals, they shared a mentality and set of values that ran flagrantly counter to the ideals of a united Europe. Rather than human rights, the rule of law, civil society and pluralism, they thought in terms of strong-arm leaders, organic society and ethnic superiority. In words and often deeds, they perpetrated intolerance, hatred and violence.

By the end of 1992, in both Eastern and Western Europe, undemocratic nationalist movements made up part of every country's political landscape. In several of the former Yugoslav and Soviet republics, radical nationalist leaderships with definite totalitarian characteristics had already come to power. In many cases, ominous neo-fascist movements emerged alongside the official structures of power. With influence dramatically disproportionate to their size, the national extremists succeeded in manipulating age-old antagonisms and territorial grudges that plunged whole societies into the abyss of ethnic hatred. In societies with weak or non-existent traditions of democracy, right-wing populists played directly on the deep insecurities facing the Eastern European peoples in their time of transition. On the streets of Dresden and Leipzig, as well as Prague and Budapest, neo-Nazi "skinhead" gangs staged pogroms against non-Aryan peoples. In Western Europe, their counterparts in Paris and Munich singled out similar targets, while the "New Right" political parties such as the Freedom Party in Austria or the National Front in France played to the same prejudices of their middle-class constituencies. In the former East bloc, extremist movements such as *Pamyat* in Russia, *Vatra Romaneasca* in Romania, the *Chetniks* in Serbia and the *Ustashe* in Croatia grew in both size and influence to the point that they no longer existed on the margins of political discourse. They were armed, fielded candidates in elections and openly vied for power.

In Western Europe, the ballot box victories of the New Right parties in France, Sweden, Germany, Austria, Italy and Belgium in the late 1980s and early 1990s jolted many democrats out of their smug overconfidence in post-war Western Europe's democratic stability. With scant political programs centered primarily on the influx of foreigners into their countries, the New Right parties captured as much as 15 or even 20% of the vote in certain cities and regions. The brunt of their xenophobic message was that it was the Arabs and the Asians, the immigrants and the asylum seekers, who were responsible for society's every problem. "Germany for the Germans!" hailed the ultra-right Republican Party, charging that foreign nationals were "taking over" Germany, depriving Germans of jobs, apartments and social services. In times of economic instability and political upheaval, it was a message that could strike sensitive nerves. Interestingly, studies show that the New Right parties' constituencies, however, were neither primarily the socially dispossessed or those who lived in areas with high concentrations of foreign nationals. Rather, a disproportionate number of right voters were middle-class with stable incomes (a high percentage men between the ages of 20 and 30). It was not their own unemployment that they were protesting — but their fear of future unemployment. Nor did they vote for racist parties because their neighbors were African. Most came into little or no contact with the peoples against whom they directed their wrath. Nevertheless, their frustration found an easy scapegoat in people with darker skin.

The New Right movement has its recent origins in the late 1970s and early 1980s, when extremist thinkers in Germany, England and France set out to construct a fresh new image for an ultra-right movement. They sought to bring the Right out of the shadow of Auschwitz and Vichy, to distance themselves from the damning stigma of the Nazi past. They discarded their jack boots and swastikas for a young, professional veneer. They dropped terminology such as "Aryan supremacy" and "*Blut und Boden*" society for their own, no less racist versions of "European unity" and "environmental protection." And, as the elections results showed, their "cultural revolution" successfully legitimized neo-fascist ideas for a whole new generation of voters, discontented with politics as usual. Yet, in contrast to those in the former East bloc, the ultra-right parties in the West seemed incapable, at least in the short term, of actually coming to power. The strength of the *Vlaam*

Bloc or of Jean-Marie Le Pen's like-minded National Front hardly seemed great enough to undermine the foundations of the democratic state in Belgium or France. Nevertheless, one must ask just what kind of democracy was it in which people of color were afraid to walk the streets at night, in which skinhead thugs burned the hostels of political asylum seekers to the ground at will? Unable or unwilling to protect the rights of minorities, did these countries then become democracies in name only? Nor could the influence of ultra-right elements on mainstream political discourse be underestimated. In Germany, for example, the hysterical demagoguery of the Republican Party and the violence of their skinhead collaborators had a profound impact on the debate over laws guaranteeing refugees political asylum in Germany. In the face of right-wing pressure, finally even the German social democrats caved in to accepting restrictive immigration laws that they had long opposed.

As worrying as the New Right's surge in Western Europe was, postcommunist Eastern Europe confronted a situation of another scale entirely. In one form or another (window-dressing such as Vaclav Havel aside), the new democracies in Central and Eastern Europe settled upon deeply conservative, nationalist leaders to take their countries into the post-Cold War era. Under the old dictatorships, conservative traditions had either been suppressed or commandeered by the ruling communist parties, thwarting the evolution of a more modern political conservatism such as that which had emerged in post-war Western Europe. Rather than embark upon a qualitatively new project, most of the nationalist leaderships harkened back to bygone eras, to myths of national prestige and prosperity. At the same time, reluctantly or not, they endorsed rash free market economic programs which brought their feeble economies to the brink of total collapse.

The nationalists' rhetoric of past injustices and lost national territory fueled expansionist ambitions throughout the region. In the Balkans, the scramble for "greater" states resurfaced as never before. The bellicose claims of nationalists for territory across their borders in turn provoked nationalist hysteria amongst their neighbors, escalating the action-reaction spiral of nationalism. The hardest-hit victims of domestic nationalism were the ethnic and national minorities. The persecution radicalized the minorities as well, convincing many that political justice was possible only within the frontiers of their mother nation-states. Other minorities, such as Gypsies, Jews, Third World students and foreign workers also found themselves excluded from the Rightists' notion of an ethnically pure nation.

The sources of and explanations for the explosion of right-wing and nationalist identification are complex. There is more than a grain of truth in the widely-accepted argument that the trend was an embrace of all that the discredited "left" regimes had outlawed — a logical swing of the historical pendulum. As soon as the lid was lifted on nationalism and religion, many people endorsed the forbidden ideologies as the clearest expression of anticommunism.

Yet, the interwoven social, psychological and economic roots of the undemocratic movements in the former East bloc were much deeper. Under the name of "socialism," the post-war dictatorships ruled over totalitarian systems with profoundly conservative modi operandi. In fact, a distinct continuity existed between the overthrown communist systems and the extreme right-wing forces that claimed to represent their antithesis. Four decades of Stalinist rule in societies with weak democratic traditions laid a fertile basis for the reemergence of historical nationalism and right-wing traditions. Despite their radical break with communist ideology, the right-wing movements subscribed to political cultures with striking parallels to those of their predecessors. The means of indoctrination — from rigid school systems to the party-controlled press — encouraged an "authoritarian personality" that could conform as readily to one all-encompassing authoritarian ideology as another. Although the peoples of Eastern Europe consciously rejected communism, many latched on to political traditions that implemented the same mechanisms that they had come to rely upon. Thus, the provincialism, intolerance and militaristic code of the single-party socialist states also defined the political cultures of the Right. Not surprisingly, in authoritarian right-wing parties throughout the region, the former secret police, regime apparatchiks and disgruntled military brass found a popular platform for their law-and-order politics. Where nationalist parties took power, the new leaderships quickly revamped the familiar structures of the Leninist state. Although different forms of parliamentary democracy replaced the dictatorships, the essence of political culture in post-Cold War Eastern Europe proved much more difficult to change.

The nationalist fervor that gripped the region also appeared to have reemerged as if it had been in deep-freeze for two generations. Indeed, the East bloc states discouraged the popular expression of national identity under the pretense of an international socialist identity. But, at the same time, Marxist-Leninist ideology alone proved insufficient to guarantee the stability of the post-war regimes. Throughout the region, more moderate communists succeeded the hardline Stalinist leaders, and national policies were adopted in every state. Within the framework of communist ideology, the states manipulated and perpetuated national identities to shore up their fragile power bases. When those nationalisms raised their heads from below — often in the form of anti-communist opposition — the states quashed them with force. The desires that the regimes encouraged with one hand, they frustrated with the other. When the walls suddenly came crashing down in 1989, a pent-up and deformed nationalism came to the fore almost overnight. In Romania, for example, where President Nicolae Ceausescu had implemented his own particular brand of "national communism," ultra-nationalists resurrected his pro-Romania rhetoric verbatim.

The lines of historical continuity also stretched much further into the past. The national populists of the early 1990s anchored their ideologies in white-washed versions of their nation's pre-communist history. In some cases, parties and movements uncritically identified with their nation's pre-1945 fascist movements, which had allied themselves with the German Third Reich during World War II. In other cases, the ruling political parties harkened back to extremely conservative, nationalist historical legacies that developed parallel to fascism.

As the jarring economic transition took its course, rampant inflation, falling living standards and high unemployment contributed to greatly increased feelings of insecurity, frustration and fear. Foreign investment and aid from the West proved to be only a fraction of what the new leaderships in the East had counted on. But even for countries with growing second thoughts about the wonders of the free market, the elected governments had tied themselves in to International Monetary Fund-dictated policies that left them precious little room to change course without paying the highest price. The discredited status of progressive left and social democratic forces enabled national populists to occupy the pressing social issues at hand. Contrary to popular wisdom in the West, Eastern Europe's nationalist Right remained deeply skeptical about capitalism, which many viewed as a modern, foreign and Jewish-led conspiracy undermining traditional national values and structures. Aside from vague populist demagoguery, however, the nationalists lacked any real economic programs of their own. Instead, the right-wing conveniently laid the blame of the people's misery at the door of the national minorities, Jews, Gypsies, Third World students, asylum seekers, refugees and so forth. Pogroms in former East Germany, Czechoslovakia, Poland and Romania claimed many lives. Anti-Semitism, which the communist leaderships had also manipulated, resurfaced in full force, finding a popular echo even in countries where only a handful of Jews remained.

A brief survey of some of the former East bloc countries provides a more detailed portrait of the Rights in those countries:

Germany: The German Democratic Republic's (GDR) 1968 constitution unequivocally proclaimed that "fascism has been extinguished" on the territory of the "anti-fascist state of workers and farmers." Yet, as in West Germany, neo-Nazi skinheads surfaced there as part of a burgeoning underground youth subculture in the 1980s. Despite official apologetics and upped repression, the state's dirty secret was impossible to conceal: young people across the GDR with shaved heads, green "bomber" jackets and high-top army boots identified with neo-fascist ideology. In the GDR, the "skins," with their affinity for violence and long hate list, often indulged in brutal attacks against anarchist punks, gays, foreigners and the police. A few defiant sociologists ventured to look deeper into the phenomenon. Their findings were startling. For one, a disproportionately high percentage of the neo-Nazis were the sons of communist apparatchiks. Second, they located a dangerous potential for right-wing identification in the majority of GDR youth.

The fall of the Berlin Wall in the fall of 1989 brought the issue of the GDR's Right into the public spotlight. Neo-fascist parties from West Germany lost no time organizing the informal extremist groups in the GDR into political parties with defined fascist ideologies. Violence against Third World peoples exploded on an entirely new level. By 1992 rarely a day went by without German press reports of attacks against persons of color or refugees from Eastern Europe. Although the actual number of active right-wing extremists on both sides of the former wall accounted for only a small percentage of the population, polls showed that large segments of the people approved of the radicals' racist motives. As the economic situation in the new federal states continued to worsen, and the citizens of former West Germany were forced to pick up the mounting costs, the future of the Right in the united Germany remained an open question.

Poland: The rise of political Catholicism in Poland saw the values of the Catholic Church become embodied in the state, as well as in political culture in general. As the defiant sanctuary for political opposition during the communist era, the Church emerged with tremendous political clout, which it did not hesitate to wield. Church-led campaigns to criminalize abortion, bring religious instruction into the schools and ban contraception dominated much of political debate in 1991–92. Even in matters outside of the Church's traditional jurisdiction, politicians admitted that they had limited power to confront the Church. Polish national populism had proponents inside the corridors of power, as well as more extreme advocates vying for power. President Lech Walesa, for one, invoked thinly-veiled anti-Semitism against his liberal opponents in the 1991 election. Right-wing political parties such as the National Party, the Confederation for Independent Poland and Party X relied upon much cruder appeals.

Hungary: In 1990, the first free election in Hungary since 1947 brought a deeply conservative, national populist government to power. The ruling Hungarian Democratic Forum (HDF), like its counterparts throughout Central and Eastern Europe, rallied around the values of nation, religion, tradition and family. At the same time, they rejected the emphasis on the individual and the free market that has united neo-conservatives in the West. In classic national populist terms, the conservatives posited the nation as an organic community, threatened by the alien, "foreign" influences of twentieth century modernism. The populists' suspicion of modernization and liberalism was effectively converted into a potent anti-Semitism, which the HDF did not hesitate to use against its liberal critics.

Where such deep conservatism defines the mainstream, nasty radical movements inevitably surface on the right side of the political spectrum. A violent skinhead movement, a fascist Arrow Cross Party and the reactionary ultra-nationalist St. Steven's Crown Party demanded the resurrection of a Greater Hungary in its pre-1920 borders. The radicals freely admitted that they were connected to a far-reaching international neo-fascist network, ranging from wealthy right-wing exiles to like-minded groups in Austria, Germany and the U.S.

Romania: After a quarter of a century under Ceausescu's draconian rule, a thriving ultra-right no less extreme took root in post-communist Romania. The severity of the dictatorship left an angry and desocialized people in its wake. The array of ultra-right parties preyed effectively on their deep anxieties, calling for military solutions to halt the country's disastrous economic tailspin. In at least a half dozen ultra-nationalist publications, the Right's proponents hysterically whipped up hate against the Hungarian minority, Gypsies, Jews, Russians and democratic intellectuals. Opinion polls showed a large segment of the population in general agreement with the ultra-right. Throughout 1991, the xenophobic weekly *Romania Mare* (Greater Romania) boasted the country's largest circulation at 600,000 a week. The rampant demagoguery claimed at least 30 victims in 1990 in Transylvania, the home of the 2 million-strong Hungarian minority, when members of the neo-fascist Romanian organization *Vatra Romaneasca* attacked a peaceful Hungarian march.

The extremists' nationalism was virtually the same as that which Ceausescu had used to bolster his popularity and fragment opposition along national lines. And the Right's leadership were familiar faces, too; former *nomenklatura*, secret police chiefs and hack intellectuals who had loyally served Ceausescu's dictatorship found a new home in the ultra-nationalist camp. In fact, the right-wing extremists forged close alliances both with the government and with Stalinist hardliners in the revamped communist party. Not surprisingly, both factions agreed that, in retrospect, the Ceausescu years hadn't been so bad after all.

Former Yugoslavia: In Yugoslavia, the violent disintegration of Tito's centralized federal state unleashed a plethora of ultra-nationalist movements. The bitter war that broke out first in Croatia and then in ethnically-mixed Bosnia-Herzegovina radicalized the region's many peoples, bringing highly nationalistic, autocratic rulers to power in almost every former republic. The determining characteristic of Yugoslavia's many right-wing ideologies was the nationalism that underpinned the logic of national independence; and, in most cases, nationalist expansion. The war transformed the republics' political cultures into militaristic war cultures, and the governments themselves into virtual dictatorships.

Yet, as the conflict plunged the south Slavs further into nationalist delirium and economic chaos, markedly more extreme, heavily armed radicals found themselves in positions of power. These extremist groups provided the most vivid example of the way in which tiny radical splinter elements can trigger emotions and movements with far-reaching consequences. Many journalists portrayed the peoples of former Yugoslavia as crazed nationalist zealots, and the conflicts of today as the result of yesterday's hatreds which only the police state had suppressed. But, in fact, the many peoples of the region had lived in relative harmony for over forty years, as friends, neighbors and often as family. Rather, it was the republics' chauvinistic leaderships and a handful of extremists who successfully manipulated the nationalities' age-old fears of one another, reviving the deep hatreds that flourished prior to 1945. Most experts, for example, claimed that the vast majority of the human rights atrocities during the wars were committed by between 1,500 and 2,000 people.

In Croatia, President Franjo Tudjman, a Partisan general turned nationalist, encouraged the explosion of an ugly Croatian nationalism that could one day turn against him. As Croatia steadily lost territory to the Serb-backed federal army in the 1991 war, the fascist, paramilitary *Ustashe* (officially, the Croatian Party of Law), or CPL, swelled in size and influence. In the 1930s and 40s, the CPL was the party of Croatia's Nazi-allied leader, Ante Pavelic, whose ferocious rule shocked even Mussolini and the German SS. In 1992, the CPL controlled Croatia's most feared frontline assault units.

In Serbia, the republic's belligerent nationalist president, former communist Slobodan Milosevic, set about the creation of a Greater Serbia at any and all costs. The nationalist fervor that Milosevic exploited so successfully in the late 1980s, however, spawned offspring even more extreme than its creator. The ultra-nationalist Serbian Radical Party (SRP), commonly known as the *Chetniks* after the pre-1945 monarchist movement, turned its original following of a few hundred into many thousand. The *Chetniks* called for a "historical Greater Serbia," which included all of Yugoslavia save for Slovenia and a tiny piece of Croatia. On the front, the *Chetniks* also made up the most fanatic units, which, theoretically at least, were under federal army command. As the SRP rose on the political scene, they came to embrace their former arch enemies in Milosevic's Serbian Socialist Party as their closest allies.

Russia: The Soviet Union's break-up fueled nationalist and ultra-nationalist movements in every former republic. Given the meteoric speed at which Yugoslavia's reactionaries came to the fore, it remained an open question where such groups as *Pamyat* in Russia and in the Ukraine, the Freedom League in Lithuania, and the Citizens' Committees Movement in Latvia, to name just a few, would find themselves by the mid-1990s. In Russia, *Pamyat* and numerous radical offshoots of the ultra-nationalist movement won followings by touting long-suppressed Russian nationalism. *Pamyat*, with its openly anti-Semitic program led the crusade for a "return" to the tradition of Russian monarchism and the values of the Russian Orthodox Church. A rival of the original 1970s-grounded *Pamyat* movement was the Orthodox National Patriotic Front Pamyat, which called for the "unity of the people and the monarchy" and the "extermination of all of the evil powers on the earth, particularly Zionism." A 1990 Moscow poll showed that 77% of those people asked harbored anti-Semitic feelings. Ethnic and nationalist hatred was also on the rise: across the former Soviet Union, the former republican borders became the object of heated dispute, igniting several wars and setting the stage for more in the future.

The process of fragmentation in the former East bloc only fueled nationalist movements in many Western countries. The flight of over two million refugees from war-torn Bosnia-Herzegovina alone promised to be just the tip of the iceberg if further wars were to break out in the Balkans and the former Soviet Union. With no end in sight, the economic collapse of the post-communist economies in Central and Eastern Europe produced an unprecedented wave of economic victims. In Germany and elsewhere these refugees were met not with hospitality, but with stones and firebombs. Did the end of the Cold War and the fall of communism make possible the realization of the ideals of a democratic, united Europe? Or did it jeopardize the economic and political stability of Western Europe, while igniting a nationalist conflagration in Eastern Europe? At the end of 1992 the terminus of the new nationalism and its radical proponents was still not in sight. Yet it was imperative that the West and progressive democratic forces not look on helplessly as the nascent new order disintegrated into lawless chaos. The mechanisms of all of the existing multi- and supra-national institutions — from the European Community to the United Nations — should have been utilized to their fullest to protect human and minority rights, as well as the sovereignty of independent states. It seemed crucial that the West also come immediately to the economic aid of the beleagured democratic forces in Central and Eastern Europe — clearly making that assistance dependent on the respect for human rights and steady progress toward democratic societies. Otherwise, it seemed that the Europe of the past might well become the Europe of the future.

14

Closing Ranks:
The North Locks Arms Against New Refugees

Bill Frelick

The new world order has ushered in a full-fledged assault on the principle that persons fleeing war and persecution ought to be allowed to escape the country where their lives are in danger and enter neighboring countries where they can receive temporary safe haven. This troubling development has been marked by three watershed events, which, taken together, and in combination with other trends, such as the harmonization of entry and asylum procedures in the European Community, constitute the most serious abandonment of the principle of asylum since before the Second World War.

The three events:

* In April 1991, 452,000 Iraqi refugees, overwhelmingly Kurdish, massed at the border with Turkey, but, with a few exceptions, were denied entry. The world looked on as images of refugees clinging to the sides of mountains flashed across our TV screens.

* In August 1991, 17,000 Albanian asylum seekers were herded like cattle on the pier in Bari, Italy, rounded up and returned without any opportunity to raise asylum claims.

* In May 1992, the United States summarily returned Haitian asylum seekers interdicted by the U.S. Coast Guard without making any attempt to determine whether they might be refugees in fear of persecution.

This chapter will look at these three events singly and together, assessing both the political and historical context that allowed them to occur, as well as their implications for the future of refugee protection.

International Refugee Law Biased Toward Maintaining State Sovereignty

At the close of World War II, as the world divided into the two camps that would wage the Cold War for the next four and half decades, a "new world order" of sorts emerged in which a class of refugees found a comfortable fit.

States signing on to the 1951 Convention Relating to the Status of Refugees agreed not to repatriate forcibly those refugees who feared persecution if returned, based on a narrow spectrum of human rights violations — "race, religion, nationality, membership of a particular social group, or political opinion."

The Convention was both explicitly and implicitly Western and Eurocentric in orientation. It explicitly limited its legal force to refugees affected by events occurring prior to 1951 in Europe, thus excluding the rest of the world's refugees from its protection mandate. Although the geographic limit and cut-off date were subsequently dropped in the 1967 Protocol, the implicit Western and Eurocentric state bias remained untouched. The notion of a well-founded fear of persecution based on deprivation of certain civil and political rights accorded easily with the Western view of Soviet-style communist repression of dissidents and minorities, accommodating the bona fide needs of those people, while at the same time enabling the West to score points in the Cold War's ideological battle by encouraging disaffected elements within the East bloc to "vote with their feet."

The refugee definition failed, however, to address forced migration resulting from deprivation of economic, social, and cultural rights, such as the right to food and shelter or the right to self-determination, causes of significant mass displacement during the past forty years. Similarly, by focusing exclusively on individualized persecution, it failed to account for warfare as the cause of most refugee movement throughout human history, including our own time.

The Convention was also biased toward preserving state sovereignty. The prerogative to determine who was — and was not — a refugee was left entirely in the hands of states. Furthermore, states maintained that they were only obligated not to return refugees who had actually entered their territory. Keep out the refugee, argued governments, and avoid the obligation to protect them against return to persecution.

Despite efforts of Western governments not to bind their hands in determining how to treat refugees and asylum seekers, in fact many of these governments proved to be generous in their refugee policies during the Cold War for refugees and asylum seekers who, by and large, were fleeing communist regimes. (However, the United States, in particular, showed a particular bias against those fleeing "friendly," noncommunist regimes.)[1]

The denial of the right to leave was among the most obvious of the failings of the communist world; extending what amounted to an open invitation to defectors and escapees kept the pressure on the eastern bloc. The Berlin Wall effectively symbolized the divided world of the Cold War era; when East Germany could no longer stem the westward flow, not only did the Wall itself fall, but the whole Soviet-bloc communist edifice crumbled.

But the commitment of the new East European regimes to democratic principles and their adherence to human rights norms, including the right to leave, have removed the sense of obligation from the West European states. Furthermore, the relative poverty and continuing economic disruption in the east, combined with the newfound freedom to travel, are strong enticements to westward migration. In effect, Western Europe has now seen the utility in reconstructing "Berlin Walls" to block entry, as opposed to deterring escape. This leads to the first of our three major denials of asylum at the dawn of the new world order.

Italy Summarily Returns Albanians

For decades, Albania was one of the world's most repressive societies. Travel in or out was highly restricted. The criminal code carried five-year prison sentences for "illegal border crossing." Many would-be refugees, however, were shot and killed at the border.[2]

Any Albanian who managed to escape was automatically regarded as a refugee and given asylum. There were two outstanding reasons for this: first, the numbers were so small that Albanians did not represent a burden to any host countries; secondly, the very act of leaving without permission subjected the emigrant to persecution if returned. No further test of the well-foundedness of the fear of persecution was necessary.

However, the pendulum has swung abruptly in the opposite direction; Western host countries have been quick to switch from near total acceptance to near total rejection. But changes in Albania have not been so abrupt.[3] In 1989 and 1990, as other East European countries rushed to adopt democratic reforms, changes agreed to by the Albanian government were grudging and limited. In July 1990, thousands of Albanians burst into foreign embassies in Tirana seeking asylum. Student protests continued for the remainder of 1990, and elections were scheduled for February 1991. As political pressures building toward the election mounted in December 1990 and January 1991, a mass exodus of refugees fled to Greece. Demonstrations increased in intensity, and the elections were postponed until March 31. In March, with uncertainty about Albania's political future gripping the country, the first mass exodus to Italy occurred. When the elections finally were held, the Socialist Party, which under other names (the Communist Party, and, later, the Party of Labor) had ruled Albania for the past 46 years, received more than two-thirds of the vote. The election results only caused further turmoil — strikes, demonstrations, food riots. In June, the government agreed to step down, and allow a caretaker "national salvation" government to be formed pending new elections. It was at this time of continuing instability that the second mass exodus to Italy took place.

The Italian response to the Albanian asylum seekers was influenced both by the end of the Cold War and by efforts to create an integrated European Community. The EC has been moving steadily toward a single market, with the free movement of people and goods across the internal borders of its members. However, the fear that a "weak link in the chain" would allow asylum seekers free access anywhere within the EC has placed considerable pressure on countries such as Italy to tighten admission controls and asylum procedures.

Accordingly, Italy adopted tougher immigration laws that resulted in the turning away of tens of thousands of foreigners at the border.[4] But these had been individuals; in March 1991, a mass influx of Albanians, some 28,000, landed at Brindisi harbor. For several days, the thousands of asylum seekers remained stranded on the docks with no shelter from the sun and elements, inadequate food and water, and a lack of sanitary facilities. After the initial shock, however, most of the Albanians were allowed to apply for asylum.

However, the authorities decided to prevent any recurrence. Among other steps, including an aid package for Albania, Italy sent their navy to interdict Albanians on the high seas and began returning them without examining their potential refugee status.[5]

But, on August 8, an old freighter, the *Vlora*, crashed the blockade and arrived at the Bari harbor crammed with thousands of Albanian asylum seekers. The dismal welcome on the Brindisi pier in March looked good by comparison with the reception at Bari. In the August heat, no toilets were provided for the 17,000 waiting on the pier, and the stench of excrement hung over them. This time Italy denied the Albanian asylum seekers *any* opportunity to present asylum claims. Thousands were herded into planes to take them back to Albania. About 2,000 who initially had been part of a group held at a soccer stadium refused to leave. They relented after being promised that their asylum claims would be considered. However, after leaving the stadium, these people were rounded up in the pre-dawn hours of August 18 and summarily deported.

Italian officials insisted that Albania was now a "safe" country and could no longer be considered to be producing refugees. This, despite continuing unrest in the country throughout the summer months. Italy simply made a blanket determination that none of the Albanians who arrived in August were refugees. And the assertion went essentially unchallenged by the community of nations which, heretofore, had paid heed to the notion that in the first instance a mass exodus of people in flight from their home country should be accepted on a temporary basis until a determination of their refugee status is made or other arrangements are reached to accommodate their needs.

The abandonment of this principle was underscored in our second watershed event, the Kurdish refugee crisis in the spring of 1991.

Iraqi Kurds: Stuck Between Frying Pan and Fire

In the aftermath of the Persian Gulf War, the most massive and sudden exodus in the 40 years since the founding of the United Nations High Commission on Refugees was stopped cold at the Turkish border. The Western coalition, rather than persuade or pressure Turkey to comply with international responsibilities and keep its border open, contrived to keep the refugees out and deny them the asylum they sought outside the borders of their home country which was persecuting them.

Under the new world order proclaimed by President Bush, a protective shield was supposedly being provided for a repressed and endangered minority in flight. In fact, true safety in the form of asylum was denied, and the assistance that did arrive came as much to shore up political alliances with friendly governments as to assist the refugees.

Turkey — a key ally in the U.S.-led coalition against Saddam Hussein — has remained among the most recalcitrant European states regarding the applicability of the Refugee Convention and Protocol. While the other European states that have acceded to the Refugee Convention have dropped its European-specific limitation, Turkey (along with Yugoslavia and Hungary) has steadfastly maintained a geographical reservation to its accession to the Convention, limiting its definition of refugees to persons fleeing Europe.

Maintaining its limit of refugee protection exclusively to Europeans, Turkey has neither recognized, nor protected, any but a minute fraction of the hundreds of thousands of Iranians who have fled to Turkey in the past decade. Refugees from Iraq, as well, are barred from consideration as refugees. Since most refugees who have sought asylum in Turkey from Iraq have been Kurds, a Turkish refugee policy that excludes Kurds fits comfortably with Turkey's repression of its own Kurdish minority.

It came as no real surprise, therefore, that when a mass exodus of Iraqi Kurds arrived on Turkey's borders at the end of March 1991, they were spurned and left to fend for themselves clinging to the sides of mountains, a picture of misery and death that briefly riveted the world's attention and stirred its conscience. A Senate staff report observed, "If the refugees had been permitted to cross the border — even by half a mile — to enter more hospitable Turkish valleys and facilities, some of the tragic loss of life could have been minimized during those desperate early days in April."[6]

Was the U.S. government's response to that suffering to use moral suasion, or indeed the more taxing pressures the United States was in a position to exert, in order to force Turkey to open its border and provide refuge? No. Turkey, the good ally, was essentially let off the hook.

Creating a safe haven zone inside Iraq was a convenient "single-edged sword" for the United States, blunt on the Turkish side, protecting its ally from any encroachment, yet razor sharp on the side jabbing into Iraq. The United States, joined by Britain and France, justified its creation of a "safe haven zone" in northern Iraq by citing UN Resolution 688 (adopted by the Security Council on April 5, 1991).

The resolution is important both for what it says and doesn't say. It frames its condemnation of Saddam Hussein's repression not in terms of the human rights violations committed against Iraqi citizens inside Iraq, but rather in terms of the "massive flow of refugees towards and across international frontiers" caused by that repression. So the concern is not primarily about Saddam's threat to the Kurds of Iraq, but rather a fear of the Kurds themselves — that their flight to other countries will "threaten international peace and security in the region."[7]

Resolution 688, therefore, should not be read as ushering in a new day for human rights against the evil of government abuse of its citizens committed under the umbrella of state sovereignty. On the contrary, the resolution affirms the "sovereignty, territorial integrity and political independence of Iraq and of all States in the area."

But Resolution 688 did make a significant advance. It insisted that Iraq "allow immediate access by international humanitarian organizations to all those in need of assistance in all parts of Iraq." In compliance with Resolution 688, Iraq did conclude a Memorandum of Understanding with the UN Secretary General's Executive Delegate Prince Sadruddin Aga Khan on April 18 that allowed the UN to provide humanitarian assistance wherever it believed necessary. Resolution 688 had made a genuine advance by expressing the consensus of the world community that international humanitarian organizations should be allowed free access to assist within Iraq. But nowhere was the U.S. Army defined as an international humanitarian organization.

Justifying their action through a strained interpretation of 688 — and without explicit authorization from the Security Council — Britain, France, and the United States created an occupied military zone in the name of international stability that was intended in actuality to destabilize and undermine the government of Iraq.

Far from being the breakthrough for human rights and humanitarian assistance to displaced persons that it was hailed as, the allied intervention on behalf of the Kurds of Iraq instead affirmed the power politics as usual.

A situation like the one in Iraq is not likely soon to be repeated. Rarely will the international community react with such a degree of unanimous condemnation as it did when confronted with Iraq's invasion of Kuwait. But a precedent has been set nonetheless that compromises the rights of refugees; most especially, the right to asylum and against forced return to conditions of political violence and persecution.

Now, we turn our attention to the Haitian crisis, which, together with the Turkish and Italian actions, creates a new set of precedents seriously undermining the right to seek asylum.

Legal Limbo for Haitian Asylum Seekers

Although the U.S. government had been interdicting and returning Haitians since 1981 with only the most cursory interviews to determine potential refugee status, after the overthrow of President Aristide in September 1991 the government briefly stopped returning those Haitians whom it interdicted.

But as the numbers fleeing Haiti grew, the U.S. government was caught in a quandary. On the one hand, it seemed reluctant to return the Haitians to an openly repressive Haiti; on the other, it had no interest in bringing them to the United States.

Under the circumstances in the post-coup period, the straightforward course of action would have been for the United States to have allowed the Haitians to land and give them the opportunity to apply for asylum. This is the practice accepted as a customary norm as the "principle of first asylum," which places a positive obligation on states bordering a crisis not only not to return refugees, but to admit them on a temporary basis.

But admitting the Haitians, even temporarily, was not an option the United States would choose. The creation of a "safe haven zone" within Haiti — the model utilized for the Kurds in Iraq — did not seem feasible. At first, the Haitians were kept on board the Coast Guard cutters, not designed to accommodate passengers, in extremely cramped conditions. Then the government came up with the idea of creating an artificial tier of first-asylum countries in the region. It began shopping around the Caribbean to create middlemen to take on the Haitians interdicted by the U.S. Coast Guard. The choices — Belize, Venezuela, and Honduras — were demonstrably less well equipped than the United States to shoulder the burden of caring for the refugees and only a few hundred were actually transferred. With the failure of that effort, the U.S. established a camp for them at the Guantánamo naval base in Cuba. The Haitians at Guantánamo were denied legal counsel; nevertheless one-third still managed to convince INS asylum officers of the credibility of their asylum claims. The Coast Guard began forcibly returning the other two-thirds who were "screened out."

A protracted legal battle intervened on several occasions over the course of the next several months to stop the forced repatriations from taking place. But time and again the government would prevail by using the argument that it could forcibly return Haitian refugees interdicted on the high seas because the Refugee Convention's ban on forced return applies only to refugees "physically present in the territory of the contracting State."[8]

In December a federal appeals court rejected the claim made on behalf of the "screened out" Haitians that they were protected by the Refugee Convention against forced return. Judge Joseph W. Hatchett wrote a blistering dissent, saying, "At the bottom of this case is the government's decision to intercept Haitian refugees on the high seas, in international waters, to prevent them from reaching United States territory. If these refugees reach United States territory, they will have the right to insist, in United States courts, that they be accorded proper, fair, and adequate screening procedures . . . The interdiction program is a clear effort by the government to circumvent this result . . . Having promised the international community of nations that it would not turn back refugees at the border, the government yet contends that it may go out into international waters and actively prevent Haitian refugees from reaching the border. Such a contention makes a sham of our international treaty obligations and domestic laws for the protection of refugees."[9]

Despite the court's green light to return Haitians who were "screened out," the numbers of asylum seekers continued to rise, and the relatively small corps of INS asylum officers at Guantánamo was not able to keep up with the flow. Rather than concede that this was a mass exodus not conducive to individual refugee status determinations and grant the Haitians temporary protected status, President Bush signed a new executive order in late May directing the Coast Guard to return Haitians summarily, with no screening to determine if they had valid fears of return.

A new suit was filed challenging Bush's order as a violation of the Convention and other laws and treaties. However, a federal judge in New York refused to grant an injunction that would have prevented the government from returning Haitians without screening them first for refugee status.

Although noting that the Haitians would face "irreparable harm" if the injunction was not granted, Judge Sterling Johnson accepted the government's interpretation that the Refugee Convention's ban on forced return of refugees was not binding on the United States. Clearly, Johnson was uncomfortable with his ruling. "It is unconscionable," he wrote, "that the United States should accede to the Protocol and later claim not to be bound by it. This court is astonished that the United States would return Haitians to the jaws of political persecution, terror, death and uncertainty when it has contracted not to do so."

Judge Johnson called the government's conduct "particularly hypocritical" since it had condemned other countries who had failed to abide by the Refugee Convention, such as Great Britain for its forcible repatriation of Vietnamese boat people from Hong Kong, whom it classified as economic migrants.

As it stands now, wrote Judge Johnson, the Refugee Convention is "a cruel hoax and not worth the paper it is printed on."[10]

Bleak Prospects for Refugees Worldwide

Like it or not, the actions of the United States with respect to refugee protection have enormous impact on the conduct of other countries. For example, the doors for hundreds of thousands of refugees from Vietnam, Cambodia, and Laos would have been closed had it not been for the generosity of the United States in taking in refugees admitted by countries such as Thailand, Malaysia, and Indonesia. When those countries wavered in their commitments, the United States was quick to exert its moral, political, and financial authority on the refugees' behalf. The United States maintained a critical posture toward the screening procedures in Hong Kong, and opposed the return of Vietnamese from Hong Kong who, after screening, were found not to meet the refugee definition.

But U.S. conduct with respect to the Haitians has clearly undermined its ability to take the moral high ground on the principle of first asylum. When Hong Kong forcibly repatriated 28 Vietnamese on December 10, 1991, the State Department expressed "regret" that the returnees had not been allowed to apply for a voluntary return program run by the United Nations. No sooner had he spoken than the State Department spokesman was confronted with the question why the United States opposes forced returns to Vietnam but not to Haiti. He was forced to say that "the United States believes that country conditions in Haiti are such that the persons who are returned will not face persecution" but that in Vietnam "the United States opposes forcible repatriation under present conditions in that country."[11]

At a House hearing in June 1992, Rep. Steven Solarz (D-N.Y.) commented, "I pity the poor American diplomat who in the future is asked to go to the British or the Bangladeshis or the Malaysians or the Thais and say, 'Respect the principle of first asylum.' There will be peals of laughter in the room. They will say, 'Who are you kidding. You guys don't respect the principle yourself. Why should we.' We are forfeiting our moral leadership here. And we are compromising our capacity to come to the defense of refugees all over the world."[12]

Already, disturbing trends have begun to emerge that hardly seem merely coincidental with the three actions discussed in this chapter. Thailand adopted a new stance with respect to its newest refugee influx. Fleeing one of the world's most repressive regimes, about 70,000 Burmese sought refuge in Thailand, yet were accepted neither as refugees nor as asylum seekers. The Thai government simply called them illegal, deportable aliens.[13] The Burmese students were subject to periodic round-ups, detentions, and forced repatriations. Thailand has "repatriated thousands of Burmese — including students and ethnic minorities — and resisted virtually every offer of international assistance."[14] There simply was no system for assessing the refugee claims of Burmese asylum seekers in Thailand; no temporary protected status that would be accorded without a refugee determination process; nothing.

The civil war in Somalia was one of the most violent and explosive conflicts in the new world order. In June 1992, when Yemen refused to allow a boat to land carrying sick and dying Somali refugees, the United States was conspicuously silent. Refused permission to land, the boat remained just off the shoreline, as its passengers began to die of thirst and heat prostration. In a three day period, at least 120 died.[15] Yet Yemen was not even publicly criticized by the United States.

As the all-out genocidal campaign was being waged against the Muslims of Bosnia, Croatia in July 1992 announced that it would close its borders unless Austria and Italy opened theirs. Instead of opening their borders, one country after another in Europe introduced restrictive visas to keep out those fleeing the carnage in former Yugoslavia.

For the first time governments began to say in a concerted fashion that the right of refugees not to be forcibly repatriated did not apply if the refugee had not been allowed to enter another country. This created a dangerous "new world order" for the world's refugees. The three watershed events we have discussed create a precedent for handling asylum seekers who may at any future point seek protection that tells governments: Keep them out. Interdict them. Push them back. Create fig leafs such as "safe haven zones" in their home countries, even if the tyrants that persecuted them are still in power. Or create legal definitions, such as "exclusion" in the United States, creating legal fictions that aliens physically present have not legally entered.

For most refugees in the years to come gaining asylum could well be a far-off dream. States will adopt the hypocritical stance that a refugee has the right to escape persecution, but does not have the right to enter. Many will remain in a twilight zone between exit and entry. This zone — whether aboard a Coast Guard cutter, a border post, a waiting lounge of an airport, or some legal construct — will not be a "safe haven" for refugees, no matter what the governments say. Those not allowed to enter will quickly slide in the direction of forced return, and the most fundamental principles for the protection of refugees will have been dismantled.

Notes

1. See, e.g., Court Robinson and Bill Frelick, "Lives in the Balance: The Political and Humanitarian Impulses in U.S. Refugee Policy," *International Journal of Refugee Law* Special Issue, September 1990.
2. *Amnesty International Report 1984* (Amnesty International Publications, London), p. 272. See also, Alan Dowty, *Close Borders: The Contemporary Assault on Freedom of Movement* (Yale University Press, New Haven, 1987), pp. 116–117.
3. See *Trimming the Cat's Claws: The Politics of Impunity in Albania*, Minnesota Lawyers International Human Rights Committee, March 1992.
4. Rory Watson and Nicholas Comfort, *The European*, May 10, 1991.
5. Interview with Clara Maria Bisegna, Consigliere Diplomatico, Del Ministro per Gli Italiani All'estero e L'immigrazione, Rome, October 21, 1991.
6. "Aftermath of War: The Persian Gulf Refugee Crisis," *Staff Report*, Subcommittee on Immigration and Refugee Affairs, U.S. Senate Committee on the Judiciary, 102nd Congress, First Session, May 20, 1991, pp. 36–37.
7. Resolution 688 (1991). Adopted by the Security Council at its 2982nd meeting. UN Security Council, S/RES/688 (1991), April 5, 1991.
8. *Haitian Refugee Center v. Baker*. Brief for the Respondents in Opposition to the Petition for a Writ of Certiorari to the U.S. Court of Appeals for the Eleventh Circuit, in the Supreme Court of the United States, No. 91–1292, October Term, pp. 10–11.
9. Judge Joseph W. Hatchett, U.S. Court of Appeals for the Eleventh Circuit, *Haitian Refugee Center v. Baker*, Appeal from the U.S. District Court, Southern District of Florida, No. 91–6060, in dissent, pp. 2–4, December 17, 1991.
10. U.S. District Judge Sterling Johnson, Jr., U.S. District Court, Eastern District of New York, *Haitian Centers Council v. McNary*, Memorandum and Order, 92 CV 1258, p. 7. June 5, 1992.
11. Barbara Basler, "Hong Kong Ousts More Boat People, U.S. Expresses Regret," *New York Times*, December 11, 1991, quoting State Department spokesman Daniel Rochman.
12. Oral testimony, June 11 hearing before the Subcommittees on International Operations and Western Hemisphere, recorded by the author, and published in *Refugee Reports*, Vol. XIII, No. 6, June 19, 1992, p. 13.
13. See Court Robinson, "Buying Time: Refugee Repatriation from Thailand," *World Refugee Survey 1992*, U.S. Committee for Refugees, pp. 23–24.
14. Ibid., p. 24.
15. "At least 120 Somalis Dead as Refugee Ship Founders," *Washington Post*, June 24, 1992.

■ PART FOUR ■

The Soviet Union and Russia

15

Defining Eras:
The Collapse of the Soviet Union

Fred Weir

The first anniversary of the failed August coup in Moscow was a depressing, rain-sodden affair.

Despite the rock bands and speakers laid on for the occasion by the Russian government, only a few thousand people showed up on Freedom Square to commemorate the chaotic 60-hour struggle in August 1991 that defeated a gang of inept hardline putschists. The mood, as damp as the weather, was a far cry from the soaring enthusiasm and exploding hopes that brought up to 100,000 mostly young people to the same place a year before to fight what most of them believed was a battle to change their society into a democratic, socially just and economically "civilized" one.

"We were duped into taking sides in a fight between bosses," said Sergei Ladonov, a 22-year old student, standing at the fringes of the small crowd. "Now life is better for them, worse for the rest of us. That's how things work."

The lessons of August, for many Russians, boil down to little more than that cynical message. The reason is basic. Ask anyone on a Moscow street Ronald Reagan's famous question: "Are you better off now than you were four years ago?" Nine times out of ten the answer comes bitterly, even despairingly, in the negative.

The deconstruction of the Soviet Union, the collapse of its economy and renunciation of its political system has been at best a mixed blessing for the vast majority of its people. Though it brought a measure of political freedom, an open press and at least theoretically greater choice and mobility for the individual, it has also precipitated near-total economic and social collapse. A bleak future, all the worse for having been unexpected, has swiftly been invading the lives of most former Soviets in the form of mass poverty, unemployment, ethnic tension and civil war.

This was not the promise of perestroika. When Mikhail Gorbachev came to power in 1985 he began to offer Soviets both a sharply critical view of their own country's past and an increasingly radical vision of a "restructured" future. He pointed to the vast potential that could be unleashed if Soviet resources were turned to peaceful development, if economic power were decentralized and the political system democratized. He often talked in the socially advanced language of empowering people in their communities and workplaces, of making the "human being the center of all planning." He also spoke hopefully of re-ordering global relations to prioritize "universal human values" and dreamt out loud, sometimes eloquently, of the possibilities for a Soviet Union "re-integrated with the mainstream of world civilization."

Gorbachev's dilemma, and the tragedy for his country, is that there was never a realistic way for the USSR to quickly rejoin the global economic and political system on anything resembling its own terms.

The reason lies in a unique historical paradox. The USSR, whatever its achievements, was constructed upon economic and social institutions that were fundamentally incompatible with those of the world economy. It never developed the strength or flexibility to compel the West to meet it halfway. Nor did it ever win sufficient allegiance from its own population to survive an extended struggle to win global acceptance in the face of the West's opposition. The only alternative, integration with the world economy on terms set by the dominant Western powers, implied liquidation of much of the market-incompatible Soviet infrastructure — a process which, like cutting a sick patient off life-support, spelled an enormous social catastrophe in the short term for the ex-Soviet population.

From the outset, the Soviet Union was an experiment whose central purpose was to effect a rapid industrialization and modernization of society. To say that is not to denigrate the role of ideology in the revolution, or its subsequent function as a rationale for the state policies of leaders from Lenin to Gorbachev, but to identify the underlying historical process. Indeed, the political framework and methods employed and institutionalized by Stalin had far more discernible roots in previous Russian history than in socialist theory.

On a world scale, the fundamental issue between the Soviet Union and Western nations, from the early days of the Russian Revolution to Gorbachev's rejection by the Group of Seven in July 1991, was not ideology alone. The conflict essentially stemmed from the Bolsheviks' determination to remove a great state and one-sixth of the earth's surface from the Western-dominated world system, closing off its markets and utilizing its vast resources for separate nation-building purposes. All hermit regimes, whatever their character, are enemies of the West.

In its own terms, the experiment succeeded in many ways. If war is the ultimate test of a society's viability and cohesion, one need only reflect upon the sharp contrast between the Russian performance in World War One and the Soviet showing in World War Two, to recognize that a profound transformation had taken place in barely twenty years.

Gorbachev's inheritance was an essentially modern state, a military super-power, with a huge economy. Sixty years before, eighty percent of Soviet people had been rural, primarily agrarian in occupation; by 1985 almost eighty percent were urbanized. The sociological profile was clearly, if idiosyncratically, that of a developed society, with a distribution of population among occupations and professions roughly similar to that found in any Western country. It was a highly-educated population, even by Western standards, that enjoyed reliable access to healthcare and a variety of other modern services — mostly not up to Western standards.[1]

The Soviet Union took an historically peculiar route to modernization, and was in consequence an unevenly developed society, with an autarkic economy and a population largely isolated from global scientific, political and cultural currents. The country's vast resources were locked into a closed economic system, which provided employment and the basics of life for all, but also wasted energy and wealth on a grand scale and, by the 1980s, seemed incapable of generating further development. The Communist Party, which had led the country's transformation by brutally centralizing and concentrating all power into the hands of a technocratic elite was, by the time Gorbachev appeared, an ossified and senile corporate body that elicited mainly ridicule, even from its members.

"Our system was an extremely abnormal one," says Alexander Buzgalin, a former central committee member of the Communist Party and now a theorist for the Russian Party of Labour. "It combined several different types of socio-economic relations in one construct. There were elements of state capitalism, very prominent in industrial relations, for instance. Together with this were many elements of pre-capitalist relations, including numerous semi-feudal controls on the population. Other elements reflected the underground development of a very primitive and corrupted market system. And there were also aspects of genuine socialism, perhaps deformed and undeveloped, but definitely present in social and economic relations.

"All these disparate elements were held together by just one force: the authoritarian-bureaucratic Party-State system."

It was also a society plagued by nightmare historical memories, of millions dead in the Stalinist collectivization drive and purges, of whole nations deported from their homelands, vast populations imprisoned, and a host of lesser crimes. All was remembered, and all complaints were aimed — accurately enough — at the Communist Party and the Soviet state.

If Khrushchev could look out upon the world in 1960, compare raw economic growth rates, and declare the Soviet Union would overtake the West within twenty years, Gorbachev in 1985 could only despair.

The hyper-centralized Party-State system may have been capable of effecting the crude tasks of modernization, but it could not address the social and political implications of post-industrial development. As late as the 1950s it was possible, at enormous human cost, to march unskilled masses of workers into the wilderness and command them to construct steel mills or hydropower stations. No one understood better than Gorbachev — who had a team of the Soviet Union's most talented social scientists advising him in 1985 — that the scientific and technological revolution then reshaping Western economies could never be assimilated in a country where photocopiers and computer modems were police-controlled devices and virtually all economic decisions for a sprawling land, eleven time zones wide, emanated from a single "control panel" in Moscow.

Western competition was not simply a theoretical challenge that might be ignored or deferred. From the end of World War II the United States, as leader of the "free world," had engaged the Soviet Union in an active, open-ended military-political confrontation. One dimension of this struggle, the arms race, utilized superior Western economic, technical and scientific resources to draw a disproportionate response from the Soviet Union. Where the United States seldom spent more than eight percent of GNP on military effort during the Cold War years, Russian economists now claim the USSR was spending as much as twenty-five percent of GNP (that figure is probably too high, and fails to reflect many civilian functions performed by the Soviet army — such as crop-gathering and road building — and the large scale consumer goods production of the Soviet arms industry). By the 1980s, the challenge had sharply intensified, with the United States introducing weapons, such as cruise missiles and Ronald Reagan's Star Wars, which almost seemed better designed for economic warfare against the USSR than for actual war.

For Gorbachev, ending the futile and exhausting Cold War with the West was a crucial political promise made to the Soviet people; it was also a matter of urgent economic necessity. He threw his immense personal energy into achieving this goal, though it gradually became obvious to everyone but him that Western leaders would only regard the Cold War as over when the Soviet Union and "Communism" were destroyed — and perhaps not even then.

One further scene-setting point needs to be made. As a by-product of its development, the Soviet Union created a vast state-supported professional strata, which comprised the intellectual and technical backbone of society, including managers, military officers and administrators. Due to disproportionate membership in the Party, in relation to other social groups, this was also the most politically active section of society. Although privileged in many ways, intellectuals and professionals had deeper historical grievances. They had suffered worst in Stalin's purges, and even in the relatively mild Brezhnev era felt the hard edge of repression and censorship more than other groups. In the republics, it was primarily the intelligentsia that kept alive the national memory and nursed the vision of independence.

As the most highly-educated, well-traveled people in their society, professionals also understood the deficiencies of the Soviet system best. They tended to compare themselves with their own counterparts in Western countries and found their lives sadly lacking by comparison. A bitter and savage joke current in Moscow salons during the later perestroika period sums up that frustration eloquently: "We are Fourth-Worlders," it goes. "First World people trapped in a Third World environment."

It was among the elite that Gorbachev — himself one of them — sought his allies. The initial successes and ultimate collapse of his program rode the wave of their changing attitudes.

What Gorbachev called "perestroika" — the bold attempt to generate a new wave of modernization in Soviet society and bring it into the global mainstream — may be roughly divided into three stages.

The first stage, approximately from 1985–88, was dominated by enthusiasm for the prospects of a regenerated and democratized Soviet socialism. Much unfinished business from the brief Khrushchev "thaw" was revived and extended, glasnost was the order of the day and the economy actually grew.

The second stage, ending abruptly in August 1991, was characterized by the explosion of national, political and social contradictions that had been suppressed in the past. The dominant mood was disillusionment with all reforms within a state-socialist paradigm. Gorbachev made increasingly frantic compromises with nationalist and democratic (i.e. free-market) forces — with Western political pressure constantly in view — while the administrative and intellectual elite began deserting him en masse.

The last stage, brought on by putsch and counter-putsch in Moscow, began with the abandonment of the Soviet paradigm altogether. It has seen the demise of the USSR, and seizure of power in the 15 former Union Republics by local (usually former communist) ethnic elites. The integrated and interdependent Soviet economy has collapsed, with devastating human consequences, while global market pressures — made explicit by a tough IMF program — threaten to reduce most of the former country to a Third World-like economy based primarily on extractive and agrarian industries.

Gorbachev's opening moves were universally hailed. He freed dissidents, began removing controls on the press, made efforts to transfer the executive power of the Party to elected legislative bodies (the 1917 slogan "All Power to the Soviets" staged a brief revival), and made eloquent overtures to the West on nuclear disarmament, security and economic cooperation. He also began to open up Soviet history to scrutiny, an important key to winning support from the intelligentsia.

Much of this was relatively easy to do, though it required tremendous political courage. For a brief, euphoric time, the long-repressed Soviet elite felt as though all its dreams were coming true.

In retrospect, Gorbachev appears never to have had a clear plan, though he did possess a powerful vision of an economically revived, democratized and voluntarily unified USSR.

"The goals of perestroika were founded in the very real potentials unleashed by the Soviet social revolution," says Oleg Malaryov, a developmental economist who strongly supported Gorbachev at the outset, but later became a harsh critic. "The first objective was to achieve a new level of modernization of the Soviet industrial plant and society at large. The second was to introduce a new dynamism into the economy by making working people the real masters of their enterprises. The third was to develop genuinely open, pluralistic and democratic social and political institutions. All of this seemed viable and capable of winning mass support."

One key paradox stood in the way. Chiefly, Gorbachev relied upon the power and authority of the Party to fulfill his agenda. He seldom made any serious effort to reach beyond the elite, to build mass support for his program, and therein lay the seeds of his ultimate defeat.

The subject of the Soviet *nomenklatura* — the Party elite — has been overly mystified in contemporary literature. At its peak, around the time of the 19th CPSU Conference in June 1988, the Communist Party had almost 20 million members. They represented the most active, capable and ambitious people from every walk of life, including captains of industry, trade union leaders, the most prominent academic, scientific and cultural figures, military officers, collective farm chairpersons, state officials and party apparatchiks. The USSR may usefully be compared to a giant corporation; the Party cadres were its executive corps.

A crucial point must be introduced here, one that contradicts much journalistic orthodoxy. Party members occupied relatively privileged positions in society, and enjoyed material and other benefits that rose with one's station. It is usually supposed that Gorbachev's harshest opponents were old Party "hardline conservatives" who feared the loss of their power and special privileges if the perestroika agenda were carried through. Indeed, they were his enemies. Though he defeated them in virtually every Party forum from 1985 to 1991, they retained enough strength to launch the abortive coup against him in August 1991.

However, the Party system not only conferred privilege, it also rationed and limited it sternly. For the well-educated but pampered, impatient and arrogant younger generation of the *nomenklatura*, Gorbachev's program swiftly lost its luster. They saw little to gain by re-orienting Soviet resources to a new wave of popular modernization, and frankly feared Gorbachev's rhetoric about giving economic power to the workers as much as "hardline conservatives" did. They rapidly grasped that one's elite status would be better preserved and extended by private property and market economics than by remaining within the *nomenklatura* system. As Alexander Buzgalin has remarked, "they quite naturally found their salvation in completing the bourgeois revolution rather than making a socialist one."

In the Republics, even to a certain degree in Russia, this section of the elite found their aspirations best expressed in a nationalist program. Though founded on force, the USSR was not an "empire" in any classical sense. In terms of political economy or constitutional structure it was a peculiar sort of federation. Indeed, many of the "colonies," such as the Baltic states, stood in an economically privileged position — i.e. they received more value in trade with the Union than they returned — a reality which is causing them acute pain now that they must adjust to life outside the system. However, the USSR was held together by authoritarian subordination, a centralized structure that disempowered and humiliated virtually everyone living within it. Most Soviet nationalities harbored profound and real complaints, and common grievances were viewed by each group through its own national prism.

It is not surprising that the best and the brightest of the communist elite began gravitating toward a populist brand of nationalism quite early on. Most of them had learned their ideology in the form of a corporate line, a means of rationalizing power. Ukrainian President Leonid Kravchuk, for example, was the top theoretician of the Ukrainian Communist Party and its chief watchdog against the heresy of nationalism. On the day following the abortive coup in Moscow, he transformed himself into the "Father of Free Ukraine" and has claimed, quite credibly, that he had been working with the Rukh independence movement from its inception almost two years earlier. Boris Yeltsin, also a lifelong Party apparatchik, underwent a more complex but similarly opportunistic metamorphosis, and has continued to mutate with the exigencies of power.

That self-seeking nationalists were able to usurp the label "democrats" for themselves is one of perestroika's many savage ironies. Most of the actual democratic innovations introduced into the Soviet Union, including free elections, separation of Party and state and Western-style civil rights, came under Gorbachev's governance and at his urging. There have been few such advances since the Soviet collapse. Indeed, in most Republics of the former USSR, including Russia, the democratic window is now swiftly closing.

Gorbachev had lost control of the anti-authoritarian struggle by 1990, when the agenda of much of the Soviet elite began clearly and sharply to diverge from his. His power base melted beneath him, as his former supporters reformulated the goals of perestroika in terms of national independence and rapid free-market reform. Both those agendas struck strong popular chords with populations sick and tired of fictitious economic progress, newly aware of the vast injustices of the Soviet past – thanks to glasnost — and struck by the apparent prosperity and freedom of the West. An idealized vision of Western life, expressed in the phrase "a normal and civilized society," became the pervasive slogan of impatient, thrusting national elites, and captured the imagination of exhausted but hopeful masses as well.

As Gorbachev fell behind the political curve and became little more than an irritation to his own constituency, he made few serious efforts to rally the still largely passive population. He belatedly endorsed the massive coal-miners' strike in 1989, lauding it as "perestroika from below," but it was Boris Yeltsin who later won the miners' allegiance by persuading them that only a truly Russian government could solve their problems. On one of the few occasions Gorbachev did turn to the people, when he sponsored a referendum on keeping the Union together in March 1991, he won a huge victory. Almost 75 percent of voters in the nine largest republics endorsed his concept of a "renewed federation." But by that time the process was so far out of his control that local elites — and the Western media as well — were able to dismiss the result as "irrelevant."

Underlying Gorbachev's failure was the inability to formulate an economic strategy to reform and regenerate the Soviet economy. The "Law on Socialist Enterprise," which came into effect at the beginning of 1988, contained some measures that could have borne fruit if enforced over time in a stable environment. Among the innovations were "Councils of the Work Collective" elected by the workers of each enterprise, empowered to make key decisions and supervise management. There were also provisions to decentralize economic decision-making, break down vertical command structures and introduce limited market mechanisms. In practice most of these measures merely increased the power of factory managers, as did later quasi-privatization programs.

"What we needed in this country, but have never had, is an economic strategy to select the most viable sectors of our industry — such as avionics, petrochemicals, engineering products, space technology, and many others — and channel major capital investment into them over several years, as well as introducing new forms of management, in order to bring them up to world levels," says socialist economist Tatiana Koryagina, who is currently a centrist deputy of the Russian parliament.

"Gorbachev talked much about the great panacea of defense conversion, but never faced the reality that vast short-term investments would be required to effect such a changeover. In consequence, most of our heavy and defense-related industries are on the verge of total bankruptcy today [September 1992]. Russia's 'peace dividend' will be the destruction of her industrial backbone with attendant mass unemployment, poverty and social unrest," she says.

One crushing problem for Gorbachev was that the USSR's long isolation from the world economy deprived it of cutting-edge technologies and access to large-scale development credits. Despite sweeping political changes in the Soviet Union, and some important progress in arms control and global security, he never made progress in convincing Western leaders to loosen the Cold War economic and technological blockade. The West remained opposed on principle to assisting any Soviet plan involving public sector development — a point underscored by Gorbachev's final, humiliating rejection by the Group of Seven in July 1991. Curiously, even after the Cold War has lost its global relevance, the West has remained hostile to aiding the remnants of the Soviet industrial establishment on any terms. Indeed, Western restrictions against exporting technology to Russia remained in force through the end of 1992, along with a range of other specifically U.S. national security instruments and sanctions against the Russian space and arms industry. It is a sobering thought, for example, that despite bringing democracy to his country and virtually capitulating in the Cold War, Mikhail Gorbachev was never granted full Most Favored Nation trading status by the United States government, though the arch-conservative Leonid Brezhnev had it in 1972.

The abortive coup in August 1991 was a particularly inept last gasp of the old system, but one that utterly discredited any residual authority of "the Union" or "socialism" in people's minds. During that brief struggle, all administrative and political authority fell to national elites. They rapidly adopted nationalist rhetoric to fill the ideological vacuum, and promised the weary people "radical reform" — defined as a better life — now that the long struggle against communism had triumphed.

The Soviet experiment staggered to its end, in utter defeat and exhaustion. History may judge whether the collapse was ultimately a Good Thing, but in the short term it can already be seen as an almost unmitigated disaster for the population.

The break-up of the Union into several new states dominated by local elites rationalizing their power in national terms has inevitably rekindled ethnic tensions and territorial disputes. The violence raging around the periphery of the former USSR is only the beginning of a bloody, drawn-out historic realignment that might come to be described as "the wars of the Soviet succession."

Division of the centralized, integrated Soviet economy has thrown all its components into long-term economic depression, from which few of them are likely to emerge as developed countries within the global division of labor. Virtually all of the social benefits that gave the Soviet population a modicum of modern existence have been withdrawn. It may have been excused as "market reform," but in fact it has been bankruptcy. For the vast majority it spelled a bottomless spiral of impoverishment.

In Russia, all these trends were sharply aggravated from the beginning of 1992 by an economic "shock therapy" program, written by Western advisers and backed by tough conditions from the International Monetary Fund. Its purpose was unambiguously to liquidate the remnants of the Soviet economy and social system as quickly as possible, while absorbing the few viable sectors of the Russian economy into the global market.

In the depths of economic ruin, the once euphoric hopes for direct economic salvation from the West have evaporated. Virtually no capital investment has been forthcoming, certainly nothing for infrastructure, and that aid which has been extended is so riddled with conditions and structured to promote Western business interests, that even the Yeltsin government had largely turned its back on it by late 1992.

Two equally bleak futures seemed to stare Russia in the face.

The first supposes indefinite continuation of the "shock therapy" program. A huge country like Russia — or Brazil, or Zaire, or India — will always have sufficient economic "critical mass" to create a good deal of indigenous small business and market activity. But under "shock therapy," Russia's industrial backbone, constructed during the Soviet modernization drive and now the life-support system for almost 50 million urban workers, appeared fated to disintegrate. According to Russian Prime Minister Yegor Gaidar, the production decline in 1992 exceeded 20%, and the avalanche had barely begun.

Some Russian political economists have begun to speak of the "Latin Americanization" of their country. They pointed to an apparently hopeless condition of poverty for the majority while the emerging rich strata exhibited all the hallmarks of a compradore business class. Wealth has primarily been earned by mediating the sale of Russian commodities — chiefly raw materials — to the world economy. Most of what the new rich were consuming was purchased back from global markets in an economic cycle that scarcely touched the majority of the population at all.

A survey by the financial weekly *Commersant* (September 8, 1992) estimated about two percent of the Russian population was able to benefit from the new economic order sufficiently to enjoy a "middle class European" standard of living. The propensity of this new elite to blow their profits in conspicuous consumption or padding their foreign bank accounts, made it unlikely any progressive, indigenous brand of Russian capitalism could ever emerge.

"What you have to remember is that we do not have a rational, thrifty, productive bourgeoisie in the nineteenth century Western sense," says Tatiana Koryagina. "The Russian new rich are a marriage of convenience between the most vigorous sections of the old *nomenklatura* and former black market structures. Their idea of doing business is to get rich quickly through easy speculation. There is virtually no productive investment occurring in this country.

"For many of these people, especially former partocrats, it is a perfectly natural progression to become corporate executives. They are comfortable as servants of a big organization. The fastest growing sector of our new rich these days is people who go to work as employees of multinational companies, fulfilling an economic agenda that is determined abroad."

The development of a Latin American-type oligarchy, floating above an angry and disillusioned mass of poor threatened popular explosion in Russia. It seemed likely that only Latin American political solutions would be able to contain this situation. Augusto Pinochet, who was claimed to have forced an economic miracle on his obstinate population became, unsurprisingly, something of an idol among many of Russia's new elite.

Russia's second possible fate is not as catastrophic, but offers no better long-range perspectives. It would begin with an effort to stem the collapse and effect a controlled merger with the world market by resurrecting some Soviet forms of economic and political management in Russia and perhaps compelling some other former Soviet republics to cooperate. An extremely powerful movement, the Civic Union, appeared in June 1992 to champion exactly that course. It represented factory managers, army officers, scientists and many other professionals who have become dissaffected with the "shock therapy" reforms — primarily because the wave of destruction is liquidating their bases of power.

The Civic Union called for a return to "strong" (i.e. authoritarian) government, systematic protectionism, massive state intervention and control over the economy and prolongation of some customary social benefits for the population.

That boils down to state capitalism, isolation and autocratic, paternalistic government. Russia, on the horns of its recurring historic dilemma, seemed most likely to revert to this traditional formula.

However, the Civic Union could not restore the Soviet Union nor recreate the options that theoretically existed for Gorbachev in 1985. It could only manage decline, and very likely reward the long-suffering Russian people with the worst of all possible worlds. It might also rekindle the Cold War, since Western leaders are likely to view this program of hoarding Russian resources and closing off markets in the search for a national road out of crisis as a straightforward reincarnation of communism.

There are some more hopeful, but far less likely alternatives. For the first time since 1917 a real democratic socialist movement — the Party of Labor — based in the trade unions and led by brilliant young socialist theoreticians such as Boris Kagarlitsky and Alexander Buzgalin, has appeared on the political landscape. However, in Russia's grim new Time of Troubles, its program of workers' self-management and democratic planning definitely lacks street appeal. And yet, if Russia's working millions could be moved into action, they certainly have the capacity to make history again. But as 1992 ended, and as the elite squabbled over which form of dictatorship was more suitable for Russia's "transition to the market," the dominant mood in the streets and workplaces was cynical resignation.

A joke told on Freedom Square during that miserable first anniversary of the abortive coup summed it up:

"What has Boris Yeltsin accomplished in one year that the communists couldn't do in 70 years? He's made communism look good."

For better or for worse, Russia appears condemned to rejoin the world economy and flow with the "mainstream of civilization." This process deserves to be closely and ruthlessly scrutinized for, in the months and years to come, it is going to tell us a great deal about the actual state of global civilization.

Notes

1. For a full and illuminating discussion of the vast sociological changes wrought by the Soviet revolution, see Moshe Lewin's unique study, *The Gorbachev Phenomenon* (University of California Press: Berkeley, 1988).

16

The Failed Soviet Coup: An Opening for Democracy, National Independence and Fascism

Leanne Grossman

This article will briefly examine why the attempted coup in the former Soviet Union in August 1991 did not succeed, and the effects of its failure on social movements and political processes in the USSR, particularly Russia.[1] The coup plotters failed because they grossly miscalculated how advanced the union's unraveling already was at the time they decided to act, misjudged the internal stability of the armed forces and misassessed how committed a small sector of the population was to shaping an open, democratic society.

The resulting decline in Communist Party power following the failed coup gave an initial boost to democratic elements and political pluralism in general. As the legacy of economic decline weighed on democratic parliamentarians in 1992, however, their leaders lost some legitimacy, and democratic forces began to fracture. Neo-Bolshevik and ultra-nationalist forces exploited the gap created by economic chaos to try to attract popular support and increase their influence on government decisions.

Why the Coup Failed

The failed Soviet coup accelerated the decline of the Soviet Union's regional hegemonic power, altering the course of history throughout Central Eurasia and the world. Staged on the eve of the ratification of a new confederation treaty which would have fundamentally freed the republics from Kremlin control, the coup plotters designed and declared the state of emergency in order to forestall the formal disintegration of the Soviet empire.

The coup plotters observed none of the three criteria specified in the Constitution for a legal declaration of a state of emergency. In addition, the coup affronted the 1990 democratically held Russian presidential and parliamentary elections as well as the direct elections for president held in June 1991. The coup was therefore denied any semblance of legitimacy due to

A Chronology of Coup Events

August 18, 1991: Late Sunday night, five members of the Emergency Committee (SCSE) place President Mikhail Gorbachev under house arrest at his Crimean vacation retreat upon his refusal to accept the state of emergency which is being declared in the USSR.

"August 18, 1991": Gorbachev's recently appointed conservative vice-president, Gennady Yanayev, assumes the presidency citing Gorbachev's "illness." Yanayev publicly declares the state of emergency and the SCSE proclaims itself in charge of the government and the country. To enforce the coup d'etat, Soviet tanks and troops assume strategic positions around the White House (the Russian Parliament) and other points in Moscow and Leningrad.

Small crowds begin to form at the White House and Russian President Boris Yeltsin condemns the coup from a spontaneous perch atop a tank. By evening, the crowd swells to 25,000 and more than one-third of these fearless *"zashchiti"* (defenders) spend the night to strengthen the barricades they have erected in defense against the Soviet Army.

Domestic radio and television stations are either closed or ordered to broadcast only central programming. Most domestic newspapers and periodicals are banned except certain government publications such as *Izvestia* and some ultra-nationalist and ultra-conservative media. Soon *Izvestia* breaks ranks and prints an issue critical of the state of emergency. Many of the banned newspapers still publish, using inferior equipment, scarce photocopy machines or presses outside of Moscow. Almost all Leningrad media defy the ban completely. Resisters among the general populace find innovative ways to publish as well as distribute and post leaflets in metro stations and other public places.

August 20, 1991: Tensions build as the *zashchiti* prepare to fend off an attack on the Russian White House, an event which does not materialize due to dissension in the army and air force high command. Rumor of an attack brings out reinforcements of Russian veterans, youth and other citizens. By this time, Russian soldiers are already defecting and refusing to take up hostile positions against their own people. In another part of Moscow, however, a confrontation with tanks leads to the death of three citizens.

August 21, 1991: Refusal by the naval high command and army generals Shaposhnikov and Grachev to follow orders from Defense Minister Yazov and other coup plotters effectively terminates the coup d'etat. Troops are ordered withdrawn and the Emergency Committee is arrested.

these blatant violations of the nascent democratic process.

To understand further why the coup failed, it is useful to look at the state of the Union in August 1991. First, the economy had continued to deteriorate rapidly despite efforts by Gorbachev to institute modest market mechanisms. Although the rate of economic growth in the USSR was declining in the 1980s, it still remained positive, hovering between four and five percent. In 1990, however, Gross National Product (GNP) dropped approximately 1.5%, and it had plummeted by a further 15% by the end of 1991: indications of a severely troubled economy.[2] Oil production, the prime source of hard currency, was declining annually; an ailing storage and distribution system allowed sorely needed food products to spoil; and the rising theft of goods by black marketeers diverted products to non-state stores and inordinately raised prices.

Second, the Baltic independence movements had advanced rapidly. In the belief that their economic resources were being sapped by the Union's depressed economy, and anxious to exert complete political control over their national destinies, the Baltic states had mobilized a powerful, non-violent mass movement for independence. Soviet leaders attempted to punish the three small Baltic states through an economic blockade. When this failed, the Soviet Army was ordered to disrupt activist strongholds of independence. Fourteen unarmed Lithuanians and four Latvians died at the hands of Soviet soldiers and special police eight months before the Emergency Committee would turn these same armed forces on Russian citizens. In spite of the consequences, Estonia, Latvia and Lithuania firmly declared republican independence and self-rule. Nationalist desires were also simmering in Ukraine and several other regions.

Meanwhile, in the all-union Supreme Soviet, factions such as *Soyuz* (Union) had formed on the principle that under no circumstances should the Soviet Union be allowed to dissolve. They were more concerned with preserving the union structure and thus Russian power than with preserving the ideology of Marxism-Leninism.[3] This self-serving motivation to preserve the empire was the raison d'être of the Emergency Committee that attempted to seize power. As *The Economist*'s Moscow correspondent noted, "Economic woe was the excuse for the coup, but the new Union treaty was its target."[4]

The armed forces acted as supporter and enforcer of the coup in order to preserve the integrity of the empire and thus the USSR's military superpower status. But ultimately it was the weakness of the military that accounted for the coup's failure. Torn internally by a high degree of inter-ethnic tension, poor living conditions and severe morale problems (reflected in a high suicide rate amongst soldiers), the Soviet armed forces proved unable to maintain sufficient unity, within either their highest or lowest ranks, to successfully carry out the coup.

The coup revealed the cynical and contemptuous nature of the conservative leaders who would summon the forces of the state once again. Yet it also uncovered their fatal weakness, their inability to recognize the power of the people in whose name they claimed to exercise authority. But the coup unleashed a torrent of resistance, at least among the courageous minority who built the barricades and stood on the lines for two days and nights, remaking history.

The Impact of the Coup's Failure on Political Processes in the USSR

The ultimate impact of the coup's failure was the erosion of political power and loss of authority of the Communist Party of the Soviet Union (CPSU). The CPSU inadvertently laid bare its exhausted, stagnant programs and leadership. For example, even in Gorbachev's first major address upon his release from house arrest, he stated that the CPSU needed restructuring. Despite Gorbachev's own inability to understand that the Communist Party had lost all credibility and was incapable of leading the country out of economic crisis, the coup forced aside communist elements in government and allowed democratic forces to play a stronger role in directing the transition to a market economy. Ultimately, Gorbachev's failure to perceive the total decline of the CPSU lost him his job.

Another significant effect of the aborted coup was to give freedom to the republics to rule themselves. Almost every republic declared independence from the Soviet Union within two weeks of the coup's failure. Some republics, particularly in Central Asia, would continue to be ruled by the domestic forces which represented the status quo under communism, although now with a determinedly nationalist character. In December 1991, the Commonwealth of Independent States (CIS) was formed, with eleven member republics. Ironically, the CIS is a much looser association than would have been the case had the coup leaders not preempted the signing of the original union treaty.

Emerging Democracy

In the pre-coup period, "democrats" included any individual or group who united to overturn Communist Party rule. Because the centrally planned economy, over which the CPSU presided, had led the country into severe economic decline, an essential element of the democratic reform platform included the necessity of instituting a market economy. While Gorbachev had introduced the concept of economic restructuring, communist bureaucrats generally obstructed economic reform efforts by refusing to release the levers of economic power; the Communist Party was held responsible for the state of the country. Therefore, for the majority of those active in challenging the system, driving out the communists became synonymous with adopting a free market economy and building democracy.

Many Western analysts attempted to demonstrate that democracy was being threatened because a totally free market was not being introduced within the first year. The equation of "democracy" with the "free market," however, represents a distortion. Free market mechanisms can actually be instituted by executive decree and do not necessarily represent democratic sentiments. In fact, most Russians did not describe their reform goal as "capitalism" as they feared its concomitant unemployment and dislocation. Rather, many people have expressed their desire for a social-democratic system that guarantees a social safety net, permits private ownership of land and employee ownership of businesses.[5]

A key strategic victory by democrats occurred in March 1990 with the elimination of Article VI (of the Constitution) that had guaranteed one-party rule. It signaled the impending downfall of the CPSU, the democratic opposition's main target. Similarly, the election of non-Communist Party representatives to the Congress of People's Deputies was unprecedented and helped build the foundation on which social movements relied to instigate change. These challenges to Communist Party control emerged from a growing organized movement for democracy. In Russia, the ascendance of the Democratic Russia Movement (DRM), which was made up of student and labor associations, clubs, individuals and other reform groups, culminated in mass demonstrations in Moscow of up to half a million people.

The DRM agitated for democratic and economic reform while forming a bloc supporting Yeltsin's presidential candidacy. Yeltsin had gained the respect of democratic forces through his actions over several years. For example, in 1987, he lost his post as head of the Moscow Communist Party for criticizing the slow pace of reform and top government leaders. Standing up for democratic policies within the CPSU throughout 1990 and 1991, withdrawing from the Party before the political winds shifted to make such an action opportune, and, finally, supporting Baltic and national independence prior to the coup, earned Yeltsin the reputation of a courageous, democratically and market-minded politician.

Despite the undemocratic aspects of Yeltsin's policies once he came to power, before and during the coup he emerged as a respected figurehead for those earnestly campaigning for self-empowerment.

The Decline of the CPSU and the Challenge for Democratic Forces

Long before the coup, the CPSU had lost most of the popular support it once garnered for its egalitarian ideology. It had not, however, lost the mandate to rule which it imposed through repression. The institutions of the KGB, internal defense ministry and the powerful party apparatus, while somewhat neutralized by Gorbachev's glasnost policy, still maintained control. But the coup's failure wrested the population from the psychological chokehold of the Party, marking a new period in which people emerged from a state of fear and impotence. One activist described this transformation while participating in the funeral procession held for the three men who sacrificed their lives during the coup attempt: "The faces of the people there were transfigured by the great relief they felt at having rid themselves of the burden of totalitarianism — freedom, peace and joy were now reflected in their faces."[6]

Within three weeks after the putsch, the Communist Party was banned. From monolith to political outcast, the institution so hated and mistrusted had become the butt of open opprobrium and freely expressed disdain. To negate the banning, representatives of the Communist Party mounted a weak judicial challenge. This action, however, further demonstrated the Party's impotence — the legal challenge in the Constitutional Court turned into a trial of the Party itself. Yet none of its known leaders had the courage to come forward to either defend the CPSU or accept responsibility for its activities.[7] Many democrats suspected that the protest of the banning was, in fact, a smokescreen by the Party's beneficiaries to attempt to regain control over property and land since confiscated by the new Russian government.

The overriding strategic victory of the democrats was naturally the defeat of the coup. It brought a genuine and deserved sense of empowerment to democratic forces. While the democrats could claim nominal power, however, key sectors of government remained in the hands of *nomenklatura* or communist bureaucrats who still controlled resources, information and ministries in many locales. Most of the approximately one-half million KGB agents who were laid off later complicated and obstructed the transition by going to work in the black market to which they could divert vast amounts of state production for personal profit.[8]

Thus, initial euphoria quickly faded for the democrats, as the responsibility for determining how to make the transition to a market system now rested squarely on their shoulders. Democratic alliances started to fracture in Russia on the question of how to institute free market mechanisms and at what pace. Yeltsin and his economic chief Yegor Gaidar, responding to advice from Western economists, have introduced "shock therapy," similar to the Polish model, which includes rapid decontrol of prices and removal of subsidies to industry that has triggered wholesale bankruptcies.

Critics have accused the economic program of comprising only "shock" and no "therapy." Opposition has progressively mounted due to concern about resulting mass unemployment, its harsh effect on the standard of living, and the popular reaction that could result from such imposed hardship.

Not only the general population felt threatened by this economic program. Bankruptcy laws and other products of shock therapy could undermine the careers of long-time industry managers and bureaucrats. For this reason, the Civic Union coalition emerged in spring 1992, in an attempt to slow the pace of economic reform. It included powerful industrialists, led by Arkady Volsky, who were attempting to preserve their own positions and their potentially threatened careers, joined by broader popular forces fearful of the drastic impact of the reforms on people's daily lives.

But in August 1992, the "radical Democrats" of the DRM split off to support the Yeltsin/Gaidar program in the belief that all facets of a market system needed to be implemented immediately. Yet another group, "Reform," sought middle ground and promoted dialogue and cooperation with communists but expressed concern about their continued control over ministries of defense, security and the interior.

The splitting debate over the nature of reform is inevitable in a post-totalitarian order. Expectations of transforming an empire and its constituent states overnight are unrealistic. The competing parties and alliances which have emerged have admittedly been immature; party programs have not been clearly formulated; blocs have been fluid; and some deputies, unsure of distinctions between blocs, have retained membership in more than one. In Russia, this primitive pluralism was evidenced by the fact that of 1049 occupied seats in parliament, 840 deputies identified with thirteen registered factions and one unregistered faction. Thirty deputies were in two factions while more than 200 remained independent.[9] Yet the evolution of parties, blocs and alliances, however fledgling, still represented a healthy step toward pluralism. However frustrating the process of developing democracy has been for its direct participants and for the millions of citizens affected by government decisions, from a distance, it has been refreshing to witness the birth of a wide range of opinion and debate where, just a few years ago, only one ideological line prevailed.

The real problem lies not in the existence of endless debate on the parliamentary floor, but in the absence of popular involvement in politics. This phenomenon is historically rooted in the hierarchical nature of communism, which sapped initiative from the average citizen and precluded their genuine participation in political life. In addition, rapid inflation has forced most citizens to scramble to find second jobs or get involved in a side business to subsidize insufficient incomes. While personal incomes did rise 600% in the first half of 1992, consumer prices rose at almost twice that rate.[10] Ironically, most people have been too preoccupied with where to find bread or whether or not they would even be paid, to give attention to the political machinations that affect their very cost of living.

There has not, however, been a total absence of citizen activism. Building a democratic, civil society requires not only the development of institutions capable of educating the electorate and conducting pluralist elections; it also depends on the cultivation of democratic interest groups that try to influence local, regional and national policymaking institutions. The environmental movement of the Soviet Union has been the strongest example of a democratically organized, nongovernmental movement. Having originated in the student "*druzhina*" (lifeguard of nature) movement of the 1960s, it created non-hierarchical, voluntary groups as an alternative to the totalitarian structures that dominated society. In 1987, when glasnost allowed informal groups to register, the Socio-Ecological Union (SEU) formed; by 1992 this movement had grown to include 170 environmental groups in 13 of the former republics.

Environmental activists have fought and won numerous battles against ecologically disastrous government plans. For example, the Georgia Greens halted construction of seven huge hydroelectric dams on the Enguri River after environmental impact studies indicated the dams would be environmentally unsound and energy inefficient. Months of demonstrations, blockades and a hunger strike by students, scientists and other citizens finally halted the half-completed project in 1988.[11] Relying on grassroots participation, the environmental movement inspired other elements of society who have been trying to transform the imbedded psychology of "what was done to us" into "what we can do for ourselves."

The Emergence of New Communist Organizations and the Red-Brown Coalition

The disintegration and banning of the Communist Party in Russia following the coup attempt forced its ideological adherents to organize outside of parliament. Factions which had competed within the old political structure adopted new political positions to gain popular backing. Some even left behind the trappings of Marxism-Leninism, attracting support for their commitment to restore the Russian empire. Several others steadfastly espoused such communist goals as "reuniting the masses under the leadership of the proletariat."[12]

Popular discontent grew as Yeltsin's shock therapy program failed to alleviate worsening conditions of daily life. Such discontent was fertile ground for those advocating a return to the security of the paternalistic communist state. To the extent that popular approval of communist ideas survived, it did so mainly in the older generation who, having lived under communism for fifty or sixty years, wanted to believe their lives and struggles had meant something. They yearned for a bygone era, finding it painful to adjust to the new social and economic disruption from which there seemed no escape. Additionally, the growing impoverishment of the overwhelming majority of Russians facing hunger and a lack of healthcare and other basic necessities, meant that many people were also yearning for the security of the old system. Young people, in contrast to the older generation, lived under a broken-down socialism for their 18 or 20 years, and therefore many felt no allegiance to or identity with the old communist system.

By December 1991, no less than ten communist groups existed in the former Soviet Union, ranging in size from a few hundred members to several thousand supporters. Some were vestiges of the CPSU, while others were new formations such as the Socialist Party of Ukraine.[13] The Bolshevik Platform of the CPSU renamed itself the All-Union Communist Party of Bolsheviks (AUCPB). Led by neo-Stalinist Nina Andreevna, the AUCPB appeared to be the largest group, claiming 35,000 supporters in nine former republics and 80 regions of Russia.[14]

The likelihood of a resurgent communist government, however, remained remote. Communist forces still represented a small minority of public opinion and most Russians laughed at or disregarded the few pro-communist demonstrators who still marched in Red Square. But in the period after the coup, some organized communist groups allied with ultra-nationalist forces. This "Red-Brown Coalition" posed a more serious threat. The effect of the coup's failure and its emasculation of the Communist Party was to throw these unnatural partners into an alliance against all forces of reform.

The coup further aroused Slavic nationalism. This is a natural by-product of losing "Soviet" identity, but, in the extreme, it represents an imperial drive to return Russia to her place as overseer of the empire. Several ultra-nationalist and fascist parties and organizations gained strength in the political vacuum left by the Communist Party's decline. The work of one such group was displayed in the southern Russian town of Samara in May 1992. Anti-Semitic signs (such as "Jews are Christ's enemies") were posted at train stops and on buildings throughout the town. While the city prosecutor declared that the signs did not call for national discord and therefore no action was needed, the regional youth newspaper disagreed and apologized for the incident and the lack of official reaction to it. Following subsequent lack of official action, a women's group removed the signs.[15]

The coup itself did not give rise to these reactionary sentiments, however. The Pamyat organization which emerged in the early 1980s became known for its vociferous anti-Semitism. By 1988, however, it had weakened and split into several groups.[16] Between 1987 and 1990, at least nine other conservative nationalist or fascist organizations formed and later tried to influence the first multi-party elections in Russia held in March 1990. A Hoover Institute study noted, however, that "Not one of the sixty-one candidates supported by the bloc succeeded in gaining election on the first ballot, and only sixteen managed to reach the run-offs. Most of those who did . . . were then rejected by voters."[17]

With respect to the growth of fascism, Walter Laqueur estimated the danger to be relatively low for several reasons, including the Nazis' abusive treatment of Russians during World War II and the immense destruction of the country by Germany. Another reason is fascism's resemblance to Stalinism.[18]

Other analysts, however, feared that the collective memory might tend toward selective amnesia, which in the midst of severe economic and social chaos could open the way to a Russian Führer. Vladimir Zhirinovsky appeared to be prepared to fill that role. The Liberal Democratic Party (LDPSS), which he helped found and formally establish in March 1990, stated its main aim as the defense of the territorial integrity of the USSR, including the Baltics. Zhirinovsky received six million votes in Russia's 1991 presidential elections, evidence of the fact that his political agenda found sympathetic ears. Later, his ultra-chauvinist platform and style weakened the LDPSS by causing a split.[19]

Whatever Zhirinovsky's limitations, he became a member of "Nashi" (Ours), a highly organized and vocal opposition, made up of former Communist Party officials, ultra-nationalists, chauvinists, anti-Semitic groups and anti-democratic forces in general. Established in December 1991 to preserve the empire and keep Russia dominant, Nashi constituted a genuine threat to democracy.

In coalition or separately, Stalinists and fascists appeared to be fighting a lost cause insofar as they aimed to recover the union of 15 republics. The republics have already taken concrete steps to affirm their declared independence such as initiating inter-republic trade and diplomacy. In addition, the only way to resubjugate the Baltics would be through force. Although 60,000 Russian troops still occupied Baltic territory in late 1992, this remained a highly unlikely scenario due to the extreme disarray of the military.

Conclusion

The failed coup d'etat in the Soviet Union unquestionably changed the fate of the entire region. At the end of 1992, one could predict that the tide of national independence would continue to surge forward as republics shaped new international relationships and national minorities increasingly asserted their identities and claims to natural resources; the Communist Party, having sufficiently discredited itself, would not return to a position of unquestioned power, although communist ideas were not altogether dead.

It seemed, however, that the democratic opening, conceived in the coup's failure, could close. Its fate depended heavily on the outcome of economic reform. The issue was whether a balanced combination of market stimulation and privatization, sufficient social protection and substantive democratic reform could be achieved before popular patience ran out completely. If patience continued to wane, social chaos could propel a frustrated and hungry populace to scapegoat national minorities and Jews, or to call for either a revanchist solution or fascist one.

Any scenario bore the indubitable mark of hardship for the people of the former Soviet Union. At best, the standard of living would continue to decline somewhat; at worst, it might be unbearable for many. The hope remained that enterprising and democratic initiatives would further expand and deepen, empowering the majority of people to reshape their lives in their own best interest.

Notes

1. The coup profoundly impacted all regions of the Soviet Union. Due to limitations of space, Russia, as the center of the former empire, is the focus of this article.
2. PlanEcon chart, "Annual Growth of GNP in Percent for the Soviet Union," in *One Nation Becomes Many* (Access: April 1992), p. 41.
3. Gordon N. Bardos, "Independent Political Movements in the USSR Since 1985," *At the Harriman Institute* (Volume 5, No. 5), p. 5. (Report on talk given by Geoffrey Hosking, February 2, 1992.)
4. "Yeltsin's Army," *The Economist*, August 24, 1991, p. 12.
5. For a thorough analysis of the evolution of capitalism as a goal of reformers, see David Kotz, "The Direction of Soviet Economic Reform: From Socialist Reform to Capitalist Transition," *Monthly Review*, September 1992.
6. Lydia Popova, "'The Faces Have Changed': Transfiguration in Russia," *Surviving Together* (Autumn 1991), p. 8.
7. Marina Shakina, "Who Is Afraid of the CPSU?" *New Times [Novoe Vremya]* (No. 23, 1992), p. 4.
8. Stanislav Levchenko, former KGB agent, interview by author, Reston, Virginia, August 27, 1992.
9. "Bloki i fraktsii rossiskogo parlamenta," [Blocs and Factions of the Russian Parliament] *Panorama* (June 1992), p. 14.
10. Sergei Suverov, "Reform in Review," *Eye on the East* (August 14, 1992), p. 2.
11. "The Georgia Greens, a Profile," *Surviving Together* (Summer 1991), pp. 20–21.
12. "What Happened to the CPSU?" *Soviet/East European Report*, Radio Free Europe/Radio Liberty Research Institute, January 1, 1992, p. 2.
13. Volodymyr Skachko, "Socialist Party, new 'left' opposition in Ukraine," *Ukrainian Weekly*, July 12, 1992, p. 2.
14. "The Right-Left Opposition," *Moscow News* (No. 29, 1992), p. 7.
15. "Anti-Semitic Signs Posted in Samara," *Monitor* (July 1992), pp. 1–2.
16. Vladimir Pribylovskii, *Dictionary of Political Parties and Organizations in Russia*, p. 59.
17. John B. Dunlop, "Russian Nationalism Today: Organizations and Programs," *Nationalities Papers* (Fall 1991), p. 163.
18. Walter Laqueur, "The Prospects of Fascism," *New Times [Novoe Vremya]* (No. 26, 1992), p. 5.
19. *RFE/RL Soviet/East Europe Report*, February 1, 1992.

17

Left Behind:
The Developing World in Russian Foreign Policy

Tatiana Vorozheikina

The end of the Cold War, the breakdown of the bipolar system of international relations and the break-up of the Soviet Union — these are the main landmarks on the new political map around which Russia is now forced to create a new foreign policy. Although Russia's foreign policymakers are working from scratch, they have been granted anything but a free hand. The priorities in this new foreign policy are largely dictated by Russia's deepening economic crisis and the spreading inter-ethnic conflicts on the territory of the former Soviet Union, inevitably causing tension and political conflicts within Russia itself. Russia's foreign policymakers are obliged to emphasize: 1) relations, particularly economic, with the developed counties of the West and Japan; 2) relations with the former republics of the USSR; 3) relations with Asian countries, such as Turkey, Afghanistan and Iran, inevitably drawn into a struggle for influence in areas of traditional Russian interests — Central Asia and the Caucasus — as well as relations with China.

The place of one or another country in the system of Russian foreign policy priorities and the desired character of relations with these countries has been interpreted in various ways by different political groups. But this system of priorities is by itself to a large degree determined by the objective circumstances which Russia now faces. In this system there is virtually no place for the countries of the Third World — most of Asia, Latin America and Africa — long one of the principal areas of struggle for international influence by the Soviet Union.

Changes in the public mood have tended to work in the same direction, pushing problems of the South to the periphery of social consciousness. The events within the country have been too formidable and dramatic, and the loss of the country too painfully traumatic for millions of citizens of the former Soviet Union, for remote problems, especially those of the poor and powerless, to hold a large degree of social interest. Although Third World issues are consistently present in domestic political discussions and are unexpectedly important in the search for a new Russian identity ("Who are we — a superpower or Upper Volta with rockets?"), the absence of the Third World in the new Russian mentality remains firm. As a result, in the place of the former internationalism and solidarity, only a hollow shell is left, to the amazement and consternation of left observers from the West.

The underlying basis for this omission did not emerge in the last several years, but much earlier, before Gorbachev's arrival on the Soviet political scene.

The East-West dichotomy, and the problem of relations with the non-Western world were a constant element in the consciousness of the Russian intelligentsia from the middle of the nineteenth century, as a result of Russia's geographical position and of the yearning for self-identification. After the 1917 revolution, the perception of this problem changed: official ideology and propaganda placed this problem on the level of mass consciousness and interpreted it exclusively on the plane of relations between the oppressed and the oppressors. Until the Second World War the hope of world revolution was associated primarily with Europe, and European countries were the principal objects of solidarity. (Germany and Spain, for example, far more than China.) After the war this role was fulfilled exclusively by the Third World — China, the newly liberated countries of Africa and, in particular, Cuba. The feeling of mutuality with the liberation movements in these countries was for the most part sincerely felt, meshing with the Soviet Union's "discovery" of the outside world and the Khrushchev "thaw." In addition, the solidarity movement fulfilled an important compensatory role in a country where the political sphere was completely absent and where the discussion of domestic problems was taboo.

The active imposition of the perception of the Third World as an ally in the anti-imperialist struggle did not turn mass consciousness in the Soviet Union anti-Western. The attitudes towards the countries and the peoples of the Third World remained, at best, the paternalistic, condescending relations of an older brother, in no way identifying himself with the objects of his solidarity. The Soviet role was to provide an idea and scheme to free these nations from underdevelopment, dependence and capitalism. This attitude was entirely compatible with the deep-rooted racism and xenophobia in Soviet society and enabled the shifts from ardent love to sharp criticism which "disobedient" Cuba fell victim to in the 1960s.

In the 1970s and the first part of the 1980s the issue of the Third World largely fell from mass consciousness (with the exception, perhaps, of the 1973 coup in Chile), becoming part of official ritual, absolutely alien to the bulk of society. The process of the extirpation of internationalism and solidarity concluded in the end of the 1980s with the breakdown of the socialist paradigm, fundamentally changing all of the structures and priorities of Soviet social consciousness.

The practical absence of the Third World in the stormy flowering of liberal-democratic journalism, and in official discourse (particularly conspicuous in the wave of openness to the West and the improvement of East-

West relations) was tied to changes of a global character. In a unipolar world the place of the Third World, its ability to influence events, is sharply diminished. The socio-economic inviability of the socialist and more broadly, the center-left paradigm, clearly becoming evident in Latin America in the 1980s, has left the Third World without alternatives. The resolution of the Third World's unique problems is forced into the framework of the liberal-capitalist model as the only existing framework. The problems of the Third World are no longer considered as specific and separate from the problems of the rest of humanity.

The fast-changing social consciousness in the former Soviet Union, hung on a Ptolemaic view of the world, inculcated by the now-defunct party ideology and propaganda, has not yet been replaced by a Copernican view. The decades of inculcation of an uncontradictory world view have remained unchanged. The idealization of the West quickly emerged following the rejection of the official Soviet stereotypes. The West was painted as a society where all of the fundamental problems facing humanity had been solved and the liberal market model as a universal and rapid means of achieving these solutions. The desire to return to the "mainstream of world civilization," as quickly as possible, largely excluded the Third World from the new social consciousness.

This tendency also grew out of the old and deeply rooted prejudices and stereotypes, which rose to the surface with the lifting of the blinders of official ideology and morals. These attitudes include dislike and arrogant condescension to people from Third World countries and an image of them as undeniably inferior and backward. On the everyday level this is seen in bursts of racist violence, the objects of which are usually African students, and Vietnamese workers and traders. In more civilized and cultured forms, this complex of stereotypes is shared by even the educated part of society and those who interact with Third World countries in a professional capacity (academics, diplomats, and workers in Soviet organizations abroad). Underlying these views are a rigid West-centered view of the world and a growing inferiority complex in relations with the West. The lower the respect of a society and its members for itself, the stronger its desire to affirm itself at the expense of those they feel are even less deserving of respect.

The new global situation and the crumbling of the bipolar world order has given birth to a tendency in part of the Russian establishment and public opinion to find in the Third World the only recently faded face of the enemy. It has become part of the commonly accepted wisdom that the principal remaining global contradiction is North-South, with the North understood as the bearer of progress and civilization, and the South as a disturber of the peace. "Predicting the development of the international situation at the edge of the millennium, it is possible to say that we expect more and more persistent efforts by countries of the Third World to obtain ballistic nuclear weapons, and that this perspective is becoming ever more realistic," wrote academic Piotr Korotkevich, a leading specialist in military affairs. "This means a sharp rise in the dangers of a large-scale ballistic nuclear conflict, provoked by some irresponsible regime to the south of our borders and the current sphere of NATO interests." Korotkevich sees an urgent need to unite the efforts of Russia with the U.S. and its allies, in order to "prevent aggression and the unleashing of a third world war" (*Nezavisimaya Gazeta*, August 15, 1992).

The solemnly pronounced rejection of an ideological world view has turned out to be, in essence, only a replacement of ideological symbols with stereotypes dominant in the West, and particularly in American mass consciousness. In this way Russia has imported a new enemy, "Islamic fundamentalism," for use both in domestic and foreign policy. In the formation of these new attitudes, part of the Russian establishment consciously appealed to the deeply held hostility towards Asian countries with a "socialist orientation" and to the Islamic peoples of the former Soviet Union. These recipients of Soviet economic aid, and other "freeloaders," are seen in the public's eye as bearing a large responsibility for Russia's current impoverishment. The development of events in Central Asia, the Caucasus, and Tatarstan have clearly shown the explosive potential of these ideas in a country with a significant Muslim population.

The most characteristic example of the reversal of ideological symbols in foreign policy is the image of Cuba, painted in the liberal mass media with the worst stereotypes of far-right American propaganda. The possibilities for sober analysis of Cuba, and the irresolvable problems of its development, have been swamped by the Russian media's normative and aggressively moralistic portrayal of the regime as the incarnation of Castro's perfidy and irrational desire to cling to power. The Russian parliament even held hearings on human rights in Cuba in 1992, although this should be unthinkable in a country in which the human rights of entire enthnic groups (i.e., Volga Germans) are still violated. The harshness of today's self-described democrats towards Cuba carries with it a strong internal psychological undercurrent. The attack on Cuba represents the final break with the reformers' own pasts, as the Cuban revolution was perceived by several generations in the Soviet Union as an integral part of the Khrushchev thaw.

This tendency in social consciousness is closely tied in with the main trends of Russian foreign policy, the priority of which is to develop an alliance with the U.S. and the West. The foreign policy conception of the Ministry of Foreign Affairs is also characterized by a split portrait of the world, with the left-over image of a barricade running down the middle. Previously the barricade divided the West from the East — the world of aggressive imperialism from that of peace-loving socialism. Now it separates the civilized democracies from "states disturbing the peace or those violating human rights, which as a rule are one and the same." As these are, for the most part, former allies of the Soviet Union, democratic Russia's place "is on the other, civilized side of the barricade." From Russia expect "genuine alliance with those who stand on the side of international law and order and who are ready to undertake the most decisive steps to support these principles" (Andrei Kozyrev, *Nezavisimaya Gazeta*, August 20, 1992).

This conception does not propose the search for enemies in the Third World. It is entirely dedicated to the inclusion of Russia, preferably as an equal, in the ranks of the world's powerful. According to Kozyrev, "a place in the ranks of highly developed nations, the leading representatives of humanity, . . . belongs to Russia by right. . . . It is clear . . . that continued autarchy instead of entrance into the community of democratic nations and correspondingly into the highly developed world economy would be equivalent to national betrayal, finally sinking Russia into the rank of third rate powers, although by her geographic position, and scientific-technical and natural resource potential, she is called to make a leap into the club of the chosen" (ibid).

The uncharacteristically straightforward eagerness to form an alliance with the powerful and rich of the planet is the bedrock of the new Russian foreign policy. Everything else, with the exception of relations with the former republics of the Soviet Union, has been subordinated to this task.

The results of this policy for relations with the countries of the Third World have been overwhelmingly negative. This is reflected in the weakening of ties with the Soviet Union's traditional partners, such as India, and the complete loss of position among those countries, which in one way or another, were allies of the Soviet Union. The rapid and passionate rejection of support for these countries and Russia's shift to the opposite "side of the barricade" damaged her prestige as a reliable ally, both among former allies and in those developing countries which never felt any special sympathy for the Soviet Union.

Even by Russia's new foreign policy criteria and priorities the results achieved in the Third World have been negligible or worse. "For example, our far too casual betrayal of Najibullah — who was moving Afghanistan towards peace more successfully than it seemed to many at the time — is a case where extreme obsequiousness towards the United States delivers a blow not only to our interests, but to theirs as well. The fall of Najibullah, which did not move Afghanistan one iota closer to peace . . . led to a dangerous destabilization of central Asia" (Pavel Palazhchenko, Dmitri Furman, *Nezavisimaya Gazeta*, October 24, 1992).

The Cuban case is distinguished by the severity of the Russian policy implemented and the inordinate attention paid to Cuban immigrants in the U.S. In this case, as well, the breaking of ties (although resulting mostly from Russia's internal economic crisis) has not yielded the desired results. In consideration of the increasingly harsh American blocade of Cuba, Russian policy has so far been counterproductive in terms of promoting genuine democratization in the country. External pressure has permitted Castro to drum up a fortress mentality and effectively block any attempts to reform the regime from within, without which any changes in Cuba will inevitably have a catastrophic and bloody character. Russian foreign policy in 1991–92 has to a great extent facilitated the island's gradual slide into a tragic dead-end.

It is worth noting that even a more restrained policy towards developing countries would hardly change the end result of Russia's actions — the practical withdrawal from the Third World. This is largely an objective process guided by the break-up of the Soviet Union, and by Russia's drastic weakening and extreme economic crisis — factors beyond the sphere of foreign policymakers.

Russia's policy of unilateral withdrawal from the Third World has also failed to generate any respect in the West and has not brought her any closer to the stated aim of entering into "the club of the chosen." Western countries, observing the growing internal problems and conflicts in the former Soviet Union, show less and less willingness to accept Russia into that club. Andrei Kozyrev's wish, expressed in a speech at Columbia University, that "in a short time we will be able to speak not of the Group of Seven plus One industrialized countries, but of the Group of Eight," seems not only utopian, but outside the realm of common sense (*Nezavisimaya Gazeta*, October 8, 1990).

In spite of the constant invocations that Russia is doomed to be a great power (*Moscow News* No. 43, October 25, 1992), Russia's loss of this status seems an obvious fact (although many draw exactly the opposite conclusion from these facts). This problem, in conjunction with the break-up of the Soviet Union, has effected the strongest and mostly negative influence on mass consciousness in Russia and has become a sort of exposed nerve for the bulk of domestic political discussions. The defects in Russian foreign policy, and its clear lack of a sense of dignity, have deepened Russia's inferiority complex, in spite of Kozyrev's stared desire to overcome it.

Russia's national humiliation, "the sell-out of the homeland" and pro-American foreign policy, have become the principal weapons in attacks on the Russian government by the unified national-patriotic and communist opposition. "Those who claim that Russia has no foreign policy aren't telling the whole truth. Russia has a foreign policy. And it is entirely comprised of prostrate servility in the company of 'civilized' states, where with quaking hearts yesterday's foreign policy clerks have been thrown by fate to the pinnacle of a country with a thousand year history. None of the 'civilized,' to make an understatement, thirst to see Russia among the great" (*Pravda*, August 18, 1992). The break-up of the Soviet Union, according to *Pravda's* Viktor Linnik, and its disappearance as a locus of power in international affairs, has extremely destabilized the world and brought the threat of war even closer. "A war, lost with the completeness with which the ex-Soviet Union lost the Cold War, has never led to peace. Remember the results of Versailles' humiliation of Germany. Already the mines have been laid under the newly created world order. The unconditional surrender of its positions by the Soviet Union, resulting from its break-up, gave birth to such untold arrogance from the victors, that this alone contains within it the seeds of future conflicts. The stronger the temptation of today's victors to decide the fate of the world, the greater the suffering that will visit nations, peoples and continents."

Great Russia, or the Soviet Union (which in this view are one and the same) is seen as the victim of an international conspiracy, aiming to destroy her economy, external political power, and spiritual health. The intentions of the national-radical position are openly revanchist. The resurrection of the trampled rights of the great power and the return to traditional Soviet foreign policy in general, and towards the Third World in particular, are openly seen as the restoration of the traditions of the Russian Empire.

It would be dangerous to underestimate the influence of these ideas, particularly in light of a large part of the population's psychological disorientation, resulting from the crumbling of the accustomed social pillars. The national-radical conception generates support by stressing just those areas where official policy prefers to remain silent or indulge in wishful thinking. It is unlikely, however, that in the present situation a wide circle of people and significant social actors will be convinced of the satanic and ill-willed intrigues of the West towards Russia, in spite of the country's long tradition of scapegoating. Apathy, exhaustion and the rapid decline in political activity limits the growth of the national-patriotic opposition and their own forces are clearly insufficient to make the leap to power and reverse Russia's foreign policy. In spite of their extreme aggressiveness and boisterousness, these forces still form only a marginal part of the political spectrum.

More significant has been criticism from within the new government establishment. An influential part of the democratic camp, including persons occupying high posts in the presidential administration and in the Supreme Soviet, have promoted alternative foreign policy visions. These proposals have been largely an attempt to steal some of the thunder from the national-patriots.

This position has been most clearly and forcefully expressed by Sergei Stankevich, a political adviser to President Yeltsin. He has disparaged the dominant "Atlanticism" in Russian foreign policy, the inordinate attention paid to the U.S. and Germany, and the quest to quickly join the G7 countries and Europe. The excessive pragmatism of the pro-Atlantic policy, he feels, should be counter-balanced by a "healthy idealism." Russia should not discard its mission in the world, which is to "initiate and support multifaceted dialogue between cultures, civilizations and nations." According to Stankevich, Russia is the "one country which absorbs both East and West, North and South, uniquely and possibly exclusively capable of enabling the harmonious combination of many different traditions" (*Nezavisimaya Gazeta*, March 28, 1992).

The main principle of Stankevich's Eurasian policy is the observation of balance in foreign policy orientations. For this, Russia should eliminate the current foreign policy distortion favoring the U.S. and Europe. The need to turn towards the East and the South, in Stankevich's view, is related not only to the altered geographical and geopolitical situation which Russia faces as a result of the break-up of the Soviet Union, but also from a sober evaluation of its current possibilities. "The entrance to the market and full integration into the system of economic relations of countries such as the U.S., Japan and the economically developed countries of Europe is highly problematic. Inescapably, and for many years, we would be condemned to the role of a junior partner, not even worth accepting. At the same time there are wider and more favorable opportunities, related to, you could say, second tier states and countries, which are at a similar historical level to us. These are countries lying to the South of our traditional partners: in Latin America — Mexico, Brazil, Chile, Argentina; in Africa — South Africa; and in Europe — Greece, and then Turkey; in Asia — India, China and the countries of Southeast Asia" (ibid).

This turn towards countries of the South, and in particular, to Latin America, appears significant and positive from the point of view of giving Russian public opinion a more realistic conception of Russia's place in the world after a period of thoughtless West-centered euphoria. The very possibility of the comparison of Russia's problems with those of the Third World, and Latin America in particular, has been seen as insulting for a country with "enormous economic, natural resource, scientific and spiritual potential." As economic difficulties and the disintegration of society deepen, the Latin American analogy has begun to be recognized in social consciousness. But this analogy has been portrayed mostly as catastrophe — the transformation of Russia into a third-rate, mafia-run, banana republic. It is obvious that these images are the reverse side of the West-centered coin and likely to interfere with a sober perception of the Latin American experience.

The development problems currently facing Russia are in actuality very similar to those which Latin America has struggled with in recent decades. The similarities include the characteristics and type of their integration into the world market and the necessity of continual adjustment to changes in the more dynamic centers of the world system. The common economic basis of transition both in Latin America and Russia is evident; the need for structural adjustment and short-term economic and financial stabilization, and a qualitative reduction of state economic control and regulation. The dominant social dilemma is also common for Latin America and Russia: the inevitable cost of economic adjustment is a decline in the living standards of the great majority, together with unemployment and the impoverishment of substantial segments of the population. Against the background of the economic crisis, democratic regimes in both regions show a high degree of political fragility. These are all aspects of the most likely Russian scenario in the near future. Acquaintance with the Latin American experience of the 1980s and early 1990s provides an immunization against many illusions and a chance to avoid many mistakes, especially in the economic sphere.

In spite of Stankevich's wishes, however, the common problems and "historic task" will hardly enable long-term economic cooperation and the improvement of Russia's market position in these countries. With the exception of defense technology, arms, and energy resources, Russia so far has nothing to offer them. It is also doubtful that ties with countries of the South "will open opportunities for Russia to win favorable geopolitical position in key regions, and with time, enter into the ranks of the world's leaders" (*Nezavisimaya Gazeta*, March 28, 1992).

Stankevich's posing of this issue demonstrates that the Eurasian policy, in his interpretation of it, is aimed at the restoration of Russia's lost superpower status, in the same way as the "Atlanticist" policy he rejects. This is particularly clear in the policies these political leaders promote in relations with the fellow republics of the former Soviet Union. These countries are seen as Russia's natural and undeniable sphere of influence where the rights of Russians are used more and more as instruments of political and, occasionally, military pressure. Even considering the positive potential of the Eurasian policy in returning Russia's foreign policy to the realities of a multifaceted world, it can hardly be seen as a step forward from "Atlanticism," as it is conceived according to the same system of coordinates. In some ways the Eurasian policy is even more dangerous because it is implicitly oriented towards the preservation of Russia's imperial traditions.

It is no coincidence that the burst of polemics around foreign policy strategy was accompanied by a growing conservative reaction to economic reforms in Russia. Encountering the realities of liberalization, public opinion quickly turned its back on the reigning liberal illusions. In spite of this, none of the major political forces, including the Civic Union, the most influential candidate for the leadership of the country, have yet proposed concrete economic alternatives to the government's program. But they still hope to soften people's overall disillusionment with reforms by implementing a more familiar and tried set of measures. One of the leaders of Civic Union, Alexander Vladislavlev writes that "the political orientation capable of uniting and mobilizing our people to active social creativity cannot be either the market or democracy . . . The most realistic . . . is the idea of the resurrection of Russia as a great power" (*Nezavisimaya Gazeta*, September 25, 1992).

Both domestic and external factors are forcing public opinion to face this extremely painful problem. But the consequences of a policy to restore Russia's superpower status, in the current situation, can be only negative. This strategy will continuously provoke conflicts with the other republics of the former Soviet Union and condemn Russia to fruitless wavering between "Atlanticism" and isolationism. There is also an obvious danger in appealing to the great power idea, inevitably pregnant with the revival of Russian chauvinism in an ethnically diverse country.

The optimal solution to these problems is likely to be found in exactly the opposite direction. In spite of all of the pain of the break-up of the Soviet Union, the loss of the superpower status gives Russia a chance to become a "normal country" and concentrate on its own very real problems. Russia can at last reject the self-satisfaction and pretensions of its special mission in the world — end its self-admiration and, its inevitable companion, self-humiliation. Russia would gain the ability to feel itself part of world rather than always either its leader or its victim.

18

Re-Imagining Tajikistan: Exclusion in the Age of Nations

Farhad Karim

The world is in the process of re-imagining itself. Sub-national and trans-national groups, previously shackled to the imperatives of imperial, super-power, and national interventions, are redefining themselves on the basis of reconstructed identities. From Québec to Kashmir, the hegemony of the deracinating centralized nation-state is being contested; and from Estonia to Eritrea, power has been wrested from oppressive state structures. These variegated movements of liberation are attempting to legitimate themselves on the basis of monolithic national identities, thus autonomy is being sought under the banner of a particular group's right to self-determination. The narration of new nations on homogenous identities is, despite its liberating rhetoric, engendering a new world order based on domination and exclusion.

The construction of nation-states on exclusive definitions of national identity is a serious threat to rights extended to individuals and groups *qua* members of a particular state.[1] Nation-states are not homogenous entities; they are composed of and fractured by a multiplicity of imbricating identities such as gender, class, religion, region, linguistic group, and ethnicity; identi-ties which are both contested and dynamic. Thus, while at the macro-level of the state, certain "national" groups may achieve political autonomy, other identitarian claims may simultaneously be ignored or repressed. For example: independent Afghanistan's mujahadeen leadership has obstructed women's involvement in the "public" sphere; "liberated" Kuwait's ruling establish-ment has denied citizenship to 89% of the resident population; post-colonial Pakistan's government has juridically prevented the participation of Ahmadis in the state as equal citizens; and post-Soviet Georgian nationalists have been complicit in the displacement of South Ossetians and Abkhazians.

The promotion of the rights of sub-national groups such as women and religious, ethnic, or linguistic minorities is deemed to subvert nationalist projects, as the national struggle is considered the ultimate struggle. Different identitarian groupings which seek to define their own spaces within and outside the context of the nation are handcuffed to the goals of the nation; goals which often render difference unacceptable. It is along the contested landscape of identitarian politics that intra-national conflicts tend to emerge.

The modern era of nations and nationalisms is fraught with numerous intra-national conflicts which challenge the ability of various nation-states to guarantee equal citizenship rights. These conflicts are often accompanied by violence, bloodshed, and extensive state repression. A plethora of explanations has been offered as to the origins of these conflicts. Some argue that intra-national conflict is rooted in traditional rivalries between ancient tribes, ethnic groups, clans, and religious sects. Others argue that this conflict is a symbol of the "breakdown" of the state. Still others argue that the problems are a result of the displacements wrought by the penetration of global capital. Yet, simple deterministic models cannot provide a nuanced explanation of the causes of the intra-national violence which is occurring throughout the world.

Intra-national violence is rooted in the historical exigencies of the construction and re-construction of the nation. The actors involved are not merely the products of transcendental ideologies and identities. Rather, they have the power to affect the world in which they live and "act purposively and reflectively, in more or less complex inter-relationships with one another, to reiterate and remake the world in which they live, in circumstances where they may consider different courses of action possible and desirable, though not necessarily from the same point of view."[2] This is not to say that class, religion, ethnicity or other identities do not inform people's actions, but that individuals' and groups' actions are not the simple product of ethnic hatred, class conflict, or religious zeal. Intra-national conflicts emerge from the constantly shifting relationships between the state and civil society, international interests and domestic needs, nationalism and regionalism, politics and economics, ideologies and identities.

The newly independent states of Central Asia, initially components of the Russian empire and subsequently republics within the Soviet Union, are experiencing a number of violent intra-national conflicts. One of the most bloody manifestations of such conflicts is occurring within Tajikistan, which is located between Afghanistan, Uzbekistan, Kyrgyzistan, and China, and has been in a virtual civil war since March of 1992. The government is attempting to stave off the complete collapse of centralized authority, various regions have declared themselves autonomous or independent, and different political groupings, mobilizing an array of ideological, nationalist, and religious symbols, are contesting the authority of the state and its bureaucracy. The immediate effects of the rampant violence that has accompanied this conflict are the deaths of tens of thousands of people, the displacement of hundreds of thousands, increasing state repression, the emigration of large numbers of non-Tajiks, and the devastation of the economy.[3]

The Tajik conflict is paradigmatic of the intra-national conflicts affecting nation-states in many parts of the world today, in that the complexity of the events surrounding this conflict is masked behind simple dichotomies. Just as the conflict in Bosnia has been interpreted as a vicious battle between Serbs and Muslims, the conflict in Tajikistan has been reduced to a dispute between Muslims and communists. A more sophisticated interpretation of this conflict is necessary. In order to elucidate the complexities of the Tajik conflict, the history of the area must be examined.

Tajikistan is a modern construct and thus it is difficult to narrate its pre-national history without reifying a Tajik identity. However, as long as one does not operate teleologically and assume that a Tajik nation always existed within this narrative, it is beneficial to historicize the various political structures that have governed the region. Historically, South Central Asia has been engulfed by various political formations in which power has shifted between a variety of groups including Bactrians, Arabs, Persians, Mongols, Turks, and Russians. In the seventh century the majority of South Central Asians were converted to Islam by conquering Arabs, and to this day the language of Islam plays an important role as both a legitimizing ideology of state power and as a subversive theology of resistance. Resistance to Arab rule in the ninth century brought state control into the hands of local dynasties and the Samanids until the eleventh century. The Samanid empire had a profound impact on the region in the realms of economic development, trade, science, philosophy, architecture, and Persian language and literature, producing a number of prominent figures such as Ibn Sina and Firdousi and creating urban cultural centers such as Bukhara and Samarkand. The political and cultural supremacy of the Persian-speaking Samanids was undermined by the subsequent dismemberment of the empire by the Seljuk Turks. Resistance to this changing political landscape was articulated through the development of numerous non-"official" *tariqah* (paths) of Islam. Seljuk rule was displaced by the Mongol invasion of Genghiz Khan, which was succeeded by his Timurid descendants. The Timurids were overthrown by the Golden Horde, which established a decentralized empire that by the eighteenth century was divided into the independent Khanates of Bukhara, Khiva, Kokand, Gissar, and Badakshan.

The geographic space that Tajikistan currently occupies (South Central Asia) was never a monolithic state representing the Tajik nation, nor was it a separate and distinct province within an empire. Rather, in contrast to myths of Oriental despotism, pre-colonial Central Asia's political systems were based on complex and shifting alliances which accommodated multiple sub- and supra-national identities. Sovereign authority was vested in symbolic centers in Samarkand or Bukhara; however, this authority was diffused over a multiplicity of power formations. The relationships between Grand Khans or Emirs and subjects of particular Khanates or Emirates were mediated by local beks, pirs, diwans, viziers, qazis, and mullahs. Therefore, while individuals were subjects of an overarching empire, they retained a multiplicity of affiliations to their locality, their religious *tariqah*, and their linguistic group.

The Tajiks who spoke Eastern Iranian dialects primarily resided either in or around the cultural and trading centers of Samarkand and Bukhara or in the eastern portion of the Emirate of Bukhara, where present-day Tajikistan exists. Tajiks, unlike Shia Persians in Persia/Iran, predominantly adhere to the

Hanafi school of Sunni Islam. The Uzbeks however, who are also predominantly Sunni, speak the Turkic language of Uzbek. They controlled the political apparatus of the Emirate of Bukhara, and lived predominantly in the western portion of the Emirate of Bukhara. Although Uzbek and Tajik are theoretically distinct identities, historically they overlapped and, for example, many Uzbeks in Samarkand and Bukhara spoke Tajik in addition to Uzbek. Linguistic affiliation as a signifier to divide communities was most important in urban centers and in cultural/intellectual circles; however, the bulk of the population tended to identify with sub-"national" identities such as locality, or supra-national identities such as religious *tariqah*. In the latter part of the eighteenth century the Russians began to advance into Central Asia where they annexed sections of Turkestan and established a protectorate in Bukhara. Indigenous groups took advantage of Russian penetration to increase their own power, and thus, for example, the Uzbek Emir of Bukhara initially sought the aid of the Russians to subdue opposition leaders and replace them with Uzbek allies. Other indigenous groups such as the Jadids sought to promote the "Western" education and science of Russia as a moderating tool against the conservative domination of the Muslim clerisy (*ulema*) and the Emir. However, on a political level, in an anti-Russian vein, the Jadids promoted pan-Turkic and pan-Islamic movements in resistance to foreign rule.

In 1917 Russian imperial rule over South Central Asia was replaced by the revolutionary Russian-controlled Tashkent Soviet. This transfer of power was resisted by conservative Muslim groups, who attempted to form an independent Turkestan separate from socialist rule. Other Muslim groups who were members of socialist organizations, such as the Union of Toiling Muslims of Ferghana, supported the establishment of Soviets in Turkestan. In the still nominally independent Emirate of Bukhara, a group called the Young Bukharans attempted to remove the Emir with support from the Tashkent Soviet. Their attempt failed due to the strength of the opposition *ulema* which supported the Emir. The *ulema* called for a revolt against all Soviet oppression in Central Asia and a movement of resistance called the Basmachi was born. Certain liberal Muslims opposed the Basmachi movement as reactionary and cooperated with the Russian revolutionaries.

The Tashkent Soviet sought to quash the Basmachi insurgency and thus extended its frontiers to incorporate the Emirates of Bukhara and Khiva; important bases for Basmachi support. The Emir of Bukhara fled to eastern Bukhara (modern day Tajikistan), established his headquarters in Dushanbe, and continued the struggle against Russia. By 1921 the Red Army had moved into Eastern Bukhara and forced the Emir to flee to Afghanistan. Indigenous people of the region who did not support the Emir initially welcomed the Red Army. However, the Red Army's later repression of the indigenous people and their denigration of Islamic symbols and institutions increased support for the Basmachi. In 1924, the People's Republic of Bukhara was carved up into the Uzbek Socialist Republic in which a Tajik Autonomous Socialist Republic was declared. Resistance continued until Soviet rule was firmly established in the late 1920s. In 1929 Tajikistan became a separate Soviet Socialist Republic and it was given a portion of the fertile Khojen district of Uzbekistan. The "Tajik" cities of Samarkand and Bukhara remained in Uzbekistan. Under Soviet rule, large scale moderniza-tion programs commenced with which the establishment of a Soviet nationa-lities policy was inextricably intertwined.

The Soviet nationalities policy sought to dismantle historic, cultural, and religious bases of community and reconstruct communities more consistent with Soviet socialist aims.[4] Lenin, with the help of Stalin, took advantage of existing divisions among Central Asians and created complex policies to break down previous affiliations, reconstruct pro-Soviet (Russian) identities, and mask this process behind the rhetoric of modernization, revolution, and liberation from exploitation. Local cultures were defined, categorized, and divided into "progressive" and "bourgeois national" elements.

The construction of a Tajik Soviet Socialist culture was focused around the development of a new Tajik historiography, the study of Persian in its classical literary forms, the development and modernization of the Farsi language and the promotion of a certain form of Tajik art. The Tajiks were firmly distinguished from Uzbeks and other Turkic groups on the basis of a Persian vs. Turkic identity. By categorizing and dividing complex and shift-ing identities and promoting a pro-Russian orientation, the Soviets were able to exert control over a large number of people.

The cultures which the Soviets redefined were not merely imposed on indigenous groups, but rather were imparted with the collusion of local elites. In the case of Tajikistan this policy enabled the break-up of supra-national sentiments such as pan-Turkism or pan-Islamism and attempted to limit the power of local affiliations. Power in Tajikistan could be gained through the category of Tajik and thus it became an important construct.

The most important result of the Soviet nationalities program in Tajikistan was the construction of an indigenous Soviet Socialist elite drawn predomi-nantly from Khojen and allied with groups in Kulyab, which became in-creasingly divorced from the bulk of the Tajik people, and particularly those from Garm and Badakshan. This elite, which dominates the Tajik Commun-ist Party and much of the bureaucracy, has a pro-Russian orientation and works with a large number of Russian and German immigrants.

During Mikhail Gorbachev's attempts at perestroika and glasnost a num-ber of Tajik nationalist and Islamist groups officially and unofficially began to articulate grievances against this elite represented by the state and sought to involve the Tajik people in reclaiming their Tajik or Muslim heritage. This resulted in clashes with the government which attempted to keep a firm hold on power. As the Soviet Union began to collapse and Tajikistan gained independence, the conflict between the various groups intensified. Massive pro- and anti-government rallies were held in Dushanbe's two public squares and finally violence erupted throughout the south of the country. The vio-lence was extremely bloody as weapons were distributed by government and anti-government forces. A variety of competing and often conflicting symbols were utilized by both sides to demarcate the other from one's own group. These symbols were rooted in groups' nationality, sectarian background and ideological affiliation. Amidst this terror, control of the government shifted from the communist leadership to a coalition government involving the opposition to the communist leadership.

The only explanations of Tajikistan's crisis proffered thus far have not elucidated the nuances of the conflict. The American press has portrayed the situation as either a conflict between Muslims and communists,[5] or as a manifestation of "ageless rivalries and feuds."[6] The Russian press, clearly immersed in Orientalist thinking, has claimed that the traditional political culture of Central Asia, which is inclined towards totalitarianism, is re-emerging due to the break-up of the Soviet Union. Thus, Tajikistan is represented as experiencing a battle between two totalitarian systems, Islam and communism. Although certain participants in the Tajik conflict have identified themselves under the banner of the Islamic Renaissance Party or the Communist Party, depicting the conflict as a clash of ideologies is ahistorical, denies the actors agency, conceals the Tajiks' heterogeneity and masks the conflict's complexity.

The break-up of the Soviet Union, resulting in the independence of Tajikistan, has left a vacuum at the level of central state authority. Therefore, at the most simplistic level, the violence in Tajikistan is rooted in a contest for state power. The major actors on this contestatory stage are those currently benefiting from the government apparatus and those seeking a re-configuration of power to include previously excluded groups. The conflict has explicitly revolved around the leadership of the communist-dominated Supreme Soviet of Tajikistan.

The Communist Party, which dominated the government and bureaucracy until recently, primarily receives support from Tajik clans originating in Khojen in the north and Kulyab in the south; Uzbeks living in the fertile Ferghana valley, Khojen city and Dushanbe; and urban-based Russians and Germans. The Communist Party has alienated other Tajiks by privileging Kulyab and Khojen for infrastructural development, promoting the power of particular clans, maintaining strong ties with Russia, supporting the Russian, Uzbek and German minorities in Tajikistan, and condemning certain Islamic leaders. Those opposed to the Communist Party have articulated their grievances through calls for returning Tajikistan to the Tajiks or indigenous Muslim rule. The project of Tajik nationalism, in its secular and religious forms, seeks a re-dispersal of power from the Russians, Uzbeks, Germans, and their indigenous allies to all Tajiks. Non-Tajik groups and Tajik collaborators are perceived to be the beneficiaries of decades of Russian/Soviet imperial rule. The various groups that oppose the communist leadership have articulated their demands for power under the rubric of Tajik nationalism coupled with particular agendas.

The main groups that oppose the Communist Party are Rastokhez, the Democratic Party of Tajikistan, the Islamic Renaissance Party, and Lali Badakshani. Rastokhez (rebirth) is a popular front movement controlled by liberal intellectuals from Dushanbe. Its members have denied participation in the violence and they have been instrumental in attempting to remove the country's hardline leaders and replace them with more "liberal" ones. The group appeared in 1989 as a "popular front" promoting the revival of Tajik culture and the Tajik language. The Democratic Party of Tajikistan, with much of its support coming from Kurgan-Tyube, lower-level government officials, and certain intellectuals, was established to promote Tajik nationalism and the development of a secular democratic state. The Islamic Renaissance Party (IRP) has support primarily in Garm, Dushanbe, and the rural areas. Its stated objectives are "not only to enable Soviet Muslims to live in accordance with the requirements of the Qur'an and Sunna but also to advance the concept of equal rights for all nationalities and humanistic ideas generally."[7] According to interviews with its secretariat, the party accepts only constitutional means of achieving its goals and explicitly rejects terrorism and extremism.[8]

The government, particularly since 1990, wary of "the threat of Islam," has been extremely sensitive to praise the "moral influence of Islam" and has taken steps to prevent superficially offending Muslim "sensibilities."[9] At the same time, a number of Uzbek and Russians have left Tajikistan, claiming a fear of religious fundamentalism and Tajik nationalism.[10] The flight of non-Tajiks from the region is affecting healthcare, education and industry. This is indicative of the control of non-Tajiks over certain industries and the governmental bureaucracy.

The final major internal actor in the opposition is Lali Badakshani. While they have explicitly called for greater autonomy for the region of Gorno-Badakshan, moderates in the group merely want increased participation at the center. Composed primarily of Pamiris, the Lali Badakshani plays an important role among the mountainous Pamirs and also in urban areas as intermediaries between the government and the opposition.

External groups have also been involved in the internal conflict. Russia, under Boris Yeltsin, has been concerned with its own strategic interests, its need for Tajik resources (particularly cotton), and the status of the local Russian population. Thus the Russians have issued stern warnings to Iran and Afghanistan not to become embroiled in the Tajik conflict. Moreover, to maintain stability (and therefore Russian hegemony), it has deployed Russian troops in Tajikistan, under the guise of a Commonwealth of Independent States peacekeeping force. These troops, which until recently were able to provide support for the Communist Party, have been used primarily to seal the Afghan border and protect strategic installations necessary for the Tajik (and thus Russian) economy. The influx of Russian troops has exacerbated the tensions between the government and the opposition. The opposition views Russian intervention as a continuation of Soviet imperial policy over the region.

Uzbekistan's President Islam Karimov, in an effort to consolidate his power over Uzbekistan, has attempted to prevent Tajik nationalist and religious elements from entering Uzbekistan. He is unwilling to share the fate of the Tajik Communist Party and be forced to share power. Thus, he has limited contact with Tajikistan, closed all Tajik language schools in Uzbekistan, stopped air travel between the two countries, and sealed the border. In Tajikistan, these actions have instilled fear in the local Uzbek population and resentment among Tajiks.

Iran's official involvement in Tajikistan has been limited to the promotion of Persian culture and education and the Muslim religion. In congruence with their interest in extending their sphere of influence over the region, Iran has supported all sides in the conflict. Various Afghani groups from Masoud to Hekmatyar have armed different Tajik groups to further their own aims in the region; Pakistani missionaries have supported the Islamic movements; the Indian and Chinese governments have expressed fear of Islamic or nationalist groups coming to power; and the Americans have indicated that they are concerned merely with "stability" in the region and thus are wary of Iranian involvement or the threat that this conflict could "spill" over into other neighboring states.

The division of Tajikistan on partisan lines, though cemented as a result of external involvements, is at a deeper level rooted in the history of the political economy of the region. The inequitable distribution of power and wealth in Tajikistan stems from Russian rule in the region. Russian colonial penetration into South Central Asia transformed the region's agrarian and industrial base. Initially the region produced a wide array of agricultural products for indigenous human consumption, livestock and trade. The American Civil War precipitated increased world prices for cotton and subsequently the Czarist regime moved into Central Asia to exploit the local agricultural system. As earlier cotton production in Central Asia did not maximize "efficiency" and "productivity" in cotton production, the Russians implemented a program to extend and expand pre-existing irrigation systems incorporating certain areas into a profitable cash crop economy. Increasing amounts of land were devoted to cotton production at the expense of subsistence agriculture and animal husbandry. The Soviet regime, determined to be self-sufficient, increased the intensity of cotton production and collectivized much of the farmland. Moreover, a large number of Russians were encouraged to emigrate to Tajikistan to manage important posts in the government bureaucracy and industry.

This shift from subsistence agriculture to a non-diversified cash crop economy left Central Asia increasingly reliant on Russia for foodstuffs. The importance of this historical legacy is witnessed today in Tajikistan's civil strife. Russian/Soviet agricultural modernization policies inequitably privileged certain regions for development and left control of wealth-generating state lands in the hands of certain groups. Groups from those regions which benefited from such processes (e.g. Khojen) support the maintenance of the Communist Party and strong links with Russia, whereas groups from regions which did not receive an equal share of entitlements (e.g. Garm) seek a redistribution of resources.

It is obvious that the breakdown in the relationship between state and civil society in Tajikistan has not been determined simply by an ideological battle between communism and Islam, but rather by a number of groups vying for political power and the redistribution of economic resources. Regional tensions coupled with the involvement of external groups have exacerbated the conflict. At an ideological level, however, the complexity of the situation lies in the dialectical relationship between identity and state construction.

The discursive terrain over which this battle is being fought is the nation. Tajik nationalists have sought to legitimate their claim to state power on the basis of the Tajiks' right to the Tajik nation. Thus, through selective appropriations of history, the Tajiks have fashioned an identity that allows them to (re)claim their country from the clutches of Russians, Uzbeks, and their indigenous allies. The ability to control the nation is grounded on a capacity to define the nation. Thus, nationalists have sought to exclude those who they deem non-Tajik.

Certain Tajik nationalists look towards Iran as a protector from the encroachments of not only Russia but also Turkestan. A sense of their Iranianness enables them to define their identity against the large numbers of Russians and Uzbeks in the region. There is a sense, among nationalist intellectuals, that they will lose their identity if ties to the Persian-speaking world are not maintained. Nationalists argue the Tajiks have lost their identity and ability to be the masters of their own destiny because the communist leadership has historically prevented them from fostering ties with the wider Persian-speaking world.

Inextricably intertwined with the nationalist project has been the retrieval of a number of "Tajik" symbols. The poetry of Iqbal, the philosophy of Nasir Khusraw, and the slogans of the Iranian revolution have all been ahistorically (re)claimed as Tajik. Tajik nationalists have also sought to tie their history to the ancient dynasties of the Samanids, who played an instrumental role in creating literary Persian. One can imagine that soon maps, censuses, and museums will appear to further reify the Tajik identity. Islamic symbols and institutions have also played an important role within certain nationalist groups. The Islamic faith and culture has strong resonances among vast sections of the population, and because of the history of its suppression in the region Islamic movements are clearly identified as anti-Soviet/communist movements.

The communist government initially supported moves to "Tajikize" Tajikistan. In 1989, in response to nationalists' demands, the government made Tajik the state language and called for replacing the Cyrillic alphabet with the Perso-Arabic script. Leninabad was renamed Khojen, and Naw Roz was declared a state holiday. However, once the government realized that the nationalists were contesting not only a Russified identity, but state power, tensions between the government and the opposition intensified. The Communist Party claims that the threat of religious fundamentalism and ethnic nationalism warrants its hold on power. They further argue that only they can prevent Tajikistan from breaking into smaller fragments.

The Communist Party's project is doomed to increasing resistance, as it has not been sensitive to the aspirations and claims of previously excluded groups in Tajik society. The opposition, in its nationalist and Islamist manifestations, is also bound to have difficulties because difference is rendered unnatural and thus the presence of Uzbeks in Tajikistan or "Tajik"

Samarkand and Bukhara in Uzbekistan, or Ismailis in Badakshan, or Khojens in control of the state apparatus will always symbolize the failure of pure Tajik nationalism. Even if the Uzbeks are forced to leave the region and Samarkand and Bukhara are miraculously incorporated into a greater Tajikistan, fractures within the nation (Ismailis, Kulyabis, Khojens) could lead to further fragmentation.

The intra-national violence in Tajikistan is rooted in multiple spheres of dominance. Dependence on Russia and a non-diversified economy, the privileging of certain regions for economic development and political control, the alienation of those who subscribe to previously disallowed Muslim or nationalist movements, the involvement of external actors, and the framing of an inequitable power structure within the context of the Tajik state have led to the increased politicization of the population. The Communist Party and the opposition groups are battling for control over the newly "independent" political, economic and intellectual structures left by Soviet rule. The communists wish to maintain this legacy, whereas the opposition groups are attempting to reconstruct some form of an indigenous non-Soviet identity that would allow a new power structure to be created.

Both groups' ventures have appealed to ideological, religious, and nationalist sentiments. One cannot deny the power of ideological rhetoric, religious symbols and perceived authentic identities. However, nationalist, religious, and ideological identities rooted in material and cultural bases form a horizon which limit contesting identitarian groupings within its space. Each respective identitarian formation subordinates and thus represses all other identities and allows/encourages the denial of their rights. Tajikistan's battling factions must search for a new accommodation, a more tolerant ethic which can respect a multiplicity of imbricating identities. If this does not occur, post-Soviet Tajikistan will continue to be drowned in the bloodshed of intra-national conflict.

Notes

1. I define rights as claims that individuals have against the institutional structures which have sovereignty over them. These claims can range from the minimal, "the right not to be tortured," to something more comprehensive like "the right to a bundle of entitlements (food, clothing, shelter, education, health care)."
2. Ronald Inden, *Imagining India* (Cambridge: Blackwell Publishers, 1992), p. 23.
3. See Bess Brown, "Whither Tajikistan," in *Report on the USSR*, May 10, 1991; "State of Anarchy," *The Herald*, November 1992; *Human Rights Watch World Report 1993*; *New York Times* (June 7, 1992, October 25, 1992, November 23, 1992, February 21, 1993); and daily reports from March 1992 to February 1993 of Radio Free Europe, *Report on the USSR*.
4. See Teresa Rakowska-Harmstone, *Russia and Nationalism in Central Asia* (Baltimore: Johns Hopkins University Press, 1970).
5. For example, see "An Islamic Awakening in Central Asian Lands," *New York Times*, June 9, 1992, p. A1, and "Reports of Massacre and Fresh Fighting Increase Tajik Woes," *New York Times*, November 23, 1992, p. A9.
6. "War Bleeds Ex-Soviet Land at Central Asian Heart," *New York Times*, February 21, 1993, p. A1.
7. Reuters, June 4, 1990.
8. Bess Brown, "The Islamic Renaissance Party in Central Asia," *Report on the USSR*, May 10, 1991.
9. Bess Brown, "Whither Tajikistan," *Report on the USSR*, June 12, 1992.
10. See "Conversations: Two Families in Tajikistan. An Empire's Retreat Strands Exiles in a Place They Call Home," *New York Times*, June 7, 1992, Section 4, p. 7.

■ PART FIVE ■

The Middle East

19

A Middle Eastern View of the "New World Order"

Rami G. Khouri

The overwhelming majority of Arabs and other Middle Eastern people greeted George Bush's unilateral proclamation of a "new world order" with a combination of skepticism, fear, and bemusement, because most of the people of the region suspected they were exempted from the provisions and the promises of that new order. We heard the rhetoric of the New World Order, but we suffered through a regional political and economic order that staggered under the unrelenting burdens of the old order.

The single most common Middle Eastern rejoinder to the rhetoric of the New World Order was to ask whether the real objective was global stability and equity, or, as we suspected, to ensure continued predominance of American ideological impulses and the materialism of that minority of the U.S. population that lived in enviable comfort? The collapse of the Soviet Union was deeply felt in key parts of the Middle East (especially Syria, Iraq, Palestine, Algeria, and Libya) where its arms supplies, diplomatic support or technical/financial aid provided an important counterbalance to U.S. aims. The collapse of this diplomatic/strategic balance opened the way for the U.S. to dominate the region and to assert more overt control of lands, people, resources and political systems it deemed vital to its interests — in the spheres of oil, financial flows, arms sales, technological dominance, and support for Israel's military superiority over the Arabs.

In the early nineties, on four separate occasions when the United States had opportunities to interact meaningfully with the rest of the world, the bottom line of Washington's objectives was made very clear. Soon after the announcement of the New World Order, both U.S. President George Bush and Secretary of State James Baker said during the Gulf crisis that one purpose of the U.S.-led military move into the Arabian Peninsula was to assure the jobs of Americans at home. One year later, during his visit to Japan, President Bush repeated his motive for that trip as being to promote jobs for Americans. And another half year later, on the eve of his departure for the Earth Summit in Brazil, President Bush again affirmed his primary responsibility as safeguarding American jobs. And as he set out for the G7 meeting of industrialized powers in Germany in July 1992, George Bush again announced that preserving American jobs was one of his key objectives. One wondered: did the new world order really mean full employment for Americans — and the rest of the world be damned?

The particular skepticism of the people of the Middle East about the New World Order reflected the fact that the region continued to suffer the severe consequences of the worst aspects of the old order: frail and fractured states, a fragmented regional order, excessive militarism and violence, stagnant or declining real standards of living, severe economic disparities, rising levels of grassroots frustration and anger, institutionalized and permanent Israeli aggression and human rights denials, Western neo-colonial exploitation, and the negative consequences of having been entangled in the regional ramifications of the Cold War. While the New World Order held out the promise of resolving regional disputes and human inequities in other parts of the world (e.g. Southern Africa, Central America, Southeast Asia, or Eastern Europe), there were few tangible signs that it could target the human needs, political rights, and national aspirations of Arabs and other Middle Eastern peoples. Instead, there were growing fears throughout the region that the New World Order was simply a cruel, white, northern euphemism for maintaining neo-colonial patterns that exploited the financial, strategic, and natural resources of a few oil-laden Arab states in the Gulf, while relegating the 95% of the rest of the Arabs, along with other regional players such as Iranians and Kurds, to a future of long-term submission to predatory and materialistic U.S. corporate dictates. The essential Arab concern was that the New World Order would simply accentuate and perpetuate the distortions, inequities, and injustices that have defined the Middle East for the last several decades, while targeting the emerging Islamic politics and nationalism of the region as the new enemy of those who wage fierce technological and economic warfare in the name of the New World Order.

If the collapse of the Soviet Union and the end of the Cold War in 1989/1990 marked the ideological genesis of the New World Order, the Gulf crisis in 1990/1991 highlighted the range of important issues that caused the Arabs to demand that a new Middle Eastern order be part and parcel of a New World Order. The Gulf crisis clearly defined and encapsulated the leading problems that have plagued the Middle East, especially the Arabs, for decades. These issues explain much of the deep anger that most Arabs expressed against the United States, Great Britain and the West in general during the Gulf crisis. They were also the major issues that lingered from the decades of the old order — and that had to be addressed by the Arabs and the rest of the world if the region was to enjoy the fruits of any New World Order. The following are the seven major causes of Arab anger in the post-Cold War era:

1. The tradition of Western militarism practiced by imperial and colonial powers. Ever since Napoleon invaded Egypt in 1798, the Arab people and lands have been subjected to a non-stop legacy of military occupation or political subjugation by Western powers. With the exception of the inland deserts of Saudi Arabia, the mountains of Yemen, and the southern regions of North Africa, every Arab country has been occupied or colonized by foreign powers during the last 200 years, whether by the Turks, British, French, Italians, Portuguese or Zionists/Israelis. Most Arabs saw the arrival of Western troops in 1990 as simply another episode of foreign troops seeking to maintain a political and economic order in the Middle East which served Western economic interests more than it served the developmental goals of the Arab people themselves.

2. **Inter-Arab economic disparities and inequities**. As a consequence of the imperial division of the Middle East after World War I, and its fragmentation into 20 different countries, some Arab countries found themselves with small populations but enormous oil and gas wealth, while others had large populations but little national income. By the 1980s, the Arab world had evolved into three different groups, defined by per capita gross national product. By 1988, according to United Nations and World Bank statistics, the per capita GNP of Arab countries ranged from a high of $15,770 in the UAE and $13,400 in Kuwait, to lows of $660 in Egypt and Yemen, $480 in Sudan and Mauritania, and $170 in Somalia. While about 20 million Arabs in oil-producing states had an average per capita income of nearly $10,000, the rest of the Arabs comprised 65 million people with a per capita income of $2,000 each and 115 million people with a per capita income of $500 each. Such extremes of wealth and poverty caused resentment and anger among the majority of Arabs who saw themselves sliding deeper and deeper into debt and chronic poverty. Many poor Arabs were angered by what they claimed was a tendency by the wealthy Arab oil producers to waste their money on foreign investments, instead of building the productive capacity of the Arab world itself.

3. **The challenge of Israel**. Ever since the creation of Israel in 1948, the Arab world has been unable to come to terms with it, either through war or peace. As Israel became stronger militarily and technologically, thanks in part to some $50 billion in U.S. aid, the Arabs seemed to become more fragmented. This allowed Israel to dominate the region militarily. This reality of a small Israeli state of some 4 million people able to check and militarily defeat 215 million Arabs caused tremendous pan-Arab humiliation. After 1980, this expressed itself in strong political sentiment or street activism against ruling Arab regimes, Israel, and the United States and the West in general.

4. **International double standards in implementing UN resolutions**. When the West put together a coalition of 30 countries and sent a veritable armada of half a million troops and thousands of warplanes to the region to implement UN Security Council resolutions demanding Iraq's withdrawal from Kuwait, the immediate reaction in most Arab minds was: why does the world mobilize so fiercely to implement UN resolutions in Kuwait, but does not react in the same manner to implement hundreds of equally valid UN resolutions in Palestine, Lebanon and Syria? Arabs rejected this double

standard of a zealous international response when rich Arabs and Western economic interests were threatened, but a nonchalant international response in the case of Israeli occupation of Arab lands.

5. Lack of Arab democracy and human rights. There was a general feeling throughout the Arab world that perhaps the main reason for the sad state of Arab affairs was the lack of democracy and human rights, and the prevalence of autocratic political systems run by individuals or families. The majority of Arabs felt that only through more democratic expression of people's wishes could the Arab world finally tap its true resources, and live in stability, dignity and prosperity.

6. A tradition of violence, turbulence and militarism. The Middle East, especially the Arab world, remained the world's most militaristic and violent region. In the 15 years to 1988, the Arab states are estimated to have spent at least $700 billion on defense and security, including some $250 billion on arms imports. On average, defense spending accounted for 21%–24% of total government spending in the Arab countries, and military expenditures accounted for 11% of gross national product. Arms imports in Arab countries accounted for an average of 17% of total imports — the highest ratio of any region of the world. The Arab countries also had the world's highest ratio of soldiers per population, averaging 15 soldiers per 1,000 population (compared to 8.7 in North America or 3 in Africa).

7. The lack of pan-Arab integration. The above factors left the Arab world fragmented, weak and dependent on foreign aid, arms, technology and food. While most Arabs felt they shared a single Arab identity comprising a common heritage, language, social traditions and religious ethic, they also felt frustrated because they have not been able to express their commonality in practical terms. As of the 1920s, Arabs states were divided by frontiers, political and economic ideologies, and standards of living. Joint Arab action was rare, especially on major political issues. People felt that Arab governments turned to their former colonial powers in the West for help before they turned to fellow Arabs. The fragmentation of the Arab world resulted in many small states that were weak on their own, even if some of them had substantial incomes from oil. The majority of Arabs saw the arrival of Western troops in 1990 as an attempt to maintain this fragmentation, to keep the Arabs separate, divided and weak, and therefore to assure the regional dominance of Israel and the global dominance of the United States and its economic interests.

The massive and pervasive Arab sense of failure directly prompted the development of several powerful political forces in the area during the past century, including Arab nationalism, Islamic fundamentalism and political activism, the quest for democratization, and the drive for more rational regional or sub-regional socio-economic integration. These trends were hastened by the distortions of the oil-fueled economic boom in the period 1974–1983. By the late 1980s, consequently, the Arab region was characterized by the following dominant realities: high population growth rates, rising urbanization, widespread poverty and gross economic disparities, high unemployment, excessive foreign debt, socially constraining economic adjustment, widespread water shortages, the threat of expanding malnutrition, rising homelessness, increasing populations of displaced persons and refugees, the first Arab boat people in Algeria and Somalia, national and political fragmentation, dependence on foreign sources of money, food, arms, and capital and consumer goods, massive intellectual and creative mediocrity, almost total political pacification of domestic populations, direct subjugation and occupation by Israel, disdain and exploitation by Western powers, and the final ravage and insult of renewed large-scale immigration to Palestine of Jews from the Soviet Union, Ethiopia and other lands.

By the 1980s, the Arab region had evolved into a parody of viable statehood and authentic nationhood. It was a painful collection of frail states that represented a failed post-1920 political order. That failed order had comprised three kinds of states: the cash-fueled state welfarism of the Gulf, the heavy-handed authoritarianism of states such as Iraq, and the light-handed authoritarianism of states such as Egypt or Morocco. All three models had failed to provide their people with the four basic needs that people expected from their states: physical security, rising standards of living, a sense of national identity based on participatory and accountable government, and the hope for a better future for one's children.

The failure of the modern Arab order was painfully symbolized in several ways. First, it was difficult to say exactly how many Arab countries existed, given the rather vague status of lands such as Somalia, Djibouti, north and south Lebanon, Palestine, northern Iraq, Western Sahara, and others. Second, the spectacle of states in ruins, on fire, or ravaged by the domestic violence of their people or government had spread to the four corners of the Arab world: Lebanon in the Levant, Kuwait in the Gulf, Somalia in the Horn of Africa, and Algeria in North Africa. And third was the agonizing spectacle of Kuwait, whose land and vessels in the period 1986–1991 flew five different flags — those of Kuwait, Iraq, the United States, the United Kingdom, and the United Nations. Countries that collapsed, or burned, or flew five flags in five years, raised serious doubts about their viability as countries, and their authenticity as national communities.

Just before and during the Gulf crisis, most Arabs had started to ask five basic, painful questions about their sad condition: how could a small country such as Israel inflict such defeat and humiliation on such a large and once powerful Arab nation? Why had the Arab world degenerated into a series of autocratic principalities ruled by the whims of self-imposed, unelected, non-accountable leaderships? Why could the West continue to meddle in the region and exploit its natural, financial, and strategic resources for its own ends? Why did the Arabs not achieve their enormous human and economic potential, but instead remained fragmented, quarreling, and politically incoherent? And why were the basic life quality and future prospects of most ordinary people in most Arab states *declining* in recent years, when the region was widely portrayed abroad as being rich?

In almost every Arab country in the 1980s, small or large numbers of people showed fearlessness and defiance in confronting their own domestic injustices, inequities, oppression, and denial, in a massive, uncoordinated but organically unified quest for Arab dignity. Each country presented a different case, and people used a variety of means to challenge domestic orders that they had deemed to be unresponsive or unacceptable, including armed struggle, Islamic fundamentalism, Arab nationalism, and calls for democracy and human rights. Even the rich Gulf societies felt such challenges, evident, for example, in the pro-democracy movement in Kuwait.

The results of the first decade of the Arab re-awakening were mixed. A few dictators or autocratic presidents were removed, including Habib Bourguiba in Tunisia, Jaafar Numeiry in Sudan, and Mohammad Siad Barre in Somalia. Assassinations of heads of state were achieved or attempted in Yemen, Lebanon, Algeria, Egypt, Syria, and Kuwait. Several countries started to move towards various forms and stages of pluralism and democratization, including Jordan, Yemen, Morocco, Algeria (until the suspension of democratization in January 1992), Egypt, Tunisia, Kuwait, and even Mauritania. Lebanon sought in its own peculiar way to work out more equitable power-sharing arrangements. There were strong calls within the Palestinian national movement for wider participation in decision-making, and both Oman and Saudi Arabia deemed it necessary to offer their people consultative councils as possible first steps towards more formal participatory politics. Power flows in Iraq, Syria, Libya, and Djibouti remained largely unchanged, and almost totally in the hands of the ruling elites that had governed for two decades.

The changes that occurred in the Arab world revealed leaderships that were forced to come to terms with their people's demands for a more responsive political order and more equitable social and economic systems. Two important new elements drove and defined such change in the 1980s: 1) a mass turning inwards by Arab populations that recognized their own domestic deficiencies and sought to redress them before attempting to confront regional or international challenges, and 2) a sense of fearlessness and defiance that saw Arabs confront their own political power structures, Israel, or, in the Gulf crisis of 1990–1991, the political, economic and military might of the West and its adjuncts in the Gulf.

The Gulf War resulted in a predictable military victory for the United States, but did not deal with any of these other issues that had been on the mind of the Arab people well before the August 1990 crisis struck. From the late 1970s, the Arab world has been dominated by two political trends: the rise of Islamic fundamentalism, and the call for democratic reforms. The seven problems outlined above gave rise to these grassroots Arab sentiments well before the Gulf crisis, and they will continue to drive Arab political trends for years. Many Arabs argued that while the war solved the question of the Iraqi occupation of Kuwait, it aggravated these other important issues, and therefore made the region less stable and more volatile than it was before the Gulf crisis.

The political split in the Arab world was stronger and more obvious by 1992 than ever before in this century, and was aggravated by the direct presence of foreign troops in Arab countries. While the immediate future remained unclear, the modern history of the Arab world would suggest that inter-Arab diplomatic dialogue would resume and the Arabs would realize that foreign military intervention could not be a long-term answer to the region's problems — no more than foreign military forces could resolve the problems of Vietnam, Afghanistan, Angola, Cambodia or other regional conflicts around the world. As foreign troops gradually began to leave the area, it seemed the Arabs would focus increasingly on resolving their key regional problems. These were the issues that had to be resolved if the Arabs were to feel that they were part of the drive towards a truly new world order. They included:

* Resolving the Arab-Israeli dispute: This was a key priority, because the unresolved Palestine problem continued to have an impact throughout the region. This impact was felt in terms of exaggerated arms spending, a sense of humiliation by Arabs far from Palestine, and complications in ties between the United States and some Arab countries that resented what they perceived to be Washington's one-sided, pro-Israeli posture. Some Arab countries used the threat of Israel as an excuse to maintain their own military regimes. Peace in Palestine, and non-belligerent or even normal relations between the Arab states and Israel, would be a major spur to economic development, tourism, trade, investment, dealing with a looming regional water shortage, and slowing down the regional arms race. Resolving the Arab-Israeli conflict on the basis of international law and UN resolutions would also spur the resolution of inter-Arab problems, such as border demarcations and water rights, and would lessen the need to turn to war to resolve local disputes.

* Democracy, pluralism and human rights: The Arab world could not be allowed to remain the only major region of the world which was not moving towards democratic rule. The Arab people made it clear that they wished to enjoy the dignity that comes from living in a democratic society that respects individual human rights. The regional tradition of political power closely held in the hands of individuals, families and military elites did not give the Arabs security, stability or development; rather, it caused people to rebel against the existing order, and to demand more equitable political systems that permitted people to express themselves and to participate in decision-making. Democratic practices had to extend beyond the political arena, to encompass cultural life, the arts, business and education, so that the full human and economic potential of the Arab world could be tapped to deal with its major challenges.

* Regional integration: The fragmentation of the Arab world into small states separated natural and human resources that should work together for the national welfare of the entire Arab world. Just as the United States would not function efficiently if the oil of Texas, the wheat of Kansas, the fruits of California, the cash of New York banks, and the steel of Pennsylvania were separated in individual countries that rarely traded with one another, the Arab world remained constrained by an inability to integrate its resources into a productive whole. The oil and cash of the Gulf states, the fertile lands of Egypt, Jordan, Lebanon and Syria, the water of Iraq and Syria, the

minerals of North Africa, the people of Egypt and North Africa and the markets of the entire Arab world needed to be integrated into a single economic dynamic that would allow the Arab world to rely on itself more and also to generate substantial new jobs and income. In 1992 only about 6% of all Arab commercial trade was carried out with other Arab countries — a sign of deep deficiencies in inter-Arab integration.

* Economic equity: If the human, natural and financial resources of the Arab world were more integrated and economically complementary, the severe economic imbalances in the region would be significantly eased. If the Arab world continued to split into a small group of very rich people and a large group of very poor ones, the region would be threatened by perpetual instability and conflict, as the poor sought to share in the wealth of the rich — by force if necessary. The rich countries of the Arab world could not realistically expect the West to send half a million troops every time one of them was threatened. Stability and security in the region would have to come from the feeling by all the people of the region that they lived in political dignity, economic equity and social justice.

* Security and arms control: The tremendous waste inherent in massive military spending needed to be reduced, if the region was to aspire to stability and peace. The hundreds of billions of dollars spent on security did not bring the region real security, but only chronic warfare. A serious regional effort needed to be launched to assure regional security requirements through means other than armaments. This could only occur after the resolution of the Arab-Israeli conflict. It also had to encompass domestic stability through political structures that reduced the role of ethnic and tribal identity, and instead allowed people to manifest their national identity as citizens of a productive state that assured all its nationals equal rights and opportunities.

* Population, water and food: In the early nineties the Arab world had one of the highest population growth rates in the world, averaging 3.8% a year, which was causing tremendous pressure on limited land and water resources. In 1930, the Arab population was 53 million; in 1992 it was 225 million, and the projected population for the year 2000 was over 260 million. The Arab world's self-sufficiency rate in food had declined steadily since 1960, from 91% to 61%. Consequently, the Arab states had to import an average of $17 billion worth of food a year, which was a major drain on often scarce foreign exchange resources. Water shortages were already a reality in every Arab country except Iraq, and were predicted to worsen steadily. Water promised to become an increasingly important source of political tension with Israel and Turkey, and prompted speculation about new inter-Arab disputes (Syria/Jordan, Egypt/Sudan, Syria/Iraq). Providing sufficient food and water for the growing Arab population promised to be the single biggest domestic challenge facing the Arab world as the turn of the century approached.

* Relations with foreign powers. The Arab states needed to formulate more balanced and mutually beneficial ties with the leading powers of the world. Economic ties, for example, could not continue to reflect an outflow of Arab raw materials, energy and cash in exchange for manufactured goods, food and arms. Joint investments were needed to promote genuine Arab

economic development that allowed Arab money and raw materials to join forces with Western technology, with the aim of promoting jobs and long-term growth in the Arab world.

The simultaneous end of the Cold War and the advent of the alleged New World Order quickly clarified the real nature of most Middle Eastern states, of which four types were now discernible: 1) the neo-protectorates of the Gulf such as Kuwait, Saudi Arabia and the rest of the Gulf Cooperation Council, which paid the West handsomely for military protection; 2) the neo-Mamluke states such as Egypt and Morocco, whose pressing domestic pressures caused them to sell their services as warriors and political adjuncts to the West; 3) the neo-mandates, such as Lebanon, Iraq, Libya, Djibouti and Somalia, states that had effectively lost control of their own sovereignty and that lived or died according to the political whims of other powers in the region or in the West; and, 4) the newly democratizing states such as Jordan, Yemen, Algeria, and Tunisia, that had embarked on a slow process of pluralism and democratization as an antidote to the previous decades of unsatisfactory and unstable statehood.

By the early 1990s, as the Cold War ended, global geopolitical realignments took their toll on the Middle East region, and talk of a New World Order filled the air. Important new questions dominated the thoughts of Arabs, Iranians and other Middle Easterners who were assessing their place in the proposed New World Order:

— Why was Islam often portrayed as the new threat to Western civilization and selectively exploited by the West when it suited them (in Afghanistan) but opposed when it did not (in Iran, Algeria, and much of the rest of the Arab world)?

— Why did some Arab governments, such as Algeria, Tunisia, Iraq, Syria, or Egypt, effectively deny their people the option to resort to God and to their Islamic religion as a refuge in times of stress, and as a vector for political change and rebirth?

— Why did the Arabs suffer continued double standards in the implementation of UN resolutions and political morality, e.g. why did the West formally protect the Kurds in Iraq but not the Palestinians in Palestine, even though two separate UN resolutions sought protection for both peoples; why did the West resort to sanctions to protest the suspension of democracy in Haiti and Peru, but not in Algeria; and why did the West demand that pluralism, democracy, and human rights should be preconditions for aid to the new republics of the former Soviet Union, but make no similar demands of Arab states that sought Western aid or protection; why did the United States politically pressure and suspend economic aid to three small, democratizing Arab states (Yemen, Jordan, and Tunisia) during the Gulf crisis, at a time when it said its intervention in Kuwait aimed to promote freedom and protect the sovereignty of small states?

— Why were the Arabs and Muslims being subjected to technological racism that denied them, but not Israelis, the opportunity to buy or develop advanced military technologies such as nuclear weapons or ballistic missile systems?

— Why were some Arab lands, such as Somalia and Lebanon, treated as if they did not exist, and were allowed to drown in their own blood after they had lost their former strategic importance? Were Arab states such as Iraq and Somalia only seen by the West as utilitarian entities, to be supported and armed in times of geo-strategic need but ignored or destroyed when the need was no longer there?

— What were the ultimate implications of a United States that continued to assert its racist self-perception as a superior culture whose highest judicial authorities gave it the right to kidnap foreign nationals and bring them to the United States for trial — whether by war (Panama) or financial inducements (Mexico)? Was American dignity more important to satisfy than the dignity of Arabs and Muslims?

In the early 1990s, as the Arab people responded to their prolonged dilemma of contemporary national mediocrity and political stagnation, the issue of redressing the injustice done to the Palestinians emerged as central to the efforts to resolve the region's many problems and set it on a new path of development, stability, and peace. This was perhaps best illustrated by the intense American and pan-Arab quest for peace negotiations in 1991 and 1992, and the use of the Arab-Israeli talks to promote parallel multilateral negotiations on regional issues such as water, security, economic development, refugees, and the environment. The historical cycle had come full circle: the denial of Palestinian rights and the prolonged Israeli occupation of Palestine were central causes for Arab failure in the three decades after 1948; Palestinian resistance in Palestine and Lebanon were pivotal factors in igniting an Arab re-awakening in the 1980s; and resolution of the Palestine problem emerged in the 1990s as the core of serious international efforts to deal with the many problems plaguing the wider Middle East.

The message that emerged from the grassroots of the Middle East since the overthrow of the Shah of Iran in 1979 was clear, consistent and reasonable: the people of the region insisted on developing societies that responded to their human rights, needs and aspirations, in line with the goals of stability, equity, rule of law, and regional integration that define the New World Order articulated by the West. If such a goal could not be achieved through the normal course of political life, it would be achieved — as it was in Southern Africa or Eastern Europe — through a combination of political challenge, military resistance, and mass civil rebellion. The people of the Middle East were demanding that any New World Order should apply equally to them as it did to other regions of the world. They insisted that a genuine New World Order should see the emergence of a new Middle Eastern regional order, based on principles of democracy, human rights, real national sovereignty, and meaningful regional integration. If the New World Order held out the promise of attaining these goals, the people of the Middle East would embrace it with enthusiasm. But if the New World Order were to turn out to be a cage in which the people and resources of the Middle East were trapped as the perpetual victims of the old order — the world's last colonies — it could only continue to elicit skepticism and resistance from a region that had clearly demonstrated its capacity for sustained struggle for dignity.

20

Dinosaur in the Tar Pit:
The U.S. and the Middle East After the Gulf War

Joe Stork

The Bush administration did not decide to go to war against Iraq in order to establish a "new world order." Quite the opposite: the decisions to confront Iraq's seizure of Kuwait, and to escalate the confrontation to war, were intended precisely to suppress this particular challenge to the old order in the Middle East, and to do so in a way that enhanced the ability of the United States to withstand less dramatic but equally fundamental global challenges to the old order arising out of the growth of rival economic powers and the decomposition of the Soviet Union. The key word for George Bush, James Baker and the other stewards of the U.S. ruling class was "order," not "new." To the extent that a "new world" was emerging, it was one in which disorder would be a defining feature, and the U.S. role would be diminished.

At the regional level, the U.S. intention was to reimpose the old order in the Persian Gulf, and to do so in a way that would short-circuit the self-evident linkages between the Gulf crisis and the Palestine-Israel-Arab state conflict. At the global level, the U.S. goal was to reassert political leadership among the leading industrialized capitalist countries, by insisting that military power still mattered in the post-Cold War equation. Finally, at the domestic level, there was a two-fold goal of "kicking the Vietnam syndrome" — domestic constraints on foreign military intervention — and forestalling competing claims on the resources allocated to the military sector.

In the Middle East, the military victory was only narrowly decisive — in expelling Iraq from Kuwait and crippling Baghdad's ability to project power outside its borders. The American conquest, coupled with the Soviet collapse, leaves the U.S. unrivaled as the preeminent power in the region, but this preeminence has brought with it complications. General Norman Schwarzkopf, while promoting his ghostwritten autobiography, defended the U.S. decision to leave Iraq's regime in power by claiming that "[h]ad we taken all of Iraq we would have been like the dinosaur in the tar pit — we would still be there, and we, not the United Nations, would be bearing the costs for the occupation."[1] This interesting admission of how the U.S. views the role of the UN notwithstanding, the U.S. is "still there," and in a situation for which the term "tar pit" seems apt.

War for Oil?

A truly "new order" in the region (with some of its fascistic overtones) might well have been the outcome of a successful Iraqi incorporation of Kuwait. There is no evidence that Iraq would have attempted further military conquests, such as Saudi Arabia. Western access to oil was never in question. But Iraq's weight in Gulf politics would have been considerably enhanced, and may have eclipsed Saudi influence within the Organization of Petroleum Exporting Countries (OPEC).

The consequences of such a realignment would have been more harmful for the United States than for any other outside power. The U.S. decision to push for war over other means of coercion, such as sanctions, rested on additional considerations, such as Washington's desire to maintain control of the Middle East political agenda. But what compelled Washington to mobilize its resources and its allies and clients so forcefully was that it had the most to lose from a shift of power in the Gulf.

The oil in and around the Persian Gulf is key to industrial economies because it is relatively inexpensive to produce.[2] In the 1950s and 1960s, the difference between production costs and market prices meant bonanza profits for the giant U.S. and European oil companies that dominated the world petroleum industry and the concessions in the Persian Gulf. In the 1970s and 1980s, OPEC successfully raised the selling price of oil — boosting its member states' own take and relative share without encroaching on the per barrel profits of the companies. A more significant structural change was the nationalization of foreign oil operations in virtually every Middle East oil producing country by the 1980s.

The costs of production in the Middle East have risen with inflation and the expansion of production, but the relative cheapness of Middle East oil remains.[3] What has changed most significantly with nationalization are the circuits of capital. To a greater degree than before, the spread between costs of production and selling price is captured by the national oil companies and ruling families rather than directly by the Western oil companies. These monopoly rents are then circulated in the form of purchases (civilian and military) and investments (wasteful and productive). These circuits benefit most the countries with the most developed international financial markets, which happen to be those countries whose companies have historically dominated international oil — the U.S. and Britain. It is this advantage that gave the U.S. the most to lose materially from any radical change in the balance of forces in the Persian Gulf.

For most oil exporting countries, population and economic structure place an immediate call on oil revenues in terms of meeting immediate consumption and investment needs. In the Middle East these countries include Iran, Iraq and Algeria. In the second category, where production and revenues significantly exceed the immediate consumption and investment needs of the society, are the family-run states of the Persian Gulf — Saudi Arabia, Kuwait, the United Arab Emirates (UAE) and Qatar.[4] These "excess revenue" countries have long-standing ties with U.S. and British banks and financial advisers, and have subscribed to the conservative investment philosophies that stress Western corporate and government bonds and financial instruments as the safest repositories for their funds.

In a regional political order dominated by a country like Iraq, those investment patterns would be different, and likely less oriented to Western priorities. This is not a matter of virtue: Iraq's vast investments in military goods and technology were not morally or politically "better" than Kuwait's or Saudi Arabia's portfolios managed out of London or New York. The point is that the locus of decision-making is different, and the allocation of funds is made within different parameters.

Not coincidentally, those oil exporters with relatively large populations and revenue needs are those (like Iraq and Libya) which have experienced political revolutions, installing populist authoritarian regimes which have restructured the political and financial links established in the earlier era of oil imperialism. Iraq's invasion of Kuwait would have eliminated a key family autocracy closely aligned with the political and financial centers of the West, and would have reduced the ability of the remaining monarchies to influence the terms of oil trade.

The other industrialized countries share with the U.S. the interest in preventing any regional or external hegemonic power from dominating the Persian Gulf. The particular U.S. interest is that within this environment of diffuse power the Saudis should play a leading role. The Saudi ruling family, in the 1960s and early 1970s, decided that the key to its longevity was its relationship with the United States, and that its interests were more or less identical to the interests of the American firms. It was a clever decision, designed to turn Saudi dependency on the U.S. into an asset. The history of OPEC has been the history of Saudi efforts to persuade or compel the more populous member regimes to also follow policies solicitous of the West. The phrase "more or less identical" is important, though, and the Saudis still have to balance this self-identification with the U.S. against competing pressures from the other leading producers, such as Iraq and Iran. Washington's spectacular deployment of military power has made that considerably easier than would otherwise have been the case.

The fact that Japan and Europe are more dependent on oil imports from the Persian Gulf than the U.S. has led some to conclude that the U.S. used this crisis as an opportunity to position itself to control the access of its chief competitors to this vital resource. In circumstances of open hostilities between the U.S. and Europe or Japan, the U.S. military advantage in the Persian Gulf would be an immense asset. Short of this unlikely scenario, however, can the U.S. parlay its military position into competitive economic advantage? Is this a factor driving U.S. policy and strategy in the region?

In the 1950s, the U.S. intervened in Iran to restore the Shah to power and defeat Iran's effort to nationalize its oil industry, in the process replacing the formerly British Petroleum monopoly with a consortium of companies with a controlling interest for American firms. In the 1990s the U.S. role as savior of the status quo in the Persian Gulf will give some advantage to U.S. firms there. The October 1992 Kuwaiti decision to buy General Dynamics' M-1A tanks rather than the British-made Challengers is a case in point. U.S. engineering and construction firms like Bechtel have done very well in the post-war reconstruction contracts. But this is qualitatively different from the kinds of advantage that U.S. ascendant hegemony could secure 30 and 40 years earlier. Japan's recent decision to privilege its growing trade links with Iran over Washington's campaign to restrict high technology exports to that country indicates the difficulty of imposing economic hegemony by military means.

Guarding the Gulf

Over the last two decades, the dynamics of uneven development and political resentment in the Persian Gulf region have given rise to Iran's revolution, Iraq's invasion of first Iran and then its invasion of Kuwait. These dynamics have compelled the United States to escalate its military role. The Gulf crisis and war of 1990–91 consolidated the trend towards direct U.S. military intervention as a necessary component in the campaign to preserve shaikhly rule, itself a prerequisite for preserving a hegemonic U.S. position in the Gulf.

"If in the next few years it again becomes necessary for the U.S. to deploy combat power abroad," CIA director Robert Gates told a Congressional committee in 1992, "the strategically vital region encompassing the Middle East and the Persian Gulf is at the top of the list of likely locales."[5] In the summer and fall of 1992, the United States had some 250 warplanes and 25,000 troops in the Persian Gulf and vicinity. Washington has signed military agreements with Kuwait, Qatar and Bahrain, and "upgraded" its agreement with Oman for prepositioning military equipment and access to "facilities."[6] "We've got ships going into ports left and right," boasts Rear Admiral Raynor Taylor, head of the Persian Gulf Task Force. "We've got ships and planes doing bilateral exercises left and right . . . Having to have a 90-day advance notice to go into Jiddah or Dammam, that doesn't exist any more."[7]

Only Kuwait eagerly sought to become an unabashed and undisguised U.S. protectorate. The UAE broke off such talks with Washington in early 1992 (but may be reconsidering following Iran's clumsy assertion of full control over the Persian Gulf island of Abu Musa). Admiral Taylor is not allowed to mention that his flagship, the USS LaSalle, is berthed in Bahrain.

Some serious complications have arisen with Saudi Arabia itself. Following the war with Iraq, Schwarzkopf recommended to Secretary of Defense Dick Cheney that the U.S. leave in Saudi Arabia six fighter wings and equipment to outfit a "heavy division." A year later, the Saudis had still not agreed to U.S. terms for prepositioning.[8] The Saudis were balking at signing the usual "status of forces" agreement that waives local jurisdiction over U.S.

troops. Perhaps they remember how Ayatollah Khomeini, as far back as in 1963, used the U.S. status of forces agreement with Iran to mobilize popular opposition against the Shah. The Saudis reportedly have agreed to greater U.S. port access, but rather than U.S.-controlled prepositioned equipment they want the U.S. to sell the equipment to them, as part of a plan to more than double Saudi troop strength to 200,000 men. At issue is whether the equipment will be under Saudi or U.S. control, and whether the U.S. would have automatic access or have to rely on the informal helpful interference of someone like Ambassador Prince Bandar bin Sultan at a point of crisis. The Saudis, it seems, would prefer to have nothing in writing.

It was a Pentagon team that drew up the Saudi troop expansion plans. Either course holds evident complications for the internal balance of forces in the kingdom. The U.S. will preposition the equipment only with a written Memorandum of Understanding governing access, but such tangible terms of reference expose the ruling family to charges by Saudi Islamist radicals that they are puppets of the U.S. The second course, expanding the Saudi military, would require conscription, which could upset the balance between the different Saudi forces (such as the regular army and the national guard) and the ruling family factions to which they are attached.

Even without any new agreement with the Saudis, of course, the U.S. capacity to intervene remains enormous. The U.S. goal has been to create a situation that would allow an even more rapid buildup than that which occurred in the fall of 1990. And Washington wants the capacity to act completely unilaterally. "Such capabilities are essential to our ability to lead, and should the international support prove sluggish or inadequate, to act independently, as necessary, to protect our critical interests," wrote Cheney in the still-secret Defense Guidance 1994–99 document.[9]

The enhanced U.S interventionary posture in the Persian Gulf is one indication of the extent to which U.S. strategy in the region has become largely a military strategy. Another indication is the scale of military sales and exports to the region — more than $24 billion in fiscal year 1991 alone. The U.S. military export drive, though, is primarily motivated not by policy or strategy but by the need for markets. One Congressional aide irreverently dubbed the Bush administration's proposed list of $23 billion in weapons sales to Saudi Arabia following Iraq's invasion of Kuwait the "defense industry relief act of 1990."[10] Military hardware, writes Brookings Institution analyst Yahya Sadowski, "is one of the new manufacturing export sectors where the U.S. is still internationally competetive."[11]

The New Old Order

The augmented military position in the Persian Gulf is the most tangible feature of Washington's strategy in the region following the war with Iraq. The other main elements are: (1) the post-war "behavioral modification" campaign directed at the Baghdad regime, and the regional complications arising from that campaign; and (2) the effort to broker multilateral talks between Israel, the Palestinians and the Arab states.

The U.S. decision to allow Baghdad to regroup militarily and defeat the insurgencies in the south and north of the country in March and April 1991 was a calculated one. Saddam Hussein could usefully serve to impose order inside Iraq, and suppress dissident forces which might threaten Turkey and Saudi Arabia. But Baghdad complicated this scenario by repeatedly challenging U.S. disarmament orders (delivered via the United Nations), and otherwise refusing to show the proper deference to "international" authority.

More serious plans to bring about the end of Saddam Hussein's rule apparently took shape in the fall and winter of 1991–92. Well-placed leaks in the major media had the Saudis urging the U.S. to take the lead in organizing a covert campaign against Baghdad along the following lines: (1) provide arms and some military training to Kurdish and Shi'a opponents of the regime who would (2) mount a limited military campaign which would force Baghdad (3) to choose between ceding control of territory at the periphery or sending out crack military units and leaving Baghdad vulnerable to a coup by dissident Ba'athi officers, who would (4) call in foreign air support against forces loyal to Hussein. "There has to be a combination of a major covert operation and a major air operation and then leave the rest to the Iraqi people," was how one "senior allied official" put it.[12]

The main proponents of this scenario seem to have been NSC chief Brent Scowcroft and his deputy, Robert Gates. But when the Deputies Committee (a crisis management team comprising second-tier representatives from the major cabinet-level agencies chaired by the NSC deputy director) asked the Joint Chiefs of Staff to develop plans for a U.S. response to a request for assistance from Iraqi military plotters, General Colin Powell's report held that success would require a "large and combined effort by U.S. air and ground combat forces." For the White House, this was the wrong answer. Powell's report was sent to the Deputies Committee for "review" and "refinement," to eliminate the prescription for a large ground commitment and to support Scowcroft's insistence that air support would suffice in such a scenario.

What has evolved is a policy that continues sanctions and provocative inspection missions, and continues to funnel funds to approved Iraqi opposition groups. Some believe this largesse has merely increased the number and pro-U.S. sentiments of groups to the detriment of their effectiveness.

The most important feature of the policy is the decision to impose a "no-fly zone" across southern Iraq, forbidding Baghdad from sending aircraft against rebel forces there. While there is no evidence that the U.S. seeks to divide Iraq, Washington has apparently concluded such an outcome is a risk worth running. Kuwaiti ruling circles understandably perceive that Iraq without Saddam Hussein is no less of a menace, given popular Iraqi support for the proposition that Kuwait is part of their country. What is new is that at least some key elements in Saudi ruling circles have come to agree that, in the words of one official, "we may need several small entities to deal with instead of attempting to preserve one Iraqi nation."[14]

Washington's failure to develop a viable policy towards Iran is likely to be the source of further conflict in the Gulf involving U.S. forces. Tehran insists that it must be brought in to any regional security arrangement in the Persian Gulf for those arrangements to be effective. The Bush administration completed a review of policy in early April 1992, and concluded that there should be no shift from a policy of confrontation and containment for the time being. Richard Haass, who directed the Bush administration's policy review towards Iran, claimed the appropriate policy is one of containment "even if it takes 70 years" (i.e., the lifespan of the Soviet Union). The sudden media attention to an allegedly extensive Iranian arms buildup, following earlier alarmist reports of Iranian "diplomatic offensives" among the former Soviet republics of Central Asia, suggests that Iran has made a quick comeback as adversary of choice in Washington.

The Kurdish Complication

If the situation in southern Iraq and the Persian Gulf is reminiscent of a familiar pattern of confrontation between the U.S. and its allies on the one hand and Iran on the other, the situation in the northern, Kurdish areas of Iran lacks any precedent. The U.S., with warplanes based in Turkey, is protecting Kurds in northern Iraq from Baghdad's military depradations, while U.S. ally Turkey uses U.S. weapons to carry out bombing raids and ground offensives in northern Iraq against its own Kurdish opponents. Iraqi Kurds are careful to insist that they seek only autonomy in a "federal" Iraq, not the independent state favored by the PKK (the major Kurdish political and military organization in Turkish Kurdistan), but the logic of their situation seems to be pushing them towards a de facto independence. At an extraordinary meeting in Ankara in mid-November 1992, the foreign ministers of Iran, Syria and Turkey opposed publicly the Kurdish "federal" project, as well as the broader opposition Iraqi National Congress. Turkey, while adopting this public stance, seems intent on imposing its own "security zone" in northern Iraq, along the lines of that set up by Israel in southern Lebanon. The bottom line coming out of Ankara is that "nothing will happen in northern Iraq that is not permitted by Turkey." Turkey's goal is to be able to withdraw thousands of Turkish troops now fighting in northern Iraq soon, leaving the task of maintaining security to Iraqi peshmergas and the Turkish air force while Turkish troops cope with the Kurdish insurgency within its own borders.[15]

Perhaps things will evolve in accordance with the scenario of the Turkish general staff in Kurdistan, but this is far from certain. The U.S. is engaged politically and militarily in a very fluid situation over which it has little control. Washington's instinct is to ally itself with Turkey, especially given Washington's reliance on Turkey to play a major role in containing Iranian influence in the former Soviet republics of Central Asia. But Ankara's human rights record against its Kurdish population could make this difficult politically. U.S. military engagement in the Kurdish areas was not something Washington sought in the first place. A similar combination of inadvertence and compulsion could well come into play again.

The Israel-Palestine Arena

The most surprising development in U.S. Middle East policy after the war against Iraq was the Bush administration's dogged effort to convene negotiations between Israel, the Palestinians and the Arab states. Washington used Israel's request for $10 billion in loan guarantees to compel the Likud regime to participate in these talks, and this U.S. pressure became a major element in Likud's electoral defeat in June 1992.

The pertinent questions are two. First, what turned the charade known as the "peace process" into actual negotiations? Second, do the negotiations amount to a cosmetic or a substantial change from the previous state of affairs?

The brief season of open discord between the U.S. and Israel, from September 1991 through June 1992, was unusual, but its significance should not be exaggerated. It was a phase in the overall recalibration of U.S. policy in the region in the wake of the Gulf War and the demise of the Soviet Union, and it was enabled, in terms of domestic politics, by the U.S. economic crisis.

The Bush administration's efforts to stage the Madrid talks and subsequent negotiations represent at bottom a U.S. acknowledgement of the "linkage" issue — that is, the insistence of Palestinians and other Arabs, not least of them Saddam Hussein, that the political future of the Persian Gulf could not be entirely separated from the dynamics of the Palestinian-Israeli-Arab state conflict. A prime concern of U.S. policy in the Middle East is to dominate the agenda, and this is a major reason why the U.S. chose war as the means of choice for confronting Iraq's aggression. To have accepted the "Arab solution" approach of Jordan's King Hussein (among many others) would have been to share the power to set the agenda. Linkage in this sense had to be rendered presumptuous and invalid.

The extent of popular support in the Arab world for Iraq against Kuwait and against the United States — against the prevailing hierarchies of power and privilege — captured the attention of the custodians of power. True, no political firestorm erupted to devour any of the Arab allied regimes, but the legitimacy of the existing order was clearly vulnerable. Once Iraq, and by extension its partisans among the Palestinians and other Arabs, had been defeated, linkage could flourish — on terms largely set by Washington.

Movement towards negotiations on Palestine represented the only serious option, if we consider the other issues that the Gulf crisis put squarely on the agenda:

* *Arms control and demilitarization*. Iraq presented a real scare, and compelled policymakers in the U.S. and elsewhere to look more seriously at various arms limitation schemes. But U.S. export imperatives have ensured that the post-war demilitarization campaign applied solely to Iraq.
* *Equity and social justice*. For the Saudis and the other Arab oil monarchs, this was a complete non-starter. The war had been fought, after all, precisely

to restore and maintain the separation of people and resources that has produced the region's glaring disparities of income and wealth in the first place. There was the further problem that the war itself had cost the Arab states collectively some $620 billion, and that even the Saudis no longer enjoyed surplus revenues that could painlessly fund a Middle East Development Bank.[16]

* *Democracy, governance and human rights.* In late March 1991, King Fahd summoned Brent Scowcroft to Riyadh to insist that Washington go *sotto voce* about Kuwaiti human rights violations. There has been not the slightest peep from Washington about the issue of political reform in Saudi Arabia itself. There has been no U.S. encouragement for Yemen's efforts to establish a pluralist, multi-party system. Most strikingly, the U.S. has not made free elections a part of the panoply of UN demands on Baghdad, despite the precedence of UN resolutions to that effect in Cambodia, for instance.

The one remaining regional issue prominently highlighted by the Gulf crisis was the Palestine question. Movement (or the appearance of movement) on this matter would serve to make the alliance of the Saudi, Egyptian and other regimes with the U.S. against Iraq appear productive, without at the same time undercutting those regimes.

The very public U.S. animosity with the Shamir government served this purpose well. There were other factors. The U.S. interest in controlling the agenda extended to Israel. Bush and Baker had long perceived the need to recalibrate the U.S.-Israeli relationship, and the Gulf War aftermath provided both the impetus and the opportunity. The purpose was to "normalize" the special relationship — a project that could only be seen as a threat by Shamir. All of this was facilitated by the very serious divisions in Israeli society and among Israel's partisans in the U.S. over the wisdom of Shamir's confrontational and belligerent approach in general and his determination to colonize the West Bank and Gaza in particular.

The negotiations, like the "peace process" before them, can be an end in themselves or a means to an end. Will the Clinton administration be content to keep talks going without really caring whether they get anywhere? The talks themselves, and the theatrics over the $10 billion loan guarantees, served the immediate need of legitimizing the ties of key Arab regimes with the U.S. Washington has not displayed the sort of urgency that suggests a larger purpose. Clinton may well defer to Israel in setting the parameters and the pace of the talks. There is little reason to think, though, that the situation would have been much different with a second Bush term.

At the same time, it is important to remember that the same dynamics which compelled the Bush administration to "normalize" the relationship with Israel are still operative. Close U.S.-Israeli military and intelligence ties will continue, but U.S. economic aid is likely to decrease. The Gulf War, furthermore, accelerated the shift in the center of gravity of U.S. Middle East policy from the eastern Mediterranean to the Persian Gulf, a trend which gives less weight to Israel as a strategic ally. In Yitzhak Rabin, Washington has an Israeli leader who understands this and who will work to maximize

Israel's advantage in this shift rather than stand against it altogether. In terms of the current negotiations, this is likely to mean some movement towards settlement with Syria and Jordan. On the Palestinian front, though, it is likely to mean further stalemate.

Concluding Premises

As Stanford University historian Joel Beinin points out, the historic bases of U.S. power in the world have been four: (1) industrial productivity, particularly in leading economic sectors; (2) the role of the dollar as the leading international currency; (3) access to and control of raw materials; and (4) military power and the means to reproduce it. Competition from other powers has trimmed the U.S. advantage in the economic spheres. Control of and access to resources remains key, but it is now mediated through regimes as varied as the family proprietorships of Saudi Arabia and Kuwait to the authoritarian populist republics like Iran and Iraq to the range of constitutional oligarchies that rule in places like Mexico and Ecuador.

The one feature that remains relatively unchanged is the military sphere. Even here, though, the facts of economic competition and national sovereignty have required the U.S. to negotiate the alliances and the tribute that make that military power useable. The United States used the UN to accomplish its purposes in the war with Iraq. General Schwarzkopf's candid characterization of the UN as a sort of all-purpose security and social service agency, suitable mainly for dealing with the messy consequences of U.S. policy, should temper any enthusiasm for the new acclaim in Washington for the world body. At the same time, it is significant that Washington *did* feel compelled to work through the Security Council as a way of legitimizing its policy, and a more gifted adversary than Saddam Hussein would have exploited that need much more than he did.

The U.S. war against Iraq has eliminated for the time being that country's capacity to act as a regional hegemon, and has left in the region a U.S. capacity to intervene militarily that is far greater than existed before. The war has not, however, dealt with the underlying political challenges that beset the region. If anything, the war aggravated the vulnerability of the regimes and intensified the sense of popular grievance against an unjust and intolerable order. The important political challenges in the Middle East in the future are going to happen within countries rather than between them. The very unsettled lines of authority in Kurdistan are a case in point, and the continued confrontation with Iran now directly engages the U.S. as its own gendarme in the Persian Gulf. In Algeria, grievances over economic welfare, corruption and political accountability have produced a condition of low-level civil war. In Egypt a similar situation exists: recent Islamist attacks on foreign tourists have escalated the crisis there significantly, as the state feels compelled to move in force to crush this challenge to one of the key sources of state revenue and foreign exchange.

In terms of the U.S. ability to continue to play a hegemonic role globally, the Gulf War did expose the fragility of a "European bloc" that could serve as an alternative Western power. This exposure of European disarray — reaffirmed by the debacle in the former Yugoslavia — extends the U.S. claim to a commanding role further into the decade. It does not, however, change the underlying trends towards a diffusion of power among the "Northern" states and the decreasing significance of military power in the overall equation.

These combined tendencies are apparent in Washington's response to the "new world" that has emerged despite the U.S., not because of it. How the Pentagon is planning to cope tells a bit about how U.S. strategists see the world and the place of the Middle East in that world. In the first-draft words of the 1994–1999 Defense Planning Guidance document, "our overall objective is to remain the predominant outside power in the region." To meet this objective, strategists have proposed reducing the existing five military theater commands (Atlantic, Pacific, European, Southern, Central) to three: Atlantic, Pacific and Contingency.[17] Where they anticipate the greatest threat is apparent: the Atlantic and Contingency commands combined would have the capacity to replay Desert Storm.

In considering the changes that have occurred at the global level, it is important not to accept at face value the self-serving claim that the U.S. "won" the Cold War, or to attribute to the U.S. defeat of Iraq changes that derived from fundamentally different factors. The "new world" that is emerging owes much more to dynamics over which the U.S. has limited influence. At the domestic level, the Bush administration's victory has been most clearly pyrrhic, as the consequences of economic crisis have undermined its hold on power. Even Bush's claim that "we finally kicked the Vietnam syndrome" has to be heavily qualified. True, Desert Storm's Nintendo-type victory — rapid high-tech spectacle with few U.S. casualties — will probably make it easier politically to launch a future war. Yet it is telling that within the administration the main opposition to further direct U.S. military engagement in Iraq, or in Yugoslavia or Somalia, has come from the Pentagon itself. And with good reason: the Vietnam syndrome lives.

Notes

1. *Washington Post*, September 20, 1992.
2. A Chase Manhattan Bank study in the early 1960s estimated that the average cost of maintaining and expanding production in the Middle East was 16 cents per barrel, as opposed to 51 cents for Venezuelan oil and U.S. average costs of $1.73 per barrel. Oil is a global commodity, and world oil prices tend to reflect average costs of production: a barrel of oil from the Persian Gulf costing 16 cents to produce sells for more or less the same price as a barrel from Louisiana or Oklahoma costing closer to $2.
3. A recent study estimated a cost of between $3,000 and $10,000 per barrel/day to bring a new field on stream in the Middle East, as opposed to between $15,000 and $30,000 in the U.S. or North Sea (*Arab Oil and Gas*, July 1, 1992).
4. The only non-Persian Gulf states in this situation have been Brunei and Libya, although the U.S.-imposed embargo of Libya, combined with the decline in revenues per barrel in the late 1980s, have rendered that country less of an exception in this regard.
5. *Washington Post*, May 31, 1992.
6. In Kuwait now there is equipment, food and fuel to outfit a U.S. battalion with M-1A battle tanks, Bradley fighting vehicles and 155 mm artillery pieces (*Washington Post*, September 5, 1992).
7. *New York Times*, July 18, 1992.

8. Some 290 M-1As, a similar number of Bradleys, and so forth (*New York Times*, August 1, 1991; *Inside the Army*, May 28, 1991; *Washington Post*, May 31, 1992).

9. *Los Angeles Times*, October 23, 1992.

10. William Hartung, "Breaking the Arms Sales Addiction," *World Policy Journal*, Winter 1990–91, p. 15.

11. *Middle East Report* #177, pp. 12–13.

12. *New York Times*, January 19, 1992. Some of the "sources" for this account apparently thought this plan naively dangerous, and hoped that publicity would thwart it, while others apparently wanted the publicity to give moral encouragement to the Iraqi dissidents.

13. *Washington Post*, February 9, 1992.

14. *New York Times*, August 2, 1992. For as long as it was useful, Washington has encouraged the notion that Iraqi Shi'a represented an Iranian fifth column, and that a "strong" regime like that of Saddam Hussein was necessary to preserve Iraq's territorial integrity against Iranian expansionism. This fear was always overblown, and underestimated the importance of Iraqi nationalism in the Shi'a sense of identity. Once the decision had been made to enforce a no-fly zone in southern Iraq, the usual cast of experts were trotted out to endorse the suddenly useful proposition that the people of southern Iraq were indeed bona fide Iraqis.

15. *The Independent*, November 6, and November 16, 1992.

16. Arab Economic Report 1992, cited in *Arab Oil and Gas*, September 16, 1992.

17. William Kaufman and John Steinbrunner, *Decisions For Defense*, Washington, Brookings Institute, 1991, pp. 33–35.

21

A Viable Partnership:
Islam, Democracy and the Arab World

As'ad AbuKhalil*

The discourse about "a new world order" is reflective of new international realities that were produced by the demise of the Soviet Union. There is no evidence of any dramatic change in U.S. foreign policy in the wake of the collapse of the Soviet empire. The U.S. has so far been reactive in formulating its foreign policy worldwide. The U.S. is showing a desire to pursue past policies without the restraints that were imposed by the Cold War: the new world order is the old one minus the Soviet superpower. The real change in the "new world" has been mostly in the realm of American official rhetoric. The U.S. government now invokes far more than it used to issues of human rights and democracy, although there has not been the slightest hint that these lofty ideals now constitute the thrust of U.S. foreign policy. The U.S. emphasizes the need for democratization, but still only in countries where the rulers are politically unfriendly to the U.S. In anti-democratic countries where the rulers are supportive of U.S. foreign policy (like the Arab states of the Gulf) the regimes still enjoy the support of the U.S., which has not been pressuring the Saudi royal family, for example, to improve its human rights record, as the American official rhetoric might imply.

The second feature of the U.S. understanding of the "new world order" is derivative of the collapse of the Soviet Union: the U.S. is no longer reluctant to use the United Nations when it proves useful for U.S. interests. The end of the Soviet factor has allowed the U.S. a free hand in the United Nations, especially given the financial leverage the U.S. has vis-a-vis that institution. The U.S., however, is not showing consistency, and has not insisted on a UN role in all cases of regional and international disputes. The U.S., for example, still prefers to exclude the UN from any role in the Middle East peace talks,

* This is an expanded version of an essay that appeared in the Winter 1992/93 issue of *Harvard International Review*. Reprinted by permission.

which are under the sole — real — sponsorship of the U.S. government, with Russia having an insignificant and largely ceremonial role. The U.S. intervention in Somalia was an example of U.S. use of the United Nations in pursuit of U.S. goals.

It is also noteworthy that the U.S. is not encouraging a democratic structure within the UN. The U.S. role in the United Nations during the Gulf War entailed tactics of pressure and coercion, as Yemen can testify. The poor and democratizing country of Yemen was punished financially by the U.S. for the "wrong" vote it cast in the Security Council against Resolution 678 authorizing the use of force against Iraq. Similarly, the U.S. is playing an instrumental role in matters of policymaking and personnel selection in the world body.

The impact of the "new world order" on the Arab world will be less the result of any new American initiatives and more the result of the demise of Soviet power which acted as a counterbalance to U.S. interests. The U.S. now finds itself free to pursue its interests in the region free from the threat of Soviet molestation and free from the threat of radical Arab states, which are preoccupied with preserving their anti-democratic regimes.

Democracy in the Arab World

Westerners often maintain that the Arab world has not been affected by popular expressions for democratic change. The absence of democracy in the Arab world and the prevalence of oppressive regimes in the region has led people to attribute the political situation to religious and cultural factors. There are several noted Middle East experts in the U.S. who insist that democracy does not exist in the Arab/Islamic context because Arab/Islamic civilization has been inclined toward authoritarian rule. These experts also argue that Islam and democracy are fundamentally incompatible. There are some who insist that the very nature of what they call "the Arab/Islamic mind" is not conducive to representative governments. This latter view, however, is too blatantly prejudicial to deserve a response.

Apologists for Arab regimes sometimes claim that this Arab government or that Arab government is indeed democratic. In reality, there is no Arab government today that can be said to be democratic. Absolutist rule seems to be prevalent in the Arab region, although there are some governments that are more absolutist and oppressive than others. The absence of democratic governments, however, should not be construed as a sign that the Arab people are themselves hostile to the concept of democracy.

Democracy, as an aspiration and not as a political actuality, is now sweeping the entire region. Over the past decade, Arab men and women have clearly voiced their deep desire for democratic changes in their respective countries. Developments dealing with democratic aspirations in the Arab world do not receive the wide sympathetic coverage that democratization movements in other parts of the world do. It is unlikely that the Western press will pay more attention to reform in the Arab world, because democratization in that area will likely produce forces and movements that, for political and not religious or cultural reasons, express antipathy to the U.S. and its interests. Unlike in Eastern and Central Europe, democratization in the Arab world is not synonymous with pro-Americanism. The Arab people are generally very critical of U.S. military and political involvement in the region, which they blame for the longevity of some of the most unpopular Arab regimes — such as the Persian Gulf regimes.

Over the past several years, political changes have taken place in several Arab countries that are now leading to democratization of one form or another. Democratization of the political system occurred in Jordan, Algeria (until the process was aborted by a military coup d'etat in 1992), Yemen and Lebanon (despite recent election irregularities and Syrian and Israeli heavy-handedness in that country). It should be emphasized that these governments democratized their systems not for their love of democracy per se but rather as a direct result of democratic movements consisting of men and women who made their desire for fundamental political changes very clear. In both Algeria and Jordan, security services used deadly force against pro-democracy demonstrators, but the news was not widely publicized in the West because of a still pervasive lingering hostility to Muslims and Arabs. Moreover, it is often mistakenly assumed that Muslims only demonstrate to show opposition against the U.S. and/or Israel.

It should be noted that Arab citizens have opposed their governments, even in Iraq, despite the ruthless oppressiveness of some Arab regimes. In February 1982, for example, the Syrian government crushed a popular rebellion in the city of Hama, killing more than 15,000 people in the process. Similarly, the Iraqi government has killed many civilians in its ongoing campaign against dissent. It is rather bizarre that the Arab people and Islamic religion are still held responsible for the tyrannical governments under which they are forced to live.

Islam and Democracy

Discussion of politics in the Arab context often focuses on the question of Islamic resistance to democracy. The characterization of Islam as "a way of life" has negatively influenced most Western analysis of Islam and politics. The idea that in Islam there is no separation between "church" and state leads people to assume that secularism is inapplicable in all regions where Muslims predominate. But any religion — more precisely, any of the three major monotheistic religions — if applied fully in the twentieth century, is incompatible with democracy and secularism. Similarly, a religion is a way of life if one attempts to apply religious laws — and only religious laws — to all facets of social life. To be sure, Islam has been used by governments for centuries for political purposes, and it has consequently affected various aspects of Muslim life. But the questions of Islam and democracy as well as of Islam and secularism are often discussed in ways that imply a peculiar anti-democratic streak in Islam.

In reality, the teachings of the three major monotheistic religions would appear anachronistic if one attempted to live today only according to religious laws. Islam, contrary to claims made by its apologists and critics, has no opinion on the central questions of secularism and democracy. It is only the strict religious orthodoxy that has been trying to force upon believers the myth of "Islamic answers to all of today's problems." The Qur'an, which is the only book accepted by Muslims as the word of God, has very little to say about matters of government. Most of the Qur'anic verses — over two-thirds according to one estimate — deal with matters of ethics and spirituality, while later Qur'anic revelations deal with everyday life. The Qur'an lacks references to politics, with the exception of some very general and vague references to *shura* (consultation) and obedience to "those in charge." These references are hardly the Islamic recipe for a better government that Muslim fundamentalists claim they are. In other words, Islam has no specific and rigid opinion regarding the most desirable forms of government or on the question of separation of "mosque" (there was no religious hierarchy in early Islam) and state. It was post-Muhammad rulers and jurists who wished to re-interpret and in some cases misinterpret Islamic texts for the purely political purpose of legitimizing governments-in-power. The marriage between the political elites and the clerical establishments in past and present day Arab politics explains the obscurantism and dogmatic adherence to a one-dimensional interpretation of Islamic sources.

The rise of Islamic fundamentalism in the Arab and Muslim worlds should not be attributed to religious fervor. The underlying causes behind the emergence of "political Islam" are not theological or religious, but rather socio-economic and political in nature. Many members of fundamentalist organizations were formerly members of leftist and sometimes atheist communist organizations. The demise of the leftist model worldwide and the resentment aimed against Arab governments left the Muslim and Arab masses with one, largely untried, practically novel model. The attractiveness of Islam rests on its ability to appeal with its language and simplicity to millions of people and on its effectiveness as a political vehicle of change. As such Islam ceases to be a body of theological teachings and becomes an ideology of provocation that is intended to embarrass and delegitimize dominant Arab governments.

Moreover, traditional Western hostility to Islam and the antipathy among most Arab people to the political, military and economic interests of the U.S. makes the Islamic weapon all the more appealing. The fixation among Western governments with "an Islamic threat" and the negative reaction to the fall of the Shah of Iran intensified Muslim anger against what is perceived to be a Western stigmatization of everything Islamic. Furthermore, many Arabs and Muslims resent the staunch Western support for the government of Saudi Arabia and other Gulf states, as well as Western identification with Israel. The Arab Gulf regimes represent to many Arabs the monopolization of a nation's wealth by a small family elite, the ostentatious squandering of government funds and the hypocritical exploitation of Islamic slogans by corrupt elites who preach one thing and practice another.

The events in Algeria in 1991–92 are destined to increase the appeal of Muslim fundamentalists in the region. In Algeria, a Muslim movement won through what was considered a relatively fair and honest election process. The military establishment in Algeria chose to cancel the election results and launch a coup d'etat that imposed a crackdown against Muslim activists. There was widespread popular Arab criticism of Western indifference to the crackdown in Algeria; Arabs now believe that the U.S. and other Western governments tolerate oppression and the annulment of election results if the victims are Muslim fundamentalists. Many Arabs charge that the U.S. is not consistent in its verbal — albeit timid — commitment to the spread of democratic ideals in the region. There is a popular perception in the Arab world today that the U.S. only cares about human rights violations in countries that are not politically friendly with the U.S. Western toleration of the Algerian coup will only reinforce Muslim/Arab suspicions about fundamental Western hostility to Islamic governments. Fundamentalists are already using the Algerian example to demonstrate the limitations of "working within the system."

The seizure of power by one fundamentalist group or another in one Arab country or another is almost inevitable. The Islamic government in the Sudan is, of course, not the product of an electoral process in which the people of Sudan expressed their support for 'Umar Bashir and/or Hasan Turabi. Rather, Bashir and the military clique seized power forcefully and against the wishes of most Sudanese. His government has already discredited the Islamic fundamentalist formula among many Sudanese, although there is no reliable survey of public opinion in Sudan under Bashir's government. Nevertheless, the Sudanese opposition movement(s) — operating both in the Sudan and outside — has become one of the strongest opposition movements in any Arab country, even though it does not have the material and military support of other movements, such as the Iraqi one, for example.

The Islamic fundamentalist movement in the Arab world is benefiting from its opposition and underground status. It gains from its distance from government; it is not tainted by association with governments. As some Arab states have succeeded in coopting leftist and nationalist opposition groups, the Islamic fundamentalist movement is regarded as a principled and independent political force. Many people also argue that fundamentalists should be given a chance to experiment with the governmental process since everybody else has tried and failed, in the eyes of the populace. The 1960s and the 1970s marked the end of the appeal of leftism and the various brands of Arab socialism in the Arab world.

It is highly likely that this decade will entail major political changes in the Arab world. Many of the authoritarian leaders are getting older, and the prospects of smooth and peaceful transitions of power are farfetched in most Arab countries, where the realm of the ruler is indistinguishable from the realm of the state. Electoral choices will produce victories in several Arab countries. But the fundamentalists have failed to devise a recipe for change that would address the acute social and economic problems faced by the Arab people. In the absence of detailed and specific programs, the terms of fundamentalist governments will be quite limited in duration.

Much of the popularity of Muslim fundamentalism stems from its anti-establishment position. Islamic fundamentalists will not be discredited until they seize power. Fundamentalist movements have been operating on the basis of catchy but hollow slogans. The slogan "Islam is the solution," which was basically the program of the fundamentalists in Algeria, will eventually lose its appeal when people begin looking for real solutions to their acute social and economic problems. The fundamentalists are mistakenly assuming that their Islamic character will shield them from criticism once they hold the reins of power. When this writer asked Sheikh Muhammad Husayn Fadlallah (the "spiritual guide" of the Party of God in Lebanon, better known by its Arabic name, Hizballah) about his program for the impoverished Shi'ites of South Lebanon, he answered, "We do not need programs. We have the Qur'an." While clerical leaders can afford to claim to rely solely on the Qur'an in their lives, poor peasants and workers cannot use the Qur'an to pay their bills and feed their children. The crisis of legitimacy for the fundamentalists will be created by their attitude toward dissent, their dogmatic view of social and economic problems and by their exclusive composition that alienates many of the qualified (non-clerical) experts and technocrats.

Arab Discourse on Democracy

The subject of democracy and openness has been the focus of Arab intellectual debates since before the demise of communist rule. The Gulf War and the weakness of the Arab regional system exposed the need for political reforms and regional integration. The opportunistic exploitation of Islam by Saddam Hussein and the Saudi royal family and the defeat of tyrannical regimes in Eastern Europe only increased the demands for democratization and regional integration. While some Western analysts still insist that Arab nationalism is dead, the popular Arab reaction to the Gulf War reflected a unified mass reaction among the Arab masses of the *Mashriq* (the East) and the *Maghrib* (the North African region) which has been rare in contemporary Arab history. The failure of Saddam Hussein's brutal invasion of Kuwait (which was presented by Hussein as "unity" with Kuwait, and a rectification of colonial territorial inventions) and the collapse of the Soviet Union made it clear that unity-through-coercion will not last. Most Arabs now understand that unity without democracy will be short-lived.

The ideological debate in the Arab world today, particularly in the scholarly writings published by the Center of Arab Unity Studies in Beirut and by publishers of Arabic materials in London, focuses on the way in which Islam, Arab nationalism and democracy can be linked together harmoniously. Strict Islamic fundamentalists refuse to recognize forces of national loyalty because they see in Islam the only acceptable bond of collective allegiance. Furthermore, some Islamic fundamentalists see in Arab nationalism a secular danger to their aim of imposing Islamic religious laws on all citizens. Even some secular Arab nationalists are now trying to appease the fundamentalists by resorting to Qur'anic language and by avoiding a confrontation with the sectarian forces in the Arab world. Democratic enthusiasts have tried to reconcile Islam and democracy by simply maintaining that democracy is consistent with Islam because the Qur'an emphasizes the necessity of *shura* among Muslims. And the fundamentalists themselves are recognizing — at least verbally — the Arab population's thirst for democracy by pledging their commitment to the electoral process. Democracy is now central as a theme in Arab novels, poetry, movies and plays. The Iraqi press is now carrying articles about democracy, not so much because the government is willing to democratize, but because the regime is trying hard to win legitimacy. All Arab governments are now making promises of democratization an integral part of their political rhetoric.

Democracy in the Arab world is now understood by Arab intellectuals and people to mean real, effective institutions. No longer will the Arabs be misled by rubber-stamp parliaments or advisory councils such as the newly established one in Saudi Arabia. Arabs are now insisting on institutional democracy. In July 1991, a group of more than four hundred *ulema*, jurists and university professors emphasized to King Fahd of Saudi Arabia in a confidential memorandum that the proposed advisory council (which the king had been promising for several years) "should not be a mere rubber-stamp formality, as is the case in some countries." Democracy in the past was stigmatized in the minds of some Arabs due to their Western colonial heritage. Arabs after World War II were too proud to accept being seen as imitators of Western models and institutions. Arabs today are clearer and more specific about their political expectations. In today's Arab writings on the subject, it is clear that democratization means Western-style institutions, parliamentary representation, a one-person-one-vote electoral system, freedom of expression for political organizations, accountability of the elected, an independent judiciary and individual rights. The hollow slogans of *shura* arrangements often used in Arab Gulf regimes will not deceive or satisfy the Arab people.

Conclusion

While there is evidence of the spread of ideas of democratization in the Arab world, there are still some strong forces at play against the democratic trend. Not only are Arab governments still violently resisting the relinquishment of power which they have all attained illegally and/or violently, but there are various groups and minorities still being oppressed in various parts of the Arab world: women and homosexuals everywhere in the region; Kurds in Syria, Iraq and Lebanon; Blacks in Mauritania and Sudan; Berbers in North Africa; Palestinians in the Gulf, Lebanon and in the Occupied Territories; Christians, particularly Copts, in Egypt; and all Jews still living in Arab lands; and in general all the citizens of the oppressive Arab regimes. The Arab world will not be free merely with the elimination of the oppressive ruling governments. It will be free only when all Arab citizens, regardless of gender, religion, sexual orientation, racial background, ethnic affiliation, tribal lineage and political identification are equal before the law. This will not be achieved until the juridical hegemony of Muslim laws (*shari'ah*) is lifted and secular status laws are finally codified.

22

The Geopolitical Realities of Kurdistan vs. Hopes for a New World Order

Mehrdad Izady

The collapse and dissolution of the Soviet Union — the last of the European empires, whose boundaries bordered on the ethnic territories of the Kurds since 1813 — has drastically affected the balance of power in their region. The disbanding of that outdated superstate has nullified many of the old rules and eased the way for the further implosion of unworkable multi-ethnic polities in the region. In addition to the old USSR, several other multi-ethnic states have broken up, while some others have fused to provide independence or unification to ethnic groups who coveted such a change of status. Ethnic demands for independence, let alone internal autonomy, are no longer taboos, and are not condemned out of hand as subversive or externally motivated.

Like all other culturally and economically oppressed ethnic minorities, it is only natural to expect the Kurds to long for independence. In an opinion poll conducted by the Center for Research of the Kurdish Library in Brooklyn, 96% of the Kurdish respondents indicated they want an outright independence, with 89% adding that cultural and civil rights or autonomy alone will not be acceptable to them.[1] Here, therefore, I will only examine the possibility, scope, and various forms that an independent Kurdistan might take with regards to its geopolitics and in the context of the new world order. Autonomy in various forms and intensity has been tried in different segments of Kurdistan in the past. It is independence that has never been tried and is most wanted by the Kurdish public.

Living as national minorities within half a dozen independent states and over a vast stretch of territory from central Anatolia to central Asia, the impact of any change in the political climate on the Kurds directly correlates to how those changes affect the governments and states in which they live (Map 1). Hence, it is obvious that it is the political status of the Iraqi Kurds that is the most fluid and promising: the "new world order" has solidified over the crushed body of the Iraqi state.

246

Map 1

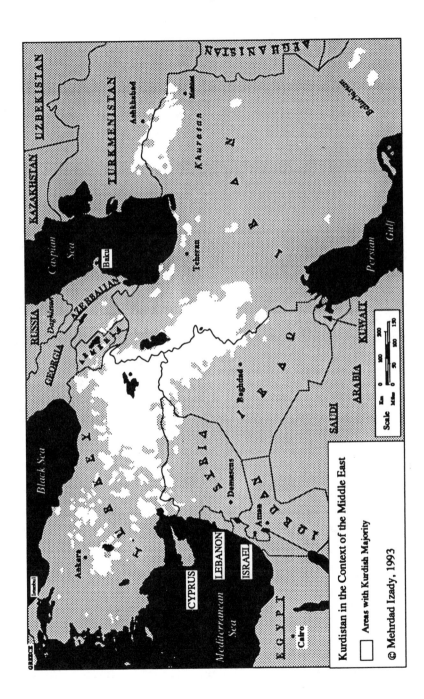

Kurdistan in the Context of the Middle East

Areas with Kurdish Majority

© Mehrdad Izady, 1993

What caused an easy independence for parts of the ethnic territories of the Armenians and Azeris, namely the demise of central (Soviet) state control over those territories, is also in existence in most of the Kurdish regions of Iraq. On the face of it, the prospects are set for the creation of an independent Kurdistan covering about a sixth of the land and a similar proportion of the total Kurdish population, i.e. Iraqi Kurdistan.

Externally, the geopolitical realities of Kurdistan place the question of independence for Iraqi Kurdistan, indeed any part of Kurdistan, under the solid and expanding shadow of Turkey, regardless of what political or military conditions obtain in Iraq. There is little need to substantiate this. A simple comparison between the reflection in the Western media of the Kurdish resistance in Turkey and Iraq should make this point amply clear. Waging the same type of struggle for their basic human and national rights, the Iraqi Kurds are heroes in the West, receiving overt Western assistance, while similar Kurdish resistance fighters in Turkey are routinely labeled as "terrorists" and "destabilizing separatists." This is simply because the former struggle is taking place on the territory of the demonized Iraq and the other in West-friendly Turkey. The Kurds in Iran and Syria are ignored completely because the West has decided to ignore Tehran and Damascus altogether. In sum, the external factor: the impact of the new world order on the Kurds is a subsidiary effect of any such impact on their home governments and needs to be studied in that context.

The internal factors affecting the Kurds involve the effective fragmentation of Kurdistan 70 years ago among five hostile world geopolitical blocs,[2] which has translated into a good deal of diversity of opinions, ethos, economic and social values among various Kurdish groups augmenting and intensifying the existing internal religious, linguistic and social pluralism that has been present among the Kurds and all other populous nations spread over vast territories.[3] The creation of a pan-Kurdish state may be frustrated as much by exasperating internal factors as by the hostile external barriers it needs to overcome.

Not since the end of the First World War has the world seen such a fluid condition in international boundaries and fundamental change in the internal politics of states on the Eurasian land mass. On that occasion Kurds turned out to be one of the major losers. Fragments of their territories were parceled out to five sovereign states — two of them, ironically, newly formed for the benefit of other neighboring ethnic groups. Much was said and written at the time about the necessity of a Kurdish state. Like the American president today, Woodrow Wilson was involved in that question, issuing statements in support of Kurdish (and Armenian and Arab) self-determination, but doing little else. Within a few years, all this had come to nought, a good deal of it because of Turkish objections and military operations (as today) and because the one disinterested Western country (England) saw the Turkish point of view and its own economic interest as superior to Kurdish aspirations for a state. In the aftermath, Kurds paid dearly through decades of bloody uprising, massacres and deportations. They also became the first nation to experience aerial bombardment of civilians (British Royal Air Force bombing of the Kurdish villages in northern Iraq, 1923–29),[4] and most recently, the first use of chemical weapons on their citizens (Halabja 1988). This bloody history of the Kurds in the twentieth century was all brought about by missing the window of opportunity of 1918–1921. Are the Kurds destined to miss this new opportunity as well?

Within 800 miles of Kurdistan now, over a score of new, ethnic-based independent countries have emerged, while two — East and West Germany and South and North Yemen — have coalesced. Three of these new states actually border on Kurdistan: Armenia, Azerbaijan and Georgia. Like the Kurds, ethnic Armenians, Azeris and Georgians had long struggled for independence, and now they are in possession of their own territories, basically by the default of the Soviet Union. What are the prospects for similar developments for ethnic Kurds? Let us look at some important statistics on various fragments of Kurdistan, and then examine what renders the Kurdish situation similar or different from these other ethnic groups, from Germany to Kyrgyzistan.

Turkey by itself contains more than half the Kurds living today. Approximately 52% of the Kurds live in that state, followed by Iran which contains about 26% of the Kurds. The Iraqi share of the overall Kurdish population was about 17% until 1975, but many years of cross-border expulsions and emigration have left Iraqi Kurdistan with barely 15% of all Kurds, and possibly as little as 12%. The Kurdish population of Syria adds up to about 5% of the total, while the remaining 2–3% are now dispersed in Armenia, Azerbaijan, Georgia, Turkmenistan, Kazakhstan, Uzbekistan and Lebanon.[5] There are also several hundred thousand Kurdish "guest-workers" and asylum seekers in diaspora, in Europe and elsewhere. From these figures, it is obvious that what affects the Kurds of Turkey is what counts for the general Kurdish future. But is it possible for the totality or a majority or the Kurds to gain independence, when this would require the implausible redrawing of boundaries of half a dozen sovereign states to accommodate the Kurds fully? What other alternatives are available and internationally practiced before, making the Kurdish aspiration for independence pragmatic?

Numerically, ethnic Kurds are larger than all other nationalities who have gained their independence through the demise of the old world order, except the Ukrainians (approximately 27 million Kurds vs. 52 million Ukrainians). Like the Armenians and Azeris, the Kurdish ethnic territories stretch over several state boundaries (Map 2). Besides the Armenian Republic, a large number of Armenians are to be found outside its borders, in Azerbaijan, Georgia and Iran, while the bulk of the Azeris actually live in Iran, with the Republic of Azerbaijan only second in the number of Azeris it represents. Southeastern Georgia is also solidly Azeri, while ethnic Azeris are also found in Russia (in the territories of Daghistan), with smaller numbers in Armenia and Turkey. The detached, Azeri-inhabited territory of Nakhichivan also belongs to the Republic of Azerbaijan. Kurds, like these two newly independent ethnic groups, are spread over several state boundaries, and in this

Map 2

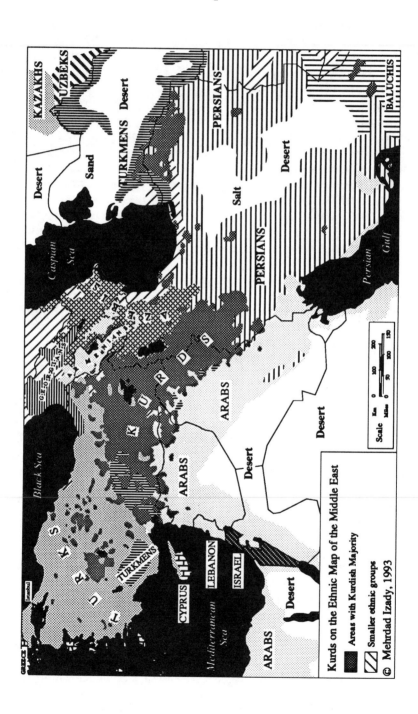

Kurds on the Ethnic Map of the Middle East

respect they are not at an initial disadvantage. In fact the phenomenon of ethnic dispersion over many political boundaries is rather commonplace in the Middle East and Central and Eastern Europe. While ethnic Arabs fill over 20 independent states, they are also found as ethnic minorities in many more. Ethnic Persians run Iran, Afghanistan and Tajikistan and live as indigenous minorities in another half dozen neighboring countries. Even the ethnic Turks, who are the most compact of ethnic groups in the area, are found also as minorities in Bulgaria, Romania, Greece, Macedonia and Serbia. In Europe, ethnic Hungarians are found in large numbers in all countries neighboring Hungary, and Germans are sovereign in four states (five, until the unification of East and West Germany), are the majority in Switzerland, and constitute large ethnic minorities from northern Italy, northeastern France and western Poland to Transylvania, Russia and Kazakhstan.[6]

There is no reason, therefore, to contemplate only a single, pan-Kurdish state covering all territories with a Kurdish majority. In fact the internal diversity of the Kurdish nation (not too dissimilar to the Arabs) may favor a multiple political status for various Kurdish populations, at least for the time being. Noting the above alternatives drawn from the experience of other ethnic groups, one can speculate about a Kurdish state that comprised only a large portion of the ethnic domain of the Kurds (like the Republic of Armenia), or even one which included a minority of their ethnic total (like the Republic of Azerbaijan). The future may augment this with many more independent "Kurdistans" (like the case of the ethnic Germans), or one independent state augmented by representation of the rest as ethnic minorities in neighboring states (like the Hungarians). It is a fact that since there also exist two large detached enclaves of ethnic Kurds outside contiguous Kurdistan, it would be impossible to include all territories with a Kurdish ethnic majority into a hypothetical pan-Kurdish state without also taking in vast numbers of non-Kurds. The two largest detached enclaves, those in central Anatolia and in Khurasan (northeast Iran in central Asia), with several million Kurdish inhabitants, are Kurdish islands in seas of Turkish and Persian ethnic domains and will have to be left out of any scheme for a pan-Kurdish state. They could only join other Kurds if they chose to emigrate from their homes of several hundred years and settle in a hypothetical independent Kurdistan. More likely, however, they will remain behind. The over two million-strong Hungarian ethnic enclave in Transylvania is similarly located like an island in a Romanian ethnic sea. It simply cannot be joined to Hungary without taking in more Romanians than ethnic Hungarians in the balance.

The demise of the Soviet Union has had the unlikely effect of placing the question of Kurdish independence again in the hands of Ankara, even for non-Turkish-administered portions of Kurdistan. This situation is only marginally different from what prevailed at the end of the First World War and caused the Kurdish aspiration for a state of their own to founder even though they came so close to attaining it. While Ankara has legally exasperated

Kurdish national dreams within Turkey, it is also actively and illegally frustrating the chance for an independent state for the Iraqi Kurds.[7] The Western power now listening to Turkey's concerns and demands is the United States. It was the British empire in 1921.

In all this, interestingly, the Iranian Kurds find themselves rather unaffected. Why so? Varied past histories, different ethnic relationships, demographic trends, and contending internal state policies vis-a-vis the Kurds have combined to render the fragments of the Kurdish nation with very different feelings and attitudes towards their own future, and have created contradictory prospects for their future. Let us look at these differences and their impact on the Kurdish future, while noting the consequences that each state with a Kurdish minority will have to face by letting go of its Kurds. Let us remember once again, that not all Kurds can be realistically let go (those dispersed in other ethnic regions) or might want to go. Four percent of those responding to the opinion survey mentioned above did not choose independence for Kurdistan at all, and many more will find it economically a bad choice to resettle in an independent Kurdistan from bustling cities such as Istanbul, Tehran, Baghdad or Damascus.

Turkey: Without its deeply Asiatic Kurdish territories and citizens, Turkey would be practically a European state, economically (rich agriculture and manufacturing exports), demographically (low, European growth rates), educationally (nearly 85% literate), politically (functioning multi-party system), and nearly geographically (part of Turkey is actually on the European continent). Such a divorce would pave a very clear road in Europe for Turkey's future, reducing or eliminating the strong objection of the other EC members to Turkey's entry.[8] There are no other important ethnic minorities living in Turkey besides the Kurds, and such a divorce would create out of Turkey a true "Country of the Turks" as the state name implies. The natural wealth of Kurdistan has been thus far no match for the cost of the upkeep of this unintegrated part of the Turkish Republic, economically, politically, and psychologically.

The strategic water resources of Kurdistan (the Tigris-Euphrates river system) would be irrelevancies to a Turkey divorced of its Kurdish territories. The Kurdish east is geologically and hydrologically distinct and detached from peninsular Turkey. Kurdish water resources are only concerns of the Arab countries of Syria and Iraq, and others farther south. Even the major agricultural-hydrological developments envisaged now by Turkey in the "East Anatolian Project" (GAP in Turkish)[9] matter primarily to Kurdistan regions and not the rest of the country, and at any rate will amount to little when set against the cost of revamping the economy and revitalizing the society in depressed eastern Turkey (i.e. Kurdistan). In giving up Kurdistan, Turkey would give up only a liability, very similar to Russia's giving up the poverty-stricken, demographically exploding central Asian republics. But can there be a meaningful separation of the Kurdish and Turkish citizens of Turkey, to allow for two new states representing totally or near-totally the Turks and the Kurds? Probably not.

Nearly half the ethnic Kurds in Turkey may now actually live west of the Euphrates River, the oft-mentioned, traditional western boundary of "Kurdistan." The flood of economic migrants, job-seekers, and those simply escaping the harsher natural and political conditions in the Kurdish mountains, should tip the balance further. Short of some draconian measures in "ethnic cleansing," any disassociation arrangements between Turkey and its Kurdish minority will leave behind millions of Kurds dispersed in the larger Turkish cities and western Anatolian provinces. A demographic revolution causing a "population explosion" within the economically and educationally backward Kurdish populations of Turkey is exacerbating this situation to the point of precluding any pragmatic way of separating ethnic Kurds from the Turks within 30 years time: there would be simply too many Kurds mixed spatially with too many Turks within the Republic of Turkey to warrant any meaningful "separation."[10] By then there will be at least as many Kurds as Turks in the state, if not actually more, and they will be living in a strongly mixed ethnic state. There may be no need for a separation, as the question will soon be "in what configuration?"

If the chances of a separation of Kurds from Turkey are thus receding, thanks to the forces of demography, why should the Turks worry about a Kurdish state outside their present borders? Mostly paranoia, mixed with the fear of repercussions for so many decades of neglecting the welfare of their own Kurds, should an independent Kurdistan emerge anywhere. However, once the Kurds are economically and socially integrated into the mainstream of Turkish state life, and the Kurdish political elite and ambitious individuals are given an equal chance of promotion in the state political and financial apparatus without having to first renounce their Kurdish identity, the fear of an ethnic explosion will recede.

We need only to look at the Iranian Azeris for a model. Perhaps proportionately as many Azeris live in Iran as Kurds do in Turkey. The bulk of the Azeris too have left the Azeri provinces and are widely scattered throughout the Iranian state, reaching the pinnacle of all political, economic, and social hierarchies without the need to renounce their Azeri identity. The emergence of an independent Azerbaijan Republic from the ashes of the Soviet Union has caused little concern in Iran, and no uprising of the Iranian Azeris to join their ethnic brethren has occurred. Treating its Kurds as the Iranians treat the Azeris, Turkey may equally need have no lasting fear of the motivations of its citizens.

Iran: Iranian Kurds are present in that state not as a result of a recent award of their territories by the colonial empires to that country. They have in fact been living in that state since at least the beginning of sixteenth century, and realistically for much longer, as they were included in many Iranian states since ancient times, sometimes run by royal houses of Kurdish extraction.[11] The boundaries that divide the Iranian Kurds from the rest of their kinspeople were set in the sixteenth century during the formative wars between the Ottoman and Persian empires. Iranian Kurds, therefore, carry with them a connection to the Iranian state far more deeply than other Kurds do to their respective states, all of which were formed in their current shape and definition only after the end of the First World War.

Being linguistically and culturally themselves an Iranic people, Kurds share with the Persians and other Iranic peoples, like the Afghans, Tajiks and the Baluchis, many fundamental elements of their ethnic identity. In fact the Kurdish, Persian and Baluchi languages are as closely related as German, Swedish and English.[12] It is difficult for a Kurd to complain of the specifics of cultural oppression by the Iranian state, since many national celebrations, beliefs, and practices of the Kurds are also those celebrated statewide in the country. With the expanding volume of Kurdish publications in Iran and now the constitutional guarantee for parallel education in the ethnic languages alongside Persian in elementary and secondary schools, fewer points of friction are found to warrant a widespread uprising or politicizing of the Iranian Kurds. Many Kurdish individuals have attained high political and social status. A Kurd, Karim Sanjabi, for example, has been heading the most important non-religious political party in Iran, the National Front, for the past few decades.

In addition to the parts of contiguous Kurdistan that straddle the western and northwestern frontiers of Iran, a very large and detached Kurdish enclave is found 700 miles away on the northeastern frontier of Iran with Turkmenistan in central Asia (Map 1). There are many more populous pockets of Kurds in the Alburz Mountains in northern Iran as well. The Iranian Kurds also constitute the most heterogeneous group of Kurds among the five fragments of greater Kurdistan, practicing many religions and speaking many distinct dialects. In any divorce, a very large number of Kurds thus would have to be left behind, or relocated. Despite all the bonds with Iran and the internal diversity, what if the Kurds in Iran chose to leave?

As the heir to the Persian empire, Iran shares some of the features of that old-fashioned empire, made up basically of a collection of distinct ethnic groups, with the Persians constituting just over half the population. Allowing the Kurds to go would break asunder along its ethnic seams the entire fabric of that ancient empire. There would be little incentive for the other dozen or so ethnic groups to stay on once the Kurds — the third largest ethnic group in the country (after the Persians and the Azeris) — were allowed to leave. Iran would cease to exist as it has for millennia. The economic implications of any such Kurdish disassociation on the Iranian state need not be contemplated, as the political and social ones are dire enough. Iran will not allow the Kurds to go, as this would be tantamount to the complete disbanding of that state. By the same rationale, if other ethnic groups, e.g. the Azeris or Arabs, break away, Kurdish independence from Iran will too become almost inevitable.

Iraq: In no other state is Kurdistan and the Kurdish ethnic group as compact and their culture and society as distinct from the other groups as in Iraq. They occupy a solidly Kurdish region in the north and northeast of the country, with very few mixed ethnic areas or internal diasporas in Arab Iraq. Nearly one-third of all Iraqi oil deposits are within the Kurdish areas, and with it the bulk of oil facilities and refineries at Kirkuk. Iraq has much more oil in its Arab south, and could hardly miss the loss of the Kurdish oil. But the loss of Kurdistan would cost Iraq dearly on other strategic grounds. Nearly all the river waters of the otherwise arid Iraq have their source in Kurdish highlands in general, and nearly half of it (the Tigris catchment area) in Iraqi Kurdistan itself. The loss of Kurdistan would place Iraq at the mercy of Kurdistan for this increasingly strategic resource. Iraq would also lose all its highland territories, and become the flat alluvial plains of Mesopotamia and parts of the Syrian desert. With the Kurds gone, Iraq would become nearly totally Arab, with a 85–90% Shi'ite majority.

With oil exporting facilities and pipelines to the Mediterranean (via Turkey and Syria) already in place, rich agricultural and mineral resources, Iraqi Kurdistan could contain all the Kurds of that state without a need for population exchanges or "ethnic cleansing." It also has one of the most highly educated Kurdish populations, well-suited for self-rule and independence. The landlocked nature of this smaller independent Kurdistan need not be a problem, as most of the countries in Central Europe are also landlocked, as are all newly independent republics in central Asia and the Caucasus, with the exception of Georgia. In fact the proximity of this Kurdistan to its market, an excellent road system to the neighboring states and Europe added to the existing oil pipelines to the open seaports, renders the landlocked argument rather meaningless.

Syria: Once cannot talk of a Syrian Kurdistan, but rather of Syrian Kurdish regions. There are three detached areas of Kurdish concentrations along the northern borders of Syria and Turkey. This was brought about when the French colonial administration of the Mandate of Syria unimaginatively took the course of the Mosul-Aleppo railroad tracks to represent its territorial boundaries with that of newly emerging Turkey. The railroad just happened to cross into and emerge out of the Kurdish-inhabited territories in three separate places!

Since these pieces cannot be joined without taking in equal numbers of ethnic Arabs as well, the Syrian Kurdish regions can only hope to merge with any hypothetical Kurdish state formed from Turkish Kurdistan. Since the chances of the latter are receding for the reasons described above, the Syrian Kurds, forming a mere 9% of the Syrian population, cannot be expected to achieve anything more meaningful than cultural autonomy from Damascus. The economic implication of the loss of Kurdish territories to Syria would be minimal; strategically, it would mean a more exposed Aleppo, which is already precariously close to the Syrian border with Turkey.

Commonwealth of Independent States: In the territories of the former Soviet Union, Kurds used to be found near the Iranian and Turkish borders in the Caucasus, and the Iranian border with Turkmenistan. In the course of the 1940s and Stalin's massive deportation programs, the entire Kurdish population of Georgia from the districts of Akhaltzikhe and Akhalkhalaki was deported to central Asia and Siberia. They are still there in Kazakhistan,

Kyrgyzistan and Uzbekistan. In Armenia Kurds fared much better, even though they came to be swamped by the expanding Armenian population, arriving themselves as war refugees from the Ottoman empire, and later from other points in diaspora. The Kurds in Azerbaijan and Turkmenistan have seen the official stripping of their ethnic identification from them. They are, however, there in force. The entire land bridge between the Armenian enclave of Ngorno Karabakh and Armenia proper is populated by Kurds, who thus have a strategic importance to both Armenians and the Azeris who would like to keep the Armenian enclave detached and within their state territories. The towns of Kelbajar, Lachin, Kubatli and Zangilan, all on the border of Armenia and Azerbaijan, are Kurdish, and have recently been caught in the crossfire of the Armenian-Azerbaijani conflict and have witnessed expulsions (nearly 20,000 Kurds in the case of Lachin city). This and other Kurdish enclaves in the Caucasus are not connected with contiguous Kurdistan, and their only concern would be a form of cultural autonomy within their respective states in the Caucasus. Altogether, there are only about 350,000 Kurds living in the CIS — although this is still double the latest official Soviet census of 1990. Obliging to Azeri and Turkmen feelings, the Kurds of those two republics had not been included in the official censuses since 1924.

While the opposition of the Iranian and Iraqi governments to the separation of their Kurdish territories is understandable, that of Turkey is far less so, especially since the ethnic mixture in that state has not yet reached the point at which division becomes impracticable. The Czechs let go of the poorer Slovaks, and the Anglo-Canadians will at any moment let go of the Franco-Canadians if they so choose. However, the Turks, Persians and Arabs, along with everybody else in the Middle East, have not reached that degree of social awareness and economic consciousness needed to put their peace, prosperity and tranquility above their preference for territory for the sake of territory, even when the latter entails a poorer economy, bloodstained daily lives of their citizenry, and the accumulation of human rights abuse cases by the day.

The Iraqi Kurds have now become politically, economically, socially and historically logical and practical candidates for independence. They have not, however, been able either to secure the crucial factor of external support, or (so far) to make their case for independence acceptable to the West, particularly the United States. To their chagrin, not much can be expected to change in the short term, since the arch foe of any expression of Kurdish existence, Turkey, has ended up on the winning side of the Cold War. What is more is that it is becoming increasingly true that what is good for Turkey in the Middle East is good for the United States (similar to the case made for Iran under the Shah). In fact, if anything Turkish status in Western eyes will continue to be enhanced, as the bloodshed in the Balkans, the Caucasus and central Asia continues and the Kurdish case becomes yesterday's news. The rigor with which pseudo-history and geography is being invented and circulated both in Ankara and the West, declaring Turkey the "key" to the

Asiatic republics of the former Soviet Union in the Caucasus and central Asia, and now the Balkans, is a strong sign that the honeymoon will continue and prosper in the future.[13]

While the prospects of independence for the Iraqi Kurds thus remain blocked, not a shred of Western support for the Kurds of Turkey can be expected in the foreseeable future either, unless of course Washington and Ankara special relations cool. The cases of the sudden fall from favor of Iran and Iraq, both once courted by the West, could repeat itself vis-a-vis Turkey. And this is not as farfetched as it seems. The speedy crumbling of the U.S.-Iran special relationship once the Shah was out of that "island of stability," can serve as an example, if not the speedy disgrace of Iraq after its invasion of Kuwait. A religious fundamentalist takeover or military adventurism by the Turks in the Caucasus, Balkans or even Iraq could all precipitate a sudden change of heart in the West, allowing the Iraqi Kurds to go their way without the detrimental factor of Ankara. This is however a big if.

Time is also a crucial factor. With the mess in the ex-Yugoslavia and the Caucasus, the vogue of ethnic groups declaring independence and rather automatically receiving support is fast fading. The Kurds, particularly the Iraqi Kurds, who are most ready for independence, seem destined to lose this opportunity as well, almost regardless of what happens to the special relationship between Turkey and the United States.

Notes

1. Vera Beaudin-Saeedpour, "Kurdish Hopes, Kurdish Fears: A Survey of Kurdish Public Opinion," *The International Journal of Kurdish Studies* 5;1–2 (1992).
2. Kurds have had the dubious distinction of being the only ethnic group in the world to have their people and ethnic territories represented in four world geopolitical power blocs (five, until the collapse of the Soviet Union and the Warsaw Pact). They are present in force in the NATO bloc (in Turkey), Arab bloc (in Syria and Iraq), and the central and south Asian blocs (in Iran and Turkmenistan). In fact, except for the Germans, Kurds were quietly the only ethnic group whose home territories served as the front line of fire for both NATO and Warsaw Pact since their formations.
3. While Sunni Islam is practiced and Kurmanji dialect spoken by a majority of the Kurds, three other dialects are spoken by about 40% of the Kurds, and non-Sunni Islam, Yazdanism, Christianity and Judaism practiced by about equal numbers of Kurds today. In this respect the Kurds are similar to the Germans, as they too practice various denominations of Christianity and speak (far less now than before the promotion of High German to the status of state standard language) many dialects of German at home.
4. Michael Gunter, *The Kurds of Iraq* (New York: St. Martin, 1992), p. 3.
5. Mehrdad Izady, *The Kurds: A Concise Handbook* (Washington: Taylor & Francis, 1992), pp. 111–18.
6. An excellent source demarcating the extent of ethnic domains of the Kurds and other world nationalities remains S.I. Bruk and V.S. Apenchenko, *Atlas Narodov Mira* (Moscow: Academy of Science, 1964).
7. Illegally, because it constitutes interference in the internal affairs of a foreign, sovereign state, namely Iraq.
8. With Kurdistan gone, there would be a marked reduction in all objections towards Turkey's entry, e.g., high birth rates and large poverty-stricken (primarily Kurdish) underclass, high cases of human rights violations (compiled, again, primarily in respect to the Kurdish situation), low economic performance (backward Kurdistan counted with more advanced western Turkey).
9. The much-advertised projected revenue from the sale of water to the thirsty countries of the Middle East downstream is in reality a minor part of the project, and its relatively small revenue unimportant in the balance.
10. Mehrdad Izady, "Kurdish Demographic Trends," *The International Journal of Kurdish Studies* 6;1–2 (1993).

11. Most recently, by the Zand dynasty (AD 1750–94).
12. Kurdish is a member of the Northwestern division of the Iranic branch of the Indo-European family of languages, distinct from Semitic Arabic or Altaic Turkish. In addition to Persian, Kurdish is naturally related to other Indo-European languages like Armenian, French, English or Russian.
13. There is nothing, for example, which relates the central Asians to Turkey other than the kinship between their languages and the state language of Turkey, and that is similar to the relationship which linguistically connects German to English, Swedish, Dutch or Norwegian. Beside being of interest to the linguists, this is not much of a relationship to invest upon. There is far more that Iran and Afghanistan have in common historically and culturally with central Asia than Turkey does.

23

Why Palestine Should Stand Up for Itself

Edward W. Said

The new world order has not been spoken about much recently. With his listless re-election campaign taking him from one opportunity to make promises to the next, George Bush, the man who revived the phrase, stopped trying to address the world at large, much less manage a coherent foreign policy. The problems, however, remain; nowhere with more depressing results and prospects than in the Middle East. Operation Desert Storm was supposed to have been the centerpiece in the new world order, that post-Cold War concept of multilateral internationalism with the U.S. as everyone's impartial big brother. The bullying triumphalism of the Gulf War itself left Saddam Hussein still in power, along with Kuwait justly restored to sovereignty, albeit relatively unimproved, its large and productive expatriate population shabbily driven out.

The invidious aspect of U.S. policy towards Iraq after the war has not only been its merciless violations of Iraqi sovereignty, nor its complete indifference to the dreadful state of Iraq's civilian population, nor even its off-again on-again policy of quarantining, threatening, destabilizing the Hussein regime (which it actually supported during the Ba'athi genocide against the Kurds), but the selectively moralistic and hectoring application of these policies.

After all, the region is full of regimes whose depredations and attacks against its own people approach Saddam's, without much of a response from the U.S. When Saudi Arabia expelled 800,000 Yemenis in 1990 and 1991, no objection was registered. Kuwait, Syria, Sudan, Tunisia, Morocco, Algeria practice human rights abuses, most of them unctuously overlooked as a result of strategic calculation and indifference. Israel, of course, remains a consistent offender, systematically abusing an entire people for years and years, all the while enjoying an annual American subsidy of between five and six billion dollars.

The inconsistencies go even further. The Bush administration proclaimed its commitment to arms reduction. This has been wonderfully convenient to do in the case of Russia, but less so in the case of wealthy governments willing to pay cash for U.S. planes and missiles. Saudi Arabia and Taiwan have been negotiating for multi-billion dollar deals that would give them the latest in jet fighters and missiles.

Towards the end of his term in office, President Bush specifically outlined a program of arms limitations for the Middle East, which has been scrupulously applied to poor Lebanon (whose struggling army really does need arms) but just as scrupulously violated for Saudi Arabia whose gigantic arsenal, now increased in size by an additional purchase of nine billion dollars in F-15s, is disproportionate with its capacity for actually defending itself.

With such profits at hand the Bush administration prudently said nothing about the new world order or about a diminution in the scale of support for the Israeli military. And nothing at all either about Israel's continuing unwillingness to sign the nuclear proliferation protocols.

That therefore leaves the "peace process" as the Bush administration's major post-Cold War achievement (charity enjoins us to overlook such minor fiascos as its Libyan policy, for instance, to say nothing of policies towards Bosnia, Haiti, Somalia, and the environment). In the great chorus of praise for James Baker for getting the parties together at Madrid and thereafter, not enough attention was paid to the anomalies and anachronisms in his approach.

In the first place the U.S. letter of invitation to Madrid specifically prevented the United Nations from playing any active role in the process. This was a rather narrow view to take for a power that had insisted throughout the Gulf War on the UN's centrality to its policy. Why then this sudden about-face? One of the reasons suggested at the time was that Israel had sensitivities about the UN's impartiality, and was therefore unlikely to approve. By any decently consistent standard of universality this argument should have been unacceptable, but it was made a precondition, which all the participants (the UN itself included) accepted. Thus Madrid was to be an American show, with the Soviet Union as dubious and purely formal co-sponsor, and a host of other countries, as well as regional and international organizations (the UN included) present as observers.

In the second place, a large number of, in my view, crippling preconditions were laid on one party, the Palestinians. There was the familiar, and yet stupidly inappropriate, prohibition of the PLO. Whatever its egregious faults, the PLO is universally acknowledged to be the representative of the Palestinian people, most consistently by the Palestinians themselves.

As Abba Eban said at the time, this sort of condition was unique to the history of conflict, that one party should be able to pick the representative of the other party. With American complaisance, this condition was accepted, even though the PLO was not only consulted at every step, but remained in fact to direct the Palestinian delegation behind the scenes. Another condition banned all but "acceptable" Palestinians from the West Bank and Gaza; no one from Jerusalem was allowed direct participation, and no one either from the population of Palestinian exiles (referred to occasionally as Diaspora Palestinians).

Final status issues, the matter of Jerusalem, questions having to do with the exiles who now constitute a majority of the Palestinian population and who linger as stateless persons for the most part in the refugee camps of Syria, Lebanon and Jordan: all these were proscribed from discussion. As the price for entry into the peace process this was rather high, but it was paid accordingly (with some ingenious attempts at circumventing the obstacles) because it appeared that there was no alternative to this U.S.-organized forum.

If there is one thing that has characterized the thinking of everyone since the end of the Cold War, it is this fatalistic sense that the U.S. provides the only forum and is court, judge, and jury of last appeal. No one needs to be reminded of how the U.S. got the Saudis and Kuwaitis to pay for the Gulf War even as it bullied, cajoled, and otherwise convinced an assortment of countries to join its UN-based coalition.

I recall that the spring and summer before Madrid I had several conversations with Italian, British, Irish, and Swedish government officials about the U.S. free hand in the war's aftermath. Why was it, I asked, that Europe didn't take more of a role? Invariably I was told that "it's their game" with a fatalistic and even supine passivity I found difficult to comprehend.

A similar attitude to Europe's rules the day in the Arab world. Egypt is now an impoverished American client, dependent on a quarterly dole (itself requiring certificates of good behavior) from the U.S. It shuffles inevitably to Washington for succor and direction. As a group, the Gulf states are wealthy, of course, but they are totally subservient to the U.S. Much the same is true of Morocco, Syria, Tunisia, whose internal problems and the absence of alternative outside patronage put them in no mood to confront or even disagree with the U.S. Jordan for its pains in trying somehow to craft an independent Arab position is regularly put through undignified ordeals, with its aid turned off by the U.S. one day, and demands for unilateral inspection pressed the next.

Always there is this strange contradiction, a persistent cultural, perhaps also emotional, hostility to the U.S., and an ineluctable yielding to it at the same time. The notion that there should be dialogue and discussion with, plus careful critique of, the U.S. occupies no significant place in the cultural economy of the Arab world. To my knowledge there is still no institute anywhere in the Arab world whose main purpose is the study of the U.S. There is not even a university department of American studies.

Consider also that most of the men (always men) who constitute ruling circles in Egypt, Iraq, Jordan, perhaps Syria, Lebanon, and the Gulf, are American-educated; far from giving them some insight into how the U.S. operates, this background seems to have given them only a sort of nostalgia for the American way of doing things, a myth that keeps them mentally in line with whatever Washington wishes, or seems to wish. If this isn't cultural imperialism I do not know what is, a Sadatian legacy without Sadat's gumption and dash. Perhaps a better phrase for it is, to borrow from the African-American movement, a nigger mentality. Look with favor on us, and we will do your bidding.

Most disheartening is the almost total unavailability of a collective Arab identity, the result of willed amnesia, on which to draw for sustenance and a healthier perspective on cultural difference. No wonder then that the gap between the bureaucratic and military elites in the Arab world (which is where the defeatism is) and the disenfranchised and disempowered is so great. And that gap of course is where the various and sundry Islamic groupings have pitched their tents.

This retreat into quietism and terminal supplication vis-a-vis a mystified idea of the U.S. is nowhere more disheartening than within the Palestinian national movement, particularly (but not exclusively) its expatriate leadership. Granted that the struggle is inhumanly uneven: no twentieth century liberation or independence movement in the Third World has had so difficult a set of enemies, has had expatriation and the total absence of sovereignty to contend with, and has had so inhospitable and treacherous a local environment to negotiate, as well as so many continuous debacles, massacres, losses to comprehend, all without a major power as strategic ally. But it still does not follow from those appalling circumstances that we needed to throw everything not just into the American basket but in the hands of so ill-suited a pair of champions as Bush and Baker.

While it is undeniable that Baker exerted himself on behalf of a Palestinian component in the peace process as no one before him, I found it quite astonishing that as secretary of state, Baker acquired a halo in the eyes of some Palestinian leaders. It occurred to none of the people that quite aside from his personal prepossessions, Baker was an official of a government whose record and actual performance all across the Middle East and the Third World stood against what Palestinians were fighting for — self-determination, human rights, social justice. Instead of hesitant, critical, and skeptical engagement on a variety of fronts with the U.S., there was, I believe, an unseemly rush to make Palestinians acceptable to the U.S., turning the whole history of our struggle and our sacrifices into so much ballast that could be jettisoned whenever an American or Israeli request was made.

Much of this stems from a radical misapprehension of how the U.S. functions as a system. It was assumed by Palestinians with no history at all of residence in or literacy about the U.S. that the U.S. was a dictatorship, and what Baker (like Hafez el-Assad, perhaps) wanted, Baker got. For at least 15 years a number of us in the U.S. have been saying to our leadership that only a parallel campaign inside the U.S. on behalf of Palestinian human rights would improve conditions, widen the context, enhance the prospects for those rights inside the peace process itself.

In order to mount such a campaign, even at a time when a significant number of Americans, including many Jews, appear to be in favor of Palestinian self-determination, there would have had to be a political resolve to do it, and to give such a campaign maximum attention, the way, for instance, the anti-apartheid movement did it, or the way the Vietnamese, Nicaraguans, and others did it in the past. We would have had to work the system, mastering the complexities of the ethnic, academic, ecclesiastical, media, Congressional, and other environments, above all working with our allies here.

But alas this has not happened. Instead there has been a long-standing wish to find someone "important" or well-placed (always a white man, by the way) whose advice and contact would be worshipfully sought or otherwise rewarded. A quick fix seemed always to be promised. Starting in the fall of 1991, the Palestinian delegation arrived in Washington, armed with the best intentions, stayed for a bit, then left, also with the best intentions. Some of these admirable people told me how disappointed they were with the U.S., as if the promises made by Baker to get us into Madrid had been believed totally, but were now shown to be what they always were, a matter of great power interest and expediency.

The Palestinian leadership's attitude even went so far as to promise further concessions and drop long-standing principles (the rights of representation, of return, and of participation for the Palestinian exile community, for instance) even as the rhetoric of struggle continued on the ground. Literally nothing was done in the U.S., the premise for that particular bit of self-denial being, as best as I can make it out, a fear that were we to do anything to challenge U.S. policy within the U.S., Bush and Baker might in the end "give" us nothing. This unattractive amiability took us as far as appearing to endorse the "Bush-Baker" ticket, as it was called by one Palestinian delegate, in the election campaign. That Bush had himself given up to the Pats Buchanan and Robertson in the meantime, or that he had handed Israel a $10 billion loan guarantee with no strings attached seemed to matter very little. The idea was to keep close to the Big Man, and to do it at virtually all costs.

I do not want to be misunderstood. I certainly supported (and still do support) Palestinian participation in the peace process, just as I have believed in and acted on behalf of co-existence for two peoples in two states in historic Palestine. I am under no illusion that there is any other way but difficult step-by-step negotiation to win us our self-determination. But in the rush to acknowledge American primacy we put aside some principles of our national history, and — worse yet — made it difficult for all Palestinians to struggle for a better life. That I think was unwise. There is now some disenchantment with the leadership in Tunis, which guides the Palestinian delegation's herculean efforts in the bilaterals. Explaining, rationalizing, above all, leveling with the people about the necessities of the peace process has not been given requisite importance. Sudden changes of position indicate volatility but not a slow and patient policy of constructive detail. High hopes followed by bitter disappointment: this tends to be the pattern rather than to act on the ground for what is right and can be achieved through planning, organization, mobilization. Worst of all, a silly factionalism sometimes undermines the common effort.

My own reading of the Palestinian struggle, and indeed of the very question of Palestine itself, is that for several decades we have been a local movement acting locally of course, but spearheading a whole series of other struggles in a movement towards greater democracy and justice for minorities, women, and other disenfranchised groups in the Arab and Israeli world. That is the real meaning of the question of Palestine. But it is one thing to try to dismantle a web of oppressive and discriminatory laws (as, for example, put in by the Israelis for the Occupied Territories) and quite another to maneuver exclusively in a space (the so-called peace process) created, maintained, and defended by the United States with the basic aim of preserving the status quo, with a few adjustments here and there.

One can see the difference between the two spheres even in the matter of language. To agitate against, say, a law that specifically prohibits Palestinians from growing a new fruit tree without a permit requires quite a different vocabulary — one that is more concrete and detailed — and a different energy than is required to involve oneself in a negotiation behind closed doors inside the U.S. State Department, which has all along been financing and supporting the Israeli occupation. You speak, act, think, so differently in the second as, in a sense, to minimize or otherwise neutralize the first.

The point is that such a result perfectly suits the Israelis, for whom the word "peace" often means something both vague and desirable from a public relations standpoint. For Palestinians, when their signatures are attached to a document, peace can be an illusory concept essentially legitimizing Israeli control over the land; what the Israelis propose now is in effect to let Palestinians run the details of their daily lives, in the fields of education, sanitation, social welfare, etc., but to keep control of land, water, security and foreign affairs in their hands. Thus autonomy for the people, but not for the land, which is a state of affairs not unlike that of the South African tribal homelands.

Without a parallel effort in the West — a massive campaign for Palestinian human rights that essentially raises the reality of Palestinian life under occupation and in exile to such visibility and power as to both illuminate and give real substance to the peace process — the negotiations in Washington can become very unsatisfactory indeed. While Israeli diplomats exchange notes and ideas with Palestinian delegates in Washington more land slips away from Palestinian hands, more people are imprisoned, more water is siphoned off.

To have expected George Bush and James Baker to put a stop to these things was about like waiting for Godot. With Clinton in office, we need to ask ourselves publicly what his particular "vision-thing" for the Middle East is. Certainly he is no more in favor of Palestinian self-determination than his predecessor was, or in a less warlike and aggressively armed Israel; besides, his administration has tacitly endorsed a stepped-up strategic partnership with Israel to offset the 72 F-15s purchased by Saudi Arabia. There isn't much that official Washington has done in the Middle East that suggests a great interest in democracy, in human rights and justice. Policy is (understandably) focused on keeping the oil flowing "freely" and the motley assortment of undistinguished dictators and clients that run the place in power.

Yitzhak Rabin has played a knowingly intelligent game during his tenure so far, in style rather like de Klerk's in South Africa — appearing flexible, showering CBMs (confidence building measures) left and right, saying exactly what Shamir never did. But power is what it is all about, and little he has said or done suggests that Israel is about to do anything more than delegate (as opposed to transferring) authority on the West Bank and Gaza. This may suit the new world order, but it flies in the face of a people which has struggled as long and as hard as the Palestinians.

The question of Palestine must not be allowed to die therefore, but it can only be kept alive as the cause of an entire people whose principles and vision really do provide an alternative to the sullen submission envisioned for us by the Israelis. We do not have a Mandela, alas, but we do have a potentially responsive constituency still in the Arab and Third Worlds, in Europe, and, yes, in the United States. Most important, as the *intifada* has shown, we are a resourceful and brave people, willing to undertake mass actions of a kind that have made a difference.

To give all that up for illusory and insufficient diplomatic arrangements, or to accept those arrangements without also transforming the context of those arrangements is, many of us believe, to give up too much too soon. There are alternatives to an unqualified *pax Americana*, and those have to be articulated both for ourselves and for Americans and Israelis to see, and then to be persuaded of patiently, methodically, tirelessly.

24

False Promises:
The Madrid Peace Process

Naseer H. Aruri

Introduction: The Antecedents of Madrid

This essay endeavors to explain the nature and objectives of United States Middle East diplomacy during the Bush presidency, with emphasis on what became known as the Madrid process and its linchpin, the Palestinian dimension. How and why was the Madrid conference convened in September 1991? What was the basis for the investment of so much U.S. political capital in that process? Why was a diplomatic reflection of the military victory in the Gulf War so important for the consolidation of U.S. gains? Why did the various parties to the conflict agree to participate and what means of pressure and persuasion were employed to guarantee their involvement? What impact did Washington's pursuit of stability have on the "peace process," and what are the prospects for the future?

Much of the construction work on the road to Madrid had already begun under Secretary of State James Baker's predecessors. In fact, the Madrid framework, governing the negotiations, represents a synthesis of previous U.S. diplomatic initiatives. The two-track approach, the self-government concept, and transitional arrangements are derived from the Camp David Accords negotiated under President Carter's auspices in 1978. The Jordanian dimension of a Palestinian-Israeli settlement is grounded in the Reagan plan.[1] The linguistic bait designed to attract the Palestinians is largely inherited from the Shultz plan, which itself incorporated the salient features of Camp David and the Reagan plan.[2]

Two characteristics are shared in common by all these initiatives. First, they were all occasioned by structural changes in either the regional or the global environment. The "de-Nasserization" of Egypt and the subsequent collapse of Soviet influence there created a strategic imperative for U.S. diplomatic action, and the outcome was Camp David. The Israeli invasion of

Lebanon in 1982 so weakened the Palestinian national movement that President Reagan declared the outcome an "opportunity" for peace, which effectively removed Palestinian national rights from the active global agenda. Having just embarked on a new Cold War against the Soviet Union and revolutionary nationalism, Reagan welcomed the opportunity to rearrange the strategic landscape of the Middle East. His plan, however, was thwarted by a junior ally with strategic designs of its own: the Israeli cabinet delivered a categorical and prompt rejection of the Reagan plan. The historic process which propelled the diplomacy of George Shultz was the Palestinian uprising (*intifada*), that began in 1987. The Shultz plan was introduced in 1988 in order to reaffirm United States custodianship over the Middle East, to elbow out other plans proposed by various segments of the international community and to protect Israel's image in the U.S., after it was tarnished by its brutal methods of suppressing the *intifada*. Hence, the strategic imperative constituted a common denominator not only for Baker's post-Gulf War diplomacy, but for the three plans which had preceded it as well.

The second and related common denominator, is that in all four cases the roles of the protagonists in the "peace process" were always overshadowed by the strategic actors and imperatives of that process. Interest on the part of regional protagonists has often lagged far behind that of the United States, thus creating a corresponding disparity between the pursuit of comprehensive peace and the search for comprehensive security. The parties to the conflict have tended not to share Washington's diagnosis that the circumstances were propitious for peaceful relations. And while Israel said "no" to the Reagan and the Shultz plans, and later renounced its own plan for elections in the West Bank and Gaza in 1989 in order to avoid a territorial settlement, most of the Arab parties opted for negotiations despite the adverse conditions in order to win favor with Washington.

The diplomatic history of the Middle East during the past two decades reveals that a half dozen U.S. administrations stood consistently in opposition to a settlement supported by an international consensus — one that would provide for an end to the Israeli occupation and a beginning of Palestinian statehood. At the same time, Israel has managed to reject every single U.S. initiative involving a territorial settlement, even when such initiatives excluded Palestinian sovereignty. The Palestinians have thus been confronted with two protagonists intent on denying them a national existence and a sovereign order. Regional and international circumstances have elevated one of the protagonists to the status of sole arbiter; hence the dilemma of the Arab parties to the Madrid negotiations. This is not to imply that U.S. and Israeli policies have been constantly and consistently in tandem. U.S. policy throughout the post-Second World War period has been preoccupied with regional stability in order to assure hegemony and facilitate unimpeded access and control of petroleum resources. Also, at the heart of this policy has been the containment of a host of domestic oppositional forces as well as external challengers of that hegemony, whose convenient address was "communism" or "Soviet aggression." That endeavor, which was classified in the category of "vital national interests," converged with the Israeli interest in reducing the influence of Arab nationalism to manageable proportions. The two interests also coincided to the extent that successive U.S. administrations viewed the disaffected Palestinians as a volatile anti-establishment group whose irredentist goals precluded their having any stake in the existing regional order.

The U.S. pursued its objectives relentlessly, despite its rather isolated position in the world community, hedging its bets on favorable global or regional circumstances in the not-too-distant future. Two historic figures were to play a pivotal role in fulfilling Washington's dreams: Mikhail Gorbachev, who presided over the disintegration of the Soviet empire; and Saddam Hussein, whose fateful decision to invade Kuwait in August 1990 gave George Bush the green light to reshape the strategic landscape of the Middle East, terminate the existing Arab political order and resolve the impasse in favor of Washington's Palestinian and Arab agenda.[3] It was a windfall for a superpower facing relative economic decline and sagging credibility, yet anxious to remain "number one."

The Global and Regional Setting for a Settlement

The strategic imperatives for a negotiated settlement, largely on U.S. terms and under U.S. auspices, were created by the effective collapse of the Soviet Union and the destruction of Iraq. The Soviet Union was transformed from chief diplomatic backer and arms supplier of the Arab states to U.S. appendage in the "peace process." Iraq was reduced from the champion of strategic balance with Israel to an impotent nation preoccupied with the preservation of its sovereignty and territorial integrity. Thus, with deterrence having suddenly vanished at the global and regional levels, the U.S. was left without any serious opposition for the first time since Nasser; ironically, the major source of irritation for its diplomatic efforts now was its own regional ally, Israel.

The dramatic transformation of the strategic and political landscape of the Middle East in the aftermath of the Cold War and the destruction of Iraq paved the way for George Bush to shape a new structure of relationships in which an Arab-Israeli settlement became a U.S. national interest. For the United States, this was the first "opportunity" to reshape the strategic balance in the Middle East without the countervailing influence of the Soviet Union and in the absence of a single Arab power professing regional responsibility for mutual deterrence vis-a-vis Israel. As for Israel, this was also the first time since the peace treaty with Egypt in 1979 that a number of Arab states seemed ready to conclude peace with it outside the framework of an international peace conference in direct bilateral negotiations and not subject to Palestinian approval.

U.S. strategic planners now envisage a post-Cold War re-division of the world, in which economic rather than military power will be the catalyst for change, and in which the Middle East, as a potential source of capital, will rest securely in the North American sphere of influence. Given that U.S. relations with Japan and the EC will have to consume the larger portion of

American energies during the next phase, a settlement of the Arab-Israeli conflict becomes not only desirable but essential from the U.S. vantage point.[4]

The Gulf wartime alliance, in which Arab active participation combined with Israeli passive support, proved to be a mere battle convenience. Translating that convergence of interests into a viable anchor for regional stability required a negotiated settlement capable of freeing the Arab states to fully embrace Washington's new political order in the region. Such a settlement would also free U.S. taxpayers from the huge burden of subsidizing the Israeli treasury in the name of security, a fact which itself continues to fuel anti-American sentiments in the region.

Moreover, as long as U.S. energy policy remains dependent on the military option, and the flow of cheap oil to the industrial world remains vulnerable to national self-assertion in the oil-producing countries, an unsettled Arab-Israeli conflict constitutes a potential threat to the desired stability. Further, legitimating enhanced U.S. hegemony in the Middle East, at a time of its relative economic decline vis-a-vis Europe and Japan, requires the kind of political settlement that would improve sagging credibility. For the U.S. to credibly claim the leadership in shaping the "new world order," it has to demonstrate not only its commitment to crush the detractors but also its willingness and ability to broker a viable peace after a prolonged impasse. To the extent that the Middle East has become more firmly entrenched in the American sphere than at any other time in the past, U.S. unilateralism has come under urgent scrutiny. Its role in the Middle East has become a litmus test of U.S. leadership in the post-Cold War world.

The Arab States

The Gulf War effectively demolished the official Arab consensus on Palestine, eroded Arab solidarity and exposed regime insecurity in the Gulf/Peninsula region. The illusion of Arab defense and the higher Arab interest was eclipsed by the spectacle of kings, sheikhs and presidents ingratiating themselves with Washington, thus enabling the U.S. to deal with them separately on the basis of narrowly construed interests, rather than as a solid bloc with a broad nationalist and Palestinian agenda.

The Arab world has become more divided than at any other time since the establishment of the Arab League. Arab solidarity against Israel has broken down, and thus an important source of pressure for Israeli concessions is in danger of being eliminated. Moreover, the indebtedness of the poorer Arab countries as well as the virtual protectorate status of the richer Arab states seems to translate into loss of relative sovereignty and leverage.[5] There is hardly any economic or diplomatic leverage left for these countries; and with the destruction of Iraq as a regional power Arab military leverage has also been eliminated for the forseeable future.

The significant thing about all these developments is that the joint Palestinian-Arab strategy developed at the Rabat Summit in 1974, based on Arab economic and diplomatic leverage and Palestinian "moderation" (a two-state solution rather than the secular democratic state concept) has been dismantled. That enabled the Bush administration to obtain Arab and Palestinian acquiescence in its framework for the Madrid negotiations tilted heavily against the Arab side.

The Gulf War also removed the question of Palestine from the top of the Arab agenda. The conventional wisdom prevailing in the West, that the Palestinians did their cause irreparable damage by identifying too closely with Iraq, was conveniently adopted by the Arab members of the war coalition.[6] Not only was the Palestinian leadership demonized for its political stance, but the PLO, which had become the embodiment of Palestinian nationalism, was disregarded and the cause itself marginalized.

Moreover, the rapid acceleration of influence of the internal Palestinian leadership in the Occupied Territories, a trend underway since the 1982 Lebanon war, was exploited by the U.S. and Israel to further marginalize the external PLO leadership in Tunis and consequently to devalue Palestinian national rights.

An example of that marginalization was the U.S. refusal to allow the PLO any meaningful diplomatic gains in exchange for its historic concessions of 1988. The Algiers Declaration of Independence and Arafat's subsequent "renunciation" of terrorism rather than "denunciation" at that time, as well as his recognition of the "right" of Israel to exist, rather than its mere existence, not only satisfied Kissinger's well-known conditions of 1975 but Reagan's additions as well.[7] And yet Washington managed quickly to find an excuse to "suspend" or, more accurately, terminate its dialogue with the PLO.

In doing so, Washington was able to extract a high diplomatic cost for the PLO in Europe and even in the Arab world. Today, the PLO no longer insists on even partial, let alone sole, representation of the Palestinians in diplomatic negotiations; it is now reconciled to merely naming the Madrid negotiators within Israeli-set limits, and is committed to the concept of a joint delegation with Jordan.

An "Opportunity" for James Baker

The outcome of the Gulf War provided James Baker with a favorable climate for negotiations, largely because of the victor-vanquished dichotomy. The war consecrated U.S. diplomacy as the sole broker of an Arab-Israeli settlement. Not only did Baker succeed in replacing the long-sought international conference with a symbolic regional parley whose main function was to legitimate the bilateral talks Israel so much desired, but his shuttle diplomacy also secured Soviet and Syrian acquiescence.

Baker's shuttle diplomacy was successful in bridging the gap between the Arabs and Israel on terms largely prescribed by the latter, yet accommodative of cosmetic changes, thus creating the illusion of a compromise. The Arab position, which was based on the necessity of an international conference, was gradually watered down with each shuttle.

On April 12, 1991, Syria and Jordan indicated their willingness to attend an international conference with the additional proviso that it should be based on UN resolutions.[8] At the same time, Israel was insisting that the conference comprise only a single, brief session, to be followed by separate bilateral talks.

Just one week later, King Hussein said that "Jordan would be very flexible when it came to the terms of [a] conference."[9] Syria, on the other hand, stood by its position, insisting on UN participation in a conference with a permanent structure, and demanding that Israel commit itself to the exchange of land for peace.[10]

On his next shuttle, May 8, Baker proposed a "compromise," whereby the conference would be sponsored by the U.S. and the then-Soviet Union, and it would reconvene every six months.[11] A UN envoy would be present but would remain silent. Although the meeting would be based on UN Resolution 242, Baker proposed that each side would be free to bring in its own "interpretation" of 242. With regard to Palestinian representation, Baker's "compromise" saw the Palestinians as part of a joint Jordanian-Palestinian delegation.

Even that "compromise" proved to be unacceptable to Israel, and was also rejected by Syria, thus prompting Baker to return to Washington and blame both parties. He did, however, emphasize that Israel's continued settlement policy was "the biggest obstacle to peace."[12] In the meantime, President Bush hinted that invitations could be issued, implying that those who failed to attend would be considered as standing in the way of peace.

On July 14, President Assad of Syria accepted the U.S. "compromise," stating that the plan was "an acceptable basis for achieving a comprehensive solution."[13] This prompted Baker to return to the region and look for additional conciliatory moves by the Arabs to entice Israel. But despite a firm Syrian commitment made to Baker by Assad in Damascus, plus a call by Egyptian President Hosni Mubarak to end the Arab economic boycott of Israel in return for an Israeli "suspension" of settlement construction, Prime Minister Shamir could only tell Baker, upon his arrival in Israel on July 21, that he needed more time to consider the matter.[14] On the same day, Jordan announced its acceptance of Baker's proposal, and together with Egypt and Saudi Arabia, offered to suspend the economic boycott.[15]

With concessions mounting from the Arab side in this manner, Israel became concerned about the outcome of a public relations battle, particularly as it developed a posture of rejectionism under Shamir. Israeli approval was thus extended finally, on July 24, but the familiar conditions were repeated: Palestinian presence at the conference was limited to non-PLO, non-Jerusalem, non-diaspora Palestinians. Those excluded amount to about 75 percent of the Palestinian people.

These major concessions were incorporated into a letter of invitation signed by the U.S. and the Soviet Union on October 18, 1991. The letter effectively replaced the UN resolutions as a framework for settling the Arab-Israeli conflict. It contained "assurances" to the protagonists, expressed in separate documents, which largely defined U.S. (not Soviet) understandings and intentions concerning the negotiations. The main principles in the joint letter of invitation are:

1. Peace must be grounded in Security Council Resolutions 242 and 338

and the principle of land for peace, in accordance with President Bush's address to Congress on March 6, 1991. It must provide for Israeli security and recognition of Palestinian legitimate "political" rights, and for Palestinian control over political and economic decisions which affect their lives.

2. The venue for the peace negotiations would be a regional conference that would lead, after a few days, to direct bilateral negotiations. The conference would have no power to impose solutions, veto agreements reached by the parties, or make decisions for the parties. It can reconvene only with the consent of the parties.

3. The negotiations regarding the Palestinians would be conducted in phases, beginning with talks on interim self-government arrangements. The interim self-government would last for five years, and during the third year negotiations would begin to determine the final status of the territories.

The private letter of U.S. assurances to the Palestinians reiterates these principles but adds a few specific points:

1. The Israeli occupation should come to an end, but that can be accomplished only through negotiations that are comprehensive and proceed along two tracks, a Palestinian and an Arab state track.

2. The United Nations would be represented only by an observer. Agreements would be registered with the UN Secretariat and reported to the Security Council. Significantly, the U.S. insisted that as long as the process continues, the U.S. would not support another process in the United Nations.

3. The Palestinians can choose their own delegation. But while the U.S. says it does not seek to determine who speaks for Palestinians, it stipulates that the delegation members must be from the Occupied Territories, agree to the two-track concept, agree to the phases arrangement, and must be willing to live in peace with Israel. No party can be forced to sit with anyone it does not want to sit with.

4. Jerusalem must never again be divided, and its final status should be decided in negotiations. The U.S. does not recognize Israel's annexation of East Jerusalem or the extension of its municipal boundaries. Palestinians from Jerusalem are excluded from the delegation but a Palestinian resident in Jordan with ties to a prominent Jerusalem family would be eligible to join the Jordanian side of the joint Palestinian-Jordanian delegation. Palestinians from East Jerusalem should be able to vote in the elections for an interim self-governing authority. Together with diaspora Palestinians, they can also negotiate on final status.

The proximity of these parameters to Israel's conditions is striking, resulting from the process in which Baker's shuttles incorporated virtually all of the Israeli position. Thus the ground rules of Madrid have not only supplanted the United Nations framework, but also earlier U.S. proposals. The self-proclaimed catalyst for peace had to conduct its brokering in Madrid and subsequently in Washington and Moscow, largely in accordance with Israeli standards. This in itself reflects the disparity between Washington's estimates of post-Gulf War Israeli and Palestinian/Arab influence and power, as well as the strategic significance of each in the post-Cold War period.

Palestinian Vulnerability

U.S. strategic planners have already made reassessments of their estimates of the Palestinian potential for regional destabilization. Deprived of a solid and unified Arab backing in the negotiations; isolated from its constituencies in the Occupied Territories, the Gulf, Syria, and Lebanon; and faced with economic, ideological, leadership and governance crisis, the PLO is seen by the U.S. administration as the weakest link. Therefore, Baker's diplomacy treated the Palestinians as unequal. There was a deliberate ambiguity in that diplomacy which left the various parties considerable room for personal interpretation and even self-delusion; it was designed to secure a unanimous consent for attending the conference. But after the opening speeches, the urge toward specificity began to replace the need for ambiguity. Baker's diplomacy began to be challenged by the aggrieved and the recalcitrant. The vague boundaries between substance and procedure, which kept Baker's mission alive, have come to be defined more closely, especially the many substantive issues thinly camouflaged as procedural arrangements. A few examples suffice:

1. The issue of Palestinian representation is not a matter of procedure; it is substantive par excellence. Baker's acquiescence in Israel's exclusion of diaspora and Jerusalem Palestinians nullified Palestinian national rights, including their internationally recognized rights of return and self-determination. Similarly, Tel Aviv's refusal to deal with the PLO reflects a concern not with terrorism, but with acknowledging the national character of the Palestinian issue — that it goes beyond the Occupied Territories. The U.S. position also lends a certain credence to the Israeli claim to Jerusalem despite the well-established international position, to which the U.S. itself is committed.

2. The numerous procedural encumbrances on the peace conference, including its designation, participants, and the limits of speech among others, are also substantive as they render the very reality of a belligerent occupation, a recognized status under international law, a sideline issue.[16]

3. The much publicized two-track approach represents a disingenuous attempt to side-step the central issue in the conflict. Issues of arms control, water resources, economic development, regional security and the environment, which make up the agenda of the multilateral talks, did not arise out of an ideological conflict between the Arabs and Israel. They derive naturally from the central issue, Palestine, which is the root cause of the Arab-Israeli conflict. The multilaterals were intended to entice a reluctant Israel; whereas the bilateral track represents the "give" for Israel, the multilateral track holds the plums, not least the de facto recognition accorded Tel Aviv by Saudi Arabia and other Gulf states and other Arab participation in the talks.

The Real Challenge and the Prospects

While the objective conditions in the post-Cold War Middle East implied a reduction of Israeli influence, the pre-Madrid concessions were made solely by the Palestinians and the Arabs. Even so, Israel still viewed the peace process as a belated threat to check its ongoing absorption of the land, atomization of the Palestinian community, and continued efforts to preempt a state-in-formation.

While moral and legal considerations were secondary to the strategic nature of Baker's diplomacy, an obvious refusal to give them at least minimal consideration constituted a basic flaw in the initiative. The fundamental moral issue which Baker's diplomacy evaded was the wrong done to the Palestinians — dispossession, dismemberment, disenfranchisement, subjugation — ills which George Bush's declared tenets of a "new world order" promised to remedy. Hence the responsibility for the plight of the Palestinian refugees was arbitrarily transferred from Israel to the world community despite UN Resolution 194 of 1948 calling for the right of return or compensation, and the fact that its fulfillment by Israel was made a condition for Israel's own admission to the United Nations. Another legal element which Baker's approach neglected was the Fourth Geneva Convention Relative to the Protection of Civilians in Times of War of 1949.

From the very beginning of the process these shortcomings of the Madrid framework and the deliberate ambiguity of Baker's diplomacy prevented the parties from making the kind of progress needed to meet deadlines. The right-wing government in Israel during Madrid viewed the peace process as an investment to buy a few more years in which Soviet immigrants and expanded settlements in the Occupied Territories would help assure an effective foreclosure on a territorial peace. Shamir put it succinctly thus: "This mass immigration aims at forming a greater Israel . . . will make Israel bigger, stronger and better . . . In the space of five years you will not be able to recognize this country. Everything will change, everything will be bigger. The strongest of the Arabs around us will be in a state of desperation and panic as they will not be able to stop the natural flow of Jewish people into their land."[17]

The attitude of the new Labor-dominated government headed by Yitzhak Rabin toward the settlements is not all that different, despite widespread publicity to the contrary. The ascendancy of Rabin to power was greeted with widespread approval in the United States and among official circles in the Arab world. The U.S. media hailed Rabin's victory as a vote for the U.S.-sponsored "peace process." An embattled President Bush, pondering his sagging popularity in the opinion polls, viewed Rabin's reemergence with great relief. The hurried dispatch of Secretary Baker to the Middle East even before Rabin's executive staff was on the job, and the invitation for Rabin to visit Bush at his family home in Kennebunkport, Maine on August 10, 1992 were more in tune with Washington's political agenda than diplomatic necessity.

Rabin's election symbolized the termination of a period of acrimony between two strategic allies. Rabin's largely quantitative, not qualitative, shift on settlements meant there was no more need for Bush and Baker to withhold the $10 billion in loan guarantees previously denied to Israel and risk losing the entire Jewish vote. Hence the decision to approve Israel's request for those guarantees was quite predictable.

Given this, Rabin, in a no-lose situation, was hailed as the peacemaker despite the lack of any real qualitative change from the Likud zealots and ideologues of the previous administration; and notwithstanding his own earlier record, all the way from the mass expulsions of Lydda and Ramleh in 1948, to the occupation of vast Arab lands in 1967 when he was chief of staff, to the anti-*intifada* "might, force and beatings" policy of 1988 when he was defense minister. The important thing is that the perception of Rabin as a man of peace itself became a substitute for reality. Hence Rabin was poised to deliver, and in fact he echoed Baker's cliche about the need not to miss the last bus when he addressed the Knesset as prime minister on July 13, 1992:

> You who live in the wretched poverty of Gaza and Khan Younis, in the refugee camps in Hebron and Nablus; you who have never known a single day of freedom and joy in your lives; listen to us, if only this once. We offer you the fairest and most valuable proposal from our standpoint today — autonomy, with all its advantages and limitations. You will not get everything you want; perhaps we won't either. So once and for all, take your destiny into your hands. *Don't lose this opportunity which may never return.*[18] [Emphasis added.]

Would the United States under a Clinton administration remind Israel that the lack of "freedom and joy" in Palestinian lives is directly attributable to its occupation?

The issue of building settlements has emerged as central in the stalled Arab-Israeli negotiations. Will Rabin's policies remove the hurdles and pave the way toward substantive talks? The Labor Party platform pledged that "new settlements will not be established and existing settlements will not be thickened, except for those in Greater Jerusalem and the Jordan Valley." Rabin himself, however, has never pledged to refrain from building new settlements. His criterion is a familiar concept in the Israeli politico-strategic lexicon: security. Concretely, Rabin's government has canceled 5,000 settlement units while continuing work on 11,000 others.

There was a time when U.S. policy on building settlements in occupied territories was in accord with international law. Up to Jimmy Carter's tenure, settlements were considered "illegal" within the meaning of the humanitarian Fourth Geneva Convention. Ronald Reagan, not especially noted in the area of international law, altered that policy when he declared that the settlements are "not illegal," a finding that was later tempered by his professional diplomats, leading to the settlements being relabeled merely "an obstacle to peace."

For the Palestinian people, the Madrid process is the only game in town, given the grim regional and global realities of the post-Cold War, post-Gulf War world. Nevertheless, it is an uncertain path, if not in fact a blind alley. Negotiations should constitute a process of conciliation, with a possible outcome already in place. In this case, there is neither an outline nor a vision of the final outcome. All fundamental issues involving borders, refugees, Jerusalem and indeed the occupation itself have been deferred. Self-government, as the sole concern of these negotiations in the immediate term, is seen by the Palestinians as the necessary link towards independence; Israel, on the other hand, has already ruled out independence, and views what it calls self-government as a mechanism to legitimate the occupation under a new and different label.

Any doubt about this strategy was dispelled by the text of the Israeli plan entitled "Ideas for Peaceful Coexistence in the Territories During the Interim Period," submitted during the March 1992 round of negotiations in Washington. Its premise seems to be consonant with parameters enunciated by former Israeli Deputy Foreign Minister Benjamin Netanyahu in December 1991: "Maximum security for Israel and minimum intervention in Palestinian life." The text of the plan makes it very clear that Israel's concept of security denies the Palestinians any overall central authority, geographical space, economic planning, legislative authority or judicial review, to say nothing of defense, foreign affairs or natural resources. The Palestinians would have their own municipal police but no state police; they would have municipal courts but not an appellate or a supreme court. They would have a semi-canton on about 5% of historic Palestine — exactly the same amount of land owned by Jews on the eve of the establishment of Israel.

The outcome of the Gulf crisis has so radically altered the balance of power in the region that it is nearly impossible for the Palestinians to achieve even their minimal goals under the U.S.-sponsored peace talks. The United States has, after all, used its Security Council veto or abstained in the voting on nearly all the 43 UN resolutions since 1967 critical of the Israeli occupation. The American "new world order" does not regard international legality as indivisible, nor does it set a single standard for the application of human rights. President Bush's vocal defense of the human rights of the Kuwaiti people, in which he included self-determination and the restoration of the unelected emir to power, will not be matched by an American call upon Israel to allow the Palestinians to choose their own representatives, elect their own government and enjoy self-determination, as required by UN resolutions.[19]

The real challenge to the Clinton administration as "catalyst for peace" will be to bridge the gap between the Arabs and Israel with definite proposals, a task which Israel considers taboo and Washington approaches with extreme caution bordering on timidity. The material conditions which propelled U.S. diplomacy toward Madrid, and the quality of change Madrid is expected to produce would have to be synchronized. That is going to depend on how specific proposals replace the initial ambiguity. It will also depend on whether Clinton's support of the Madrid process will be matched by a necessary shift in the well-known substantive positions of the U.S. Only then will the real U.S. definition of Resolution 242 be known. It will be a real test of the post-Cold War relationship between Israel and the United States.

Notes

1. For a description and analysis of the Reagan plan, see Naseer Aruri and Fouad Moughrabi, "The Reagan Middle East Initiative," *Journal of Palestine Studies* vol. 12, no. 2 (Winter 1983), pp. 10–30.
2. The Shultz plan was proposed in February 1988. See State Department, Bureau of Public Affairs, *U.S. Policy in the Middle East*, Selected Documents No. 27 (June 1988).

3. For the regional and global significance of the Gulf War, see Tom Naylor, "American Aims in the Persian Gulf," *Canadian Dimensions* (March 1991), pp. 34–37; James Petras, "The Meaning of the New World Order: A Critique," *America*, May 11, 1991, pp. 512–514; Noam Chomsky, "U.S. Gulf Policy," *Open Magazine*, January 18, 1991, pp. 1–17; Chomsky, "What We Say Goes: The Middle East in the New World Order," *Z Magazine* (May 1991), pp. 50–64; and, in general, Phyllis Bennis and Michel Moushabeck (eds.), *Beyond the Storm: A Gulf Crisis Reader* (New York: Olive Branch Press, 1991).

4. On the relationship between the U.S., Europe and Japan, see Lester C. Thurow, "Money Wars: Why Europe Will Own the 21st Century," *Washington Post*, April 19, 1992, p. C1; also Steven Greenhouse, "U.S. and the World: A New Economic Order Is Ahead," *New York Times*, April 29, 1992.

5. See Yahya Sadowski, "Revolution, Reform, or Regression? Arab Political Opinion in the 1990 Gulf Crisis," *Brookings Review* (Winter 1990–91), pp. 17–21.

6. For a sample of Western media opinion, see Stephen Howe, "The Palestinians: Back to the Wall," *New Statesman and Society*, August 24, 1990; Anthony Lewis, "Desperation and Folly," *New York Times*, January 21, 1991; see also editorial in the same issue, entitled "Sure Losers: The Palestinians."

7. See Aruri, "The United States and Palestine: Reagan's Legacy to Bush," *Journal of Palestine Studies* vol. 18, no. 3 (Spring 1989), pp. 3–21.

8. *New York Times*, April 13, 1991.

9. *New York Times*, April 21, 1991.

10. *New York Times*, April 24, 1991.

11. *New York Times*, May 9, 1991.

12. *New York Times*, May 23, 1991.

13. *New York Times*, July 15, 1991.

14. *New York Times*, July 22, 1991.

15. Ibid.

16. See W. Thomas Mallison and Sally Mallison, *The Palestine Problem in International Law and World Order* (New York: Longman, 1986); Raja Shehadeh, *Occupiers' Law: Israel and the West Bank* (Washington, D.C.: Institute for Palestine Studies, 1988), second edition.

17. *New York Times*,

18. *Jerusalem Post*, July 14, 1992.

19. For a discussion of the double standard, see Norman Finkelstein, "Israel and Iraq: A Double Standard in the Application of International Law," *Monthly Review* (July/August 1991), pp. 25–53.

25

Israel and the New World Order

Mattiyhau Peled

The title of this paper should be read as an antithesis. Whatever may have been the meaning or intention of the concept of "a new world order," it could not have referred to the problems posed or faced by Israel in relation to its neighbors. Under the most sympathetic interpretation, the idea of a new world order, as far as the Middle East is concerned, could mean the creation of conditions which would eliminate the danger of another eruption of an unmanageable crisis that might require a concerted international military intervention. It is significant that no similar ideas were put forward after the crises of the Falkland Islands, Grenada, Panama or any of the Middle Eastern wars of 1967, 1973, 1982 or the internal wars in Lebanon, nor indeed, after the first phase of the Gulf War, between 1980–1988. Although in all but those actively involving Israel, superpower involvement was essential, no-where was it felt necessary or advisable to propose a new world order as a consequence. As for the Israeli-Arab wars, they were all terminated with some kind of international mediation which fell within the concept of customary aid provided to belligerents in local conflicts. It was only the very peculiar circumstances of the final phase of the Gulf War that brought forth the call for a new world order.

These peculiar circumstances are related to the new system of international relations as they were evolving at that particular moment. The Iraqi invasion of Kuwait took place just as the foreign ministers of the U.S. and the Soviet Union were conferring in Russia and it took them by surprise. None of them had any reason to be worried about the supply of oil as a result of the Iraqi takeover of the Kuwaiti oilfields, since Iraq could do nothing with it except sell it. But they had every reason to be worried about the dangers involved in the liberty taken by minor powers to use force in a local conflict without the consent of either of the superpowers. To Israel the reaction of the United States to the Iraqi demarche was thoroughly welcome, since Israel would never launch an attack on any of its neighbors without prior U.S. consent.

Therefore it could remain passive during the crisis. Thus, to the extent that the new idea sprang out of circumstances which had not touched Israel's relationships in the region it is hard to see how the new order concept — whatever it might mean — could affect Israel or relate to its problems.

Israel's central problem with its neighbors is one of recognition and acceptance. If all the countries in the region miraculously announced their recognition of Israel's legitimacy and acted upon it, the raison d'être of the Arab-Israeli conflict would disappear and a settlement would soon be achieved. Such recognition would oblige Israel to withdraw from the territories occupied in 1967, which have always been seen — except in marginal quarters — primarily as a mortgage to be released when peace is achieved. In other words, in this context the problem is not one of security but of peace. It is a typical problem born of the Cold War era and is not susceptible to a solution except in terms of the circumstances which had brought it into being. The call for a new world order is aimed at providing a measure of security to all countries in the region within their de facto borders and under their present regimes. This may not have been officially or authoritatively stated, but to judge by the actual steps taken to implement it — such as the unprecedented outpouring of modern weapon systems to the countries of the region — this conclusion is inescapable. The whole framework of the concept is oriented toward the creation of a situation in which no disturbance of the existing order would be possible. This is supposed to be "new" only in the sense that it should be impossible at any time in the foreseeable future for any country to jeopardize the established order of its neighbors.

Such expectations were current also before the Gulf War but their realization was constantly threatened under the conditions of the Cold War system. At its core was the desire of each of the major antagonists to take advantage of any weakness in the other with the purpose of upsetting the order cherished by the opponent. Instability was sought after and the supply of arms to trusted satellite states was one of the major means of ensuring that no opportunity to hurt the antagonist would be missed. It so happened that as the second phase of the Gulf War was unfolding the Cold War was already over and the United States could obtain the cooperation of the Soviet Union both in opposing Iraq and in forcing it out of Kuwait — a development which would have been unthinkable only a few years earlier. In fact this is where Saddam Hussein made his cardinal mistake: not reading correctly the new international map. He failed to appreciate the fundamental change which enabled the international community to take a unified position in favor of the status quo.

This new era was ushered in with gusto, with the international community feeling elated about it. This could be seen not only in the unity demonstrated at the United Nations, but also in the disproportionate size of the military force assembled against Iraq. It was certainly not the actual military needs that dictated the "order of battle" built up for the operation. After all, the quality of the Iraqi Army was well known to military observers who watched its performance during eight years of the most mismanaged and incompetently-led war in modern history, the Iran-Iraq war. The artificial aura of invincibility given to the Iraqi Republican Guard, whose fame as an out-standing fighting force was entirely fictional, stemmed not from a mistaken intelligence evaluation but from the need to justify the desire for a huge concentration of forces. The size of the allied forces was required not to fight the Iraqis but to highlight the significance of the moment.

Once the demonstration had been held, and the full meaning of the post-Cold War era was brought home, everything else was reduced to insignificance. The huge debt owed by Iraq to its rich neighbors was suddenly forgotten, even though it was the Gulf states' refusal to excuse a large part of it, in consideration of the service Iraq had rendered them by containing the threat of Khomeinism, which had caused the invasion of Kuwait in the first place. The call to the Kurds and Shi'ites of Iraq to rise up in arms was soon found ill-advised as the unity of Iraq was rediscovered as a fundamental asset for the region's stability. Even the democratization of the regime in Kuwait was left as an unimportant issue to be dealt with at the convenience of its authoritarian ruler.

Examined against the reality of the event that brought forth the concept of the New World Order, it is clear that it was meant to set new norms for the settlement of problems arising from post-Cold War situations; it was never meant to apply to issues born in the previous era. Therefore, the initiative taken by Secretary of State Baker to revive the dormant Israeli-Arab peace process — whose origin as well as the problem it was supposed to resolve, belong to an entirely different international reality — only appeared to be connected to the Gulf War and the call for a "New World Order" produced by it. In essence it had nothing to do with the preceding events, and in fact developed entirely separately from them.

The history of the Israeli-Arab conflict has come to be regarded as one revolving around the problem of Israel's security only because the Arab refusal to admit the legitimacy of Israel was linked to a threat to dismantle it when the opportunity arose. The most obvious policy mistake of the Arab leadership over the years lay in their inability to modify their position on the question of Israel even after finding out that it was beyond their capability to destroy it. The inevitable conclusion drawn by Sadat, that since the Arabs could not destroy Israel they had better make peace with it, proved to be beyond their reach. They therefore allowed the conflict to deteriorate into one seemingly about secondary issues, principally the question of security. It has been clear all along that Israel could not threaten the security of the Arab countries just as the Arab countries could not threaten Israel's security. They could cause each other much unpleasantness but their overall security has been guaranteed over the years both by the constant supply of arms and by an international constellation which assured both sides of political equality before the international community.

When James Baker began his initiative he had, theoretically, two alterna-tives. One was to seek a solution to the root problem, which for Israel is that of recognition, and the other was to deal with the secondary problem of security. He should have understood that beginning the revived peace process with the intention of resolving the security problem would lead to a dead end. Perhaps he had considered other approaches, but the one which he failed to adopt was that of returning to the Camp David Accords. The unique quality of those Accords can now be better appreciated in the light of international developments that have taken place since then. President Sadat's initiative, which was motivated by his desire to take the Arab-Israeli conflict, as far as Egypt was concerned, out of the Cold War tangle and deal with it as a problem of recognition and acceptance, led to Camp David. His success can be seen, among other things, in the formulae of these Accords with regards to the Palestinian question. They provided specifically for an ultimate resolution of the question "in all its aspects," through Palestinian self-determination — after a period of autonomy as a transitional phase for five years — to be based on "the legitimate rights of the Palestinian people." There is no other document, with Israel as a signatory, that is so explicit on this issue. Indeed, Prime Minister Begin soon regretted signing the document, and many believe that his pathetic retirement from politics was due to his inability to live down what he came to consider as the unforgivable mistake of Camp David. In fact, soon after returning from Camp David he managed to deprive the Palestinian provisions of the Accords of their original meaning by subjecting them to a distorted interpretation. He thus succeeded in delaying indefinitely any action required by the Accords on this issue. But when Baker started his initiative he was not bound by any such semantic maneuvers of Israel's and could certainly have argued that the Accords, being the source of the process he meant to revive, should be adhered to and taken as a starting point. In them there was no reference to the artificial separation of the Palestinians living in East Jerusalem from the rest of their people, nor was there any differentiation between Palestinians living in the Occupied Territories and those in the diaspora, nor was there any specific exclusion of the PLO from the peace process. Therefore, adhering to that document would have avoided the maddening complications caused by Israel's insistence that all these novelties be accepted as ground rules for the revived process.

As a matter of fact Baker adopted another document as the basis for his initiative, namely the Israeli "peace plan" of May 1989, which incorporated all these new conditions. That "peace plan" is fundamentally incompatible with the Camp David Accords. It is unclear whether Baker fully grasped the differences between the two documents. The Accords had, as their main goal, guaranteeing recognition to Israel as a prerequisite for achieving peace and thus facilitating a solution to the Palestinian problem; the Israeli "peace plan" had as its goal the guaranteeing of Israel's security in a situation of non-recognition and continuous hostility.

It is arguable that if Baker had ever considered taking the Camp David Accords as a starting point he must have decided that there would be no chance of getting Israel's consent, and he therefore looked for something more likely to be acceptable to Israel. But what he in fact achieved was a process that could proceed nowhere. Perhaps there was also a psychological explanation for Baker's preference: the "peace plan" was couched in terms much more congenial to the trend of thinking inaugurated by the concept of a "New World Order," in that it aims at maintaining the status quo rather than changing it.

It was convenient to blame Shamir's intransigence for the poor results achieved in the process. But the fact is that the May 1989 plan represented a bipartisan Labor-Likud position. Rabin even claimed, correctly, its authorship and has claimed that Shamir, by attaching his name to the plan, actually plagiarized it. And indeed, as soon as Rabin assumed the office of prime minister he announced that he would adhere to the Madrid framework. In Madrid Shamir made it clear that Israel's notions with regard to the Palestinian problem, as formulated at Camp David, had been superseded by Israel's subsequent interpretations. This clearly meant that the new terms, spelled out in the Israeli "peace plan," would be binding on all participants. And this was also exactly the position taken by Rabin. Thus it is clear that the process has been geared to deal with matters of security, as if this were the real issue of the Israeli-Arab conflict. This fit well the Israeli line of thinking: that as long as its concept of security is not guaranteed nothing else is negotiable. Several attempts to put the process back on the right track were abruptly derailed by Israel. Thus the most promising proposal of President Mubarak — to call off the Arab economic boycott of Israel in return for Israel's undertaking to suspend all settlement activity in the Occupied Territories — was turned down as a mere ploy to divert attention from the security issue.

The difference between the Camp David provisions for a transitional period of Palestinian autonomy and those of the Israeli "peace plan" is fundamental, and Rabin's persistent attempts to depict both documents as complementary were entirely misleading. The former envisaged a gradual transition from occupation through Palestinian autonomy to independence, whereas the latter envisaged autonomy as the end-product which would in fact gain for Israel Palestinian legitimization of an indefinite occupation. There is no doubt that the Palestinians have understood the difference between the two documents. But they seem to have been trapped by their traditional denunciation of the Camp David Accords. Therefore they avoided the argument that the new rules contradicted the provisions agreed to at Camp David, while insisting on ground rules emanating directly from those provisions.

This is the point where American ruling was crucial. In fact Baker preferred the Israeli "peace plan" to that of Camp David and exerted all his influence to persuade the Palestinians that this was their best chance. The Palestinians had great difficulties accepting Baker's proposals. Sometimes it seemed as if they were really impressed, not so much with Baker's arguments, as with the wisecrack attributed to Abba Eban, that the Palestinians never miss an opportunity to miss an opportunity, and were reluctant to provide another proof of the tendency. But leaving aside the question of how historically true that witticism is, it is clear that they allowed themselves to be lured into the process knowing that it held little hope for them.

The extent of loss to the Palestinians in the present peace process can be clearly seen by examining the true significance of the multilateral talks. This was a feature of the renewed process that was entirely unprecedented. It was added to the process as a concession to Israel's demand that the Palestinian issue be taken up only as part of the broader issue of Israeli-Arab relations. Clearly this was designed to avoid a recognition of the uniqueness of the Palestinian question which could then be defined as a mere appendage to the Israeli-Jordanian complex. The very question of Palestinian autonomy was thus considered as part of an eventual solution to Israel's conflict with Jordan. The Palestinians tried desperately to make the best of a bad job by making a Jerusalemite the de facto head of their delegation, with whom the Americans had to deal. They openly consulted with the PLO leadership, thus demonstrating that in fact the Israeli demands, though formally acquiesced to, had been rejected in practice. However, it became clear that while the talks were taking place, and throughout the indefinite transition period of autonomy, Israeli settlements in the Occupied Territories would expand and flourish, that control over land and water would remain in Israeli hands, and as long as the transition period lasted the Palestinians would have no legislative authority of their own.

The actual configuration of the process was quite obvious. The restrictions it imposed on the Palestinians were clear, just as it was clear that nothing of importance was likely to emerge from the process. But the question remained: why did Israel prefer a process that was aimed only at consolidating its security in a hostile environment, to one which would have brought it closer to peace, that is to Arab recognition? No less important is the question of why the U.S. supported the Israeli position when it knew very well that this could not lead to a resolution of the Arab-Israeli conflict? As for Israel, its consensual view of the future required that it maintain the borders of "Greater Israel," which are roughly those of the territory under its control at the start of the Madrid talks. According to Israeli thinking, such a situation would give it security and, in time, also recognition. But as long as territorial aggrandisement was not accompanied by Arab recognition then the former was preferred. The American position may not have been fully in agreement with that of Israel, but the two met at one essential point: maintaining the status quo as a goal of the first priority. And this meant, in the first place, denying the right of the Palestinians to a state of their own. Just as the U.S. shied away from the possibility of creating a Kurdish state in Iraq, even if it meant allowing Saddam Hussein to stay in power, so it shied away from the idea of a Palestinian state and preferred a situation in which there was no real solution but which held out the promise of maintaining the status quo. And as long as Israel and the U.S. were agreed that a Palestinian state should not be allowed to come into being, everything else was of secondary importance. The U.S. probably wanted to see Jordan eventually regain some of the West Bank, and was driven by this consideration to oppose massive Jewish settlements in it. But Israel, even under its Labor-led government, planned to pour into the West Bank some 50,000 additional settlers before the end of 1993 — raising the number of Jewish settlers to close to a quarter of a million — and to use American aid for that purpose just as it had done since the early seventies. The Americans also knew that new immigrants, primarily from the former Soviet Union, would form a sizable portion of these settlers, and that for this reason a lot of money would be invested in the territories to provide jobs for the new settlers close to their habitat.

The massive Soviet immigration was certainly one of the outcomes of the post-Cold War era; it was allowed by the Soviet government in order to qualify as a legitimate member of the "Free World." No other considerations guided its conduct in this matter. Western governments, who pressured the Soviets to allow the emigration of Jews, never felt obliged to allow these immigrants into their territories. (The exception was the United States, where a quota was fixed enabling a limited number of Jewish emigrants from the former USSR to settle in the U.S.) But it was a great relief to all those governments to find out that Israel actually welcomed their non-humanitarian attitude towards the emigrants, which deprived them of the right to settle in a country of their choice. And while Israel exerted great diplomatic efforts to block the emigrants' ways to other countries, it prepared to channel them mainly into the Occupied Territories. This policy was a logical outcome of Israel's fear that demographically its hold over the Occupied Territories would otherwise remain tenuous. The new wave of immigration came at a time when human resources in Israel for massive migration into the territories had dwindled and the influx of newcomers was therefore seen as an urgent national interest. The feeble attempts made by the U.S. to stop the plan were haughtily brushed aside. And it became clear that with American loan guarantees additional money would become available to further implement the plan. The reason was obvious. In the light of the 1992 U.S. presidential campaign, and after the historic rivalry between the United States and the USSR had been eliminated, it became clear that aid to Israel was primarily a function of U.S. domestic policy. This had been true all along; now the fact could no longer be concealed by arguments which sounded valid in the Cold War era.

Given the historic failure of the Israelis and the Americans actively to seek a solution to the Arab-Israeli conflict, the question had to be asked: was there another way of dealing with the problem? The answer is that the alternative was provided back in 1983 in the UN General Assembly's resolution calling for an international peace conference for the Middle East. That conference should be attended by Israel and the Palestinians, as well as the Arab states directly involved in the conflict, along with the five permanent members of the Security Council. Such a conference would conduct its deliberations on the basis of Resolutions 242 and 338, and whatever the parties agree to would be backed up by the Security Council. Should the parties agree that a transition phase of Palestinian autonomy is necessary this would be carried out; but clearly this would not be considered the final goal.

The idea of dealing with the problem by means of a machinery provided by the UN has been described by Israel as unrealistic due to Israel's perception of the UN as essentially a prejudiced and an inefficient organization. But whatever the merits of this argument in the past, it is clear that, in the post-Cold War era, the UN has become the main instrument for dealing with crises left over from the previous era. The action taken against Iraq was certainly the most impressive case and showed that the UN could be an effective instrument of punitive action against countries that violate the new era's norms. But the UN has proved capable of serving as a peace-making instrument as well, as was demonstrated in Cambodia, for example. The new role of the UN in conflict resolution could be the most significant feature of the New World Order, and it should be invited to play an active role in the Israeli-Arab conflict. But significantly, the UN has been specifically excluded from the American-initiated peace process, thus emphasizing that this conflict, born in the Cold War era, still has to be dealt with in terms of that era. So, although the U.S. and Russia have cooperated in sponsoring the process, they have both been reluctant to allow the UN any say in the matter.

But if the Madrid talks were to fail, as seemed very likely, the possibility remained that the issue would eventually be turned over to the UN, where a new start could be attempted. This in itself would be meaningful progress, since it is inconceivable that under UN sponsorship the conditions imposed by Israel on Palestinian participation would be accepted. But more fundamentally, turning the responsibility for leading the process over to the UN would indicate that the problem had been re-defined in the correct terms: namely, how to bring about an end to the occupation, mutual recognition and acceptance, rather than how to preserve the status quo.

26

Concentric Circles:
The U.S. and Israel After the Cold War

Naseer H. Aruri

The major realignment of the strategic and political landscape of the Middle East, which led to a virtual recolonization of the Arab East, provided the U.S. with an opportunity to shape a new structure of relationships in which a settlement to the Arab-Israeli conflict became a U.S. national interest. The major task now facing the U.S., as the undisputed hegemonic power in the region, is how to convert what it views as an historic opportunity into a concrete diplomatic achievement.

The Gulf War of 1991 consolidated the hardline forces in Israel, placed the Israeli peace movement on the defensive, causing its faint voices to drown in the tidal wave of rapidly rising right-wing forces, fueled by a violent shift in the Palestinian *intifada*. The crisis also provided the Israeli government with a natural pretext to clamp down on the *intifada* in an atmosphere of near total freedom from the international scrutiny.[1] Under cover of the Gulf crisis, Israel simply embarked on the destruction of *all* the achievements of the *intifada* over the preceding three and a half years in the diplomatic, political, economic fields and in healthcare and social organization. It was an opportunity to cripple the evolving Palestinian infrastructure, which had already been dealt a serious blow a decade earlier in Lebanon.

The Gulf War also provided Israel with an opportunity finally to impose its own diplomatic framework on any negotiations that it was expected to join. In fact, it was the only party to the ensuing Madrid peace talks whose demands were not scaled down for the sake of a compromise, but were elevated instead. Consider Israel's refusal to entertain Secretary of State Baker's suggestion of a mere freeze on building illegal settlements in the Occupied Territories rather than the suppression or cessation of such activities mandated by international law. Israeli demands did not encounter significant U.S. opposition. The emerging U.S. strategy in the aftermath of the war was to shift the emphasis away from the Palestine/Israel dimension —

which had characterized previous peace plans, such as that of Reagan (1982), Shultz (1988) and the Shamir-Baker-Mubarak proposals of 1989 — and to pursue instead a "two-track" solution. Although this was defined as a simultaneous pursuit of Arab-Israeli and Palestinian-Israeli agreements in parallel negotiating tracks, Prime Minister Shamir argued that only after Israel had achieved peace with the Arab states would it feel confident enough to discuss the West Bank and Gaza.[2] This did in fact represent a change from his earlier insistence on Arab recognition of Israel as a precondition for entering any peace talks that would ultimately lead to talks between Israel and the Palestinians;[3] but, nevertheless, the two-track approach, which provided for multilateral negotiations on environmental issues, water, refugees, economic development and arms control along with the bilateral talks, assured Israel a de facto recognition from the Arab states attending the "multilaterals," such as Saudi Arabia and the other Gulf states. Such de facto recognition was not even contingent on the fulfillment of Israeli obligations to the Palestinian people, or to Syria and Lebanon.

The second part of post-Gulf War Israeli strategy was the replacement of the international peace conference, which had been called for in Security Council Resolution 338, with a regional conference hosted by the U.S. and the USSR. Not only did this strange concept diminish the importance of Resolution 242 (long considered the cornerstone of any just solution to the Arab-Israeli conflict) but it effectively flouted its real meaning and value; in the process it rendered a 45-year old legal record, enshrined in countless UN resolutions, virtually irrelevant to the framework of the negotiations. Unlike the peace processes in El Salvador and Cambodia and the earlier negotiations to solve the Iran-Iraq conflict and the war in Afghanistan, Middle East negotiations came to be governed totally outside the context of the United Nations. A token UN observer was invited to the conference, but he was committed to humiliating silence.

In addition, Israel placed a number of other conditions which were accepted by Baker, sold to the Arabs and incorporated into what became known as the Madrid framework. Salient among these were the following:

— The Soviet Union had to establish "full diplomatic relations with Israel and agree to the meeting ground rules demanded by Israel," in order to qualify as co-sponsor.[4] These ground rules included Israel's insistence that "all that would be discussed at first with the Palestinians is an interim settlement involving self-government." Final status talks would begin three years later.

— That an opening statement at such a conference by the U.S. had to refrain from delineating any plan for a settlement.[5] In fact, James Baker was already on record as saying that he opposed presenting a plan. It will be recalled that he went out of his way to emphasize that his "Five Points" of 1989 were simply a "proposal," and not a "plan."

— That in view of the limited purpose of the conference, which was to have been a one-time event to launch direct negotiations and pave the way for discussing Israel's autonomy plan, participation would be limited to Palestinians living in the West Bank and Gaza, and would specifically exclude those living in East Jerusalem, in Israeli jails and the four million living in the diaspora.

Furthermore, Israel expected the U.S. to persuade the Arab states to agree that the regional conference lead immediately to direct negotiations in the two tracks; that the "meeting have no power to impose solutions on the parties, or to pass judgement or agreements reached in bilateral negotiations";[6] and that Resolutions 242 and 338 would not determine the outcome of the process. Israel also demanded that the PLO should have no role at any point in the peace process, a position which the U.S., the Arab states and even the PLO itself accepted. Had the PLO insisted on representing the Palestinians, the United States and the Arab states were ready and willing to promote an alternative leadership in the Occupied Territories to negotiate a peace based on the new balance of power in the region. The tools intended for that scheme included Israeli measures to ease some restrictions and "improve the quality of life" with Saudi petrodollars and U.S. orchestration. The deteriorating economic conditions in the Occupied Territories, created by Israel's draconian measures during the Gulf crisis, were counted upon by the three parties as the catalyst that would prod the Palestinians toward their scheme. A U.S. official traveling with Baker on one of his early shuttles in the region was rather unsubtle about the utility of Saudi money and Israeli measures:

> There are political ways, ways designed to sort of create more of a sense of political support for Palestinians who would be stepping forward. There are financial ways, especially given the level of economic deprivation and difficulties in the territories now.[7]

The Gulf War was clearly viewed by Israel and the Zionist movement as an historical juncture that could associate a number of Arab states with its long-standing objective of removing the national rights and grievances of the Palestinian people from the diplomatic agenda. Disqualifying the PLO from the process was calculated to be the first significant step toward achieving that goal.

The strategic shifts in the region and the world had two seemingly contradictory effects on Israeli hegemony. Unlike the Arab states, which were left with virtually no leverage, Israeli influence was in fact enhanced. U.S. Defense Secretary Dick Cheney reconfirmed the U.S. commitment to the security of Israel and its military advantage in May 1991, and a new package of military and economic aid was announced during his visit there. And yet, Israel's strategic relationship to the U.S. in the aftermath of the Cold War seemed to require some updating. The Soviet eclipse created a new opportunity for Baker, and produced an added imperative for such a reassessment.[8] A diminished Soviet "threat" is said to be incompatible with the notion of a strategic asset, or a cheap NATO; to some people, Israel has begun to look more and more like an expensive liability.[9] The American public has become less inclined to give foreign aid, after the removal of the "Soviet threat" from Washington's foreign policy lexicon, and as domestic needs have assumed urgent and renewed concern in the midst of recession. A *Wall Street Journal-*

NBC public opinion poll, which revealed that the percentage of Americans who would give aid to the Soviet Union (58%) exceeded that of those who would give to Israel (44%), was rather significant.[10]

And yet, the likelihood of an improved strategic relationship remains powerful. An Israeli-U.S. alliance adapted to post-Cold War conditions will not be based on the obsolete "Soviet threat," but on Israel's continued willingness and ability to offer the United States a strategic base in the Eastern Mediterranean to respond to regional conflicts. Israeli strategists suggested in interviews with the *Washington Post* that Israel "will present itself to Washington as a figurative home port in a sea of regional crisis."[11] The Haifa port is gradually and consistently accommodating larger U.S. naval vessels; meanwhile the United States is interested in prepositioning enough equipment in Israel for a mechanized battalion. And, already, Israel has served as a testing ground for equipment, a research and development center, and a weapons purchaser and supplier.

Now that the Pentagon has come up with new ideas for American "security policy" in the post-Cold War era, Israeli military planners are at work trying to find a role and ensure strategic significance. The concept of "strategic asset" — of which Israel is the prime example — will not only be retained by the U.S., but will also be reshaped and adapted as the Pentagon continues to imagine new enemies to fight. In March 1991, the *New York Times* published a leaked draft policy statement attributed to senior Pentagon officials, that foresaw a single superpower world. The United States is seen as the world's only policeman and no combination of allies or enemies is to be permitted to challenge that role:

> We will retain the pre-eminent responsibility for addressing selectively those wrongs which threaten not only our interests, but also those of our allies and friends, or which could seriously unsettle international relations.[12]

The Pentagon visionaries apparently imagine a future with a battered Iraq invading Kuwait and other oil states in the Gulf. They anticipate major battles for the U.S. there, in the Korean peninsula, in Panama, probably the Philippines and Europe. There is practically nothing in the document about taking serious steps towards collective security.

This context will likely prove to be fertile ground for Israel's own military planners, who have long awaited an opportunity to bridge the gap between U.S. global orientation and Israel's regional orientation. In their view, the post-Cold War United States will be more amenable to Tel Aviv's longstanding thesis that regional threats supersede the global, and that therefore Israel's interests in the region and those of the U.S. may coalesce in the coming years. The absence of Soviet-related scenarios could lead both countries to focus on regional problems. With turmoil in Algeria, Somalia and Sudan, uncertainties in Libya, Central Asia and the Gulf, and a full-scale war in Yugoslavia, the Pentagon authors of the future war scenarios might well find an able and willing Israel a suitable platform — "The biggest aircraft carrier in the Mediterranean," as one senior Israeli official put it.

Israel's strategic relevance for future U.S. endeavors would be enhanced by leaps and bounds in the context of an Arab-Israeli diplomatic settlement. Israel would no longer have to be kept out of Gulf "security" matters. Its regional role would be confirmed and expanded to include the Mediterranean, the Gulf and Central Asia. It would become a vanguard in the coming crusade against what is known in the West as Islamic fundamentalism and extremism. It would be in the forefront in the fight against "terrorism," the spread of nuclear weapons and weapons of mass destruction to countries of the South, and might use its own terrorist methods and nuclear blackmail to achieve U.S.-Israeli mutual objectives. It would also try to seduce the Central Asian states with agricultural technology — the United States is already providing huge amounts of money for an Israeli project involving the export of agricultural and irrigation know-how to Central Asia.

The strategic relationship is also being rebuilt in the area of shared intelligence, as well as servicing U.S. 6th Fleet naval ships and military aircraft stationed in Europe. All U.S. F-15 planes are now serviced by the Israel Aircraft Industries, while the government-owned Israel Shipyards regularly services and repairs U.S ships at Haifa. The U.S. Navy has allocated funds for expanding the port of Haifa, dredging the harbor and strengthening the piers.

Such joint ventures in military and non-military matters would reconfirm the special relationship and reinforce the strategic alliance. Israel would re-emerge as regional enforcer for the sole superpower, and thus continue to be a strategic asset beyond the Cold War and the dissolution of the Soviet Union. On the eve of Rabin's first visit to the U.S. as Israeli prime minister, his foreign minister, Shimon Peres, challenged the view that Israel's strategic importance has diminished:

> If previously we had to confront the Russians, now we have to confront the situation . . . Because the best peace paintings, hung on deteriorating walls, will fall down. We need different walls, not just different paintings. And I think it is in the interest of the U.S. to see the Middle East reconstructed.[13]

Such regional "reconstruction" is expected to have a much better chance of success with Rabin at the helm in Israel. His pragmatism and sensitivity to relations with the U.S. qualify him as a more suitable partner for the Pentagon strategists than Shamir, whose obsession with outmoded ideological notions was a serious barrier to such cooperation. Rabin's practical approach is more consonant with Washington's subtle requirements for forging a *pax Americana* under the guise of a "new world order." Rabin's August 1992 meeting with Bush at Kennebunkport was pivotal in the creation of a framework for redefining and broadening the post-Cold War strategic cooperation which Shimon Peres alluded to.

Although this analysis reveals that a new chapter is being opened up in the relationship between the United States and Israel, it by no means implies that Israel in the post-Shamir, post-Cold War era is being given *carte blanche* by its strategic ally. The fact is that while the strategic relationship is being renewed, it is also being clarified. American interests after the Cold War are not exactly the same as those during the Cold War. Access to Gulf oil and protection of Israeli security remain, as expected, among the United States's primary interests in the region. Victory in the Cold War and the Gulf War, however, has enabled the United States to establish unrivaled dominance in a previously contested area. American inclinations toward a single superpower world will be enhanced by using that dominance to exercise influence over its principal allies of the Cold War period. The Middle East therefore, becomes a critical testing ground for what George Bush called the "new world order." Rearranging the regional order under these conditions implies a need for a settlement of the Arab-Israeli conflict. That endeavor also puts the onus on Washington to avoid being blatantly biased. American stewardship in the region is going to require a viable settlement that reflects the irreducible minimum of Palestinian national aspirations and Arab basic requirements.

Herein lies the challenge to the Palestinians and the Arabs: the so-called new world order demands a higher level of regional conformity to Washington's global interests. The aspirations of potential regional hegemonic powers will be circumscribed if they are perceived as friendly, and destroyed if they appear hostile, like Iraq. That means friendly Israel, the foremost regional ally of the U.S., will not have the same degree of strategic independence that it used to enjoy in the past. It will have to conform to the broader and updated concept of U.S. interests. But it will still be strategically relevant.

Notes

1. For details, see the weekly bulletin of the Jerusalem Media and Communication Center for the period of the Gulf crisis.
2. *Boston Globe*, March 4, 1991.
3. Peter Waldman, "Israel Drops Recognition as Peace Talk Condition," *Wall Street Journal*, March 6, 1991.
4. Thomas Friedman, "Israel Backs Plan for Single Session on Mideast Peace," *New York Times*, April 10, 1991.
5. Ibid.
6. Mary Curtius, "Israel Says It Would Meet Arab States, Palestinians," *Boston Globe*, April 10, 1991.
7. Mary Curtius, "Saudi Arabia Has Halted Funding of the PLO, Baker Is Told," *Boston Globe*, April 12, 1991.
8. For a discussion of the U.S.-Israel relationship, see Naseer Aruri, "The United States and Israel: That Very Special Relationship," *American-Arab Affairs* No. 1 (Summer 1982), pp. 31–42.
9. See, for example, Glenn Frankel, "The East-West Warming Trend Has Chilling Implications for Israel," *Washington Post National Weekly Edition*, December 25–31, 1991.
10. *Wall Street Journal*, October 15, 1991.
11. *Washington Post*, July 28, 1992.
12. *New York Times*, March 8, 1992.
13. *Christian Science Monitor*, August 3, 1992.

27

Lebanon and the New World Order: Restoration of the Old Lebanese Order

As'ad AbuKhalil

The collapse of the Soviet Union has produced a new international situation in which the U.S. enjoys vastly more freedom of action. This new international situation is now being called by the U.S. the "new world order." This term, however, is inaccurate because the term implies a change of policy on the part of the United States. There is no indication (under Bush and under the new Clinton administration) that the U.S. has changed its foreign policy principles. Rather, the U.S. has merely reacted and adjusted to the new international context with far less restraints for American foreign policy.

The talk about a "new world order" masks a desire by some U.S. officials to promote past policies under a new banner. It is important for U.S. foreign policymakers to rationalize their actions and statements through the invocation of principles of human rights and democracy. The universal trend of democratization, which — contrary to assertions made by some Middle East experts in the U.S. — is affecting the Arab world where popular voices for liberty and equality are loud and clear, has forced the U.S. to take cognizance of the popularity of ideas of freedom. It is not cynical to suggest that principles of democracy and human rights have never been the major determinants of U.S. foreign policy. There were some attempts made during the presidency of Jimmy Carter to emphasize human rights in foreign policy, but these attempts were partial and inconsistent at best. There has been a trend in U.S. foreign policy to emphasize the need for democracy but only in countries ruled by groups or rulers who are opposed to U.S. policies.

Lebanese have often exaggerated the significance of Lebanon in world affairs. One Lebanese poet, Yunis Al-Ibn, once described Lebanon as: *hal kam arzi 'l-aj'in al-kawn* (a few cedars that have preoccupied the universe). In reality, Lebanese have been more responsible for their fate and for the destiny of their country than they wish to believe. The various conspiracy theories favored by most Lebanese to explain the protracted civil war were all too convenient to blame outsiders for Lebanon's acute problems. Many Lebanese sincerely refused to believe that a ferocious civil war like the Lebanese one was largely the product of Lebanese wills. The complexity of the Lebanese problem and the multiplicity of international and regional players, of course, confused many Lebanese and many observers of Lebanon.

The fall and disintegration of the Soviet Union did not have a direct impact on the Lebanon situation. The most important effect of the new changing international situation has to do with Syria's changing pattern of regional and international alliances. It was the end of the Soviet Union that pressed President Hafez al-Assad to reconsider his former network of alliances and to review his relationship with the United States. It was the new relationship between Syria and the U.S. that had the most lasting impact on the Lebanese scene. Assad seemed to have chosen a different outlook vis-a-vis the U.S. in the wake of the end the Cold War. No more was Syria able to exploit superpower rivalries for its own advantage. Assad felt compelled to associate himself with the U.S. and its Arab Gulf regimes in order to enhance the financial standing of Syria and to extract possible concessions from Israel. His long-standing strategic doctrine *at-tawazun al-'istratiji* (strategic balance) was dealt a severe blow because Russia was not interested in meeting the military demands of the Syrian regime.

The "new world order" emerged, so to speak, from the womb of the Gulf War. Syria decided to align itself with the American-led coalition, and was consequently able to extract a concession from the U.S. on the Lebanese question. While world attention was focused on the Gulf situation, the Syrian regime decided to end the power of General 'Awn, who was still holed up in the presidential palace in Ba'abda, Lebanon. The decision to crack down against General 'Awn's forces was, of course, influenced by the world's indifference to 'Awn's bombastic rhetoric. 'Awn's alliance with the Iraqi regime did not win him any additional friends either. The defeat of General 'Awn cemented the ties between Syria, Saudi Arabia, and the U.S. There developed a consensus among them that the agreement of At-Ta'if represented the best chance for a formula that could institutionalize meaningful political reforms. The problem, however, was that the accords of At-Ta'if merely changed the arithmetic in the formula for the distribution of political power on a sectarian basis, but it did not at all alter the underlying principle of the sectarian distribution of political power.

The impact of the "new world order" on Lebanon was felt more strongly in the area of Saudi-Syrian relations. The two countries have been feuding for over a decade over the Lebanese problem; indeed early in the civil war the Saudi regime supported the Phalangist coalition because it was concerned about the specter of a communist Lebanon. Syria was also unwilling to share any power in Lebanon with any Arab — or non-Arab — country. Saudi Arabia, in order to please Syria, had to abandon any desire of spreading its influence in Lebanon, with the exception of some generous donations to Saudi-supported politicians and organizations. The Saudi-Syrian alliance during the Gulf War ushered in a new era in the history of the Lebanese civil war; it allowed for the selection of a Saudi citizen (Rafiq Hariri) as prime minister, although Syria had opposed his nomination for years because it feared Saudi political hegemony in Lebanon. The prime ministership of Hariri should be seen as the product of the new era in Syrian-Saudi relations, where Saudi Arabia is allowed to enjoy some political influence in Lebanon in return for financial payments to the Syrian regime. (There are no reliable estimates of Saudi aid to Syria since the Iraqi invasion of Kuwait.)

The demise of the Soviet Union affected Lebanon insofar as some communist Lebanese and Palestinian organizations and parties in Lebanon lost a major backer. The perceived bankruptcy of the Soviet model discredited the agenda of communist parties in the Middle East. Some communist parties (including Yasir 'Abd Rabbuh's branch of the Democratic Front for the Liberation of Palestine (DFLP) and some North African communist organizations) abandoned Marxist-Leninist ideology and chose to promote themselves as socialist parties with nebulous ideologies. The attachment to Marxism-Leninism became a heavy burden to bear in much of the Arab world.

Soviet financial and military backing had been instrumental in the preservation of Lebanese and communist bureaucracies; after the break-up of the USSR, the Lebanese Communist Party, for example, was forced to close down the daily edition of its newspaper *An-Nida'* for financial reasons after decades of publication. Lebanese and Palestinian organizations had also enjoyed direct and indirect Soviet military backing in the course of the civil war. So shattered was the Lebanese Communist Party, that its strong leader George Hawi decided to resign and leave political life altogether.

The "new world order," however, did not create a political environment in the Middle East that is sympathetic to U.S. economic and political interests. On the contrary, the U.S. heralding of the new world order coincided with the intensification of Arab popular antipathy to U.S. interests. The plight of Iraqi civilians, Western inaction in the Bosnian war, the cancellation of the Algerian elections to the indifference — if not the glee — of the Western world because the victors were Muslim fundamentalists, the continued U.S. support for pro-U.S. undemocratic regimes, and the continued sufferings of the Palestinians all increased Arab resentment against the U.S., despite the increase in the number of Arab regimes willing to support the U.S.

Lebanon was no exception. The rise of Islamic fundamentalist groups in Lebanon discouraged the Lebanese government from going too far in its alliance with the U.S. It should be noted that the Lebanese government was far more restrained in its support for Kuwait during the Gulf War than was Syria. Lebanese public opinion, which has an outlet in the relative freedom of the press, expressed sympathy for the Iraqi people, and the Syrian desire for a symbolic Lebanese military presence in the Gulf for the "liberation of Kuwait" was never fulfilled. Instead, the Lebanese government found itself in a position where it had to please the Syrian government and Saudi Arabia without provoking the Lebanese population, which was clearly unsympathetic to the Kuwaiti cause.

The military intervention by the U.S. also added to the suspicion by many Lebanese that civil wars and wars in general can not go on unless the U.S. wants to continue. Those conspiracy theorists in Lebanon became convinced that the Lebanese civil war represented an American wish, if not an American conspiracy hatched by Henry Kissinger (as many Lebanese still believe). The decision by the U.S. to deploy troops in record numbers in a far away place ostensibly to implement UN resolutions was contrasted in the minds of many Lebanese and Palestinians with the U.S indifference to the unimplemented UN resolutions dealing with the Lebanese and Palestinian situations. Furthermore, many Lebanese who lived through the Israeli invasion of Lebanon in 1982 could not understand why the Western world had not shown any enthusiasm for intervention against Israel at that time. In many ways, the Gulf War and the talk of a "new world order" increased Arab (including Lebanese) public disenchantment with the U.S.

Nevertheless, there is one link between the discourse about the "new world order" and the situation in Lebanon. There is evidence that interest in democratization and the creation of a civil society is as strong in Lebanon as it is elsewhere in the Arab world, despite the lack of attention paid to it by the Western media. The pluralistic legacy of the Lebanese political system, the relative freedom of the press, and the presence of dozens of publishing houses in Lebanon has only reinforced the appeal of democratic reforms. In Lebanon, however, democratization has been limited by virtue of the sectarian considerations which often promote specific, authoritarian agendas.

Finally, it should be noted that the reform efforts of At-Ta'if do not aim at the creation of a new political system in Lebanon. Rather, these efforts are limited to the resurrection of the old order according to a new mathematical formula. Sectarian tags and consciousness still prevail in the minds and the constitutional laws of Lebanon, and Syria seems intent on pushing its agenda in Lebanon with little consideration of internal opposition. The 1992 elections in Lebanon, which are an unreliable measure of Lebanese public attitudes and preferences given the successful boycott by most Christians of the elections and the various irregularities that marred the electoral process, were used to legitimize the Syrian political role in Lebanon. Furthermore, Israeli occupation of parts of South Lebanon, and the continued Israeli bombing raids against Lebanese and Palestinian targets — with very little concern for civilian lives — do not seem to bother the "new world order," which is supposedly based on the rule of law and on the necessity of implementing UN resolutions. In this respect, the fact that the UN resolutions calling for Israeli withdrawal from South Lebanon have yet to be implemented is a forceful reminder to the Lebanese that while some may talk of a new world order, in this part of the world the old order is still very much in place.

■ PART SIX ■

Africa

28

Marginalization or Renewal?
Africa in the New World Order

William Minter

In a June 19, 1992 editorial, the *Washington Post* appealed for action to save the tens of thousands dying in Somalia, asking rhetorically "Why will the world not pay attention?" During the month preceding and the month following the editorial, however, the *Post* carried only 8 articles on Somalia, averaging 420 words each, as compared with 26 articles in the same period on Bosnia, averaging over 800 words each. There were sixteen front-page stories on Bosnia, but only one on Somalia. Altogether the influential Washington newspaper published more than six times as many words on Bosnia as on Somalia.

The *Post* was not the worst offender. Over the same period the *New York Times* published almost nine times as much copy on Bosnia as on Somalia, and National Public Radio aired six times as many stories. Television coverage was even more disproportional. In late July and August of 1992, public attention and media coverage of Somalia increased, as the United Nations and the U.S. finally moved to step up relief efforts. But the change was late, fell far short of the scale of the human tragedy at issue, and was unlikely to be sustained.

In Bosnia, as in Somalia, the great powers appeared unwilling to avert the worsening tragedy. But at least the world was watching, and the response was greater. The difference is a paradigm for Africa's place in the "new world disorder" of one superpower and economic inequality, in which Darwinian struggles to survive and compete have largely supplanted ideological wars, and in which international institutions faced overwhelming new demands with shrinking resources.

Somalia, where drought and famine was accompanied by the breakdown of any semblance of political order, is an extreme case. But other African crises were also relegated to the margins of public attention, media coverage and policymakers' agendas. Positive developments were equally neglected.

The U.S. public was almost totally unaware of an unprecedented ferment of popular democracy movements, creative efforts at conflict resolution, and the search for new development paths by African intellectuals and grassroots groups (see box at the end of this chapter).

With the end of the Cold War, the motives for much negative U.S. intervention in Africa disappeared. But it seemed to be replaced by what Council on Foreign Relations analyst Michael Clough has termed "cynical disengagement." Both Africans and the international community were looking to the remaining superpower for leadership and support. In some cases middle-level U.S. officials with Africa responsibility played constructive roles with respect to conflict resolution, support for democratic change or provision of needed relief. But the overall policy displayed no recognition of past U.S. responsibility for creating present crises and no sense of urgency about resolving them. It was a posture that could only be generously described as "benign neglect."

The consequences were heavy. They included continued U.S. tolerance of violence in South Africa and dictators like Mobutu in Zaire and Banda in Malawi. U.S. policymakers were disastrously sluggish in responding to the crisis in Liberia as well as Somalia, and indifferent to Moroccan abuses of a referendum agreement in occupied Western Sahara. Washington, meanwhile, failed to bolster African grassroots groups taking initiatives for democratization and development around the continent. And the U.S. was still throwing its weight behind dogmatic free-market structural adjustment programs which punished the poor and had little chance of success even in their own restricted terms of macroeconomic growth.

The configuration of issues for different African countries varied enormously. The political and economic landscape in Somalia was not the same as in South Africa or in Zaire. Nor did Mozambique's painful quest for peace, Tanzania's efforts to cope with economic marginalization, or Nigeria's military-directed transition to civilian rule all fall into some common African pattern that could be summarized neatly to make up for the absence of sustained coverage and public information. But throughout Africa, the failure of old paradigms was forcing peoples and governments to confront fundamental issues: violence and security, democracy and participation, sustainable development and inequality.

For Africa, it was not only — or even primarily — the collapse of the Soviet Union and its social model that was forcing this rethinking. It was above all the practical failure of the post-colonial order: of states with ideologies from right to left; of despots or pragmatists without ideology; and of the bilateral and foreign donors who often prescribed the policies for African states.

There was no agreement on the details of solutions, which in any case differed from country to country. But some consensus on general principles was evolving among Africa's intellectuals, grassroots groups and leaders inside and outside of government. One element of this consensus was that any solution must involve *both* fundamental reforms in African state and society *and* international willingness to support this process without imposing yet another variant of inappropriate external guidelines and undemocratic bureaucracy.

Africans were not asking the world to prescribe solutions or provide all the resources for dealing with them. But Africa's structural dependence still ensured that, in case after case, what the outside world did — or didn't do — weighed heavily on the success or failure of local initiatives. A few cases from selected countries will illustrate the point.

Violence and Peace-Making

In Somalia in 1992, as in Liberia, the collapse of a dictator long backed by the United States was followed by disintegration, as reprisals between armed groups and the absence of working government accentuated ethnic or clan divisions. There was general agreement in Africa, as well as internationally, that in such extreme cases the international community had to find some way to make up for the lack of effective national sovereignty. The question was how to do it, and who should assume responsibility.

Liberians trusted in their "special relationship" with the United States, only to see Washington wash its hands of responsibility. A force from the Economic Community of West African States played the key role in restoring a modicum of order there. In the case of Somalia, located in the conflict-ridden Horn of Africa, there was no subcontinental regional organization to play this role. Critics rightly faulted the Organization of African Unity and the Arab League, of which Somalia was a member, for failing to take the lead. But the United Nations and the United States, with far greater resources to cope with the crisis, also failed to respond promptly.

In other contexts the international community was not being called on to intervene, but simply to bring pressure to bear against regimes involved in promoting violence. The most notable case was southern Africa. There international sanctions helped force Pretoria to release Nelson Mandela and begin new reform initiatives in 1990.

After that success, however, the international community and Washington in particular turned a blind eye to the ongoing violence instigated by South Africa's covert military assets both inside South Africa and in Mozambique. More than 7,000 people were killed in South African townships between January 1990 and the end of 1992. The June 17, 1992 massacre of over 40 people at Boipatong was only the latest and the best publicized incident. At the grassroots level the violence in some areas became a matter of back-and-forth retaliation between migrant workers in hostels organized by Chief Buthelezi's Inkatha, and township dwellers loyal to the African National Congress.

Nevertheless, reports by Amnesty International, the International Commission of Jurists and other human rights observers stressed that (1) the initiative for violence most often came from the government-allied Inkatha warriors, (2) there was massive documentation for inaction, partiality and cover-ups by the security forces, with no evidence of serious reform efforts by top officials, and (3) the de Klerk regime showed no interest in exploring available evidence of direct involvement of the security forces in instigating the violence.

Aid from South Africa from official or unofficial sources also continued to fuel the brutal Renamo attacks on Mozambican civilians, as did access by Renamo to Malawi and support from private right-wing groups in the United States. For more than two years of peace talks, Renamo found excuse after excuse for not signing a ceasefire. Even if a hoped-for October 1992 ceasefire deadline was met, recovering from the legacy of violence would be an enormous task.

In these two related cases, African and other international organizations, such as the Organization of African Unity, the Frontline States and the Commonwealth, responded to requests to put pressure on the South African government and on Renamo. The Frontline States, the alliance of southern African states which long coordinated the diplomatic campaign against apartheid, spoke out. But the realities of world power were that it was pressure from the United States and other major powers that counted. Such action was belated, weak and emasculated by bias in favor of the de Klerk regime.

In a landmark meeting of former and current African leaders in Kampala, Uganda in May 1991, the delegates adopted a proposal to establish a continent-wide Conference on Security, Stability, Development and Cooperation in Africa, analogous to the Helsinki process in Europe. They recognized that instability in any African country threatened other countries as well, and called for collective measures and structures for conflict resolution.

Neither establishing such a general organizational framework, nor dealing with the multiple crises that would not wait, were easy tasks. There were no African states which combined sufficient internal stability and continent-wide influence to give strong leadership on more than the particular issues which most directly affected them. Africa-led initiatives at conflict resolution, if they were to work, would need strong reinforcement from the United Nations and the rich countries. Judging by the record, the post-Cold War tendency seemed more likely to be perfunctory attention by Washington and the international community in general, as well as persistence of a pattern of holding former U.S. clients to lower standards of human rights.

Democracy and Dictatorships

Despite the wave of democratization movements around the world and in Africa, the South African white minority regime and aging Cold War relics such as President Mobutu of Zaire, Banda of Malawi and Moi of Kenya clung to power in the early 1990s. In some countries, such as Zambia, incumbent leaders retired gracefully after election defeats. But even when free and fair elections were held, substantive and sustainable democracy also depended on building institutions of popular participation. Without that, "democracy" would be a game of elites. And it would lose legitimacy as it failed to address fundamental problems of ordinary citizens confronted with round after round of belt-tightening and burgeoning corruption.

In terms of general rhetoric, the United States supported democracy. But U.S. policymakers largely closed their eyes to the unfulfilled promises and persistent stalling tactics of their undemocratic client regimes. Congressional mandates calling for support to grassroots groups and popular participation were scarcely reflected in the budget priorities or policy prescriptions which made up U.S. policy in practice. Money allocated to promoting "democracy" was largely directed to the technicalities of balloting or to simplistic assumptions that democracy was best promoted by advice from American contractors on emulating the American way of doing things. Top officials continued to dismiss concerns for human rights and popular participation as "feelgood" rhetoric, irrelevant to the pursuit of the U.S. national interest.

In South Africa, the negotiations at the Congress for a Democratic South Africa (CODESA) stalled, in part over the government's failure to stop the violence but also because the de Klerk regime still wanted to build a white-minority veto into a future constitution. Although buried in complex verbiage, the fundamental issue was whether the existing regime would be guaranteed the perpetual right to veto actions of a popularly-elected government. Combining such legal provisions with the regime's de facto control of the military and the bureaucracy, affirmative action would be blocked and white privilege preserved indefinitely. In their infatuation with de Klerk's image of reformer, however, U.S. policymakers and the media virtually ignored these substantive questions, in favor of pious urgings to all parties to keep talking.

In Zaire, the National Conference planning a transition to democracy existed uneasily with Mobutu's insistence on his control over army and government. The process seemed always to be on the point of breaking down. But the Bush administration refused to listen to public and Congressional demands to tell Mobutu definitively good-bye.

Around the continent the democratic agenda was being defined by popular movements and intellectuals. It included competitive elections and legal protection of human rights. But it also stressed that sustainable democracy had to go beyond such formal institutions to provide for participation by the wider public, in the context of sustainable and equitable development policies.

Drought, Famine and Sustainable Development

By the early 1990s few argued, as many did in the early post-independence years, that political rights had to wait on economic development. The predominant view was that democratic participation was one of the fundamental requirements for achieving development. But the inverse was also inescapably true: economic failure endangered whatever democratic advances were made.

It was difficult to exaggerate the depth of the economic crisis facing almost all African countries. Although most African governments adopted structural adjustment programs as demanded by international financial institutions, these programs did not restore vigorous macroeconomic growth or modified structures of dependence on exports of primary products. Moreover, they increased the vulnerability of the majority of the population. Natural disasters and conflict accentuated and revealed the underlying economic weaknesses, but they did not create them.

In Mozambique, as in many other countries, the structural adjustment program mandated cuts in government spending, keeping wages down and reducing the number of government employees, while allowing prices to rise with currency devaluation. Health, education and other services were devastated. Corruption grew enormously, as few even high-level managers could afford to live on their salaries. Skilled workers were drained away to the private sector, or to work for international aid agencies. In hard currency, a chauffeur at a Maputo embassy earned more than a top-level civil servant. Meanwhile, 3,000 foreign technicians, many on World Bank or bilateral donor contracts, earned $180 million in 1991, roughly three times the wage bill of the entire Mozambican civil service of 100,000, including teachers and health workers.

Mozambique, a country at war and one of the poorest on the continent, was an extreme case. But the structural adjustment packages had similar effects in dozens of other African countries.

The famine in southern Africa which began in 1991, following the worst failure of rains in this century, threatened almost 18 million people with starvation or severe malnutrition. Over 20 million people were also at risk of famine in northeastern Africa, particularly in conflict-ridden Somalia and Sudan. The United States was contributing relief, although the programs needed more funding and more high-level attention. But the fundamental issue was long-term policies that promoted sustainable development, including food self-sufficiency, for African countries.

The southern African drought provided a dramatic example of the negative influence of the short-sighted policies promoted by external advisors. In the late 1980s, Zimbabwe built up a large surplus of grain, as part of the Southern African Development Coordination Conference's plans for food security. Just before the drought, the Zimbabwean government, with U.S. and World Bank encouragement, sold off the stockpile as "uneconomic," and even lowered prices for corn while raising prices for export tobacco. Farmers planted 40% less corn, with the result that when the drought hit Zimbabwe had to import expensive grain from the U.S.

As in the political arena, there was no simple economic solution. But there was an emerging African consensus that, in contrast to orthodox structural adjustment programs, sustainable development had to emphasize investment in Africa's human resources, transform institutions in both the public and private sectors, and move away from the inherited dependence on export of primary products which were inherently vulnerable to world-market fluctuations.

Africa's Problems . . . African Initiatives

One of the few success stories of the post-independence era was that the expansion of education produced a new generation of educated Africans. In comparison with the period immediately following colonial rule, there were far more human resources to supply skills, creative solutions and leadership within both the organizations of civil society and the state.

But just as with the most neglected regions and social strata within advanced free-market societies, the operations of international markets and international decision-making institutions sucked these resources away from where they were needed. Many of Africa's best-trained men and women went into political or economic exile overseas. Pursuit of individual self-interest was rewarded, whether or not it benefited the African economies and societies. Promising initiatives by dedicated individual leaders, grassroots groups, political movements and even government bureaucracies were left to founder, deprived of resources or even the moral support of international attention.

For those seeking to understand and respond to African initiatives, there is no substitute for learning the details of particular countries and movements, from the African National Congress in South Africa to those involved in promoting National Conferences in Zaire and other French-speaking countries (see box). But there were also general statements, attempting to build an Africa-wide consensus, that deserved the attention of outsiders. In addition to the Kampala statement on security issues by African leaders, mentioned earlier, the Economic Commission for Africa pioneered an alternate framework to structural adjustment programs. And a continent-wide conference initiated by grassroots groups issued the African Charter for Popular Participation.

The end of the Cold War, which had so blighted international involvement in the African continent, had to become the opportunity for creative new initiatives. The urgency of the human crises were undeniable. Nor was there a shortage of creative African proposals for what needed to be done. Judged by the record of the "new world order" up to the end of 1992, however, labels like "cynical disengagement" or "benign neglect" seemed the most likely to stick.

Africa's Problems . . . African Initiatives: A Sampling of Lesser-Known Examples

* In almost every African country, new non-governmental human rights monitoring groups emerged, expanding their operations despite limited international assistance and occasional government harassment. Such groups were particularly active in Nigeria and Kenya, and stressed the importance of the rule of law as well as the need for free elections.

* In Benin, the Congo, and Mali, pro-democracy movements culminating in "National Conferences" bringing together civic groups, religious groups, politicians and others resulted in elections of new leaders. The National Conference phenomenon, with varying degrees of success, became a model for almost all French-speaking African countries.

* The activist Greenbelt Movement, founded by Wangari Maathai in Kenya, mobilized 50,000 women to plant trees, and actively protested environmentally damaging government projects.

* After the overthrow of General Mengistu in Ethiopia in 1991 the new Ethiopian government and Eritrea, a territory which had fought for decades for independence, agreed to settle the independence question by a peaceful referendum in 1993. Both governments were making good-faith efforts at reconstruction, with only minimal international assistance.

* African ministers of health, confronted both with the AIDS epidemic and with repeated budget cuts, sponsored an International Conference on Community Health in Africa, meeting in September 1992 in Brazzaville. The conference was designed to bring together grassroots groups with government officials and technical specialists, to concentrate on health mobilization measures that could be adopted without increasing national budgets.

* In Mozambique, with its overwhelming and chronic food crisis, relief officials continued to stress that emergency food aid had to be accompanied by efforts at reconstruction: seeds, tools, supplies for education and health programs. Despite the failure of international agencies to match emergency relief with support for these long-term needs, people in refugee and resettlement camps made their own efforts to survive. Families took in orphans, and displaced teachers set up schools under trees.

29

The Future in Black and White:
U.S.-South African Relations After the Cold War

Bernard Magubane

At a moment like this, when moral passions are running high, certain truths need to be re-asserted very firmly. South Africa is so important to the Western world, economically and strategically, that violent revolution there, resulting in chaos and disruption, is quite as much against Western interests as it is against the interests of the indigenous whites. Ideally, the West would like to see a controlled and orderly progression towards multi-racial democracy, but if the choice is between revolutionary change and no change at all, then the West will, and must, come to terms with the latter rather than risk aiding or abetting the former. It follows from this that neither black Africa nor the Soviet Union should be left in any possible doubt that the United States will not tolerate external support for the cause of black revolution.
— Peregrine Worsthorne, *Sunday Telegraph* (London), June 20, 1976

Even as the Cold War has been declared dead with the demise of communism in the Soviet Union and its satellites in Eastern Europe, the United States is grooming Botswana as a forward staging base for U.S. military forces in southern Africa. What does this strategy say about U.S. intentions in the region? To answer this question a sober assessment of the twelve years of the Reagan-Bush administrations is imperative.

Post-World War II U.S. foreign policy is full of case studies from which we can draw lessons of what any U.S. administration is likely to do: Vietnam, Cuba, Grenada, Nicaragua provide important clues. In Vietnam, the U.S. squandered billions of dollars, lost fifty thousand lives of its own young men and women, maimed many more, destroyed the fabric of a peasant society. Why? All in the name of containing communism! It is almost fourteen years since the Vietnam War ended, and Washington was, until Operation Desert Storm, still struggling to rid itself of what is called the Vietnam syndrome.

The relation between southern Africa policy in particular and the more general issue of U.S. policy toward communism and the USSR was central to the whole policy of so-called "constructive engagement" with South Africa which characterized the Reagan years. Constructive engagement was not about helping the black populations of South Africa and Namibia rid themselves of the oppressive and exploitative white minority regime, but was founded on the desire to preempt what Cold War ideologues called "Soviet-backed revolutionary change." A cynical injection of the "red scare" turned what was a straightforward issue of ending oppressive white minority rule in South Africa and colonization in Namibia into a strategy of incorporating South Africa as a respected member of the Western defense system in the struggle against so-called "Soviet expansionism." Behind the sweet-sounding phrase "constructive engagement," U.S. policy was aligned even more openly with the goals of the apartheid regime, under the pretext that this was the only way this notorious regime would be "nudged" to reform itself.

When giving testimony before the Senate Foreign Relations Committee during his nomination, Reagan's Africa envoy Chester Crocker outlined the key elements of the policy that he would pursue during his tenure. Among other things he said that the policy on Africa would:

1. Support regional security.
2. Ensure for the U.S. and our allies fair commercial access to essential petroleum and non-fuel minerals.
3. Promote U.S. trade and investment in Africa.
4. Foster basic human liberties in keeping with both our principles and our long-term interests and objectives.[1]
5. Cooperate with our Western allies and friends in Africa to deter aggression and subversion by our adversaries.

Crocker was at pains to emphasize the point that:

Our political relations with Africa must be guided by our interests, both global and regional . . . Together with Zaire, southern African countries play an important role in meeting U.S., European and Japanese requirements for critical minerals . . . The challenge this administration accepts is to develop policies throughout southern Africa that enhance our interests and impede opportunities for our adversaries . . .

How were these goals to be achieved? According to Crocker, "It would clearly be unwise to rule out military instruments of our policy in Africa or anywhere else . . . the challenge to U.S. policy is to acquire and retain a level of influence commensurate with our interests, strategic, political, and economic."[2]

The goals that the Reagan administration set for itself in southern Africa were complex and ambitious, and involved the military doctrine of coercive diplomacy. According to this doctrine, a nation can sometimes achieve certain limited political objectives by combining carefully measured doses of military force with diplomacy against an adversary who resists one's demands, while "negotiations" are continued. In some cases, inducements of aid or other incentives may be offered. The idea is that an adversary may be "persuaded" to accept one's demands when enough military pressure has been applied, and when suitable inducements are offered.

From 1981 to its humiliating 1987 defeat at Cuito Cuanavale, South Africa, encouraged and abetted by the Reagan administration and its allies, embarked on an aggressive exercise of military diplomacy which would leave Angola and Mozambique in economic shambles; and the rest of the frontline states subject to sustained sabotage by the agents of South Africa, with millions of dollars lost.

The Anti-Apartheid Act of 1986

In 1986 the Comprehensive Anti-Apartheid Act was passed by Congress over Reagan's veto. The passage of the Act must be understood in the context of the events sketched out above, and the escalating pressure within the United States for stronger action against apartheid; this pressure came from student activists, Jesse Jackson and the Rainbow Coalition, the demonstrations from Trans-Africa, and various church-related demands for divestment. The act effectively repudiated the policy of constructive engagement in South Africa. In Section 4, the act sets out as its principal purpose a "comprehensive and complete framework to guide the efforts of the United States in helping to bring an end to apartheid in South Africa and lead to the establishment of a non-racial democratic government." The act also works out the priorities of the executive branch by defining what U.S. policy must be "toward the government of South Africa, the victims of apartheid and other states in southern Africa."

The act, according to Winston Nogan, reflected a widely held perception in the opinion of policymakers within Congress that the white minority — in spite of almost 60 years of trying — was no nearer to its goal of establishing its hegemony in southern Africa; moreover, within South Africa itself its ability to rule over the black majority was slipping and could not be maintained indefinitely.[3] The striking thing about the act, he goes on, is that it "mirrors the survival of the national phobia of anti-communism, a prominent feature of the political climate in the U.S. since World War II . . . A pervasive concern of the Act is fear that the national liberation movement of South Africa is controlled, or might be controlled by elites with communistic ideological affiliations. Indeed, a leitmotif of the Act is the fear that liberation in South Africa will ultimately be a victory for international communism."[4] The act reveals deep-seated U.S. suspicions about the African National Congress (ANC), especially its alliance with the South African Communist Party (SACP). In U.S. foreign policy under Reagan and in the Anti-Apartheid Act there were hints that if the ANC repudiated its alliance with the communists it could be acceptable as a negotiating partner. But in general the fear remained that if communists were a significant force in the ANC, the West would have no guarantees that they would not subvert a future ANC-led government.

Besides giving the president discretionary powers to implement the very act which supposedly repudiated his previous policy toward South Africa, another glaring loophole in the act was to leave in place and legitimate the cooperation between the U.S. security forces and those of the apartheid regime. Nogan underlines this obvious contradiction:

> Therefore, as a matter of public policy, and in unprecedented fashion, intelligence collaboration with the South African government has been legitimized. South Africa is keenly interested in the deployment of ANC operatives as well as the strategic and tactical thinking of the ANC leadership. Since the prime object of the South African security system is to monitor and destroy the liberation movements, especially the ANC, there is a serious question whether mutual trust can be established between the liberation movement and the U.S. government in light of this intelligence collaboration. It cannot be forgotten that Nelson Mandela was an early casualty of CIA collaboration and betrayal to the South African security policy.[5]

The End of the Reagan Era

As Ronald Reagan reluctantly prepared for what to the people of southern Africa was a welcome and a graceless departure from history, Chester Crocker, the architect of the failed constructive engagement policy, embarked on a flurry of diplomatic activity to help bring about the departure of Cuba's internationalist forces and the defeated and dispirited South African expeditionary forces from Angola, and to bring about the independence of Namibia.

In 1981, when the U.S. had linked the independence of Namibia to the withdrawal of Cuban forces from Angola, South Africa's diplomacy achieved a major breakthrough. In November of that year, the Johannesburg *Financial Mail* wrote that "South Africa pressed the right diplomatic button when it dropped the issue of UN impartiality and concentrated on the Cuban presence as a point of negotiation, thus finding common cause with the U.S." From then on the U.S. and South Africa would maneuver not only to link the withdrawal of Cuban troops and advisers, but to rebuild and support the UNITA movement of Jonas Savimbi in Angola. On the latter issue, South Africa's General Malan would declare jubilantly that "Angola is one place where the U.S. can roll back the Soviet/Cuban presence in Africa."

It was in this context that Crocker's diplomatic efforts took place in the late eighties, and in which the aims of South Africa and the Reagan administration vis-a-vis the ANC began to emerge. According to *The Independent*:

> If the Angolans, and their Cuban and Russian backers agree, the chief prize for Pretoria in the current U.S.-sponsored negotiations may not be the removal of Cuban troops from Angola but the collapse of the ANC's military campaign, and the delivery of the ANC to the negotiating table. There have been serious doubts that South Africa has any intention of ending its 68-year-old rule of Namibia. The prospect that the ANC would be forced to negotiate might be the ultimate prize which could persuade them to give up the territory (May 1, 1988).

The question of the closure of ANC bases in Angola soon became moot, as the Angolans agreed to close the ANC bases there. In a speech observing the

77th year of the founding of the ANC, its president, Oliver Tambo, announced that the ANC would close its bases in Angola in order to facilitate the independence of Namibia. The non-aggression pact brokered by the U.S. and signed in 1984 between Maputo and Pretoria had also led to the expulsion of the ANC military wing from Mozambique. The *Financial Times* observed that the decision stunned the ANC, angered some of the black-ruled states of the region, and provoked private misgivings within Mozambique's ruling Frelimo party (September 15, 1988). But as subsequent developments were to show, although the pact failed to end South African support for the Renamo rebels, it proved critical in Mozambique's campaign to win Western economic, humanitarian and military aid.

On Angola, Chester Crocker continued to insist that the U.S. would continue its support for UNITA as long as the Soviet Union's aid to the Angolan government continued. Crocker's linkage plan and South Africa's demand regarding the ANC meant that the U.S. and South Africa had other agendas. After the December 1988 agreement on the independence of Namibia and the withdrawal of Cuban troops from Angola, the U.S.-financed war in Angola escalated, at tremendous human cost to the Angolan people.

Representative Ron Dellums of California criticized the policy of funding UNITA, saying that such actions flew in the face of democratic ideals and open conduct of foreign policy. From the debates, it was obvious that:

> Many policymakers recognized and were sympathetic to the reality of changed world conditions symbolized by the end of the Cold War. Even many who supported the administration's funding of "UNITA freedom fighters" against the "Soviet-backed Marxist-Leninist MPLA," recognized the stagnant quality of the old arguments. Persistent overtures by the government of Angola and the new international climate will continue to condition the legislative environment and possibly result in further shifts in policy.[6]

These sentiments were ignored by the Bush administration. For instance, in March 1991 the Seventh Congress of UNITA was held at what is called Kwame Nkrumah military base in southern Angola. During the Congress, Walter Kansteiner, the American envoy, read to the assembled delegates a message of support from President George Bush, who expressed his support for UNITA during the transition to multi-party democracy. Jonas Savimbi is said to have made every effort to represent the U.S. position of general support as "a more precise backing for Savimbi himself as a future president of Angola."[7]

The historic posture of the U.S. as well as the administration's vigorous determination to support Savimbi showed that what was at issue in Angola was the installation of a regime that could guarantee U.S. access to that country's enormous resources. Despite administration claims that they were primarily interested in peace in Angola, in practice U.S. policy in resource-rich countries is to ensure a "free" hand in exploiting these areas. It is a policy that has a long history in Latin America, Asia and Africa since the process of decolonization began in 1957.

The Release of Nelson Mandela

Developments in South Africa since the release of Nelson Mandela on February 11, 1990 have been so far-reaching and swift that there has barely been time to make a considered judgement of how these changes will alter or influence U.S. policy. Mandela's 1990 historic visit to the U.S. was immediately followed by President F. W. de Klerk's own visit. According to Bernard Trainor, in a special *New York Times* article, during the de Klerk visit there were no plans for a rally in Yankee Stadium, for T-shirts, or for mayors and other politicians to line up and embrace him. The only crowds President de Klerk could expect were those to protest his visit:

> But Mr. de Klerk can count on a warm center of support in the White House. While Mr. Mandela has been a hero to the masses, Mr. de Klerk is officialdom's champion. During Mr. Mandela's visit, officials in the Bush Administration were eager to praise Mr. de Klerk. And President Bush once told a reporter of his warm regard for Mr. de Klerk even though the questioner did not ask about him.

Trainor gives two reasons for the White House support for de Klerk; the first was his lifting of the embarrassing ban on the ANC and beginning the process of negotiating South Africa's future. The second reason, he says, is habit:

> Except for the brief period in the 1970s when the Carter Administration excoriated the South African Government, Washington has sought to maintain solid relations with South Africa, mindful of its strategic location, its valuable minerals and its anti-Communism. The Central Intelligence Agency may have helped South Africa capture Mr. Mandela 28 years ago, according to recent published reports that the Administration did not dispute. Until a few years ago the United States showed little diplomatic interest in the African National Congress. During the Nixon Administration, the United States Ambassador to South Africa visited Robben Island, the island prison off Cape Town where Mr. Mandela and other political prisoners were held. He went as a guest of the South African Government — not to visit Mr. Mandela, but to shoot birds, which some of the prisoners were obliged to fetch for him.

Trainor notes how during the Reagan era, the State Department was solicitous of South Africa's white leaders as a matter of clearly defined policy:

> There was always a whiff of self-congratulation in the Reagan policy on South Africa. Administration officials were pleased with themselves for not yielding to popular emotion to condemn South Africa, a course they described as unproductive.

In the meantime, Congress, responding to popular sentiment, enacted economic sanctions against South Africa over President Reagan's veto and Vice-President Bush's opposition, although the latter later conceded they may have helped push the South African government to its subsequent negotiating position. Trainor also says that the Bush administration was concerned that de Klerk was moving faster than many whites would tolerate.

"The officials discount the possibility of a coup, but they worry about his political support leaching away." Trainor goes on:

> Although American officials admire Mr. Mandela, they believe Mr. de Klerk is more important, and his departure from the scene would most upset prospects for peaceful change. In this, the Bush policy toward South Africa resembles nothing so much as the Administration's policy toward the Soviet Union and Mikhail S. Gorbachev — a near-total reliance on the man in power staying in power.

The Changing Situation Within South Africa

Following the defeat of a Nationalist Party candidate, in a by-election in Vereening, de Klerk called for a referendum, for March 17, 1992. In an 85% poll, white voters voted by a margin of 2 to 1 in favor of shaping a new constitution that would enfranchise the black population and thus begin the process which will lead to the transfer of power to the majority. This was nothing less than a political and social earthquake. White minority rule, black exploitation and powerlessness have been a way of life in South Africa, enshrined in law since 1910. Generations of whites were bred to believe that God had ordained white supremacy and black inferiority; that black demands for freedom were at best ridiculous and at worst a communist plot.

How do we explain this vote which will lead to a white surrender of political if not economic power? This was not a mere decision to let a minority have civil rights, as in the American South when in 1964 the Congress passed the Civil Rights Act. It was a decision to let the overwhelming majority— 80% of the population — have human rights. The result initiated a process that must sooner rather than later result in political power for the majority.

The strategic objectives of the ANC, before its unbanning on February 2, 1990, were based on a delicate balance and a particular relationship between various dimensions of the struggle, which included underground work, the armed struggle, sanctions, and isolation of the white minority regime at the international level. And the goal of the struggle was defined as the transfer of power to the people of South Africa. What then were the implications of entering negotiations with the white minority regime that had overwhelming military power? The process of negotiation no doubt introduced a new element into the overall struggle.

The willingness to negotiate on the part of the ANC is in fact not that new. In 1949, before it adopted the Program of Action that would lead to the Defiance Campaign of 1952–1954, the ANC had called on the government to convene a national conference to discuss the adoption of a democratic constitution for the country. Before convening the Congress of the People at Kliptown in 1955, where the Freedom Charter was adopted, the ANC had again renewed its call on the regime to rethink its refusal to sit down with the representatives of the people to work out a new charter for the country.

On December 17, 1961, following the persistent refusal of the regime to enter into negotiations with the representatives of the people, the ANC issued an historic statement which declared war on the white minority regime. The ultimatum stated:

> The time comes in the life of any nation when there remain only two choices— submit or fight. That time has now come in South Africa. We shall not submit, and we have no choice but to hit back by all means in our power, in defense of our people, our future, and our freedom.

These were momentous words, and they rang loud and clear in the capitals of the world. Therefore, it was a new milestone when on August 7, 1990, the ANC suspended the armed struggle with this terse statement:

> The African National Congress is now suspending all armed actions with immediate effect. No further armed actions and related activities by the ANC and its military wing will take place.[9]

The original question faced by the ANC — to submit or fight — had come up again, nearly three decades later, and it was found that it could be fundamentally reformulated. So dramatically had the situation been changed by de Klerk's speech of February 2, that the ANC leadership concluded that there was indeed a third option, an alternative to the stark choice of 1961. The ANC did not have to submit, and it did not have to fight. It could negotiate.

In assessing developments after February 1990, the ANC has come to this further sobering conclusion: As decent as Mr. de Klerk may be, the ANC cannot base its strategy for the future of democracy solely on the integrity of those in power. The regime did not come to the negotiating table because of a change of heart. On the contrary, it agreed to talk because the crisis of apartheid compelled such a decision. Therefore, the ANC's capacity to deepen this crisis and ensure that those in power are dissuaded from the temptation or intention to derail the process of "peaceful transition" has had to inform present and future strategic considerations.

In this rapidly changing political context, however, calls for the continuation of the armed struggle, whatever the tactical advantage of doing so from the point of view of negotiation strategy, may result in substantial social anxiety. They can easily be seen as having the potential of jeopardizing a perceived gain in the legitimate effort to lessen an historical burden. The symbolic effectiveness of continued commitment to armed struggle may be compromised by the sense that the racist government has made a major departure from its past actions of restricting political activity. The ANC does not want to seem unreasonably wedded to an old position where the appearance of resourceful newness is required. The psychological need for change, it has realized, must be accommodated, irrespective of the validity of established positions. In other words, the ANC has realized that:

> A reflex resort to an established position may represent a kind of trap: the unintended trap of a self-evident moral advantage. It can blunt the capacity for initiative and resourcefulness. A response must be found that rides on the wave of

what is no less than an historical gain, that exposes limitations while opening up new avenues.[10]

Those avenues lie in the ANC's unequivocal commitment to democratic principles and a Bill of Rights that would restrain the arbitrary action of the state. Thus, instead of guaranteeing group rights, the future constitution would be based on guaranteeing individual rights.

The ANC Conference, July 2–7, 1991

The 48th ANC conference held from July 2–7, 1991, attended by some 2,000 delegates, and the first to be held in South Africa since 1959, was historic in every sense of the word. The delegates represented different theaters of struggle and varied agendas, and they gathered to see if they could harmonize those agendas and strategies. The conference challenged the organizational abilities of the ANC as nothing else in its experience. The hope of the event's organizers was to leave the conference not only with a fighting machine, but also with a coherent organizational thrust.

The delegates represented constituencies that were in a fighting mood, who wanted an ANC determined to confront the regime in every arena, and they got their wish. The ANC emerged from five days of deliberation a much more united and more determined movement. From a movement governed for almost thirty years from London, Lusaka and Robben Island, the ANC received legitimacy to act for its constituency on the strength of mandates from its grassroots support throughout the country. It skillfully welded the exiled leadership to the assembly of tough, internal activists and created a purposeful machine which now has its eyes firmly focused on its historic goals. The threatened factionalism did not materialize.

The decision on the ANC's military wing, Umkhonto Wesizwe (Spear of the Nation) (MK), proved uncomfortable to many ANC detractors, including the regime. The conference not only decided to give MK representation on the National Executive Committee (NEC), but also to keep it in constant combat readiness, to encourage MK to establish structures throughout the country, and to widely celebrate its 30th anniversary. MK was instructed to hold a conference inside South Africa, which it did; it was attended by the newly elected president, Nelson Mandela, and other members of the NEC. Another key conference decision was that the ANC remain a liberation movement, instead of becoming a political party. In other words, the ANC is in the struggle not for the liberation of its constituency only, but for the liberation of all oppressed South Africans. The ANC had every reason to be satisfied with its first congress in the country in more than 30 years.

Congress for a Democratic South Africa (CODESA)

This, then, is the background to the convening of CODESA. Following the ANC conference, the mass democratic movement under the leadership of the ANC experienced a high level of confidence and unrivaled militancy. In the meantime the Inkatha Freedom Party had been damaged and discredited, following the revelations that some of its activities were funded by the apartheid regime. The shake-up in the government following the Inkatha revelations undermined de Klerk's credibility. Then came the massive strike on November 4 and 5, 1991 called by the trade union movement and the ANC to protest against VAT (value added tax). The scale of the two-day strike provided a glimpse of the support the democratic movement under the leadership of the ANC enjoyed.

What has been going on in South Africa since February 2, 1990 can be described as the normalization of defeat on the part of the white oligarchy. The process has been tedious and at times confusing. There has been a great deal of petulance and grand-standing on the part of the Pan-Africanist Congress (PAC) and Inkatha, but the process of negotiations has gone on. The de Klerk regime seeks a constitutional formula that will guarantee white economic privileges, while the ANC wants a democratic government that will immediately begin to address the accumulated injustices of a hundred years. Between those poles it is not difficult to discern a workable compromise.

From the vantage point provided by the study of the history of African struggle since the ANC was formed in 1912, the current negotiations in South Africa are a great success. The willingness of the regime to sit down with the ANC and its allies to discuss the modalities of the transfer of power to the majority was an acknowledgement that the revolutionary impetus set in motion by the 1976 student rebellion had become irreversible; it rendered the country literally ungovernable without the ANC and its allies. The ANC's insurrectionary slogan of 1986 — "Make apartheid unworkable and the country ungovernable" — has been crowned with success. The regime has been forced to repudiate forty years of apartheid — by no means a small achievement.

Regional Implications

The advent of majority rule in South Africa will have significant international and regional importance. The democratic government that inherits power will have an impressive economic, scientific, and technological capacity, quite capable of making South Africa into a center for regional integration: grouping countries with rich mineral, power, water, and timber resources, with a relatively developed transportation infrastructure, and nuclear capabilities as well. As a member of the OAU, finally freed from the vestiges of colonialism, South Africa could become a major international player.

Over 100 million people — a quarter of sub-Saharan Africa's population — reside in the southern states of Angola, Botswana, Lesotho, Malawi, Mozambique, Namibia, Tanzania, South Africa, Swaziland, Zambia, and Zimbabwe. The World Bank's categorization of nations according to per capita income supports the generalization that this is sub-Saharan Africa's most economically productive region. Six of the countries — South Africa, Zimbabwe, Swaziland, Botswana, Angola, and Namibia — are among sub-Saharan Africa's fifteen strongest economies.

Moreover, unlike any other region of sub-Saharan Africa, the countries in the south are remarkably compatible in their judicial, financial, and institutional infrastructures. With the exception of Portuguese-colonized Angola and Mozambique (which are only gradually building closer ties with the local commercial network), all have similar tax structures, commercial codes, property laws, judicial processes, accounting systems and business styles, as well as common languages. Although a common currency does not exist, in practical terms the freely convertible South African rand serves a similar purpose in most of these countries.

Besides the well-known mineral resources of South Africa itself, the other countries of southern Africa produce significant quantities of minerals: oil, copper, diamonds, gold, nickel, ferro-chrome, cobalt, steel, asbestos, coal, chromite, zinc, tin, iron ore, silver and lead. The most valuable are oil (Angola); diamonds (Botswana, Namibia and Angola); copper (Zambia and Zimbabwe); gold (Zimbabwe); nickel (Zimbabwe and Botswana); ferro-chrome (Zimbabwe) and cobalt (as a by-product of copper production Zambia, Zimbabwe and Botswana). In some of these cases SADCC (Southern Africa Development Coordinating Council) member countries produce significant proportions of total world output.

The transformation of South Africa into a non-racial, democratic society is going to confront the West with crucial problems. Historically both Europe and the U.S. enjoyed substantial economic benefits from apartheid South Africa. Pretoria's destabilization kept African states divided and fragile. The effect was to lock these states into unequal relationships with South Africa and Western imperialism and to deprive Africans of the right to direct their own political and economic destinies. In its destabilization campaign South Africa was aided and abetted by the Reagan and Bush administrations.

Mongosuthu Gatsha Buthelezi, leader of the Inkatha Movement, was a frequent visitor to the Reagan and Bush White Houses and a recipient of funding from the National Endowment for Democracy, a federally funded program, in spite of the well-known link between Inkatha and township violence. When in July 1992 the *Weekly Mail* disclosed that the de Klerk regime had funded some of Inkatha's activities aimed at destroying the ANC, President Bush went out of his way to absolve de Klerk, instead of condemning the funding.

South Africa and the IMF took advantage of the destruction of the economies of Angola and Mozambique, forcing those countries to abandon their efforts at "socialist" development and to adopt capitalist development, complete with privatization.

It was disclosed recently that the U.S. is involved in contingency planning to "contain" any political damage to the West that may result from the end of apartheid in South Africa. Plans include the building of a one billion rand air base development project at three sites in Botswana, which the U.S. could use for direct intervention in post-apartheid South Africa in the event of its acting against the interests of U.S. foreign policy. The main base will be at Monopole, near the South African border. The U.S. initially denied the reports, but the evidence is accumulating that the U.S., even as the Cold War has come to an end, has major plans for a post-apartheid South Africa.

Botswana, with an armed force of 7,000 personnel and a small air force, does not need a state-of-the-art air base. Recently it has been disclosed that some 45 officers from the Botswana Defense Force are being trained in the U.S. And the "Voice of America" has installed a new transmitter there, replacing the one destroyed in Liberia. In January 1992, 200 elite U.S. airborne troops staged joint exercises, code-named Operation Silver Eagle, with the Botswana Defense Force near Gaborone. These developments are underlined by a strategic vision in Washington, where the end of the Cold War has seen a renewed emphasis on the need to project U.S. strategic power into resource-rich areas of the world.[11]

In South Africa, among other things, the U.S. is demanding that Pretoria run down its arms industry before the political transition takes place, so that it will not fall into the "wrong hands." The U.S. is putting pressure on South Africa to abandon its satellite launch program, because it could be converted into a missile program. The U.S. extended its arms embargo against South Africa as a warning to Israel of the sort of tough action it could take, and specifically to force Israel to abandon arms cooperation with South Africa. The U.S. intervened recently to force Saudi Arabia to abandon a massive arms contract it was about to sign with South Africa, to prevent Saudi Arabia from becoming less dependent on the U.S. and to ensure that the South African armaments industry gets starved of business.[12]

Conclusions

The collapse of Soviet communism has deprived both the U.S. and South Africa of their main ideological rationale for intervention overseas. This, according to Rob Nixon, became apparent in November 1991, when Margaret Thatcher urged Europe to defend Croatia from the Serbian "communist onslaught" and when Inkatha's executive member Musa Myeni warned that South Africa was "suffering under an emerging African National Congress dictatorship backed by communists all over the world" — nobody listened.[13]

Since the end of World War II, anti-communism in the U.S. and South Africa had become a moral crusade against what President Reagan called the "Evil Empire." Now South Africa and the U.S. are left bereft by the demise of this well-tried ideological pretext, which justified their imperial intervention in the domestic affairs of other countries. As Nixon puts it:

> Since its ascent to power in 1948, the National Party has relied upon anti-communism as its most versatile justification for all manner of domestic repression and regional imperialism. The Suppression of Communism Act of 1950 — which inflicted four decades of unrelieved suffering on South Africans — gives some sense of the protean referents of the label "communist" under Nationalist rule. An organization could be banned or a person detained, imprisoned, or executed as a communist if they sought, in the eyes of the law, to bring about "any political, industrial, social, or economic changes within the Union by the promotion of disturbance or disorder, by unlawful acts of omission or by means which include

the promotion of disturbance or disorder, or such acts or omissions of threat." A communist was further defined as anyone who "aims at the encouragement of feelings of hostility between Europeans and non-Europeans."[14]

With the arrival of the Clinton administration, the United States faces a region in economic ruins, with aspiring dictators and warlords like Buthelezi, Dhlakama and Savimbi either on the rampage or making threats of warfare, with millions of people dead or uprooted, all the result of twelve vicious years of racist instigation in the name of "anti-communism" from the Reagan and Bush administrations.

But the new administration also finds a confident African National Congress with the political upper hand preparing for power, a young Namibian government beginning to harness that nation's resources, and governments in Angola and Mozambique still holding out the hand of friendship to the United States, despite the wars of terror supported by the U.S.

While it is too early to see the direction the Clinton administration will take, there are a few signs of a positive approach. The invitation extended to Mandela by the Clinton administration to be an official guest at the inauguration, and the strong criticism of Savimbi in the first week of the administration show, as Bill Keller of the *New York Times* points out, that the fate of Africa has a sense of irony (Jan. 17, 1993).

Notes

1. Note that "basic human liberties"(undefined) are only of interest insofar as they do not interfere with the main U.S. aim of keeping Africa within the imperialist orbit and maintaining U.S. access to and exploitation of the human and material resources of the continent.
2. Committee on Foreign Relations of the U.S. Senate: Hearing on the Nomination of Dr. Chester Crocker, May 4, 1981.
3. This section owes a lot to the comprehensive analysis of the various clauses of the act by Winston P. Nogan, "An Appraisal of the Comprehensive Anti-Apartheid Act of 1986," in *The Journal of Law and Religion*, Vol. V, 1987, No. 2, pp. 327–365.
4. Ibid., p. 360.
5. Ibid., pp. 363–64.
6. *Washington Notes on Africa*, Winter 1990, p. 4, Washington Office on Africa.
7. *Africa Confidential*, April 6, 1991.
8. *New York Times*, July 10, 1990.
9. *Weekly Mail*, August 10–12, 1990.
10. Ibid.
11. "South Africa: Uncle Sam Moves South, While Namibia Remains Buckled by Its Colonial Past," *Work in Progress*, no. 83 (July-August 1992), p. 5.
12. *Cape Times*, February 14, 1992; *Johannesburg Star*, February 15, 1992.
13. Rob Nixon, "The Collapse of the Communist–Anti-Communist Condominium: The Repercussions for South Africa," *Social Text* 31–32 (1992), p. 245.
14. Ibid., pp. 246–247.

30

Namibian Independence:
The New World Order Welcomes Africa

Joseph Diescho

"The current state of world affairs hardly encourages confidence and optimism about our common future, and one does not need to be a cynic to hold this view."
— Theo-Ben Gurirab, Namibia's first foreign minister, at the Forty-Seventh Session of the United Nations General Assembly in New York on October 6, 1992.

On March 21, 1990, Namibia achieved political independence after more than seventy years as Africa's last colony. After the Namibian people waged a war for independence for twenty-three years, the world reached a consensus on Namibia's right of self-determination based on an unprecedented style of decolonization. As South Africa, the colonizing power, was for decades treated as a pariah state, the consensus was that Namibia was to become independent under the auspices of the United Nations.

Namibia did indeed achieve its political independence under the United Nations peace plan which was agreed to in September of 1978 in United Nations Security Council Resolution 435, but real independence remained out of reach due to Cold War geopolitical and ideological considerations.

The implementation of the United Nations peace in 1989 came as a result of the new rapprochement between the superpowers of the time. In other words, the independence of Namibia was more a reflection of the end of the Cold War, than it was a commitment of the international community to the right of self-determination of the African people of Namibia.

Namibia is also a *cas vivant*, a tale of where Africa stands after the ideological battle between the superpowers, which robbed members of the Eastern European communities of their freedom, but, ironically, benefited the liberation struggle in Africa. For a country like Namibia, the collapse of the Soviet system meant that a key political and economic option, however flawed, was removed. But further, the discourse about how to challenge the system of exploitation was undermined by the collapse of a model of economics and ideology that could serve as an alternative to what the capitalist West offered.

Essentially, Namibia's independence could best be described as: (a) only as much of a victory for the Namibian people as it was for the system which the Namibian people fought against for years — a system characterized by stark racial domination, economic exploitation, and socio-cultural alienation with attendant white power, wealth and control on the one hand, and black poverty and dispossession on the other; (b) a sound warning to Africa as a whole regarding the paucity of options available to any African country attempting to determine its own fate and avoid succumbing to the political interests of the so-called advanced Western countries; and (c) the reassertion of the United States, whose corporate agenda has now been fully embraced by its former ideological opponent, as the superpower pace setter of development, the model for and leader of social and economic change.

Hence what Namibia has become is unlike what many people who fought for independence expected or wanted. It is a situation where those who were supposed to be the decision-makers have become mere managers of a crisis largely beyond their control — a crisis which serves the interests of the North even better than colonial Namibia during the Cold War. From the constitution to political culture, Namibia is being governed without the sense of urgency that spurred the struggle for liberation, and from a position of tremendous weakness. Namibia's frailty is part and parcel of the "New World Order," which continues the marginalization of Africa, this time under *pax Americana*.

The idea of a "new world order" is by no means new when it comes to countries and people on the periphery. Much has been done to them by others in the name of a new and better world system. The creation of the League of Nations of 1919/20 after the First European Tribal War, and the United Nations Organization after the Second European Tribal War which ended in 1945, were both monumental attempts by the so-called developed world to secure a better order for humankind, prevent war, and in their own parlance, make the world secure for democracy. And yet, it still took devastating guerrilla wars and uprisings in Africa to bring about self-rule and eventual independence.

From an African point of view, the idea of the "new world order" has to be viewed against a tapestry of racial domination, economic exploitation and cultural alienation, and nothing in the new pronouncements suggests any significant change to that. The real questions that ought to be posed are: when did the old order end and the new start, who decided, and by whose authority is the new one to take shape? For Africa, the big question is: what role will Africa play that is different from the past?

Namibia's political independence came at the end of what was aptly described by many African economists as a "wasted decade." Africa as a whole was increasingly marginalized, and the dramatic events in Eastern Europe in 1989–1990 further eclipsed Africa across the range of arenas — economic, political, strategic, financial and public information. Eastern

Europe captured the imagination and compassion of governments and people of the world, at the expense of older struggles for human rights, freedom, and democracy that were still going on in Africa.

The world was in attendance, as observers, when Namibia made the most profound move towards democracy in the history of Africa. But the Berlin Wall came tumbling down on November 9, 1989, the third day of Namibia's first ever democratic and free and fair elections. This led to the eclipsing of the African story; so much so that Namibia's contribution to the process of democratization in Africa received less attention than was really due. But in one sense, the collapse of superpower rivalry just when the Namibian Constitution was drafted can only be seen as a blessing in disguise. It forced all contending parties to abjure outside sponsorship and rely on their internal resources and turn to, rather than against each other, to find a working solution for their country.

But Namibia's achievements at the beginning of the new world order give little reason to celebrate Africa's opportunities in the new era. The first democratically elected government in Namibia and its people have had to accept what they were against, collaborate with people they knew were responsible for their years of degradation, and accept an international economic reality antithetical to the hopes and aspirations of the majority of the people.

The evolution and conduct of the first freely elected government of Namibia, with regard to its policy of national reconciliation and the manner in which national and international issues are identified and determined, was shaped by the process of decolonization that gave rise to Namibia's independence just when the bipolar world was deconstructing and Africa's share of the international economic pie was shrinking even further. Resolution 435 itself placed limitations on Namibia's independence and subsequent program of reconstruction. Proxy wars between the superpowers around the world were winding down as the Soviet Union and the United States embarked on a new era of detente. The signing of the tripartite agreements between South Africa, Angola, and Cuba in New York on December 22, 1988, took place within that context. South Africa's war against Angola was to come to an end, as was its colonization of Namibia. This disintegration of southern Africa's Cold War was to have wide ramifications for Namibia's road to political and economic independence. The Namibian liberation movement, SWAPO, wanted to gain the maximum out of these less than optimum conditions.[1]

While expecting negative reaction to Namibia's imminent independence from conservative white people living in Namibia, SWAPO leaders — as a result of their own experiences living in exile in other African countries, especially Angola, Mozambique, and Zimbabwe — understood how important the white population would be in building a viable economy in Namibia. With the implementation of Resolution 435, essentially a formula for the West to safeguard its own interests in southern Africa, SWAPO staggered towards the end of its own war with South Africa. It led to only partial victory for the liberation movement, SWAPO in particular, and Namibia's exploited African people in general. The events of April 1, 1989 which led to well over 300 deaths of Namibian soldiers by South African gunfire, reflected SWAPO's final expression of dissatisfaction with and mistrust of the United Nations process.[2] In the eyes of SWAPO and of many Namibians, the signs grew more ominous. South Africa stood poised to systematically stab SWAPO with the poisonous dagger of support for the Western-oriented Democratic Turnhalle Alliance (DTA), in order to prevent SWAPO from gaining the two-thirds parliamentary majority required to impose its own constitutional framework. In the meantime, apartheid ensured that only white people in the colonial administration controlled the skills and expertise that SWAPO or any new government would need in order to build a strong and independent country.

During those first months of the implementation of Resolution 435, SWAPO remained determined to carry through its struggle for justice and equality, but at the same time, its leaders understood the importance of pragmatism. They would have to accommodate themselves to the white power structure in order to protect and maintain the infrastructure that South Africa had built for its administrative bureaucracy and military. Moreover, SWAPO was determined to do all that it could to preserve a climate of peace and stability, which it saw as a necessary precondition for introducing development programs. Many members of SWAPO, especially those who had lived in Angola and Mozambique, were all too familiar with how debilitating and draining a post-independence military conflict could be in a place where the former colonial administrators have stockpiled firearms and foodstocks. That is to say, that if the pre-independence colonial white civil servants were not appeased, the stability which Namibia now enjoys would have been hard to achieve. It was this realization that led the Central Committee to make national reconciliation the cornerstone of SWAPO's election manifesto.[3]

As the international climate changed, and the world became less polarized between the socialists on the one side and the capitalists on the other, SWAPO found it necessary to adapt itself by appearing less radical. In order to gain international acceptance and support, SWAPO's policy of national reconciliation became a matter of survival. The SWAPO leadership was confronted with the reality that they would have to construct a government that catered to black people and white people alike, without overtly challenging the historical foundations of racial inequality and their resulting disparities of economic and political power.

As the independence process progressed under the sponsorship of the United Nations, South Africa continued to wage violence against the Namibian people, especially in the north near the Angolan border. The Southwest African Police (SWAPOL) and its special paramilitary counterinsurgency unit *Koevoet* continued to roam the countryside with impunity and many Namibians throughout the country were harassed and intimidated.[4] In a message to all, but especially white, supporters of SWAPO, Anton Lubowski, the highest ranking white SWAPO official, was assassinated several weeks before the November 1989 elections.

For many the social climate during those heady days before the elections and leading up to independence on March 21, 1990, was still one in which people were encouraged to change their attitudes. For the first time in modern Namibian history, black people and white people listened to one another. Opposing parties began to communicate with one another as did different ethnic groups. In this way, national reconciliation was at its best, a dynamic process of balancing interests.

But while the theme of national reconciliation created a spirit of unity during the electoral process, it was at best superficial. Once in power, the new SWAPO-led coalition government of Namibia pursued a goal of stability without the social transformation necessary to heal old wounds and address historical inequalities born of years of colonial rule. In other words, those policies implemented by the government served to appease the wealthy white portion of the population, most of whom were South African citizens nervous about their futures both in Namibia and South Africa. Moreover, in mollifying such persons, the government relied on the loyalty and willingness to wait of those who had supported SWAPO for 23 years, mainly poor black people. For black Namibians, the period of national reconciliation has come to mean patience and tolerance, while for white people it means business as usual: namely, privilege and control.

The fact of the matter is that the new government's economic and social policies, adopted after the bitter struggle for freedom, equality and an alternative to the inequitable economic system in the country, are somewhat antithetical to the goals of justice and social equity as articulated during the struggle itself. Economic exploitation of the majority by the few, racial domination of the blacks by the whites, and the disparities between the rich and the poor are still in place and the contradictions remain charged.

The sudden enforced reliance by SWAPO on the business sector cannot lead to the emancipation of the exploited blacks in the country. In the past, there was a strong alliance between that same business sector and colonialism and apartheid. It was business and international finance that legitimated racism and exploitation while ignoring black grievances and delegitimating resistance. Now suddenly, business has changed, and overnight forged a close alliance with the Namibian political elite. Business leaders are now viewed as the harbingers of change and black upward mobility. The point is that most whites, especially those who control the business sector, are willing to give up symbolic political power, but not ideological influence or economic power. This is where the most difficult battle remains to be fought. It will be a dangerous blunder for African people across the continent to forget that the market, as such, does not guarantee social progress or social protection, especially where the market economy has been the engine behind the colonial economic exploitation, and political and cultural repression that are too familiar a tale in all Africa.

Essentially, reconciliation should be a process of denunciation and annunciation. It should be a process of distinguishing good from evil as forcefully as possible. It should be a point of reflection and assessment by naming the evil, identifying and assigning the wrongdoing — a point of reckoning. The struggle for national independence should go beyond simple issues of colonialism, the need for self-rule and formalistic party or state control with commandist structures of decision-making, and should encompass the struggle against domination, exploitation, and hunger at all costs.

The best thing the leadership can do under these very trying circumstances would be to abjure a view of the world in terms of the tired Cold War division between capitalist and communist models. It would be far better to hold capitalism and socialism in constructive tension in order to get a synthesis that is better for the people. To succumb to the apparent capitalist triumphalism is to misread history, and an oversimplification of a much larger issue. First of all, neither capitalism nor statist communism has succeeded when viewed from the perspective of the marginalized nations of the world. Secondly, the oppressive condition that fueled the struggle for independence was that of capitalism, not of communism. How can newly unchallenged capitalism now suddenly rescue the people of Namibia from that bondage and exploitation which was largely created by capitalism in the first place? Thirdly, Western propaganda that all socialism has failed because of the recent experiences in the USSR and the Eastern bloc is too unfair to the vast experiences of the people in the Two-Thirds World where their daily anguish can be placed at the door of capitalist plunder and deceit, and is barely attributable to socialist failure. If anything, the very regimes whose brand of socialism has "failed" have been more than helpful in the quest for liberation of the marginalized peoples of the world. It would be fairer to history to say that it is indeed too early to say that the failure of socialism implies the success of capitalism, as everything is in great transition at this stage. All one can say with certainty is that the world will be very different ten years from now. Fourthly, socialism has not failed in the Two-Thirds World, and has a fair chance of being an attractive and alternative ideal as long as there is capitalism.

In fairness, it is too early to tell exactly what the Namibian government's economic policies are, and how they will impact the future economy of the country. But it is clear that without a well thought-out plan with which to undertake development, there can be no real progress. If everything is left to the free market economy, there may be commodities, but no freedom and no equality. The sudden zeal for a free market is unlikely to help the very constituency that does not have access to capital. One cannot be a capitalist without capital.

A SWAPO constitution adopted as late as 1983 stated very clearly that the movement was committed to establishing a non-exploitative, non-oppressive, and classless Namibian society. This economic view was echoed in SWAPO's election manifesto in 1989:

> As a movement committed to the values of social justice, solidarity and public interest, SWAPO does not conceal its belief in the moral superiority of socialism over capitalism. Egalitarianism forms the basis of its vision of a just social order.
>
> Under a SWAPO government, Namibia will not allow the status quo to continue whereby the structure of the economy is tailored to the needs and demands of foreign and local private capital. Change will have to be brought

about. The present unjust state of affairs characterized by the supremacy of foreign capital, on one hand, and the total subordination of national capital formation, on the other, will have to go.

SWAPO's economic policy on ownership relations is that there will be state, cooperative, joint venture and private participation in the economy. The state will have ownership of a significant part of the country's economic resources. No wholesale nationalization of the mines, land and other productive sectors is, however, envisaged in the foreseeable future.[5]

SWAPO has clearly made drastic changes as the organization moved towards power. It dropped most of its earlier platform as political realities changed all over the world. In fact, the pressure on SWAPO to reassure the West and an international community that is inherently skeptical of the chances of democracy in Africa, was to show that SWAPO did not intend instant nationalization or redistribution of wealth in Namibia. The pressure led to the newly-elected President Sam Nujoma delivering an inaugural speech that was primarily directed at a foreign audience. The entire speech was in English. He spoke on behalf of the Namibian people, not to or with them.

In February of 1991, the Namibian government convened an internationally publicized Private Sector Investment Conference. The conference was part of the government's strategy for dealing with its image in the international economic order, and also in part to manage the crisis that was engulfing Namibia economically. But if what happened at the conference is anything to go by, the government's economic agenda clearly neglects crucial social sectors by, for example, relying almost entirely on the assumption that foreigners could deliver an economic miracle of massive investment, thus providing employment for the majority of Africans. Again, this is wishful thinking on the part of a small and relatively insignificant country like Namibia, given the post-Cold War Western donor fatigue with respect to Africa and the new needs of people in Eastern Europe who happen to be white. One of the lessons that developing countries in Africa seem not to have learned is that neither democracy nor development come from donations from outside.

The collapse of the socialist bloc will have an especially adverse effect on countries that cannot look to the United States for help with their socio-economic and political problems. Neither the Cold War nor its demise is inherently good for the Two-Thirds World. Needless to say the existence of the Soviet Union provided the people of the Two-Thirds World with a counterweight to the power of the United States, and they could take advantage of one or other of the superpowers by playing them off against each other.

The end of the Cold War leaves the world with nothing but *pax Americana* — an apparent triumph of the capitalist system. Two-Thirds World nations will have to find their own solutions, and not depend on any large nation. As the African proverb goes: When two elephants fight, it is the grass that dies; when the two elephants embrace, it is the grass that dies; the only time the grass survives when the elephants are there is when they relieve themselves on the grass.

There are other factors that complicate the Namibian economy after independence. The first important factor is the historical reality of the 23-year SWAPO-South Africa war. This war of independence has left the Namibian and the entire southern African economy devastated for a long time to come. Statistics of the 1980s have shown that about 10% of the Namibian population was forced into exile, leaving many families dislocated, most of them without their usual providers. Many men, especially the young and able-bodied, fled the country in fear of the South African soldiers. Many teachers fled the country too when they chose to be on the side of students.

Because of the war, too many subsistence farmers were caught in the crossfire. As a result, many food producers abandoned their land, a factor which rendered the vital countryside economically unproductive. The people who were once self-reliant became less free and less capable of planning their economic activities and future. They were lured away from the countryside and flocked to shantytowns near urban centers in order to be safe from "terrorism" and to maintain a sense of community. This forced many people to seek employment with the military. The South West Africa Territorial Force became the largest employer, and recruited publicly from high schools all over the country. Those who joined were paid exorbitant salaries in addition to other benefits, such as housing, cars, health facilities, and quick promotion that was unprecedented for blacks with their level of education. While in the military, young blacks were accorded some modicum of respect by junior white soldiers, something that meant a great deal to people accustomed to degrading treatment by whites. This is an important factor in understanding what made the spying industry, led by the paramilitary anti-SWAPO squad *Koevoet* — with its huge branches *Ezuva* in Kavango, *Etango* in Owamboland, and *Namwi* in Caprivi — such an attraction for the young men who remained in the country at a time when the South African education system collapsed. On this state of affairs, Robert Gordon wrote insightfully:

> Traditional life has been wrecked by the war. Draconian enforcement of the curfew has effectively altered activities of social significance such as cooking, beer brewing and outdoor evening activities. Many who previously had broken the 7 to 7 curfew with impunity no longer do so. Encounters with security patrols and checkpoints are part of the daily routine. Counter-insurgency wars are psychologically gruelling not only for the troops but especially for the populace . . .[6]

After independence, there remains much mistrust that could easily create internal battles, especially when triggered by ethnic and tribal misunderstanding. The long struggle led by SWAPO was in part characterized by the refusal to recognize ethnic and tribal differences as a normal makeup of any society. After independence, any attempt to acknowledge the historical heterogeneity of the Namibian population would smack of South Africa's apartheid.

The presence of United Nations forces in the country for over a year created a false vision of Namibia's economy. Thousands of Namibians who were never paid well before, suddenly received extraordinary salaries that could never be matched by a poor young nation such as Namibia. Drivers, typists, interpreters, cleaners, secretaries, security guards and others received temporary salaries set at UN levels. After the departure of the UN Operation, thousands of people faced tremendous economic loss.

During the illegal occupation by South Africa, the majority of Namibians, namely the Africans, were deprived of any economic opportunity. The whites, only 6% of the population, owned virtually all the land. This is still the reality after independence. Article 16 of the Constitution protects the rights of those whites who had the land, and the only way the government can get the land back is by buying it from those who had acquired it under an evil system.

The migrant labor system is still intact, and by all accounts will stay in place despite the contribution of Namibian migrant workers to the liberation struggle. For the longest time to come, Africans will remain condemned to the lowest paying jobs. The per capita income disparity between whites ($16,500) and Africans ($750) in Namibia is one of the worst in the world. The top 10% of the population receive more than 55% of the total income, and the poorest 40% only about 6%. The government seems willing, at least temporarily, to accept the migrant labor system. In an interview with the German newspaper *Die Welt*, on March 20, 1991, and in response to a question of what guarantees the Namibian government could give to German investors, the Namibian prime minister responded:

> First of all, Namibia is stable, peaceful, and a multi-party democracy. Second, they [businesses] can repatriate DM10 million and their profits. That is guaranteed by a law (Protection of Foreign Investment Act) . . . In addition, there are incentives such as tax deferrals, and a cheap workforce . . .[7]

Despite Namibia's great potential, the country's economy stagnated in 1990, the year political independence was attained. 1991's recession in South Africa reverberated throughout the region, and impacted Namibia especially hard. In addition, the poor performance in these years is partly due to the falling world prices of the main mineral exports, lack of rains in some parts of the country, and steep increases in the price of oil in the last period of 1990 due to the Gulf crisis. Namibia is also vulnerable to the current recession inside South Africa, by being inextricably tied into Pretoria's monetary system. Against this background, the Namibian government's room for maneuver becomes increasingly restricted.

On December 28, 1990, the Namibian government passed the Foreign Investment Act No. 27 of 1990, by which it wanted to assure the international financial community that the government was no longer committed to SWAPO's earlier positions. It gave assurances that Namibia was committed to safeguarding the capital and interests of foreign investors. In essence, the Foreign Investment Act was geared to lure international business, not to regulate exploitative behavior. The Foreign Investment Act was actually passed before there was a Labor Code, and this Act did not include any guarantee of a minimum wage to protect the already exploited Namibian workers from new investors and their greed.

The constitution writers who hurriedly put together the document bowed to Western wishes and made the sudden switch to the notion that the protection of property rights would be the solution to all Namibia's problems. This transformation on the part of a movement that fought to end exploitation and inequality is understandable in light of Africa's position in a world reconfiguring after the collapse of Soviet and European socialism. However, from the vantage point of those who have been so abused by the heartless free market ethos, this style of pragmatism leaves much to be desired.

Furthermore, South African blackmail tactics continue to undermine Namibian independence. Before independence, and when it became clear to South Africa that SWAPO could win an election in Namibia, many state-owned concerns were privatized. The irony is that until SWAPO's victory was imminent, Western states endorsed the arrangements in which everything was owned by the white government. But those governments sided with South Africa in the effort to privatize everything before independence, for fear that the state under SWAPO would own and turn everything socialist.

After independence, Namibia, small as it is, is a mirror image of where all of Africa is politically and economically after the fall of the Berlin Wall. There is even more to the marginalization of Africa today. The industrialized world is wont to pay more attention to Eastern European situations like Yugoslavia where — not to make light of the plight of innocent people in that country — more attention and resources went than to Somalia in Africa. Throughout 1992 more people died in one day in Somalia that died in a month in Yugoslavia. The first African United Nations Secretary-General, Boutros Boutros Ghali, criticizing the immediate Western response to Yugoslavia and lack thereof to the crisis in Somalia, noted that the civil strife in Yugoslavia was a "war of the rich" and those dying in Somalia were poor.[8]

In conclusion, it has to be said that race is still a factor in the shaping of this "New World Order." People of Africa and the Arab world in particular have perhaps more reason to feel *Angst* than celebration as the "New World Order" takes hold. In South Africa and the Middle East, where the oldest racial and national struggles continue unresolved, the lines of Western support still run along racial lines rather than ethical and principled lines of democracy, human rights, the rule of law and equity. For example, Israel gets more U.S. unconditional aid than the whole of Africa put together. Post-communist, post-colonial Eastern Europe gets a level of response that Africa could never get from industrialized countries, no matter what the gravity of the situation. To illustrate this situation, Nelson Mandela came to the United States after 28 years of imprisonment by a racist regime. President Lech Walesa of Poland came to the United States after leading a successful struggle against a communist regime. Mandela received more moral support but left with little financial support. Walesa received less visible moral assistance, but left with huge financial support.

Be that as it may, the reality that Namibia's independence, hard-won as it is, has been eclipsed by events in Eastern Europe should not be a bad sign altogether. The lesson for Namibia, Africa, and perhaps the entire Two-Thirds World of the South, is that in order for them to be the true shapers of their countries and destinies in the New World Order, there is going to be hardship in the short run, but the benefits of the end of the Cold War are likely to be great in the long run. The people who have been sandwiched between two rival ideologies will hopefully come to rely on none but themselves if their countries are to create national and economic development and systems of governance that will work for them, and not on behalf of others to whom political elites are forever beholden.

It has to be reiterated that the New World Order as it is propounded by the United States at the beginning of the 1990s is no different from the Old World Disorder that brought the world to its current state. African people were abused on their land as the missions of civilizations went on to bring them into the order of enlightenment, and they were transported as slaves to the Americas, to the New World Order of the time. The end of the Cold War era, ironically, has deprived Africa of strategic importance to the superpowers. Despite political rhetoric in the camps of the so-called developed nations, there has not been any sign of the peace dividend for Africa and the poor people of the world after the end of the Cold War. It is now time for Africa to make this new era beneficial to itself and its own interests.

Namibia, the best democracy in sub-Saharan Africa, could take the lead in looking inward, domestically, in terms of its resources, natural and human, and regionally in southern Africa. Namibia has the foundation of human rights, the rule of law, and fundamental liberties that should now undergird the development of Africa's potential for building democracy, prosperity and stability, ingredients of a working and evolving economy in the twenty-first century. However it may be viewed in the West, Namibia is not marginal to Namibians, and Africa is not marginal to Africans.

Notes

1. The imminent end of the Cold War was not the only limiting factor. Resolution 435, adopted in 1978, was a watered down version of Resolution 385 of 1976, which did not provide South Africa with the role of being in charge of the independence process.
2. On April 1, the day on which the United Nations plan and the ceasefire agreement between South Africa and SWAPO were to become operative, an unknown number of SWAPO cadres crossed into Namibia at a time when they were not supposed to in terms of the tripartite (Angola, Cuba and South Africa) agreements of December 22, 1988. SWAPO's move into Namibia was an expression of frustration with the whole United Nations plan that placed South Africa, the colonizing force, in charge of the decolonization process and allowed South African soldiers to be inside Namibia whereas SWAPO was not allowed to have its soldiers on its own territory. This was an issue that SWAPO had pressed for ten years before the implementation of Resolution 435. On March 31, 1989, SWAPO wanted to make its presence known by doing something that would technically be a violation of the agreements. It was SWAPO's attempt at *realpolitik* to try to force the United Nations to create bases for SWAPO fighters on Namibian soil, and an attempt that, if successful, would have boosted SWAPO's image in the United Nations-supervised elections. SWAPO's move is understandable as an expression of frustration at the fairness, not the legality of the process.
3. National reconciliation is not a Namibian invention. Zimbabwe adopted it on gaining independence in 1980, albeit with greater strength in that it was still possible for a developing country to play tough with socialist rhetoric. The Namibian government did not have even the power of sloganeering at the time they moved to the top.

4. *Koevoet* is the Afrikaans word for crowbar. Known as *Ezuva, Etango* and *Namwi* (The Sun) in local languages, it was created in the early 1980s by South African military intelligence to mobilize the local population against SWAPO and the idea of independence under the United Nations plan. In its efforts to win the hearts and minds of the local population, soldiers took Namibian teachers, nurses, civil servants and students and put them through semi-secret classes and workshops at locations far away from their homes.

5. SWAPO's election manifesto: *Towards an Independent and Democratic Namibia: SWAPO's Policy Positions* (1989).

6. Robert Gordon, "The Praetorianization of Namibia," *TransAfrica Forum*, Vol. 6, No. 2, Winter 1989, p. 21.

7. *Die Welt*, March 20, 1991, pp. 6–7.

8. *New York Times*, August 3, 1992.

31

The Emerging Maghreb:
North Africa and the New World Order

James A. Paul

On July 8, 1990, just three weeks before the Gulf crisis began, General Colin Powell, Chairman of the U.S. Joint Chiefs of Staff, arrived in Morocco for high level talks. His trip also took him to Tunisia and to Egypt, where he met with top military and government figures in private discussions. Two days after Powell left, on July 15, police chiefs of the North African trade association states met in Algiers for an "exchange of information."[1]

These events suggest the changing political landscape of North Africa at the beginning of the New World Order. Governments once keen to emphasize their independence and autonomy have openly coordinated their military policy with the world's most powerful state. And as economic conditions have worsened and mass oppositions threatened, governments have anxiously reinforced their security apparatuses, turning "regional cooperation" into an engine for repression rather than economic growth.

The Gathering Storm

Two decades before, North Africa had seemed a bastion of Third World radical nationalism with a promising economic future. Enriched by oil, gas, and phosphates, and endowed with fertile agricultural lands and well-developed infrastructure, the region seemed destined for prosperous development, and leadership in the proposed New International Economic Order.[2]

By the time General Powell arrived, North Africa's economic and political scene had altered dramatically. Living standards, long on the rise, had started to decline. Deeply indebted governments, in urgent need of foreign currency and investments, were selling off state companies and decontrolling their economies. Draconian austerity measures, imposed by Western bankers, ravaged the meager living standards of the poor. And amid the decline of socialism and nationalism (discredited as official state ideologies), Islamic religious movements stood at the forefront of the opposition.[3]

The disintegration of Soviet communism and the emergence of a U.S.-dominated global order contributed to these changes and hastened their pace, but the shift had been underway for many years. For over two decades, one North African government after another had reduced the role of the state in the economy,[4] and conceded more freedom to political oppositions.[5] But reforms had not reignited economic prosperity or established a healthy political pluralism. Quite the opposite. Only Libya had resisted this process — cushioned from political and economic pressures by its great oil wealth, its small population and its tough, idiosyncratic regime.

By the time the Soviet system collapsed, many governments and societies in North Africa were already in crisis. Existing development efforts had failed to meet the urgent needs of society — economically, culturally and politically. Algeria, for example, former standard-bearer of radical nationalism, witnessed an alarming unraveling of daily life in its capital city, Algiers — the public transportation system barely functioned, elevators and telephones were frequently inoperable, water and electricity were only sporadically available, food was scarce, and housing was hopelessly inadequate for the rapidly-growing population.[6] The public viewed the ruling party, the FLN, with contempt and rarely believed the official news organs. By 1990, the government had run so short of foreign exchange that many state factories lay idle for lack of vital inputs. According to a former prime minister, a decade of bribery and corruption had cost the national treasury no less than $26 billion — the equivalent of the entire foreign debt.[7]

The statist nationalisms, though tragically inept and corrupt, did not collapse under their own weight. Perhaps under other circumstances they might have discovered a means of political renewal. But the World Bank, the International Monetary Fund (IMF) and other international lenders kept up a steady pressure for "structural adjustment" throughout the 1970s and 80s — pressure which the governments increasingly could not resist.

In the optimism of the 1970s, many governments and state companies had borrowed heavily to fund major development projects. Then, in the 1980s, the world economy weakened, and European markets closed, as the EC tightened its inner unity. Even North African workers (source of precious remittances) were no longer welcomed by the neighbors across the Mediterranean.[8] Saddled with high-interest debt payments, hobbled by declining export prices, and faced with rapidly expanding populations, the North African governments scrambled to attract Western aid and investments — anything to create jobs and get their economies moving again. But strings were attached: deep structural changes to make their economies more compatible with international capital, more fully integrated into the world market. Eventually, quite reluctantly, and sometimes after intense internal debates, governments gave in, starting a cycle of far-reaching reforms that sharply reduced the living standard for the majority of their populations.

Privatization, Market Prices, and the Cruel New Order

When Soviet and East European communism collapsed, North African advocates of state-centered economic development could no longer count on economic aid or diplomatic support from a friendly power to the north. Local capitalists and their political allies took courage and pressed harder for reforms. International bankers turned up the heat. So, as economic problems within North Africa intensified, the movement of privatization, decontrol, and price reform speeded up dramatically.

In Morocco, 1990 was a year of price hikes and further cuts in social programs. The king also promulgated a sweeping new law on privatization of state enterprises. In 1991, the government finally announced plans to sell more than a hundred businesses, banks, hotels, factories and other properties, including distribution and trade monopolies, worth hundreds of millions of dollars.[9] The government also passed a law creating a new tax-haven offshore banking zone in the northern city of Tangier, a move requiring tens of millions of dollars in special infrastructure costs. And on September 15, 1991, the king announced that the dirham would soon be freely convertible, yet another step in the effort to throw open Morocco's economy to foreign investment.[10]

Algeria followed a similar trajectory. In April 1990, having run out of cash to pay for its imports, Algeria also signed its first major agreement with the IMF, obtaining emergency loans in exchange for currency devaluation, price decontrols, currency reserves and other "adjustment" measures. The decontrol of prices set off sharp increases in the cost of bread, cooking oil, sugar, semolina, cooking gas and other necessities. Not long before, such a shift would have been unthinkable in Algiers, but under the gun of the international lenders, the government had little choice.

The president of the National Assembly resigned after delivering a speech harshly critical of the reforms and several top members of the ruling party quit, but — with the backing of President Benjedid — the program went ahead: the governor of the national bank announced that the dinar would soon be convertible, the government declared that hundreds of state enterprises would lose their subsidies, and the parliament passed a law privatizing public agricultural lands. As price decontrols continued, the cost of living shot up, nearly doubling in 1990–91.

Noureddine Ait Laousine, a former chief of the national oil company, declared that the dramatic oil and gas nationalizations of 1972 had been a "mistake," and proposed the direct sale of Algeria's major oil and gas fields to foreign companies.[11] The government eventually published a new and very open investment code in late 1991, encouraging foreign companies to enter Algeria's oil and gas exploration and production.[12]

These and other reforms offered a bitter pill to the great majority of the North African population. The statist systems had worked badly and needed serious change. But the IMF medicine may have been worse than the disease. Poverty and unemployment rose sharply as governments raised prices, slashed education and social programs, and shut down state factories. In

Algeria, where the shift came most suddenly, the trauma hit most severely.

Supporters of the reforms argued that the pain of transition would soon be followed by greater growth and more efficiency, benefiting everyone. The public reacted with skepticism and anger. Mass protests threw politics into the deepest region-wide crisis since independence. Morocco seethed with resistance in the summer and fall of 1990 and exploded in riots in mid-December; demonstrations constantly rocked Algeria in the same period, and in mid-October of 1990, after steep new price increases went into effect, bloody clashes between rioters and security forces shook Constantine, Algiers and dozens of other cities.[13]

The protesters' fury targeted not only high government officials but also the traders, speculators and middlemen who had made millions in the new economic climate. Peasants marched in Algiers against speculators who had profited by buying up state lands. Students demonstrated in Fez against profiteers. Fancy cars, sumptuous homes and elegant nightclubs enraged those living on the edge of survival. People turned with desperation towards the ascetic moralism of political Islam.[14] Economic "freedom," with its gaping class differences, had led to an impasse.

Desert Storm Deepens the Crisis

The Gulf War — opening salvo of the New World Order — deepened the North African crisis. In most countries, it sharpened economic problems, fired the fervor of Islamic and secular oppositions and increased governments' dilemma of having to navigate between the pressure of their Western bankers and the indignation of their own mass publics. Everywhere it served as a stark reminder of *disorder* in the New World Order.

Egypt, once the most independent and firmly nationalist state in the region, now bankrupt and deeply dependent on the United States, gave swift and unconditional support to the Washington-led coalition, sending a contingent of 35,000 troops, and providing substantial diplomatic assistance to the U.S. coalition-building effort. With the help of Gulf monarchs and other affluent allies, Washington offered penniless Egypt a rich reward: grants and loans totaling more than $2 billion, $10 billion in forgiven loans, and $14 billion in rescheduled borrowings — totaling half the foreign debt.[15] Egypt was also rewarded diplomatically. The Arab League moved its headquarters back to Cairo from Tunis. And an Egyptian candidate won election as secretary general of the United Nations.

But Egypt paid a high price. Though President Hosni Mubarak found considerable public support for his Gulf policies, intense opposition arose. The Muslim Brothers in particular drew strength from their militant opposition to Western intervention in the Gulf. Hundreds of intellectuals and journalists denounced the government. And riots broke out at the universities, notably Cairo's Al-Azhar. In response, the government cracked down, jailing thousands of its opponents.

Egypt also faced an economic crisis as a result of the Gulf War: tourism dried up, exports lagged, and more than a million Egyptian expatriate workers returned penniless from Iraq and Kuwait. With hundreds of thousands of families deprived of their means of subsistence, the country as a whole grew more dependent than ever on foreign assistance. Egypt's political troubles in the period ahead would reflect these social tensions.

In exchange for the favorable treatment of its debt, Egypt struck a deal with the bankers at the end of the hostilities. It agreed to harsh conditions for economic reforms, including steep price hikes in energy and transportation, cuts in social services, a new consumption tax, and a radical deregulation of agriculture which threatened to push hundreds of thousands of peasants off the land. High domestic interest rates and eventual privatization of public firms were also part of the package. As a result, most Egyptians have suffered a drop in their standard of living, the textile sector (one of Egypt's largest) has been in deep decline, and the economy as a whole has entered a sharp recession.[16] The economic crisis has further deepened the political crisis.

Morocco also agreed to support the coalition — with a token commitment of troops. Within weeks, Western lenders and Gulf funders gave Morocco its reward: debt refinancing totaling $6 billion, as well as special war-related aid grants and loans worth hundreds of millions more. But King Hassan's regime won little public support and faced intense criticism for its pro-coalition policy.

Morocco's most powerful opposition party (the USFP) and one of its largest trade unions (the CDT) led a campaign which linked Western intervention in the Gulf and Western-imposed economic austerity measures — denouncing them both.[17] When students went on strike in Fez in mid-December, the whole country exploded with strikes and riots, reflecting the depth of anger and outrage at what was seen as a combined economic and political assault. A shaken Hassan eased some austerity measures and promised constitutional revisions, but security forces attacked protesters mercilessly, killing dozens and arresting thousands of political activists, especially among the Islamic movements.

Three governments — Tunisia, Algeria and Libya — opposed the intervention of Western military forces in the region.[18] With strong public sentiment opposed to the Western coalition in all three countries, even conservative Tunisia could not risk joining the coalition forces or giving its verbal support to the Western campaign. In some measure, these countries proved their capacity for continued independence of action in a world increasingly influenced from Washington. But they paid a high price.

Regimes in both Tunisia and Algeria discovered that they had forfeited the enormous economic benefits of coalition partnership, while still losing ground to Islamic opposition forces. In both countries, throughout the fall of 1990, Islamist forces and police clashed in bloody battles leading to many arrests. As in Morocco, opposition to economic austerity measures overlapped with opposition to Western intervention in the Gulf, fueling the fire of anti-government forces. In Tunisia, the alarmed government finally clamped down in October, jailing thousands of activists and sharply curbing press and speech freedoms. In Algeria, the anti-war protests led directly into the victory of the Islamists in the June municipal elections — and the government repression that soon followed.

Only Libya, beyond the reach of debt and aid pressure, and without a tolerated opposition movement, emerged from the Gulf War without sharpened internal conflict and economic crisis. But its hour of reckoning was soon to come.

The United Nations and the Campaign Against Libya

Not long after the end of the Gulf War, the United States and Britain launched a campaign of destabilization against the Libyan regime of Muammar Qaddafi. Coming so soon after the battle against Saddam Hussein in the Gulf, this second campaign was seen by most North Africans as an intolerable intervention. Even Egypt, the U.S.'s faithful ally, tried to head off a clash that embarrassed and humiliated nationalist sentiment throughout the region and uneasily recalled the U.S. bombing of Libya's two largest cities in 1986.

As in the past, Libya stood accused of vague charges of "international terrorism." In mid-November 1991, a British court handed down indictments against two Libyans, accused of responsibility for bombing a U.S. airliner over Lockerbie, Scotland in 1988. One day later, the French accused Libya of responsibility in another aircraft explosion in 1989. Only a few months before, Western intelligence experts had mentioned Syria and Iran as responsible for these incidents and most observers saw the new charges as politically motivated.

The U.S. and British governments demanded that Libya turn over the two men for trial, or risk international sanctions. When Libya refused, citing the lack of an extradition treaty, the U.S. and Britain moved to impose sanctions. Both Washington and London made it clear that their ultimate goal was to oust the Qaddafi regime.

The moves against Qaddafi demonstrated both the enormous power of the United States in the New World Order and the limits of its power. Washington wanted to crush the Libyan regime with a UN-sponsored oil embargo and possibly even a trade embargo as well.[19] Against the wishes of most member-states, the UN eventually voted sanctions, but the U.S. failed to obtain the harsh sanctions it wanted. Its resort to heavy-handed diplomacy only strengthened the position of Europe — in North Africa and in the UN itself.

Germany and Italy came out as a staunch opponents of sanctions, because of their close economic relations with Libya. With help from China, the Maghreb states, and many others, the Europeans exerted their influence to block or water down the U.S. sanctions package. As a result, the U.S. needed over four months to build support for even a mild sanctions package, consisting of blocked air links, an embargo on arms sales and reduced diplomatic representation. The Security Council finally voted these sanctions — Resolution 731 — on March 31, 1991. To Washington's embarrassment, China almost cast its veto, and one-third of the Security Council members — including Morocco — abstained on the vote.

Libya had been chastened, however, and the Maghreb states reminded once again of their vulnerability. The United States and Britain, armed with awesome military and financial powers, continued to push for tougher measures, in hopes that they could force Qaddafi to step down and turn over Libya to a more conciliatory, pro-Western regime.

Governments, Oppositions and Renewed Repression

In every country except Libya, new political parties had attained legality in the late 1980s, new organizations had come into being, and governments had been forced to tolerate considerably wider political expression. Movements for human rights had broadened their influence. Groups to defend women and minorities had gained legality and public attention. New publications had emerged. But, above all, powerful Islamic mass movements had burst upon the political scene.

As long-entrenched governments fought to preserve their power, opponents demanded an increasing share in the political system. In early 1990, it seemed that major political changes were inevitable, given the scale of the social crisis. In Morocco, opposition parties and trade unions posed King Hassan the most serious challenge of his 29-year rule. In Tunisia, where ailing President Habib Bourguiba had just been ousted after 32 years in power, the government of President Zine al-Abidine Ben Ali sought to revive the flagging fortunes of the ruling Neo-Destour Party; but a growing opposition movement, led by a strong Islamist party, demanded the right to govern. In Algeria, the most dramatic political opening of all saw over fifty new political parties and hundreds of new newspapers and magazines emerge; even leaders of the ruling FLN admitted that their once-powerful party was effectively "dead."

Islamic politics held center stage, especially in Tunisia and Algeria. With inspiration from Egypt and Iran, money from Saudi Arabia, and leadership from zealous young intellectuals, North African Islamic movements filled a widespread need — for a sense of commitment and belonging in the midst of the social crisis. Working through small base groups in local communities and mosques, their influence spread rapidly as traditional politics failed to provide meaning, purpose and material satisfaction to most of the population. Civil servants, professionals and intellectuals joined the movement, along with students, workers and the unemployed.

But the Islamic movements faced determined opponents. Not only were the governments keen to stamp them out. But secular political forces saw Islamists as a threat to democracy and social diversity. In Morocco and Algeria, Berbers refused the Islamists' programs for Arabization;[20] in Egypt, Copts resolutely opposed Islamization; everywhere, substantial numbers of women rejected the Islamists' restrictions on dress and public life; many others disliked the Islamists' militant asceticism and the Islamic insistence on a single standard of behavior.

In Algeria, Islamists attacked women in the streets for not adhering to conservative codes of dress and conduct.[21] And when Islamists won Algerian local elections in 1990, they abolished mixed schools for boys and girls, closed down movie theaters and cafés, and separated men and women in municipal offices. A fierce debate began in the government and the army over whether democracy would best be served by allowing the Islamists to assume power.

Paradoxically, Islamists made least headway in Morocco, North Africa's most religious country. King Hassan kept Morocco's Islamists in check by emphasizing his own religious leadership as "Commander of the Faithful." He called conferences of religious scholars, maintained close relations with the Saudi monarch, King Fahd, and built a gigantic new mosque in Casablanca — persuading most Moroccans that he was more legitimate than any of his religious opponents. Morocco's Islamists also faced arrest and notoriously harsh treatment. And they had to compete with a vigorous secular opposition.

In Algeria, Tunisia, and Egypt, however, rigorously secular governments, with weak oppositions, had left a large political space for the Islamic movements to take root. As governments relaxed restrictions on political organizing, the Islamists grew rapidly and hoped soon to take power.

Tunisia's Islamic Tendency Movement, later known as al-Nahda, put forward a radical social form of Islam that won wide popularity. But President Ben Ali, backed by the army and the security forces, launched a tough crackdown against his Islamic opponents. The first wave of arrests, in October 1990, detained as many as ten thousand in prisons and camps throughout the country. Then, in May 1991, Interior Minister Abdallah Kellal announced that the government had discovered a "diabolical plot" against state security and many more arrests followed. Altogether, authorities detained as many as 30,000 Islamist activists, mistreating and torturing thousands. Islamists were not the only targets. In the summer of 1992, the government forced the Tunisian League for Human Rights to disband.

Algeria's political opening saw even more drama. In early 1990, Algeria had become the freest country in the Arab world. As dozens of parties competed for public support, the Islamic Salvation Front (FIS) won Algerian municipal elections in the spring of 1990 and it later gained large majorities in the first round of parliamentary elections in November 1991. Amid continual unrest, a deep split between Islamists and secular forces, and the worsening economic crisis, the army finally intervened to "save democracy" in early January 1992, ousting President Benjedid, arresting the Islamic leaders, and imposing a new government with emergency powers. Armed Islamic militants battled security forces in the wake of the takeover and authorities imprisoned thousands of Islamists, many in concentration camps deep in the desert. As violence escalated, assassins gunned down the new president, Mohammad Boudiaf, in June 1992, as he delivered a nationally-televised speech. Islamist attacks on police patrols and acts of sabotage against government offices and public buildings created an atmosphere of siege and drew still more fierce repression by the security forces.[22]

Egypt, too, saw a serious upsurge of Islamic militancy and violence in this period, including widespread attacks on security forces and on Christian Copts in Upper Egypt and in Cairo itself. In July 1992, the Egyptian parliament passed tough new anti-terrorism laws and the government launched a major crackdown, with security forces making tens of thousands of arrests.

Throughout North Africa, expectations of democratic change evaporated. Familiar regimes remained in power in every country, with the help of the military and security services; thousands of Islamists languished in jail. By late 1992, governments had outlawed dozens of associations and parties, imprisoned leading oppositionists, and again imposed tight restrictions on the press. The democratic opening was over.

The New World Order and the Future

The New World Order produced unprecedented economic, social and political turmoil in North Africa. The harsh privatization and austerity programs, combined with the effects of the Gulf War and Libya's destabilization, left populations and political systems reeling.

What, then, is North Africa's future? Will there be further economic crisis and austerity or successful capitalist development? Islamist fundamentalism, violence and repression or an emerging pluralist democracy? The answer depends in large measure on developments outside the region itself: the state of the world economy and the development of Europe are particularly crucial to North Africa's future.

In 1992, European attention is directed eastward, towards the newly-accessible reservoir of cheap labor and a promising new array of investment opportunities. But Europe also cannot afford to ignore its neighbors to the south. Their poverty and instability pose security concerns; their potential as producers and markets offer tempting possibilities to European businesses. So EC institutions and governments have already intervened to dampen the effects of the North Africa crisis, by offering new loans and assistance. On March 21, 1991, former French Prime Minister Michel Rocard called for "intense French participation" in the modernization of Algeria and its North African neighbors.[23] As former colonial power in Morocco, Algeria and Tunisia, the French have been especially keen to build links to North Africa. But the Germans, the Italians and the Spanish are not far behind.

When the European economy rebounds, the ties to North Africa will almost certainly increase all across the EC. Already, gas pipelines link the two shores of the Mediterranean. European companies are investing in privatized North African firms. Tourism and trade ties continue to grow. And more than two million North Africans live and work in Europe.

For better or worse, North Africa is being pulled into Europe's orbit. But proximity to the world's richest zone may not guarantee North African prosperity, except perhaps in the very long term. In the meantime, growth will be slow and North Africa will remain an impoverished reserve of cheap labor and raw materials — Europe's Mexico. Continuing global recession and further austerity will fuel the fires of Islamism and insure the repressive military response. North Africans are bound to see the New World Order as a long nightmare, comparable only to the dark era of colonialism itself.

Notes

1. *Maghreb Mashrek/Monde Arabe* No. 130 (October–December 1990), p. 142.
2. 1970 was the year Muammar Qaddafi came to power and claimed the mantle of Abdel Nasser as champion of Arab nationalism. Two years later, Algeria nationalized its oil and gas resources, and called for a New International Economic Order to redistribute global wealth. Even in Morocco, ruled by a pro-Western monarchy, opposition political pressures forced the government to nationalize foreign landholdings, assume state control over trade and "Moroccanize" a number of major foreign-owned companies.
3. A synthesis of nationalism and socialism provided the ideology of the anti-colonial movement in all the countries of North Africa. After successfully ousting the colonial rulers, new governments sought to diminish Western economic control and promote more rapid economic development by nationalizing industries and otherwise promoting state control over the economy. This approach was enormously popular at first, symbolized by Abdel Nasser's triumphant nationalization of the Suez Canal in 1956. By the 1970s and 80s, the economic problems of the new system had become apparent and the new states seemed increasingly oppressive in their own right. As a result, official state ideologies mobilized less and less support from the public as time went on.
4. Egypt's shift came after the death of Gamal Abdel Nasser, in the early period of his successor Anwar al-Sadat. Its first expression was Law 65 of 1971 on foreign investments. By 1977, government initiatives to remove price subsidies, under pressure from the IMF, had led to serious riots. In Tunisia, the shift was marked by the downfall of economic czar Ahmad Ben Salah in 1970. Seven years after the ruling Neo-Destour Party added "Socialist" to its name and began to build a state-centered economy, President Bourguiba repudiated the leftward course and put Ben Salah on trial for treason. Privatization began slowly in 1981 and a major agreement with the IMF in 1986 speeded up the process of "adjustment." Morocco's shift was marked by its IMF agreements in the late 1970s, forced by high military expenditures and the plunging price of phosphates. By 1979, a few state enterprises had already been privatized. In Algeria, the death of President Boumedienne and the coming to power of Chadli Benjedid in 1979 proved the beginning of disengagement from state-sponsored development and the slow introduction of liberal economic policies, but Algerian economic reforms were mostly delayed until 1989 and after. See John Waterbury, *The Egypt of Nasser and Sadat* (Princeton, 1983); Ilya Harik, "Privatization et développement en Tunisie," *Maghreb Mashrek/Monde Arabe* No. 128 (April–June 1990), pp. 3–26; Zakya Daoud, "Privatisations à la marocaine," *Maghreb Mashrek/Monde Arabe* No. 128 (April–June 1990), pp. 84–89.
5. In Algeria, the region's most dramatic political opening began with the new constitution of February 1989 and the law on multi-party politics of July 1989. Within less than two years, 120 new publications and 60 new political parties had come into being. In 1990, Algeria enjoyed unprecedented freedom of association and expression.
6. Unlike many areas of the Third World, North African population growth has not begun to enter the period of transition to lower fecundity. Rapidly-increasing population puts a specially heavy pressure on resources. Algeria, with 4% annual growth, has the highest rate. See Djilali Sari, "L'Indispensable maitrise de la croissance démographique," *Maghreb Mashrek/Monde Arabe* No. 129 (July–September 1990), pp. 23–46.
7. Former Prime Minister Abdelhamid Brahimi announced on March 26, 1990 that bribes and kickbacks on foreign contracts had amounted to $26 billion during the previous decade. The current prime minister, Mouloud Hamrouche, inadvertently confirmed the scale of the scandal when he argued that Brahimi was wrong and the corruption was "only" several billions. (*Le Monde*, May 11, 1990.)
8. When Greece and Spain were included in the EC, their fruit and vegetable produce took precedence over the produce from North Africa, which lost its preferential place in the market in France. Similarly, the prospering production of thread and cloth in North Africa, particularly in Morocco, lost much of its market after the European "multifiber" agreements.
9. The state in Morocco owned a share in approximately 700 enterprises, including a controlling interest (over 50%) in some 220 companies. Of these, 112 were identified for privatization, including the country's five largest banks. All, or nearly all, of the state enterprises will likely be sold off eventually. The largest private owner, and greatest beneficiary of privatization, is King Hassan himself.
10. The Egyptian pound, long tightly controlled, has similarly been allowed to move towards free market rates and President Mubarak announced in the fall of 1992 that (like the dirham) it would become freely-convertible in 1993.
11. Algeria's president, Chadli Benjedid, initially supported this proposal, which involved the sale of some 25% of Algerian reserves. The Hassi Messaoud field was to be sold immediately to raise $6–8 billion.
12. Algeria was not the first Middle East country to move in this direction. Both Iran and Iraq, eager for foreign funds to rebuild after their war, began privatization of oil production in the late 1980s.

13. These movements recalled previous uprisings over IMF-imposed austerity programs: 1965 in Morocco, 1977 in Egypt, 1981 in Morocco, and 1983–84 in Morocco and Tunisia.
14. An Algerian intellectual wrote in early 1992 that the Islamic movement "represents the final hope that the raging citizens cling to, when they feel betrayed, abandoned and deceived by the state. It responds to a kind of collective fantasy, a sort of desperate obsession, which takes form amid great social and cultural misery." (Lahouari Addi, "Algérie, le dérapage," *Le Monde Diplomatique*, February 1992, p. 20.)
15. See "Power, Poverty and Petrodollars," *Middle East Report* No. 170 (May–June 1991), esp. Yahya Sadowski, "Arab Economies After the Gulf War," pp. 4–10.
16. Fawzy Mansour, "L'Egypte découvre le prix de sa docilité," *Le Monde Diplomatique* (September 1992), p. 23.
17. Many Egyptians supported Mubarak against Iraq because Egyptian workers in Iraq had been subject to abusive treatment there, deprived of the right to remit their earnings home, and then suddenly deported en masse.
18. The campaign was led by the Union Socialiste des Forces Populaires (USFP) and the Confédération Démocratique du Travail (CDT). See M. al-Ahnaf, "L'opposition maghrébine face à la crise du Golfe," *Maghreb Mashrek/Monde Arabe* No. 130 (October–December 1990), pp. 99–114.
19. Space does not allow discussion of the most interesting question: why the U.S. and Britain were so keen to take on Qaddafi. Most obvious was his refusal to accept the economic and political tutelage of the West. But another matter is worth considering: the Libyan National Oil Company had built up one of the most important downstream systems in Europe, challenging the Anglo-American oil majors and posing a new model for all oil producers. Was the effort to destroy Qaddafi aimed at rolling back his nationalist oil policies as well?
20. Many Berbers prefer to use their own languages or French — the colonial language that is still very widely used in North Africa — rather than Arabic. Morocco and Algeria both have large Berber populations.
21. A full page ad in the French newspaper *Le Monde*, signed by French and Algerian intellectuals, appeared on May 7, 1990, calling on the Algerian government to take steps to protect women from the new Islamic "climate of terror."
22. Some of the most militant and violence-prone Islamists had participated in the civil war in Afghanistan. When the Cold War ended, the Soviet-supported Afghan government finally fell and the Islamic guerrilla movements in Afghanistan lost much of their foreign aid. The Algerians then returned to their country and began to put their guerrilla training to use against their own government. They became known as the "Afghans." About the same time, the Islamist government of Sudan began to train guerrilla forces. North African governments have also charged Iran with complicity in training anti-government forces.
23. *Le Monde*, March 22, 1992.

32

Crises in the Horn of Africa: Persistence of Cold War Legacies

John Prendergast and John Fieno

Throughout the last two decades, the Horn of Africa has been increasingly scarred by famine, war, and political instability. In 1992, the United Nations estimated that more than 23 million people faced starvation in the northeast corner of the continent, and similarly extraordinary numbers of people were reported at risk throughout most of the 1980s.

At the root of this human tragedy is the interface between drought and war. Millions of people who survived because of centuries-old coping mechanisms have been displaced by war or repeated drought, making them completely dependent on emergency relief programs. Subsistence and surviv-al, not development, has become the primary preoccupation in the Horn of Africa.

In the early 1990s, the political map of the Horn was in transition. By late 1992, the Horn had three recognized governments in Sudan, Ethiopia, and Djibouti; two separate, unrecognized governments in what was known as Somalia (the Republic of Somaliland in the North and Somalia in the South); a territory awaiting a referendum to determine its future, Eritrea; and major opposition movements in Sudan (the Sudanese People's Libera-tion Army, SPLA) and Ethiopia (the Oromo Liberation Front, OLF). Political instability and the series of wars in the region have interrupted any serious efforts at economic development or a solution to regional famine.

The Horn of Africa, which is half the size of the continental United States, has an overall population of 75 million; nearly half of them are fifteen years of age or younger.[1] Most live in extreme poverty: almost two-thirds of the population — 50 million people — live below the poverty line established by the UN. In Ethiopia, 65% of the population has an annual income less than US $375 (the United Nations' benchmark for poverty); in Somalia, 70%; in Sudan, the figure reaches 85%.[2] Worse, the future seems to become more bleak. The World Bank estimates that the Horn of Africa will have 195 million people by the year 2025. This population explosion, coupled with a serious lack of economic improvement and the devasting depletion of the natural resource base, threatens catastrophic consequences in the future.

On the national level, these statistics translate into mass suffering. Over 7.5 million Sudanese were considered at risk for starvation through the first half of 1992; malnutrition among young children is at least 40% in many areas of the country.[3] Even if food is available, most rural and urban dwellers cannot purchase food because of its high price. In Ethiopia and Eritrea, external food relief was provided to eight million people in 1992. Countless millions continue to be vulnerable to life-threatening illnesses because of the inaccessibility of medicines or clean water. As a result of years of civil war in Sudan and Ethiopia, large groups of refugees and internally displaced live on the edge of survival.

In the recently partitioned Somalia, 4.5 million people, mostly women and children, live in hunger. As war has raged in Somalia, many areas have no healthcare or clean water whatsoever. Agriculture and livestock production has fallen sharply. With at least half a million mines surrounding major Somali cities, any attempts at reconstruction have been greatly inhibited.[4] Djibouti and Kenya reel under the weight of large influxes of Ethiopian and Somali refugees. Djibouti has an unemployment rate of 36% and faces recent civil unrest.[5] Kenya has experienced a major drought in the north in 1992, placing nearly one million people at risk of severe food shortages. Under the weight of drought and conflict in the Horn, public infrastructure and social welfare systems have completely broken down, which has left the poor and hungry utterly helpless.

The Horn of Africa has experienced rapidly increasing movements of people across borders. Ethiopia hosts nearly 600,000 refugees, with roughly 15,000 from Sudan and the remainder from Somalia. In addition, Ethiopia awaits the return of more than 340,000 Ethiopian nationals who fled its recently concluded civil war. Moreover, thousands of Eritrean refugees are returning from the Sudan to participate in the Eritrean referendum on independence. More than two million displaced Somalis await their return home from Ethiopia. Already 100,000 Somalis have come home. Sudan hosts 750,000 Ethiopian and Eritrean refugees, not including the quarter of a million Ethiopians who have returned to their country.[6] By the end of 1992, the United Nations expects nearly a half million more refugees to enter Kenya in order to escape wars in Ethiopia, Somalia, and Sudan.

Militarization and the Culture of Conflict

Armed conflict has paralyzed post-independence Africa and has paralyzed almost all efforts at economic development; this is especially true for the Horn of Africa. Moreover, warfare in the Horn exacerbates food shortages, causing the deaths of untold non-combatants. War disrupts every level of agriculture: planting, harvest, milling, and distribution. Wars also displace hundreds of thousands of people and obstruct relief programs which could prevent most famine deaths. During wartime, food may be used as a weapon:

one army may prevent the transport of food in order to starve the enemy. Under these circumstances, civilians always perish first.

The wars which have caused persistent famines in the region are grounded in authoritarian political systems, unequal distribution of assets, and centralized development processes. All were exacerbated by Cold War rivalries. Although countries of the Horn are among the poorest in the world, military spending in the past decade has dominated domestic expenditures, accounting for over half the fiscal budgets of Ethiopia, Somalia and Sudan. Ethiopia, under its former dictator, Mengistu Haile Mariam, spent over $700 million annually on its army. Sudan continues to spend $1 million per diem on its war against the SPLA.[7] These resources could have been used for economic development and famine prevention activities.

Most of the region's conflicts have consisted of civil wars, although Ethiopian and Somali forces clashed in 1977–78, during which time the United States and the Soviet Union swapped client states. (Moscow had supported Somalia in the 1970s but switched clients when Somalia invaded Ethiopia.) Regimes in Ethiopia, Sudan, and Somalia have all assisted insurgents in neighboring countries' civil wars. As these internal conflicts continued and casualties steadily increased, insurgent forces and ruling armies became more polarized, thus reducing the possibility of negotiated settlement and national reconciliation.

The problems of the Horn of Africa cannot be reduced, as some commentators would like, to tribal or religious differences. The roots of the civil wars lie in the colonial rule of the British and the Italians and the monarchical rule in Ethiopia until 1974. Instead of promoting social harmony, colonial administrators and Ethiopian monarchs intensified ethnic and religious tensions by favoring some groups at the expense of others. As this strategy divided the local population and allowed for dictatorial rule, economic and political inequities linked to ethnic origin or religion endure and undermine these modern nation-states.

Further, the discriminatory distribution of external military and economic aid to the post-colonial, post-monarchical governments has reinforced established social cleavages and created more political instability. The Isaaq in Somalia, the Tigreans in Ethiopia and the Dinka in Sudan exemplify ethnic groups which suffered outright discrimination. Consequently, they erupted into some of the most violent rebellions in modern African history.

Since independence, government armies across the Horn of Africa have been the main beneficiaries of foreign aid programs. During the Cold War, the Horn's dictators were assets to the superpowers, and military aid was the most facile instrument for the cooption of African leaders. Since power in the Horn came out of the barrel of a rifle, the modernization of these countries was stunted radically: agriculture continued to operate in peril; industrialization did not receive adequate resources; infrastructure deteriorated; and health and education systems broke down under the weight of war. An opportunity for development and a higher standard of living after independence was wasted, and a crisis of immeasurable human suffering would unfold.

The Causes of Famine

A primary reason for the continuing famine in the Horn has been manipulation of Horn governments by external powers, whether victimized in the context of the Cold War or Middle Eastern politics. In return for their client status, authoritarian rulers extracted exorbitant amounts of weapons and aid from the United States and the Soviet Union. For example, Ethiopia received $1 billion annually from the Soviet Union in the 1980s; likewise, Sudan and Somalia received large sums from the United States.

A second cause of famine is the political issue of legitimacy in these countries. The principal sources of legitimacy for most regimes were its external financial and military supporters and the countries' urban populations. Inside these countries, regimes attempted to pacify city elites with pro-urban policies, namely food subsidies and low farm-gate prices. Accordingly, the rural areas suffered.

Further, regimes in the Horn have resorted to repressing their own citizens in order to hold power. Amnesty International and Africa Watch have compiled extensive records of the systematic repression of dissent during the reign of Siad Barre in Somalia, Haile Selassie and Mengistu in Ethiopia, and Gafaar Nimeiry and Omer el-Bashir in Sudan. The nature of these authoritarian regimes helped to cause the severity of the famine. A third reason for continuous famine lies in the decision of Horn governments to promote single-product exports and impose state-controlled or state-coopted marketing systems. These nations, under the tutelage of foreign sponsors, pursued policies which favored large-scale, capital-intensive, export-oriented agriculture. However, the international market for their export products crashed in the 1980s, and the Horn's economies never recovered. For example, Sudan, with the encouragement of the World Bank, converted some agricultural production from sorghum to cotton. In the early 1980s, the cotton market crashed due to an oversupply of cotton on the world market and the development of cheaper substitutes, and Sudan's formal economy reeled.

The foreign exchange generated by profits has either serviced debt or purchased weapons. Most governmental and World Bank investment has been in profitable, environmentally unsound, commercial export agriculture rather than small-scale production for local consumption. Despite the persistent threat of famine throughout the 1980s, Sudan exported food to the European Community.[8] Besides chronic food shortages, the resultant environmental degradation is rapidly destroying the productive capacity of the land through deforestation, decreasing soil fertility and increasingly irregular patterns of rainfall.

Finally, dependence on food aid is a lingering issue in the examination of the causes of famine. John Block, the United States Agriculture Secretary during the Reagan administration, stated, "Food is a weapon, but the way to use it is to tie countries to us. That way they'll be far more reluctant to upset us."[9] Food aid has been an instrument of cooption. Accordingly, donors with agricultural surpluses may quietly prefer to provide food aid rather than rehabilitation assistance. (Constant dependency on food aid makes Horn countries more pliable to donor wishes.) This has led to an undermining of the Horn's agricultural base. Somalia, a nation that could feed itself in the mid-1970s, became a major recipient of Western food aid throughout the 1980s and even before the war had become one of the most food import-dependent countries in Africa.[10]

The Changing Face of Geopolitics in the Horn of Africa

In the 1980s, geopolitical realities prevented any fundamental rethinking of American foreign policy in the Horn of Africa. Washington's preoccupation with the Soviet Union translated into a foreign policy determined almost exclusively by Cold War considerations. In the Horn, geo-strategic concerns were heightened as the West feared that the Iran-Iraq War would jeopardize oil supplies. From Washington's perspective, the Soviet Union's close ties to Ethiopia, Libya and South Yemen posed a danger to the Red Sea lanes which transport a significant amount of the world's oil supply. As a counter to the Soviet presence, the United States supported equally despotic dictators: Gafaar Nimeiry in Sudan and Siyad Barre in Somalia.

As the superpowers' clients were set against one another, geopolitical rivalry was paramount in the Horn. However, the end of the Cold War has offered hope for a new approach to the region's endemic problems. This hope was placed on hold after the Persian Gulf War returned the Horn of Africa to the strategic chessboard. When Sudan supported Saddam Hussein in the conflict, Western and United Nations relief workers pulled out of the country.

Ethiopia has also remained a place of strategic importance. After a popular insurgency toppled the Mengistu regime, the top U.S. State Department official on Africa commented in the *New York Times*: "Ethiopia's position at the gateway to the Red Sea opposite a key U.S. ally, Saudi Arabia, makes it of strategic interest to Washington even though the confrontation with the Soviets is now over."[11]

In the post-Cold War Horn of Africa, Middle East countries have attempted to fill the political vacuum left by the superpowers. These countries are jockeying for influence in a region rich in natural resources and susceptible to Islamic fundamentalism. Natural resources in the Horn provide the economic incentive for the involvement of Middle East countries. Strategic commodities such as oil, water, and grain represent goods of tremendous regional value. The involvement of Egypt, Israel, Saudi Arabia, Iran, Iraq, and Libya in the region partially results from a desire to influence the utilization of these vital resources. These countries usually trade oil and/or weapons for access to these resources. For example, Iraq sent military hardware to Sudan in exchange for grain, even though famine was raging in the latter.

Religion is the other major reason for the Middle East's involvement in the region. Iran and Libya view themselves as the principal promoters of the spread of Islam in Africa. Libya preaches a moderate form of Islam; the Shi'ism of Iran is more religiously orthodox. Both continue to finance militant organizations in the name of Islam. The Iranian Hizballah and the Libyan Islamic Legion both train personnel in Sudan, the first country in the Horn of Africa to be ruled by Islamic fundamentalists. Egypt, Saudi Arabia, and Israel, threatened by this tide of Islamic fundamentalism, have strangely become political bedfellows. All have sought to destabilize the fundamentalist regime in Sudan by covertly supporting its opponents. Also, Israel has collaborated with successive Ethiopian governments because of concerns about the plight of Ethiopian Jews.

Conclusion

External assistance has contributed more to the problems of the Horn rather that to their resolution. Foreign aid received by the Horn's dictators may have provided short-term legitimacy but did not help long-term development or political stability. Horn governments or factions will continue to be beseiged by foreign powers attempting to coopt them with military, economic or humanitarian aid, while their people suffer in extreme poverty.

On the other hand, emerging Horn leaders such as Ethiopia's Meles Zenawi, Eritrea's Isias Aferwerkie, and Sudan's Omer el-Bashir all are preaching a much more self-reliant vision of the Horn's economic future. Whether these new paradigms for self-reliance and self-determination are strong enough to withstand foreign intervention is uncertain. What does seem certain is that despite continuing cycles of famine and civil conflict, Horn populations no longer seem willing to peacefully accept the exclusionary, despotic political and economic systems that predominated during recent decades. In some cases, such as Eritrea, this may result in a new model of locally defined political and economic development. In others, such as Somalia, long-term militarized anarchy may follow.

"Humanitarian intervention," underway in Somalia and proposed for southern Sudan, is another factor which requires closer analysis. New rules regarding sovereignty will be tested in vulnerable regions such as the Horn.

The Horn will also be on the cutting edge of experimentation in governance; i.e., new models of participatory, decentralized government in Ethiopia and Eritrea. The rest of Africa is closely watching the approaches to democratization which the Transitional Government of Ethiopia and the Provisional Government of Eritrea have undertaken. The declared Republic of Somaliland is also being watched while it considers options such as local elections or a national referendum.

Most importantly, the entire region of the Horn of Africa is marked by a serious depletion of asset and natural resource bases, which will lead to further cycles of local and national conflict. Rebuilding these bases, through environmental restoration, agricultural rehabilitation, livestock restocking, micro-credit schemes, and other initiatives aimed at local farmers and pastoralists must go hand-in-hand with national efforts at conflict resolution and democratization if the New World Order is to bring peace to the Horn.

Notes

1. The World Bank, *World Development Report 1990*, Washington, D.C., 1990.
2. United Nations Development Program, *Human Development Report 1990*, New York, 1990.
3. UN Special Emergency Program for the Horn of Africa (SEPHA), *Consolidated Inter-Agency Appeal*, September 1991, p. 8.
4. Ibid.
5. Ibid, p. 44.
6. Overseas Development Council, "Politics and Refugees: Crises in the Horn of Africa," a briefing paper by the Congressional Staff Forum on International Development, November 4, 1991.
7. Anthony Lake, *After the Wars*, Overseas Development Council, Washington, D.C., 1990, p. 180.
8. Gayle Smith, "The Hunger," *Mother Jones*, October 1991, p. 61.
9. Senate Agriculture Committee Hearings, nomination of John Block, 1981.
10. *World Bank Agricultural Report*, Washington, D.C., 1987, and *World Bank Discussion Paper on Somalia*, Washington, D.C., 1986.
11. *New York Times*, May 30, 1991.

33

Reaping the Whirlwind:
Somalia After the Cold War

Chris Giannou

From the Balkans to the Caucasus, Central Asia and beyond, ethnicity and nationalism monopolize political debate in the post-Cold War world. Peoples demand sovereignty and self-determination on the basis of their sense of cultural identity and natural nationhood. Ex-Yugoslavia and the ex-Soviet Union are presented as seething cauldrons of ancient racial, ethnic and religious hatreds, suppressed for a few decades only through the policies of totalitarian regimes. Even liberal democracies with linguistic communities, as in Belgium and Canada, are not immune. Xenophobia raises its ugly head in the heart of Europe with ever increasing frequency. Former state structures are in constant tension with local "nationalism."

This essay will argue that Somalia proves that linguistic, cultural, religious, ideological and ethnic differences are not necessary for the outbreak of civil war and the decomposition of the nation-state. State structures may well disintegrate when the culture of the nation-state is imposed from without or when it is not the outcome of the natural social and political evolution of that society. It is the legitimacy of the international nation-state system that is in question. Post-colonial and post-imperial nation-states were taken for granted as being *the* social and political expression of self-determination while the ideological conflict of the Cold War dominated the world. But there is an ideological bias in this unitary nation-state model of expression itself. The only independence thinkable was, and is, the nation-state. This is the culture of imperialism.

In Africa, the sense of "natural" nationhood can best be claimed by Somalis. Somalia is not only one of the rare countries on the continent which is ethnically, linguistically and religiously homogeneous; not all ethnic Somalis live within the Somali state and, as a result, this situation has given rise to the longest lasting and most powerful irridentism in Africa: two wars with neighboring Ethiopia and the original non-recognition of the independence and sovereignty of Kenya. Genealogy, through a system of segmental lineage, is the defining criterion of the Somali social system; an individual is defined by his or her genealogical tree. The total corporate genealogical tree of Somalia constitutes the Somali "nation" — in effect, the overly extended family — and provides for its founding myth: legendary Arab sheikhs descended from the family of the prophet Muhammad landed on the Somali coast 1,000 years ago, married with local women, and thus founded the major clan confederations. The perceived unity of the Somali "nation" was an ancient "mechanical" community of identity and not a modern "organic" community growing naturally through various inter-relationships over time.[1]

But Somalia exists no longer. The land has splintered into a mosaic of clan-ruled regions. Civil war and civil strife ravage the country. State institutions have disintegrated and the traditional authority of clan elders and religious leaders put into question, effectively disestablished. Civil society has unraveled and the traditionally neglected rural clansmen take revenge on their urban relatives. Reinforced clanism has forced society into devolution, with the emergence of ever smaller communities of identity and social solidarity. War's destruction and insecurity have paralyzed the economy and the country's infrastructure has fallen apart or been looted. Drought has hit, followed by famine.

Perniciously, the world media, at first, neglected Somalia entirely, and then focused only on the starvation (skeletal little African babies) and the anarchic insecurity. The journalists' attention then zoomed in on the next chapter in a brave new world order in which an American-led expeditionary force (marines bravely fighting off the glare of TV spotlights on the shores of Mogadishu, for want of Tripoli) intervened in the name of humanitarian principles. But Somalia since the end of the 1980s represents far more in reality than the cliché of "just another devastating famine in an African country incapable of feeding and governing itself." The unexpected, and precedent-setting American troop deployment is designed to achieve much more than the purportedly "humanitarian" goals that the American public has been led to believe motivated it.

Somalia poses significant political and humanitarian challenges: What is the legitimacy of the nation-state system? What is the capacity of a society to transform itself to fit into externally imposed structures and institutions? What is the ability of international legitimacy, in the form of the United Nations, to respond in a timely fashion to impending social and political catastrophes? What is the ambiguity, and hidden agenda of armed, unilateral "humanitarian intervention" in creating a "kinder and gentler" new world order?

Return to the Water Hole: The Natural vs. the National

Semi-nomadic pastoral transhumance defined traditional Somali society. More or less large groups of people trekked, according to the season, between the Haud highlands of the Ethiopian Ogaden and the water sources of the Indian Ocean coast. Nomad families moved with their camels, goats and sheep in search of water and pasturage. During a drought year, conflict over water or forage could, and often would, erupt between different groups, representing a collective need and collective decision to fight for survival. Should a clansman kill someone, the contending elders would meet, and the clan would pay compensation to the victim's group. The fundamental unit of society was/is the *mag* or *diya* (paying-unit): the blood money compensation group. Blood money compensation, in the form of an agreed number of camels, is paid, not by the killer but by his *mag*, and not to the immediate family of the victim, but to the group that would be called upon to pay in similar circumstances. The result is that "kinspeople act in concert instead of as individuals," according to the Somali sociologist and historian Said Samatar. "In their personal autonomy, Somalis are extremely individualistic; in their attribution of privilege and obligation, they are inflexibly collective-oriented."[2] Traditional pastoral society, therefore, ignores individual culpability, responsibility and accountability. Security and responsibility are collective; a vital condition for survival in a brutally harsh climate and geography.

Related *mag* groups form *reer*; kindred *reer* give rise to family lineages, subclans, then clans and finally the six great clan confederations. This segmental system gives rise "to the collective predilection to internal fissions and internecine sectary conflicts as well as of the unity of thought and action among Somalis — a unity that borders on xenophobia."[3]

This was how Somalis organized their society before colonialism, when the entire population was nomadic and pastoral. The coastal cities were perceived as foreign enclaves, the work, first, of Persian and Arab traders, followed by Portuguese, British, French and Italian explorers and colonizers. With colonialism, more and more Somalis moved into the cities; but the bulk of the population remained outside the system and continued its traditional way of life.

Colonialism imposed centralized structures and fortified urbanization; coercive policies maintained order in the cities; manipulation of clan elders and rivalries served in the countryside. Privileges and revenues devolving from the colonial economy were distributed according to clan divisions. A Somali elite, as a function of the colonial administration, also took shape. After independence in 1960, the state attempted to incorporate all of the population and the entirety of society. Somalia was the only country (along with the Cameroons a couple of years later) on the continent to counter the "balkanization" of Africa, as former Italian Somalia and British Somaliland united to form the Somali Republic. Somalia found itself in the vanguard of contemporary African politics in another distinct way: the republic was originally a parliamentary democracy.

Although Somalia has a homogeneous population, the schismatic clan system defines the society; unlike what most people believe, the centralized unitary Somali nation-state and free elections did not reduce, but simply reinforced, divisive clan consciousness. The logic, mentality, social structures, and human realities of the society were foreign to the nation-state. The criterion for the establishment of the nation-state is a "national vision" or national consciousness, an ideological factor as a people sharing a common future involving a common historical project, thus leading to an organic nation. Somalis never developed such a consciousness for working together within the confines of the state. The only historical project they shared was pan-Somali irridentism: the mechanical nation lived on; the organic one failed to develop. The traditional emotional appeal of pan-Somali nationalism, and irridentism — a centripetal social force — was counterbalanced by the centrifugal force, equally traditional, of clanism.

If in the desert clans fought over water holes, in the city of the post-colonial nation-state clans fought over the biggest water hole of all: the state, its institutions and its power to dispense the spoils of foreign and military aid. Nepotism, corruption, inefficiency, non-ideological political discourse, clan politics ruled Somalia. A constantly-shifting alliance of clans in power and another constantly-shifting clan opposition dominated the republic. One either partook of the watering hole or one did not, but the entire concept of the centralized nation-state was never put into question as long as the clans alternately partook of power.

Compare Somalia's parliamentary past with the powerful popular demand for more public accountability and popular participation that many African countries have witnessed over the last several years, leading to a peaceful and democratic transfer of political power in several. In others, the process has been flawed, and the protest movement reinforced as a result rather than crushed. This contrasts with the clan-based system that condoned collective action and distribution of the spoils of the state and shunned any individual responsibility or culpability for mismanagement or corruption. The old structures and mentality of nomadic Somali existence remained to haunt the nation-state.

The division/unity dialectic, centripetal/centrifugal balance, was further reinforced by the military regime that overthrew the parliamentary republic and its clan-based, clientele politics. When Siad Barre, "an obscure police officer from a minor clan," (as a popular adage had it) overthrew parliament and instituted a military dictatorship in 1969, the population celebrated. Pragmatism and charisma marked the early period of the regime which gave rise to an important popular mobilization and such progressive social policies as the establishment of the Somali tongue as a written language which permitted a widespread literacy program in a national language rather than in those of the colonial era. The effort to improve the lot of women with the foundation of the Somali Women's Association resulted in the concomitant campaign against the practice of female genital excision. Alongside the rhetoric of Somali "scientific socialism," the campaign against clanism helped to increase the centralization of social structures and state institutions. This latter campaign against clanism attempted "to replace archaic, divisive lineage loyalty, by productive revolutionary allegiance to 'the nation.'" Siad Barre vowed "to eradicate social balkanization and fragmentation into tribes and sects . . . to bring about an absolute unity."[4]

Unity at home, the denunciation of divisive clanism, had, as its corollary, the unifying ideology of Greater Somalia irridentism. This ideology led Siad Barre into the disastrous Ogaden War. In the Cold War context of 1977, the outbreak of hostilities between revolutionary post-imperial Ethiopia and scientifically socialist Somalia produced the "great superpower flip-flop": Soviet technical and military advisors left Somalia to replace their American counterparts in Addis Ababa while the U.S. took the place of the USSR in Mogadishu. (The Somali military performed well, but ultimately suffered a crushing defeat at the hands of Cuban troops airlifted in from Angola.) After years of Soviet assistance, the Somalis then enjoyed hundreds of millions of dollars of American and Western aid, distributed by the regime along clan lines. The culture of dependency, and corresponding opportunism thus created over the decades of Cold War rivalry, would play havoc with the efforts of relief aid workers in 1992.

The Somali defeat in the Ogaden War caused the military regime of Siad Barre to lose legitimacy in people's eyes. The war was not entirely Barre's doing. Rather he was pulled into it by the activities of a guerrilla group which had widespread support, and it was an immensely popular enterprise; however, this did not spare Barre from criticism in losing the war. The people turned, in clan-based opposition, against Barre's clan which had lost the war. No Somali could accept the collective guilt of the nation in pursuing Somali irridentism; instead Somalis placed the blame on the collective, the clan coalition, in power.

In reaction, and to retain power, although Siad Barre maintained the much publicized official campaigns against "tribalism," his own politics became entirely clan-based and ever more tyrannically coercive. Siad Barre held on, aided by cynical Cold War calculations and manipulations.[5]

The room for maneuver finally became very narrow. Too many clans found themselves out of power too often or did not participate sufficiently in the distribution of the spoils system and repression became more violent, ending with Siad Barre's leveling by air bombardment of the second largest city, Hargheisa in 1988. A popular uprising in Mogadishu between December 1990 and January 1991, and the pressure arising from the various armed opposition groups closing in on the city, resulted in the overthrow of the Siad Barre regime. A power vacuum ensued.

The leaders of the opposition groups then simply fought amongst themselves to see who would gain control of the state and who would replace the dictatorship of the former clan coalition by the dictatorship of their own clan. But the popular rejection of the Siad Barre dictatorship transformed itself into the rejection of centralized authority imposed by any "other" clan. Thus, another level of conflict appeared in the form of warlords intent on seizing control of central state power and imposing another unitary state with themselves at its head against a multitude of warlords who seized power in their regional fiefdoms and did not want to give it up to the center.

Somali society found itself unable to cope. Clan competition erupted into open warfare on several fronts reflecting warlord conflict. Four months of street fighting and shelling destroyed Mogadishu. Social checks and balances disappeared. The traditional authority of clan elders no longer held sway with the warlords or the armed bands of disabused rural dwellers, "camelboys," who left their homes and occupied the cities. The warlords brought the camelboy-warriors to the cities to overthrow the Barre regime and then lost control of many of them.

The country fragmented, institutions disintegrated and major parts of the economy ceased to function. Internal refugee migrations sorted the population into defined regions along subclan lines. Massacres and looting became commonplace. Drought hit and the cyclical Somali famine became a devastating, catastrophic mass starvation. Humanitarian emergency food aid, and the salaries and rentals paid by the aid agencies became the new booty of clan rivalry and warfare: a new water hole.

The "Anarchy": A Systematic Social Devolution

How does a segmentary clan system function when the imposed unity of the nation-state crumbles? In spite of its ethnic homogeneity, Somali society is so deeply schismatic that the community of identity keeps changing according to the conflict at hand or the stakes involved. At times, this collective self-image is the "nation": "Somalia against the world," or more pertinently against imperial Ethiopia or colonial Britain, Italy and France. At another level, the division of power in the centralized structures of the colony or the post-colonial nation-state, the community of identity devolves from the "nation" to the clan federation. When the centralized structures no longer exist, the collective self-image transmutes once again, to the clan, or subclan, level. And when the society, in the midst of the tumult of civil strife, faces drought and starvation, the basic unit of social identity recedes still further; the community of identity becomes ever more restricted and narrow, the ties of social solidarity tighter — it is a question of life and death. Now, when one talks about "my people," the identification of the individual through ties of social solidarity may well be to a very restricted social unit.

The continuing civil war is due to a few warlords who hope to impose their rule, and consequently the rule of their clan, on any new state structure. The warlords distribute weapons but do not pay salaries; the booty of war — looting, pillage, rape — are the combatants' reward.

But this inter-clan, inter-factional civil war constituted the least of the fighting in the country just prior to the arrival of the multinational forces in December 1992. Most of the "security problems," the anarchy, occurred when the camelboy warriors were not fighting rival clans. They occupied the cities, the sites of privilege, traditionally developed at the expense of the rural areas. They then took their revenge on the urban population, even those of their own clan, in the form of class conflict, through banditry, squatting or looting luxurious dwellings and public buildings, including schools and hospitals. Any looting or killing for personal gain immediately created conflict amongst subclans, then sub-subclans. Discipline was impossible to enforce. Traditional clan elders and religious officials had little influence; since the warlords did not distribute salaries, they appeared, at times, to be the hostages rather than the leaders of their own men.

By 1992, the salaries and rents paid out by the relief and aid agencies represented the only functioning economy remaining in many parts of the country. Food represented the only commodity of any value. The agencies would hire a certain number of men, often unemployed "camelboys," by now urban warriors, as security guards; the unhired became looters. The two groups were often interchangeable. Military activity in the agriculturally rich provinces prevented planting and harvesting and, compounded by drought, the famine became more severe. The brutal formula of everyday life became: "have gun, will eat." Although some looters stole because of hunger, this was not always the case. In Baidoa, at the height of the famine with upwards of 500 people dying every day, the situation before one's eyes was simple and stark: anyone with a gun was well fed; no one who was starving had a gun.

The clan instinct of survial lay at the root of the security problems. The argument that, "This food is to save *your* people from starving," did not work with the armed young men. Those were not "his" people; they were from another clan. The plea that, "We must save the children. They are the future of society," had no meaning. If the children survived and the young adults died, the children, as orphans, would have no clan identity. If the adults survived, they could always have more children. The armed bands would take the looted food itself, or convert it into currency via the merchants who then sold the food in the marketplace, and helped their clan to survive.

Even after the worst of the famine, or in areas not badly affected, the looting and extortion, as a function of intra-clan competition, continued. In Belet Huen, about 200 miles west of Mogadishu by the Ethiopian border, the International Committee of the Red Cross (ICRC) used two leased civilian C-130 Hercules airplanes to airlift food from March 1992 onwards. This effectively prevented this region from suffering the same catastrophic consequences that befell Baidoa, where warlord military activity rendered the city inaccessible to relief agencies for many months. In late summer, a multinational airlift began moving food into Belet Huen. It used many military C-130 Hercules with self-imposed rules and regulations concerning cargo weight and flight rotations, instead of the two civilian ones, to deliver the same quantity of food. The ICRC had been leasing trucks from a local contractor to carry the food from the airstrip to their warehouse. The arrival of many more airplanes with various national designations — all carrying ICRC food, nonetheless — was the pretext for a second contractor to present himself. He said this was a different action from the ICRC's, and he wanted a part in the "spoils." Each contractor, representing a group of different subclans, split into ever dwindling segmentary units. Eventually, two weeks later, forty-four contractors were vying, often with weapons, to deliver the same ICRC food from the airstrip to the warehouse. No one from amongst the forty-four groups represented by the local contractors was starving at that time; the starving population in the region were to be found amongst the unarmed refugees who had flowed into the previously calm area of Belet Huen, drawn by the food distribution. Thus, the intensification of the relief effort, when done inefficiently, increased the incidence of security problems: shooting, looting, armed extortion and attempts at blackmail.

It is in this context that rehabilitation of the economy and the institutions of society is a *sine qua non* for any restabilization and political reconciliation in Somalia. The United Nations-mandated multinational expeditionary force and UN troops are supposedly, in a fuzzily defined way, to occupy, disarm, restore law and order, feed, heal, repair and make function the infrastructure. There is no recent precedent for an enterprise of this magnitude; not even the UN presence in Cambodia goes this far.

Are social peace and stability in Somali society unrealizable goals? The picture remains very bleak, and although colonization and decolonization, Cold War rivalry and the "culture of dependency" all play a part in and bear some responsibility for the disaster that is Somalia today, there is also a profound contradiction at work in Somali culture. Imposed systems — colonialism, parliamentary democracy and the nation-state — have never really suited Somali realities, and Somali society has never really undergone the radical transformations necessary to fit them.

Lessons to Be Learned: The Saga of Sahnoun

The International Committee of the Red Cross issued an urgent appeal in December 1991, saying that "mass starvation was imminent in Somalia." The response was virtually nil. Another appeal appeared in March 1992. The response was minimal until August, when images of starving children began to appear in the Western media. The international response, then, was more important, but inadequate. International public opinion, watching the American-led multinational military airlift, and the UN agencies, and non-governmental organizations (NGOs) that mobilized to face the situation of mass starvation, thought that the problem was famine. Too many foreign aid and UN workers simply did not understand Somalia, did not understand the politics, did not fully grasp the connection between relief efforts and security problems. Food distribution and healthcare programs were inefficient, even incompetent, as a result.

There is one important case where a UN official attempted to face the realities of Somalia. Mohammed Sahnoun, the UN secretary general's former special envoy to the country, is a distinguished and experienced diplomat who has dealt with problems as intractable and complex as Lebanon's civil war and acted as intermediary for negotiations concerning American hostages in Tehran. Sahnoun represents well the jealously guarded national dignity of anti-colonialist Algeria, and he gained widespread respect amongst all Somali factions. He had a brilliant plan, starkly simple and well-adapted to Somali realities. It also respected people's dignity, and was totally unorthodox with respect to traditional international peacekeeping and rules of legitimacy. His solution took as a given that one had to build on the clan system that had undermined the unitary state, a system that was the basis of the continuing civil conflict, and was not about to disappear.

Sahnoun wanted UN troops to distribute uniforms and salaries to the local militias — the gunmen, "camelboys," security guards, looters. They were to serve as an officer training corps to discipline the militias and turn them into local police forces, thus beginning the task of local institution building. Sahnoun knew that Somalis had to participate in the restabilization of their own society; that only Somalis, eventually, could successfully disarm Somalis. By distributing salaries, the plan would have addressed the economic component of the security situation that was the cause of all of the looting in a country that had little left of an economy except for international relief aid. Sahnoun also proposed an extreme decentralization of administrative structures, legitimizing the de facto "cantonization" of the country into subclan fiefdoms and recognizing the dozen Somalias and Somalilands that effectively existed on the ground if not on the map. The unitary nation-state would have to give way to an extreme form of decentralization with fiefdoms living in peaceful co-existence once they felt that they had nothing to fear from the hegemonic designs of other clans. They could then negotiate regional cooperation and coordination agreements to which any or all could freely accede.

To give any other meaning to "national reconciliation" in the Somali context would be to court another disaster even more catastrophic for the Somali people in the not too distant future. However, it took months for the Security Council to finally agree to send 3,500 UN troops to Somalia under Sahnoun's plan for the country, and he had no support or leverage in his negotiations with the warlords that an effective UN relief effort would have given him.

The plan was never implemented. There was no budget to pay for uniforms and salaries, and Ambassador Sahnoun's public criticism of UN agency incompetence and the inadequacy of the international response to Somalia's crisis was so eloquent that it resulted in his forced resignation. The situation deteriorated, or was allowed to deteriorate, to such an extent that massive military intervention was necessary, simply to feed the people. The culprits responsible for the deterioration were presented as: insecurity, opportunism, extortion, stemming from the bands of armed, uncontrolled, qat leaf-chewing youth, the warlords and their merchant financiers. The NGOs and UN agencies, and the international press corps, were the biggest and loudest lobbyists pushing for a military deployment, pleading for "the right and duty of humanitarian intervention."

And so it came to pass. The West, a century after classic colonialism brought "civilization to savage peoples," today brings humanitarian food and medicine, under armed guard, to an "anarchy-stricken" people. Even more morally ambiguous than the first colonization of Africa, this end-of-the-millennium re-colonization is presented as the only way to feed and heal the victims of Somalia's plunge into destitution and anarchy. It may well be one way safely to deliver food and medical supplies; it is probably not the only way. It is one way of re-ordering Somali society; how successfully, is another question. There are probably other ways; this was the challenge of Sahnoun's plan.

Sahnoun's extreme decentralization, turning the *de facto* regional clan fiefdoms into *de jure* cantons, responded to the historic and human realities of

Somalia, and was an impressive alternative model. Somalis have a way of doing things: their way. Sahnoun understood it and wanted to use it, with UN help, to restabilize Somali society on its own terms, using Somalis as the principal instrument.

The Sahnoun saga and the intricacies of New York-based UN corridor politics raise some fundamental questions. Can populations actually involved in a conflict, under the aegis and legitimacy of the UN, help put an end to that conflict? If so, then the role of the United Nations, as well as the scope of national sovereignty must be rethought. UN trusteeship, originally a model for bringing colonies to independence, may well provide the cadre for humanitarian and political intervention. This would involve a new role for the UN system and necessitate new, more efficient, structures, as well as a new decision-making process. Its application would also have to be universalized; one cannot establish trusteeship over Somalia, Liberia or Zaire, and do nothing about Bosnia, Kosovo or the Israeli-occupied territories of the Gaza Strip and the West Bank.

The artificiality of post-colonial nation-states, not to mention the successor ethnic states of the former USSR and Eastern Europe, is one of the main sources of instability in the world today. The ramifications of accepting artificial and arbitrary boundaries as the causes of that instability are widespread: for example, what should be the basis for self-determination in the demographic leopard skin of the Balkans or the Caucasus? The nation-state, ethnic state or something else?

Last but Not Least: Geo-Strategic Politics

The precedent-setting foray into Somalia of tens of thousands of American troops, accompanied and then followed by tens of thousands of others, all under the aegis of United Nations resolutions, raises other questions. What is the responsibility of the United Nations Organization when there are no institutions in a country which embody national sovereignty? How and when can the international community undertake military/humanitarian intervention in the name of international law and "universal" principles? What is the legitimacy of the international system of nation-states in the post-Cold War world order of things when most conflicts themselves arise from the inadequacy of the nation-state model? And what is the proper role of the media in setting the parameters of public discourse and in determining policy? Somalia receives major attention, belatedly; Liberia does not.

Although the American public may have assumed altruism behind U.S. interventionary policies in Somalia, one must never forget that, in reality, the situation was allowed to deteriorate and the worst of the starvation was over by the time the military was deployed. Other factors behind the intervention include: 1) saving the Pentagon budget after the Cold War; 2) proving that the UN could not function effectively without direct U.S. military involvement (implying that the UN could be forced into becoming a simple annex of the State Department); 3) the need to deploy against militant Islamic radicalism simultaneously in the Persian Gulf and in the Horn of Africa (the Sudanese government's response to the landing of the Marines was most telling: they called it "Christian imperialism"); 4) creating a precedent of "humanitarian intervention in a setting of civil strife" in a region of the world where the West does have vital strategic interests (which leads to the question of how this will affect U.S. policies towards Zaire and South Africa); 5) using intervention to suppress "tribalism" and return the region to the so-called normality of the unitary nation-state and end disruption in neighboring Ethiopia, Djibouti and Kenya; 6) doubtless the oil in northeastern Somalia, being developed by the U.S. Continental Oil Company (CONOCO), also had an impact on this intervention.

Lastly, there is good old geo-strategic politics. In the same way that the Straits of Gibraltar are the strategic passage between the Atlantic and the Mediterranean, so the Bab el Mandeb, at the northern tip of Somalia, is the strategic passage between the Mediterranean, via the Suez Canal and the Red Sea, and the Indian Ocean. The U.S., with its influence over Morocco, and Great Britain on the Rock of Gibraltar hold strategic sway over the shores of the Atlantic-Mediterranean bottleneck. The U.S. and the French are similarly positioned to control access to the Red Sea.

Historically, Great Britain controlled this part of the route to India by its garrisons in Aden and British Somaliland, while the French Foreign Legion is still ensconced in Djibouti, the *Française des Somalis*. Then Secretary of Defense Dick Cheney made it abundantly clear, as U.S. troops moved into Somalia, that American warships would patrol the Somali coasts for some time to come — even when and if the internal feuding of Somalis ends. UN soldiers will take over from American troops in Somalia, but 5,000 of the latter — responsible for logistics and a rapid deployment force — will remain. The U.S. has gained another foothold to the southwest of the Arabian peninsula and the Suez Canal — a major new platform for intervention into the Arabian oilfields and southward into the African mines of strategic minerals. The humanitarian venture into the Horn of Africa can be seen as simply another chapter, after the Gulf War, in the further positioning of U.S. forces around Saudi Arabia and the reinforcement of the strategic logistics of the U.S. Central Command, successor to the Rapid Deployment Force. In the post-Cold War period, delivering humanitarian aid has provided the Pentagon with a popular means to deploy its ships and hardware near the Gulf. The marine landing, with camouflage fatigues and painted faces, on the beaches of Mogadishu was a "military exercise," totally inappropriate for the humanitarian task at hand, unless the real task was simply another military maneuver. One can argue that the longer Somalia remains unstable, the more a case can be made for a continued U.S. presence offshore at the mouth of the highly strategic Red Sea.

Somalia was never just a country with catastrophic famine, and the international response was never just an altruistic humanitarian one. The people of Somalia have reaped the whirlwind of history: self-imposed, but also determined by forces completely beyond their control.

Notes

1. See I.M. Lewis, *A Modern History of Somalia* (Boulder, Co.: Westview Press, 1988).
2. Said Samatar, *Somalia: A Nation in Turmoil* (London: Minority Rights Group Report, 1991).
3. Ibid.
4. Lewis, op. cit.
5. S.R. Shalom, "Gravy Train: Feeding the Pentagon by Feeding Somalia," *Z Magazine* (February 1993).

■ PART SEVEN ■

Asia

34

India: Non-Alignment Gives Way to U.S. Alliance

Praful Bidwai

India — erstwhile leader of the Non-Aligned Movement, one-time vocal critic of Western politics of global domination and U.S. hegemonism, and suspect in Washington's eyes since the days of John Foster Dulles — has readied itself to become a supporter of one version of the New World Order, and a friend and partner, if not quite an ally yet, of the United States. A major reorientation in New Delhi's posture has been gradually and quietly wrought by successive governments since the late eighties. The P.V. Narasimha Rao government has been building on that base both to establish a decisive and complete break with India's earlier pursuit of an independent, non-aligned foreign policy, and to formalize a new relationship of proximity with the West, in particular the U.S.[1]

Dramatic as it is, the shift in India's orientation has been buttressed by far-reaching rightward changes in domestic social and economic policy, New Delhi's search for conservative solutions to the country's debt-led economic crisis, and by new perceptions amongst its policymakers of India's place in a post-communist world. Above all, Indian policymakers have been driven by the search for "security" (within the South Asian region) and "stability" (of India's borders), which is compatible with the option *not* to reform and recast India's relations with her neighbors, in particular Pakistan, into a more balanced, equitable, non-adversarial mold.

However, although the forces that favor a Westward realignment of Indian policy are numerous and powerful, and while the political establishment has already advanced considerably in that direction, resistance to the move should not be underestimated. That resistance, itself closely linked to considerations of political legitimacy, has put a question-mark over the long-term sustainability of India's new orientation.

India's Westward turn has been starkly evident since the Gulf War, itself a turning point in relations with the U.S. In the months preceding the war, India, in violation of its professed policy favoring the resolution of international disputes through non-military and multilateral means, did not criticize Resolution 678 of the UN Security Council, authorizing the use of force against Iraq. In effect, it supported the U.S. strategy to bypass the General Assembly in discussing the Iraq-Kuwait issue and was complicit in Washington's hijacking of the UN. Worse, New Delhi actively supported the Western war effort when, in January 1991, it allowed U.S. warplanes to refuel in India en route from bases in East Asia. This was dictated not so much by strategic necessity or logistical considerations — several other, equally suitable, if not more convenient, staging points were available, including Diego Garcia and Singapore — as by New Delhi's willingness to send out the political message, and in a demonstrative way, that it had executed a change in its stand and now no longer opposed an avoidable war led by the U.S. against a Third World country.[2]

Since those early months of 1991, there has been closer political, strategic and economic "cooperation" between New Delhi and Washington, under the latter's tutelage. The U.S. has accorded favorable treatment to India in multilateral economic institutions such as the World Bank and the International Monetary Fund, on which India has been highly dependent for loans and concessional finance. Important differences between the two governments on issues such as intellectual property rights, especially patents, have narrowed, thanks to India's greater "flexibility."[3]

Washington has repeatedly commended New Delhi for the market-oriented radical economic policy changes that it has embarked on. And despite recession and the state of its economy, the U.S. continues to be the largest investor in India, accounting for the lion's share of (admittedly modest) new foreign investment proposals, with companies such as Kellogg, DuPont and General Motors taking the lead.

The two governments have sought to smooth out the rough edges in their political relationship. This has typically taken the form of New Delhi acquiescing in, and tacitly or overtly supporting Washington's scheme of things in international relations. Thus even after joining the Security Council in January 1992, India has been a virtually silent spectator to U.S. maneuvers in, and manipulation of, the United Nations, resulting in a drastic reorganization of its secretariat, the placing of pro-Western officials in key positions in UN agencies and, most important of all, the virtual dismantling of the organization's development function.[4]

On contentious issues such as sanctions against Libya, New Delhi has elected to abstain rather than oppose U.S.-sponsored motions, in departure from its professed policy and well-established traditional position. Even where overt U.S. pressure was brought to bear upon it, New Delhi's response has been muted or low-key.

An example of this was the December 1991 agreement by India to sell a relatively small quantity (100,000 tons) of rice to Cuba, a long-standing friend whose leaders continued to enjoy a measure of popularity in India. The U.S. Department of Agriculture made no effort to disguise its displeasure at this proposal and told India, itself in the market for wheat, that it would not be entitled to purchase subsidized wheat from the U.S. Under Washington's pressure, New Delhi all but annulled the Cuban agreement in early 1992. This drew a good deal of flak from a substantial section of Indian public opinion, as well as the domestic political opposition, which saw it as an unconscionable compromise of national sovereignty, besides the betrayal of a friend in need. In the spring of 1992, a broad-based committee of left-wing political leaders, artists and intellectuals started to organize a campaign to collect voluntary donations of rice for shipment to Cuba. Ultimately, under the pressure of public opinion, the government decided that it would be impolitic to renege on the deal. However, it took care not even to hint that U.S. pressure had been at work in early 1992.

In return for its "cooperation," New Delhi has received Washington's support for its claim to a special, preeminent status in South Asia, and, very importantly, general if tacit endorsement of its handling of the problematic situation in Kashmir. The U.S. does not support the Indian stand — which itself sits ill with the 1971 Simla agreement between India and Pakistan to resolve all disputes through negotiations, and which New Delhi has often invoked — that Kashmir is an inalienable part of India and that its accession to the Indian Union, shortly after Independence in August 1947, is not negotiable. However, the U.S. has been extraordinarily careful not to criticize New Delhi's violations of civil liberties and human rights in the Kashmir valley, certainly not publicly. It has also urged Pakistan to withdraw support to secessionists and anti-Indian militant groups which Islamabad has armed and trained.

In matters strategic, Indo-U.S. cooperation has become unprecedentedly close despite differences on the nuclear proliferation issue and occasional criticism of India for export of dual-use chemicals and military technologies to West Asia and North Africa.[5] Even before the Gulf War, New Delhi had decided to effect a major shift in the source of supply of major weapons systems away from the former USSR. Soon afterwards, it embarked on a close military partnership with the U.S. Thus it accepted an agenda of strategic realignment based on what have come to be known, after a former commander of the U.S. Army in the Pacific, as the "Kicklighter proposals." These include combined Indo-U.S. training activities, regular exchange visits by chiefs of staff, joint conferences, staff talks and army management seminars, and regular joint exercises and information exchange. A significant joint naval exercise in the summer of 1992 marked a high point of this new "cooperation," which has gone well beyond the terms of the much talked about but for long irrelevant 1971 Indo-Soviet treaty of peace and friendship, even in its heyday.

These exercises were indeed a far cry from the bitter tensions symbolized most starkly by the dispatch of aircraft carrier *USS Enterprise* to the Bay of Bengal in 1971 at the time of the Bangladesh war, in a clearly threatening gesture. The putative gain for New Delhi from the new phase of "cooperation" has been U.S. acknowledgment of India as the power center of South Asia and a junior partner of the United States.

The process of reaching either a new regional compact or a wholly new cooperative relationship between India and the United States has not been without strain or misunderstanding on both sides. India has been treated as a special case, but within a larger framework dictated by the United States. New Delhi has been told that it cannot possibly hope for a relationship of equality with the U.S. It has accepted this, however reluctantly. The United States has used a combination of persuasion, threats and coercion to achieve major changes in the Indian stand on regional and international issues. The U.S. has recognized India as the preeminent power in the region, but broader global concerns for Washington have limited the privileges that might otherwise have come to India in consequence of the special relationship.

A major area of disagreement has persisted on the nuclear weapons issue. While the U.S. has favored an agreement for nuclear restraint between India and Pakistan (which it has been prepared to guarantee), eventually leading to the joint signature of the Nuclear Non-Proliferation Treaty (NPT) of 1968, India has remained firmly opposed to the latter on "principle" — in reality, primarily because it does not wish to close the nuclear weapons option.[6]

The U.S. has sought to put on the bilateral agenda of discussions with India and Pakistan an arrangement well short of the NPT, but involving the capping of Indian and Pakistani nuclear weapons capabilities. In mid-1991, it endorsed — and according to some strategic analysts, actually initiated — the proposal formally made by the Pakistani prime minister, Nawaz Sharif, for a five-nation conference on nuclear weapons in South Asia (including, besides India and Pakistan, the U.S., the former USSR and China).

India first summarily rejected the proposal as a version of the NPT "through the backdoor"; it also reiterated its opposition to a regional (as distinct from a global) approach to nuclear disarmament and to the discriminatory nature — itself an indisputable fact — of the NPT, which legitimizes the existence of five nuclear-weapons states without imposing a specific time-bound obligation on them to undertake disarmament. However, there have been indications that India's stand on a regional nuclear restraint plan might not be immutable. In early 1992, it agreed to discuss the matter further in strictly bilateral (with the U.S.) talks, although not in a five-nation framework. Hints were later dropped that what is on the cards is an agreement for capping South Asian nuclear weapons capabilities at their 1992 level: this would implicitly acknowledge India's superiority over Pakistan.[7]

India is not entirely averse to discussing the proposal at greater length, but the bottom line, retaining the weapons option, remains.

Under the Bush non-proliferation agenda, divergence on the nuclear issue did lead to tension, as in mid-1992 over the issue of the sale of Russian cryogenic rocket engine technology for the Indian space program. The U.S. administration, peeved over the deal, which it claimed would violate the missile technology control regime (MTCR), imposed sanctions against the Indian Space Research Organization (ISRO). India contended that the engines were unfit for use in military rockets/missiles and would not breach MTCR requirements; it further offered not to transfer missile technology to other countries. The Russians affirmed, for what it was worth, that they would stand by the deal. The sanctions have remained in place. But, remarkably, rancor has been altogether missing from the whole Indo-U.S. contention.

Clearly, Indian policymakers, keen not to miss out on what they perceive, probably over-optimistically, even wishfully, as the likely benefits of a cooperative, albeit subordinate relationship, with the U.S. and the fruits of the "unipolar moment" (such as it might be), have proved extremely accommodating and eager.

Domestically, the new orientation has been ruthlessly pushed through without as much as a policy-planning paper, detailed discussions between the concerned ministries, or Cabinet deliberations, let alone public or parliamentary debate. The two successive governments which have promoted the new turn have both had a minority representation in parliament. The second administration, headed by Prime Minister P.V. Narasimha Rao, lacked a popular mandate for such a wholesale change of major policies.

However, Rao has not been alone in his keenness to pursue the new policy agenda; he has found a relatively (if newly) powerful and willing ally in the shape of the far- or hard-right, Hindu-chauvinist, anti-secular, militant Bharatiya Janata Party, the second largest parliamentary force. The BJP, always hostile to the former communist states and suspicious of Islam, has generally been pro-American and clearly favors the new orientation. Without this valuable support from the right, it is difficult to believe that Rao, whose policies have faced a good deal of opposition from within his own party, could have been so persistent.

The U.S. role in domestic Indian politics has remained much smaller than, say, in Pakistan, where the American ambassador has maintained a remarkably high profile and has popularly, if with bitter irony, been referred to as the "Viceroy." However, it has been growing at a rapid pace. There is reason to believe that weak governments and leaders in India have recently tended to use U.S. endorsement of or opposition to policies as a clinching argument for or against them and as a lever vis-a-vis their opponents. The prime beneficiaries here have been the right-wing of the ruling Congress Party and of course the BJP. They have been the only forces that have stood, although not always openly, for a pro-Western, pro-American realignment of Indian policy.

The impetus for the realignment lies in five long-term factors and processes. First, the end of the Cold War, the dissolution of the Warsaw Pact and the Soviet collapse have decisively altered the context in which Independent India has conducted its foreign policy. The Soviet Union as a countervailing power to the West has disappeared, cutting the ground from under India's traditional refusal to align itself with either bloc and her ability to play one bloc off against another. This has especially been the case in international fora such as the UN, which have traditionally been important for the conduct of Indian diplomacy, with its high moral tone and its appeal to the non-use of force in international relations. The end of the Cold War has also meant that conflicts in the Third World, an essential constituency for India, have decisively changed in character. The West's (and especially the U.S.'s) overwhelming power in the post-Cold War world has reduced the scope for Indian diplomacy focusing on the countries of the South. In the so-called

New World Order, India could no longer convincingly claim to be a special spokesperson for the forces of independent, self-reliant development opposed to colonialism, racism and hegemonism, as it once did.

Second, a major premise of Western, particularly U.S., post-war policy — the essential viability of the state communist system — has been rendered invalid. The United States need make no more allowances for noncapitalist, nonmarket political systems or seek to accommodate the concerns of the Third World. This has only added to New Delhi's sense of a loss of moorings. Suddenly, the Development Agenda — the pursuit of the goals of self-reliant, need-based, endogenous, equitable, ecologically sound, balanced development, or growth with distributive justice, in terms of which the Third World sought in the past to argue its case for a new international economic order — has been put on the back burner. Its content seems to have become irrelevant in relation to cold-blooded calculations of brute strength and market-based power. This has meant a certain narrowing of India's options. But Indian policymakers have tended to draw the most extreme, negative conclusions from it: accept the new currency of power in a unipolar world, one without alternatives; or perish.

Third, non-alignment has been coming apart in its specific organizational form. By 1992 such pillars of the Non-Aligned Movement as Yugoslavia and Egypt could only figure in a nostalgic account of its past. The point is that India has failed to build an alternative structure to the Non-Aligned Movement. The organizational difficulties into which NAM has run have impelled New Delhi to draw a cynical conclusion: its earlier strategy of combining the pursuit of the national interest with non-alignment has become simply unviable. Since the early days of Indian independence, non-alignment has come to mean two things. At one level, it was a doctrine and a rejection of the division of the world between two power blocs. At the other, it was also synonymous with a specific foreign policy orientation of maneuvering between the two blocs. India successfully combined the two, especially under Nehru. Until the early nineties, including Rajiv Gandhi's time (especially 1987–89), some combination of the two furnished a relatively stable base for Indian diplomacy. That link has been broken under the Narasimha Rao regime in the post-Cold War period.

Fourth, a rift has opened up between the United States and Pakistan. Not only have "strategic consensus" and joint management of the mujahedeen operation in Afghanistan ended, but the end of Cold War alignments means that Pakistan's place in the U.S. strategic scheme has shrunk. A segment of New Delhi's policymakers has sought to insert India into that vacuum. This is not to argue that Indian policymakers have all agreed that New Delhi should seek to replicate during the nineties Pakistan's role as a "frontline" state during the eighties: far from it. Most would settle for nothing less than American acknowledgment of India's preeminent, leading and unique status within the South Asian region and that too as a democratic state, and hence one to be greatly preferred over (at best) semi-democratic Pakistan. But they have been equally keen that the opportunities opened up by the breach in the Pakistani-U.S. alliance should not be missed. Such opportunities seemed likely to grow under the Clinton administration if it replaced the Bush regime's emphasis on non-proliferation with the rhetoric of democratization. This would be the case especially if Islamabad established closer relations with the newly independent, predominantly Muslim, CIS states of Central Asia. What better chance for India than to be an easy, "natural" ally of the world's sole superpower?

Finally, there has been a major change in the Indian elite's perceptions of the country's place in the world, determined partly by domestic considerations and partly by external factors. This place has steadily contracted in size and importance; the political dimensions of India's role have been reduced largely to economic parameters. That is, India would be able to command attention only to the extent that it could become a roaring "Asian tiger" economically. To that end — self-evidently the appropriate goal — India had to become the U.S.'s junior partner. It was of course extremely unlikely that such a partnership would furnish to India the kinds of advantages that, say, Japan, South Korea or Taiwan once benefited from (e.g. relatively low levels of defense spending till the seventies or eighties). It is even more improbable that economic links with the U.S. would open a privileged avenue to rapid industrialization and obviate the need for thoroughgoing domestic social and economic reform, measures to achieve better income and assets distribution and eradication of abject poverty, or for mass literacy and creation of a broad base of skills, etc. However, it is characteristic of the elite's obsessive search for quick fixes and shortcuts, and its essential myopia, that it believes jumping on to Washington's economic bandwagon would somehow eliminate the need for those reforms.

The effect of all these developments has been plain: India, which for so long — under the irrepressibly moralistic, left-inclined Jawaharlal Nehru, the implacable Indira Gandhi, the maverick Morarji Desai and the unreliable Rajiv Gandhi — defied U.S. tutelage, has finally come around. As a result, the United States can put a blanket over the entire history of its own shortsighted South Asia policies and proceed to reorder its relations with India, although this time not in furtherance of Cold War considerations.

Also implicit in this is a resigned acceptance by the Indian elite of the reality that with the disappearance of the USSR as a superpower, the possibilities of an "independent" course for the Third World have ended. This "realism" has prevailed because India's foreign policy was no longer based on the Nehruvian model of a domestic project of planned modernization and egalitarian development. Under Nehru, India's claim to a high status in the world community was based on the originality and grandeur of the Great Indian Project, which aspired to build a modern, open, prosperous, democratic and egalitarian society that would combine planning and judicious state intervention with the market and private initiative, within a relatively autonomous, non-dependent framework. Now that project itself has been all but jettisoned.

One major factor explains this shrinking of vision: the Indian elite has been willing to accept a subordinate and purely regional status for the country within a U.S.-prescribed framework of "stability" (read stable external and internal borders) and "democracy" (i.e., isolating semi- or undemocratic Pakistan), because it is no longer assured of its authority in South Asia or confident of holding the country together on the basis of persuasion and consensus. Washington could have made a serious miscalculation, however. In pushing India hard towards an overtly, indeed slavishly, pro-American stand, it underestimates the strength of Third World nationalism and socialism in India. Its pressure is liable to generate a hostile reaction and further divide a strife-ridden society, perhaps contributing to making it less governable.

However, can this orientation be sustained in the medium or long run? Quite apart from the "external" constraint — the unviability of the U.S., itself in economic and political decline, as (the sole) superpower in a polycentric world — and the lack of unanimity even among conservative Indian policymakers that a middle-ranking or regional power such as India could best promote its interests through an alliance with the U.S. rather than, say, with Germany or Japan, or other states or groups of states, there remains very importantly an "internal" constraint or limiting factor too. This derives from the history of Indian nationalism, and the values of the Independence movement, which have continued to influence public perceptions of contemporary politics and remain fundamental to the political legitimacy of any party or regime in the country.

These values militate against any notion of dependence upon or subservience to a great power, especially a superpower whose dominance involves oppression and exploitation of the weak. The political culture of Indian democracy, warts and all, is such as would deny legitimacy to any project that compromised on national sovereignty or involved subservience to an alien power. Instinctively, as it were, Indian politicians' rhetoric tends towards patriotic hubris and nationalist assertion vis-a-vis great power dominance.

This suggests a wide disparity between mass and elite concerns. Equally, it opens up possibilities of resistance to efforts at India's Westward reorientation. The resistance is itself linked to and part of a larger process in Indian society and politics involving a search for alternatives to the dominant elitist, dualist, inegalitarian model of growth implicit in the "free market"-oriented, neo-liberal policies of the "structural adjustment" variety being pursued in the early nineties. Whether the resistance is successful or not is, then, a function of the larger process. But its reality cannot be denied — nor its potential to unravel India's American alignment.

Notes

1. This has been extensively documented in the Indian press. In particular, see my "India Lurches Towards U.S.," *The Times of India*, New Delhi, Bombay and other editions, September 24, 1991; also "India's Passage to Washington," *The Nation*, New York, January 20, 1992.
2. This was first reported in late January, more than two weeks after the first planes were refueled in Bombay. See my "Refuelling a Political Message," *The Times of India*, January 29, 1992.
3. At one stage, in early 1992, New Delhi came close to signing the so-called Dunkel draft of proposals on the Uruguay Round in GATT, which would have meant a drastic alteration of India's existing IPR, in particular patent protection, regime, itself the product of a prolonged public debate in the

country during the fifties and sixties. However, faced with some spirited opposition from numerous public interest groups, as well as from sections of domestic industry, the government appointed a committee of ministers which heard several representations and decided to submit a report to parliament; at the time of writing, parliament has yet to debate the issue.

4. In the spring of 1992, the Group of 77 (developing countries) registered a strong protest against these changes to the secretary general's office, to no avail. Among the changes were the abolition of the UN Center on Transnational Corporations, and the appointment of Governor Thornburgh, known for his hard-right views, to a key job in the secretariat.

5. See, for example, Michael R. Gordon, "U.S. Accuses India on Chemical Arms," *New York Times*, September 20, 1992.

6. For a discussion of the nuclear policies of India and Pakistan, see Achin Vanaik and Praful Bidwai, "South Asia Case Study," in R. Cowen Karp (ed.), *Security without Nuclear Weapons?* SIPRI/OUP, Stockholm and London, 1990.

7. Estimates of Pakistan's capability and the strength of its facilities vary widely. While a few estimates based on Western intelligence reports suggest that Pakistan has already crossed the nuclear threshold, the majority are more ambivalent; no one considers the two countries to be equal. India's capacities in the field are long established, considerably more broad-based, and in all probability far greater. Not only did the country explode a Nagasaki-type fission device in 1974; it has since stockpiled large amounts (variously estimated, but probably adequate for several fission bombs) of unsafeguarded plutonium.

35

Prospects for Korea After the Cold War

Richard Falk

In one sense the torments of Korea during the last several decades are a more direct consequence of Cold War bipolarity than any outcome in the post-1945 world order aside from Yalta's assignment of East Europe to the Soviet sphere. Korea in a manner that is yet to be rectified was not only made geopolitically dependent in the course of its supposed liberation from Japanese rule in 1945, but its peoples were wrenched apart in a geopolitical agreement with the Soviet Union, supposedly only to handle the Japanese surrender process, but quickly solidified by the formation of antagonistic states organized along lines according with the occupying power's identity. The ensuing story is familiar, and is by no means purely tragic. The South Korean economic record is an Asian miracle second only to Japan's in magnitude. At the same time, however, Korea became a testing ground for superpower resolve, and as such, a potential flashpoint for World War III, a face-off that assumed menacing proportions at various times of crisis and near-crisis. Aside from Germany, Korea was the next most likely candidate to be the setting of nuclear devastation. Korea definitely became a global strategic arena, leading governments in both parts of Korea to relinquish crucial aspects of their sovereignty in the security sphere, although not to an equal degree.

This primal reality of Korea's recent history gave rise to the common sense expectation that since the Korean division was so clearly a product of the Cold War, then the ending of the Soviet/United States encounter would lead directly and quickly to the restoration of Korean unity and sovereignty in accordance with the dynamics of self-determination exercised by the Korean people as a whole. This expectation seemed especially plausible in light of European developments in 1989, most spectacularly the surprisingly rapid reunification of Germany. But common sense is rarely helpful as a predictor of behavior in international political life, and undoing the division of Korea, given its experience of warfare, ideological tensions, and military suspicions now seems less likely to occur as an automatic sequel to Cold War realities. Actually, the German experience may have been as much chastening as inspiring for Korean observers, particularly revealing the high costs of economic merger given the high degree of success on the capitalist side and the utter failure on the communist side.

Despite the persistence of the status quo in Korea there are hopeful signs at both the level of geopolitical involvement and of the internal political dynamics of both Koreas. Under no circumstances will the demilitarized zone crumble dramatically in the fashion of the Berlin Wall, but possibly the two Korean governments, with a degree of encouragement from larger countries, especially the United States, can carry forward a process that brings both peace and unity. A signpost in this direction is, of course, the already historic document of December 13, 1991 entitled Agreement on Reconciliation, Nonaggression and Exchanges between South and North (Korea) signed in Seoul.[1]

A distinct image of evolution toward Korean peace is based on the possibility of accommodation without reunification. Such a normalization of division could be read into the politics of both North and South Korea that underlay the simultaneous admission of the two Koreas into the United Nations after 45 years of stalemate over the issue on August 8, 1991. Unlike the German Democratic Republic, North Korea's leadership in the late 1980s was neither visibly challenged from below nor was its leadership ready to renounce its claims to govern. Even more than China, North Korea seemed determined to ignore the Soviet collapse and the Gorbachev phenomenon and remain on its path of statist socialism. In this view, if things were to go badly, the future of the Korean peninsula could be one of heightened tensions despite the relaxation elsewhere. In 1991 North Korea seemed to believe that the evolving imperatives of *juche* (self-reliance) required the development of a nuclear weapons capability. Even if there has been an apparent negotiated move away from such a development, the possibility of extending the antagonist division of Korea into the post-Cold War era cannot yet be excluded, nor is it necessarily inconsistent with developing in the years ahead more cordial relations between the two Koreas that could include high levels of trade and travel. Uncertainty abounds.

The difficulty of assessing Korea's future is definitely compounded by the role of outside political and economic forces. Korea is simultaneously virtually autonomous as a zone of conflict, while remaining a pawn in larger games, especially between the U.S. and Japan, but also engaging China, and in time, Russia. This essay attempts to clarify the bearing of this larger game on prospects for peace on the Korean peninsula.

I. The Setting

Throughout the Cold War the present cast a long shadow on the future. Important changes in the details of international relations occurred, of course, but largely by stages that gave ample forewarning, and with the notable exception of China, these changes were at the margins of world order. Throughout the period there were recurrent challenges to the bipolar structures, but these were mainly neutralized, although sometimes at great social and political costs. The Korean War was one such challenge. The Hungarian uprising of 1956 was another. The Cuban Missile Crisis was yet another. None of these developments, or several others that could be mentioned, altered the core bipolar reality: the East-West encounter, the two superpowers, a preoccupation with the avoidance of World War III, and the puzzle of containment and co-existence.

In contrast, during the last five years a series of extraordinary surprises have reshaped our entire sense of international reality: Eastern Europe broke free from the Yalta system, Germany reunited overnight, the Cold War ended, and the Soviet Union dissolved into its constituent parts. The cumulative weight of these changes stimulated some to adopt grandiose lines of conjecture. Perhaps none impacted more strongly on the political imagination than did Francis Fukuyama's provocative interpretation, "The End of History?" With the retrospect of only a few years, Fukuyama's radical stance seems itself to have been tied far too closely to a Eurocentric Cold War mindset, supposing that with the discrediting of communism and the collapse of the Soviet challenge, the essential unfolding of the historical process had attained its final stage, and would itself come to a halt. On reconsideration, Fukuyama's interpretive line confirms how entrapped the political culture of the West had become in the particular qualities of its own recent past; his essay pretentiously illustrates the general failure of the public mind to distinguish between Cold War history and history![2]

The Gulf War abruptly challenged the complacency of the overall assessment that associated the withdrawal of the Soviet Union from geopolitics with the emergence of world peace, perhaps a time when boredom would come to replace anxiety as the basic attitude toward international life. President George Bush used the Gulf crisis to stake a post-Cold War claim for American leadership beneath the alluring banner of "the new world order." Such a claim on behalf of U.S. leadership seems confused in intention, mixing an idealistic appeal to establish collective security on the basis of international law and within the framework of the United Nations, with a unilateralist insistence that the UN, especially the Security Council, is primarily relevant as a vehicle for U.S. foreign policy. The destructiveness of the Gulf War, especially its devastating impact on Iraqi civilian society, and its inconclusiveness in relation to promoting democratic tendencies within Iraq or establishing conditions for regional peace, persuaded even those who celebrated the military victory as it occurred in 1991 against any longer calling attention to the overall outcome a year later. Surprisingly, even George Bush was reluctant in the last months of his presidency to confirm his dedication to a new world order. Despite this, a preoccupation with change of global scope has made it inevitable that there will be many attempts to depict the emergent overall international situation with as much coherence as possible; that is, in effect, to depict or propose "the new world order," not as an American project as set forth during the Gulf crisis, but as a new stage in the evolution of geopolitics, or even as a fluid process with several main possibilities for regional and global restructuring, but none yet clearly ascendent.

The Pacific region was far less susceptible to Fukuyama's generalizations than elsewhere. For one thing, the Cold War pivot had been the confrontation in Europe, despite the offsetting and chastening reality that the main wars of the era were located in Asia. For another, the internal democratizing challenges directed at communist regimes succeeded in the European setting, while being blunted in Asia. Finally, the ideological fault-lines of the Cold War have yet to disappear in Asia, considering the persistence of several communist regimes, most notably that of China. With the breaching of the Berlin Wall, the European agenda arising out of the East-West split was resolved; only details remained. But in the Pacific the divisions of Korea and China persist, and the destiny of Indochina is far from resolved. Tibet remains entrapped within China. In addition, the Philippines continues to experience a major internal revolutionary struggle that is perceived through a Cold War optic of communism versus "authoritarian liberalism." Burma is governed by a brutal military autocracy. Indonesia remains ruled by an authoritarian military regime whose legitimacy rests partly on its anti-communist roots. In other words, for the Asian Pacific region it seems wildly premature to treat the Cold War era as over except in the limited sense of the disappearance of a bipolar dimension and of a Soviet strategic role.

What certainly can be said is that the momentous global developments culminating in the replacement of the Soviet Union with a precarious anti-communist entity called the Commonwealth of Independent States has profound, yet ambiguous, implications for Asia, some of which are already becoming apparent. There is no longer a Soviet dimension present in the regional politics of the Pacific, and the American dimension is in the process of adaptation, as was evident during George Bush's January 1992 visit. This process of adaptation has created definite new openings for peace and stability, most dramatically in relation to the future of the Korean peninsula. It has altered the strategic calculus with respect to Korea, reducing the likelihood of the recurrence of warfare and enhancing both the prospects for and the problematic character of reunification.

At the same time, it is erroneous to extrapolate mechanically from the changed global circumstances. There is a temptation, for instance, to treat the beginnings of dialogue in Korea as a direct effect of the end of the Cold War (in its core U.S./USSR sense). But other more concealed factors must also be relevant, including the perceived circumstances of the two Koreas. There has been considerable recent speculation that Pyongyang has reached out more constructively mainly because of North Korea's economic failures and because Kim Il Sung wants to complete his historical mission by presiding over some sort of Korean rapprochement while he is still alive. It may also be that Seoul's receptivity to dialogue with the North expresses concern about the prospect of an American military withdrawal from the region or an acute anxiety, possibly encouraged by Washington, with the urgency of preventing North Korea from acquiring nuclear weapons. In other words, the specific Korean response to a new global circumstance may reflect the primacy of factors indigenous to Korea; but this is difficult to demonstrate, especially given the tendency of governments to keep their true motivations for policy shifts as hidden as possible, and for policies on complicated issues to arise from compromises among factions in the ruling elite. Especially if these shifts of approach arise from either weakness or fear, the real grounds of policy will be misleadingly explained at an official level. In addition, the complexity and interrelatedness of relevant factors makes it impossible to explain why a certain new approach to the Korean conflict seems to be surfacing at the present time. What can be concluded with confidence is that the collapse of bipolarity is a small part of the unfolding Korean story.

There is also the problem of taking account of the suppressed "Japan factor": to what extent do recent Korean initiatives reflect anxiety about Japanese regional ascendancy? In this regard, even North Korea could be worrying about the consequences of a substantial reduction in the U.S. regional presence. How relevant to current policy choice by Korean leaders is the memory of the current generation of Korean leaders of the period of Japanese occupation between 1910 and 1945? In this respect, for surprisingly similar reasons, the two Koreas might seek unity as a means to enhance security, fearing Japan more than each other in the new conjuncture of forces. Such a line of reasoning acquires added plausibility because the immediate risks of Japanese domination are less military than economic and cultural, and hence more difficult to defend against.

Another dimension of relevance concerns the evolving revised arrangements among the regional great powers — the United States, the former Soviet Union (now Russia), China, and Japan. Each of these actors has a complicated relationship to the Korean story, and is undoubtedly in the process of clarifying its priorities and reflecting upon its options. The United States, in particular, is seeking less economically costly ways of sustaining its regional influence, and this may incline Washington to encourage peace and accommodation in Korea as an alternative to persisting in readiness for renewal of peninsular warfare. This American effort to reduce its security burdens in the Pacific while maintaining its leadership role, which could well be defined as including the containment of Japan economically, strategically and militarily, may be of particular importance in the current Korean circumstance.

Such a cluster of considerations also apparently reflects wider regional concerns that economic pressures might lead the United States to withdraw from, or at least reduce, its security role in the Western Pacific, producing a geopolitical vacuum that would either be filled by Japan or generate a destabilizing struggle between China and Japan for regional primacy.[3] In such an atmosphere, there arise incentives to find ways to reconcile a U.S. security presence with budgetary pressure to reduce the costs of U.S. overseas commitments.

II. The Korean Opening

Although it is artificial to separate internal Korean perceptions and conditions from the wider historical patterns that help shape the Korean reality, emphasis will be placed on Korea as seen from without, and especially by the U.S. government. It is important to realize that the U.S. commitment to Korea is not woven into the fabric of U.S. political life in the manner of Israel, Europe, or Central America. At most, the Korean relationship is symbolic of American intentions in the Pacific, especially the degree to which the U.S. will sustain Cold War-era commitments. In my view, the primary restructuring energy at work in U.S. leadership circles is the shift from an anti-communist posture focused on containing the Soviet Union to a regional stabilizing role that is guided by an overriding concern in the Pacific — especially northeast Asia — about Japan that could move either in the direction of partnership or antagonism. It would be wrong to equate this concern with a replacement of the Soviet Union by Japan as "enemy" of the United States. The new posture is not yet even explicitly anti-Japan, but it is sensitive to a drift of geopolitical circumstances that could make an anti-Japan option of great strategic importance in the years ahead.[4] I would interpret the readjustment in U.S. basing arrangements in the Pacific from this perspective — both the unexpectedly weak resistance in Washington to the Filipino drive to close American bases, and the choice of Singapore as a partial alternative. Again without overstating, the geopolitical focus of this strategic redeployment is to place American naval forces astride the Straits of Malacca (through which 80% of Japan's oil and one-third of its trade passes), a move that can be construed either as protective of Japan's lifeline or threatening to it. What seems evident is that from the U.S. viewpoint its primary interest at this stage is to restructure its relationship to Japan, preparing for either renewed alliance or an intensifying economic conflict.[5]

Fitting Korea into this larger setting is, at this stage, a still unsolved piece of the geopolitical puzzle, but it is an important piece. President Bush's visit to Seoul in January 1992 just prior to arriving in Tokyo was expressive of this importance. U.S. diplomacy was definitely supportive of the recent moves toward reconciliation on the Korean peninsula, although displaying a certain ambivalence as well. On the one side, the U.S. government has been generally favorable toward regional conflict resolution ever since 1988, partly to reduce its overall defense burdens, partly in response to the changes taking place in Moscow, and partly as a means of increasing regional and global stability. In this regard, encouraging the two Koreas to heal their wounds carried forward a global trend, and one regionally manifest, especially with regard to Cambodia. Secondly, in the American political mind, the division of Korea and the Korean War are closely associated with the worst phases of the East-West struggle. With the Cold War ended, the strategic relevance of Korea as a crucial test of containment, as applied to Asia, came to an end. In this regard, getting drawn into a recurrence of Korean warfare would now seem absurd from the perspective of U.S. national interests, particularly if it imposed dollar costs and risked American lives. Thus, American diplomatic priorities are generally supportive of a Korean peace process; but with two, possibly three caveats.

The first caveat relates to nuclear proliferation. The United States, especially in light of the Gulf War, is deeply committed to preventing the acquisition of nuclear weapons by potentially hostile countries in the South.[6] U.S. pressure on North Korea to discontinue its nuclear weapons program in a manner subject to international verification by IAEA procedures and its willingness to remove its own nuclear weapons long deployed in the South, to stop annual war games with South Korean armed forces, and most of all, its willingness to abandon its policy of neither admitting nor denying the presence of nuclear weapons in South Korea are moves consistent with this altered set of goals. From one perspective, the focus on the nuclear weapons issue raises tensions, even the possibility of an American military strike against North Korea's nuclear facilities. But in another, this focus has paradoxically contributed to the peace process, removing nuclear weapons from Korea altogether (at least for now) and acceding to North Korea's role as a bargaining partner. The seeming resolution of the nuclear weapons crisis was achieved not by fiat, but by diplomatic pressure and threat, some compromise, a credible degree of mutuality, and an apparent abandonment of nuclear weapons ambitions by the North. Perhaps the U.S. government would have redeployed its nuclear weapons in any event, but their removal in exchange for North Korean acceptance of IAEA inspections seemed like a genuine diplomatic bargain. The bargain having been struck, including the involvement of South Korea in the process, meant that for the first time a real trilateral relationship based on cooperation more than conflict had been established.

The second caveat concerns the uncertain and contradictory effects of a Korean peace process on China and Japan. Korea can be seen from the U.S. perspective either as a bargaining chip in conflictual relations or as a security buffer in some emerging conception of regional order. As a bargaining chip, unresolved Korean relations limit Japan's influence in the region, and heighten its security concerns, perpetuating a sense of dependence on the United States. As a buffer, a reunified Korea might enhance Japanese overall regional influence or, contrariwise, act as a brake upon Japanese regional expansion. Much depends on the nature of the relationship between Korea, China, and Japan that evolves, as well as with the new Russia. At one extreme is a bonding of these three Asian powers as a balance against U.S. hegemony; at the other is a competitive series of efforts by Japan to bond closely with the U.S., thereby sharing the benefits and responsibilities of a regional hegemonic order. In effect, the regional flow is likely to move toward either a new species of bipolarity or a new variant of hegemony or unipolarity.[7]

It is in light of these two caveats that one is reluctant to project a steady linear process that culminates in a peaceful process of Korean reunification. Either the re-emergence of the nuclear weapons issue or the linkage perceived to wider regional and global concerns, especially U.S.-Japan relations, could obstruct the evolution of Korean policy in unpredictable ways (even leaving aside uncertain impacts of domestic forces in both Koreas). Ambivalence stemming from such concerns possibly explains President Bush's reported pressure on Seoul to slow down the accommodation dynamics with Pyongyang until it receives firmer commitments on the nuclear weapons issues.[8] Such pressure seems more closely connected with clarifying the wider reality in the Pacific than to guard South Korea against some hidden pitfalls of accommodation. It accords also with reported Korean convictions that various foreign governments have varying interests in keeping Korea divided.[9]

III. Common Security for Northeast Asia

There are no obvious implications for Korea that arise from the termination of the Eurocentric phases of the Cold War. This process has an influence in the Pacific region, but the cumulative character of this influence is impossible to discern as yet. Part of the difficulty arises from contradictory perceptions and adjustments. The two Koreas could move toward separate nuclear self-reliance or toward reunification at this stage. There is a supportive geopolitical logic for either direction of adjustment, given the possibility of either U.S. geopolitical withdrawal or of deepening hegemony. Similarly, the uncertainty surrounding the future U.S.-Japan relationship can be interpreted in contradictory ways — as fostering the status quo or as generating pressures toward Korean peace and stability. In effect, a geopolitical analysis is inconclusive in the extreme at this time because of cross-cutting, unresolved pressures in an unusually fluid situation.

Similarly, a normative analysis based on international law and the UN. The claims put forward during the Gulf crisis, principally by the U.S. government, that "a new world order" is emerging around the authority of the UN and international law, seem irrelevant to the present circumstances of the Pacific. There is no firm indication that such a strengthening of the organized world community is likely to occur, or if it did, whether it would have a discernible impact on the Korean circumstance. The most relevant speculation here, too, concerns whether Japan's influence is to be contained in the region, and if so by whom. Perhaps, in this regard, especially if the United States lessens its commitment to Korean security per se, but increases it with respect to the containment of Japan, UN collective security could conceivably provide Korean diplomacy with an instrumentality. Such speculations are so fragile as to be almost worthless, except possibly to explore the range of future configurations of policy choice and security threat.

What seems most helpful at this stage is to foster a regional climate conducive to Korean self-determination. First of all, such a climate presupposes deference by the United States, especially, but also by Japan, China, and Russia to the realities of Korean sovereignty. Secondly, Korea should not itself get drawn into the conflictual elements of emergent arrangements in the Pacific, and should seek to emphasize a passive geopolitics with respect to the United States, Japan, and China. Such an evolution of policy is laden with history, and is especially related to the U.S. role in South Korea during the Cold War period. The Korean future, to the extent that it moves toward reunification and peaceful relations, needs to emphasize independence and sovereignty, proceeding by way of dealignment so far as Seoul is concerned. Obviously such a path needs to be taken carefully, by stages, on the basis of reciprocal developments in North Korea. One line of approach which draws on the experience of the Helsinki Process (Conference on Security and Cooperation for Europe) would be to combine this stress upon independence and sovereignty with firm mutual commitments regarding human rights and democracy, including annual sessions of bilateral review and accountability.

This recommended approach also presupposes maximal Korean diversification with respect to international trade — both exports and imports. In the period ahead, the real path to political independence is likely to involve economic and even cultural policies far more than weapons and boundaries.

Whether this course of Korean evolution is feasible in the short-run will depend on its overall endorsement by both leadership cadres in Korea and by those states in the region with the greatest stake (that is, the United States, Japan, and China; and probably, in the years to come, Russia). Such a positive prospect is far from likely — the United States seems too deeply engaged, the two governments in Korea remain too suspicious of one another and both probably fear a political evolution that mandates democracy and human rights, and Japan seems too ambitious economically and culturally to allow such Korean independence to evolve unchallenged.

In essence, some moderating of tensions in line with recent North/South initiatives is desirable and even quite likely to gain modest momentum, but not sufficiently so to establish the basis for reunification or a demilitarized peace; furthermore, the external players, with their cross-cutting goals, are likely to encourage a modest degree of progress, but not more. To go further will depend on real social forces in South and North moving powerfully and in a sustained manner on behalf of democratization and human rights. Put differently, reunification-from-below is the most likely positive scenario if the goal is a reunified Korea that is not drawn destructively into some new geopolitical maelstrom in the region. That is, Korea needs to look forward as well as backward. Otherwise, the danger of becoming once again a pawn in the regional chess game currently taking shape is considerable.

As suggested at the outset, the prospects for Korea remain enmeshed in a complex of interlocking political forces that are being regionally restructured, mainly in response to the collapse of the Soviet challenge and the virtual disappearance of an ideological axis of conflict. But this restructuring could proceed smoothly toward a regional balance or it could move awkwardly toward some new confrontation between antagonistic forces. Similarly, in Korea, the two polities could move toward a redefinition of the status quo on a milder basis, or embrace a genuine transformative politics; but if the latter, then the dynamics of democratization must exert a far more decisive influence on state/society relations, especially in the North, than is now evident.

A reformulation of policy options in relation to Korean reunification seems opportune at this stage. The German experience with reunification should induce caution, especially in Seoul, about a rapid, all-at-once, process. Nevertheless, the yearning for the recovery of Korean unity remains strong. Balancing these considerations suggests the encouragement of a process of normalization as a prelude, perhaps carried on for a decade or longer, to reunification. Normalization conceived as a deepening of interaction, ranging from tourism and family life to trade and culture. Normalization may make the transition to a reunified Korea far less traumatic than otherwise, and build trust at societal, as well as at governmental levels. In this spirit, it would be helpful to drop reunification as the core element in a Korean peace process, and work more directly on the intrinsic virtues of engendering a dynamic of normalization.

Anticipating the future is rarely fruitful, but it seems especially hazardous during this period. Both the pressure of internal social and political forces from below and of external geopolitical forces from without are exceedingly difficult to assess in relation to any specific set of substantive concerns. During the Cold War, basic structures of conflict were kept stable through the clarity of bipolar implications. Projecting the present — the only skill of social scientists — seems at this juncture to offer the least likely scenario for the future. Even the fictive musings of literary and utopian sensibilities have more to offer, but not in a specific enough manner to guide policy and expectations. In this regard, confessions of humility and uncertainty are to be welcomed.

Against this background it is possible to consider anew the Korean prospect, acknowledging the excitement of the openings, the confusions wrought by an ambiguous and complex indigenous, regional, and global setting, and the essential opaqueness of the causal grid that accounts for the behavior of states.

Notes

1. For text see *The Korea Herald*, December 14, 1991.
2. Fukuyama's more comprehensive line of interpretation is now available in book form. Fukuyama, *The End of History and the Last Man*, New York, Free Press, 1992.
3. C.f. "Asia in the New Age," Special Report, *Time*, January 27, 1992, pp. 6–19.
4. For a strong argument as to the inevitability of a U.S./Japan clash in the Pacific, see George Friedman and Meredith Lebard, *The Coming War with Japan*, New York, St. Martin's, 1991.
5. Note that this concern is linked to, but distinct from, the worry by Pacific countries about Japanese regional hegemony; it is possible that the U.S. could concede this hegemony in exchange for a favorable restructuring of the global aspects of the U.S.-Japan trade and financial relationship.
6. This concern was accentuated by apparent intelligence failures in relation to Iraq that evidently grossly underestimated the scope of Saddam Hussein's nuclear weapons development programs, and thereby have influenced U.S. policymakers in this period to fear that the nuclear weapons program of a country under suspicion, such as Korea, may be far more extensive than meets the eye.
7. In the Pacific, the geopolitical realities during the Cold War were always more multipolar than elsewhere (especially after the Sino-Soviet split) and more unipolar than elsewhere (considering the relative supremacy of the U.S. vis-a-vis the Soviet Union).
8. The main press reports emphasize U.S. concerns that South Korea obtain clearer reassurances on the inspection provisions that would implement the December 31, 1991 Joint Declaration for a Non-Nuclear Korean Peninsula. *New York Times*, January 7, 1992.
9. E.g., Donald Kirk writes of Japan's manipulation of commercial ties with both Koreas as a way to exert influence, especially in its more substantial relations with the South. See Donald Kirk, "For Some, Dreams of a Single Nation," *International Herald Tribune*, December 20, 1991.

36

Risking Cambodia:
The UN Brokers a Flawed Peace

Ben Kiernan *

During the Pol Pot period, from 1975 to 1979, Cambodia was subjected to probably the world's most radical political, social and economic revolution. The country was cut off from the outside world, its cities were emptied, its economy was militarized, its Buddhist religion and folk culture destroyed, and 1.5 million of its eight million people were starved and massacred, while foreign and minority languages were banned and all neighboring countries were attacked.

Thus an international conflict was intertwined with genocide that provoked a civil war. On May 10, 1978, Phnom Penh radio broadcast a call not only to "exterminate the 50 million Vietnamese" but also to "purify the masses of the people" of Cambodia. When Cambodian communists rebelled in the Eastern Zone, Pol Pot was unable to crush them quickly. Over the next six months, more than a million easterners were branded as "Khmer bodies with Vietnamese minds," and at least 100,000 were exterminated by Pol Pot's forces.[1] In 1979, surviving leaders of the Eastern Zone dissidents (like Hun Sen and Heng Samrin) succeeded Pol Pot, once Hanoi had driven his Khmer Rouge army into Thailand.

The Cambodia-Vietnam conflict had started in 1977, with Pol Pot's regime staging repeated savage raids into Vietnamese territory, massacring thousands of Vietnamese civilians and causing hundreds of thousands to flee from their homes.[2] Hanoi's complaints to this effect were corroborated at the time by both U.S. intelligence reports and the testimony of Vietnamese

* This abridged, updated version of "Deferring Peace in Cambodia: Regional Rapprochement, Superpower Obstruction" is reprinted with the permission of the Institute of International Studies, University of California, Berkeley, publishers of *Beyond the Cold War: Conflict and Cooperation in the Third World*, edited by George W. Breslauer, Harry Kreisler, and Benjamin Ward, Berkeley, 1991, pp. 59–82.

refugees fleeing abroad from the war zone, and they have since been extensively documented from both sides of the border.[3]

After Pol Pot's regime refused to negotiate peacefully or accept international supervision of the border,[4] Vietnamese forces intervened and overthrew it in early 1979. Western rhetoric aside, Hanoi's invasion of Cambodia was not "aggression" (unprovoked attack). Vietnam's immediate reason for intervention was self-defense. China joined Cambodia as an aggressor state when Pol Pot's ally Deng Xiaoping retaliated against Hanoi with his own invasion of Vietnam.

Vietnamese troops remained in Cambodia, offering to withdraw only in return for two concessions: the exclusion of Pol Pot's forces from the country, and the ending of the new Chinese threat to Vietnam itself. China, the Association of Southeast Asian Nations (ASEAN) and the West, on the other hand, demanded an unconditional Vietnamese withdrawal, recognized the ousted Pol Pot regime as the "legitimate" representative of the Cambodian people, and rearmed and supplied its forces. With this aid and in the sanctuary of Thailand,[5] the Khmer Rouge rebuilt an army of about 25,000, and in 1982 were joined in a coalition government-in-exile by two small Western-backed groups nominally loyal to Norodom Sihanouk (the ANS) and Son Sann (the KPNLF).[6]

Nevertheless, from 1980 Hanoi began withdrawing its advisers, and in 1982 began official partial withdrawals of its troops, as the new Cambodian government consolidated its position. As we shall see, Vietnam successively dropped its two conditions for a withdrawal, which it completed *unilaterally* in September 1989. The State of Cambodia forces have since held the country, belying Western predictions that a collapse would quickly follow any withdrawal. (A mid-1987 Australian intelligence assessment, for instance, had put the chances of a Vietnamese withdrawal by 1990 at "1 in 300," in which case the Phnom Penh regime would last only "seven months.")

In their ten-year occupation, the Vietnamese not only established a full-fledged Cambodian government led by Khmer nationalists,[7] but also trained a large Cambodian defense force. The three levels of the army — national, regional, and local — probably mustered over 100,000 regular troops and 200,000 militia. They were hard pressed in 1990, but later accounts suggested that the military situation had again stabilized.[8] The opposition seized a swathe of remote territory on the Thai frontier, but all cities and populous rural areas remained under Phnom Penh's administration. The Khmer Rouge posed a serious military threat, but one that united most Cambodians against it. The economy became the most pressing problem for Phnom Penh with the end of Eastern European and much Soviet aid in 1990.[9]

The 1985 fifth congress of the ruling People's Revolutionary Party had formally legalized and endorsed the private sector. Later economic reforms in Cambodia included the privatization of agricultural land, housing, and the industrial and commercial sectors. Political reforms made Buddhism the state religion, legalized Christianity, officially declared neutrality in foreign policy, and changed (at Sihanouk's request) the official name of the country and the flag. Cambodia remained a one-party state, although Hun Sen favored a multi-party system for a post-war Cambodia.[10]

The Cambodia conflict has been played out on three levels: the national, regional, and great power levels. Within Cambodia, the military balance has favored the incumbent State of Cambodia. In the UN Security Council, its opponents have had hegemony. But at the intervening regional level, the forces are fairly evenly divided. Southeast Asia's ten nations are politically diverse, none has overall preponderance, and few can be ignored. Those who have sought a solution to the conflict can be found on both sides of the ASEAN-Indochina divide, and unlike in the UN Security Council, none of the Southeast Asian countries readily identifies with the remaining obstacle, the Khmer Rouge. The only lasting solution to the Cambodia conflict is to be found in Southeast Asia.

Washington has sought not a mere independent Cambodian government, but an *anti-Vietnamese* one. According to the *Far Eastern Economic Review* of September 7, 1989, "Thai officials believe that, despite its publicly expressed revulsion towards the Khmer Rouge, the U.S. has been quietly aiding the Khmer Rouge war effort for several years." One senior Thai official said: "We would like to see a lead against the Khmer Rouge taken by the U.S. . . . ."

After ten years of U.S. opposition to its role in Cambodia, Vietnam withdrew. The Hun Sen government did not collapse. Then Washington moved the goal posts. "Hanoi has an obligation to do more than just walk away," Assistant Secretary of State Richard Solomon now said. Thus began the search for a "comprehensive settlement." The United States called on Hanoi to force another change of government on the Cambodians, one that would appease Pol Pot's Khmer Rouge, if not return them to positions of power. Washington's policy demonstrated that it would not reduce its support for the genocidists or take any action against them, before their only Cambodian opponents, the Hun Sen regime, were first displaced from power.

The Region and the Great Powers

"I do not understand why some people want to remove Pol Pot," Deng Xiaoping said in 1984.[11] "It is true that he made some mistakes in the past but now he is leading the fight against the Vietnamese aggressors." In May 1989, Prince Sihanouk revealed to foreign diplomats that Deng had threatened to "fight" him should he abandon his alliance with the Khmer Rouge.[12] Chinese support for the Khmer Rouge, including a large delivery of weapons in mid-1990[13] despite a previous undertaking to cut arms supplies in return for Vietnam's withdrawal,[14] has remained strongest. China has provided the Khmer Rouge forces with $100 million per annum, according to American intelligence, and in late 1990 began supplying them with T-59 tanks, 24 of which had arrived by October. *Jane's Defence Weekly* described the Khmer Rouge tanks as "the most significant increase in firepower the resistance to the Vietnamese-installed government has ever received."[15]

The USSR, while continuing to supply Vietnam and Cambodia at reduced levels (aid to Vietnam fell by 63% in 1990),[16] rapidly lost interest in the region, owing to Vietnam's mismanagement of its aid and Soviet domestic problems. The Soviet Union, according to Steven Erlanger of the *New York Times*, "no longer has the money or, seemingly, the will to project an ideology onto developing countries anywhere."[17] The "virtual Soviet military withdrawal" from Cam Ranh Bay in Vietnam underscored that lack of interest.[18]

On the other hand, three major planks of American policy towards Cambodia remained unchanged. The U.S. veto of aid, including UN, World Bank, and International Monetary Fund aid to Cambodia,[19] U.S. support for a Khmer Rouge role, and U.S. military support for the Khmer Rouge's allies ($17–32 million per annum),[20] all continued despite the Beijing massacre of June 1989, the Vietnamese withdrawal from Cambodia in September 1989, and Washington's policy "shift" of July 1990.[21]

Unlike the affected regional countries, great powers can afford to ignore for years the damage their policies inflict on small nations. A British diplomat expressed this distance when he remarked on Cambodia in 1986, "We're only talking about six million people."[22] France, too, like the United States, was unenthusiastic about any settlement arrived at independently in Southeast Asia.[23] And given the choice, China naturally blocked isolation of its Khmer Rouge client, as well as resisting moves toward regional concord, demonstrating its preference for a balkanized Southeast Asia with "many roads to Beijing."

For over a decade, official Western support for Deng Xiaoping's China spilled over into Western support for his protégé Pol Pot. Former U.S. National Security Advisor Zbigniew Brzezinski says that in 1979: "I encouraged the Chinese to support Pol Pot . . . Pol Pot was an abomination. We could never support him but China could."[24]

They both did. The United States, Brzezinski says, "winked, semi-publicly" at Chinese and Thai aid for the Khmer Rouge after their defeat by Hanoi. Washington also pressured UN agencies to supply the Khmer Rouge. In *Rice, Rivalry and Politics*, the major study of the relief effort for Cambodian refugees in Thailand, Linda Mason and Roger Brown, graduates of the Yale School of Management, revealed: "The U.S. Government, which funded the bulk of the relief operation on the border, insisted that the Khmer Rouge be fed." They add: "When World Relief started to push its proposal for aid to the Khmer Rouge, the U.S. was supportive, though behind the scenes . . . the U.S. preferred that the Khmer Rouge operation benefit from the credibility of an internationally-known relief organization." Congressional sources also cited a figure of $85 million for U.S. aid to Pol Pot's Khmer Rouge since 1979.[25] This may explain why, under U.S. influence, the World Food Program alone handed over $12 million worth of food to the Thai army to pass on to the Khmer Rouge. "20–40,000 Pol Pot guerrillas benefited," according to former Assistant Secretary of State Richard Holbrooke.[26] Mason and Brown note that the health of the Khmer Rouge army "rapidly improved" throughout 1980. "The Khmer Rouge had a history of unimaginable brutality, and having regained their strength, they had begun fighting the Vietnamese."[27]

In May 1980 the CIA produced a "demographic report" on Cambodia which denied that there had been *any* executions in the last two years of the Pol Pot regime.[28] (The toll from executions in 1977–78 had in fact been around half a million people.) In November 1980, then-deputy director of the CIA, Ray Cline, made a secret visit to a Khmer Rouge camp inside Cambodia.[29]

In the diplomatic arena, the United States led most of the Western world to line up behind China in support of the Khmer Rouge. The Carter and Reagan administrations both voted for Pol Pot's representative, Thiounn Prasith, to occupy Cambodia's seat in the United Nations. He did so until late 1990, and in 1992 continued to run Cambodia's UN Mission in New York. As of 1992, no Western country had voted against the Khmer Rouge in the twelve years that their tenure had been challenged.

In 1981, at an international conference on Cambodia, then U.S. Secretary of State Al Haig dismayed the Southeast Asian countries by backing China's firm support for the Khmer Rouge. The next year, the United States and China cooperated to force the exiled Cambodian leader Prince Sihanouk to join a coalition with Pol Pot. The Reagan administration then justified the Khmer Rouge flag flying over the UN in New York by reference to its "continuity" with the Pol Pot regime.[30]

In 1983, Secretary of State George Shultz described as "stupid" the efforts of Australian Foreign Minister Hayden to encourage dialogue over Cambodia.[31] In 1985, Shultz visited Thailand and again warned against peace talks with Vietnam. According to the *Bangkok Post* of July 13, 1985, "A senior U.S. official said Shultz cautioned ASEAN to be extremely careful in formulating peace proposals for Kampuchea because Vietnam might one day accept them."

Washington's fears were realized. Rapprochement in Southeast Asia, particularly between Thailand and Vietnam, facilitated the Vietnamese withdrawal and allowed the prospect of a settlement of the Cambodia question. The key remaining issue was the future of the Khmer Rouge, armed to the teeth by Deng's China, to whom Washington has given "most favored nation" status.

By contrast, the Bush administration threatened to punish Thailand for its defection from the aggressive U.S.-Chinese position. As the *Far Eastern Economic Review* put it on March 2, 1989: "Officials privately warned that if Thailand abandoned the Cambodian resistance and its leader Prince Norodom Sihanouk for the sake of doing business with Phnom Penh, it would have to pay a price. 'Thailand should consider whether the total value of any new Indochinese trade would even cover the U.S. trade access privileges it still gets under the Generalized Special Preferences,' one administration official said." Soon afterwards, the U.S. ambassador in Thailand stated that the Khmer Rouge could not be excluded from the future government of Cambodia.[32]

The removal of the negotiations from a regional forum to the great power forum in Paris, with the introduction of a unanimity requirement, gave the Khmer Rouge both direct superpower backing and a veto over resolution of the conflict. At the International Conference on Cambodia in Paris in August 1989, James Baker restated his proposal to return the Khmer Rouge to positions of power. The Conference failed to foster a Sihanouk-Hun Sen alliance against the Khmer Rouge. As the *Economist* put it on September 30, 1989: "The talk among the delegates is that the American State Department torpedoed the deal."[33]

Roger Normand, fieldwork editor of the *Harvard Human Rights Journal*, obtained the contents of some of Pol Pot's confidential speeches, recorded in briefing notes taken by Khmer Rouge commanders who defected in 1989.[34] They show Pol Pot's conscious use of the veto the West had given him over the negotiation process through its push for a unanimous "comprehensive settlement." In 1988, Pol Pot secretly revealed plans to "delay the elections" until his forces "control all the country," when his officials "will lead the balloting work." In this secret briefing to Pol Pot's commanders, Khieu Samphan, his delegate to the negotiations, added: "The outside world keeps demanding a political end to the war in Kampuchea. I could end the war now if I wanted, because the outside world is waiting for me, but I am buying time to give you comrades the opportunity to carry out all the tasks . . . If it doesn't end politically, and ends militarily, that's good for us." Here Pol Pot interrupted, saying that "to end the war politically" would make his movement "fade away": "We must prevent this from happening."

Yet the struggle for peace continued. After the breakdown of the Paris talks, *Asiaweek* reported on October 13, 1989: "The only sign of settlement is a conference of the four factions along with ASEAN and Vietnam, suggested by Thailand's fence-mending Prime Minister Chatichai Choonhavon . . . Washington, whose say-so is important, has indicated that it disapproves. That has put a damper on the plan." The United States then also opposed Thailand's proposals for a ceasefire and establishment of neutral camps to protect Cambodian refugees from the depredations of the Khmer Rouge and their allies.[35] According to diplomatic correspondent Nayan Chanda, writing in the *Christian Science Monitor* on June 13, 1990, Washington "politely dismissed" even Japan's peace plan, which called for "elections in Cambodia with a limited UN participation."

On July 18, 1990, Washington announced its readiness for talks with Hanoi over Cambodia, a modicum of humanitarian aid for children there, and a vote against the Khmer Rouge coalition for Cambodia's United Nations seat. Although Washington later began direct talks with Phnom Penh, U.S. leaders were aware that they could rely on the forthcoming UN "Perm 5" Plan (agreed on July 17) to absolve them from casting the promised vote against the Khmer Rouge. U.S. goals had not changed: displacing the Hun Sen regime and returning the remnants of Cambodia's pre-1975 regimes to power. These non-communist factions were not able to translate twelve years of covert and overt U.S. and allied military aid into significant military power. So in the absence of a settlement with Phnom Penh, their ambitions remained dependent on their Khmer Rouge partners inflicting critical damage on the State of Cambodia. This looked an easy road to follow, but it was blocked further ahead. Any Khmer Rouge defeat of Phnom Penh would likely have turned Khmer Rouge aggression against their coalition allies, whom they privately regarded as enemies.

Nevertheless, the American search for leverage over Cambodia's future demanded two things. First, increased power for its non-communist protégés. U.S. policy remained wedded to the hope of Sihanouk and Son Sann riding to power on the back of the Khmer Rouge. Washington continued to aid them despite the explicit contrary undertaking of Under-Secretary of State for Political Affairs Robert Kimmitt, when he explained the policy "shift" on July 18. When asked: "Are you telling the non-communist resistance to pull away from Pol Pot, or the United States will desert them?" Kimmitt replied quite clearly: "Any time they are in any form of association with the Khmer Rouge, that makes U.S. support no longer possible."[36] Nevertheless Washington extended overt and covert aid to Sihanouk and Son Sann's forces despite their unabated cooperation with the Khmer Rouge. Sihanoukist commander Kien Van boasted in early October 1990 that the Khmer Rouge would provide him with 2,000 troops for an attack on Siemreap, as well as 12 tanks plus jeeps, trucks, and heavy weapons provided by China to the Khmer Rouge in the previous two months. Sihanouk's son Norodom Ranarridh added, as if he had been warned to keep Washington's secret: "I have to say very frankly, and Washington will criticize me again — that against Siemreap the Khmer Rouge will be the major attacking forces . . ."[37] U.S. policymakers pursued a calculated risk of assisting an eventual Khmer Rouge takeover, and prospects for another genocide.

Second, the United States naturally had more leverage over Cambodian discussions held in a great power forum, than in the more finely balanced regional environment. If necessary to maintain U.S. leverage, Washington favored a great power forum, allowing the Chinese their say as well. That too entailed a continuing Khmer Rouge role.

These two factors prompted the search for a "comprehensive solution," as designed by the U.S. with the other Permanent Five members of the United Nations Security Council. As American hopes for influence remained wedded to Khmer Rouge ambitions, Washington's policy refused any reduction in its continuing support for the Khmer Rouge until the only Cambodian opponents of these genocidists were first displaced from power.

The Regional Diplomacy

The regional players had very different ideas. In 1983 Bill Hayden, Australia's new foreign minister, identified the two key issues dominating the Cambodian conflict. These were: the problem of a threatened Khmer Rouge return to power, and the need for a Vietnamese withdrawal. Hayden launched an effort to "facilitate dialogue" on the Cambodian question.

Indonesia encouraged this effort, even expressing the vain hope that Australia would restore its aid program in Vietnam. In February 1984, Benny Murdani concluded a third visit to Vietnam with the statement that Hanoi posed no threat to Southeast Asia. He also recognized that Hanoi's invasion of Cambodia had been undertaken in self-defense, "to maintain

Vietnam's own existence" against Pol Pot's attacks.[38] Soon after, Hanoi made a new diplomatic proposal, which Indonesia's foreign minister, Mochtar Kusumaatmadja, called "a significant step forward." The Thai foreign minister, Siddhi Savetsila, also welcomed unspecified "new elements" in Hanoi's position.[39]

In 1985, Hanoi, after capturing all twenty of the Khmer Rouge and allied camps along the Thai-Cambodian border, dropped its demand that the Chinese threat would have to end before any full Vietnamese troop withdrawal from Cambodia. In early March 1985, Hayden visited Hanoi, and heard further Vietnamese proposals from Foreign Minister Nguyen Co Thach, which Hayden claimed were "a considerable advance."[40] Indonesia's Mochtar concurred that there had been another "advance in substance" in the Vietnamese position.[41]

While in Vietnam Hayden had had a meeting with Hun Sen, becoming the first of many regional leaders to meet the Cambodian premier. Hun Sen told him: "We are ready to make concessions to Prince Sihanouk and other people if they agree to join with us to eliminate Pol Pot." Hun Sen later announced that the Vietnamese troops would all leave Cambodia by 1990, or earlier if there was a settlement. (The previous date set by Hanoi had been 1995.)

Vietnam now insisted only that the Khmer Rouge be prevented from returning to power. This meant that the Cambodian problem could from that point be resolved within Southeast Asia, principally by Thailand, which could cut off sanctuary and supplies to the Khmer Rouge, and Vietnam, which could withdraw the rest of its own troops. China's cooperation in a settlement was no longer necessary. However, China (and, as we shall see, the United States) disagreed.

But in July 1988 the first round of the Jakarta Informal Meetings (JIMs) took place, attended by all ASEAN and Indochinese countries, and all Cambodian factions. This meeting leapt a major hurdle, the refusal of the Cambodian sides to meet face-to-face, each having long insisted it would negotiate only with the foreign backers of the other. In Jakarta the ice was broken by having the Cambodian parties meet first, with the Southeast Asian supporters of each then joining the conference.

The "consensus statement" from the meeting, released by the new Indonesian foreign minister, Ali Alatas, stressed the two problems Hayden had identified: a Vietnamese withdrawal (promised for 1990), and prevention of "a recurrence of the genocidal policies and practices of the Pol Pot regime." In April 1989 the Vietnamese undertook to withdraw by September 1989. Sihanouk and Hun Sen met again in Jakarta the next month. They reached general agreement, and Sihanouk said he was prepared to go it alone without the Khmer Rouge should they prove recalcitrant.[42] However, he reneged on this undertaking immediately after leaving Jakarta.

The Prince had lost his nerve, becoming a genuine puppet of the Chinese and the Khmer Rouge. As the last Vietnamese troops were pulling out, Sihanouk called for a civil war in Cambodia to overthrow the Hun Sen government, threatening Cambodia's people with "danger to yourself" unless they rallied to his coalition to "avoid the charge of treason" after its victory.[43]

The third Jakarta Informal Meeting, in February 1990, broke down over the Khmer Rouge objection to use of the word "genocide" in the final communiqué. Although it had appeared in previous statements, the Khmer Rouge now opposed its inclusion, insisting instead on mention of "Vietnamese settlers," to which Hun Sen and Vietnamese Foreign Minister Thach objected. The Australian foreign minister, Gareth Evans, then proposed placing an asterisk next to each disputed phrase, with a note that these had not been agreed upon unanimously. Hun Sen and Thach agreed to this compromise. But the Khmer Rouge refused, and the talks broke up.[44] Again, Sihanouk and Son Sann had declined to break with the Khmer Rouge.

In Tokyo in June 1990, Sihanouk did go ahead in ceasefire talks with Hun Sen, despite a Khmer Rouge boycott. He signed an agreement on "voluntary self-restraint," and subsequently named six members of the non-communist forces to an agreed twelve-member Supreme National Council, with Hun Sen naming the other six. But again, Sihanouk tore up this agreement after the Khmer Rouge expressed opposition.[45] The Pol Pot-Sihanouk-Son Sann coalition has long held firm. Sihanouk revealed in September 1990 that he "would agree to anything the Khmer Rouge wanted."[46]

But meanwhile the policy of Thailand, the "frontline state" most threatened by Hanoi's 1979 removal of the Pol Pot regime, shifted. Thailand's first elected prime minister since 1976, Chatichai Choonhavon, held office from 1988 until he was ousted in a military coup in 1991. During this period, sensing advantage in the accelerating Vietnamese withdrawal, Bangkok moved closer to both Hanoi and Phnom Penh, hoping to turn Indochina from "a battleground into a trading ground." In Southeast Asia, the Cambodian issue is the major one dividing the region, and the momentum developed for a settlement.[47]

The Southeast Asian consensus favored a settlement that would exclude both Vietnamese troops and the Khmer Rouge — potential common ground with Hanoi. And the Tokyo meeting of Cambodian parties went ahead without the Khmer Rouge.

These advances were possible because the great powers, particularly China and the United States, were not involved. But there was no settlement precisely because of Chinese and U.S. rejection of any such move to exclude the Khmer Rouge. The great powers continued to offer the Khmer Rouge a veto, which has been regularly exercised.

Prospects

The "Perm 5" proposal of August 1990 called for the United Nations to introduce civilian personnel to "supervise or control" five key ministries of the State of Cambodia, and hold elections under the scrutiny of UN troops who were supposed to disarm and cantonize all four Cambodian armies. Reflecting U.S. and Chinese interests, this proposal entails risks for Cambodia.

Gone is the Jakarta forum's earlier provision against "a recurrence of the genocidal policies and practices of the Pol Pot regime." The UN General Assembly first watered this down in November 1989, to "the universally-condemned policies and practices of a recent past." Even that euphemism now reads blandly: "Necessary measures should be taken in order to observe human rights and ensure the non-return to the policies and practices of the past." In effect, the Perm 5 have condoned genocide.

Within days, the UN's Human Rights Subcommission decided to *drop from its agenda* a draft resolution on Cambodia. This resolution had referred to "the atrocities reaching the level of genocide committed in particular during the period of Khmer Rouge rule," and called on all states "to detect, arrest, extradite or bring to trial those who have been responsible for crimes against humanity committed in Cambodia," and "prevent the return to government positions of those who were responsible for genocidal actions during the period 1975 to 1978." "The sub-commission's chairman, Danilo Turk of Yugoslavia, decided to drop the text from the agenda after several speakers said it would render a disservice to the United Nations after the five permanent members of the UN Security Council issued a joint plan this week aimed at ending the fighting . . ."[48]

The 1991 version of the UN plan attempted to give Pol Pot's Khmer Rouge "the same rights, freedoms and opportunities to take part in the electoral process" as any other Cambodian, and specifically to "prohibit the retroactive application of criminal law."[49] The Perm 5 have signaled to future genocidists that the worst they can expect is to have their opponents disarmed and removed from office, and to face them in unarmed combat with immunity from prosecution.

Yet there was no serious UN attempt to spell out how the Khmer Rouge forces are to be located, supervised, "disarmed" or "cantonized." This will be much more difficult to do to the Khmer Rouge, who are located in remote, jungled areas, than to the Hun Sen army which defends fixed bases, cities and populated areas. During the 1989 Paris Conference, the Khmer Rouge successfully kept the UN military investigation mission away from their secret military camps.[50] The likelihood now is that any effective disarming will be lopsided and will favor the Khmer Rouge. Even if all the Cambodian armies are in fact disarmed, the process would most disadvantage the Hun Sen army, easily the largest (over 200,000, compared to its opponents' combined 50,000). Thus genocidists, who threaten to repeat their crimes against humanity,[51] would undergo less UN control than those who have opposed them. This may be the reason China agreed to the proposal.

The Khmer Rouge are not willing to hand over their arms, only to hide their troops if necessary.[52] A settlement that does not effectively disarm them is illusory. Popular support does not exist to offer the Khmer Rouge hope of power by peaceful means, and they could merely bide their time before attempting a coup, a return to insurgency, or "death squad" activity.

As part of a new effort to break the Cambodian deadlock, Japan made three new proposals in early 1991: UN monitoring from the start of a ceasefire, expulsion from the settlement process of any group which violated the ceasefire, and establishment of a special commission to investigate the Khmer Rouge. In Bangkok on March 18, 1991, U.S. Assistant Secretary of State Richard Solomon criticized Tokyo's proposals, as "likely to introduce confusion in international peace efforts." The next month, the new military strongman in Bangkok, Suchinda Krapayoon, told a visiting U.S. senator that he considered Pol Pot a "nice guy."[53]

In June 1991, the four Cambodian parties assembled in Jakarta once more. Sihanouk and Hun Sen agreed for the second time that the former would head the Supreme National Council, and the latter would be deputy chairman. The next day, once again, Sihanouk announced that his Khmer Rouge allies had rejected the agreement.[54] The possibility remained that this scenario might recur even though a UN Peace Plan was eventually signed in Paris on October 23, 1991.

Two weeks after signing that agreement, Khmer Rouge forces in Pursat province attacked a Cambodian village and massacred 60 men, women and children there. In January 1992, Khmer Rouge troops made a concerted attack on 25 villages in Kompong Thom province. They mortared and burned down "whole villages," killed 13 people, wounded 18, and drove 10,000 from their homes. Diplomats said that this "was the worst violation so far."[55] Far worse was to come, culminating in the Khmer Rouge breach of the Paris agreement by their failure to disarm any of their troops. On May 31, 1992, Khmer Rouge forces "attacked a UN cantonment site where government troops had gathered to surrender their weapons to UN officials. The UN troops immediately fled . . ." The Phnom Penh troops took up a defensive position and held the Khmer Rouge at bay, while shelling continued. On June 1, Khmer Rouge forces held a UN officer, Captain David Wilkenson, "at gunpoint" for nearly two hours.[56]

On June 10 the director of the UN Transitional Authority in Cambodia (UNTAC), Yasushi Akashi, announced that he had received a letter from the Khmer Rouge stating that their army "was not in a position to allow UNTAC forces to proceed with their deployments" in Khmer Rouge-held areas. Akashi described this as "a clear breach of the Paris agreement," and therefore "unacceptable."[57]

At what point will the Khmer Rouge be denied "the same rights, freedoms and opportunities" as any other Cambodians?

Notes

1. Ben Kiernan, "Genocidal Targeting: Two Groups of Victims in Pol Pot's Cambodia," and Chanthou Boua, "Genocide of a Religious Group: Pol Pot and Cambodia's Buddhist Monks," in P. Timothy Bushnell, et al., eds., *State-Organized Terror*, Westview, Boulder, 1991, pp. 207–40.
2. See, for instance, Bernard Edinger, "Cambodians Behead Vietnam Villagers," AAP-Reuter, *The Asian* (Melbourne), November 1977, p. 11.
3. According to *Asiaweek*, "Most intelligence analysts in Bangkok agree that Cambodian raids and land grabs escalated the ill-will . . . until peace was irretrievable" (September 22, 1978). See also Ben Kiernan, "New Light on the Origins of the Vietnam-Kampuchea Conflict," *Bulletin of Concerned Asian Scholars* 12, 4 (1980): 61–65, esp. p. 64, and *How Pol Pot Came to Power* (London, 1985), pp. 413–21.
4. Hanoi's proposal of February 5, 1978 offered a mutual pullback 5 kilometers each side of the

border, negotiations, and consultation as to an appropriate form of international supervision. Phnom Penh rejected this.

5. See Ben Kiernan, "Kampuchea: Thai Neutrality a Farce," *Nation Review* (Melbourne), May 24, 1979.

6. Both Sihanouk and Son Sann reported being pressured by the United States to join the coalition with Pol Pot. See Ben Kiernan, "Kampuchea 1979–81: National Rehabilitation in the Eye of an International Storm," *Southeast Asian Affairs 1982*, Institute of Southeast Asian Studies, Singapore (Heinemann, 1982), p. 187, and David J. Scheffer, "Arming Cambodian Rebels: The Washington Debate," *Indochina Issues*, no. 58, June 1985, p. 4.

7. For more recent information on this, see Steven Erlanger, "Political Rivals Jockey in Phnom Penh," *New York Times*, August 11, 1990.

8. The *Far Eastern Economic Review* reported on July 19, 1990: "Government forces may be poorly paid and badly trained, but they have shown a marked willingness to fight in recent engagements." The *New York Times* on July 22, 1990 quoted Pol Pot's ally Prince Norodom Ranariddh as saying that "it seems we may have lost on the battlefield."

9. Steven Erlanger reported from Phnom Penh in the *New York Times*, August 6, 1990: "No credible analyst or official here sees any imminent political or military collapse. The main concern, they say, is the economy, which the Khmer Rouge is trying to disrupt. Economic collapse could lead to the kind of panic that would quickly undermine an army that is *still holding its own*." [Emphasis added.]

10. In an interview with U.S. National Public Radio on July 27, 1990, Hun Sen said: "Once we reach a political solution, a multiparty system will be automatically adopted . . . to allow all political parties to participate in an election. I know we can be asked why we do not allow a multiparty system at this time. I'd like to argue that we do not want to fight simultaneously on two fronts, for the danger facing the Cambodian people is not the question of a multiparty system or a one-party system, but the return of the Pol Pot genocidal regime."

11. Nayan Chanda, "Sihanouk Stonewalled," *Far Eastern Economic Review*, November 1, 1984, p. 30.

12. Gareth Porter, "Cambodia: The American Betrayal," unpublished paper, 1989.

13. *New York Times*, May 1, 1990.

14. This undertaking was given by Chinese premier Li Peng on a visit to New Zealand in January 1989.

15. "Sihanouk: No Council without K. Rouge," *Bangkok Post*, July 23, 1990. *New York Times*, July 19, 1990. "Khmer Rouge Receive Chinese Tanks," by Nate Thayer, Associated Press Writer, AP, October 7, 1990. *Indochina Digest*, No. 90–40, October 6–12, 1990.

16. *Far Eastern Economic Review*, August 30, 1990, p. 65. See also *New York Times*, April 16, 1990.

17. Steven Erlanger, "Cambodians Face Loss of Eastern Aid and Trade," *New York Times*, August 12, 1990.

18. Nayan Chanda, "For Reasons of State," *Far Eastern Economic Review*, August 2, 1990.

19. See Steven Erlanger, "Cambodians Face Loss of Eastern Aid and Trade," *New York Times*, August 12, 1990.

20. *Far Eastern Economic Review*, July 12, 1990, p. 14. $7 million of this is overt "non-lethal" military aid. Another $10 million is said to be provided by Singapore in "military hardware and other supplies." *New York Times*, July 19, 1990, and also July 8, 1990.

21. See Ben Kiernan, "Pol Pot Stomps in Deng's Footsteps, and with US Support," *Sydney Morning Herald*, July 13, 1989, and "US Policy Turn on Cambodia is Incomplete," London *Guardian*, July 23, 1990.

22. Eva Mysliwiec, personal communication, 1987. See her book, *Punishing the Poor: The International Isolation of Kampuchea*, Oxford, Oxfam, 1988.

23. See, for instance, "France in Bid to Gag Report on Cambodia," *The Australian*, February 26, 1990.

24. Elizabeth Becker, *When the War Was Over* (New York, 1986), p. 440.

25. Letter from Jonathan Winer, counsel to Senator John Kerry, Member of the U.S. Senate Foreign Relations Committee, to Larry Chartienes of Vietnam Veterans of America, October 22, 1986, citing "information from the Congressional Research Service." The details cited included U.S. aid to the "Khmer Rouge" for "development assistance, food assistance, economic support, and in smaller amounts for the Peace Corps, narcotics enforcement and military assistance." This was later denied by the U.S. State Department, while the Congressional Research Service reportedly transferred its employee who provided the statistics.

26. William Shawcross, *The Quality of Mercy: Cambodia, Holocaust and Modern Conscience* (New York, 1984), pp. 289, 395, 345.

27. Linda Mason and Roger Brown, *Rice, Rivalry and Politics: Managing Cambodian Relief* (University of Notre Dame Press, 1983), pp. 136, 159, 135.

28. *Kampuchea: A Demographic Catastrophe*, National Foreign Assessment Center, Central Intelligence Agency, May 1980. For critiques of this document, see Michael Vickery, "Democratic Kampuchea: CIA to the Rescue," *Bulletin of Concerned Asian Scholars* (BCAS) 14, 4 (1982): 45–54; and Ben Kiernan, "The Genocide in Cambodia, 1975–1979," BCAS 22, 2 (1990): 35–40, and references cited.

29. "Thais Furious at Cambodians for Disclosing Visit by Reagan Aide," *Los Angeles Times*, December 5, 1980. I am grateful to Jack Calhoun for this reference.
30. See Ben Kiernan, "Kampuchea 1979–81," *Southeast Asian Affairs 1982*, and John Holdridge (U.S. Department of State), Hearing before the Subcommittee on Asian and Pacific Affairs of the Committee on Foreign Affairs, House of Representatives, 97th Cong., 2nd sess., September 14, 1982, p. 71.
31. "Peace Plan 'Stupid'—U.S. Rap," *Herald* (Melbourne), June 28, 1983.
32. Moreover, U.S. Secretary of State James Baker actually proposed the inclusion of the Khmer Rouge. Mary Kay Magistad, "Khmer Rouge are Closer to New Chance at Power," *Boston Globe*, April 17, 1989.
33. When the Paris Conference on Cambodia foundered in August 1989, Washington "reiterated its support for a Khmer Rouge role in a transitional government" (Associated Press, *Bangkok Post*, September 1, 1989). As a result of U.S. support, the Khmer Rouge emerged strengthened from the failed conference.
34. For some of the contents of these speeches, see Roger Normand, "The Teachings of Chairman Pot," *The Nation*, August 27, 1990; also Roger Normand and Ben Kiernan, "Khmer Rouge Poised to Gain from U.S. policy," letter to the *New York Times*, August 6, 1990; and Ben Kiernan, "US Policy Turn on Cambodia Is Incomplete," and "Medieval Master of the Killing Fields," London *Guardian*, July 23 and 30, 1990. I am grateful to Normand for making this information available.
35. Paul Wedel, United Press International (UPI), "US Opposes Proposed Ceasefire in Cambodia," May 14, 1990.
36. *MacNeil-Lehrer News Hour*, PBS-TV, July 18, 1990, interview with Jim Lehrer.
37. "We will have seized Angkor Wat and Siemreap by January at the latest," Kien Van predicted inaccurately. "Khmer Rouge Receive Chinese Tanks," by Nate Thayer, Associated Press Writer, AP, October 7, 1990. *Indochina Digest*, no. 90–40, October 6–12, 1990.
38. *Age* (Melbourne), March 16, 1984.
39. Ibid., March 16, 19 and 27, 1984.
40. Ben Kiernan, "Kampuchea: Hayden is Vindicated," *Australian Society*, August 4, 8, 1985, pp. 20–23.
41. *Age*, March 21, 1985.
42. "Sihanouk to Return as Cambodia's Head of State," and "Move to Dump Khmer Rouge," *Sydney Morning Herald*, May 3 and 4, 1989.
43. Kelvin Rowley quotes Sihanouk's speech on September 24, 1989, broadcast on the Voice of the National Army of Democratic Kampuchea: "You must get rid of the regime immediately. . . . Rally to the tripartite forces of our resistance movement before it is too late, so that the real patriots . . . can undoubtedly see that you are also patriotic. By so doing, you in Cambodia can avoid the imminent danger to yourself. . . . It is impossible this time for me to defend you." I am grateful to Rowley for this reference.
44. Roy Eccleston, "Evans Plan Stumbles over an Ugly Word," *The Australian*, March 2, 1990.
45. *Far Eastern Economic Review*, July 19, 1990, p. 14.
46. *Indochina Digest*, No. 90–37, September 15–21, 1990.
47. For the background to this regional feeling in the common post-war anti-colonial struggles, see Ben Kiernan, "ASEAN and Indochina: Asian Drama Unfolds," *Inside Asia* 5 (Sept.–Oct. 1985): 17–19.
48. *Agence France Presse* report from Geneva, August 30, 1990.
49. UN Security Council statement on Cambodia, released January 11, 1991, pp. 24, 27.
50. Michael Haas, "The Paris Conference on Cambodia," *Bulletin of Concerned Asian Scholars*, 23, 2, 1991.
51. In a secret 1988 briefing to his commanders, recounted by defectors to Roger Normand, Pol Pot blamed most of his regime's 1975–79 killings on "Vietnamese agents." But he defended having massacred the defeated Lon Nol regime's officers, soldiers and officials. "This strata of the imperialists had to be totally destroyed," he insisted. In "abandoning communism" now, Pol Pot added, his movement discards its "peel," but not the fruit inside. "The politics has changed, but the spirit remains the same." The Khmer Rouge predict their return with this slogan: "When the water rises, the fish eat the ants, but when the water recedes, the ants eat the fish."
52. Normand's Khmer Rouge defector informants quote Pol Pot as saying in 1988: "Our troops will remain in the jungle for self-defense," in the event of a settlement.
53. Senator Bob Kerrey, testimony before the U.S. Senate Foreign Relations Committee, April 11, 1991.
54. *Sydney Morning Herald*, June 3 and 4, 1991.
55. *New York Times*, January 21, 1992, and "Peace Accord Violation Leaves 13 Dead: Khmer Rouge Forces Attack Villages," *Financial Times*, January 21, 1992.
56. *Cambodia Peace Watch*, 5, 1, May 1992, citing UPI, May 30 and June 2, 1992; *Indochina Digest*, June 5 and 12, 1992; and "Khmer Rouge on the Attack," *Australian*, June 2, 1992.
57. *Indochina Digest*, June 12, 1992.

37

Vietnam in the New World Order

Ngô Vĩnh Long

On March 9, 1991 when President George Bush announced victory over Iraq and declared that a "new world order" had begun, he also added: "By God! We've kicked the Vietnam Syndrome once and for all . . . We promised this would not be another Vietnam. And we kept that promise. The specter of Vietnam has been forever buried in the desert sands of the Arabian peninsula."[1]

What has this new world order got to do with Vietnam? In the context of the post-Cold War world, American aggression in Vietnam, and the Persian Gulf, it means that the United States, as the only remaining military super-power, can now presumably impose the old imperial order on Third World countries at will. In spite of all the Cold War rhetoric, the Vietnam War was fought mainly to teach people elsewhere in the world the lesson that revolutions do not pay; and that even if a nation managed to regain its independence, the United States and its allies would make it impossible for them to rebuild their country and develop their economy. This was the reason for the embargo, the use of the "Chinese card," and many other policies to punish Vietnam after 1975. James Fallows, former President Jimmy Carter's chief speech writer, was only partially correct when he wrote in March 1991 that: "The real reason the embargo persists, of course, is that we lost the war. That is also the reason that, although we can forgive the Soviet Union and Nicaragua, we can't forgive Vietnam — even though it is a relatively well-behaved country now, with economic reform plans as impressive as most in Eastern Europe."[2]

Now, almost two years since the statements of President Bush and Mr. Fallows, Vietnam's good behavior and impressive economic reforms have not seemed to make much of a difference in terms of its relations with the United States. A recent statement by a deputy secretary of state in the new Clinton administration, Clifton Wharton, to the effect that there were preconditions attached to a normalization of relations between the United States and

397

Vietnam, caused some concern in Hanoi. In response, on January 25, 1993, the spokesperson of the Vietnamese Foreign Ministry made the following remarks at a press conference:

> Vietnam always holds the view that relations between countries should be based on mutual respect, equality, mutual interests and non-intervention in the internal affairs of each other. From this principle, Vietnam regards a normalization between Vietnam and the United States as having no preconditions. Vietnam is ready to normalize relations with the United States because this will satisfy the interests and desire of the peoples of the two countries as well as the interest of peace and stability in the Southeast Asian region and in the world . . .
>   Vietnam has always regarded the MIA [Missing In Action] question as a purely humanitarian issue which has no linkage with any political issue. This is also something that was agreed to by the United States and Vietnam when the special American presidential envoy [former Chairman of the Joint Chiefs of Staff General John Vesey] visited Vietnam in 1987. Vietnam has and will actively cooperate with the United States on this humanitarian issue and hopes that the American side will live up to the spirit of its agreement with Vietnam.[3]

It is not yet clear whether the Clinton administration preconditions adhere to the four-stage "road-map" for normalization that the Bush administration announced in 1991. This road-map — or roadblocks to be more precise — outlined specific requirements concerning the POW/MIA and Cambodian issues that the Vietnamese had to overcome. So far the Vietnamese side has met all the requirements of the four phases except the one which states that the last known POW/MIA discrepancy cases — which totaled 31 when the U.S. Senate Select Committee on POW-MIA Affairs released its final report on January 13, 1993 — had to be resolved before the U.S. would recognize Vietnam. Meanwhile, the United States has yet to meet half of its obligations under Phase II of the plan, which supposedly began once UN peace-makers were established in Cambodia. In this phase the United States was to: 1) Send high-level delegations to Hanoi for talks on normalization of relations; 2) allow U.S. telecommunication links with Vietnam; 3) allow signing of U.S. commercial transactions meeting basic human needs in Vietnam; 4) work with others to help Vietnam eliminate barriers to international financial institutions (IFI); 5) allow U.S. firms to open commercial offices in Vietnam; and 6) lift all restrictions on U.S. non-governmental organization projects in Vietnam.

Phase III supposedly was to begin once UN procedures and the Cambodian settlement process were well in place. In this phase the U.S. is to: 1) Open a diplomatic office in Hanoi and invite Vietnam to establish one in Washington; 2) fully lift the trade embargo; and 3) support IFI aid meeting basic human needs in Vietnam. Phase IV begins once the objectives of the U.S.-Vietnam 2-year effort to resolve POW/MIA issues have been achieved and the UN-certified elections take place in Cambodia (scheduled for May 1993). In this final phase the U.S. is to: 1) Establish ambassadorial-level diplomatic relations with Vietnam; 2) consider granting most-favored-nation status to Vietnamese trade; and 3) favorably consider IFI assistance for non-basic human needs projects in Vietnam.[4]

Given the unprecedented cooperation by the Vietnamese government on POW/MIA issues — which included allowing U.S. investigators to forage through classified files in their archives for any information on POWs and MIAs, and to open any door at their equivalent of the Pentagon to the various American POW/MIA delegations to search for any evidence of Americans having been kept there — the *New York Times* editorialized on December 18, 1992:

> No major POW-MIA issues remain unresolved. On Cambodia, the other U.S. test for normalization, Washington says that Vietnam is cooperating fully with UN peace efforts.
>
> Normalization wouldn't eliminate U.S. leverage over Vietnamese behavior; Washington would still have the power to grant, withold or condition most-favored-nation tariff status.
>
> To defer rapprochement until after Bill Clinton becomes president is to invite recriminations from some veterans' groups that resent Mr. Clinton's efforts to avoid the draft. That World War II veteran and Vietnam hawk George Bush could do his country a patriotic favor by finally, honorably, ending America's longest war.

After commenting on how the Senate Select Committee had given authoritative answers on MIAs, another *New York Times* editorial on January 14, 1993 commented: "Washington can now prudently go ahead on normalization."

Given the fact that there are now still some 80,000 American MIAs from World War II and nearly 9,000 from the Korean War, and the fact that the Vietnamese still have about 300,000 MIAs of their own, their cooperation in looking for a small number of Americans in such a large and difficult terrain has been regarded by many as truly incredible. But there are many Americans who still share the sentiment of Senator Bob Smith, the vice-chairman of the Senate Select Committee, when he said on September 22, 1992: "My peace movement would have been to make them [the countries of Indochina] a parking lot at the end of the war, but unfortunately that didn't happen."[5] Many of these people have argued that there is still a need to maintain pressures against Vietnam until it goes the way of the ex-Soviet Union and Eastern Europe. Hence the Bush administration not only did not begin the normalization process, but also maintained the broad prohibition against most trade with Vietnam.

The key question is whether continued American pressures will cause the socialist system in Vietnam to collapse and what impact such an eventuality would have on the stability of the already troubled Southeast Asian region. Answers to the first part of the question can be found in the nature of Vietnam's reforms and its relations with its Asian neighbors as well as with the U.S.'s European allies.

The first significant reforms began in mid-1979, partly to meet the challenge of the "proxy war against Soviet expansionism" conducted against Vietnam by China and the United States. The Cold War atmosphere and rhetoric also helped China and the United States to rally their allies and other Southeast Asian countries to honor the American embargo, to cut economic aid and to reduce commercial activities with Vietnam. Thus, in spite of about

U.S. \$2 billion a year in military and economic aid from the Soviet Union and Eastern European countries by the mid-1980s, the military expenses of having to keep about a half million soldiers along the northern border and another quarter million in Cambodia to fight against the Khmer Rouge and the other two anti-Phnom Penh factions, created a huge budgetary deficit which in turn caused hyper-inflation and other economic and social problems. As a result, at its Sixth National Congress in December 1986 the Vietnamese Communist Party (VCP) adopted a comprehensive reform program called *doi moi*, which literally means "change and newness" and which has been commonly translated as "renovation." But because of the continuing war with Pol Pot and conflict with China, the stresses and strains caused, among other things, food production to decrease and inflation to reach about 30% a month by early 1988.

All this forced the government to institute yet another series of reforms in 1988, which were even more fundamental and far-reaching. In the economic sphere this meant an unprecedented shift toward a market economy:

> Some of the main policies included payment of wages and salaries on a straight cash basis, pricing of inputs to state enterprises on the basis of costs, permission for private manufacturers to employ up to ten workers (later increased), abolition of internal customs checkpoints, a revised Foreign Investment Law, virtual decollectivization of agriculture, elimination of virtually all direct subsidies and price controls, increased autonomy for enterprise managers, devaluation of the dong to market rates, elimination of the state foreign trade monopoly, separation of central banking from commercial banking, provision for foreign participation in banking, reduced restrictions on private enterprise, creation of export processing zones for one hundred percent foreign owned enterprises, legislation on shareholding and corporations, dismantling major elements of the central planning and price bureaucracies, a fifteen percent government workforce reduction, and return of businesses in the south that had been nationalized in 1975 to their former owners or relatives. Discussion was underway in 1991 on proposals for a real estate tax, stock market, and bankruptcy law.[6]

The program quickly brought about some intended results in spite of drastic cuts in aid from the Soviet Union and Eastern European countries. By the beginning of 1989, inflation was reduced to about 6% a month and then to about 3.5% by May. Agricultural production reversed its downhill slide to achieve a 4.1% growth rate in 1988 as opposed to 1.3% in 1987. Overall, economic growth attained a reasonable rate of 5.8% in 1988 as opposed to only 2.2% in 1987. By the end of 1989 and the beginning of 1990 inflation was reduced to about 2% a month. In 1989 grain production totaled 21 million metric tons, as compared to 18 million metric tons in 1988. There was a significant rice surplus and so Vietnam was able to export 1.5 million metric tons of milled rice, but only at extremely low prices because of lack of markets due to the U.S.-imposed trade embargo that was still honored by many of its allies.[7]

The Vietnamese leaders realized, therefore, that economic, social and political stability in Vietnam required a solution to the Cambodian situation and the conflict with China, as well as access to international markets and foreign aid, which are closely related. Confident that it had already helped Cambodia back on its own feet, in early July 1988 Vietnam pulled its entire military command and half of its remaining troops out of Cambodia, placing the rest under Phnom Penh's command. By the end of September 1989 Vietnam's withdrawal of its military forces from Cambodia was complete.

Meanwhile, however, the May 1989 Tiananmen Square massacre of "pro-democracy" demonstrators in China created much discussion at the highest levels in Vietnam about the nature of the Vietnamese reforms. Many top Vietnamese leaders, some reformers among them, agreed with the Chinese position that too much democracy too soon would create anarchy and instability which in turn would compromise the economic reforms. The more radical reformists argued that a market economy had to go hand in hand with democracy and pluralism. At the seventh Central Committee plenum in late December 1989, Tran Xuan Bach, ranking politburo member and a leader of the radical reformists, read a speech urging simultaneous application of strong market economy measures and acceptance of bold democratic and pluralistic policies. Bach's view was rejected by the majority as being danger-ous and provocative toward China. Bach was subsequently ejected from both the Central Committee and the politburo without being given the customary face-saving position of "adviser." Foreign Minister Nguyen Co Thach, a like-minded reformer who saw the need for pluralism at home and multipolar relations abroad (i.e., balancing everybody off against each other, including China) asked Bach to be an adviser and researcher at the foreign ministry. As a result of this, Thach was strongly denounced at the ninth party plenum in August 1990 as "right leaning."[8]

Fearing that the looming shadow of China would darken the future of the reforms in Vietnam and needing some support to balance Chinese influence, Thach arrived in the United States in September 1990 for talks with Secre-tary of State James Baker and other U.S. officials. However, the Americans insisted on a "comprehensive" political settlement of the Cambodian situa-tion — which was precisely China's position of forcing the Khmer Rouge-dominated coalition on that hapless country — and a full resolution of the MIA/POW issue as conditions for normalization of relations between Viet-nam and the United States. Although Thach got nothing for his efforts, he nevertheless accepted without any hesitation a U.S. proposal to station a permanent U.S. office in Hanoi to deal with efforts to account for U.S. MIAs. Thach was to pay dearly for this unreciprocal gesture and misjudge-ment. He was relieved of his positions as a ranking member of the politburo and foreign minister at the Seventh Party Congress in late June 1991. He was in fact one of three persons whose heads China specifically demanded if Vietnam wished to have normalization of relations with China.[9] Even so, it took repeated kowtowing by many high-level Vietnamese delegations, in-cluding the November 1991 visit to Beijing by Vietnamese Communist Party General Secretary Do Muoi and Prime Minister Vo Van Kiet, before China deemed that it was time for normalization.

However, with the demise of the Soviet Union and the clearly pro-China stance of the Bush administration, Vietnam has had to pay a heavy price for detente with China. A few examples will illustrate this point. The first has to do with the dispute over the Spratleys, a group of islands which are situated on top of an estimated 13 to 17 billion tons of gas and oil in the South China Sea and which are claimed by the Philippines, Malaysia, Brunei, Taiwan, Vietnam and China. Vietnam's position is close to those of the other ASEAN claimants, which is to shelve the sovereignty issue and jointly explore and develop the resources in the archipelago area. China had said on several occasions that it would do likewise. But on February 25, 1992 China passed a law claiming all the islets in the area as well as reaffirming its sovereignty over the neighboring Paracel islands (which China took from the Saigon regime in January 1974). Then, in the words of Nayan Chanda of the *Far Eastern Economic Review*:

> The next Chinese move came in May when Peking [sic] announced that it had signed a contract with a U.S. oil company, Crestone Energy Corp., to explore oil in a block contiguous to an offshore Vietnamese oil field. The president of Crestone has claimed that the operation will be protected by the Chinese navy. In June China landed troops on a reef claimed by Vietnam and set up a "sovereignty post."[10]

In addition to Chinese government claims, thousands of Chinese merchants also poured into the border town of Mong Cai in Quang Ninh province and practically turned it into a Chinese trading town and smuggling center. Several hundred million U.S. dollars worth of Chinese goods enter Vietnam every year through Mong Cai and Lang Son and flood the Vietnamese markets as far south as the Mekong delta, causing Vietnamese manufacturers to complain loudly and frequently about Chinese dumping.[11]

It was against the above background that Hanoi sent a high-level delegation led by former General Secretary Nguyen Van Linh to try to iron things out with China. The November 1991 China-Vietnam normalization agreement stipulated that disputes between the two countries would be settled peacefully through negotiations. High-level officials in Hanoi and some of the aides who accompanied Linh to Beijing informed this writer in August 1992 that China told the Vietnamese delegation that the northern border issues could be discussed but the Spratleys situation was non-negotiable. However, the thunderous slap in the faces of the Vietnamese was that, as they were being ushered out, the representatives of the Crestone Energy Corporation were led into the same room to sign the contract. This contract covers nearly 10,000 square miles between the western part of the Spratleys and the Vietnamese coast which the Vietnamese said was an extension of Vietnam's continental shelf and not even part of the disputed area of the Spratleys.

China's high-handed methods and its actual military capabilities — it is the least threatened but most fully armed nation of East Asia — caused concern as well as serious factional disputes in Vietnam. Nayan Chanda reports that "Some of Vietnam's leaders, especially senior politburo member Gen. Le Duch Anh had counted on ideological solidarity with China's hardline leadership to give Vietnam some respite on the Spratleys front."[12] High Vietnamese officials informed this writer in January and August 1992 that

Chinese leaders repeatedly told Vietnamese delegations to China — including those led by Le Duch Anh, Do Muoi and Nguyen Van Linh — that Vietnam should form a coalition with China and North Korea to provide a "tripod" (*the chan vac*, literally "three-legged urn position") to uphold socialism in Asia. China was afraid that the presence of pluralism and participatory democracy immediately south of its border would provide a bad example for its citizenry and would help undermine its politically repressive system. And the repeated Chinese pressures seemed to have worked. The resolution of the third plenum of the Vietnamese Seventh Party Congress — which met from June 18–29, 1992 — followed the Chinese line almost word for word when it came to the question of "national security." It calls on the nation to "be highly vigilant and to resolutely fight all schemes and connivances at peaceful evolution [Chinese code word for democratization] and other destructive activities by enemy forces."[13]

Prime Minister Vo Van Kiet and some other leaders, however, saw in the crude behavior of China opportunities to develop closer ties with other Southeast Asian countries and to integrate the economy of Vietnam into a regional and global economy so as to promote peace and stability in the region. In late 1991 Kiet visited Singapore and signed a series of diplomatic and commercial agreements which resulted in U.S. $550 million in bilateral trade during the first 6 months of 1992. Kiet followed up the trip to Singapore with a visit to Indonesia, Malaysia and Thailand from January 20–23, 1992 and again a series of agreements were signed. By February 1992 about 50 companies from Indonesia, Malaysia, the Philippines, Thailand and Singapore had invested U.S. $220 million in 54 projects alone. And this represented about 14% of the total investment already under operation in fields such as petroleum, seafood products and processing, agricultural and forest products, hotels, and banking activities. The biggest investor in terms of dollar amount was Singapore. But Indonesia had the largest number of projects, and the Indonesia Bank invested U.S. $27 million in coal production. Petro-Vietnam and Petronas of Malaysia had the only joint venture in oil exploration and production among the Southeast Asian countries.[14] By contrast, in spite of the size of its economy, the total amount of trade between China and all the ASEAN countries was only about U.S. $7 billion in 1991. Direct investment on the part of Southeast Asian countries in China was also small.

China clearly does not have the economic muscle to tell ASEAN countries how to behave towards Vietnam in the post-Cold War world. China could, however, exert enough pressure on Vietnam to modify its overtures towards other Southeast Asian countries. And this was precisely what happened in the summer of 1992. Many high officials in Hanoi told this writer in August 1992 that Prime Minister Vo Van Kiet could not muster any support that summer to make official follow-up visits to ASEAN countries. So in late July and early August 1992 he had to visit Thailand and Malaysia as a private citizen, and signed a series of trade agreements he called "understandings."[15] Kiet's visits, however, opened up cooperation with ASEAN countries which was solidified by Vietnam's signature on the ASEAN Treaty of Amity and

Cooperation on July 22, 1992 at the ASEAN Foreign Ministers Conference in Manila.[16] This was one of the most important events in the relations between Vietnam and other Southeast Asian nations in the last several decades.

Vietnam's relations with the European Community also improved. A series of agreements on economic, scientific and technological cooperation as well as agreements on textile and trade were signed from May to October 1992. The EC allowed Vietnam to export U.S. $250 million worth of textile goods to Europe. France became the fourth largest trading partner as well as the fourth largest foreign investor in Vietnam. In 1992 Vietnam attracted U.S. $4 billion in foreign investment. Meanwhile, Japan decided to renew its overseas development aid to Vietnam after a fourteen year hiatus and gave Vietnam a loan of U.S. $370 million at special low interest rates. Japanese aid is of particular political and economic significance because Japan had always towed the U.S. line on the trade embargo as well as on loans.[17]

On September 24, 1992, the day after he was re-elected to a second term by the National Assembly, Prime Minister Vo Van Kiet held a press conference in which he made the following remark:

> The American trade embargo has not limited our relationship with neighboring countries and has not restrained increasingly open relationships between us and other countries. If the United States lifts the trade embargo we will have more favorable conditions for development, but we will also have new difficulties and complexities. Nevertheless, our policy is to try our best to normalize relations with the United States. This will not be just beneficial for Vietnam and the United States but also for peace and stability in the Southeast Asian region. I want to stress again that our efforts at renovation are not dependent on the American trade embargo.[18]

In the 1992 year-end report to the National Assembly Kiet said that in 1992 Vietnam met and surpassed all planned quotas approved by the National Assembly. GDP increased by 5.3% over 1991, industrial output increased by 15%, grain production increased by 9% to reach 24 million metric tons, direct foreign investments increased by 75%, government receipts increased by 82%, export increased by 19%, and inflation was reduced from 70% a year for 1990 and 1991 to about 18% a year since March 1992. Therefore, Kiet concluded that not only did Vietnam survive the crisis years of 1990–1991 when aid from the former Soviet Union and Eastern European countries completely dried up but with better economic performance it would be able to attract more foreign aid and foreign investment in the future.[19] In 1992 Vietnam exported 2 million metric tons of rice and became the third largest rice exporter in the world. What was very significant was that the northern and central regions were able to export rice for the first time. Vietnam was also able to export 5.5 million tons of crude oil in 1992, most of it to Japan. As a result, for the very first time since unification, Vietnam gained an export surplus of over U.S. $80 million.[20] Even more important is the fact that the market-oriented reforms seemed to be functioning increasingly smoothly. All wages and prices are now determined by the market, with the exception of electricity and water which are still being subsidized by the state. And corruption and smuggling, which are non-intended results of the market economy, have been systematically tackled by all levels of the government. In 1992 3,000 corruption cases and 50,000 smuggling cases (mostly from China and Cambodia) were discovered.[21]

In conclusion, while the hostile policies of the United States against Vietnam have neither caused the regime in Vietnam to collapse nor isolated Vietnam completely from the world community, they have served to increase China's leverage and influence on Vietnam and to hinder the process of democratization there. To what extent Vietnam will be pushed into China's orbit or forced to follow the Chinese model will depend greatly on Vietnam's relations with both Asian and European countries, and on a new Clinton administration policy. The United States should discard the illusion that it can still impose solidarity on its allies in continuing to punish Vietnam in this post-Cold War world. Furthermore, ASEAN countries are now quite leery of China, not least because of its occupation of the Spratleys and its fantastic military buildup. Japan has also become quite nervous about Chinese intentions, especially given the fact that oil supplies to Japan from the Middle East have to be transported along sea lanes close to the Spratleys.[22] The first test of American intentions will come in April 1993 when the International Monetary Fund (IMF) will again review loans to Vietnam. By that time Japan and France will have helped Vietnam pay its arrears and the United States will have no more justification for blocking loans to Vietnam. If American delegates at the IMF can keep their mouths shut, then a new chapter in relations with Vietnam may finally open. If not, the United States may have an interesting time with her allies. President François Mitterand of France has expressed his opinions quite clearly by making the first state visit of any French head of state to Vietnam for nearly half a century. And he brought along a couple of hundred businesspeople with him to drive the point home.

Notes

1. *New York Times*, March 10, 1991.
2. James Fallows, "Vietnam Shut Out," *Atlantic Monthly*, March 1991.
3. *Quan Doi Nhan Dan* (Army of the People, the official daily of the Vietnamese armed forces), January 26, 1993, p. 4.
4. Robert G. Sutter and Robert L. Goldich, "What Would Constitute the Fullest Possible Accounting of POW/MIAs? Current Issues and Possible Approaches for U.S. Policy," in *The Challenge of Indochina: An Examination of the U.S. Role* (Congressional Staff Conference, May 8–10, 1992, The Aspen Institute, Vol. 7, No. 3, 1992), pp. 33–34. See also *New York Times*, October 24, 1991.
5. "POW Charge Denounced by Kissinger," Associated Press report of the Senate POW/MIA hearings, September 23, 1992.
6. William S. Turley and Mark Selden (eds.), *Reinventing Vietnamese Socialism* (Boulder, Co.: Westview Press, 1993), p. 7. The studies collected in this volume, by authors from Vietnam, North America and Australia, contain the most detailed discussions of the reforms in Vietnam to be found anywhere to date.
7. Douglas Allen and Ngô Vĩnh Long, *Coming to Terms: Indochina, the United States, and the War* (Boulder, Co.: Westview Press, 1991), p. 57. Chapter 2 of this volume, entitled "Postwar Vietnam: Political Economy," gives an overall description of the reasons for and the nature of the reforms.
8. Thanh Tin, *Hoa Xuyen Tuyet* (Flowers Rising Through Snow), (Saigon Press, PO Box 4995, University Station, Irvine CA 92716: 1991), pp. 152–54. This is the memoir of Colonel Bui [Thanh] Tin, deputy editor-in-chief of *Nhan Dan* (People's Daily, the central organ of the

Vietnamese Communist Party), and the man who officially received the surrender of Saigon from General Duong Van "Big" Minh in 1975. Colonel Tin left Vietnam for Paris in September 1990, where he issued an open letter criticizing the party for mishandling economic and political developments in Vietnam at the time.

9. Turley and Selden, op. cit., pp. 202–203.

10. Nayan Chanda, "Treacherous Shoals," *Far Eastern Economic Review*, August 13, 1992, p. 15. There are several detailed articles on the subject of the South China Sea in this issue.

11. For details, see the July 21 and July 30, 1992 issues of *Tuoi Tre* (Youth), the official newspaper of the Vietnamese Youth League, published in Ho Chi Minh City.

12. Chanda, op. cit.

13. For a transcript of the resolution, see *Tap Chi Cong San* (Communist Journal, official monthly of the Vietnamese CP, published in Hanoi), July 1992, pp. 3–5.

14. *Lao Dong Chu Nhat* (Sunday Labor, a weekly magazine published in Ho Chi Minh City), Spring 1993, p. 11.

15. Ibid.

16. *Toui Tre*, Spring 1993, p. 5.

17. Ibid.

18. *Toui Tre*, September 25, 1992.

19. See *Vietnam Business* (a bilingual magazine published in Ho Chi Minh City), Vol. 3, No. 1, January 1–15, 1993, pp. 13–14.

20. *Lao Dong Chu Nhat*, Spring 1993, p. 11; *Thoi Bao Kinh Te Saigon* (Saigon Economic Magazine), January 14–21, 1993, pp. 6–7.

21. *Lao Dong Chu Nhat*, Spring 1993, p. 11.

22. See *Far Eastern Economic Review*, July 9, August 6, August 13, and September 24, 1992 for Chinese economic and military activities and capabilities in the South China Sea, and for discussions of the reactions of ASEAN countries and of Japan to China's recent activities in the area.

38

Post-Cold War China: The New Realities

Law Wing-Sang

Whether the Cold War can best be analyzed as a rivalry between two opposing ideological systems or simply as a strategic competition between two superpowers is bound to be a complex issue.[1] The involvement of China in this chapter of post-war history only serves further to complicate the equation. The case of China seems to suggest, however, that the national-strategic considerations of the superpowers rather than genuine ideological rivalry are the defining characteristics of the history of the Cold War. Over the last four decades, China has reformulated its identity several times vis-a-vis the ideological parameters of the Cold War and, thereby, shifted its strategic position more than once. And despite, or perhaps because of the fact that China has survived the waves of communist collapse in the late eighties, it is unlikely, at least in the short term, that the discourse of the Cold War will cease to be part of the constitutive imagery of Chinese politics and society.

In the 1950s, China's participation in the Korean War undoubtedly aggravated the American fear of the spread of communism in Asia. This Cold War thinking, epitomized by the notion of the "domino effect," entirely shaped American foreign policy through the mid-seventies, culminating in the Vietnam War. As far as China was concerned, the direct result of the confrontation with the U.S. in Korea was a long period of isolation, which helped to prolong American intervention in Taiwan: the deep freeze in U.S.-China relations resulted in the continued recognition by the U.S. of the nationalist (KMT) government in Taiwan. The geo-strategic importance of Taiwan explains the U.S. policy of containment which effectively barred China from participation in world affairs for more than two decades.

However, what China suffered was in fact a double isolation, since its relationship with the Soviet Union had also foundered in the late fifties. It was not until Nixon came to power with a new assessment of Cold War strategy in the U.S. that China's isolation began to come to an end. The result

407

was a new triangular game, to replace the former two-way conflict. Mao's dispute with Khrushchev over the orthodoxy of communism ironically turned out to be the beginning of a process whereby China became an expedient Western "ally." Of course, American moves to court the Asian communist giant did not signal ideological concessions, still less the end of the Cold War. On the contrary, American strategic interests were paramount behind the language of detente, in which the "China card" could be played to further Western goals.

This strategic rapprochement between China and the U.S. had the effect of facilitating historic change in the whole course of the Chinese project — ironically, given Maoism's deep-seated militant attitude toward capitalism, and its belief in the inevitability of a third world war. Mao's China, however, refused to be restricted to its designated position in the Cold War: ideological commitment was not allowed to exhaust the range of options available to it. On the contrary, Maoism's apparent pessimism allowed China to justify its purely strategic actions in defending itself against the "socialist-imperialist" USSR, which could then be portrayed, in apparent agreement with U.S. propaganda, as the more menacing threat.

Although Mao claimed that his model of independent foreign policy was applicable to Third World national liberation struggles more generally, in fact the specificity of China's situation — in particular its formidable military capability — disallowed any simple extrapolation of this "model" beyond the Chinese context. Nevertheless, there was a kernel of genuine Third-Worldism in Mao's China; this disappeared, however, in the search for an alternative to Cold War deadlock. If the discourse of China as leader and paradigm for the Third World survived the end of the Mao era, it did so only as empty rhetoric, taking its place in the emerging Dengist nationalist-statist regime. Displaced from its original claim to be part of a larger global popular struggle, the narrow Chinese nationalism of Deng has irreversibly changed the meaning of "socialism" in the People's Republic of China.

Deng: Reformism or Socialism?

The era of reform in China began in the 1980s, built upon Deng's hegemonic project with the twin goals of maintaining communism as orthodoxy, and realizing the dream of "prospering the nation and strengthening the army" (fu-guo-qiang-bing). By retrieving China's pre-communist national-chauvinistic impulse, Deng's reform project actively excludes elements not amenable to statist discourse.

In the course of this project, the notion of "socialism" has been unceasingly redefined throughout the last decade. In direct opposition to the Maoist revolutionary project, "socialism" has been interpreted to mean merely "the liberation of economic productivity"; in this way, it can legitimize almost any measures in the chase for economic prosperity. Thus adherence to socialist principles has become no more than a facade which serves to justify the continuation of party rule.

Certainly, Dengism is a kind of pragmatism. However, it does not follow from this that China is prepared to implement a fully-fledged technocratic agenda which would potentially make the ideological old guard redundant. On the contrary, despite its phenomenal success, reform in China has been a process of muddling-through, a series of compromises between the power-loving aged rulers and the younger opportunists who are concerned more with entrenching personal and sectoral privileges. And without an effective political and legal framework to keep corruption and malpractice in check, reform programs have provided a myriad of opportunities for the abuse of power and privilege.

The privileges of party officials have been secured and expanded largely through the domestication of public assets and the exploitation of bureaucratic loopholes. Despite occasional vain attempts by grassroots political movements to root out corruption, the Chinese Communist Party is now deeply immersed in generational, regional, and sectoral splits. These divisions have usually been simplified by foreign observers, and portrayed as a split between "reformers" and "conservatives"; such an analysis is at best a half-truth, and at worst a complete distortion of the situation within China.

The real issue is not the ideological differences involved in competing versions of "socialist principles"; indeed the discourse of socialism serves merely as a cover for underlying personal or sectoral power struggles. As long as the communist monopoly on power is not challenged, the terms "reformer" and "conservative" are merely ever-shifting strategic positions to be occupied or opposed depending on prevailing power relations. The Tiananmen Square massacre, for example, demonstrated that the so-called "reformist" element in the party was in fact a complete misnomer; they preferred to maintain the gerontocracy in power in the hope that it would naturally decay in time leaving the "reformers" in power, rather than put themselves at risk in an intra-party showdown. Moreover, and more importantly perhaps, so long as Deng does not abandon his reform and modernization project, the reformists can increase their power within the current system by utilizing unregulated favoritism — misnamed "special policies" — which are effective in securing and entrenching localized interests at the expense of the prodigious but inefficient state apparatus. And although they may have minor differences with the "conservatives" in areas of economic policy, politically both groups are allied in their need for a "stable" China backed by the powerful state machinery of coercion, in order to curb nascent popular demands.

Given that there may remain some differences between the technocratic-authoritarian (misnamed "conservative") and the market-authoritarian (misnamed "liberal-reformist") approaches to the pace of reform in the economic and ideological arenas, it seems that the current "open door policy" is adequate to unify the ruling power bloc. It is largely through the so-called "special policies" that the motor of Chinese economic growth is driven, and from which the privileged class derives major benefits.

Although the proliferation of Western influences caused by the opening up of Chinese society has been generally unwelcome, the continued insistence of the old guard on cultural purity has gradually been giving way. What is really felt to be challenging now is not Western consumer culture, but rather the pluralist political aspirations which have accompanied it. As the notion of ideological or cultural purification becomes increasingly alien to the mass of the people, party rule can only be secured by material concessions based on economic liberalization. Such a process has been audacious but can only be effective in the short term; in the long run the policy can only guarantee support to the extent that people feel they have a share in it — a feeling which was shattered by popular discontent and uprising in the late eighties. No one knows how long the current compromise can be maintained. Socio-political and ecological tensions inherent in the reform program have already reached dangerous levels; the lack of accountability and democratic input can only aggravate these tensions, creating a potentially explosive situation.

In a manner not dissimilar to the path taken by most ex-communists in Eastern Europe, what Deng has done for China is to turn socialism into a misnomer for nationalist-statism. The difference from Eastern Europe comes in the orientation of the nationalist impulse. In Eastern Europe nationalism purports to represent an historic identity suppressed under Soviet tyranny; in China, by contrast, nationalism serves more as an apology for the continuation of party rule. This is a relatively new phenomenon: in the eighties the discourse of nationalism seemed to hold the possibility of expressing dissent, and it was conjured up as the platform common both to party reformers and the younger elites who advocated a thoroughgoing political transformation in China. The Tiananmen massacre, however, signaled clearly that the state-supervised nationalist discourse would not tolerate the kinds of freedoms the young people were hoping for. After the tragedy, the nationalistic voice has become synonymous with the "new conservatism," the priority of which is the defense of the status quo. Arguing for the stability "needed" for national development, "neo-authoritarianism" has become the tacit paradigm of the elites and party ideologues, such as He Xin, whose thought reflects a new but predictable phase of Deng's hegemony over contemporary Chinese thought.[2] While the East Asian "authoritarian road to development" is gaining currency in Chinese elite strata, other dissenting voices are marginalized, silenced and repressed.

It is difficult to predict the future of Dengism in terms of the length of time it can maintain the existing balance of forces. The most crucial determinant will be the extent to which the unity forged by this hegemonic project will survive the death of Deng himself. The ideological integrity of the party has already been irretrievably lost after the Tiananmen massacre and the massive corruption in the reform era. Although the central state still holds its grip on power, internal fragmentation and splits have gradually intensified, signaling the beginning of an era of local and regional politics. The national party leadership will become less and less effective in regulating the social and economic divisions which will increasingly manifest themselves along class, regional and ethnic lines. Barring genuine political reform to curb or regulate these fragmentary currents, Deng's death will very likely unleash powerful forces in favor of restructuring the state. What remains uncertain is the form which this restructuring will take. Deng's political imagery of nationalist-statism will probably have to form the basis of any future plausible statist projects, be they "market-Stalinist" or cautiously technocratic. Nevertheless, the capacity of nationalism to unify the Chinese political project will continue to diminish, although it would be premature to predict its final demise. Since there is virtually nothing which could curb the growing regionalism, it seems certain that any new regime will be characterized by a coalition of regional forces. The viability of such a regime, however, depends substantially on the international environment, to which I shall now turn.

China, Russia, and the West

In the area of foreign relations, the early and mid-eighties were a time of conciliation for China. At that time the notion of an imminent world war between the superpowers was considered to be a thing of the past. Celebrating the coming of the "age of cooperation," China seemed finally to be entering the era of "peaceful co-existence" which Khrushchev had heralded two decades earlier. Now, however, China's conciliatory attitude was at odds with the heightened Cold War tension of the early Reagan era, and it could not disguise Sino-Soviet tension, although the issue was then interpreted in more nationalist terms. The conflict with the Soviet Union finally ended toward the end of the Gorbachev era, and the normalized relationship which resulted will probably continue in the nineties, even though the Soviet Union has ceased to exist. The only danger would appear to be from separatist movements in China's north western border provinces, spurred on by the newly independent Central Asian Muslim states.

Although the end of the Cold War has generally lessened pressures from the north, China remains troubled by its relations with the West. Ever since Tiananmen Square, China can no longer present itself as a credible partner of the West. The geo-strategic importance of China has also shifted after the collapse of Eastern European communism, making it more vulnerable to Western scrutiny. Although Deng's pragmatic open door policy has created a new-found land for Western capital, the Western powers have reason to worry about the kind of regime they are helping to promote with their financial investments. Pressure now exists for much tougher action against China, now considered by the West to be one of the worst offenders when it comes to human and minority rights. China was fortunate to have a strong ally in the White House in President Bush; it remains to be seen whether President Clinton will turn his strongly-worded criticism of China during the 1992 campaign into action now his administration is in place. For instance, the addition of conditional clauses on human rights to the annual granting of Most Favored Nation status would have a serious impact of China, which would see such action as part of a Western plot to destabilize it.

So far, China has been able to reassure itself, particularly since its leaders believe that the Cold War anti-communist alliance has already begun to crumble. China has a tendency to project its own image of national competition as the only possible language of post-Cold War global politics. In evaluating its own position in the new international configuration, China has been relatively complacent, banking on its rapid economic growth over the last decade, and the sheer size of its market ready for development. China is also tempted to see itself as irreplaceable in the next so-called "Pacific Era," as the key to global capitalist profits. In view of the economic problems the West has been facing, China believes that the Western nations will be much more concerned with developing the Chinese market than with pursuing ideological ideals.

However, although the incorporation of China into the international market is no doubt in the interests of global capitalism, one should not overstate the importance of the Chinese market, given the ample investment opportunities available elsewhere, such as Mexico and Eastern Europe. In addition, China may be mistaken in assuming that the determining factor in such equations is the presumed trade benefit to the Western nations, given the protectionist atmosphere prevalent in the shrinking capitalist economies. Hostile images of China resisting external criticism could be played up to arouse further opposition in the West, and in support of the exclusion of Chinese competition from American and EC markets.

China has tried not to interpret the end of the Cold War as the final triumph of capitalism (in which it is at least partly right), and at the same time refuses to recognize that the global call for democracy and the protection of human rights is not simply an ideological cover for rampant capitalism. In fact, the Western statist discourse of triumphal capitalism is undoubtedly antithetical to genuine democracy — but to the Chinese leadership, long schooled in Cold War thinking, it is hard to tell them apart. Yet deliberate misinterpretation of the call for democracy as part of a perceived "anti-China chorus" will tend to serve as a self-fulfilling prophecy, fueling Western hostility toward China in an ever-increasing spiral of accusation and denial.

China, Asia, and the United Nations

In international fora such as the United Nations, China used to speak as the self-appointed "leader" of the Third World. China spoke the language of non-alignment, criticizing global arms sales and the nuclear race between the two superpowers (although China had an ambiguous relationship with the Non-Aligned Movement itself). The threat posed by the heavy Soviet military buildup along the Sino-Soviet border gave China's criticisms of the Cold War a particular edge. However, the end of the Cold War has stripped China of this status. China's actions at the UN now appear more clearly to be promoting its own interests. The new focus on regional problems has also put China's own arms sales in the spotlight; missile sales to Saudi Arabia, Pakistan, Syria, Iran, Iraq and other countries have greatly irritated the West. In view of the power vacuums left in many regions after the end of the Cold War, a powerful China may also be an unwelcome image to many of the Third World countries who perceive a potential Chinese threat.

At the level of ideology, in contrast to Maoism which had a theory as well as an historical vision with regard to Third World struggles, the Third World now views China as the paradigm of the failed socialist path to development. Moreover, the nations of the global South are increasingly fragmented in the post-Cold War era, making it all the harder to speak with a singular Third World voice. China's ailing credibility could not be better illustrated than during the Gulf War. Although China used the rhetoric of anti-imperialism, its actions rendered such talk hollow-sounding indeed; in particular, China's failure to use its veto in the crucial Security Council vote on the use of force against Iraq.

On the issue of the North-South division, China historically has sided with the developing countries. However, now that China conceives itself as catching up with the industrialized nations of the world, its support for the poorer nations of the South has become half-hearted at best.

In an attempt to seek a more diversified set of alliances, China is eager to shake off its ideological straitjacket in foreign relations. The recent establishment of formal diplomatic relations with South Korea — before the U.S. had granted similar recognition to North Korea — demonstrates China's sensitivity to the post-Cold War regional power balance. China sees this period of global restructuring as the opportunity to build a stronger regional power base in Asia. However, the role that China might play in the region still causes anxiety in other Asian states. Most of the ASEAN countries, except perhaps Singapore, remain to be convinced that China will not be the next hegemonic threat in the region. Given historic suspicion of China, and given the sensitive issue of the power and status of these states' ethnic Chinese, much is still to be done before "more than normal" relations can be established. With the memory of China's "war of punishment" against Vietnam still fresh, together with the destabilization brought about by China's support for the Khmer Rouge in Cambodia, China's image as a peace-loving neighbor is far from secure. China's arms sales to Myanmar (Burma) have also been badly received within ASEAN. And although these countries would not be so concerned about finding fault with China over human rights issues, there remains the potentially explosive problem of the multinational sovereignty dispute over the Nansha Islands (Spratleys) in the South China Sea. Any escalation of the situation will pose an acute dilemma for China, which will be forced to respond aggressively given that Deng's only claim to legitimacy is a version of Chinese nationalism.

Improving relations with Japan would obviously provide a useful counterweight to Western pressures, since Japan is seen by China as a more reliable trading partner and alternative source of investment capital than the West. It seems at present as if the two countries are seeking to forge a tentative diplomatic partnership in order to reinforce their influence in international fora. Beijing would likely help promote Japanese interests at the UN, while Tokyo would lobby for China within the Group of Seven elite industrialized nations. China is certainly eager to consolidate a Sino-Japanese alliance because Japan, which is perceived to share the same "authoritarian" culture, is more tolerant of China's misdeeds in the areas of democracy and human rights. Apart from this, the history of Japan's economic growth is believed to be transferrable to the Chinese context. The only obstacle to wider Sino-

Japanese cooperation seems to be a profound wariness, based on historical experience, of a possible revival of Japanese militarism prevailing inside China and throughout the East Asian region.

China and Hong Kong

Today, it seems that China's most dependable ally in defending its free trade status may well be Hong Kong. The most successful areas of growth produced by China's open door policy are located in the southern coastal regions, which have greatly benefited from their proximity to Hong Kong. Hong Kong, although championed by the West as a model of the laissez-faire capitalist state, has in fact effectively merged economically with China, and serves as its major source of investment capital. Possible Western sanctions against China would not only hurt Chinese businesses, but would also adversely affect the economic future of Hong Kong. It is for this reason that Hong Kong has acted as a kind of buffer for the authoritarian leadership in China against international censure, thereby diluting the confrontation between China and the West.

Apart from this "use" of Hong Kong as a bargaining chip in Sino-American relations, the existence of Hong Kong (together with Taiwan) has had a huge impact on development within China, as large amounts of Hong Kong and Taiwanese capital have found their way into Chinese counties and towns. In contrast with the economically backward interior regions of China, the relative prosperity of the coastal areas has created a self-sustaining politico-economic region. China is also heavily implicated in this politico-economic zone, since many Chinese provincial governments have substantial investments in Hong Kong. In the run-up to 1997 — when China will regain sovereignty over the British colony — Chinese investment has already surpassed that of Britain. Among the economic links between the two regions, many are disguised interests of the Chinese elite, particularly the descendants of party officials, the so-called "party princes" (*tai-zi-dang*), who are de facto the most influential interest group in Chinese politics. Aided by loopholes and favoritism from their parents and family members who are high-ranking party officials and bureaucrats, neither market mechanisms nor state administration can explain or regulate their power. But with regional and local factors increasingly important both politically and economically, this group is likely to have a profound influence on the future of Hong Kong.

Given the Cold War siege mentality which is still pervasive within the Chinese communist regime, the liberal environment in Hong Kong poses a considerable challenge to Chinese authoritarian rule. Millions of people in Hong Kong have demonstrated against the suppression of the pro-democracy movement in Beijing, and many continue a pattern of protest and civil disobedience; in response, China has been trying hard to stop these "subversive elements" from turning the idea of "one country, two systems" into a wedge which could rekindle the democratic movement in China. The transition period before the handover of Hong Kong to China has been dominated by Chinese pressure to prevent leaders of the democracy move-ment from winning local elections in Hong Kong. However, the recent electoral victory of parties with platforms calling for greater democracy has sent a warning signal to Beijing. The Chinese response has been to intensify their cooption activities, courting the conservative colonial elite class in an attempt to form a shadow ruling alliance in Hong Kong — an alliance which, however, cannot gain popular support.

From the late eighties onward, Beijing's interventionist policy toward Hong Kong has greatly irritated the Conservative government in Britain, causing it to abandon its appeasement policy toward China. With the arrival in 1992 of a new governor, Chris Patten, London has readjusted its position vis-a-vis the pace of democratic change in Hong Kong. A new proposal for wider representative elections is now before the Legislative Council for approval; China has responded with threats. The issue is interpreted by China as part of a British plot to continue colonial rule after 1997, and even as the beginnings of a new Cold War against China, and thus Chinese reaction promises to be harsh. This, in turn, seems likely to elicit reciprocal hostility on the part of the West.

The issue of Hong Kong is certain to have a wide-ranging and lasting impact on Chinese politics — and on East Asian politics more generally — since apart from being a large international trade and financial center in the Far East, Hong Kong is also on the front line geopolitically, as Berlin once was — a "free city" in the heartland of authoritarian rule. Although the substantive issues no longer involve sharp ideological distinctions between capitalism and communism, it is likely that any struggle over Hong Kong would still be conducted in language reminiscent of the Cold War.

Conclusion: Cold War Rhetoric in the Future

To China, the Cold War was never just a conflict between ideological positions; this is as true for Deng as it was for Mao. However, the imagery of the Cold War is ubiquitous in shaping China's conception of itself and its relation to others. A certain paranoid attitude has always underpinned the ruling elite's image of the world; this has had the effect of denying speaking roles to the notions of liberty, democracy, human dignity, and international cooperation. If one effect of the Cold War was to stifle people's imagination, foreclosing any third road dominated neither by Moscow nor Washington, then it seems that such suffocation continues in China — paradoxically, given China's historic claim to represent precisely that alternative path. Although the content may have changed, the rigid and dogmatic mentality of the Cold War is alive and well in Deng's China.

Notes

1. See, for example, Fred Halliday, "The Ends of Cold War," and Edward Thompson, "The Ends of Cold War: A Rejoinder," in Robin Blackburn, *After the Fall* (London and New York: Verso, 1991).
2. He Xin, *China and the World at the Meeting Point of Two Centuries* (Sichuan: People's Publishers, 1991).

■PART EIGHT■

Latin America

39

On Its Own:
Cuba in the Post-Cold War Era

Medea Benjamin

Perhaps nowhere else in the Third World did the collapse of the Soviet Union and Eastern Europe create as much chaos as it did in Cuba. When the U.S. imposed a trade embargo against Cuba in 1960 — an embargo which the Cubans say has cost them more than $20 billion in lost trade[1] — Cuba became dependent on the socialist bloc for the vast majority of its trade. At the time that the Soviet bloc began to collapse in 1989, a full 85% of Cuba's trade was with those nations.

Cuba's greatest dependency was on oil — 90% of the island's oil came from the Soviet Union. But Cuba, a predominantly agricultural country, was also dependent on the socialist bloc for feeding its people. In return for its sugar, tobacco, citrus and nickel, Cuba imported Soviet wheat, East German powdered milk, Bulgarian chickens, etc. Cuba also depended on the socialist bloc for its transportation, from Russian Ladas to Hungarian buses. Even Cuban-made goods were produced in factories tooled by the Soviets and Eastern Europeans.

At the same time, the U.S. government took advantage of Cuba's woes and the Soviet Union's weakness to intensify its efforts to put an end to Cuban socialism. The U.S. began tightening up the loopholes in the 30-year-old blockade and putting increased pressure on U.S. allies not to trade with Cuba. By 1990 the Cuban government declared it was facing two blockades — one from the U.S. and the other from the former Soviet Union, since trade with former Soviet Republics was virtually blocked due to the reigning chaos and their changing priorities. This "double blockade" led to shortages of everything from aspirins to zippers; but the number one shortage was oil. Cuba previously exchanged one million tons of sugar for almost seven million tons of oil. The Soviets received Cuban sugar at prices below the Soviet costs of sugar production and Cuba received oil at prices below the world market rate. But in 1991 Russia decided to trade with Cuba at world market prices, meaning that a million tons of Cuban sugar was worth only 1.3 million tons of oil.

Now that Cuba could no longer trade sugar for oil at the same advantageous terms, it had to drastically slash its oil imports by more than half. By the end of 1989 the economy was in tatters. Imports plummeted by 60% between 1989 and 1992, and Cuba's Gross Domestic Product was slashed by an alarming 25%.[2] The standard of living which the revolution had previously guaranteed its people was in serious jeopardy. While Cuba was formerly the only country in Latin America to have eliminated hunger,[3] severe food shortages threatened that precious achievement. All food became rationed, and there were times when the government could not guarantee every item on the ration.

Another of Cuba's most precious achievements — its world renowned healthcare system — was also threatened by shortages of medicines and supplies. While Cuba produced the majority of its own medicines, many of the raw materials were imported and Cuba lacked the hard currency to purchase them. A paper shortage meant a dearth of children's textbooks. Scarce building materials led to a severe curtailment of new housing construction and a deterioration of the already existing housing stock. The transportation system, already abominable, got worse. The number of bus routes in Havana was slashed from 100,000 per day to 10,000 per day, and there was little fuel available for private cars.

The dizzying rate at which living standards plummeted left many Cubans in a state of shock. What started out as inconveniences — harder to get a bus to work in the morning or standing in longer food lines — soon turned into real hardships. The government — which euphemistically labeled this crisis the *"periodo especial"* or "special period" — devised an emergency plan to reduce the use of energy and other imports, bolster food production, and increase hard currency earnings. Citizens were urged voluntarily to reduce their use of electricity, and the power was cut in different neighborhoods at different times of the day to economize. Offices turned off their air conditioners and elevators; entire factories and work centers that were not considered essential were closed, with the workers transferred to other priority efforts.

The transportation system underwent what is probably the world's most rapid and extensive overhaul from motorized vehicles to non-motorized vehicles. Over one million bicycles were imported, mainly from China, and Cuba began building four bicycle factories. The government planned to distribute two million bicycles — about one for every five inhabitants — by the end of 1992. And in the countryside, tractors gave way to oxen and trucks were replaced by horse-drawn carts. Massive cuts were also made in the use of imported pesticides and chemical fertilizers. To save hard currency, Cubans implemented biological pest controls, organic fertilizers, greater crop rotation and creative intercropping to replenish the soil. The use of medicines and medical supplies was rationalized. People with chronic illnesses were given first priority, getting a card that entitled them to pick up their monthly supplies at the pharmacy. Herbal remedies, known as "green medicine," fast became substitutes for imported drugs.

While many of these import-saving measures created hardships for ordinary Cubans, they also had a positive side effect: they turned Cuba into an ecologist's dream. Fewer buses and cars led to cleaner, quieter streets. Bicycle-riding and low-fat diets (due to meat shortages) meant that people were trimmer and fitter. And the decreased use of pesticides and chemical fertilizers resulted in a safer food supply.

In addition to slashing imports, another government priority in coping with the economic crisis was to increase food production. Some land used for export crops was switched to domestic food crops and new lands were put into production. Tens of thousands of urban workers were encouraged to go to the countryside for two-week shifts to plant and harvest. And city dwellers began cultivating their own private and community gardens to help cope with the food shortages.

The government's third priority was to find ways to earn more hard currency. The world market price for sugar — traditionally the island's largest source of export earnings — was so low that it did not even cover production costs. Furthermore, by reducing access to farm machinery and transportation, the oil shortages affected the sugar harvest, making 1992's harvest one of the lowest in 15 years. With the combination of low prices and small harvest, sugar export revenue was expected to be under $1 billion in 1992, compared to $3.9 billion in 1991.[4] The prices for other traditional Cuban exports, such as coffee and tobacco, were low as well.

A much more promising source of future dollars was the sale of medical products discovered through Cuba's advanced research in biotechnology. These products, such as their meningitis-B vaccine, streptokinase (which can limit damage from a heart attack), treatment for skin burns, interferon, and AIDS testing kits, have been sold mainly to Latin America, particularly Brazil. In 1990, they accounted for some $200 million in hard currency earnings.[5] Many Cuban officials predicted that by 1993–1994, hard currency earnings from biotechnology products would outstrip all other hard currency earnings except those from sugar, nickel and tourism.

But Cuba's biotech industry was still in its infancy and faced fierce competition from multinational corporations. Its detractors claimed that Cuba lacked the testing, marketing, packaging and financing skills to break into a world market dominated by large multinational corporations. In addition, U.S. pressure to stop countries from buying Cuban products further obstructed Cuba's efforts in this field.

Another possible source of significant income was nickel. Cuba's nickel mines, among the richest in the world, were badly in need of renovations. A Canadian company was rumored to have agreed to invest an enormous sum of $1.2 billion, potentially doubling Cuba's nickel exports to $900 million by 1994.[6]

A real wild card in Cuba's economic future was oil. In 1992 Cuba produced a small amount of low-grade oil, but it had signed contracts with French, Swedish, Brazilian and Canadian companies to explore for oil. There was growing confidence that in 5–7 years Cuba could become an important oil producer.

The most controversial area in Cuba's post-Soviet economic strategy was tourism. In desperate need of quick cash, the Cuban government turned to the island's greatest natural resource — its gorgeous beaches and glorious weather. Its campaign to attract Canadian, Latin American and European tourists led to a major leap in the number of foreign visitors — from about 250,000 in 1988 to some 400,000 in 1991. Gross income earnings during this same period doubled from $150 million to $300 million.[7]

The renewed emphasis on tourism, however, was accompanied by a host of problems. Tourism led to a resurgence of prostitution (nowhere near the level of pre-revolutionary Cuba, but prostitution nonetheless) and a fierce black market in dollars. Tourists were molested on the street by people wanting to change money or buy something for them in the dollar store. Another harmful effect of tourism was an increase in crime. Cuba was once known as one of the most crime-free societies in the world. While violent crime remained rare, petty theft increased dramatically.

But the worst "side effect" of tourism is that it created a two-tiered society in Cuba — the privileged foreigners and the unprivileged locals. In an effort to absorb the tourist dollars, the government created tourist stores, tourist restaurants, tourist nightclubs, tourist hotels, even tourist taxis — accessible only to foreigners with hard currency. Some Cubans felt that this "tourism apartheid" had subverted the whole purpose of the revolution, which was to promote equality. Others countered that unlike other countries, tourist income in Cuba did not go into the hands of a few wealthy business tycoons, but went to keep up the healthcare system, the schools, the food supply. But even many Cubans who understood this argument were irked when they saw the island's best resources going to coddle foreigners while their own lives grew more difficult every day.

A final question about tourism is whether it would really bring in the amount of money Cuba needed. While Cuba was getting a lot of tourists from Canada, Western Europe and Latin America, its most natural market, of course, was the United States. Five to six million U.S. tourists traveled to the Caribbean each year, but U.S. law restricted them from going to Cuba. Until the U.S. government allowed its citizens to visit the island as tourists, the Cuban industry would never be able fully to develop.

Capitalists Welcome but not Capitalism

In a scramble to find new trading partners, Cuba redoubled its efforts to cultivate commercial ties with other Latin American countries, particularly Brazil. While the U.S. continued to block Cuban entry into the Organization of American States, by the 1990s Cuba had diplomatic or consular relations with every country in Latin America except Costa Rica, Dominican Republic, El Salvador, Guatemala, Haiti, Honduras and Paraguay.

Trade with China also skyrocketed, jumping by 300% from 1988 to 1990.[8] In fact, by 1992 China was Cuba's second largest trading partner after Russia, followed by Japan, Spain and Canada. The Cuban government also opened up its economy to foreign investors as a way to find sorely needed sources of capital. A joint venture law passed in 1982 allowed foreigners up to 50% ownership and tax-free investments. In 1987 the law was further liberalized, including a guaranteed three-year return on investments and no restrictions on profit repatriation.

The bulk of the foreign investment is in tourism. Spanish entrepreneurs, for example, invested over $100 million in building five-star hotels. During 1991, investors branched out into other areas, including biotechnology, pharmaceuticals, nickel, oil, textiles, construction and food processing. By mid-1992, Cuban officials claimed there were some 200 joint ventures, with many more being negotiated.[9]

While the Cuban government opened up to foreign investment, it remained firmly against the greater use of market mechanisms internally. Critics of the government contended that the only way to revitalize the economy and break away from the inefficiencies of state bureaucracy was to allow for the greater use of private initiatives, particularly in the service sector. They called for markets where farmers could sell directly to the customers instead of selling solely to the state. They spoke of family- or worker-owned restaurants and cafeterias to overcome Cuba's exasperating food service.

The official line on giving freer rein to private initiatives was that Cuba tried that route in the early 1980s, way before perestroika, and it didn't work. During those experimental years, private farmers' markets were opened, where farmers could sell their surplus at whatever price the market would bear. Home owners could sell their property to others without the state as intermediary. Licenses were given out to plumbers, carpenters and other skilled workers to work for themselves. Artisans were permitted to sell their crafts directly to the public in street fairs. The flirtation with the free market was, however, shortlived. Goods from the state sector were siphoned off into the private sector, and the markets fostered income inequalities that the government was unwilling to tolerate. In 1986 the farmers' markets were closed, the private selling of homes was also banned, and fewer licenses were given out to freelance workers.

Many Cubans, however, felt the problem was not the market mechanisms themselves, but the way in which they were handled. The government failed to institute proper controls. If it had set ceilings on prices, or if the sellers were licensed, regulated and taxed, the markets might have worked. As it was, the experiment left a bad taste in the mouths of government officials. Maintaining virtually total state control of the economy, however, not only led to inefficiency but to a thriving black market. Almost the entire population was engaged in the black market in some fashion or another. With endemic shortages of basic items, the black market was often the only way to get a meal on the table or shoes for the kids.

This problem, however, had to be set against the danger that opening up the economy during such a difficult period could lead to the downfall of Cuban socialism. The income inequalities that would undoubtedly ensue could create massive resentment among the people and delegitimize the government.

Political reforms

While the Cuban government was reluctant to institute major market reforms, it was also reluctant to institute major political changes. The island continued to be governed by a one-party state with the same leader — Fidel Castro — in power since 1959. But with the breakdown of the Soviet bloc, Cuba began to make political changes in its system that marked significant breaks with certain aspects of its past.

In October 1991 the Communist Party held a congress at which it initiated several reforms. People of religious faith were welcomed into the party as a way to make the party more inclusive. Many young people were elevated to high positions, including the Politburo, to give youth a greater say in the party's future direction. Voting for local party leadership was changed to direct, secret balloting instead of voice vote. It was also recognized that the party had become too involved in the affairs of the state. This meant that Cuba's highest legislative body — the National Assembly of People's Power — tended to "rubber stamp" party-led initiatives rather than debating and making decisions on its own.

As part of an effort to strengthen the National Assembly, the party recommended that national delegates be elected by direct vote. Previously, neighborhood representatives were directly elected; they in turn elected the provincial delegates, who then elected the national ones. Direct elections for the National Assembly was seen as a way to give people more of a say in national issues. While there would still be only one party and very limited campaigning, people could, theoretically, vote for candidates who were opposed to the present system. "If the people were counter-revolutionary, if the majority of the people were counter-revolutionary," insisted Fidel Castro, "all they need do would be to nominate counter-revolutionaries and the majority of the delegates would be counter-revolutionaries opposed to the revolution and socialism."[10] Although such a scenario seemed highly improbable if not impossible, the reforms were not insignificant. If these elections — which started in 1993 — could truly give a voice to people of various political persuasions, they could become important indicators of public opinion and vehicles for increasing public involvement in policymaking.

But direct elections for the presidency was a stickier issue, mainly because it involved the role of Fidel Castro. It was impossible to gauge the support for Castro in the absence of independent political polls and presidential elections. But it is obvious that many Cubans equated "Fidel" with the revolution itself and feared a change in leadership during such unstable times. Even a 1992 report by the U.S. Army War College concluded, "In spite of the current crisis, Castro still retains a substantial base of popular support among the Cuban public, and many of those who do not actively support him see no viable alternative."[11]

With Fidel Castro continuing to play such a pivotal role, no one in Cuba seemed to envision presidential elections within the next few years. The few who speculated about such elections saw them as coming about during a post-Fidel transition period. The first step would be direct elections for delegates to the National Assembly, with the National Assembly electing the president for perhaps a five-year term. Then at the end of that term there might be direct presidential elections.

Most sensitive of all, however, was the issue of a single vs. multi-party system. While only a few years before Cuban leaders seemed ideologically opposed to a multi-party system, by 1992 many were saying they would not be opposed to having several parties — but only after the United States stopped harassing Cuba. They said that as long as the U.S. was trying to sabotage the present government, Cuba could not afford the luxury of a multi-party system. They felt the Cuban government could never compete with the money and propaganda the U.S. would pour into opposition parties, and that Cuba would not only lose its socialist system, but its national sovereignty as well.

The U.S. Tightens Sanctions against Cuba

Believing that Cuba was on the verge of collapse, the United States began further to tighten the sanction screws, waging a fierce campaign to stop any loans to Cuba and to prevent U.S. allies from dealing with Cuba. The U.S. scared off potential investors with its pressure tactics. It strongarmed Japan into cutting purchases of Cuban sugar; bullied a Spanish firm into dropping a multimillion-dollar investment in tourism; and prevented the Brazilian airline VASP from upgrading Cuba's airline. In April 1992 President Bush closed U.S. ports to third-country vessels carrying goods or passengers to or from Cuba. And in yet another escalation of the economic and ideological war against Cuba, the Cuba Democracy Act, which was passed by Congress in 1992, further restricted Cuba by reducing economic assistance to countries that trade with Cuba; prohibiting U.S. subsidiaries from trading with Cuba (U.S. subsidiaries did $700 million worth of trade with Cuba in 1991, mostly food and medicine); and making it easier to prosecute individuals and groups that break the embargo.

In the wake of the U.S. invasion of Panama and the Gulf War, Cubans also had good reason to fear direct military aggression from the United States. The U.S. stepped up war games in the region, including maneuvers at the island's Guantánamo base. And at least partly in response to Cuban-American pressure, U.S. leaders made a series of bellicose pronouncements about the urgent need to "restore democracy" to Cuba. (In George Bush's acceptance speech at the 1992 Republican Convention he proclaimed his desire to be the first president to set foot in a "free Cuba.")

Cuba's response to this increased external pressure — a natural response for any nation under attack — was twofold. One was to prepare for war: the army and militia underwent intensive mobilizations; tunnels and bomb shelters were being dug all over the country. The other response was to close ranks and crack down on dissent. The handful of human rights groups that had sprung up in the 1980s were enjoying unprecedented freedom in 1989. They held frequent interviews with the foreign press and traveled abroad criticizing the Cuban government. But the space for dissident activity narrowed considerably in the early nineties. Those who advocated the over-throw of the Castro regime had no legal means to organize or propagate their views. You could talk all you wanted about how rotten the system was, but if you organized to remove it, you'd probably wind up in jail.

In 1992 there were over a dozen dissident organizations in Cuba that had a few hundred declared members. Some of them worked closely with U.S. government officials, and took a hard line of advocating no talks while Fidel Castro remained in power. Others were more conciliatory — they wanted to see an overthrow of socialism but felt the U.S. should begin talks with Castro to bring about gradual reform. The dissident groups tended to be more well known outside Cuba than inside. This was partially because they did not have space to organize openly in Cuba, but it was also due to the fact that people were much more concerned about dealing with day-to-day economic prob-lems than they were with long-term political change.

While there was little space for those advocating a complete overthrow of the system, there did seem to be a widening of the definition of "revolution-ary" to include people who would have liked to see major changes in government policy while maintaining the basic principles of socialism. A new term, "revolutionary dissident," began to crop up to describe this type of person, who might previously have been labeled a "counter-revolutionary."

A revolutionary dissident would support Fidel Castro and Cuba's socialist agenda but might, for example, think that cafeterias and restaurants should be privately owned, or that markets where farmers could sell their goods directly to the public should be allowed. A revolutionary dissident might speak out against corruption in the Communist Party, Cuba's nuclear power plant, or the sorry state of the Cuban press. While such an opening of the political discourse may have seemed slight to an outsider, in the Cuban context this represented a great leap forward.

But the greatest obstacle to a more tolerant revolution remained U.S. policy. The United States wanted to see greater polarization. It was hoping that the economic crisis would lead to more dissent, which would lead to greater political repression, which would lead to a popular uprising.

There was certainly much demoralization. Many Cubans wondered why they should go to work when they often sat idle for lack of inputs, particular-ly when getting to work was so difficult, when extra hours a day were needed to wait on lines for food, and when there was so little to buy with the money you made. Young people got demoralized when they could not find jobs in the fields they were trained in, and were forced to take lower skilled jobs in tourism or agriculture. In some ways, the very success of the revolution in creating a well-educated, sophisticated citizenry meant that it had become more difficult to ask people to conform to more limited opportunities.

But people were not rioting in the streets, as they had done in so many other countries around the globe when people's standard of living dramati-cally drops. Was that because Cuba was a police state? While Cuba was certainly a tightly controlled society, it was not as repressive as dozens of countries — from China, to Thailand to Guatemala — where people risked their lives to face government tanks.

One reason Cubans had not risen up against the government is that they saw no better alternative. Most people were repulsed by the rich, white Cuban-Americans who had raised billions to buy up the island's assets in a post-socialist era. They also looked at the chaos and economic dislocation in the former Soviet Union and Eastern Europe and wondered whether their lives would be any better without socialism. They were certainly not inspired by their poor capitalist neighbors such as the Dominican Republic or Haiti.

While some had not risen up against the government for lack of an alternative vision, many others were simply supporters of the government's path. Unlike Eastern Europe, Cuba's revolution was homegrown; it overthrew a hated dictator; and it brought concrete benefits to the people. And while Marx and Lenin might no longer provide the inspiration they once did, Cubans seemed to have a boundless sense of nationalism — a nationalism rooted in Cuba's independence leader José Marti and nurtured by a burning desire to maintain Cuba's sovereignty from the clutches of the United States. It thus became nationalism — not socialism — that fueled the Cuban revolution.

By 1993, some estimated that about 70% of Cubans still supported the revolution; others said the figure was closer to 50% — and falling. But among the revolution's supporters were well-educated, articulate Cubans who were enthusiastic and creative in devising ways to overcome the economic morass and prove that socialism could really work. They were tremendously excited about the possibility of building a truly independent nation — one that was not dependent on any superpower for its survival.

At the very time when the Cuban revolution was facing its greatest economic challenge ever, it had the opportunity of adapting in a way that would ensure its continuity. While foreign pundits kept predicting the revolution's imminent demise, vast numbers of Cubans were intent on proving the pundits wrong.

Notes

1. Cuba Info Newsletter, May 18, 1992.
2. Andrew Zimbalist, Cuba Update, September 22, 1992.
3. Medea Benjamin et al., No Free Lunch: Food and Revolution in Cuba Today, Grove Press, 1988.
4. San Francisco Chronicle, May 13, 1992.
5. James Petras, In These Times, April 1–7, 1992.
6. Andrew Zimbalist, Cuba Business, February 1992.
7. Donna Rich et al., New Opportunities for U.S.–Cuba Trade, 1992.
8. "Let Them Eat Coconuts," The Economist, February 3, 1990.
9. Miami Herald, May 17, 1992.
10. Fidel Castro, In Defense of Socialism (New York: Pathfinder, 1989), pp. 80–81.
11. Donald E. Schulz, "Cuba and the Future," Strategic Studies Institute, U.S. Army War College, January 16, 1992.

40

El Salvador's Peace Process: Stumbling into the New World Order

*Ana Guadalupe Martínez**

The negotiating process in El Salvador unfolded during a period that was defined by the disappearance of the socialist camp, the weakening and the final dismemberment of the Soviet Union, the growing isolation of Cuba and the defeat of Nicaragua's Sandinista Front at the polls. All the external factors that might have been expected to support the FMLN side in the Salvadoran balance of forces were either swept away or left without influence. Even the socialist countries, which regardless of any direct involvement had provided a measure of support just by existing and providing a semblance of balance on the Security Council and in international power relations, disappeared from the equation.

With its supposed foundations washed away, the FMLN at the end of 1989 was exposed on the new world stage as a genuinely national force. Only with enormous popular backing would it be able to keep up the political and military balance of strength that would make real negotiations possible.

At the same time, opinion in the United States was turning against the more warlike strains that supported continued unconditional support to the Salvadoran army. The decline in the levels of foreign aid from the United States, thanks in part to that country's economic crisis and in part to the Salvadoran army's profound disgrace — not to mention its increasingly obvious inability to deliver a military victory — was decisive in forcing the government into real negotiations.

Moreover, negotiation became a possibility because of the political, military and social equilibrium that the FMLN was able to establish, within which to propose the changes that were ultimately agreed to. The resulting balance, an impasse in military terms, was a clear political victory for the Salvadoran opposition.

* Translated from the Spanish by Ted Kuster.

The peace that was won, therefore, was a result of the confluence of pressure from the international community and an enormous groundswell of popular support at home.

If there is a single unarguable lesson to be learned from the Salvadoran civil war, it is that the war was a product of social and political conditions. To recognize that reality was taboo to the first and second Reagan administrations, but after November 1989, a month that saw an unusual string of world-shaking events, there was finally no dodging it. The Berlin Wall fell November 9, precipitating the final break-up of the socialist bloc. And in El Salvador, the Cold War counter-insurgency fantasy of a war against the United States by Cuba and the Soviet Union by way of Nicaragua finally collapsed as well.

Two days later, the FMLN opened a general offensive across the country, centered on San Salvador, the capital city. It was a rude awakening for the United States, which for nine years had thought its military, economic and political support for successive Salvadoran governments had managed to weaken and isolate the FMLN while professionalizing the army and helping build an impregnable modern state in El Salvador.

The November offensive did not simply throw the army into a military crisis. It also effectively canceled the operating line that the FMLN no longer had the military strength or the popular backing required for a serious challenge to the Salvadoran government.

In the midst of this offensive, as an act of war, the army massacred six Jesuit priests and two women who worked for them. The dead were personalities of great prestige, especially Father Ignacio Ellacuria, the rector of the Catholic University, who was well known for his work in support of a negotiated solution to the war. This multiple murder finally changed the balance of opinion in the U.S. Congress in favor of a shift in the administration's El Salvador policy. The campaign to question U.S. aid to El Salvador enlisted the open assistance of such powerful figures as Sen. Christopher Dodd.

The subsequent decline in the level of U.S. assistance, along with the army's shattered reputation, were the key international factors that moved the war toward a truly negotiated resolution.

Pressure to Negotiate

At the end of November, with battles raging and the capital besieged by the FMLN, the search began for a ceasefire to avoid further civilian casualties. The governments of France and the former Soviet Union, along with several Latin American powers, opened private initiatives to seek an end to the violence.

The Salvadoran government and its army, unwilling to enter any negotiations with their rear guard occupied, refused to stop the war until the guerrillas had been dislodged from the capital. As a result, the fighting in San Salvador dragged on another month and a half and kept the Salvadoran issue on the front burner at a number of international fora — most importantly the Central American presidents' December 8 summit meeting, where the region's leaders unanimously urged Salvadoran President Alfredo Cristiani to accept the good offices of the United Nations to get a real negotiating process off the ground.

Three days earlier, the United Nations secretary general's office had contacted the FMLN's leaders to probe their willingness to accept serious United Nations-sponsored talks. The FMLN offered the secretary general two basic considerations: (1) the chief goal of negotiations was to transform the country and not simply to end the war and disarm the FMLN; and (2) the civil war involved a member state of the United Nations and a firm ally of the United States, which meant the secretary general must even the equation by bringing in the support of other countries.

An Unprecedented Role for the United Nations

Mediating a civil war in a member state was a new experience for the United Nations. The original approach was simple: stop the war, separate the forces, and negotiate. For the FMLN, however, it was crucial that the war not be said to be officially over until there were solid commitments to reform.

The first contacts between Alvaro de Soto, the secretary general's personal representative, and the government and the FMLN, in early January 1990, were to establish the framework for negotiation. In a "pendulum" methodology, Soto met alternately with Cristiani and the FMLN and gradually sought to bring the two sides' positions closer together.

The point of greatest discord during the first phase was whether to agree on a ceasefire first and then negotiate, as the government demanded, or to negotiate the issues and then talk ceasefire, as the FMLN wanted. For the government, without the war to worry about, there would be all the time in the world to address — or not — the opposition's demands. For the FMLN, the war was the chief source of pressure for reform, and it could only stop when the political understandings were solid enough to ensure the transformation of the country.

An agreement of how to negotiate was reached and signed April 4 in Geneva — it could not be signed at the United Nations headquarters in New York because the U.S. government refused to issue visas to the FMLN negotiators. The U.S. approach reflected a last-ditch hope that the Salvadoran government could somehow take military advantage of the time the talks had bought to impose the kind of resolution that would constitute an FMLN surrender.

Soto, meanwhile, to the horror of the government side, opened a series of meetings with representatives of all the Salvadoran political, social, religious and business sectors, in search of an objective overall framework to consider the range of issues that the talks had to resolve. Soto's unique initiative was a critical part of the ultimate success of the peace talks. There were issues on which no rapprochement seemed possible; without denying the two main parties their own positions on each point of the agenda, the United Nations team was establishing that it could itself offer positions and lead the talks on that basis.

In an infinitely complex process, the United Nations team reached interlocking agreements on changes and reforms in state institutions, the army, the security forces, the courts and the electoral system, and created altogether new institutions around a national attorney general for human rights and a new civilian police force. This was possible only because the United Nations accorded equal standing to both main parties, without giving any extra weight to the government side for being a United Nations member state.

The United Nations had been persuaded that political, economic and social changes were urgently needed in their own right in El Salvador — otherwise the war might be stopped for now, but there would be no lasting peace.

The UN was able to take the new initiative because all parties, especially the United States, became convinced that El Salvador needed change, and that negotiations offered the best opportunity to provide incentives. Its success lay in the consensus achieved both nationally within El Salvador, as well as internationally reflected in the Security Council. Crucially, of course, the end of the Cold War stimulated the environment conducive to negotiations.

At the time of writing, five months after the peace accord was signed, the battle centers on whether it will ever truly take effect. This, in turn, will determine whether El Salvador inherits a broad version of democracy or a restricted one. Only if wholesale military reform, changes in the justice system and a new national civilian police force can be achieved, will there be room to strengthen civil society, subordinate the military to civilian power and put an end to impunity.

The institution with the most power to lose if the agreements are carried out is the armed forces, while civil society has the most to gain. The fundamental aspect of the agreement in this period is the subordination of the Salvadoran army to civilian power, and to determine a single function for the army: to protect the sovereignty of the country. This new constraint on the military will allow the emergence of institutions representing the interests of the broad population of Salvadorans. The FMLN will continue as the force pushing for change within its capacity to offer proposals; this means it must be flexible in its approach to other contending social forces.

A New Role for the United States

Peace, to the United States, is synonymous with pacification. The extent to which the Salvadoran process will consist of pacification, as opposed to real social change, will depend on the forces the broad progressive movement is able to assemble to keep the change element viable. With U.S. support for the peace accords relatively solid, their success is mainly a question of the strength of the bloc in their favor.

U.S. policy is focused on consolidating peace, understood as a set of political, military and economic changes that are significant but not so profound as to threaten the position of the country's natural U.S. allies. U.S. support for bringing the FMLN back into the country's institutional and civic life therefore carries some clear conditions, which are visible in the rebuilding programs the U.S. is willing to sponsor through its Agency for International Development. To qualify for aid, programs must be designed by the contracting organization and not by the FMLN itself.

It is clear that the United States will attempt to heavily influence the organization of the new civilian police force. It is just as clear that the AID program of reinforcing municipal government in the areas of heaviest conflict, where the FMLN has its deepest popular backing, is an effort to win through the reconstruction plan what could not be won by force of arms. And it is clear that Arena, the current governing party, holds the franchise for U.S. electoral support. U.S. policy is clearly still threatened by a left that can stay united and take advantage of the new conditions created by the peace agreements.

The U.S. government still sees a Central American government of the left as a dangerous possibility, as witness the recent threat to cut off remaining U.S. aid to the Nicaraguan government for "too much Sandinista influence." The end of the Cold War has changed nothing about the U.S. view of Central American leftists as ideological enemies. Despite a slightly more flexible approach, there is still no room in the U.S. world view for the forces of transformation that could balance the power of the right and help bring their societies together.

In the end, though, that world view creates no clear U.S. policy for the long term. It appears the U.S. is assessing its approach to left forces on a case-by-case basis. In the case of El Salvador, there is ongoing dialogue with representatives of the political structure (the State Department) and others (including the Justice Department) who are cooperating with Salvadorans in the creation of a new national police force. But the policy is being implemented by functionaries, many of whom were shaped by their years in a Cold War environment. Not surprisingly, many of them reflect the old view that those on the left remain enemies. Whether their anachronistic view continues to be influential in U.S. policy circles remains to be seen.

41

Back to the Future:
The United States, the Sandinistas and the
Changing World Order

Alejandro Bendaña

In Nicaragua, the most sustained military intervention by the United States against a small country since the Vietnam War came to an abrupt halt as a result of the electoral defeat of the Sandinistas in February 1990 and the peaceful transfer of government power to the U.S.-backed coalition of forces headed by Violeta Chamorro.

For the majority of Nicaraguans, perhaps the greatest difference between the "old" and "new" world orders was *not* the end of the historical contest between a revolutionary option embodied by the Sandinistas and a hegemonic one represented by Washington, but rather the transformation of the battleground in which political and economic warfare prevailed over military means.

The FSLN (Sandinista Front) had lost an election and not a war. Yet just as the revolutionary process in Nicaragua did not begin with the takeover of state power, neither did it automatically end upon losing it. Unlike what had happened in Eastern Europe, the civil dismantling of a "socialist-oriented" government did not entail the collapse of the Sandinista party organization and influence; the FSLN captured 42% of the vote, and even though a considerable period of disarray was in store for the FSLN, it behooved the government to recognize its status as the single most powerful party in the country, the largest single voting bloc in the legislature, in control of important municipalities, with representation on the Supreme Electoral Council and the Judiciary, and with considerable influence over the social movements including organized labor, not to mention over the army and the police.

And unlike what subsequently took place in El Salvador, Angola or Mozambique, the Sandinista army was not defeated or forced into a stalemate; it was practically uncontested in the field and was not subject to negotiated or violent dismantlement. Coming to office within an institutional political-electoral framework established over ten years of revolution, Chamorro's government was both constitutionally and politically bound to respect the army and its internal structure. Although the Sandinista army would uphold its constitutional loyalty to the new government, even to the point where many Sandinistas felt uncomfortable, the fact was that the new government could not count on a repressive instrument of its own to carry out the counter-revolution some of its partisans and Washington demanded.

The United States has failed to accomplish its objective of destroying the Sandinista Front. It had, however, deprived the Sandinistas of state power by forcing them to hold an election on a very uneven electoral playing field. The question now was whether this limited accomplishment would suffice in a post-Cold War order where the outright destruction of the left was no longer on the agenda.

Could both the left and the United States continue to wage their contest on a civic terrain as the FSLN, perhaps the first of others to come, born as a guerrilla movement, hurled into power by a violent insurrection, now assumed the role of a respectful legal and loyal opposition? Would a new maturity and what some called the political modernization of the left be met half way by the United States to produce a new, unprecedented respect for political pluralism in Nicaragua and Central America, a region where pluralism had previously been defined by Washington as encompassing only parties from center to right?

Sandinistas v. Washington: Phase One

No doubt the weakening of the Soviet Union and the abdication from its role as geopolitical counterweight to the United States explains the "international climate" that after 1988 propitiated settlements to what the U.S. ethnocentrically denominated "regional conflicts." Superpower rivalry did play a part in the Nicaraguan and Central American conflict, as did superpower cooperation in ending it, but Nicaraguans and Central Americans played the most important part.

The military failure of the contras, the Iran-contra scandal, and the prospect of policy changes with a new administration in Washington, prodded the Sandinista government to seize the Esquipulas peace process, initiated in August 1987, as a vehicle for making political concessions that in its opinion would make it impossible for any new administration to continue with the belligerent policies of the old.

The Sandinistas were not losing the war but they could not win it in a clear-cut fashion, allowing demobilization of the defense machinery, as long as the contras could count on secure bases in Honduras and a vital lifeline to Washington. Low intensity warfare was being waged on both sides, and it was essentially political in nature as each government calculated that the other would find it domestically impossible to continue the war. The Reagan administration had to contend with Congress and public opinion, and the Sandinistas with the enormous economic and social costs of sustaining the military effort.

Following the Baker-Shevardnadze meetings in September 1989, the Soviet foreign minister visited Nicaragua and prevailed upon his hosts to accept the "suspension" of arms shipments. By this point, however, the negotiations and the electoral process were already irreversible, as the Sandinista government fought to find a way out of the conflict at the least possible political price. What was more devastating then the arms cut-off was the fact that by 1988 the old Soviet bloc could no longer continue crucial oil deliveries and economic subsidies.

In what many came to regard as a disastrous decision, especially in an electoral context, the Sandinista government imposed a drastic "stabilization" program in a desperate effort to end a 32,000% inflation rate and stave off economic collapse. Sandinista technocrats hoped that the "surgery without anesthesia" would meet the old and new world Western conditions for obtaining economic assistance. The Bush administration, however, remained equally determined to block all external funding. In the end, the Sandinista government paid a heavy domestic price as the plan hit the poor especially hard, without winning the support of Nicaraguan and foreign capital.

Supposedly, Soviet "cooperation" made it easier for the Bush administration to shift away from solely military means, to utilize the Esquipulas regional peace initiative and complement diplomatic with military pressure, maintaining the contra army intact throughout the electoral campaign — in effect indicating to the Nicaraguan people that the only way out of war was to throw the Sandinistas out of office.

Still the Soviets were to pride themselves on having induced the U.S. to publicly support the regional peace process and to state that Washington would respect the outcome of a free and fair election in Nicaragua. The sincerity of such a commitment, of course, could only have been tested in the event of a Sandinista victory. Instead, the unexpected election victory of Chamorro forced the Bush administration to abandon its planned challenge to the legitimacy of the election.

But the weight of global factors should not be exaggerated. The presence or the absence of the Soviet Union or of Cuba does not constitute a complete restraint on U.S. policy in Central America. Far from inducing the United States to modify its interventionist conduct there, perestroika and the subsequent Soviet collapse simply allowed the U.S. to place more stress on new political, ideological and economic interventionist modalities.

Sandinistas v. Washington: Phase Two

For different reasons, both the United States and the FSLN threw their support behind the Chamorro government. Washington's presumption was that the economic would prevail over the political: that the new government's own neo-liberal inclinations, its pro-U.S. sympathies and undisguised need for economic assistance would force it to pursue a counter-revolutionary path, eventually relegating the Sandinistas to the dustbin of history. Bush hoped to continue to accomplish by civic means what Reagan had failed to achieve militarily.

The FSLN calculation was that the political and the social would prevail over the economic. When Daniel Ortega said that the Sandinistas would "govern from below," it was a stark proposition that the loss of state power did not mean the loss of the revolution. Not simply because revolutions that depend more on state power than on the people's power are not revolutions at all, but also because in the context of an adverse international economic and geopolitical setting, perhaps the best thing that a revolutionary movement could do would be to avoid governing, at least until a better global balance of power permitted a governing revolution a chance of survival.

Some, like Ronald Reagan or Jesse Helms, believed that the Sandinistas had thrown the election and were up to their old tricks. Chamorro's technocratic government was doing some new thinking of its own: the combination of economic support from the United States, military support from the Sandinista army, and FSLN collaboration in politically neutralizing social protests would ensure stability for a political scheme of humanitarian capitalism.

Herein lay a test of the new world order. If the Chamorro government could pull off its balancing act, a clear signal would be sent to El Salvador and Guatemala that peaceful political change was possible, and that the U.S. would stand by negotiated agreements that took into account the grievances which had led to popular armed opposition in the first place. The Central American left was being asked to renounce armed struggle in return for a real chance to participate in a reformed political structure with at least partly adequate security and economic guarantees.

But if, on the contrary, the United States was to insist on counter-revolution and on blocking the government-Sandinista *modus vivendi*, the chances for a new political order in Central America would be dealt a serious blow. Popular forces in El Salvador and Guatemala could come to the conclusion that signing a peace accord with their governments was tantamount to bargaining with someone that could not deliver.

This test is still being played out in Nicaragua. In what some believe to be the new modality of revolution, armed conflict has been resolved without a clear-cut victory for either side. The struggle continues for social change and income redistribution, for an alternative political project which must be waged against a neo-liberal governmental project supported by the United States and the global market system. It is a struggle that also has to be waged within the popular camp itself, inasmuch as there is no shortage of techno-crats and disenchanted leftists who have resigned themselves to "the fact" that a non-capitalist alternative to accepting the neo-liberal logic is no longer possible economically or viable electorally.

In this sense, the complex and ideological contest between the United States and the Sandinistas was also taking place within the Sandinista camp. The revisionist assumption, both in Washington and among some Sandinis-tas, was that the global and national changes would force both parties to reassess their historical relationship, to take note of Sandinista electoral good behavior, and cooperate in providing support for the Chamorro government.

The Economic Battle

The FSLN had an interest in supporting a political-institutional structure that it indeed had helped to create and which theoretically offered the Sandinistas a chance to come back to office. This meant in effect supporting the Chamorro government's reconciliation platform. On the other hand, the same government was pursuing a "liberal" economic program that followed and even exceeded the standard structural adjustment requirements laid down by the international banks and the U.S. AID — wreaking havoc on a population that had already suffered ten years of war and economic blockade.

As a price for their support the Sandinistas placed two demands on Chamorro's government: respect for the agrarian and urban reforms carried out over the previous decade, and no upsetting of the command structure of the police and the armed forces. The point was to provide economic and security guarantees for all who had benefited from the revolution. An understanding was reached with the Chamorro government, which was willing to strike bargains in order to buy time and stability.

The deal was unacceptable to Chamorro's partisan coalition. Most members of her electoral ticket, including Virgilio Godoy, the vice president, and Alfredo Cesar, the president of the legislature, demanded that the government proceed swiftly and drastically against the FSLN and its legacy, instead of slowly and in stages as strategized by Antonio Lacayo, Chamorro's son-in-law and virtual prime minister. By the end of 1991 the FSLN and the old UNO coalition legislators had switched places, the first becoming a supporter of the government and the latter its strongest opposition.

In the legislature the right-wing parties repeatedly came close to pushing through an agrarian-counter-reform bill and opening the way for all the old owners to reclaim their property in the courts. No less than one out of four Nicaraguans were threatened with being dislodged from their homes, urban lots or farms.

Evidently, more was at stake than simply the property issue. For months the extreme right and the United States had been demanding that the government assume a tougher stance against the Sandinistas. There was little tolerance for what the rightists termed the "co-government" between Lacayo and the Sandinistas, where differences were negotiated and concessions made and offered.

The abrupt attempt by the UNO coalition to defy the heart of the major changes of the last ten years forced the Sandinistas to match their negotiation efforts with public pressure on the streets. In what could perhaps become a new modality of post-Cold War revolutionary strategy, negotiations and mass actions were interwoven, as the FSLN learned that the two were not always mutually exclusive: to reduce itself to traditional political party opposition tactics — as some in the FSLN demanded — was to wage battle with one hand tied behind its back. But to take up purely confrontational stances more appropriate for a liberation movement — as other Sandinistas demanded — was to risk antagonizing other segments of the population whose support could be crucial in an electoral contest.

If the government caved in to the right-wing pressure on the property question, as it was ideologically inclined to do, a social explosion was sure to occur. If the cooperatives and industries now in the hands of workers' collectives were to be returned, this meant in effect that a counter-revolutionary economic structure was being implanted which in time would reverse the revolutionary leverage and consciousness established since the overthrow of Somoza.

To many the stakes at hand were much greater than those at the moment of the election: the FSLN had lost the election, but if it lost on the property question (and on the military one), then the Revolution was also being buried.

A reversal of the agrarian reform entailed a loss of political and economic space for the popular sectors — in effect it meant the United States and the old right would achieve by economic means what they had failed to do by military and electoral means. Defending popular interests entailed defending a model of popular participation in the economy. A considerable gain in this regard was for the Sandinista-influenced National Labor Federation to have secured, following two general strikes, governmental recognition for collective property rights for workers and farmers of state enterprises in the process of privatization.

The view of the United States of course was that privatization should work to the benefit of individual private enterprise, that is to say to the benefit of the already wealthy who were eager to acquire properties. For the FSLN the issue was one of economic democracy. The gains of the revolution were expressed in new forms of social and economic organization sustained by material holdings; were those material holdings to disappear, so too people's capacity to organize and sustain a non-capitalist consciousness would be undermined, unless people themselves rallied to defend their acquired rights.

The fundamental contradiction has yet to be resolved, and perhaps it is in the interests both of the socialist-minded model of most Sandinistas, and of the neo-liberal capitalist model of the government, that it should not be resolved at the expense of total social and political breakdown from which both would suffer. Sectors in the United States and on the extreme right, of course, were willing to take that risk. Judging by the severity of the economic crisis, and the spontaneous mass response to the right-wing offensive, there is new hope that moderation will prevail. The question is: who will define the terms of moderation, of reconciliation?

Back to the Cold War in Washington

Much of the ambiguity of the first two years of the Chamorro government was traceable to its prolonged honeymoon with the Bush administration. The Nicaraguan government soothed the administration in Washington in the same way it tried to placate the FSLN: telling them what they wanted to hear about the property question and the security forces. The promises to the Sandinistas, were, of course, irreconcilable with the promise of sure but gradual change made to Washington.

During the honeymoon, the Chamorro government received the political and financial benefits of the doubt. Over the course of this period the Bush administration, represented in low-key fashion by Ambassador Harry Schlaudeman, had as a principal objective the steady reduction in influence of the Sandinista Front, which remained the largest and most coherent political organization in Nicaragua. This meant shoring up the Chamorro government and the right-wing private sector to compete and eventually eradicate Sandinista influence.

The U.S. has been successful in helping the government achieve relative economic stability. Foreign assistance, of which the U.S. is by far the largest provider, explains current monetary stability and the boom in commerce; nonetheless national production and private investment has lagged far behind. This poses a problem for the U.S. inasmuch as it has no intention of indefinitely sustaining its relatively large subsidy to Nicaragua.

Neither is the U.S. happy with the political return on its investment. The Chamorro government has tended to insure political stability by securing Sandinista support at the expense of the right-wing parties in the UNO coalition. By mid-1992 there were unmistakable signs that the Bush administration had lost its patience with this arrangement.

In Washington's view, the danger was that the "co-governing" arrangement threatened to become permanent. Evidently this did not fit in with the new world order, particularly in an election year when the Bush administration found itself hostage to the clamor of the old pro-contra bloc in Congress.

Still professing general support for the Chamorro government, the Bush administration either exploited or promoted Congressional objections, led by Senator Jesse Helms, to the appropriation of funds that had already been authorized by the Executive. Helms openly denounced the Chamorro government as a mere puppet of the Sandinista Front and claimed that U.S. monies were being squandered and channeled to Sandinista organizations.

In essence, the U.S. sought to undermine the working relationship between the Sandinista Front and the government — a relationship which had entailed costs and benefits for each. By June of 1992 the Nicaraguan government began hurriedly returning properties, including some which had belonged to Somoza family interests. Furthermore, police and army units were ordered to occupy and evict workers who were in control of property still under dispute or which they refused to give up.

These actions amounted, in many cases, to clear violations of the FSLN-backed agreements signed between the government and the principal unions some months earlier. The government was also going back on its promise not to admit any Somoza-related property claims. In practical terms this meant giving the large capitalists the security guarantees that they were demanding, including the reversal of accords with organized labor and the Sandinista Front.

In September 1992 the government sacked the Sandinista chief of police and dismissed six top police officials, all in the hope of placating the Bush administration and Senator Helms. Sandinista leaders were furious at the cave-in, but there was little they could do about it. Washington stepped up demands for the head of the chief of the army and Daniel Ortega's brother, General Humberto Ortega. Quite clearly, the United States continued to insist that it was more important to insure the loyalty of armies than of governments in its own backyard. The Chamorro government, for its part, insisted that substantive "reorganizations" were underway, and that countries like Spain were providing support for the "professionalization" of the security forces. The battle was on not only for the top posts but for the "hearts and minds" of the military and police bodies which, by and large, continued to feel an identification with the poor and the Sandinista cause. And unless the government disbanded the entire police and army, the likelihood is that one Sandinista officer would replace another.

During a one-day visit to Managua in January 1992, Secretary of State Baker had been typically blunt in spelling out U.S. terms to Chamorro. Capitalist investment required respect for private property, respect was the product of security, and security could only be attained by a "non-partisan" security force. In other words, until and unless the economic structural adjustment was complemented with a political and security adjustment, then a capitalist recovery and stability could not be attained. After two years of struggle and negotiation, one could come to the conclusion that the Sandinista revolution, while weakened, had not been reversed — rather, its multifaceted influence in Nicaraguan civil and political society had served to impede the U.S. and the government from advancing as rapidly as wished in imposing its new world agenda on Nicaragua and on the Sandinista Front itself.

42

"The Only War We've Got": Anti-Drug Campaigns in Washington's Latin America Strategy

Jo-Marie Burt and Ricardo Soberón

"*The Latin American drug war is the only war we've got.*"[1] These words, spoken in 1989 by General Maxwell Thurman, then head of the Panama-based U.S. Southern Command, signaled a fundamental shift in U.S.-Latin American relations. The Cold War — which dominated Washington's perspective toward Latin America for over forty years — was officially over, and a new war — the "war on drugs" — had begun.

In the 1980s, drug abuse had become a critical domestic problem in the U.S. Cocaine abuse was on the upswing, and violence attributed to drug use had reached alarming levels. George Bush stated in the 1988 presidential campaign that drug abuse was "the toughest domestic challenge we've faced in decades." Arguing that the "cheapest and safest way to eradicate narcotics is to destroy them at their source," Bush promised to "wipe out crops wherever they are grown and take out processing labs wherever they exist."[2] Under the Bush administration, U.S. policy toward Latin America — focused in the 1980s on Central America and the "communist threat" — shifted toward the Andean region, where 90% of the world's coca leaf, the main raw ingredient in the processing of cocaine, is grown.[3]

The Bush administration announced its new drug control strategy in September 1989. Under the Andean Initiative, $2.2 billion was to be allocated over a five-year period to Peru, Colombia and Bolivia to combat drug production and shipping. The Andean militaries were to be the main allies of the U.S. in the upcoming battle against drug trafficking, reflecting a dramatic reorientation of U.S.-Latin American military relations. Total U.S. military assistance to the Andes increased six-fold between 1989 and 1990 (see table 1). By 1990, the Andean government and armies had become the largest recipient of U.S. military and economic aid in all of Latin America.

Table 1

ANDEAN STRATEGY NARCOTICS-RELATED FUNDING (in millions of dollars)							
	FY 1989 Actual	FY 1990 Estimate[1]	FY 1991 Request	FY 1992 Plan	FY 1993 Plan	FY 1994 Plan	Total 5-Year Plan
COLOMBIA:							
Military Assistance[2]	$8.6	$40.3	$60.5	$60.5	$60.5	$60.5	$282.3
Economic Assistance	$0.0	$3.6	$50.0	$50.0	$50.0	$50.0	$203.6
Law Enforcement[3]	$10.0	$20.0	$20.0	$20.0	$20.0	$20.0	$100.0
DEA Support	$4.2	$4.4	$4.4	$4.4	$4.4	$4.4	$22.0
TOTAL	$22.8	$68.3	$134.9	$134.9	$134.9	$134.9	$607.9
PERU:							
Military Assistance[2]	$2.6	$36.5	$39.9	$39.9	$39.9	$39.9	$196.1
Economic Assistance	$1.3	$4.3	$63.1	$103.1	$103.1	$103.1	$376.7
Law Enforcement	$10.5	$19.0	$19.0	$19.0	$19.0	$19.0	$95.0
DEA Support	$4.3	$6.8	$6.8	$6.8	$6.8	$6.8	$34.0
TOTAL	$18.7	$66.6	$128.8	$168.8	$168.8	$168.8	$701.8
BOLIVIA:							
Military Assistance[2]	$5.8	$33.7	$40.9	$40.9	$40.9	$40.9	$197.3
Economic Assistance	$4.0	$40.7	$95.8	$130.8	$130.8	$130.8	$528.9
Law Enforcement[3]	$10.0	$15.7	$15.7	$15.7	$15.7	$15.7	$78.5
DEA Support	$4.0	$6.6	$6.6	$6.6	$6.6	$6.6	$33.0
TOTAL	$23.8	$96.7	$159.0	$194.0	$194.0	$194.0	$837.7
TOTAL ASSISTANCE:							
Military Assistance[2]	$17.0	$110.5	$141.3	$141.3	$141.3	$141.3	$675.7
Economic Assistance	$5.3	$48.6	$208.9	$283.9	$283.9	$283.9	$1,109.2
Law Enforcement[3]	$30.5	$54.7	$54.7	$54.7	$54.7	$54.7	$273.5
DEA Support	$12.5	$17.8	$17.8	$17.8	$17.8	$17.8	$89.0
GRAND TOTAL	$65.3	$231.6	$422.7	$497.7	$497.7	$497.7	$2,147.4

1. The obligations projected for FY 1990 are approximate and adjustments may be made during the course of the year. They include Byrd Amendment reductions.

2. Military assistance includes both Foreign Military Financing (FMF) and International Military Education and Training (IMET). FY 1990 IMET projections are: Colombia, $1.5 million; Peru, $0.5 million; and Bolivia, $0.5 million. FY 1991 IMET projections are: Colombia, $2.5 million; Peru, $0.9 million; and Bolivia, $0.9 million.

3. The Law Enforcement category for FY 1990 includes $38.2 million in International Narcotics Matters (INM) funds as well as a portion ($16.5 million) of the $125 million in FMF appropriated for counternarcotics programs in Section 602 of the Foreign Operations, Export Financing, and Related Programs Act for FY 1990.

Office of National Drug Control Policy — June 20, 1990

Rather than focus on preventive measures at home such as education and treatment, the Bush administration invested millions of dollars on a military strategy in the jungles of South America that — presumably — was intended to resolve the problem of drug abuse by reducing the available amount of drugs on U.S. streets. Each year between 1988 and 1992, approximately 70% of funds allocated by the Bush administration to the drug war were invested in supply-reduction efforts, primarily overseas.[4] And at home, more money was spent on increased police forces and prisons than on treatment and drug prevention. The "war on drugs," as the very terminology suggests, is conceived of principally as a criminal problem requiring police and military intervention; drug abuse is considered only secondarily as a problem of health and education.

Yet, the feasibility of a supply-side approach to combating domestic drug abuse has been seriously questioned from the start.[5] Drug abuse is essentially a problem of consumption, not supply, according to most analysts. The logic of the marketplace — where there is demand, supply follows — ensures a steady supply of illicit drugs to U.S. consumers. The statistics offered by various government agencies confirm these arguments: three years after the anti-drug Andean initiative was launched, eradication and interdiction had had little impact where it counts most — on U.S. city streets. For example, in a 1991 report, the Drug Enforcement Agency (DEA) noted that high quality cocaine was easily available to U.S. consumers, and that the total production of cocaine had increased from 361 tons in 1988 to 1,100 tons in 1991.[6] Another government agency, the National Institute of Drug Abuse, reported that the number of Americans using cocaine in 1991 increased to 1.9 million (from 1.6 million in 1990) — an 18% increase, despite Bush's intentions to decrease cocaine use by half.[7] Other statistics speak for themselves: hospital emergency rooms have noted a dramatic increase in cocaine- and heroin-related visits; between April and June 1991, 25,370 such visits were registered, a 30% increase from the corresponding period in the previous year.[8]

But the Bush administration's drug policy in the Andes has not only failed to resolve the problem of drug abuse at home. It has also exacerbated conflict in a region marked by high levels of violence, related not only to drug trafficking but also to guerrilla activities and state-sponsored counter-insurgency operations. By establishing counter-narcotics operations in areas where entrenched guerrilla movements operate (principally Peru and Colombia), the U.S. has not only pursued ineffective drug control policies; it has also fed insurgency by focusing on a repressive drug control strategy that alienates local populations and pushes them into the arms of guerrillas willing to protect them from those who would destroy their livelihood. And by seeking out Andean militaries as its main partners in the "drug war," the Bush administration has allied the U.S. with forces known to be involved in egregious human rights abuses as well as drug-related corruption. In Peru, for example, 44% of U.S. training since 1989 has been designated to counter-insurgency units, including the Sinchis, police forces well-known for their human rights abuses.[9] Cases of corruption within the military in all three Andean countries abound.[10]

U.S. counter-narcotics assistance has also created serious tensions between military and police forces in Peru and Bolivia. In Peru, institutional jealousies are notorious between the two forces, and military units have even fired on police forces engaged in counter-narcotics activities. A report of the Inspector General's Office notes that U.S. aid to the Bolivian military was designed to reduce tensions between the police and the military (the latter was angry over substantial U.S. aid to police forces). The same report also notes the fear in Bolivia that a revitalized army might become a threat to fragile democratic institutions and feed human rights abuses and corruption.

Thus, the problem is not only one of limited efficacy in fighting the domestic drug war on the Andean front. It is also a question of the impact of U.S. policy in a region racked by internal conflict, fragile democratic institutions, and abusive and corrupt military forces. Observers have noted several adverse effects of drawing Andean military forces into the U.S. drug war. First, it has assured immunity for members of the military implicated in specific human rights cases — a kind of trade-off for military participation in a mission they do not perceive as their own. Second, it has fostered corruption in the Andean military forces. Given the magnitude of the international drug trade, the danger of corruption is always present; in countries like Peru and Bolivia, where government functionaries who are on the front line of the drug war earn salaries of less than $500 per month, the risk is even greater. Finally, prioritizing the involvement of Andean militaries undermines the U.S. government's own stated objective of promoting democracy in Latin America by strengthening the hand of the military vis-a-vis fragile civilian institutions. Emphasis on the drug war is so intense that the U.S. government has even been willing to justify authoritarian attitudes on the part of Andean governments in the name of pursuing the drug war.[11]

The Evolution of U.S. Drug Policy

In the 1980s, international drug policy was essentially considered a problem of law enforcement. Based on a supply-side approach to combating drug abuse, U.S. policy focused on restricting the supply of illegal drugs in the U.S. by eradicating coca fields, destroying processing labs, and interdicting drug shipments to the U.S. The DEA became actively involved in drug control in the Andes (and elsewhere, most notably Mexico), providing police aid and training. In 1983, the DEA helped establish special counter-narcotics units in Bolivia and Peru, which increasingly looked less like police forces and more like paramilitary squads.

By the mid-1980s, the viability of this law enforcement approach was increasingly questioned in Washington.[12] Local police forces, even with their enhanced paramilitary character, were no match for well-armed drug traffickers. Several Washington policymakers began calling for the participation of U.S. military forces, as well as their Andean counterparts. The first critical step in this direction was Ronald Reagan's signing of a National Security Directive in 1986 that declared drug trafficking a threat to U.S. national security.

The Pentagon initially resisted an increased role in fighting drug trafficking: the mission of the military, it was argued, was to confront challenges to national security; drug trafficking was a criminal issue, to be dealt with by police forces. But public panic over drug abuse meant steady pressure to bring the military into the picture. In 1988, over the objections of Joint Chiefs of Staff Chairman Admiral William Crowe, President Reagan and Congress allocated $439 million to the Defense Department in Fiscal Year

1989 (FY89) for the drug war. But it wasn't until the end of the Cold War —
and the threat of resulting budget cuts — that the U.S. military whole-
heartedly embraced the "war on drugs."

When George Bush assumed the presidency in 1988, it was evident that
the law enforcement approach to combating drug trafficking was far from
successful. Nonetheless, the Bush administration continued to operate under
the assumption that controlling the drug supply was the "cheapest and most
efficient" way of combating drug abuse. Rather than reevaluate the tenets of
this dubious supply-side approach, the Bush administration decided that a
more aggressive military involvement was necessary to match the firepower
of the narcotraffickers. The U.S. military would provide the intelligence,
equipment, and training; the Andean militaries would provide the on-
the-ground forces to attack the drug-trafficking network "at its source."

Under the Bush administration, the U.S. engaged in a steady military
buildup in the Andes. Funds allocated to the Defense Department tripled in
three years from $439 million in FY89 to $1.2 billion in FY92, and the
Pentagon is now the leading Federal agency involved in aerial and maritime
detection of drug traffickers.[13] The U.S. Southern Command (Southcom),
based in Panama, has also been in on the buildup. According to *Newsweek*,
Southcom fields 500 U.S. soldiers in counter-narcotics training and intelligence missions in the Andes (and Central America), with 80 stationed
permanently in Colombia, the home of the world's most powerful drug
mafias. Army Green Berets train police and military forces in Bolivia, Peru
and Colombia in jungle warfare, while Navy Seals offer instructions on
riverine operations. The Army's super-secret counter-terrorist unit, Delta
Force, has allegedly trained the Peruvian Army in counter-insurgency tactics.
Tactical Analysis Teams work with the DEA and the CIA to assemble
dossiers on trafficking organizations, and an impressive network of radars in
the Andean countries has been established to detect air flights.[14] This
impressive buildup made it difficult to believe Bush administration officials
who maintained that the U.S. was not involved in counter-insurgency
operations in the Andes.

A New Enemy: "Narco-Guerrillas"

But militarizing the drug war is only partially due to perceived police failures
and shrinking Pentagon budgets. It also has its roots in the "narco-guerrilla"
theory, which defines drugs as an "external enemy," much as communism was
demonized during the Cold War.[15] And, like the Cold War, the solution is
focused in far-away countries via military involvement. According to the
"narco-guerrilla" theory, guerrillas build up their war booty by protecting
drug traffickers; thus any blow to guerrillas is a blow to traffickers. This
simplified version of reality overlooks several facts. It is true that guerrillas
attempt to benefit from the drug trade: in Peru, the Sendero Luminoso
(Shining Path) guerrilla movement protects peasant growers and acts as
intermediaries with traffickers, ensuring fair prices. But two very different
logics are at work: while Shining Path maintains a strict Marxist-

Leninist-Maoist ideology and rejects the system of capitalist production, the drug cartels are model examples of capitalist accumulation, albeit of illicit origin. The two groups act in concert at times in terms of very specific necessities and interests, but they are neither synonymous nor "partners." Thus, lumping guerrillas and drug traffickers into one category, as the narco-guerrilla theory does, is not only inaccurate; it leads to ineffective and even counterproductive strategies for combating drugs.

More specifically, the narco-guerrilla theory exaggerates the links between guerrilla groups and drug traffickers, and ignores the extensive relationships between traffickers and sectors of the military, especially in drug-producing areas. In the case of Colombia, for example, there are reported links between some guerrilla groups and drug trafficking, principally in terms of war taxes levied on traffickers and coca growers. However, the links between traffickers and right-wing paramilitary squads have been far more extensive: traffickers have joined local landowners in squashing any opposition, with advice, financing and arms provided by the armed forces.[16] And substantial hostility has existed between some guerrilla groups and trafficker organizations.[17]

In Peru, the Shining Path guerrillas are indeed involved in the drug trade. However, their involvement is not focused on drug production itself; rather, they act as intermediaries, protecting local farmers — for a fee, or "war tax" — from abusive security forces, government functionaries in charge of coca eradication, and drug traffickers. By ensuring "fair" prices for farmers, Shining Path has assured itself a solid social base. However, this cuts into the profits of the traffickers, which has led to serious conflicts of interests between the two groups. At the same time, the grave economic situation in Peru makes it difficult to succeed with an essentially repressive counter-narcotics program that is not complemented by effective development programs. The Peruvian military itself has argued that counter-insurgency and anti-narcotics production operations are incompatible: it is impossible to gain the support of the local population — crucial to undercut their support for the Shining Path — by attacking the economic base of the region through anti-narcotics operations.[18] And, like Colombia, there are important ties between drug traffickers and the Peruvian armed forces: it is the military that allows traffickers to use public airstrips (for a hefty fee), and the Peruvian military has actually attempted to impede anti-narcotics activities on several occasions.[19] In one of the most notorious incidents, military units fired on local police and DEA agents engaged in anti-narcotics operations in the Upper Huallaga Valley.[20]

Conceptual Flaws, Different Realities

The tragic statistics of continued cocaine abuse in the U.S. attest to the failure of a militarized strategy to control drug supply abroad. The Bush administration argued that more time was needed, and that failures were due to Congressional interference. Using McCarthyite tactics, Bush administration officials even suggested that Congress members who opposed its Andean strategy were "soft on drugs" and tacitly supported drug traffickers.[21] But the problem is neither too little aid nor too little military involvement. In reality, the problem lies in the conceptual flaws of the Bush administration's overall drug control strategy.

The supply-side approach. Experts on international drug policy have long considered a supply-side approach to controlling drug abuse to be fundamentally flawed.[22] Market mechanisms, they argue, provide a powerful stimulus for the drug trade which is driven principally by consumer demand for drugs, rather than by the available supply of drugs.

Moreover, suppressing the supply of cocaine is a difficult if not impossible task. On the international market, agricultural products from the Third World cannot compete against subsidized goods from the industrialized world. Coca is virtually the only crop that is economically feasible in countries like Peru and Bolivia where more than fifty percent of the population lives in a state of critical poverty. This situation explains the fact that when coca is eradicated in one area, farmers go further into the jungle to grow it, and when trade routes are cut off, new ones are established. A U.S. embassy official in Peru conceded that eradication and interdiction efforts have been ineffective: "anti-narcotics operations undertaken with the support of the armed forces have led to the dispersion of laboratories and coca cultivation zones in the Upper Huallaga Valley."[23] Anti-narcotics measures have not, in fact, eliminated the underlying causes of illegal coca production. Instead, they have fostered the proliferation of coca growing areas and the laboratories used to process the coca leaf into paste and eventually into cocaine.[24]

The drug trade is stimulated by a deep economic crisis in the Andean region, where farmers earn up to ten times as much growing coca leaves than for any licit crop. In addition, coca is an easy, inexpensive crop to grow, and it has a secure market. Unlike traditional crops like corn, which require land rotation and have only one harvest per year, coca has four harvests yearly, and does not require rotation. Coca brings higher prices than any other traditional crop, and does not require traveling to distant markets to sell. As one Peruvian coca farmer stated: "The buyers come to the farm to take the coca leaves. If I grow another crop, I have to take it to the marketplace and spend money in transport. That doesn't happen with coca."[25]

Moreover, apparent successes in controlling the drug supply abroad — and feeling the effect on U.S. streets — have been short-lived. For example, in mid-1990, as a result of the Colombian government's offensive against the powerful Medellín cartel, the price of the coca leaf dropped substantially in production areas like the Upper Huallaga Valley in Peru and the Chapare in Bolivia. Pointing to lower coca prices in the Andes and higher cocaine prices in the U.S., then Drug "Czar" William Bennett declared that the drug war was being won. This was the effect sought by the U.S. and its Andean allies according to the Declaration of Cartagena signed in February 1990:

> . . . an integral struggle against drug trafficking will drastically alter the market for coca and its derivations and will reduce the price paid for them. To the extent that this struggle is successful, those who dedicate themselves to the cultivation of coca

and its paste will seek to supplement their income either by crop substitution or seeking new jobs. We will collaborate toward the objective of finding activities financed internationally to produce these alternative incomes.

However, within eight months coca prices climbed steadily back up, and cocaine prices fell. The problem was two-fold. In the Andes, a viable crop substitution program — including a secure marketplace — was not forthcoming, and farmers were forced to sell their coca crops at lower prices.[26] To recuperate lost income, farmers had little option but to *expand* their coca cultivation, and some began elaborating coca paste. In the meantime, in the U.S., cocaine prices dropped within a year of the offensive against the Medellín cartel, as rival cartels filled the gap in supply. As former Colombian President Virgilio Barco once said, the only law that narcotraffickers comply with — religiously — is the law of supply and demand.[27]

The militarization of drug control policy. The Andean Initiative has also been criticized for prioritizing a militaristic approach to what is essentially a social and economic problem. As mentioned above, the Bush administration oversaw an unprecedented military buildup in the Andes, and it actively solicited the involvement of local military forces in the "war on drugs." Several observers have pointed out the dangers of involving local military institutions in the U.S. anti-drug effort. By bringing the military in, the U.S. sends the message that it has more confidence in the capacity of the military to handle the international drug problem than in traditional law enforcement agencies such as the police and the court system. It also strengthens the hand of militaries known for their human rights abuses and corruption, with dire consequences for fragile democratic systems.[28]

The Bush administration indicated that it was indeed willing to overlook the abusive human rights record of the Andean militaries as long as they were willing to participate in its drug war.[29] In July 1991, President Bush issued a determination that Peru met the human rights conditions necessary to receive U.S. anti-narcotics-related assistance.[30] The determination stated that "neither we nor major human rights groups within Peru believe that the democratically elected government of Peru is engaged in a consistent pattern of gross violations of internationally recognized human rights." The National Human Rights Coordinating Committee, a coalition of Peru's principal human rights organizations, immediately expressed their consternation to the U.S. embassy:

Your own State Department Report pointed out that in 1990 the number of extrajudicial executions and forced disappearances increased and that not a single member of the Armed Forces has been convicted of such practices in the eleven years of violence that our country has suffered. The situation of impunity has continued under the Fujimori government . . . [H]uman rights violations are not isolated events — as could happen anywhere in the world — but are the result of a pattern of conduct consistently used by the security forces, whose Commander-in-Chief is, constitutionally, the President of the Republic . . .[31]

In response to the Peruvian military's poor human rights record — as well as the Bush administration's signal of bad faith — Congress suspended the 1991 anti-narcotics aid package earmarked for Peru until President Fujimori announced a series of measures to improve the human rights situation just prior to a visit to Washington in September 1991.[32] Congress lifted the freeze on the aid package, but continued to withhold $10 million destined to the Peruvian Army, the "most notorious abuser of human rights among the security forces,"[33] until further human rights conditions were met.

It is difficult not to draw the conclusion that in insisting on sending anti-narcotics aid to Peru, more than the drug war was at stake. The Shining Path guerrilla movement seemed to be steadily gaining ground to the point that, by early 1992, there was fear in Washington that they could take Lima within a year. This contrasted dramatically with a government and state that seemed on the verge of collapse. In this context, the U.S. had much at stake in Peru beyond the drug war: a Shining Path victory could destabilize the entire region. During Congressional hearings on Peru in early 1992, Bernard Aronson, then Assistant Secretary of State for Inter-American Affairs, compared Shining Path to the genocidal regimes of Hitler and Pol Pot. Arguing for increased U.S. involvement in Peru, Aronson stated:

> Sendero Luminoso is unlike any other insurgent or terrorist group that has ever operated in Latin America . . . Make no mistake: if Sendero were to take power, we would see this century's third genocide . . . [T]he programs we support in Peru today are not counter-insurgency programs . . . *But they also contribute to strengthening the government's economic, administrative, and military capacity to confront and defeat Sendero* . . . [T]here is a case for closer engagement with Peru. The plain fact is that while drug trafficking is our top interest in Peru, the Sendero Luminoso [sic] is a direct threat to the government's survival. *Peru's insurgencies threaten more than democracy and prosperity — they pose serious obstacles to all aspects of an effective counter-narcotics strategy . . . They threaten democracy in Latin America and the prospects for regional economic integration and trade.*[34]

The Bush administration may not have intended to get involved in the war against Sendero in Peru. Nonetheless, the logic of a militarized drug war brought it to the point where it justified closer involvement with the Peruvian military in *its* primary mission — subduing the Maoist guerrilla movement — in the name of fighting the drug war.[35]

Different priorities in the U.S. and the Andes. The Bush administration's Andean strategy has also been criticized for failing to consider the vastly different priorities pursued by the U.S. and the Andean nations, as well as the often contradictory objectives pursued by different institutions within both the U.S. and the Andean countries. Within the U.S., a fragmented policy process — originally designed to prevent the accumulation of power in one branch of government — often means that different agencies, and even the separate wings of government, are pursuing very different objectives. The drug war has been no exception. Congress has been more concerned with issues related to human rights than the Executive branch, as the Bush administration's certification of Peru in 1991 suggests. The DEA has often been at odds with the Defense Department, as each has a different conception of how the drug war should be fought and what objectives need to be prioritized. Within the Andean governments, similar institutional conflicts exist, particularly between the military and police forces. With such contradictory objectives and conceptions, finding a coherent strategy in combating drug trafficking is highly problematic. It is even more complicated given the vastly different priorities of the U.S. government and the governments of Peru, Bolivia and Colombia.

Perhaps the greatest point of divergence between the U.S. and its would-be Andean allies lies in the terrain of the economy. For the U.S., drug trafficking is the cause of serious social problems, and it does not provide important economic benefits. For the Andean countries, however, particularly Peru and Bolivia, the drug trade provides critical resources at a time when these countries are experiencing the worst economic crisis in their history. The crisis — marked by massive under-employment, a serious recession of the productive apparatus, and the collapse of productive sectors such as mining and agriculture — has been further exacerbated by economic adjustment programs that in the long term promise to cure overly protectionist economies but in the short term lead to increased unemployment and aggravate the recession. In this context, it is not difficult to understand the hesitancy on the part of Andean governments over coming down too hard on drug trafficking. In Peru alone, the drug trade provides over $1 billion a year in revenue, at a time when inflation, recession, and other ills threaten to undermine the country's political stability, already jarred by a powerful guerrilla movement that has cost the country $23 billion in losses (a sum larger than Peru's foreign debt). Defeating the drug trade would not only undermine these countries' economies, it would also create social unrest among the tens of thousands of peasants who depend on coca production for their livelihood. Neo-liberal economic policies — ironically touted by the U.S. as the solution to the region's economic problems — exacerbate the problem: in Bolivia in the mid-1980s, thousands of miners were laid off; many found their only economic refuge in the Chapare region growing coca.

Despite these different priorities, Andean governments are forced to play the U.S. drug game because they desperately need economic aid, even if it is directed primarily toward balance-of-payment supports to help balance government budgets and meet international debt payments rather than toward economic development programs.[36] The Bush administration took advantage of the vulnerability of Andean governments in this regard, tying future economic aid to cooperation in the drug war in Peru and the eradication of coca crops in Bolivia. The contradictions of U.S. policy are notable in this regard: while the U.S. has argued that the Andean nations require solid economies (read: IMF-style structural adjustment programs), it has linked economic assistance more to cooperation in the drug war than to objective economic necessities in the Andes.

But the problem is not only economic: the region is also plagued by entrenched guerrilla movements which have masterfully played upon peasant discontent in the wake of police eradication programs to win local support. The contradiction is most clear in Peru, where the military has repeatedly stated that its main priority is combating the Shining Path guerrillas, not the drug war.[37] As Peruvian Army General Mario Brito, who briefly headed the Political-Military Command in the Upper Huallaga Valley until he was seriously wounded in an ambush by another guerrilla group, the Tupac Amaru Revolutionary Movement (MRTA), stated:

> If we attack drug trafficking, we will turn the local population into our enemy. Then instead of one enemy, Shining Path, we will have three: Shining Path, the local population who will then support [them], and the drug traffickers, who will then provide [them] with resources.[38]

The main priority of the Peruvian military — as well as its counterpart in Colombia, which has been combating various guerrilla groups for over thirty years — is counter-insurgency, not the drug war. The U.S. has clashed with the Peruvian military over this issue on more than one occasion.[39] And as noted above, fighting on both fronts is not only counterproductive; it may actually feed drug trafficking *and* insurgent movements.

By focusing on an essentially repressive approach to controlling drug supply in the Andes, the U.S. has involved itself in volatile regional conflicts that are unlikely to end anytime soon. We do not believe that the Bush administration cynically invented the drug war as a cover to intervene in civil conflicts in Peru and Colombia.[40] Yet, it should be noted that the U.S. has committed itself in word and deed to counter-insurgency wars in both countries. In July 1991, the Bush administration signed a bilateral agreement with the Peruvian government which specifically commits the U.S. to the war against Shining Path based on the premise that counter-insurgency is a justifiable part of counter-narcotics activities. In Colombia, U.S. assistance earmarked for anti-narcotics efforts has been used for counter-insurgency operations unrelated to anti-narcotics activities, despite the specifications of the International Narcotics Control Act of 1990.[41] And in Bolivia, where no insurgent group of significance is active, some U.S. military officials view the strengthening of the armed forces and the repression of the coca trade as essential to *precluding* future guerrilla activity.[42]

Conclusion: A New Agenda

The U.S. "drug war" is based on the mistaken premise that a pressing domestic issue can be resolved militarily in the far-away jungles of South America. It fails to consider the vastly different priorities of the Andean governments whose armies have been designated by the U.S. to fight this "drug war," and it ignores the essence of the economic and social problems faced by Peru, Bolivia and Colombia that feed drug trafficking. By focusing on the Andean armies as its main allies in the drug war, the U.S. has militarized Andean society and in many cases further exacerbated the violence in the region. It has also allied the U.S. with corrupt and brutal military forces. Finally, by committing U.S. agencies to fighting the drug war at all costs, U.S. policy runs the risk of assuming other commitments — such as fighting a counter-insurgency war in Peru — that could prove quite costly and difficult to abandon in the not-too-distant future.

Drug abuse in the U.S. is essentially a problem of economics and public health that needs to be addressed in terms of broader preventive programs and treatment and rehabilitation centers. Drug trafficking in the Andes is, at its core, a social and economic problem that needs to be addressed via solid development programs that give local farmers real alternatives to growing coca as well as humane economic policies that do not overlook the social costs of macro-economic "adjustments." It is toward these priorities that an effective U.S. counter-narcotics policy must be directed. Otherwise, for Andean farmers, the incentive for growing an illicit crop will continue to exist, and, for Andean governments, the objective need for the drug economy will continue to exist. And without considering the complexities of Andean realities, any U.S. policy is bound to exacerbate problems related to violence, drug trafficking, and weak democratic institutions.

It is time for a new agenda in U.S. drug control policy. With the election of Democrat Bill Clinton in 1992, there is an historic opportunity to reevaluate old policies, and reorient Washington's approach to dealing with a devastating domestic problem. The first priority should be at home: urban development and jobs to improve life chances in inner cities, and more programs focused on drug prevention and treatment. Insofar as the U.S. continues to be involved in fighting the drug front in Latin America, it should de-emphasize military involvement, and focus on an integrated approach that considers the "Four D's": democracy, development, drugs, and debt. Without considering each of these aspects in a holistic manner, U.S. international drug policy is bound to fail. Without development alternatives drug control policy cannot move forward. Without debt relief, dependence on the drug economy will likely grow in the Andes. And supporting a militaristic policy that endangers fragile democratic regimes in the name of the war on drugs is, in the final instance, ultimately self-defeating. The Clinton administration has the opportunity to forge a new Andean policy based on common concerns between the U.S. and its Andean allies. Without a truly multilateral strategy that considers local priorities and problems, U.S. drug policy in the Andes is destined to end in failure at home and disaster abroad.

Notes

1. As cited by Coletta Youngers, "The War in the Andes: The Military Role in U.S. International Drug Policy," Washington Office on Latin America Briefing Series on International Drug Policy, December 14, 1990. This statement was made prior to the Iraqi invasion of Kuwait and the subsequent Gulf War. While several observers have noted that the Gulf War signified a shift in U.S. military priorities, it was a temporary one. Moreover, U.S. involvement in the Latin American "drug war" has continued to escalate since the Gulf War.

2. As cited in Peter Andreas, Eva Bertram, Morris Blackman, and Kenneth Sharpe, "Dead-End Drug Wars," *Foreign Policy*, Winter 1991–1992, p. 108.

3. The coca leaf has been an integral part of Andean highland culture for centuries. Coca is used for ritual as well as medicinal purposes, and it is an important source of reciprocity as well as a form of payment. With the growth in demand for cocaine in the U.S. and Europe, coca production expanded rapidly in Peru and Bolivia, from about 50,000 acres in 1974 to approximately 500,000 acres in 1989.

4. For figures between fiscal year 1988 (FY88) and FY92, see table 1A in *Clear and Present Dangers: The U.S. Military and the War on Drugs in the Andes*, Washington Office on Latin America, 1991, p. 8; figures for FY93 cited by Andreas et. al, op. cit.

5. See for example Peter Andreas and Coletta Youngers, "U.S. Drug Policy and the Andean Cocaine Industry," *World Policy Journal*, Summer 1989, pp. 529–561.

6. "WOLA Declares Anti-Drug Strategy Fundamentally Flawed," Press Release, Washington Office on Latin America, February 25, 1992.

7. "The Newest War," *Newsweek*, January 6, 1992.

8. *Washington Post*, December 19, 1991, pp. 1, 4.

9. General Accounting Office, "U.S. Programs in Peru Face Serious Obstacles," October 1991, GAO/NSIAD–92–36.

10. *Clear and Present Dangers*, p. 101.

11. The U.S. immediately cut off all but humanitarian assistance to Peru in the wake of President Fujimori's "self-inflicted" coup in April 1992. However, after Fujimori held elections for a Constituent Assembly — primarily to win acceptance by the international community, which had cut off aid in the wake of the coup — the U.S. re-established most counter-narcotics assistance to Peru. Yet, few observers would argue that democratic rule has been restored: the autonomy of the Congress vis-a-vis the Executive is dubious, and the judicial system is under the virtual tutelage of Fujimori and his entourage. Yet, in the name of continuing its anti-drug efforts in Peru, the Bush administration has chosen to overlook these "details" by reinstating U.S. assistance. For an analysis of the April 1992 coup, see Jo-Marie Burt, "Peru: Facade of Democracy Crumbles," *Report on the Americas* 26:1, North American Congress on Latin America (NACLA), July 1992.

12. For a more extensive analysis of the evolution of U.S. policy, see Coletta Youngers, "The War in the Andes," op. cit.

13. The number of hours of U.S. Atlantic Commission planes engaged in drug flights has increased seven-fold in two years (1989: 5,400 hours of drug flights; 1991: 37,000 hours). "The Newest War," *Newsweek*, January 6, 1992.

14. Ibid.

15. This section draws on the excellent analysis of the narco-guerrilla theory presented in chapter 3 of *Clear and Present Dangers*.

16. See "Colombia Beseiged: Political Violence and State Responsibility," Washington Office on Latin America, International Drug Policy Brief #3, May 1991.

17. For example, in 1981, following the kidnapping of Martha Nieves Ochoa, sister of a leading Medellín cartel leader by the guerrilla group M-19, the cartels and local landowners created a paramilitary death squad, "Muerte a Secuestradores" (MAS — "Death to Kidnappers"), in retaliation. MAS was responsible for numerous killings throughout the 1980s of union and peasant leaders suspected of supporting the guerrillas. See *Clear and Present Dangers*, pp. 58–61.

18. High-ranking Peruvian military officers stationed in the Upper Huallaga Valley have even expressed open support for coca growers' federations in order to win over the local population from the Shining Path guerrillas. In Uchiza, the military under the leadership of Army Gen. Alberto Arciniegas was able to regain the population's confidence only after it promised to allow coca cultivation and prohibited the police (in charge of eradication programs and feared for their frequent abuse of farmers) from operating in the area. There have been serious clashes between the U.S. government and the Peruvian military over this issue.

19. Even after Fujimori's coup in April 1992, when he ordered that personnel of the Peruvian Air Force take over all airports in the Upper Huallaga Valley, drug traffickers continue using public airstrips regularly.

20. *Clear and Present Dangers*, pp. 63–64.

21. *Washington Post*, September 18, 1991. It is interesting to note that Fujimori used the same arguments when he dissolved Congress and the Judicial branch in April 1992.

22. See especially Coletta Youngers, "The War in the Andes: The Military Role in U.S. International Drug Policy," and Peter Andreas et. al., "Dead-End Drug Wars."

23. Interview by author as cited in Ricardo Soberón, "The War on Cocaine in Peru: From Cartagena to San Antonio," Washington Office on Latin America, Issues in International Drug Policy Brief #6, August 7, 1992.

24. Known as the "balloon effect," this dispersion of illegal drug production has occurred in previous anti-narcotics campaigns in Turkey and Mexico. In the Andean drug war, drug production has become increasingly decentralized and has shifted from Colombia to Peru and Bolivia, while processing and trans-shipment have increased significantly in Brazil, Venezuela, and Ecuador. *Clear and Present Dangers*, p. 105.

25. Liz Mineo, "La coca prospera mientras fracasan las políticas," *Expreso*, December 25, 1992, pp. 12–13.

26. *Drug Trafficking Update*, Andean Commission of Jurists, Lima, August 14, 1990 and October 9, 1990.

27. As cited by Róger Rumrill, "El mayor estimulante del narcotrafico," *La República*, November 18, 1992.

28. Bolivia and Peru have suffered frequent alternations between civilian and military rule since independence from Spain. While Colombia has lived under a stable civilian regime for over thirty years, the military retains important reserves of power via state-of-siege decrees, declared almost perpetually over the past three decades. The self-declared coup of Peruvian President Fujimori in 1992, with the explicit support of the armed forces, would seem to confirm this hypothesis.

29. The militaries of Peru, Colombia and Bolivia have all been implicated in the systematic abuse of internationally recognized human rights. For specifics on each country, see: *Colombia Besieged: Political Violence and State Responsibility* (Washington Office on Latin America, 1989); *In Desperate Straits: Human Rights in Peru After a Decade of Democracy and Insurgency* (Americas Watch, 1990); and *Bolivia: Neoliberalismo y derechos humanos* (Comision Andina de Juristas, 1988).

30. The International Narcotics Control Act of 1990 stipulates that prior to receiving U.S. anti-narcotics related security assistance for FY91 to any Andean country, the president must issue a determination that security forces in each country are not involved in the systematic violation of human rights, allows the investigation of alleged human rights abuses, and the government has control over police and military forces.

31. Letter by Peru's National Human Rights Coordinating Committee to the U.S. Ambassador to Peru, dated August 1, 1991, published as Appendix C in Coletta Youngers, "Peru Under Scrutiny: Human Rights and U.S. Drug Policy," Washington Office on Latin America, Issues in International Drug Policy Brief #5, January 13, 1992.

32. Several observers have noted that Fujimori announced these measures precisely to convince the U.S. Congress of his good intentions toward improving the government's human rights records in order to obtain U.S. funding. Sadly, however, the announced policies have not been fully implemented, and the human rights situation has continued to deteriorate. See Coletta Youngers, "Peru Under Scrutiny: Human Rights and U.S. Drug Policy."

33. Letter by U.S. Senators Patrick Leahy and Christopher Dodd to Assistant Secretary of State Lawrence Eagleberger, dated September 24, 1991.

34. Statement of Bernard W. Aronson, Assistant Secretary of State for Inter-American Affairs before the Subcommittee on Western Hemisphere Affairs, House Committee on Foreign Affairs, March 12, 1992: emphasis added.

35. The situation has changed since the September 1992 capture of Shining Path leader Abimael Guzman and the capture or death of other key Shining Path leaders. For the first time, Shining Path military actions do not correspond to a clear political strategy, and while few observers suggest that the movement has been completely defeated, it is no longer considered an imminent threat to the existence of the Peruvian state. It is too soon to tell how the U.S. will interpret this event, and whether it will modify its policy in response.

36. In FY91, U.S. aid figures to Peru were broken down as follows:
$24.85 million in U.S. military assistance;
$52.7 million toward the Peruvian budget deficit;
$4.5 million toward small industry aid programs; and
$1.9 million for development projects in the Huallaga region.

37. For an excellent account of Shining Path involvement in the main coca-growing regions of Peru, and the subsequent contradictions in anti-drug and counter-insurgency policy, see José E. Gonzales, "Guerrillas and Coca in the Upper Huallaga Valley," in David Scott Palmer, ed., *Shining Path of Peru*, St. Martin's Press, 1992, pp. 105–126.

38. As cited in Youngers, "The War in the Andes . . . ," p. 21.

39. Army Gen. Alberto Arciniega, head of the Political-Military Command in the Upper Huallaga Valley in 1989, aggressively supported coca growers and opposed eradication efforts, effectively undermining Shining Path's social base and re-establishing military control over the region. The U.S. government — irked by open military support for coca growers and the obvious problems this created for its drug war — accused Arciniega of drug-related corruption and pushed for his removal from the area. See José Gonzales, "Guerrillas and Coca in the Upper Huallaga Valley."

40. The fact that anti-narcotics priorities have been the primary if not the sole guide to U.S. action in the Andes — as the case of Arciniega suggests (see footnote 39) — is illustrative in this regard.

41. For more details about the unauthorized channeling of anti-narcotics assistance to the counter-insurgency war in Colombia, see *Clear and Present Dangers*, especially pp. 51–55.

42. See *Clear and Present Dangers*, p. 57.

43

Haiti: At the Crossroads of Two World Orders

Yanique Joseph

October 12, 1992 marked the 500th anniversary of the arrival of Christopher Columbus to the American continent. This, as has been recalled over and over in countless commemorations and critical evaluations of this event, was the defining moment of North-South relations for the 500 years that were to follow. Those relationships were to be the cornerstone of the long period of colonialist domination by Western nations of the Americas (which became the model for domination in Asia and Africa) and the neo-colonial period that followed. In retrospect, we can say it was really one continuous era with two phases: *the old world order.*

December 5, 1992 marked 500 years since the arrival of Columbus on the northwestern tip of Haiti, after having landed, most assert, first in the Bahamas and then in the Dominican Republic, which shares the island with Haiti. And shortly before that date in late 1992, tens of thousands of Haitians, from all over the United States, had marched ten miles across New York City, stopping traffic on the Brooklyn Bridge and massing across the street from the United Nations. They were marking the one-year anniversary of the overthrow of Jean-Bertrand Aristide on September 29, 1991, the liberation theologian who won Haiti's first democratic elections in December of 1990, at the head of a popular movement for profound social reforms; the demonstrators were demanding Aristide's restoration. If any struggle typifies the thorny impasse which is created when a dying world order conflicts with a possible new one unable to break through, it is the Haitian one.

As a symbol, Aristide was a threat to the existing order in the Caribbean and Latin America, predominately a region of states with democratic facades bolstered by menacing armies. Aristide had headed a struggle which demonstrated that, once again, a Third World nation was challenging the prevalent imperial socio-political relations. After his deposition, Aristide, the constitutionally-elected president, was consigned to wander through a number of nations seeking public support for his return to complete his five-year mandate.

At first the Western nations and organized bodies such as the UN and the Organization of American States (OAS) condemned the coup and placed a formal commercial and diplomatic embargo on Haiti, in an apparent repudiation of the leaders and backers of the putsch. But subsequent events, in particular the tortuous negotiations that were allowed to languish while what became "the Haitian crisis" festered, revealed tacit approval, by the Western nations and most of the OAS, for the removal of the popular leader. Aristide supporters had thought that the embargo, the main weapon of the pro-democracy movement, would take just three months to bring the renegade government to its knees. It soon became obvious that it was not really being enforced; instead, rich businesspeople and high officials in the army and the government were profiting from the inflated prices which resulted from the scarcity of goods.

Moreover, on the diplomatic front, the expressions of support for Aristide's restoration were not matched by political realities. During his wanderings, Aristide was afforded all the honors of his presidential office by his host states, including the U.S., whose government was in fact covertly doing everything it could to prevent his restitution. His government officials were allowed to control embassies and consulates abroad, and recognized at official international meetings, while the de facto regime which emerged after the putsch was allowed to consolidate its hold over Haitian territory. As negotiations dragged on, punctuated by demonstrations by the Haitian pro-democracy movement in key cities in the U.S., France, and Canada, invisible but powerful hands helped to craft a painstaking scenario where both camps — the legitimate government in exile and the de facto regime inside Haiti — were played off against each other.

What resulted from this jockeying, was however, clear as a verdict. The agreement signed by Aristide and the leader of a rival political party widely reputed to have been part of the inner circle which conspired to overthrow him — the famed "Protocol Agreement of February 23, 1991" — was ignored by the de facto government, which convened a gathering to issue its own "consensus" decision. This package represented a compromise between sectors wielding power: high-ranking army officers, rich businesspeople wishing to preserve their monopolies, ambitious politicians, and assorted profiteers. They united behind Marc Bazin, a former official of the World Bank and the American favorite during the elections of December 1990. Bazin was installed as prime minister and the office of president was left vacant. The Vatican was the first and so far the only government to recognize the Haitian de facto government.

In his United Nations speech, one year after the coup, Aristide was to say: "What scandal is this? What would the attitude of the Vatican have been if Haiti had been inhabited by white people? What would the attitude of Pope John Paul II have been if Haiti had been Poland?" However, the day after, hundreds of Haitians demonstrating in front of the U.S. State Department were received at St. Patrick's Cathedral in New York City, a key symbol of U.S. Roman Catholicism, for a mass where a young priest delivered an impassioned political sermon.

Faith in the dream of democracy and liberation from hunger and social oppression would overcome death, even that of Aristide himself if need be, he told them. The large numbers of Haitian residents in New York City — overwhelmingly Catholic — could simply not be ignored, even by the Catholic Cardinal O'Connor, who has long lent his weight to conservative causes as a key and vocal player in New York City politics, at a time of dwindling church members and priests, particularly in the U.S. This is what explained the statement by Father Guy Sansaricq, who officiated at the mass, and at the end thanked the cardinal for having said that the "doors to the Cathedral" were open to the Haitian community and that they were to consider it as their own. Sansaricq, after an association with a group of liberation theologians who went on to become prominent in the popular democratic movement, pioneered the Charismatic movement within the U.S. Haitian community. This movement, emphasizing personal transcendent spiritual experience, has grown within the Catholic Church, in parallel with liberation theology. The Catholic Charismatics in the U.S. include hundreds of Haitian adherents who have been meeting annually at their own regional congresses since the eighties.

So it is not only political movements which have been knocking at the door of the "new world order." Movements within religious institutions, especially an international one such as the Catholic Church which played a defining role during the colonization of the Americas, are adding to the clamor for profound reforms in the system of relationships between power centers and the dependent and oppressed nations of the South. The association with the "progressive church," or the "people's church," led by liberation theologians and dedicated seculars, enabled the Sandinista political movement to broaden its social base, and to take power in Nicaragua. Fifteen years later, it was this alliance between the progressive church and the Lavalas movement that would result in Aristide's electoral victory. Aristide used the Lavalas concept, as the popular democratic movement in Haiti is called, to symbolize the "popular human flood" which would sweep the dictatorship away during his short but almost breathtakingly successful electoral campaign preceding his landslide victory with 67% of the vote. The U.S. favorite, Bazin, received only 14%.

The Lavalas movement, an electoral coalition of popular organizations, including many small political parties, was the culmination of what had been in fact a long, protracted struggle for profound social reforms in Haiti. Despite temporary setbacks, the movement gained more and more momentum and experience under each short-lived military regime after Duvalier. This movement gained significant political space after the routing of the Duvalier dictatorship in 1986. The "Ti Legliz" movement or "people's church," led by articulate liberation theologians, was able to take advantage of the organizational network of Catholic churches both in urban centers and in the countryside. This represented one of the largest sectors of the Lavalas movement.

During his electoral campaign and after his triumph, Aristide emphasized themes which helped to define broad orientations for the movement: participatory democracy, decentralization, non-violence and spirituality (liberation theology). Strategic allies of the Lavalas coalition, part of the broader democratic movement, included left-of-center political parties such as the Front for National Democracy and Change (FNCD), which backed Aristide in the elections, and the Movement for the Organization of the Country (MOP). The MOP was founded by Aristide's historical predecessor, Daniel Fignole (with whom Aristide is often compared), who was overthrown by the Haitian army, paving the way for the first Duvalier regime in the 1950s.

These organizations were responsible for mass mobilization and organization during this protracted democratic revolution, which followed an anarchist-populist pattern. Large sectors of the population organized themselves in neighborhood, self-education, and defense committees. However, the lack of a structured political party or coalition committed to popular interests was an important factor. The popular democracy movement, which gained strength from the time Jean-Claude Duvalier was ousted through short-lived interim regimes, had converged in the broad and loose Lavalas electoral coalition. But the largest political organization of that coalition, the FNCD, which officially ran Aristide as a candidate, was itself a loose and incoherent alliance of left-of-center politicians. Many of them saw state power as a means to form a political clientele and consolidate middle class aspirations rather than as an instrument to speed reforms for the poor and clean out the remnants of Duvalierism. Small left groups with a more stable history of ideological defense of the peasantry and workers' interests, while influential in mass organizations, failed to become an influential force within the newly developed parliamentary system.

Indicating its limitations, the FNCD remained silent when legislators demanded a hefty salary of $7,000 a month and balked at Aristide's offer of $2,000. Moreover, many former Duvalierists managed to gain seats in parliament, which they used to regain influence.

To attempt to offset the FNCD's centrism and foot-dragging on approving popular reforms, as well as the structural weakness of formations with firm popular options, Aristide and his close associates moved to form a new party. It was also to be named Lavalas, which further alienated his former electoral backers and also confused many of his supporters. Aristide was also challenged from his left, by supporters who unrealistically demanded a speed-up in his attempts to root out former Duvalierists in the administration or failed to understand why he had little choice but to make some compromises with international institutions such as the IMF. What emerged was a beleaguered regime struggling, without the support of a strong institutional left, to enact popular reforms after almost 200 years of entrenched corruption and dictatorship, and facing the enmity of powerful ruling groups, as well as indifference and sabotage by international actors.

It is undeniable that the pressure of world powers, in particular the United States, played a key role in pressuring former Duvalier associates — still numerous in government and other institutions during the five-year transitional period after the fall of the dictator — and the army to refrain from disrupting the electoral process as they did during November of 1987. The

U.S. government cut off aid to the transitional military regimes of generals Namphy and Avril. Reforms to "professionalize" the army were undertaken with pressure from the U.S. — but this entire process was designed to benefit Marc Bazin. Bazin was spurned by the great majority of the Haitian people, not only because of his conciliatory stance toward Duvalierists, but also because he was "pro-American" to the point of implying that as long as he had U.S. support, the backing of the Haitian people was insignificant. The historical surprise was that with mass mobilization, the Haitian people were able to use these reforms which restrained the army to elect a candidate of their own choosing.

In the final analysis, Aristide's regime was overwhelmed by too numerous hostile forces in a world context difficult for progressive, self-reliant Third World governments. It is widely believed that steps taken by the Aristide-Preval government to mount a major literacy campaign (Preval was Aristide's prime minister), to enact an agrarian reform, and to rout drug trafficking, particularly in the army, frightened Haiti's entrenched elites. However, the international context also bears some important features providing the Haitian pro-democracy movement with some maneuvering room. One of the most critical factors is the presence of sizable Haitian immigrant communities in centers of influence such as the United States and France, which make it more difficult for those nations to give outright recognition to the de facto government which reversed the democratic process, and to legitimize the counter-revolution.

In July of 1992, the Aristide camp convened a meeting in Miami to discuss how to respond to what was recognized as the internal consolidation of the de facto regime. Since Bazin had been the U.S. favorite, he also seemed to symbolize U.S. opposition to the return to power of Aristide and the Lavalas movement. From that meeting, there emerged the Presidential Committee, which took the path of accepting to negotiate with Bazin. This had previously been considered unthinkable by the Lavalas movement, since it amounted to legitimizing the de facto government which had emerged after the coup. It put on the agenda the possibility of a government in which Aristide was the nominal but powerless figurehead and Bazin, the de facto prime minister, held actual power. This would also mean the power to implement a social agenda closer to U.S. dictates instead of the profound social reforms Aristide and the more grassroots-oriented sectors of the Lavalas movement had stood for.

Frequent trips by Bazin and other high officials of his government to consult with strongman Balaguer in the Dominican Republic underscored the maintenance of the system of near-slavery under which tens of thousands of Haitian sugar cane cutters are forced to toil in Dominican plantations, a system Aristide had challenged in his first speech at the United Nations, shortly before his ouster. The Haitian army is kept supplied with weapons by third party countries such as the Dominican Republic. The refusal to grant asylum to post-coup Haitian refugees by the U.S. and, in one case, by France, scandalized public opinion inside and outside those countries. Both the treatment of the Haitian refugees and the repeated violation of the embargo led even mainstream newspapers such as the *New York Times* to accuse the

Bush administration of complicity with the Haitian army, and to call for an end of support to what it called "thugs." Alarm about the continuing repression grew as it was seen to be fueling the exodus of refugees, which had slowed to a trickle during Aristide's seven-month government.

As Aristide and his close entourage made concession after concession, they were ultimately faced with having to consider the possible "compromise" of sharing the government with their sworn enemies. A basic contradiction remained insurmountable: the continuing reign of terror imposed by the army — which in fact had final authority — and its visceral opposition to Aristide's physical return to Haiti. Prior to the arrival of an observer team from the OAS, three young men, members of a newly formed political organization in the Lavalas movement, had been gunned down by the army as they put up posters of Aristide.

Aristide and his entourage have maintained that the murderous opposition of the army could be solved by pressure from the U.S. government, by the withdrawal of U.S. support for not only the army but the very general who led the coup, Raoul Cedras. In a message to the OAS in August of 1992, Casimir, the Haitian ambassador, called the army the representative of "internal colonialism." From hiding, Gerard Jean-Juste, a priest and coordinator of the pro-Lavalas grassroots coalition called "The Tenth Department Organization," called for the dismantling of the Haitian army in a message of support for the September demonstrations commemorating Aristide's ouster.

The verdict is again clear — the stalemated negotiations have only given the army time to eliminate as many Aristide partisans as possible and are a clear signal to Aristide that, should he return, his safety is by no means assured. In the early days after the coup, high-ranking officials of the Haitian army stated that Aristide would be killed if he attempted to return. As a titular but powerless head of state, Aristide would, even if the Haitian army could be made to agree not to take his life (there would be no guarantee paramilitary forces would not), be powerless to enact any reforms, however desperately needed within the near future in an ecologically devastated, demographically unbalanced and militarily dominated Haiti.

There *is* in fact an urgent need for a new world order, if the rapid social and ecological decline everywhere is to be arrested, especially in the context of global economic stagnation. If the concept has come to be regarded with cynicism, it is only because it has been distorted. In countries of people of African descent, the need for a world order which allows societies to break free of the self-destructive policies of irresponsible elites as well as an equally self-destructive strategy of economic development imposed by international forces, is *immediate*. In much of the Black world, fascistic dictators and corrupt armies left over from the old world order wage fratricidal wars or war against their own people. In many of these lands, the desert is advancing and social and economic breakdown is allowed to fester, as the examples of Liberia and Somalia demonstrate, sometimes until complete collapse. The Yugoslavian tragedy equally underlines this urgency. Entire societies and cultures collapse in the vacuum left by weak and ineffective global institutions and a system of law and order based on narrow interests and backed by the naked technological might of one superpower.

So at the crossroads of a dying world order and an emergent one of new possibilities for North-South relations, the Haitian crisis is replete with the ironies and pains of the chaos and incoherence of millenial transition. Hardened and entrenched powerful international elites wedded to militarism use their might to prevent an essentially non-violent movement from gaining long-overdue liberation from a tyranny which has lasted nearly 200 years. Just as a changing international context and growing social movements for world order and ecological survival gain enough momentum to make profound changes in North-South relations possible, the forces of monopoly and privilege, oblivious to the ecological catastrophe at their doorstep, seek to retain a model of the nation-state as a prized booty to plunder to the point of suicidal collapse. An organized and self-conscious Haitian diaspora is emerging in Western capitals with the potential for significant economic support to a country known for devastating poverty. This, coupled to significant political support, could help Haiti break free of the near-slavery system that undergirds sugar production on the island. Yet this is also when the political representatives of the forces of counter-revolution and arbitrariness in Haiti seek to consolidate their power, by allying with a Dominican government eager to maintain the current system of exploitation of Haitian "*braceros*." For the first nation-state to have emerged from a revolution against slavery, this is the greatest of ironies.

If the duplicity of the Western nations and the international community of nation-states in general, in tolerating the restoration of the system of lawless repression, illustrates the absence of will by the powerful to move or even define a new world order, by contrast, the Haitian Lavalas movement represents the will of the Third World oppressed needed to offset the inaction of the comfortable, and to move the wheels of history forward as the world lurches toward a new millenium. If the Haitian popular democracy movement succeeds in turning defeat into victory, it will be because it will have clearly articulated a strategy which plays on the vulnerabilities of the dying world order. Such a victory could provide the precedent for a genuinely new world order: the need for new North-South relations which permit the devastation of the South to be addressed in an overall world context of economic revitalizaton; the need for global security which prioritizes peoples' basic rights over the arbitrariness of repressive nation-states or narrow economic interests and ideologies; the need and possibility of moral renewal in long-standing international institutions of organized religion; the need to contain volatile race conflict; and the need to end the worldwide refugee crisis.

■PART NINE■

Europe

44

Eastern Europe:
Prospects After Communism

Bogdan Denitch

The unfolding revolutionary transformations of Eastern Europe and the Soviet Union during 1989 and 1990 represented both the general and the terminal crises of the state "socialist" systems ruled by communist parties. They also represented a massive general retreat from, and finally a rout of the old officially long-held and brutally defended claim that some kind of utopia was being built in the Soviet Union and Eastern Europe. There are few cases in history of an established regime collapsing so utterly, so swiftly and with so little resistance. The quick defeat of the abortive coup by Soviet hardliners against the continual dismemberment of Soviet communism and the USSR itself in August 1991 marked the degree to which the old system had died. Even a reformed version of communism can no longer be revived. The fate of democracy, pluralism and economic reforms are far less certain.

The political and ideological retreat included a widespread denial that there was any validity whatsoever to the communist experiment, which has come to be almost universally blamed for the obvious technological, economic and political backwardness of these societies. It is also held responsible for the retrograde political cultures which are proving to be so vulnerable to authoritarian populism, militant clericalism and intolerant xenophobic nationalism. It is blamed for the economic disaster which has devastated agriculture, given birth to a herd of white elephants in industry and created an ecological wasteland.

The long decades of suffering, repression and sacrifice caused lasting damage to the societies of Eastern Europe and the Soviet Union. Eastern Europe and pre-revolutionary Russia had been food exporters; east central Europe and Czarist Russia had lively cosmopolitan artists, respected scientists and an intelligentsia which was an established participant in a general European culture. Much of that was devastated by long decades of mismanagement, misdevelopment, and repression. What was achieved was paid for

465

at enormous political, ecological and economic cost. Essentially, the positive achievements consisted of rapid and massive urbanization combined with industrial development. There were also some real advances in vastly expanded education, a crude but universal welfare state and massive social mobility. To these must be added real improvements in the legal, social and economic condition of women, which are now in grave jeopardy throughout the region. But even those genuine achievements of communist states were corrupted by crass privilege and favoritism on behalf of a greedy party elite, a politocracy, or *nomenklatura*.[1]

A key argument on the current political scene is how to finish the demolition job. How much pain in the form of unemployment and a fall in social and living standards is unavoidable, and how much is politically tolerable? There is also the question of who, if anyone, is to be punished for the catastrophe, and who is best suited to carry out the restructuring of these economies and societies. Unfortunately many of the leading candidates for that job also propose to enforce religion in schools, outlaw abortion in societies where contraception is not easily available, deal with unemployment by pushing women out of the workplace, and re-introduce censorship. They also propose a massive purge of present and former communists, the dismantling of the party institutions and press, and in some cases even outlawing the party itself.

It was communist ideologues and their fellow travelers as well as many critics of those systems who agreed that the existing communist regimes represented some, if not the only, "really" possible variants of socialism. Conservative anti-communists agreed, with enthusiasm, that communism in power was indeed the logical heir of socialism; some would even say that it was the inevitable heir of the great democratic revolutions. The very idea of socialism itself must now be redefined in a new language, making clear that it can only exist as part of the extension of political democracy and individual freedom, both of which require social welfare and substantial equality among citizens, and has little in common with the former statist authoritarian regimes.

Defining the East European States

My own preference is for a label which would clearly indicate that the East European societies were new social formations, radically different from either the previous authoritarian capitalist dictatorships, or from any projected socialist or workers' states. I prefer the term "politocracy." To put it at its simplest: whatever class was in power, it was clearly not the working class, even though the new political elites did continue to use and manipulate, albeit ever more routinely and cynically, the language and symbols of a common socialist tradition.

That social and political system was exported throughout Eastern Europe by the Soviet armies when they defeated Nazi Germany and its allies, after the end of the Second World War. It was imposed on some of the East European states from the top down, and survived essentially as long as Soviet military power was there to underpin it. Even Yugoslavia and Albania, where local Communist Party-led partisan resistance movements won power through a bitter civil war combined with a war against the Nazi occupiers, initially benefited from the support of the Soviet Union through the post-war treaty settlements of Yalta and Potsdam which legitimated their victories.[2]

Intellectual and moral responsibility for both the realities of and fantasies about these systems — self-defined and widely accepted as variants of social-ism — was laid at the door of socialism itself, both as a project and as a world view. This is in no small part because a number of Western Marxists and socialists continued to refer (and do to this very day) to these societies as socialist. By the sixties this was usually accompanied with some modifier such as "currently existing socialism" or simply as "state socialism."

These societies, at least those ruled by classic-type communist parties,[3] have each maintained an essentially similar class in power. These mature or decaying politocracies evolved a wide range of possible political forms with more or less autonomy for independent organizations and trade unions, and greater or lesser political rights and individual liberty, just as capitalist societies include a wide range of variants, from dictatorships and authori-tarian states to pluralist welfare-state democracies. The great difference is that while bourgeois societies include parliamentary pluralist variants, the politoc-racies never did, and could not.

The Collapse of a World System

Future historians may well decide that the gray, dull Brezhnev era during the seventies represented not a decline but the high watermark of communism as a world system and the Soviet Union as a superpower. That era may retroac-tively even look like the good old days of stability and gradually increasing prosperity in the face of the new post-communist perils in what was once the Soviet Union.

How distant all that seems today! And yet François Revel's and other scenarios of the certain collapse of democracies and inevitable victory of communism were written only yesterday. Statements and speeches since the *anno mirabilis* 1989, both by the communist reformers and Russian leaders, confirm in detail some of the most relentlessly harsh criticisms of these systems by both internal and external opponents. No observer of the current widespread visceral hatred for the old communist system, and all of its symbols and language, in former communist-ruled countries, can fail to wonder whether any type of socialism at all, even a socialism identified with the social democracies of Western Europe, has escaped deep injury by the identification of communist one-party tyranny as a variant of socialism.

One slightly optimistic sign is the large number of newly born parties, as well as re-born and remnants of old pre-communist socialist parties, claiming the name "social-democratic" throughout Eastern Europe and the former Soviet Union. They are requesting some kind of recognition from the Social-ist International. In this quest for some kind of legitimacy, the new and re-born parties are joined by more or less transformed, chastened and reformed sections of the old communist parties. There must be *some* reason for this frantic scramble throughout 1990 and 1991 for social-democratic credentials. Some local political actors must believe that such an identity is of practical value today, and a promising investment for the future.

The Delegitimation of a Political and Ideological System

It is questionable if even two or three decades of generous aid from Western Europe would be able to help to clean up the economic and social problems which the post-communist regimes have inherited. It is even more questionable if aid on such a scale will be available. Germany will have its resources tied down trying to integrate an economically and ecologically devastated former East Germany. After all, *these* former East Europeans vote in a unified Germany and thus have to be paid urgent political attention to. How much Western aid will be left over for helping other East European states and the former Soviet Union is anyone's guess. The first priority will be aid to Russia, and that will be for security reasons, as well as the massive natural resources which are potentially available.

All this does not augur well for the immediate economic prospects of Poland, the Czech and Slovak states, Hungary, the former Yugoslavia, Bulgaria and Romania. Albania's prospects are even worse. The trouble is that the relatively better off East European countries cannot expect a fraction of the aid which the wildly aroused expectations of their populations require. The fact that those societies are now far more open only means that the drastic contrast between their living standards and those of Western Europe are now all too clearly visible. A demagogic yellow press keeps rubbing the difference in and encourages unachievable demands for immediate increases in living standards. One of the major reasons for getting rid of the communist regimes was to become a part of "Europe"; for the population that means achieving a "European" (read: Western) living standard, almost immediately — hopefully without having to develop capitalist working habits.

Unrealistic hopes have been aroused, some quite irresponsibly, that quick solutions can be achieved by an act of political will. It should be reasonably clear that *none* of these countries is likely to become a part of "Europe," if that means entering the European Community, before the end of the century. At best, what is open is the hope for some type of half-way house process where a gradual increase of contacts and ties with Western Europe takes place. The EC *will* almost certainly try to help, but the amount of aid which is probable does not begin to approach what is needed for the expectations of the peoples of former communist countries to be satisfied.

What they expected was that their living standards would radically improve after communism. To date they have not; on the contrary, they have dropped, in the European East, in some cases drastically; moreover, it is universally predicted that things will get still worse before they get better. The only debate is, how much worse, and for how long a period of time. With the old communist repressive regimes and the potential military threat of the Warsaw Pact both gone from the scene, Western Europe and the

United States have considerably less interest in the former communist countries. Less interest, unfortunately, translates into less urgent pressure for aid. Potential immigrants are no longer courageous political refugees seeking well deserved political asylum. Instead they have become "mere" economic refugees representing economic costs and social problems, and as such have far less of a claim on hospitality. Neo-fascist anti-immigrant mobs in Germany underline this new perception.

It will do no good for the East Europeans, quite accurately, to insist that they are and have always been a part of a general European culture. That claim is abstract, and tolerance for economic immigrants with strange languages and customs has never been high in Western Europe, particularly in times of economic stagnation and low growth. The possibility that growth will rise sufficiently to make a difference to the millions of East Europeans who want to live better — now and not in the indefinite future — is remote. The world economy is stagnant and no dramatic change is expected soon.

The New Beginnings in Eastern Europe

The former communist societies are facing a crisis which must be urgently addressed without delay. The trouble is that new overall political systems *and* the social policies *and* such minor details as new constitutions, electoral systems, and new civil services *and* new political parties *and* independent trade unions *and* habits of tolerance for political and ethnic minorities all have to be built from scratch, or, at the very least, re-invented — all at the same time.

That is, both the economic and political systems have to be radically restructured while taking care of some of the most banal but urgent priorities in some of the countries, such as feeding the population and providing enough heat, fuel, and medical care for basic survival. In the case of the former Soviet Union and Romania, the situation threatens to get out of control and become catastrophic. In former Yugoslavia, of course, the situation *has* become catastrophic. The political breakdown has gone so far that a murderous war is being waged by Serbia — aided by the former Yugoslav Army — against Bosnia-Herzegovina and Croatia.

Eastern Europe now has no generally accepted notion of the common good for which voluntary discipline and sacrifices will be made now that the old repressive structure capable of commanding compliance is gone. The question is: in which directions will these societies move? Far from catching up and surpassing the advanced capitalist nations, Eastern Europe and the former Soviet Union are in acute danger of at least temporarily plunging into the Third World.

A whole generation of political and economic reforms had their day in the sun throughout the region. Hungarian and — before the civil war broke out — Yugoslav economic reforms showed that a considerable degree of marketization of the economy was possible while still maintaining social ownership. For that matter, while considering the great *flexibility* of the market as an allocator and as an engine of economic growth it should be pointed out that

Austria, for example, while undoubtedly an example of a capitalist and market economy, is one with a large sector of the economy nationalized or under public ownership. Thus private ownership and the market are not necessarily inextricably linked. Hungary and Yugoslavia also illustrated that while marketization weakens the central authority of the state, it does not automatically lead to pluralism and democracy. What it does do is to add other players with new social and political bases to those who contend for political power. Powerful and successful managers and technocrats joined the political cadres in the now expanded ruling elite, as a distinct and self-conscious part of the ruling establishment, with distinct interests. This led to at least a limited elite pluralism and competition; in turn that provided space for some politics. To be sure, it was an oligarchic politics with limited players, but in this it was no different from the politics of most of Western Europe at the beginning of this century.

Conflicts within the ruling elites about alternative ways to modernize the economy and society produced cleavages in the previously monolithic systems, cracks in a previously solid wall through which new players could enter the game of oligarchic politics, initially as allies of existing cliques and factions. This was, for example, the way in which segments of the so-called humanist intelligentsia — writers, journalists, social scientists and economists — got pulled into elite conflicts, usually on the side of the technocratic modernizers and reformers.

In turn, other parts of the elite turned to ever more dangerous power games and alliances by bringing in, very cautiously at the outset, workers and the popular urban masses, more often than not against technocratic reformers. The appeal was to egalitarian populist rhetoric and to real or imagined nationalist grievances.

There was one master grievance: over the years the East European regimes became increasingly autonomous and even national, but this remained essentially within the boundaries of what the Soviet Union would tolerate. Nationalism thus emerged as the alternative to these regimes; that is why the most popular parties which have emerged in post-communist states have tended to be nationalist. It was often reinforced with religion. Both nationalism and religion lend themselves to an organic politics of identity, unlike abstract political ideas, which need time to reach broad layers of population. The politics of identity rather than of program are more likely to survive and spring up as mass movements after long years of communist rule.

Beyond Elite Reforms to Contested Elections

All of the new governments, and most of their oppositions are at least formally committed to economic reforms, which will introduce elements of the market into the economy along with some mix of state, social, cooperative and simply private ownership. All post-communist East European regimes claim now to be democratic. To be sure, that claim to democracy is flawed by the current confusion of the dominant or majority national group and the citizens of the state, throughout the region. It is as if all East

European — and many ex-Soviet — nationalisms had adopted a "Zionist" view of their respective nation-states. That is, defining the state as the national state of the dominant people; others are tolerated, at best. This makes democracy the instrument of national majorities against others.

There is little sensitivity about the need for religious tolerance, or indeed any separation of church and state among the post-communist national populists who have won power in many of the countries. Women's hard-earned gains under the old communist regimes are very much in jeopardy throughout the region. A very real danger exists that post-communist governments could end up as nationally intolerant, clerical, obscurantist regimes in which democracy is reduced to formal regular elections. What keeps the new regimes from being even more intolerant today is the hope of eventual integration into Europe. That means that pro-human rights and democracy pressures can have at least some effect.

After the first joy at the toppling of communist regimes, popular euphoria and mobilization began to dry up practically overnight. There is no new alternate vision of the common good in these societies. After communism, what? A republic led by former dissident poets, playwrights and historians? Good — and then what? What is it they are expected to do after pushing the former communist appointees and *nomenklatura* into political (we hope only political) oblivion. Once that particular catharsis is over, there remain some basic economic questions and decisions which have to be made. There the problems begin.

The free market — which most of the former opposition, and former communists, have fallen in love with as an idea — is very abstract indeed. Everyone, including the old communist cadres, today favors all the good things associated with the market — a plentiful supply of world-quality goods, at a decent non-gouging price, with a minimum of petty bureaucratic interference by the state. Almost everyone is also for rewarding hard work and initiative, even with higher incomes, provided that it does not result in rewarding those who have the connections or relatives in the right places, as too often seems to be the case.

Very few people in Eastern Europe are in favor of limiting the distribution of health and education based on the ability to pay. Almost no one is willing to accept massive prolonged unemployment. No one, that is, except the new post-communist governments, their economic advisers, the techno-managers domestic and foreign, and the journalists supporting the now increasingly admired "hard cure." The "hard cure" comes in many forms, from the dangerously utopian plan to privatize the Russian economy in 500 days, to the so-called fire-sales of previously nationalized enterprises in Po-land and Hungary, where former communist managers sometimes meta-morphose overnight and become the new owners. It includes even the more reasonable, but still draconian, assaults on inflation. These solutions to the urgent problem of hyper-inflation have caused considerable pain to whole sectors of the economy, and have hurt especially the population dependent on incomes which have been either frozen or controlled.

The effect of making the local currencies convertible has been to open up the economies to imported consumer goods. By the fall of 1990 there was no black market either in goods or currency. On the other hand, once insignificant income differences necessarily mean more when there are attractive things to buy, in the increasingly well-supplied shops, whose goods are ever less accessible to ordinary wage earners. An economic cure which essentially requires holding down or even lowering real wages for most people, cutting down on social entitlements, and at the same time consciously increasing the real and visible incomes and consumption of the upper strata is social dynamite. All the more so, because the newly rich in these societies are not necessarily, or even usually, identical with the powerful, or those whose wealth is the result of socially useful hard work.

Without a sufficient sense of national community to make sacrifices acceptable, sneaking suspicions, usually justified, prevail; suspicions that the artful dodgers and new rich of these societies are not sacrificing. It is clear that the lion's share of the sacrifice is expected from the workers. Worse, *after* the sacrifice what is generally offered is some kind of a Mexicanized economy which will be the backwater of Europe, with ever increasing class and income cleavages. To be sure, just as in Latin America, the East European countries will now be formally completely independent of their own old superpower. There will also be very high unemployment and a great dependence on, and thus subordination to, international financial institutions like the IMF and the World Bank. It is not surprising that this does not inspire mass enthusiasm, particularly among the present or future unemployed.

Political Alternatives in Eastern Europe

In post-Soviet Eastern Europe an increasingly surly sense of political malaise pervades a landscape covered with broken promises. The new fragile multiparty parliaments have had no chance yet to develop new norms of behavior appropriate to new political alignments. Everything seems to be both possible and permissible in a political milieu where nationalist populist parties and movements compete for power and where the atmosphere is full of potential political pogroms against the former communists. That same nationalism and populism — East European varieties of Peronism — can equally easily turn against national minorities, disliked neighbors or even against those who enrich themselves too quickly under the new regimes.

Some previous heroes of democratic dissent may show cloven hooves. Many of the valiant fighters against communist authoritarian rule will turn out to be ethnic nationalists, demagogic and irresponsible populists, or intolerant religious authoritarians. More mundanely, they may turn out to be merely power-hungry parochial political opportunists, or mediocre self-promoting politicians. Democracy is after all a system in which quite ordinary people, not moral or intellectual giants, can play a role, sometimes even hold power. This commonplace fact is extraordinarily hard to accept for some previously underground heroic leaders, and the critical intelligentsia in general.

In the new post-communist democracies, for too many "democracy" means untrammeled majority rule (of *the* people, or the largest national group), unleavened by tolerance of diferences, national minorities or dis-agreement. Nationally-charged populism is now widespread in Poland, Hun-gary, Romania and at least in the two largest republics of former Yugoslavia. What is at stake today in former communist countries is not an intellectually stimulating seminar on transitions from authoritarian to democratic societies. What is being decided are the fates of real-life economies — and, more to the point, societies increasingly sick of austerity and shortages. No proposals have surfaced which do not explicitly involve considerable doses of pain. Most of that pain will have to be borne by the workers, who are those least responsible for the present economic mess.

In response, given the political predilection of much of the region to nationalism-charged populism, it can be predicted that social demagoguery will be substituted for much less available economic solutions. That demago-guery will most easily be directed against the real or imagined enemies of "the nation" — other national groups, minorities, freemasons, Jews, the Vatican, former communists, present leftists, liberals, foreigners and the other usual suspects.

The alternatives to that demagoguery are difficult and will require the building of a civil society and democratically rooted mass social movements, trade unions and political parties. Those in turn require rebuilding a political public sphere, the acceptance of a *general* political community or a modern day equivalent of a polis, where there is sufficient sense of community that certain sacrifices can be accepted. In other words, to turn away from the notion of politics as a realm where there is no common good or interest, where instead hard-edged homogenous groups, most probably based on ethnicity or nationality, struggle against each other. To move the emerging post-communist political culture towards such a conception of politics is a hard task, and it requires a democratic and egalitarian movement — in other words a modern democratic socialist movement.

The future is uncertain, but it seems that Orwell's nightmare in *1984*, as stated by the negative hero, O'Brien, that the future is a boot smashing into a human face forever, is for the moment, an unlikely outcome. That, at least, is a relief. Having said that, however, it must be added that the road of transformation of authoritarian societies in Eastern Europe and the former Soviet Union into stable democracies is likely to be a long and troubled one.

Notes

1. *Nomenklatura* is the formal system which prescribes the position, obligations and privileges of the officials engaged in decision-making processes in communist politocracies. Security and promotion are guaranteed in return for discipline and obedience.
2. Pedants can validly argue that the communist seizure of power in Czechoslovakia in 1948 was an exception, in that a genuinely massive communist party seized power in a scenario appropriate to an advanced industrial society. The Czech party, with the aid of its unions and fronts, did seize power without direct Soviet armed help. However, the reality of Soviet power in the region demoralized the non-communist democrats, while also giving enormous confidence to the communists.
3. I distinguish here between Third World revolutionary regimes which have often used Marxist-Leninist rhetoric and symbols but without a mass communist party, under whatever name, and genuine communist party regimes.

45

Germany: Mired in a Slough of Despondence

John Borneman

I

The collapse of the Soviet bloc and Marxist-Leninist ideology in 1989 along with defeat of the Third Reich and fascism in 1945 were the two most significant events of this century — certainly for Europeans, if not the world. For Germans, who were both creators and victims of these two orders, "1989" opened up new possibilities both to re-compose and resignify their domestic relations and to re-position themselves in a shifting international order. Bucking the world-wide trend following the end of the Cold War for states to dissolve or break up into smaller components, Germans again followed their historical *Sonderweg* (special path) and united, in this case two formerly adversarial states, economic systems, and peoples. Yet, three years later the optimistic expectations of a unified Germany and of its emergence as a more assertive power within a growing and united Europe have proven misleading. Comparing Germany in the fall of 1992 to the Germanys in the fall of 1989, it/they are indeed an altered state, mired in a slough of despondency.

When I first began research in Berlin in 1984, people joked about John F. Kennedy's 1961 impassioned declaration at the Wall, "*Ich bin ein Berliner*" — "I am a jelly doughnut." In the year after the Wall came down, people laughed at Helmut Kohl, who everyone at that time suspected would become "Chancellor of Unity," for supposedly saying to George Bush, "Can I say to you you?" — "*Darf ich Sie duzen?*" People make fun of what they are fond of. By 1992 Berlin had become a humorless place. With a single sheriff, new rules, and different stakes, Berliners do not find their oneness a laughing matter. In fact, the absence of unity, the starkness of strengthened antagonisms, has reinforced their sense of singularity. Contrary to expectations that with unity the anxiety would be gone, Germans are still not *merely* one nation among other nations, one people among other peoples. At this time, what they exactly are, other than an enlarged state, can only be answered in the negative.

In the short term at least, unification has failed. The vast majority of East Germans and an increasingly anxiety-ridden West German population have been unprepared for, and thus quite unhappy about, the course of events since formal unity. In the heady months following the opening of the Wall, Helmut Kohl and his Christian Democratic Party made a speedy unification enticing by promising that it would involve no suffering or pain: all East Germans would be as well or better off than before; West German prosperity would be unaffected by the absorption of the East. The government's inability to fulfill this promise bitterly disappointed both sides. Of course, people never blame themselves for their own gullibility. There were opposing voices, such as Social Democratic Party leader Oskar Lafontaine, who warned of the high cost. Or Karl-Otto Pöhl, the head of the Bundesbank, who resigned when Kohl would not heed his warning that an immediate economic union of the sort proposed (and carried out) would be disastrous for the East German economy.

This said, I do not mean to imply the existence of a plausible alternative to Kohl's basic unity plan. Given the unpredictable situation in the Soviet Union in 1989–1990, Kohl rightly embraced the opportunities offered by the historical moment — to free East Germans from Soviet domination. Rather, one might question the way in which he turned unity into an issue to manipulate for the purposes of re-election. If Kohl had leveled with the people and asked for sacrifices from the beginning, it is likely that Germans of all ilks, businesspeople and common people, would have been receptive. Instead Kohl promised a "blossoming landscape" within two years, which would come about with the simple introduction of "the market" and his own re-election.

II

It is also obvious, with the benefit of hindsight, that the East German political leadership would never have managed to solve their problems alone. There never was a possible "third way" between "socialism" and "capitalism." This leadership had steadily resisted acknowledging the malfunctioning and disintegration of its centrally planned and administered economy. Throughout the 50s that economy had been unable to keep pace with West Germany, ultimately mandating that a wall be built to keep its skilled workers from fleeing to the West. By the early 70s rigor mortis had set in. Unable to jump start growth with Honecker's proposed unity of the social and economic aspects of policy, East Germany was forced to seek credit in the West just to maintain a semblance of progress. And during the 80s the debt accumulated, without substantial changes in the administrative structure of the economy and political system that might have enabled the regime and its people to pay back the debt. Fearful of any hint of political instability and unwilling to yield any top-down political control to local initiative, the regime preferred instead to imagine that it knew both what the people wanted and what they would settle for. Under these circumstances, East Germans became masters at articulating needs which their state could not satisfy, and they were constantly stymied by that state in any initiative they made to fulfill those needs on their own.

By the mid-80s, Gorbachev's reforms in the Soviet Union heartened those East Germans interested in substantive changes at home. Church groups, environmentalists, human rights activists, and many intellectuals embraced perestroika and glasnost, understood as economic restructuring and democratization. Their widely shared goal up to November 9, 1989, was not a united Germany but a better socialism. Yet the more it seemed likely that Gorbachev might succeed in enacting his reforms, the more the leadership of GDR took great pains to distance itself from him. A series of well-publicized confrontations between the regime and oppositional groups in 1987 and 1988, as well as noticeable signs of economic collapse, created a crisis of authority in the aging political leadership. By the summer of 1989, Poland and Hungary had already initiated a series of reforms that effectively removed them from the socialist camp. Most dangerous for the GDR were the open border policies in those countries. With open borders to the West, the East German regime could no longer contain its people. The flight of 500 young East Germans across the Hungarian border into Austria, on August 8, 1989, initiated an ongoing flood from East to West that eventually led to the opening of the Wall on November 9. Through this writing (September 1992) approximately 2,000 East Germans are still resettling weekly in West Germany.

Only after the Wall was opened on November 9, 1989, could most East Germans visit the West. Though they expected to see a higher standard of living in the West, they were overwhelmed by the extent of the discrepancy between their standards and those of their Western counterparts. Neither the principles of "democracy," "democratic values," nor "freedom" influenced much the behavior of East Germans in this interim period. In the five months between December 1989 and September 1990 that I spent in East Berlin, I never once heard a conversation about democracy which I had not initiated — outside of the opposition groups organized around human rights issues. On March 18, 1990, in the first fully free Eastern European election since the end of World War II, the groups most responsible for the revolution and least "tainted" by the communist regime received less than 4% of the popular vote. Over 48% of the East Germans voted for a conservative coalition of three parties, represented by the initiative of Chancellor Helmut Kohl. Yet this election violated the legal principles of sovereignty and self-determination that were so conspicuously touted as marking the superiority of liberal regimes. West German political parties openly influenced the election results, pouring in 7.5 million D-Marks to support and create parties favoring their own explicit national goals. In any case, the majority of East Germans clearly indicated that they wanted to become part of the Federal Republic, and fast. On July 1, 1990 the economies were united, and three months later the GDR was reorganized and absorbed into the FRG.

III

West German post-war identity was based on an entirely different social contract: the ability of the political system to deliver economic goods, meaning to protect Germans as consumers and to integrate them into the West. Central to this agreement between the state and its citizens were three symbols: the D-Mark symbolizing prosperity; the *Grundgesetz*, or Basic Law of 1949, symbolizing constitutional stability; and anti-communism, which enabled a continuity with the Nazi policy of anti-Bolshevism and united the West Germans against "the East." The first two symbols, on the other hand, signified radical breaks with the Nazi period. With unity, and the collapse of the East bloc in 1989, the consensus underlying all three symbols dissolved.

Unity with the East Germans meant a movement East instead of West, both through the incorporation of part of the East into Germany, and in the anticipated decline in the standard of living or threat to prosperity for many West Germans. Furthermore, the proposed European monetary union, part of the Maastricht Accords, threatened to deprive the (West) Germans of control over their national symbol: the D-Mark. The debate over the Basic Law of 1949 was another contentious issue imbuing most West Germans with a sense of loss. With the accession of the German Democratic Republic into the Federal Republic, according to Article 23 of the Basic Law, the united Germany is obligated, per preamble, to summon "the entire German *Volk* in free self-determination to complete the unity and freedom of Germany." This means that the constitution was, according to the founding fathers, to be renegotiated and submitted to some sort of popular vote if unity ever came about. The suddenness with which both the D-Mark and the Basic Law — pillars of a 40-year-old social contract — were to be taken away caused many West Germans to think twice about all the hoopla surrounding unity.

Moreover, the dissolution of the Soviet Union and the GDR denuded anti-communism of its appeal. Add to that the withdrawal from Europe of the United States, seen as the protector which guaranteed Germany's integration into the "West." The collapse of this Cold War triangle — evil USSR, good USA, innocent Germany caught between the two — cast Germany adrift. The Cold War Germanys had abstained from an active role in world politics except to the extent they served as proxies for the two superpowers. Their domestic policies were often a function of foreign policies, which, in turn, were largely written by foreign states. The new Germany, democratic and embedded in a larger Europe, had to find a new balance between prosperity at home and peace abroad. Its search for new moorings was not a smooth cruise, but a voyage through uncharted waters.

In sum, one can understand why the ideological fervor for unity was never as great in the West as in the East. West Germans had been the privileged ones following World War II. They were split off from the poorer, more backward areas of Germany, and then were beneficiaries of the Marshall Plan that initiated the *Wirtschaftswunder* (economic miracle of the 50s).

Additionally, the Western European alliance had integrated them in a stable, relatively democratic order.

Thus West Germans experienced unity not as completion or oneness, but as loss or slippage. It is absolutely misleading to conceive of unification, as is most often the case, in terms of a kinship metaphor. East and West Germany were neither siblings nor a divorced couple united after a long separation, but had, in the 45 years following the war, assumed different, often opposite, social, political, economic, and cultural trajectories. They had become two separate peoples, two imagined communities, and they remained so even after unification. Most Cold War institutions had, in fact, treated the citizens on the two sides as enemies. The extensive private gift-giving by West German citizens that characterized the Cold War years — mostly "luxury" goods like cigarettes, nylons, coffee — was done primarily out of guilt, not because of some abstract sense of "kinship" or "good will." The givers received not only tax credits for their largess, but also a feeling of satisfaction from belonging to the superior Germany. The significance of this feeling for overcoming the guilt due to participation in the Third Reich is not to be discounted. It was one way in which many West Germans dealt with their prosperity. Conversely, the East Germans could only receive — more gifts, more guilt, more gifts, more guilt — or (falsely) project that guilt onto someone else, namely, the West German gift-givers.

Forty years later, when the Wall came down, all that most East and West Germans shared was language. And even there, differences in dialect or word choice could often be used to distinguish between sides when necessary. Most of the elderly generation that was emotionally tied to unity were already pensioners. And their shared memories were of the triumph and *Zusammenbruch* (collapse) of the Third Reich, with only a few left who had participated in the turbulent and divisive Weimar years. They too, though, were and are split by their post war experiences, which makes them remember the two world wars and Weimar and the Third Reich as substantially different histories.

IV

Much of the responsibility for the success of unity and failures of unification can be attributed to how the politicians subordinated economic and cultural problems to short-term political (ergo, electoral) calculations. The rush to unity was based on several key false assumptions: 1) that West German businesspeople would prioritize patriotism over profit, and invest in East Germany merely because it was "German"; 2) that union of the economies and governments would soon lead to a relatively frictionless cultural unity; 3) that because the present hegemony of the West was assumed to be temporary, political annexation without an open airing of the terms of division and of unity — merely a process of discursive will-formation — would not permanently cripple a fusing of the two peoples. West German businesspeople followed sound economic principles over patriotism and invested in the old FRG rather than in the old GDR. Accentuated cultural divisions rather than a unified nation followed economic and political unity. The hegemony of the West did not diminish after unity, but appeared to have provided a base for a more permanent structural superiority.

Armed with these false assumptions, East Germans looked to the West as a miracle daddy with all the right answers, and West Germans willingly presented themselves in this light, as *Besserwessis* (know-it-all Westerners). Rallying behind what Jürgen Habermas has appropriately called *"D-Mark Nationalismus,"* political leaders, with the majority eagerly following, engaged in their first great delusion when they enacted the currency reform on July 1, 1990. As it turned out, introduction of West German currency into the East not only inflated the value of East German products, but dried up the markets for these goods by giving East Germans money to buy the long-coveted goods from the West. Result: closed businesses and unemployment reaching 40% in the East.

A second great delusion was that the East German economy (basically 25,000 state or quasi-state properties) could be quickly and non-contentiously "privatized" by a para-public (read: non-political) agency, the Treuhandanstalt. In charge of reorganizing, listing, evaluating, managing, and selling properties owned by the state, the former Communist Party (and other East German parties who decided to give up their property), trade unions, and the state security apparatus (the Stasi), the office of the Treuhand was so contentious that its first president was murdered by terrorists. By early 1992, it had closed every conceivable type of business, ranging from pharmacies, bookstores, hotels, clothing shops, to resorts. Regardless of how one might want to judge its performance — and, under the circumstances, by most accounts it performed remarkably well — it acted as a single authority without being held accountable to another democratically elected institution.

At the same time as the Treuhand was set up, politicians in Bonn decided on the principle to be applied to property disputes: they favored return of property over restitution. One of the major reasons put forward for this policy was that the government did not have enough money to pay for restitution; thus return was more economically feasible. But for whom? On this question, politicians in Germany following World War II and in the other former East European states following the Cold War turned the formula around: they favored restitution over return. In the former GDR, 1.09 million applications for restitution had been filed for 2.47 million objects, most being for either real estate or land. As of March 1992, the courts had settled merely 4.4% of these disputes. The huge backlog, in turn, was contributing to a delay in possible investment in the East due to the insecure status of most property. And since most East German judges had been fired, there was an extreme shortage of qualified judicial personnel to research and resolve the disputes.

Going into unity, very few Germans on either side had anticipated this set of problems. Most East Germans assumed an easy assimilation, while most West Germans assumed life would go on as normally, and comfortably, as in the past. Ossis, as those in the East are called, never imagined themselves part of a conquered land. The accidental opening of the Wall and collapse of the old regime signaled for the majority that they had won, thrown off the yoke of an autocratic gerontocracy. "Wir sind das Volk!" was a victory message. They were no longer subjects to be ruled but agents of history. For the majority, this view of agency did not last much beyond the date of formal unity.

The West Germans, on the other hand, never pictured themselves in the role of colonizers. They were more surprised by unity than those in the East, and initially they were supportive of and generous to those in the East. Yet the further one goes West from the border, or from Berlin, the more insulated people seem from the altered states to the east. And Kohl had assured them that this "normality" would be possible. Unity's bottom line was that no one would have to pay! Those who volunteered to move to the East and contribute to the restructuring — most refused to go even when their companies pressured them — were paid in kind: oftentimes more than twice as much as their East colleagues for the same work. Additionally, many Wessis, as West Berliners/Germans are called, enjoyed the unanticipated "unity bonus" of inheriting some of those 2.5 million objects from their uncles, aunts, or grandparents.

In this context, where a colonial relationship — economically, culturally, and politically — was being imprinted on East and West, it was not surprising that personal contacts between the sides began to decline in number. To give an obvious anthropological example, take marriages between East and West Berliners in 1991. As is typical of former dowry societies, women may move up the ladder, but women will rarely marry men from a group lower on the hierarchy than they are. As hierarchies break down, cross-status marriages tend to increase. Thus we might predict that given the increased dominance of West over East, marriages between Western women and Eastern men would be rare and getting rarer. This is, in fact, the trend. Of the 16,000 marriages in Berlin in 1991, only 46 West Berlin women married men from East Berlin. By comparison, 100 West Berlin women married men from Africa. Conclusion: Ossi men were at the very bottom of the status hierarchy for Wessi women.

This example is not meant to illustrate that West Berliners/Germans made few distinctions between foreigners and themselves. On the contrary, discrimination against foreigners and cultural xenophobia intensified in both East and West after unity. As the internal hierarchies became more pronounced, scapegoating of external enemies was commonly resorted to in efforts to unite the "native" group. The point I wish to make is that Ossis were also increasingly considered to be foreigners by Wessis, especially as the status differential between the two became more transparent and permanent. Wessis often justified discriminating against Ossis by accusing them of smelling, of being dumb, of not working diligently enough. Ossis often responded like they did to authority figures in the former GDR: as whining supplicants, a behavior that elicited only disdain in the West. In the search for orientation in this new forest of signs, some East Germans were already resorting to nostalgia, beautifying their past in a way that downplayed its injustices and repressions.

Moreover, the Ossis were by no means united among themselves. Unity resulted in the dominance of the West German state as the sole *Rechtsstaat*, contrasted with the *Unrechtsstaat* of the East. This particular representation delegitimated any attempt to differentiate in reviewing the transactions and interactions in the history under that regime. Indeed, forty years of East German illegality became a commonplace assumption. Many East Germans were by no means, however, done with their histories. They saw a future in legality as contingent on a necessary working through, rather than flight from, their experiences. Thus we witnessed an understandable preoccupation with the Stasi, an attempt to reckon with a society in which one-third of all people were spied upon by someone close to them. Prosecution of the former rulers and border guards, despite the difficulties inherent in such an attempt, was also part of a general effort to secure "justice" under changed conditions of legality. More than 50,000 former GDR citizens claimed to be victims of the GDR judicial system; 7,776 filed claims for compensation or rehabilitation, of which only 1,700 had been resolved by March 1992. Furthermore, an estimated 1.5 billion marks were being demanded in damages due to harm suffered under the GDR. These concerns of the East, which sowed divisions among the Ossis and lamed them to the point that they were unable to be future-oriented, had a different function in the West. Wessis often used these conflicts to reassert their own unity and their own sense of difference and superiority: in their eyes, the East Germans were tainted by both Nazism and Stalinism, while they themselves, having lived only under legality, had the obligation to teach Ossis the superior principles of market efficiency and democracy.

V

For the enlarged Germany in the enlarged Europe, its post-Cold War state was oddly incongruous with what Germans had imagined unity would be like. Neither the absorption of East into West Germany, nor the re-integration of Central Europe into "the continent," nor the break-up and defanging of the Czarist-Leninist Russian-Soviet empire, nor the accelerated unity of Western Europe, relieved the Germans of their historical *Angst*: to be an exceptional people in the center of Europe. Their position within Europe, due largely to historical experience and to their disproportionate, if earned, economic weight, was indeed an inescapably exceptional one, though Germans no longer consciously strove for a *Sonderweg*.

Being in the middle again, Germany began to receive huge numbers of refugees from an East and Central Europe riven by war, genocide, concentration camps, and last but not least, relative poverty and economic dislocation. And Germany's friends in the West, its fellow European Community members, were proving equally contentious — obstructionist, many Germans would have said — when it came to reckoning with problems of the continent, though, of course, the means of resistance or the assertion of "national will" remained peaceful. Further, NATO, the military pact that enabled Europeans to hide behind American (im)morality during the Cold War, had truly lost its raison d'être — but members of the EC, to say nothing of a future enlarged one, could not agree on an alternative.

What frightened the Germans most about the new world order was disorder in the East, particularly the agony of the former Yugoslavia and the USSR. They experienced every convulsion produced by this disorder — migration, war, human rights violations — directly as electroshock therapy, as a cattle prod to the memory. Given Germany's own only-too-recent role as Master Criminal of the World, Germans wanted to think of themselves as reformed. Indeed, they were often profoundly convinced that they had learned — and thus other humans could too — from history. Yugoslavia's uncivil war was a continuing reminder of the violability of the two basic principles most Germans held to be inviolable: a rejection of war as an instrument of policy, and the protection of minority rights as a precondition of the right to national self-determination. Of all the Europeans, Germans had perhaps the greatest difficulty digesting that this violation was happening within Europe, home of the Enlightenment, civilization, progress, history.

One aspect of the German response to their own history and to these current crises was to accept refugees from troubled areas. For example, as of July 1992, Germany alone had accepted 200,000 refugees from Bosnia-Herzegovina (by comparison, Spain and Italy had accepted none; Austria, the next most receptive, had accepted 50,000). Moreover, approximately 1,000 refugees were flowing into Germany daily from other parts of the troubled globe.

Once in Germany, these refugees were sent to cities and towns of all sizes in the various provinces, divided up proportionately according to a federal agreement. Resentment against these stateless peoples increased at the same rate as loss of employment among Germans. And since joblessness was being suffered disproportionately in the East, the reaction to the refugees, including violent attacks on and murders of "perceived foreigners," firebombing of homes for asylum seekers, escalated dramatically in the East. Of course, one should not lose sight of the well-known fact that much of this violence in the new space of the East was being organized and financed by thugs and money belonging to the West German right and to the less-known fact that violence against perceived foreigners is growing in the West also. It is also important to emphasize that the migrations from Eastern Europe and the former USSR were likely only just beginning. They were still small in comparison with the migration flows produced by World War II. Then, Europe generated 50 million refugees, 12 million of whom were German. By comparison, the wars in Yugoslavia have produced 2.4 million refugees, in Iraq 1.8 million Kurd and Shi'ite refugees. Moreover, Europe and North America accept only 12% of all the world's refugees; the other 88% go from poor land to poor land. Viewing this refugee flow from an historical perspective does not, unfortunately, change the reaction to it. Indeed, the West Germans were wrong in demanding of their East German compatriots a *Vergangenheitsbewältigung*, coming-to-terms with the past. What was needed is a *Gegenwartsbewältigung*, coming-to-terms with the present. A changed reaction, a getting out of the slough of despondency, would only be possible when the diverse histories and concerns of East and West were fully acknowledged and respected, with an orientation to understanding the nature of these differences rather than clinging to the illusion of unification.

46

After Yugoslavia

Sonja Licht

After almost two years of a terrible civil war, even the name of my country — Yugoslavia — has been turned into a frightful notion. Tens of thousands of people have already died. Hundreds of thousands more have lost their homes and become refugees. According to the figures from the end of October 1992, the number of refugees is close to 2.5 million, almost half of them children. Hundreds of cities and villages have been destroyed. In the *Appeal to Stop the War in Yugoslavia*, issued by the Helsinki Citizens Assembly (HCA), it was stated that "in the region that used to be Yugoslavia, war is becoming a way of life. Values have been turned upside down. Criminals are turned into heroes and patriots. Adolescents are taught to be killers."[1]

The war in ex-Yugoslavia is causing one of the most dangerous crises in the post-Cold War world, and endangers not only the peaceful and democratic transformation of the Balkan region, but also the process of democratic integration of Europe. Many people wonder how such a terrible war could happen in the country which used to be known for its multicultural, multi-religious, multi-ethnic identity, and often referred to as Europe in miniature. Why is the transition toward democracy turning into a bloodbath in the country which for the people from all the other communist countries seemed closer to the idea of Europe than any of the members of the communist bloc?

There have been many attempts to answer these and similar questions, and many analysts will try to find the right explanation in the years to come. The above quoted Appeal states: "The causes of this war are varied and complex. They include the disintegration of state structures; the legacy of past wars both national and global; the suppression and manipulation of cultural identities; the breakdown of political ideologies; the economic and social hardship associated with the transition to a market economy; and, above all, the pent-up anger generated by years of totalitarian rule. All of these factors are present in other post-communist countries and there are signs of the 'Yugoslav virus' elsewhere in Eastern Europe, especially in some of the ex-Soviet republics. And in Western Europe, brutal attacks on asylum-seekers and immigrants suggest that racism, xenophobia and chauvinistic nationalism are not only post-communist phenomena. The war in Yugoslavia could be a harbinger of the spread of violence throughout Europe. The war is teaching us how fragile and dearly bought are peace and civic values."[2]

It is important to stress a few historical facts concerning the creation and existence of Yugoslavia. This state was created in 1918, after the defeat of the Austro-Hungarian empire in World War I, and the Ottoman empire by the end of the war. Parts of the country such as Slovenia, Croatia and Bosnia and Herzegovina were ruled by the Habsburgs, while other parts, Serbia, Montenegro and Macedonia, were ruled by the Ottomans. Although the idea of a South Slav (Yugo-Slavia) state was born in the 19th century, it was only after the defeat of these two strong empires that these nations could, for the first time after one thousand years of their existence in the Balkan region, create a common entity. But the new state was born in pain. Serbia and Montenegro were the only two independent nation-states before World War I and fought against the Austro-Hungarian army and its allies, while many Croats and Slovenes fought for the Austro-Hungarian forces.

With the creation of this new state East and West met. The newly formed Yugoslav state consisted not only of several different South Slav nations, but also of three major religions: Greek Orthodox, Roman Catholic, and Islam. The differences were visible in people's religious affiliation, as an important element of everyday life — as it always is in rural cultures. But they were visible, also, in major economic, cultural and political distinctions between regions. In some regions, particularly the most backward ones, the state was experienced almost as a hostile power.[4] While the Serbian ruling circles expected to benefit within the new state from the fact that the Serbs were the winners in the war and suffered the heaviest casualties (almost one-third of the Serbian nation was killed on the battlefield or died due to the hardships of the war), the Croat and Slovene political elites joined the new state only as a transition to nationhood; they hoped to gain independence through Yugoslavia rather than under the shadow of some other great power. From the very beginning of its existence Yugoslavia was faced with the conflict between those who viewed the Yugoslav idea as a way to achieve a democratic federation of separate states, and those who understood it as a transitional stage toward a unitarian nation-state or separate nation-states. It has to be stressed that among all constitutive nations there were advocates of both currents.

This conflict was one of the basic reasons why during World War II the struggle for liberation from the German, Hungarian, Italian and Bulgarian forces was accompanied by an extremely rough civil war. It was both inter-ethnic (between different ethnic groups, especially in Croatia and Bosnia and Herzegovina) and ideological (especially in Serbia, Bosnia and Herzegovina, and Montenegro, between the partisans, led by the communists, and the Chetniks, led by forces loyal to the old regime). This civil war resulted in the deaths of hundreds of thousands of Serbs at the hands of the Ustashe forces of the puppet fascist state in Croatia, with mass atrocities committed by Muslims, Serbs, Hungarians, and Albanians against each other.

As the partisans were the most numerous and the most disciplined and determined fighters against the fascist forces, they succeeded in winning a genuine support among the people. Thus, contrary to other East European countries, the communist system in Yugoslavia was not imposed from outside. It is well known that it was in some aspects different from the other communist systems, especially after Tito broke with Stalin, but its basic features were still the same. With the slogan "brotherhood and unity," with the creation of six republics (Serbia, Croatia, Slovenia, Bosnia and Herzegovina, Montenegro and Macedonia) and two autonomous provinces within the Serbian republic (Vojvodina and Kosovo), and with the recognition of Muslims as a separate nation the communists succeeded in restoring trust and cooperation between different ethnicities. However, as all identities except ideological loyalty were profoundly suppressed, as cultural pluralism and some forms of cultural democracy were imposed from above and always carefully controlled by the party apparatus, all the unresolved national problems and tensions were pushed under the carpet. When the communist oligarchy started to lose its legitimacy, after a whole series of experiments with reforms without genuine democratic changes, it turned toward statist decentralization in the 1970s. This decentralization turned the communist oligarchs into national elites, who jumped on the horse of nationalism as their last resort of legitimation. This process marked the beginning of the end of Yugoslavia.

The HCA's Appeal is quoted here because it proves that this European civic approach understood much sooner than the official one that the war in Yugoslavia is not a discrete phenomenon per se, a unique development which could be explained by some stereotypical explanation, such as "this is a struggle between democracy and totalitarism," or even worse "a struggle between good Croats and bad Serbs." The war in Yugoslavia is the result of an extremely complex set of factors, originating from the very history of this country. In addition to the problems stemming from Yugoslavia's creation out of very different national units, a second set of factors was generated by the specific nature of the communist system which dominated the entire life of Yugoslavia for 45 years. The development of the Yugoslav crisis was, moreover, strongly influenced by the political role Yugoslavia played in the Balkan region, and with the different geopolitical interests of various larger countries. The last two have been increasingly important as the process of the breakdown of Yugoslavia has become a fact of life.

The role Yugoslavia played in the Balkan region was very specific. It was the most multi-ethnic, multi-religious, multicultural country in the region, with a more developed pluralistic and democratic policy toward minorities than any other, including those who were not dominated by communist rule, such as Greece. Yugoslavia provided an example of how the federalist principle, even in very unfavorable political circumstances, is possible in this region, where the opposite, the principle of nation-states based on ethnic purity was not only the reason why the very term "balkanization" was created, but also led to almost permanent rivalries between these states in the past. Yugoslavia could play a very important role in the transition period if it could be transformed into a democratic federation. It is well known that the minority policies of Romania, Bulgaria, Greece, and Albania are unacceptable for a democratic Europe. They could be changed, and some changes were already on their way, within the efforts to develop a process of Balkan integration (which is the first and, probably, the most important step on the road toward a real integration of this region with the rest of Europe).

Unfortunately, these efforts were interrupted by the Third Balkan War. Instead of being a source of stability, Yugoslavia became the cause of great instability. All the Balkan countries are closing up, their minorities feel more and more endangered, weapons are arriving in the region instead of economic resources, and at the end of 1992, the danger of an overall Balkan war is becoming more and more real. It has also to be stressed that while the region was peaceful and calm the Balkan peninsula stopped being the "powder keg" of Europe, and the dominant countries were not interested in getting involved in this part of the world. As soon as Yugoslavia started to fall apart all of this changed. The Balkan peninsula might, once again, put the whole of Europe in flames, and there are many countries which have now discovered a very special interest in getting involved in the present and potential future divisions within this region.

Only ten days after the war started in Yugoslavia, on July 7, 1991, the HCA organized a meeting in Belgrade devoted to the topic "Disintegration of Yugoslavia — Integration of Europe." Close to 150 people from all over ex-Yugoslavia, including almost 40 from other European countries, the U.S. and Canada, gathered in Belgrade for a day to express their deep concern and to exchange their thoughts about the first war to start in the middle of Europe after the end of the Cold War.[4] This was not a simple demonstration; it was a very serious warning to Europe. At the Belgrade meeting Zdravko Grebo from Sarajevo stated that "Bosnia and Herzegovina cannot exist without Yugoslavia, and Yugoslavia cannot exist without Bosnia and Herzegovina." He predicted a terrible catastrophe if both Yugoslavia and Bosnia and Herzegovina fell apart as the result of the creation of ethnic states. Ernest Gellner warned about the dangers of self-determination as a major principle in a situation where nation-states are to be constituted in still semi-rural countries without democratic traditions. Konstanty Gebert from Poland urged the European Community to take immediate steps toward incorporating into the EC structures all those parts of then still existing Yugoslavia which were ready to follow the path of peace and democracy. The participants of the Belgrade conference emphasized that the crisis of Yugoslavia was the crisis of Europe, and that only if this were understood could something efficient be done to prevent a tragedy with immeasurable consequences. It was not understood!

The very same day, by mere coincidence, there was another gathering held in the country. At the Adriatic island of Brione the representatives of the EC met with Yugoslav political leaders to sign what was to be the first of several dozen agreements on the ending of hostilities. If they had listened to what was being said in Belgrade they would, probably, have reacted by saying that the representatives of civil society were overstating once again. This is the opinion all those who have been concerned about the deepening crisis of Yugoslavia and other post-communist countries have been hearing for a long time. This is the view all those who have been concerned about the rising post-communist chauvinist nationalism are faced with all the time as well.

European political leaders and opinion makers did not understand that the "velvet revolution" might turn into its opposite if the trends toward democracy were not immediately supported by serious economic and political aid; they did not understand that the sudden breakdown of totalitarian systems does not guarantee an instant democratic transformation. The East European dissidents, together with some sections of the intelligentsia, were dreaming about becoming a part of United Europe. The majority among them believed that the urge toward democracy in the post-communist societies would be so strong that it would overcome all the obstacles in the transition period. However, they did not realize that the decades of totalitarian rule destroyed not only the economic and political infrastructure of their societies, but also created a totalitarian state of mind. The people in these societies became used to living in a collectivist society, without a concrete social experience of individual rights and responsibilities. They also became used to the fact that their public and private lives had nothing to do with each other. Their public life was determined by ideological patterns and slogans, while their private life was the only marginal and limited space where they belonged to themselves. The absence of civic values and responsibilities, indeed the absence of civil society itself, have also left these societies without a genuine need and respect for tolerance and solidarity. The totalitarian assumptions, combined with a structural economic crisis, the slow and painful process of building pluralism and democracy without any experience of civil society, and already present strong nationalist sentiments generated by the fact that all national feelings and specific identities were suppressed by the communist regimes, created a fertile ground for a strong post-communist racist, ethnic and religious nationalism.

This nationalism was only stimulated by the fact that in many countries communism was understood and explained as a system imposed by the Soviet Union, brought by the "tanks of the Red Army." This explanation was partially true in some areas, but what is often ignored, especially after this system broke down, was that a great majority of the population adopted this system as its own, and took an active part, to various degrees, in perpetuating its life. One of the pillars of the post-communist nationalism is also to be found in the "official nationalism" developed by the communist regimes themselves, which became especially strong in the period when it became obvious that they were losing their ideological legitimacy; this was especially true in Yugoslavia and Romania. This is why genuine communists, such as Slobodan Milosevic of Serbia, Franjo Tudjman of Croatia or Leonid Kravchuk of Ukraine transformed so easily into post-communist nationalists. On the other hand, the belief that all those who were anti-communist, by that definition, represented a better, even democratic, alternative provided strong support both within the East European countries and abroad to anti-communist nationalists, such as Alija Izetbegovic of Bosnia and Herzegovina and, for the time being, even Zviad Gamsahurdia of Georgia.

Sometimes it seems to me that for Yugoslavia it is already too late. Not only because so many people have already died, because hundreds of thousands and even millions have become homeless, jobless and even countryless; but also because the feelings of hopelessness, fear, hatred, revenge are destroying the remnants of mutual trust. How could multi-ethnicity be restored in a country where cities, villages, even families have become divided along ethnic lines? How could multi-ethnicity be restored in a country where, only 50 years after a major civil war which also involved a genocide,[5] another civil war is taking place, with the possibility of even worse genocides? The obsession with ethnic states has resulted, finally, in "ethnic cleansing" everywhere the war spreads, done, more or less, by all sides.

One of the basic values of a modern, democratic Europe is multiculturism, multi-ethnicity. The most often used slogan when one walks down the long corridors of the Council of Europe or the European Parliament is "living together." Of course, one should not forget that there is a long history of creation of nation-states in Europe, and that there is a long history of ethnic cleansing, from Spain to Sweden. But this happened before Europe became a symbol of unity in diversity; this was a Europe of divisions, of wars. This happened, as Ernest Gellner often reminds us, when the Western European countries were in the phase of the creation of nation-states. And now, after the breakdown of the communist governments, after the breakdown of the Soviet empire, the region from the Baltics to the Adriatic is, according to Gellner, entering the same phase. The first results of this process are to be seen in the former Soviet Union and the former Yugoslavia. The strengthening of nationalist movements, the creation of nation-states, was seen at one point by many Western analysts, politicians, even human rights and peace activists as a liberating process. The nationalist movements in post-communist countries were understood almost as a complement to the anti-colonialist movements in Africa and Asia, and as the strongest force of liberation from totalitarianism. At the European Nuclear Disarmament (END) convention, held in Helsinki and Tallin in 1990, many people argued strongly against the thesis that the peace movement should oppose the nationalist movements because they might endanger not only the process of transition toward democracy in the post-communist countries, but also the creation of a new peaceful and democratic order in Europe and the world. Only a year later in Moscow, at the next END convention, almost half of the speakers and workshops dealt with the danger of new conflicts created by belligerent nationalist and chauvinist forces. Those who were advocating the emancipatory potential of nationalism in the post-communist systems had forgotten that most of the nationalists were thinking about these new states not primarily in terms of how to make them part of a united, democratic Europe, but how to achieve strong borders, powerful armies, and even how to enlarge the countries they already controlled.

This is the process which we are witnessing in the former Yugoslavia;

these are the objectives which led to civil war, to the efforts to partition Bosnia and Herzegovina. The creation of nation/ethnic states out of ex-Yugoslavia has already resulted in the creation of strong national armies. We have all witnessed the terrible acts of violence the Yugoslav Federal Army (JNA) and other national armies have been committing during this war. We have also witnessed the especially dreadful atrocities done by different national paramilitary forces. The number of people in these armies is already greatly outnumbering the JNA. What are these armies going to do if peace is, finally, accomplished or even imposed? Will they simply agree to live in the unadvantageous (for them) conditions of a post-war period, or will they need new wars to legitimize their existence? Who will have the strength to disarm them? At this moment, no doubt, nobody is seriously thinking about these questions, because the most important objective is to stop the war. Although this must be the main and most immediate aim, it is also absolutely necessary to consider all these issues if the world wants to prevent the "Yugoslav virus" from spreading.

The Yugoslav crisis did not bring along only the Serbian or Croatian national questions, i.e. the political tendencies to create a Greater Serbia or Greater Croatia. It now includes the Macedonian and Albanian questions, as well as the very complex problem of how to solve the national aspirations of the Muslim population, which is living in four different parts of ex-Yugoslavia — Bosnia and Herzegovina, Serbia, Macedonia and Montenegro. And these "questions" are snowballing one after the other. Hungarians are already scared to enter Slovakia with cars with Hungarian license plates, although only a few months ago almost everybody was sure, in both Bratislava and Budapest, that there would be an open, or at least soft, border between Slovakia and Hungary. The Romanian, Hungarian, and Slovak nationalists are talking more and more about mutual territorial claims based, of course, on "historical" rights. The same is happening all over the former Soviet Union. Cross claims and minority-majority hostilities are following each other in the Baltics, in the Transcaucasus and even within the Russian Federation.

The question *What is to be done?* is becoming more and more complicated to answer. It is obvious that the only way to fight chauvinist nationalism, ethnic militarism, and ethnic cleansing is through development and democracy. The question of *how to achieve* this is more difficult. Western Europe might choose the politics of isolationism, the model of "fortress Europe." Western Europe could, of course, try to divide the European continent with a Mexican-style border. It could bring soldiers to protect these borders from the influx of refugees, the number of whom would amount to millions if not tens of millions, if civil wars and ethnic cleansing become not the exception but the rule in the post-communist world. However, this kind of division of the European continent is, first, impossible to realize from a practical, logistical point of view. Second, it would destroy the democratic perspective not only outside "fortress Europe," but inside it as well, because this concept implies a new militarization of this "fortress," forced assimilation and even ethnic cleansing of all those who are not "Europeans"; in short the "Yugoslavization" of Europe. If this grim prospect is to be avoided, if Europeans are determined to realize the essence of the notion of "living together" they have to: first, try to understand the full complexity of what is happening in the former Yugoslavia and other post-communist countries; second, be ready to sacrifice part of their living standard in order to help these countries overcome their worst economic and political difficulties; third, develop strong civil societies which would be able to control their own political leaders who are from time to time ready to make very rash decisions in the name of some imagined or real "national interest." The war in Yugoslavia has proved that there is no political or national interest which could be worth so many human lives and so much suffering. It has also proved that any short-sighted politics based on the so-called national interest, which is to be achieved by manipulation and violence, endangers the lives of the people on behalf of whom this interest is executed. The war in Yugoslavia is also the best proof that the world desperately needs an integrated, democratic Europe, a Europe of tolerance and solidarity; a Europe which will be able to help the post-communist countries achieve a transition toward democracy, to help them by opening and not by closing its gates. For these aims to be achieved not only European institutions and politicians have to change their behavior, but indeed every single European citizen. There is no European identity without a responsible well organized European civil society, promoting human rights, inter-ethnicity, and, above all, democracy.

So far we have witnessed something else entirely. We see the EC and its major countries (especially Germany) approach the Yugoslav drama with partisan interests and clientism. We see ignorance march hand in hand with arrogance. We have witnessed the persistent inability to develop an appropriate and consistent policy in a situation that desperately needed and expected one. EC and, later, the U.S. and the UN demonstrated a biased and unbalanced approach to the subject of the conflict in Yugoslavia, as well as to the results of this conflict.

What is needed now is a balanced and thoughtful approach, which will, first, do everything possible to stop the war; second, punish all the villains, especially the war criminals from all sides and, third, help the people to restore as soon as possible a normal life. For these steps to be achieved it is essential to bring extremely strong pressure to bear on all warring parties: Serbia and Croatia, Bosnian Serbs, Croats and Muslims, as well as on all states which are in certain direct ways involved in the conflict (Turkey, Germany, Austria, Albania, Greece, Bulgaria, Hungary, etc.) to stop all the activities which are contributing to the conflict in Bosnia and Herzegovina, or which could contribute to the spreading of the war to other parts of the region. The leaders of all three constitutional nations in Bosnia and Herzegovina (Muslims, Serbs and Croats) should be forced to end all military operations and start searching for an acceptable solution in a peaceful and democratic way. Talks under the supervision of UN and other international organizations are absolutely essential. The international community must make it absolutely clear not only to the warring sides in Bosnia and Herzegovina, but to warmongers in all parts of the former Yugoslavia and around the world, that the only way national aspirations can be achieved is through peaceful agreements, by preserving the basic values of humanity. This is why it must discourage all those who dream about future violent, unilateral solutions, both on the internal and international political scenes, and support those who are ready to restore the basic principles of the Helsinki Accords, who are ready to struggle to bring back ethics and human values into politics.

Notes

1. *Appeal to Stop the War in Yugoslavia* (HCA Newsletter: Prague, 1992), No. 3, p. 6. This appeal was part of a series of HCA activities leading up to the Citizens and Municipal Peace Conference, held in Ohrid on October 5–8, 1992. The appeal was signed by dozens of well known public figures from the former Yugoslavia, Europe and the U.S.
2. Ibid.
3. For more details, see Sonja Licht, "The Yugoslav Experience: The Failure of Reform without Democracy," *New Politics*, No. 3 (Summer 1989).
4. Participants at the conference included Adam Michnik and Bronislaw Geremek from Poland, Ernest Gellner from Britain, Gert Weisskirchen from Germany, Laszlo Rajk from Hungary, Aleksander Langer from Italy, and Milovan Djilas from Serbia.
5. According to estimates of historians and intelligence services in the U.S. and Europe, somewhere between 600,000 and 1,000,000 Serbs died at the hands of the Independent Croat State, a puppet fascist country, during the period 1941–45.

47

EC Unification: Causes and Consequences

*Tony Benn**

I'd like to start by trying to look at what we're told has happened. We're told that "the West has won the Cold War." The Soviet Union, as we know, has disappeared: "Communism has been totally defeated, and so indeed has socialism." This is what we have been told. The United States is triumphant everywhere. The Gulf War has taught the Muslims a lesson they might not have learnt at the time of the Crusades. Francis Fukuyama has written a book to say that history has ended. I was in Calcutta the day the book came out, and I could just imagine the hungry people on the streets of Calcutta cheering at the thought that history had ended, and they would always be poor, always be hungry, and they had no prospects of a better future.

It's against this background that we've had to discuss the future of our continent. I think it is helpful for understanding where we are, and where we're going, to spend one moment on where we came from. So allow me to say a word about the Europe of the twentieth century. The years between 1900 and 1914 were years dominated by three white men. The King of England, the Kaiser of Germany, and the Czar of Russia: they ran the world. And they had one other thing in common: they were all the grandsons of Queen Victoria. And none of the great bourgeois liberal politicians cared, as long as you were being repressed by one of Queen Victoria's grandsons; because that made it all right. That really was the world order that many people now in their eighties and nineties remember from their childhoods.

Then you had the enormous event of 1917: the Russian Revolution. And whatever may have happened since, and whatever view you may take of the Russian Revolution, it *was* the greatest event of the twentieth century. Because it released, however imperfectly, into a world that had been run by kings and conquerors and landowners and capitalists, a government that was committed to different objectives. And from 1917 to 1939 all the rest of the

* This article was adapted from a speech he gave in Geneva in the spring of 1992.

European governments mobilized in order to destroy the new Soviet Union. The French, the British, and the Americans sent an army into Russia in 1920 to destroy the revolution. Mussolini developed fascist policies to destroy communism at home, and to frustrate what they thought was an extension of the Soviet Union. If you look at the leaders of pre-war Europe, they were a pretty grim bunch: Hitler, Mussolini, Franco, Salazar, Pilsudski, Field Marshall Mannerheim, King Michael, King Carol, King Zog, Neville Chamberlain. They were a terrible crowd of right-wing people, united primarily by the desire to obliterate, forever, the ideas of socialism.

But Hitler went a bit too far: he attacked Russia. And when the Russians asked for support, they got the support of Churchill, and then you had the wartime alliance, where you had the Americans, the Russians, the Chinese and the French all fighting the Germans. But that wartime alliance was really a sort of accident. I think there were many people at the top in the West who privately believed we were fighting the wrong war, with the wrong allies, against the wrong enemy. As soon as the war ended, the Cold War began almost exactly as it had been left off in 1941. The atomic bombs were dropped on Nagasaki and Hiroshima not to bring about the surrender of Japan — because Japan had already offered to surrender — but to warn the Russians that the West had weapons of overwhelming power. That was what caused the thousands of deaths in those two Japanese cities.

From 1945 until 1989/90 and the end of the Cold War, all the combined efforts in the West were devoted to building an anti-communist alliance. We were told the Red Army was intending to move into Western Europe. I never believed it. How could the USSR, with all its problems, occupy the Federal Republic of Germany, France, Italy, and Britain? It was a ridiculous idea. But it was used in order to control us; so that if anybody in Britain, for example, criticized the government, they said, "Ah ha, you are working for the KGB, you have been sent here by Brezhnev." And therefore they used the foreign enemy, as George Orwell always said they would, in order to repress domestic dissent.

Fascism in Europe was the product of the slump of capitalism. In 1929, there were one million unemployed in Germany. In 1932 there were six million unemployed in Germany and that brought Hitler to power. The failures of capitalism, the failures of the left to offer an alternative, and sectarianism on the left; these factors combined to produce despair, and people looked for a strong leader who would put it right. That slump in the 1930s was ended by rearmament, which was the way in which Western Europe came back to full employment. It was all public expenditure: unemployed people were put to work building aircraft, ships, tanks, and guns. At the end of the war that boom continued a little bit, but it was a boom caused by a continuation of the war economy, aimed at peacetime reconstruction.

The Soviet Union was feared for its ideas, and for the fact that it did actually provide some support for anti-colonial struggles. I very much doubt whether India and Pakistan and Algeria and Vietnam and Nigeria would ever have been freed if there had not been a powerful anti-imperialist country, namely the Soviet Union, in existence.

The West responded to this by building two structures, both of them designed to protect capitalism. The Common Market, forerunner of the European Community, was set up to give capitalism a chance to survive on a larger continental scale. NATO was established to defend it and to provide American forces that would protect U.S. interests.

The real fear of Western policymakers was not that the USSR would actually invade militarily, but that the ideas of communism and socialism would spread naturally as a result of the chaos and destruction rife in Western Europe after 1945.

Therefore the political strategy that was adopted was, firstly, to underwrite the European social democratic parties, in the interests of making them reliably anti-communist; and, secondly, to divide the world trade union movement by precipitating a split so that anti-communist unions could be established as rivals to the communist-led unions.

A great deal of energy and, more importantly, money was pumped into these projects by the CIA and other Western intelligence services. The right-wing unions in the U.S. and Europe were encouraged to set up the International Confederation of Free Trade Unions (ICFTU) and separate it from the communist-led World Federation of Trade Unions (WFTU). Similarly efforts were made to prop up social democratic parties to counter the burgeoning communist parties of Europe, especially in Italy, where the U.S. made it clear that it would not tolerate "the historic compromise" which would have brought the Italian Communist Party (PCI) into a coalition government. In West Germany the Social Democrats were allowed to enter into a coalition with the ruling Christian Democrats. In exactly the same way, two social democrats, Felipe Gonzalez and Mario Soares, were actively assisted in their bids to take power after the falls of Franco and Salazar in Spain and Portugal, even though the real long-term opponents of the fascists in those two countries had been the communists.

When I was born, in 1935, twenty percent of the world was governed from London. Now, of course, Britain is an American colony, with 30,000 American troops based in Britain. The U.S. has 2,000 bases and nearly a million troops (apart from the Gulf War) around the world. Imperialism is like an elephant: it's difficult to describe, but very easy to recognize. And what we are witnessing is of course American imperialism, replacing the imperialism of the past.

We all have to ask ourselves some very important questions about what happened. Socialists, especially, have to look back on that Soviet period and ask what went wrong, and why. Russia was attacked in 1914, they were attacked in 1920, and they were attacked in 1941. They were under continuous threat throughout the Cold War. But internal factors were also crucial: there was under Stalin an horrific terror, no question about it. In the Soviet Union Stalin's terror left behind a severe repression of dissent, and a bureaucracy which was quite incapable of developing the full talent of the Soviet people, who were highly educated and with enormous intellectual and technical skills. The system was centralized and inefficient, and above all, they bankrupted themselves with military expenditure. I think that is the key to the collapse of the Soviet system. They spent between thirty and seventy percent of their national income on weapons; no country can survive on that level of military expenditure.

As a matter of fact the two countries which are most successful today — Japan and Germany — are partly successful because they have small military budgets, because the conquering nations in 1945 would not allow them to rearm. This burden of military expenditure has made the United States the biggest debtor in the world. The American troops in the Gulf were, in fact, mercenary troops, largely paid for by the king of Saudi Arabia. This great empire, this apparently victorious American empire, is actually very vulnerable. And in Britain, too, many problems can be attributed to the high level of military expenditure.

The end of the Cold War produced other important changes in the strategy of Western governments, and these necessarily began to affect relations between the new European Community and the U.S. and Japan, which came to be seen more as competitors for economic dominance than as partners in resisting communism.

The mighty U.S. had defended the West after World War II, but it had also dominated it economically, industrially, politically, and culturally. This began to stimulate resentment against America, first expressed by General de Gaulle, whose post-Second World War anger at being ignored in Roosevelt's plans culminated in the withdrawal of French troops from NATO. That anti-Americanism spread more widely as the economic crisis deepened in the 1980s and 90s, and trade conflicts began to surface at the GATT talks, especially on the question of agricultural support, centering on the Common Agricultural Policy of the EC.

Similarly Japan, with its low military budget and its centrally directed economic policy implemented by the Ministry of Trade and Industry (MITI), grew to be a serious rival to the power of Europe, with its planned trade surplus and the way in which Japanese capital moved in to buy up European businesses.

The economic slump, meanwhile, had sharply reduced the influence of the European communist and socialist parties and trade unions, to the point where bankers and industrialists began to see a way to re-build the EC as a superpower able to hold its own against both the U.S. and Japan; plans even began to be drawn up for a European military capability, based on the Western European Union (WEU), which could stand alongside NATO, and even apart from it.

The Gulf War, which showed the U.S. able and willing to intervene in the Middle East in order to safeguard its oil supplies, and, more to the point, to shore up its role as oil guarantor for Japan and Europe, also caused some anxiety in Europe, even though no country in the Community supported Saddam Hussein. The idea of a federal Europe, independent of the U.S. both economically and militarily, began to gain ground. It is possible to date back some of the thinking that lies behind the Maastricht Treaty to these factors. Maastricht, of course, would convert the European Economic Community into a full-blown European Union, culminating in a single European curren-cy and a central European bank.

Now the idea being propagated is that we should move the whole of Western Europe into this new fortress, this new euro-federalism, where all power would be concentrated in Brussels, where nation-states would become cantons or provinces in this new federation, or fortress, with our own nuclear weapons. The French have their *force de frappe*; we have borrowed a few American nuclear weapons in Britain and called them an independent deter-rent. Put them together and the EC would be strong enough to stand up against America — with whom we have many trade arguments over agricul-ture — and against Japan. This is the new European nationalism which is emerging and it is happening at a time when capitalism is itself in crisis.

It is very interesting to me that we should be concentrating all our attention on the collapse of the communist economic system, which has been absolute, when it may only have been the weakest link in a world economy which is also in crisis. We see the U.S. with mass unemployment and unsolved social problems, we've seen Le Pen grow in France, we've seen the rise of nationalism and xenophobia in Germany, we see all sorts of recrudes-cence of nationalism, and this is really caused by the slump in global capital-ism. It is not just a recession — a little blip which will correct itself. This is a slump possibly of similar proportions to that which we experienced in the 1930s.

One of the reasons for this is that capital is completely free while labor is completely shackled, by legislation against the trade unions, and because labor cannot move across the world. With EC unification, the free movement of labor is supposed to exist within the integrated Europe, and European capital can go where it likes worldwide. But there is no parallel provision for the free movement of labor in and out of the Community, and the tightest immigration controls are being established to enforce these rules.

This policy actually stimulates, and then uses, racism and xenophobia to divert attention from the effects of the slump, so that foreigners get the blame for unemployment, for example, instead of the system which causes it. The most vivid example of how this works may be found in the way that British capital both financed and then made huge profits from the apartheid system in South Africa, while, at the same time, immigration controls ensured that no black South Africans were able to obtain visas to work in Britain.

This is how the new European Federation will deepen the racial divisions in the world. Its reorganization of the global economy will reinstate the very system that underpinned Victorian imperialism after Britain used its early industrialization first to impose control over its colonies.

One of the reasons the West has welcomed events in the Soviet Union, therefore, has nothing to do with encouraging democracy in the former Soviet Union. Rather, it is because the Soviet Union has a highly skilled workforce which can be exploited by Western companies recolonizing the old Soviet Union to make profits for the West; exactly as it does in the Third World.

Running capitalism from Brussels is unlikely to be any more successful than running communism from Moscow. It's too centralized and too bureaucratic. The Commission that runs the Common Market is not elected: the ministers who make the laws meet in secret (I was on the Council of Ministers for five years, and its president once). It is the only parliament in the world that meets in secret to pass its laws. And my fear is that just as the attempt to centralize communism under Moscow ended with nationalism, this will end in nationalism too. When the system breaks down, and I think it will, then instead of blaming the Treaty of Rome, people will say, "It's the Germans, it's the French, it's the Italians," and you'll return to the situation we had before World War II.

I also fear, now that the former Soviet Union is in effect joining Western Europe and the white races, that we're taking a massive step towards what will be a racial division in the world; where the whites, including the Russians, band together to keep out the Third World, and even perhaps to recreate the panic of a hundred years ago of the "yellow peril," where the Japanese and the Chinese were thought to be about to come together, and dominate the world.

These are very dangerous tendencies, and I want to suggest some of the ways in which we might approach them. First of all we have to show solidarity, based on a moral view of the world, which is the foundation of any political order. Without a moral base, in the end the whole thing is just a nationalist game.

The second requirement is that people must have access to some analysis of what is happening. And since the media in modern bourgeois societies are engaged in manipulating opinion, and emptying political dialogue of its content, we have to fill the vacuum with our own explanations. One of the failures of social democratic politics is that social democratic parties have become managers instead of becoming teachers, and they've left thousands and thousands of acres of ideological and moral territory absolutely empty, to be filled by the philosophy of the extreme right.

The third thing we have to do is to make demands on the system: for work for everybody, a decent home for everybody, lifelong education for everybody, lifelong healthcare, dignity when we're old, and peace.

Then we have to look at the very important question of democracy, especially in relation to technology and power. Democracy is a word widely used and much misunderstood, but it is part of the most urgent constitutional task of our time. Go back to the beginning of the century and look at the technology that existed then. The fastest that people could travel was on a train at sixty miles an hour — now the space shuttle can travel at 25,000 miles an hour; the largest audience one could address in 1900 was through a megaphone — now one can address the whole world through the satellite system; the largest number of people one could kill at any one time in 1900 was with a maxim machine gun — now one can obliterate hundreds of thousands or millions of people (about two hundred thousand were killed in about a week during the Gulf War in 1991); the quickest calculator was a little abacus with beads — now you can make millions of calculations a second. This century has seen such an explosion of technical power that the critical question is: who is going to control it?

Technology centralizes power everywhere. Over the course of my life I have developed five simple democratic questions. All powerful people — whether the chairman of IBM, or Robert Maxwell, or Jacques Delors, or Mr. Brezhnev — should be asked five questions. What power have you got? Where did you get it from? In whose interests do you exercise it? To whom are you accountable? And, how can people get rid of you? That is the most important question. Until people with power can answer that last question, one does not have a democratic society. That framework must provide a new structure for Europe, and a structure for a new world order.

The question is not whether one is pro-European or not; the question is what sort of Europe? I do not believe that the Treaty of Rome can conceivably provide answers to these questions. Ways must be found of harmonizing by consent and agreement rather than by dictating from above. For example it is unacceptable to have capitalism entrenched in Europe's constitution. The French constitution is based on liberty, equality, and fraternity; the American constitution on life, liberty, and the pursuit of happiness; the Treaty of Rome is based, instead, on the free movement of capital and labor within the Community.

The basic principle it enshrined was that there should be no national legal restraints that could hinder the right of capital to move to wherever the greatest profits could be made. This disregarded the economic and social impact that such capital flows might have, either on European nations facing an outflow of money, or on the Third World nations that could find their own domestic industries being bought up by European capital, with low wages paid, and the profits repatriated to European corporations.

It is a capitalist constitution, entrenching capitalism in Europe in the same way Pakistan is entrenching Islam, and the Russians entrenched Marxism. A constitution cannot absolutely exclude, by law, alternative ways of solving problems.

Finally we have to look at the United Nations itself. The United Nations after World War II was the world's great hope. But it is now dominated by the United States. The Security Council does what the U.S. wants through bribery, bullying, and pressure. The Gulf War was not a UN war: Perez de Cuellar was not even told the war had begun. It was an American act of aggression in the clothing of the UN. And if capital can move freely, and the media can communicate across the globe, and we can travel so quickly, and the military can move, and we can calculate so quickly, there must be a concomitant democratic structure for the United Nations. We should demand popular elections across the globe to choose a UN General Assembly, responsible for planetary protection and development. The Security Council should not be a group of former superpowers: it should be transformed into a democratic body and the secretary general should be responsible for it.

Finally what is the agency by which all this may be brought about? There must be a way of making links across the nations of the world between working people, of forging a new International, pluralist in character, which brings together the non-aligned countries. This must lead to a real new world order, because it is those countries, the nations of the South, who represent the dispossessed, and who must win the confidence and support of people in the U.S. and Europe and all over the world in what are called the industrialized countries. That is the task we have to achieve. It is so urgent we must set a target of making real progress before this century is out.

48

Combating Entropy:
British Decline in the American Century

Tim Watson

[Britain]'s not a bad country . . . It's just a mean, cold, ugly, divided, tired, clapped out, post-imperial, post-industrial slagheap covered in polystyrene hamburger cartons.

— Margaret Drabble, *A Natural Curiosity* (1989)

For the people of Britain, the new world order of the 1990s has so far only meant an intensification of an old cultural, economic, and social phenomenon: British decline. In the 1890s, (imperial) Britain had the world's highest per capita GDP; by the end of the 1980s (post-colonial) Britain's position in this global league table had plummeted to seventeenth, and was still falling. Such raw economic statistics can give a sense of the scale of British decline vis-a-vis the rest of the industrialized world, but they give no indication of the extent to which the experience and discourse of decline have permeated almost every cell of the British cultural and social formation. Indeed, one commentator, Martin Woollacott, has gone so far as to argue that the myths and traditions of the nation "ha[ve] even been remodelled in such a manner as to incorporate national decline itself in an emotionally satisfying way. It could almost be said that we British have become worshippers in a 'cult of decline.'"[1]

This, however, is not the whole story. One need only note the way that British politicians, artists, and intellectuals have consistently called for (and sometimes claimed to represent) national renewal and the end of decline to recognize the deep disenchantment and dissatisfaction embedded in British culture. Patrick Wright has described the way in which history has come to be seen as entropic in Britain, a gradual but inexorable leaching away of earlier power and glory: this is the paramount fact of contemporary British life.[2] While some have responded with resignation or even, as Woollacott suggests, with a kind of masochism (a position not uncommon on the British

501

left), most have attempted to resist this entropy, to reverse British decline, to put (as Margaret Thatcher famously declared) the great back into Great Britain.

While, on the face of it, the need for political and cultural renewal is unarguable, the ways in which that project has been attempted in Britain in recent years have been disabled by a fatal flaw: a powerful sense of nostalgia which determines that any model for British renovation has to be found in a mythical national past, the time when Brittania ruled the waves (not to mention a quarter of the world's population). The need for a new order cannot escape the futile desire to preserve and resurrect the old one. The result is a brutally deformed and anachronistic culture: a people wallowing in the trappings of a vanished imperial age, while sinking deeper into the mire of national immiseration.

I want to argue in this essay that as long as this version of the past remains dominant in Britain, the prospects for the future are grim indeed; however, there are signs, as yet attenuated, that this warping historical perspective is beginning to lose its grip on the British social formation. When, at the beginning of 1993, a revisionist biography of Churchill was published in Britain, it achieved widespread attention for its attempt to demythify the man who has remained an unassailable icon of British strength.[3] This suggests that Britain may finally be ready to give up its collective fantasy of superpower status, and subject its own history to serious scrutiny. This conclusion, however, must be tempered by the recognition that Charmley's book attacks Churchill partly on the grounds that he forced Britain to give up its colonies (and therefore its world power) by bankrupting the nation in the Second World War. The shifts taking place within Britain are contradictory and complex, and it is by no means certain that the progressive elements can coalesce in order to create a new culture on the ruins of the old.

New Right Hegemony

It is no small irony that a ruined society should be one of the legacies of more than a decade of Thatcherism, given that the New Right's stated goal was to arrest Britain's long-term decline. Thatcher came to power in 1979 by associating the left, and the British Labor Party in particular, with British decline, mobilizing the parlous state of the British economy (the 1976 IMF loan was a crucial negative symbol here), and the powerful myth that the trade unions "ran the country." Thus monetarism came to figure as a modernizing, progressive force — in contrast to the outdated modes of the labor movement, portrayed as anti-democratic, inefficient and paralyzing. The key to Thatcherism's success, however, was its ability to combine this discourse of late capitalist progress (the newness of the New Right) with a simultaneous reach back into the national past, bathing in the reflected glow of an older, quasi-feudal order which conservatives have always been able to claim as the very essence of Britain.

Thatcherism, therefore, was remarkably successful in imagining itself as representing both continuity with an essential British tradition (expansionist, military, aristocratic), and discontinuity with the immediate past ("Labour Isn't Working," as the Tories' infamous 1979 poster campaign had it). The interests of increasingly globalized capital were welded to the more parochial goals of the British middle class and skilled working class — the latter, upwardly mobile and virulently nationalist, were crucial in securing Thatcherism. This hegemonic bloc didn't begin to break down until the early nineties. Once this hegemony had been established by Thatcherism, it was reproduced at least in part by the identification and defeat of threats to British interests — external enemies, in the case of the inglorious slaughter which constituted the Falklands/Malvinas War of 1982 and, of course, the "enemy within," crushed during the miners strike of 1984–85.

Thatcherism, however, was not just a massive confidence trick perpetrated on the British people: its discourse of aggressive individualism ("pulling yourself up by your bootstraps") would not have gained currency if it had not resonated with people's feeling of disempowerment at the tactics and policies of a British left which was (and remains) for the most part corporatist, bureaucratic, and paternalistic. For instance, the Tory policy of selling municipal housing to sitting tenants was opposed zealously by the Labor Party in an attempt to shore up its local power bases, with the result that it looked as if the left stood in the way of people improving their material conditions: it was in areas like this that Thatcherism was not merely populist, but genuinely popular.

However, such acknowledgements should not obscure the fact that the Thatcher government's political rhetoric was often massively at odds with its policy and practice: its anti-statist, individualist discourse, for example, went hand in hand with an extreme centralization of state power and an obsession with official secrecy. Thus, while Thatcher and her ministers talked eloquently of encouraging local initiatives, they had no hesitation in responding to the leftist populism of municipal councils in London and elsewhere by simply abolishing them.

Nowhere was this disjunction between rhetoric and results more in evidence than in the economic arena. While persistently heralding the dawn of a new era in British economic history, Thatcher in fact presided over the acceleration of national economic decline. From 1979–83, through a combination of world recession and spectacular mismanagement, Britain lost a quarter of its manufacturing base, acquired structural mass unemployment, and began running a huge balance of payments deficit. Despite the consumer-led, credit-fueled boom of the mid- to late eighties, the British economy never recovered from this hammer blow. Indeed, Chancellor Nigel Lawson ruefully admitted later in his autobiography that, despite his triumphalist claims during his tenure, there had in fact been no economic "miracle" in Britain. For the millions of Britons struggling near or below the poverty level in 1992 when Lawson's book appeared, this news could hardly have come as a great surprise.

The Forward March of Thatcherism Halted?

What finally brought down Margaret Thatcher herself was the accumulated tension between her nationalist (and even xenophobic) rhetoric, and the transnational needs of British capital, particularly in the European context. Thatcher's belligerent anti-Europeanism may have served her friends in the City of London and large corporations well for a time, when it meant extracting concessions from the other EC member states, exempting Britain from various regulatory mechanisms (for example, Thatcher's wild assessment of the mostly innocuous workers' rights proposal, the Social Charter, which she called "a Marxist document," allowed Britain alone to opt out of its provisions). Eventually, however, Thatcher's anti-EC outbursts came to represent an obstacle to the free flow of capital through the European market; while she talked of the need to protect British "sovereignty" from the "bureaucrats in Brussels," British financial and corporate managers began to feel they were losing out to their German, French, and Italian counterparts. Thatcher stuck obstinately to her "defense" of the British nation-state against yet another set of enemies; other elements in the British ruling elite, however, saw the nation-state itself as an increasingly untenable and anachronistic concept in the age of global capitalism, and they overthrew the prime minister with breathtaking ruthlessness.

Baroness Thatcher, however, has been having the last laugh. Her successor John Major and his government — the bland leading the bland — have stumbled from one disaster to the next, as the whole neo-conservative project which Thatcher herself initiated has begun to unravel in the most spectacular way. (The Conservatives' eclipse has been matched only by the failure of the British left to capitalize on it.) Despite a fourth consecutive general election victory in April 1992, the Conservative Party seemed powerless to prevent what appeared increasingly to be the death throes of the British polity.

What makes this crisis seem different from all the other crises which Britain has suffered and overcome in the past, is that social and economic failure is now accompanied by the virtual bankruptcy of the key symbols of continuity with the good old days (which have always served to counteract short-term hardship in Britain, as elsewhere). Thus 1992 was the House of Windsor's *annus horribilis* (or, as *The Sun* put it, "One's Bum Year"); the wigs and robes of the British courts began to look like ridiculous pageantry given the series of spectacular miscarriages of justice (the Guildford Four, the Maguire Seven, the Birmingham Six, the Tottenham Three, the Cardiff Three, the list goes on . . .); the House of Lords, Margaret Thatcher notwithstanding, stood revealed as a relic of an earlier age, a bastion of unearned privilege and wealth completely out of touch with the everyday suffering of the British people; when Chris Patten took over as governor of Hong Kong in May 1992 his first symbolic act was to forego the pageantry of empire at his inauguration, testimony to the very outmodedness of his office and of Britain's residual imperial possessions.

As Britain struggled through the worst recession since the 1930s, one which some economists began to predict could never be overcome,[4] "tradition" began to lose its appeal as a source of identification and started to look more like a dead weight on the country's back. It was as if the signifiers of the national past, long venerated for their magical ability to conjure up models of success, were finally to be held accountable for failing to deliver that success. With their historical blinders slipping from their eyes, the British people drew on another indigenous tradition: a radical egalitarianism which loves to cut the rich and powerful down to size. If the queen is the richest woman in the world, then why doesn't she pay taxes like the rest of us? When Windsor Castle was badly damaged by fire in November 1992, the fault lines of the struggle over national history were plain to see: some bemoaned a terrible loss for the "national heritage," but others complained that taxpayers were being asked to foot the bill.

Coal Not Dole, Revisited

This changing orientation towards the national past was nowhere more evident than in the response to the government's October 1992 announcement that it planned to close 31 of Britain's 50 remaining coal mines, laying off 25,000 miners. Despite the scale of the pit closures, the government expected little more than token opposition to the plan; they believed that the National Union of Mineworkers (NUM), resoundingly defeated in the 1984–85 miners strike, was too weak to mount a successful challenge to the government's program. Therefore, the storm of public outrage and protest which greeted the October announcement shocked the government profoundly, forcing it rapidly to shelve the plans while, in time-honored political fashion, a face-saving "review" took place. As far as Britain's ruling elites were concerned, this was a full-blown Hegelian ruse of history. The miners, long the scourge of Britain with their militancy and ability to influence national policy, were dramatically reborn as the victims of a callous, uncaring regime oblivious to the suffering of working people; Arthur Scargill, leader of the NUM, found himself transformed overnight from a demonic, Stalinist dictator to the champion of the downtrodden.

And yet, however stunning the reversal was, it was also testimony to the persistence of a vernacular tradition which refuses to equate the history of the Establishment with the history of the people of Britain. Tony Benn, discoursing endlessly and eloquently about the Diggers, Thomas Paine, and the suffragettes, no longer seemed like a voice crying in the wilderness, but as the representative of a genuinely British tradition. As commentator Martin Kettle put it, referring to the movement which galvanized opposition during the depression of the 1930s: "We are back in step with the Jarrow march."[5]

However, what got lost sight of in the general euphoria in the labor movement surrounding the miners, was the way in which this radical, often suppressed current in British history can mesh seamlessly with that other, "official" national tradition which it apparently opposes. If nothing else, this is the lesson of Labor in power in post-war Britain: the ceaseless assimilation of resistant traditions into the fabric of the nation. The much vaunted social democratic "consensus" which dominated British parliamentary politics through the 1970s managed to bring the history of the labor movement (Jarrow march and all) into the fold of national history, one more item in the repertoire of past glories to be drawn on at will.

The result is an official opposition which is as backward looking as its conservative opponents. The defense of the miners, for example, was so successful partly because coalmining represents a residue of Britain's once invincible strength as a manufacturing, industrialized nation. The final assault on an industry which in 1947 employed over 700,000 miners, and which, as recently as 1984 still provided jobs for 150,000, came to signify an attempt to destroy the memory of Britain as a great power, a nation built on the success of heavy industry: mining, shipbuilding, steel. The British left, almost as much as the right, exhibits a sometimes uncontrollable yearning for long lost national prosperity. It should be remembered that it was a Labor prime minister, Harold Wilson, who said in 1964, "We are a world power, and a world influence, or we are nothing"; in 1993, it was a Conservative foreign minister, Douglas Hurd, in response to pressure to reverse cuts in defense, who proclaimed the new realism of the right in post-Cold War Britain: "We cannot be everywhere, and we cannot do everything."[6]

Britain in a Unipolar World

Since at least the Suez debacle in 1956, British foreign policy has been marked by this dualism: an acceptance, however reluctant, of a junior role in world affairs, particularly as regards the United States, coupled with a wildly overinflated rhetorical projection of British power. Thus, throughout the Cold War, successive British governments clung zealously to the notion of the country's "independent nuclear deterrent," while recognizing privately that both the technology and the command and control facilities for the nuclear capability were in the hands of the U.S. military. In the Gulf War of 1991, viewers of British television and readers of British newspapers could be forgiven for believing that the British Army was taking on Saddam Hussein singlehandedly, while in reality British involvement was dwarfed by the massive U.S. military force.

This strategic-rhetorical split has created a complex and contradictory relationship between Britain and the U.S. On the one hand, Britain's clinging to the coat-tails of the Americans as a means to shore up residual global influence (primarily, during the Cold War, within NATO; now, more precariously, in the UN) has led to the trumpeting of the "special relationship" between Britain and the U.S.; on the other, a long-standing and sometimes virulent anti-Americanism has taken root in British culture, manifested in recurrent public anxiety over being "invaded" by American influences, figured as consumerist (Drabble's hamburger cartons), low-class (TV, Hollywood), and violent (panics about crime in Britain are always accompanied by references to the horrific prospect of ending up "like America"[7]).

It seems likely, after the end of the Cold War, that such anti-Americanism will only increase its purchase in Britain, especially given the country's changing orientation (however painfully arrived at) towards Europe and away from the Atlantic alliance. One striking example of this is the way in which, even before the end of the Gulf War, euphoria gave way to revulsion in Britain as pictures of the allied massacre of fleeing Iraqi troops on the road to Basra shocked the British public; the anti-Americanism implicit in this reaction was made explicit in the inquest held into the deaths of nine British soldiers killed by "friendly fire" from an American A-10 plane towards the end of the Gulf War. The surprise verdict of unlawful killing in the case and the lack of seriousness with which the American military greeted that verdict, prompted widespread public outrage in Britain. Although, with the end of the Cold War and a gradual U.S. military withdrawal from Europe, Britain may no longer feel itself merely to be a glorified American aircraft carrier, unchallenged U.S. military-strategic hegemony will bring to the surface other unresolved Euro-American tensions, particularly in the area of trade. Although Britain is still attempting to be on both sides of this struggle, courting the U.S. at the same time as it becomes more fully integrated into the EC single market, eventually it will have to face up to the primacy of Europe.

After Maastricht

The future of Britain, at every level of both state and civil society, lies in Europe. However, although this state of affairs is so well recognized as to have become a political banality, there remains widespread bewilderment in Britain as to the meaning of that state of affairs. Increasing EC economic and political integration, particularly in the context of the end of the Cold War, requires an historic shift in British political culture away from the "special relationship" with the U.S. and, more particularly, away from the Little England attitude which persists in regarding the nation-state as the primary locus of economic and cultural activity. That historic shift has not yet taken place. While it is evident that the European nation-state in its traditional formation is not about to disappear from the scene, and that the prospects of a genuinely federal Europe are remote, it is nevertheless true that British isolationism in the face of accelerating economic, cultural and political ties in the rest of the EC can only have the effect of further marginalizing a country and a people that has always felt itself to be on the fringes of Europe.

In this context, the almost farcical events surrounding Britain's withdrawal from the EC exchange rate mechanism (ERM) in September 1992 serve as a warning. Britain's membership of the pan-European currency regulation organization (which aims to avoid major fluctuations in exchange rates between EC member currencies, in anticipation of an eventual single currency) was incompatible with John Major's policy of making the pound a symbol of national sovereignty. By pledging never to devalue the British currency, the prime minister and the chancellor, Norman Lamont, demonstrated that they had not learnt the lessons of Thatcher's demise. Gestures of old-style nationalism, especially in the economic sphere, are futile and self-defeating in an age of transnational capital. The humiliating events of September 16, 1992 — when the Bank of England spent $15 billion and raised interest rates 5% in a vain attempt to prop up a falling pound, followed by British withdrawal from the ERM and de facto devaluation — proved that even the macroeconomic policies of individual nation-states are no match for the corporate managers of global capitalism.

If the British state finds itself out of touch with the exigencies of this new European order, there are signs that at the level of civil society, by contrast, the orientation towards Europe is beginning to take place. Among young British people especially, an identification as "European" is emerging which would have been unimaginable in the mid-eighties; alongside this new identity there is a growing sense of a pan-European culture which is indigenous and not merely an assimilation of American cultural products and icons.[8] Political groups are increasingly seeking to forge links with similar groups in the rest of Europe; this is especially true of movements which do not fit into traditional party politics: environmentalists, anti-racist groups, feminists, gay and lesbian activists. And even though there has been little public energy put into European issues by the trade union movement since European Commissioner Jacques Delors' triumphant appearance at the TUC conference in 1988, there is at least some evidence that a European labor consciousness is evolving — the first signs of life for the British labor movement, all but decimated since 1979.

The Break-Up of "Britain"

Since the Second World War, many have predicted the final collapse of the British state — history has proved them all wrong. It would be foolhardy, then, to forecast once again the death of Great Britain. Nevertheless, it seems inevitable as the turn of the century approaches that both local and global movements (economic and political) will be increasingly influential, and that the realm of the strictly national will steadily shrink, even if it does not wither away entirely. This new order is going to have profound effects on the people who live in the various regions and nations which have gone by the name of "Britain."

If it is possible to discern encouraging long-term trends, particularly in relation to Europe, it is also true that in the short term the future looks bleak. Environmental degradation, a shattered infrastructure, the continued erosion of basic social welfare provision, a widening gap between rich and poor, racial intolerance, deep cultural demoralization: after nearly fifteen years of Conservative government, these are the phenomena which characterize Britain in the new world order. And as the massive windfall of revenues from North Sea oil — over $150 billion in the period 1979–91 — begins to exhaust itself, it is clear that the road to renewal in Britain is going to be long and very hard.

I want to argue, however, that the historic changes taking place within Britain and across the world, while driven for the most part by the interests of global capital and U.S. geopolitics, also open up the space for a re-imagining of politics and culture in Britain. Old familiar values are now open to question, and in the midst of the British wasteland there are green shoots of recovery to be seen. At last, the heterogeneity of the cultures and peoples of Britain is becoming an accepted part of the public sphere. There is increasing space for the assertion of previously excluded identities, so that being Black, or Scottish, or gay, or all three, is no longer incompatible with being "British"; at the same time, and in conjunction with the global shifts outlined in this essay, the category "British" is becoming less and less the primary arena of identification for many people in Britain. Of course, these changes bring with them a new set of political problems — in particular the tendency of identity politics to lapse into parochialism and exclusivism — but it is in the working through of these challenges that a new political culture could come into being.

Already we can say that certain deformations of the culture of Britain are being displaced. The imperialist nostalgia which Thatcher mobilized is no longer tenable in Britain, not least because of the presence and increasing visibility in the country of millions of people who can trace their own history back to former British colonies, and who will not allow a history of domination and exploitation to be misconstrued as a story of glorious adventure. In retrospect, the Falklands/Malvinas War can be seen as sounding the death knell for imperialist posturing, the nadir of British foreign policy rather than its finest hour.

This breakdown of accepted, and indeed cherished symbols of national belonging leaves confusion and disorientation in its wake: this is one aspect of the contemporary crisis in Britain. Along with that sense of bafflement, however, comes a feeling that everything is up for grabs, that there is the chance to shape the contours of a new culture in Britain; or, to be precise, many new cultures, which reflect and enable diversity rather than attempting to subsume it under a monolithic national construct.

The last thing Britain needs is yet another program for national recovery which yearns for a lost glory. A changing world offers the possibility for critical reflection and the chance to face up to new realities: Britain is no longer a great power and it must cease to think like one. The age of grand geopolitical strategy is irrevocably past for Britain; instead of mourning its loss, the people of Britain can make that fact the starting point for a new culture without illusions. In a world dominated by global capital and U.S. military power, delusions of national grandeur will serve only to consolidate national decline.

Notes

1. Martin Woollacott, "Britain's Blessed Trinity," *Marxism Today* (September 1990), p. 16.
2. Patrick Wright, *On Living in an Old Country: The National Past in Contemporary Britain* (London: Verso, 1985), p. 70.
3. John Charmley, *Churchill: The End of Glory* (London: Hodder and Stoughton, 1993).
4. See, for example, Wynn Godley, "No Cause for Optimism," *New Statesman and Society*, July 17, 1992, pp. 18–19.
5. Martin Kettle, "Moral Outrage in Middle England," *The Guardian*, October 17, 1992, p. 22.

Index